Building Net Sites with Windows® NT

An Internet Services Handbook

Jim Buyens

Addison-Wesley Developers Press
Reading, Massachusetts • Menlo Park, California • New York
Don Mills, Ontario • Harlow, England • Amsterdam
Bonn • Sydney • Singapore • Tokyo • Madrid • San Juan
Paris • Seoul • Milan • Mexico City • Taipei

Many of the designations used by manufacturers and sellers to distinguish their products are claimed as trademarks. Where those designations appear in this book, and Addison-Wesley was aware of a trademark claim, the designations have been printed in initial capital letters or all capital letters.

The author and publisher have taken care in preparation of this book, but make no expressed or implied warranty of any kind and assume no responsibility for errors or omissions. No liability is assumed for incidental or consequential damages in connection with or arising out of the use of the information or programs contained herein.

Library of Congress Cataloging-in-Publication Data

Buyens, Jim.
    Building net sites with Windows NT : an Internet services handbook
  / Jim Buyens.
        p.   cm.
    Includes index.
    ISBN 0-201-47949-4
    1. World Wide Web servers—Handbooks, manuals, etc.   2. Microsoft
Windows NT—Handbooks, manuals, etc.   I. Title.
TK5105.888.B89   1996
005.7'13—dc20   96-11363
                                                         CIP

Sponsoring Editor: Kim Fryer
Project Manager: John Fuller
Production Coordinator: Ellen Savett
Cover design: Robert Dietz
Set in 11.5-point Minion by ST Associates

1 2 3 4 5 6 7 8 9 -MA- 0099989796
First printing, June 1996

Addison-Wesley books are available for bulk purchases by corporations, institutions, and other organizations. For more information please contact the Corporate, Government, and Special Sales Department at (800) 238-9682.

Find A-W Developers Press on the World-Wide Web at:
http://www.aw.com/devpress/

To the homeless, seriously mentally ill persons of America.
Why is it that our society discards victims of these disorders to the gutters
and jails while lavishing health care dollars on victims of other,
less debilitating afflictions?

Contents

PREFACE   xvii

CHAPTER 1   **Internet Applications and Support Services**   1
             1.1 Application Services   1
                 1.1.1 World Wide Web (HTTP)   1
                 1.1.2 CGI and SSI   4
                 1.1.3 WAIS and Other Search Engines   4
                 1.1.4 FTP   5
                 1.1.5 Archie   5
                 1.1.6 Gopher   5
                 1.1.7 Veronica   7
                 1.1.8 E-Mail   8
                 1.1.9 List Servers   9
                 1.1.10 News   10
             1.2 Support Services   11
                 1.2.1 DNS   11
                 1.2.2 Network Security   12
                 1.2.3 User Login Security   14
                 1.2.4 File System Security   14

CHAPTER 2   **Why Use Windows NT?**   15
             2.1 Weaknesses of Other Operating Systems   15
                 2.1.1 UNIX   15
                 2.1.2 OS/2   16
                 2.1.3 Netware   16
                 2.1.4 Client Operating Systems (Windows 3.1,
                       Windows 95, Macintosh)   16
                 2.1.5 Mainframe and Minicomputer O/Ss   17
             2.2 Strengths of Windows NT   17
                 2.2.1 Microkernel Architecture   17
                 2.2.2 Multitasking   18
                 2.2.3 Portability   18
                 2.2.4 Scalability   18
                 2.2.5 Reliability   18
                 2.2.6 Security   19
                 2.2.7 Familiarity   19
             2.3 Why Use Windows NT at an Internet Site?   20
             2.4 What about Microsoft Windows Networking?   20
                 2.4.1 Microsoft Windows Networking   20
                 2.4.2 Windows NT File and Print Sharing   22
                 2.4.3 Windows NT Distributed Administration   22
                 2.4.4 NETBIOS versus Internet Names and Name Resolution   23

                2.4.5 Workgroups and Windows NT Domains   25
                2.4.6 Obtaining Windows Networking Browse Lists   25
        2.5 Windows NT Server versus Windows NT Workstation   27

CHAPTER 3   **Planning Your Site**   **29**

        3.1 Provider Segments   29
        3.2 Service Provider Roles   31
        3.3 Applications   31
                3.3.1 Full Service   32
                3.3.2 Limited Service   32
                3.3.3 Specialized Service   33
                        3.3.3.1 Secure Transactions   33
                        3.3.3.2 Credit Card Numbers   33
                        3.3.3.3 Partitioned Data (Pay-Per-View)   34
        3.4 Developing a Business Plan   34
                3.4.1 Customer Identification   34
                3.4.2 Customer Needs   35
                3.4.3 Customer Profiles and Numbers   35
                3.4.4 Services Required   36
                3.4.5 Support Plan   36
                3.4.6 Cost Model   37
                3.4.7 Product and Pricing Strategy   37
                3.4.8 Marketing Plan   37
                3.4.9 Business and Capacity Plans   38

CHAPTER 4   **Selecting Equipment**   **39**

        4.1 CPU Type and Speed   39
        4.2 Sizing RAM   41
        4.3 Choosing the I/O Bus, Disks, and Peripherals   42
        4.4 Choosing a System Bus   44
        4.5 Network Adapter(s)   46
        4.6 Fault Tolerance and Reliability   47
        4.7 Specific Recommendations   49

CHAPTER 5   **TCP/IP Fundamentals**   **51**

        5.1 Origin of TCP/IP   51
        5.2 Advantages of TCP/IP   51
        5.3 How TCP/IP Stacks Up   53
        5.4 Address Structure   59
        5.5 Routable versus Nonroutable Protocols   60
        5.6 Overview of TCP/IP Routing   61
                5.6.1 Address Resolution and Routing   61
                5.6.2 Subnetting   65

5.7 Port Numbers and Connections   66
5.8 Typical Configuration Settings   69
5.9 Domain Name System   69
5.10 Registering Your Site   71
5.11 Locating Standards Documents   72

CHAPTER 6   **Selecting Communications**   **73**

6.1 Introduction to Circuit Types   73
   6.1.1 Switched Circuits   74
   6.1.2 Packet Services   74
   6.1.3 Dedicated Circuits   75
6.2 Dial-Up Circuits   75
   6.2.1 Modem Management and Modem Banks   77
   6.2.2 Introduction to SLIP and PPP   79
   6.2.3 Dial-In Routers   80
   6.2.4 Windows NT Remote Access Service   81
6.3 Switched Digital Connections   82
   6.3.1 ISDN   82
   6.3.2 Switched 56   84
6.4 Dedicated Digital Circuits   85
6.5 Packet-Switched Networks   86
   6.5.1 X.25 Circuits   86
   6.5.2 Frame Relay Circuits   89
   6.5.3 Asynchronous Transfer Mode   91
      6.5.3.1 ATM Concepts   91
      6.5.3.2 Use of ATM for Data Applications   92
      6.5.3.3 Congestion Management   92
      6.5.3.4 LAN Emulation   92
6.6 Future Options—Cable TV and Telco   95
6.7 Local Area Networks   97
6.8 Internet Site Configuration   99
6.9 Client Software   100
   6.9.1 Sources of Client Software   100
      6.9.1.1 DOS   101
      6.9.1.2 Windows 3.1   101
      6.9.1.3 Windows for Workgroups 3.11   102
      6.9.1.4 Windows 95   102
      6.9.1.5 Windows NT   102
      6.9.1.6 Macintosh   103
      6.9.1.7 OS/2   104
      6.9.1.8 UNIX   104
   6.9.2 Supporting Client Software   104

CHAPTER 7	**Installing and Administering Windows NT**	**107**
	7.1 Preparing and Certifying the Hardware	107
	7.1.1 Physical Assembly and Location	107
	7.1.2 Pre-Installing MS-DOS	109
	7.1.3 Diagnostic Shakedown	109
	7.2 Initial Setup Options	110
	7.2.1 Disk Partitioning	112
	7.2.2 File System	114
	7.2.3 Computer and Domain Names	115
	7.2.4 Network Settings	115
	7.2.5 TCP/IP Settings	117
	7.2.6 Completing Initial Installation	121
	7.3 Testing and Refining the Installation	122
	7.4 Allocating Disk Space	122
	7.5 Creating User Accounts	126
	7.5.1 Windows NT Domain Account Structure	126
	7.5.2 Setting User Account Policies	128
	7.5.3 Managing User Rights	129
	7.5.4 Managing Audit Tracking	130
	7.5.5 Managing Trust Relationships	130
	7.5.6 Creating User Accounts	131
	7.5.7 Creating Groups	133
	7.5.8 Other User and Group Operations	134
	7.5.9 Setting File Permissions	136
	7.5.10 How Many Passwords?	138
	7.6 Advanced TCP/IP Configuration	138
	7.6.1 Multiple Network Adapters per System	139
	7.6.2 Multiple IP Addresses per Network Adapter	140
	7.6.3 Static IP Routing	144
	7.7 Installing Remote Access Service	149
	7.7.1 Equipment for Remote Access Service	149
	7.7.2 Installing the RAS Software	149
	7.7.3 RAS Configuration and Administration	155
	7.7.4 Dialing Out with RAS	155
	7.7.5 Managing RAS Dial-In Services	160
	7.8 Installing Internet Information Server	160
	7.9 Applying System Maintenance	164
CHAPTER 8	**Installing and Configuring DHCP and WINS**	**167**
	8.1 Operating Concepts and Standards	167
	8.1.1 DHCP Principles	167
	8.1.2 WINS Principles	169

	8.2 Installing DHCP and WINS	170
	8.3 Administering DHCP	171
	8.4 Administering WINS	175
CHAPTER 9	**Installing and Configuring Domain Name Service**	**179**
	9.1 Operating Concepts and Standards	180
	9.1.1 Configuring a DNS Server	181
	9.1.2 The DNS Server Boot File	182
	9.1.3 The DNS Zone Database Files	184
	9.1.3.1 DNS Zone Database Control Statements	184
	9.1.3.2 DNS Zone Database Standard Resource Record Format	184
	9.1.3.3 DNS Zone Database Standard Resource Record Types	185
	9.2 Relationship to WINS	189
	9.3 Sample Installation	189
	9.3.1 Obtaining and Installing MetaInfo DNS	190
	9.3.2 Configuring MetaInfo DNS	191
	9.3.2.1 Reviewing Sample Configuration Files	191
	9.3.2.2 Modifying Sample Configuration Files	196
	9.4 Testing and Problem Resolution	200
	9.5 Ongoing Management	206
CHAPTER 10	**Installing and Configuring FTP**	**207**
	10.1 Operating Concepts and Standards	207
	10.1.1 Security Concerns	209
	10.1.2 Disk Organization and Management	211
	10.1.3 Internet Conventions	211
	10.2 Installing the Windows NT FTP Service	212
	10.2.1 Installing a Basic FTP Server	212
	10.2.2 Enhancing Security	220
	10.2.3 Configuring Advanced FTP Parameters	221
	10.2.3.1 MsdosDirOutput	222
	10.2.3.2 MaxClientsMessage	224
	10.2.3.3 Greeting Message	225
	10.2.3.4 ExitMessage	225
	10.2.3.5 AnnotateDirectories	225
	10.2.3.6 LogAnonymous, LogNonAnonymous, and LogFileAccess	225
	10.2.3.7 LowercaseFiles	226
	10.2.4 ResKit 3.51 FTP Configure	226
	10.2.5 Performance Management	227
	10.2.6 Remote Management	228

10.3 Internet Information Server FTP Service 228
  10.3.1 IIS Service Configuration for FTP 229
  10.3.2 IIS Messages Configuration for FTP 229
  10.3.3 IIS Directories Configuration for FTP 230
  10.3.4 IIS Logging Configuration for FTP 231
  10.3.5 IIS Advanced Configuration for FTP 233
10.4 Testing and Problem Resolution 234
10.5 Ongoing Management 235
  10.5.1 Space Management 235
  10.5.2 Content Management 236

CHAPTER 11   Installing and Configuring Gopher   237

11.1 Operating Concepts and Standards 237
11.2 Installing and Configuring EMWAC Gopher 240
  11.2.1 Installing EMWAC Gopher 241
  11.2.2 Configuring Alias Files for EMWAC Gopher 243
  11.2.3 Automating EMWAC Alias File Maintenance 248
11.3 Configuring and Managing IIS Gopher 250
  11.3.1 IIS Service Configuration for Gopher 250
  11.3.2 IIS Directories Configuration for Gopher 251
  11.3.3 IIS Logging and Advanced Configuration
        for Gopher 253
  11.3.4 IIS Gopher Alias Configuration 253
    11.3.4.1 Defining Menu Names for Local Files 254
    11.3.4.2 Defining Menu Names for Local
            Directories 254
    11.3.4.3 Defining Links to Other Gopher Servers 255
    11.3.4.4 Viewing Existing Gopher Tag Information 255
  11.3.5 IIS Gopher Type Assignments 255

CHAPTER 12   Installing and Configuring POP/SMTP Mail Service   257

12.1 Operating Concepts and Standards 257
  12.1.1 SMTP Message Forwarding 257
  12.1.2 POP (Post Office Protocol) 262
  12.1.3 SMTP Message Structure 262
12.2 POP/SMTP Alternatives 267
  12.2.1 Internet Message Access Protocol 267
  12.2.2 Gateways from Other Systems 268
  12.2.3 X.400 269
12.3 Sample Installation 269
  12.3.1 SMTP Software Installation 270
  12.3.2 DNS Configuration 270

12.3.3 SMTP Software Configuration   273
12.3.3.1 Environmental and Routing Settings   273
12.3.3.2 Setting Up User Accounts   278
12.3.3.3 Preparing to Run NTMail   279
12.3.4 POP Client Configuration   281
12.4 Testing and Problem Resolution   282
12.5 Ongoing Management   284

CHAPTER 13   **Installing and Configuring a List Server**   **287**

13.1 Operating Concepts and Standards   288
13.2 Sample Installation   288
13.2.1 Creating a List Manager Address   289
13.2.2 Creating a List   292
13.3 Problem Resolution and Ongoing Management   298

CHAPTER 14   **Installing and Configuring USENET News Service**   **301**

14.1 Operating Concepts and Standards   301
14.1.1 NNTP (Network News Transfer Protocol)   303
14.1.2 Standard NNTP Commands   310
14.1.3 Selected Nonstandard News Commands   311
14.1.4 NNTP News Article Header Types   313
14.1.5 NNTP Server Operation   316
14.2 Sample Installations   318
14.2.1 Installing DNEWS   320
14.2.2 Installing NNS   327
14.3 Ongoing Management   332

CHAPTER 15   **Installing and Configuring HTTP**   **335**

15.1 Operating Concepts and Standards   335
15.1.1 HyperText Markup Language   336
15.1.2 Uniform Resource Locators   338
15.1.3 HyperText Transfer Protocol   339
15.1.4 Advanced HTTP Features   346
15.2 Sample Installations   347
15.2.1 Preparing for HTTP Server Installation   348
15.2.2 Installing and Configuring EMWAC HTTPS   348
15.2.3 Installing and Configuring Netscape
Communications Server   351
15.2.4 Installing and Configuring O'Reilly WebSite   371
15.2.5 Configuring Microsoft Internet Information Server   382
15.3 Ongoing Management   386
15.3.1 Setting Up an HTTP Server User Account   386
15.3.2 HTTP Service Start-Up   388
15.3.3 HTTP Data Directory Management   388

CHAPTER 16	**Advanced Web Services**	**391**
	16.1 Clickable Image Maps	391
	16.2 CGI — Introduction to HTML Forms and Tables	399
	16.2.1 HTML Forms	399
	16.2.2 HTML Tables	401
	16.3 CGI (Common Gateway Interface)	402
	16.3.1 Writing Standard CGI Programs	405
	16.3.1.1 hello.pl — An Introductory Standard CGI Program	406
	16.3.1.2 iconlib.pl — Passing Input Data via the Command Line	409
	16.3.1.3 grape.pl — Passing Form Data to a CGI Program	413
	16.3.1.4 Notes on Working with perl and Debugging Standard CGI Programs	426
	16.3.2 Writing Windows CGI Programs	426
	16.3.3 The <ISINDEX> Tag	429
	16.3.4 Netscape Server Application Programming Interface (NSAPI)	429
	16.3.5 Internet Server Application Programming Interface (ISAPI)	430
	16.3.6 Other CGI Approaches	432
	16.3.7 Security Concerns with CGI Programs	433
	16.4 Server Side Includes	434
	16.5 Database and Transaction Processing	436
	16.5.1 General Considerations	439
	16.5.2 Preserving State Information	440
	16.5.3 Record Locking	441
	16.5.4 Microsoft IIS Database Connector	442
	16.5.4.1 Logging IIS Activity Directly to SQL Server	443
	16.5.4.2 Using Internet Database Connectors to Summarize Log Data	445
	16.5.4.3 Providing HTML Form Input to Queries	449
	16.5.4.4 Linking One IDC Query to Another	453
	16.5.4.5 Additional HTML Extension (.htx) Facilities	455
	16.6 Client Site Programming	456
	16.6.1 Java	456
	16.6.2 JavaScript	457
	16.6.3 OLE Controls and Document Objects	459
	16.7 WAIS and Other Search Engines	460
	16.8 Performance Issues	465

CHAPTER 17	**Backup and Recovery**	**467**
	17.1 Backup Strategies	467
	17.1.1 What to Back Up	467
	17.1.2 Backup Media and Drives	469
	17.1.3 Backup Software	470
	17.1.4 How Often to Back Up	471
	17.1.5 Backup Retentions	471
	17.1.6 Media Storage and Rotation	472
	17.2 Installing a SCSI Tape Drive	472
	17.3 Running Windows NT Backup	474
	17.4 Running Scheduled Jobs	481
	17.5 Testing	484
	17.6 Ongoing Management	484

CHAPTER 18	**Security**	**487**
	18.1 Internet Security Risks	487
	18.2 Motives for Attack	488
	18.3 Methods of Attack	489
	18.4 Dangerous Applications	490
	18.4.1 FTP	490
	18.4.2 TFTP	492
	18.4.3 Telnet	492
	18.4.4 X Window System	492
	18.4.5 Finger	493
	18.5 Establishing a Security Policy and Stance	493
	18.6 Types of Prevention	494
	18.6.1 Network-Level Security Protection	494
	18.6.2 Host-Level Security Protection	498
	18.6.2.1 Avoid Risky or Unneeded Protocols and Services	499
	18.6.2.2 Don't Advertise Services, Computer Names, or User Names	499
	18.6.2.3 Tighten User Account Security	500
	18.6.2.4 Protect Privileged Accounts	500
	18.6.2.5 Enforce File System Security	501
	18.6.2.6 Close Back Doors to System Process Authority	501
	18.6.3 Digital Envelopes and Signatures	502
	18.6.3.1 Encryption and Decryption	502
	18.6.3.2 Digital Signatures	502
	18.6.3.3 Obtaining and Using Digital Certificates	503
	18.6.3.4 Securing Internet Mail	506
	18.6.3.5 Securing HTTP Transactions	508

18.7 Secure Electronic Commerce 509
18.8 Configuring Secure Web Page Delivery 511
    18.8.1 Securing Pages with Netscape Servers 512
    18.8.2 Securing Pages with WebSite 516
    18.8.3 Securing Pages with Internet Information Server 518
18.9 Log File Management 519
18.10 Viruses 521
18.11 Backups 521
18.12 The Maginot Line 522

CHAPTER 19   **System Management Principles**   **523**

19.1 Environmental Management 523
19.2 Technical Management 524
    19.2.1 Performance Monitoring 525
        19.2.1.1 Windows NT Performance Monitor 525
        19.2.1.2 SNMP Management Systems 527
        19.2.1.3 Protocol Analyzers 530
    19.2.2 Event Logging 535
    19.2.3 Capacity Planning 537
    19.2.4 Adding Computers 538
19.3 Procedural Management 539
    19.3.1 Routine Procedures 539
    19.3.2 Change Control 539
19.4 Content Management 540
19.5 Saws and Axioms 541

CHAPTER 20   **Supporting Your Users**   **547**

20.1 Start-Up Documentation and Procedures 547
20.2 Reference Documentation and FAQs 548
20.3 Setting Expectations 549
20.4 Good Surfing 550

APPENDICES

A Supplier List 551
B HTML Fundamentals, Structure, and Syntax 561
C Achieving Fame and Glory 567
    C.1 Developing Attractive Services and Image 567
    C.2 Getting Listed on Internet Search Engines 568
    C.3 Getting Links from Other Sites 569
    C.4 Headers, Addresses, and URLs 569
    C.5 Creating Awareness in Newsgroups 570
    C.6 Monitoring Activity and Feedback 570

D Legal Issues   571
   D.1 Legal Status—Service Provider or Publisher?   571
   D.2 Private versus Public Sites   572
   D.3 Location Issues   572
   D.4 Types of Objectionable Materials   573
   D.5 Copyrights and Patents   573
   D.6 Guardianship of Client Data   574
   D.7 Limits of Liability   575
E About the CD-ROM   577

BIBLIOGRAPHY AND REFERENCES   **579**

GLOSSARY   **581**

INDEX   **597**

Preface

For me, the Internet began on a Saturday afternoon in September 1994. The prior evening I'd purchased a copy of *Microsoft Systems Journal* and read an article by J. Allard and Steven Sinofsky titled "Getting Wired into the Internet: A Crash Course on FTP, Gopher, Web, and More." For the first time, I found information that was neither all hype nor knee deep in UNIX. (UNIX is a fine operating system, as Greek is a fine language. Nevertheless, I choose to avoid dealing with either of them.)

Armed with locations from the article, I dialed into the office, Telnetted to a UNIX workstation, and opened FTP sessions to Scotland, North Carolina, Illinois, Indiana, Minnesota, and Hong Kong. You can probably guess the sites. A few hours later, I'd downloaded the files from the Internet to the UNIX workstation, then from the workstation to my home PC. I had no servers to connect to, but I found I could open Web pages from my local file system. Within a few more hours, I'd bashed one of the sample pages into a personal home page. Creating more pages was easy with a Word for Windows template I got from Chinese University of Hong Kong.

As a Windows NT LAN administrator, I was pleased to discover the freeware EMWAC Web server and had it running within a few weeks. It became the perfect way for PC users to publish internal company information in a paperless way accessible from both PCs and UNIX, our primary platforms.

The global Internet hype continued, not just in the computer press, but everywhere. Almost overnight, tech support BBSs became passé and Web sites took over. Companies everywhere put up firewalls and provided employees with ready access to outside information; so did we. Network addresses started appearing on billboards, in general print ads, on the radio, and at sporting events. Network addresses! Who ever thought we'd see a network address advertised at the Super Bowl or the NBA finals?

By early 1995, I'd decided that within a few years no one could be a credible computer networking professional unless he or she had intimate knowledge of the Web, its protocols, and its applications. I got a PPP account and started lurking on newsgroups. After a while, I found the courage to post a few answers I was certain about; then I noticed that questions and products discussed one week would be questions and discussions again just a few weeks later. I also got tired of people saying Windows NT couldn't do this or that when others had discussed actually doing it just a few weeks earlier. So, I started my Windows NT Web Server Tools page, kept posting to newsgroups, and eventually got listed in *LAN Times* and *PC Week*. That's also how my editor, Kim Fryer, discovered me and how I came to write this book. Who says you can't make money on the Internet?

I was wrong about every networking professional needing Web expertise within a few years, though. It happened in a few months.

Who This Book Is For

Of course, this book is for anyone wishing to provide one or more Internet services using Windows NT. This is also a good book to read if you're not sure what operating system you want to run; it'll give you a peek at how things look from a Windows NT point of view and provide some valuable knowledge and techniques along the way. Finally, it's for anyone who just wants a better understanding of how Internet services work from a server and wire point of view.

Some segments with an interest in this book include

- Entrepreneurs seeking to become profitable Internet Service Providers (ISPs). This is currently practical but may become less so as large competitors gain market share and the cost of end-user bandwidth drops. However, small ISPs can derive considerable income from services such as installing dedicated Web sites for others and creating Web pages. These are likely to remain locally provided services, not taken over by large Internet access providers.

- Hobbyists who want a presence on the Web—one they operate themselves. Internet services have so many advantages that many dial-up BBSs are closing or becoming Web sites.

- Corporate Web sites placed on he Internet to promote the company's image, distribute advertising, provide automated technical support, solicit job applicants, and so on.

- Commercial sites (those directly implementing commerce on the Web). For example, various publishers and booksellers have established Web sites that allow users to search for books by title, author, subject, date, and so on, and order them on-line. Any industry or business that uses direct marketing is a candidate for this type of site.

- Intranets serving users on a private network. Many companies find this very useful for disseminating corporate information such as policy and procedure, organization charts, project write-ups, and hints and tips for computer users. Increasingly, Internet technology is an easier and more cost-effective approach to document distribution and groupware than products like Lotus Notes.

Organization and Approach

Information in this book appears in the order you would use it when building a site. Chapters 1 and 2 provide an overview of the major Internet services and reasons for implementing them on Windows NT. Chapter 3 offers suggestions in formulating an attainable mission and business plan before committing physical resources. Chapter 4 discusses hardware requirements, including features that make server hardware different from single-user workstations.

Chapters 5 and 6 review TCP/IP and communication lines, respectively. Chapter 7 deals with installing Windows NT, particularly the TCP/IP and Internet-related elements. Chapter 8 presents DHCP and WINS, two Windows NT facilities that automate administration of TCP/IP addresses on local networks. This chapter will be of particular interest to sites adding or expanding a TCP/IP "Intranet."

Chapters 9 through 15 discuss the most commonly demanded Windows NT Internet services: DNS, FTP, Gopher, Mail, list servers, News, and, of course, HTTP (the server that creates the World Wide Web). These chapters consist of two main parts: theory and practice. The first part describes generally how the service operates and what it expects of both the client and the server. The second part provides an installation overview using one or more products as case studies. There are two reasons for this approach:

1. Given the time required to write, edit, print, and distribute a book of this type, it's likely that every product discussed will be obsolete or superseded before you have a chance to read about it.

2. Even if obsolescence weren't a factor, you are much better off knowing how an application like Internet E-Mail works than you are knowing precisely how to configure one version of one product. Given "big picture" understanding and a manual, you can get any such product working in short order.

Chapter 16 describes a number of advanced World Wide Web techniques: clickable image maps, CGI programs, Server Side Includes, Java, JavaScript, database interfaces, and more. Coverage of these complex topics is necessarily brief yet imparts a firm sense of the concepts involved and helps decide which to investigate further. The chapter includes working examples that appear on the accompanying CD.

Chapters 17 through 20 are the homestretch and cover backup, security, system management, and user support. In short, they explain, after you get your site running, how to keep it that way.

This book isn't a software comparison or review; magazines, with their shorter publication cycles, are much better at that. The products all appeared serviceable, but so do many others; reasons for choosing a specific one often included accidents of timing and which products gave the best screenshots. There are no endorsements here, except for Windows NT.

When possible, I've included sample, demo, shareware, or freeware copies of software on the CD. This is for your convenience, but, by the time you read this, newer versions will likely be available on the net. Please read the license terms for each product carefully; there are no licenses bundled with purchase of the book.

I've made every effort to provide simple, concise explanations and meaningful examples. If a concept eludes you, try running the examples on your own system. When you get them working, modify, break, and fix them. The light bulb *will* come on; trust me on this.

Acknowledgments

First, thanks go to my family: my wife, Connie; my son, Justin; and my daughters, Lorrill and Lynessa. I love you all and sincerely appreciate your giving me time to finish this project. And yes, now I'll have time to fix the faucet, clean up the yard, and take down the Christmas lights.

Many thanks also go to my Mom and Dad, Marcella and Harold. Thank you both for a lifetime of love, support, and guidance. I think of you often, Mom, and you too, Dad. Ruth, thanks to you, too. And yes, now I'll have time to call more often and maybe even visit.

I thank my boss, Russ Becker, as well. Thanks, Russ, for understanding my occasional distractions and absences. Tell Ron Henry I appreciate his patience, too. And yes, now I'll have time to finish those projects you wanted and fix those glitches.

To my coworkers I apologize for always being in a rush and for occasionally being preoccupied when they stop in my office. This includes Corey Bodzin, Leah Gruenert, Linda Foster, Diane Higgs, Perry Mumme, Dave Seeman, Brian Thiel, Eve Smith, Jay Wilson, Cindy Baca, Alena George, Brian Jantz, Valli Leonard-Barnes, Sherry Roark, Dale Wolf, Curtis Overall, Franco Farina, Tom Shults, Bob Bosart, Juanita Holley, Bob Rusden, Phil Kaiser, Brad Kidd, Dave Lubeck, Steve

Parish, Dave Dale, Mark Rowland, Steve Spaulding, Mike Thomas, Jeff Simpson, and many others. Thanks also, folks, for your help, advice, and understanding along the way. I apologize for the bad jokes and war stories. Diane, be sure and say hello to John for me. And yes, now I'll have time to investigate those problems you brought me and I threw onto the backlog.

Thanks to the many people who assisted in granting permission to include screenshots, product information, and software. This includes Louise Rohde Bernardi, Jeff Coffler, Jeannine Cook, Brian Dorricott, Lisa Gaudet, Roger C. Greene, Edward Halsted, Elena Hammond, Taz Higgins, Brian Kendig, Jim Laurel, Donald LaMure, Christina Lessing, Nikki Locke, Bob McGonigle, Pedro Mendes, Jason Morse, Chris P. at Netwin Support, John Pearson, Eli Shapira, Scott Schoonhoven, and Kevin Thau. And yes, now I'll have time to look more deeply into your products.

Last but certainly not least, I thank my editor, Kim Fryer, who discovered me and walked (nay, ran) me through the process of creating this book. Thanks Kim; it never would have happened without you. And yes, now I'll have time to work on those proposals you wanted.

Contacting the Author

My E-Mail address is buyensj@primenet.com. Feel free to write but please understand I can't provide technical support for products, even those I mention in the chapters. Likewise, my resources for investigating specific problems and issues are quite limited. I'm interested in any errors or omissions you may find here, though, and will appreciate suggestions regarding the contents of a future edition.

To the best of my knowledge, there is no interlakken.com—at least not at the time of this writing. I invented interlakken.com for purposes of example and verified there was no match at InterNIC or Lycos. Don't look for such a site on the Internet or try to send mail there.

You can browse my personal Web page at www.primenet.com/~buyensj or my company's page at www.agcs.com. You can also search for me or this book on Addison-Wesley's Web site, www.aw.com.

Good luck with your project. You've chosen a great operating system as its foundation.

About the Author

Jim Buyens is the senior PC-LAN administrator for AG Communication Systems, a leading provider of telephone switching equipment and software. An early champion of TCP/IP connectivity, he designed a coast-to-coast corporate network that includes 25 Windows NT servers and over 1,000 client PCs. He was an early champion of World Wide Web applications for internal use and now manages a corporate Web site at www.agcs.com.

Mr. Buyens achieved a Bachelor of Science degree in Computer Science at Purdue University in 1971 and a Master of Business Administration at Arizona State University in 1992.

CHAPTER 1

Internet Applications and Support Services

As demand for the World Wide Web (WWW) has grown, so has the desire to provide Web services. This is more complex than might at first appear because the Web consists not of a single service but of a collection of many. Table 1.1 lists services Web users can directly invoke using Uniform Resource Locators (URLs) and a Web browser such as Netscape or Mosaic.

A full-service Web site may need to support all these applications, plus a variety of support functions such as DNS (Domain Name Service), IP routing, dial-in, user account management, billing, backup, and performance monitoring and tuning. The primary objective of this book is to help you understand, install, and manage such services.

Whether you're building a new site, expanding an existing one, or just keeping a site running, you need a clear understanding of your site's mission and how the services you provide support it. This book's second objective, no less worthy than the first, is to help you understand how each service might benefit your users or your customers.

1.1 Application Services

This section provides an introduction to services end users interact with directly. In contrast to support services, which appear in Section 1.2, application services support clients that present front-end interfaces directly to the end user. In short, application services provide the functionality users see.

1.1.1 World Wide Web (HTTP)

The Web has risen past the status of a computer program; it's now a worldwide phenomenon. By most accounts, it has become the most prevalent application on the Internet. It's amazing that this has occurred for a program with only three basic functions:

Table 1.1 Uniform Resource Locator Service Identifiers

Identifier	Description
ftp	File Transfer Protocol
http	HyperText Transfer Protocol
gopher	Gopher protocol
mailto	Electronic Mail
news, nntp	USENET News
telnet	Interactive terminal sessions
wais	Wide Area Information Server

1. A highly constrained text formatter.

2. A bitmap viewer supporting two formats, with the preferred one being under patent dispute.

3. A simple mechanism whereby the cryptic address of a page can be associated with hot text on another page.

The result is something like Figure 1.1.

The Web is truly an application whose strength is simplicity. It is patently easy to use: Just point and click. It is platform independent. Its lack of security and chargeback mechanisms means users can traverse the Web at will. Its lack of authoring features, which many find constraining, at least keeps authoring simple. Finally, delivering Web pages is simple and is not hardware intensive; one Web site (www.microsoft.com) reports satisfying 500,000 Web page requests a day using one (hefty) Windows NT PC.

Web browsing is a fairly simple client-server application. The client generally provides a single front-end and is called a *Web browser*. Netscape Navigator, Microsoft Internet Explorer, and NCSA Mosaic are the most common browsers. The client asks a server for a page by giving the page's file name and directory path. The server transmits the named page from its file system to the client and determines all fonts, colors, and page layout. If there are pictures on the page, the server transmits their location to the client, and the client downloads the images when it's ready to display them.

The World Wide Web is a rather nebulous thing—a large, very loose collection of clients, networks, applications, and servers. Servers are categorized by the specific application they support. Thus, the server application that distributes Web pages is generally called an *HTTP server*, not a Web server, because "Web server" isn't a specific term.

HyperText Transfer Protocol (HTTP) is the set of rules that describe how clients and servers on the Web interact. Web pages are published in HyperText Markup Language (HTML) format.

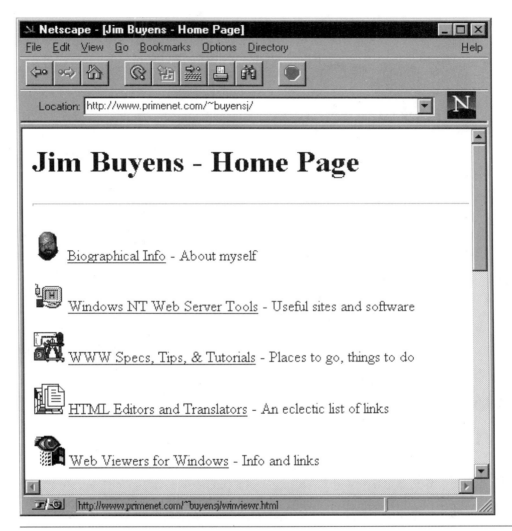

Figure 1.1 A Random Page from the World Wide Web

The Web has experienced tremendous growth on the Internet; virtually all large companies, educational institutions, government agencies, and professional organizations now have pages. Web publishing can be an outstanding, cost-effective way to distribute public information about an enterprise—informaton such as company background, annual reports, announcements, contact lists, sales and product information, and technical support.

Many organizations are also setting up HTTP servers on internal networks not accessible to outside users. This is a great way to distribute company policy, organization charts, phone lists, service directories, even computer support tips and techniques.

1.1.2 CGI and SSI

The Common Gateway Interface (CGI) allows a Web browser to invoke programs on the server by specifying the name of an executable program rather than the name of an HTML file. The executable performs application-specific processing and writes HTML for response to the remote user.

CGI works very well with the "forms" feature of HTML, which allows clients to enter data on a Web page using standard dialog elements. This supports a wide range of applications in addition to simple page publishing—applications such as database query, data entry, form submission, and remote device control.

The Server Side Include (SSI) feature also involves programs running on the server, but SSIs are triggered as HTML is sent to the user. When the HTTP server detects an SSI command in outgoing HTML, it suspends the transmission and runs the program specified by the SSI command. The SSI program sends its output to the remote client, and then transmission of the original page resumes. Server Side Includes are handy for jobs like updating and transmitting "hit" counters, "most popular" lists, server statistics, and other variable data that don't require input from the client.

1.1.3 WAIS and Other Search Engines

Text lookup is a very common CGI application. The query universe may be a collection of text articles, all Web pages at a particular site, or all pages on the entire Web. Users typically enter keywords and other lookup codes on a form, click a "submit" button to get a list of matching documents, and then select listed documents for viewing.

Systems that index files on the local file system are the easiest to develop because no network programming knowledge is required. WAIS (Wide Area Information Server) is one such system. WAIS was designed as an independent client-server application but is now generally invoked through a Web browser. An indexing program scans files in the local file system at scheduled times; this index is then used to satisfy user queries. There are two freeware versions of WAIS and one commercial version.

Search engines such as WebCrawler and the World Wide Web Worm (WWWW) index Web pages obtained via the Internet rather than a local file system. This is an excellent approach because location independence is a key precept of the Web; a user shouldn't be required to know what server something is on in order to find it. Also, such systems are self-maintaining to the extent that examining HTML links on one server generally reveals links to other servers; examining those servers reveals links to still more, and so on.

Another search engine category includes document management systems enhanced with HTTP server functions. Such systems are typically designed to operate independently of the Web and then are enhanced with optional HTTP-based front-ends.

1.1.4 FTP

File Transfer Protocol (FTP) is one of the oldest and most popular Internet applications. All it does is copy files from one computer to another, but it does so very well and in more environments than any other approach. FTP is the primary means used to distribute software, graphics, and other electronic documents around the Internet.

FTP originally had a cryptic command-line interface borrowed heavily from UNIX. More recently, numerous Graphical User Interface (GUI) front-ends have appeared, making FTP easier for mortals to use. Browsers such as Netscape Navigation and Mosaic can perform FTP downloads to the client.

1.1.5 Archie

The Archie, Gopher, and Veronica applications were much talked about before emergence of the Web. Now, they're generally in decline.

Archie maintains a database of file names located on any number of FTP sites. These are typically "archive" sites containing libraries of public files—hence, the name *Archie*. If a user doesn't know which archive site contains a needed file, an Archie search may be capable of finding one.

Searches in Archie are exclusively by file name, never by keyword, application type, or description. This, together with extremely slow search times, has impeded widespread use of Archie. Web services such as Yahoo, Lycos, and Virtual Software Library have almost completely replaced it.

1.1.6 Gopher

Gopher is a distributed document search and retrieval system. It allows users to browse, search, and retrieve documents residing on any number of servers.

Gopher was developed at the University of Minnesota, whose athletic teams are known as "The Gophers." There appears to be no other logic to the name *Gopher*, except perhaps that it "goes for" files.

The Gopher protocol and software follow a client-server model. The server provides menus and transmits files, while the client provides display services and receives files sent by the server. Stand-alone Gopher clients are still available, as are character-mode clients you can Telnet to, but Web browsers are now the most common Gopher clients. Figure 1.2 shows a typical Gopher menu displayed by Netscape; Figure 1.3 shows the same menu displayed by HGOPHER, a public domain Gopher client.

Each line in a Gopher menu is a selectable item representing a file, a command, or another menu. There's no requirement or convention that menu items point to objects on the same server; in fact, jumping from one system to another is quite transparent and common. The sum of all Gopher information everywhere is frequently called *Gopherspace*.

Gopher presaged the Web in its transparent access to multiple systems and its ability to describe and index files and documents prior to delivering them.

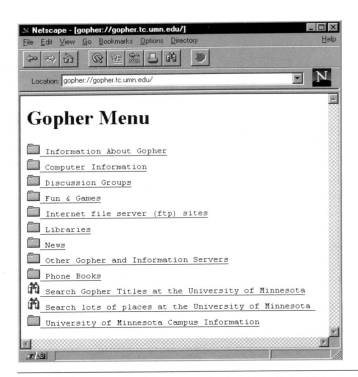

Figure 1.2 University of Minnesota Gopher Menu Using Netscape

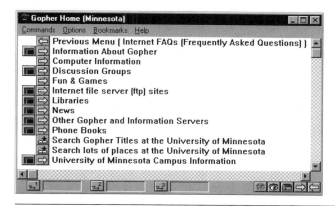

Figure 1.3 University of Minnesota Gopher Menu Using HGOPHER

Descriptions are limited to one line, however, and there's a sharp distinction between menus and documents. Most new development is happening with Web pages, not Gopher, but the existing Gopherspace remains alive and kicking.

1.1.7 Veronica

Veronica is reportedly an acronym for Very Easy Rodent-Oriented Netwide Index to Computerized Archives (Liu et al. 1994). As Archie indexes FTP sites, Veronica indexes Gopherspace. Figure 1.4 shows a typical Veronica query; Figure 1.5 shows the result.

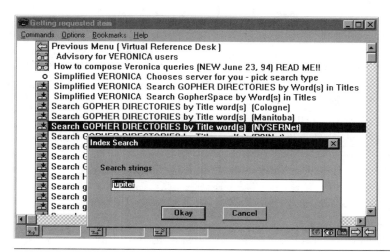

Figure 1.4 Initiating a Veronica Search

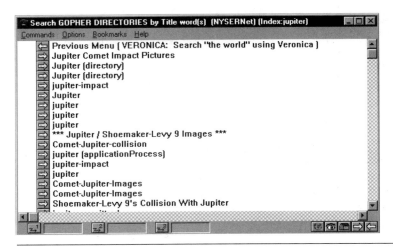

Figure 1.5 Result of a Veronica Search

Veronica servers are large and few. These servers periodically download the index of all the Gopher servers they know of and then run a Jughead program (what else?) to form a master index. This process also detects new servers referenced in the indexes of known servers. *Jughead* supposedly stands for Jonzy's Universal Gopher Hierarchy Excavation And Display (Liu et al. 1994).

A program called *Maltshop* retrieves a list of known servers from an authoritative site, checks them for availability, and automatically creates Gopher pointers to the active ones.

Amazingly, there seem to be no programs called Reggie, Betty, or Grundy.

1.1.8 E-Mail

Electronic Mail is another Internet application experiencing rapid and continuous growth. E-Mail is fast, reliable, cheap, effective, and worldwide; using it can be a transforming experience. See Figure 1.6.

E-Mail, as used on the Internet, is a distributed client-server application based on two protocols: Simple Mail Transfer Protocol (SMTP)and Post Office Protocol (POP). Clients use SMTP for sending mail and POP for receiving it. Servers support these client functions and also use SMTP for exchanging mail among themselves via the Internet. Servers may also exchange mail via dial-up modem using UNIX-to-UNIX Communication Protocol (UUCP).

Internet E-Mail addresses such as president@whitehouse.gov consist of two parts: a local part (which precedes the "@") and a domain part (which follows it). When a server receives mail addressed (via the domain part) to another server, it uses one of several methods to forward the message at least one step closer to that server.

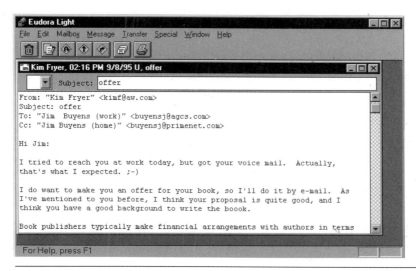

Figure 1.6 An E-Mail Message (Using Eudora Light[1])

Messages consist of two parts: a mail envelope and envelope contents. The mail envelope contains the addresses processed by the Message Transfer Agent (MTA) and is never seen by the user. The second part of the message, the envelope contents, also consists of two parts: the header and the body. The header contains the original sending and receiving addresses, the subject, the date and time sent, and so on. The body contains the actual message, but this too may be subdivided if attachments accompany the message.

SMTP/POP E-Mail shares only high-level resemblance to mail systems such as X.400, Microsoft Mail, and cc:Mail. A gateway must be used to connect these "foreign" mail systems to the Internet.

1.1.9 List Servers

E-Mail MTAs use a powerful feature called *aliasing* to translate the local part of addresses. This converts generic addresses like postmaster@domain.com and admin@domain.com to the actual address of the current postmaster or administrator. Aliases can also support simple mailing lists by translating one address into several addresses.

[1]Eudora Light is a trademark of QUALCOMM Incorporated.

Some mailing lists, however, are too large and volatile to be handled as aliases; they may contain thousands of recipients and require dozens or hundreds of changes daily. A *list server* handles such lists easily.

A list server is essentially a robot mail handler. When it receives mail addressed to one of its lists, it remails the body portion to all current list recipients. Users can typically add themselves to a list by sending the list server a message with "subscribe *listname*" as the subject or first body line. The list server reads the sender's address out of the message header and adds it to the specified mailing list. Unsubscribing is just as easy; users simply send mail stating "unsubscribe *listname*."

1.1.10 News

USENET News is a distributed, replicated, discussion group system. If the word *News* in the name of this service makes you imagine an electronic newspaper or newsletter, you're in for quite a shock.

News is organized roughly by topic into thousands of *newsgroups*. The newsgroup comp.infosystems.www.servers.ms-windows, for example, is probably of interest to readers of this book. Thousands of news servers around the world carry this newsgroup. Anyone with access to one of these servers can post an article to comp.infosystems.www.servers.ms-windows. The news protocol then replicates the article to all other news servers carrying that newsgroup. All users of those servers may then read it—at least all users who monitor that newsgroup.

News software run by end users is generally called a *newsreader* despite the fact that such software not only reads news but also posts articles and sends mail.

News servers exchange articles using the Network News Transfer Protocol (NNTP). Newsreaders also use a form of NNTP to obtain articles from the local news server and to post articles; this form of NNTP is the Network News Reader Protocol (NNRP).

Within newsgroups, articles are members of "threads." A thread begins with a new posting and includes all replies made to it, all replies made to those replies, and so forth. The news server typically stores the threading information in a "news overview" (or "nov") database. Newsreaders can retrieve threading information for a given range of articles using an "xover" command; however, this is typically something the newsreader does automatically and is not a command the user must issue.

The great thing about USENET News is that you can post a question or an opinion about any topic and get responses from all over the world. Unfortunately, responses to dumb questions and inflammatory opinions may be quite derogatory. The best approach is to start out as a *lurker*—that is, a read-only user. Once you're comfortable with the tone and level of expertise expected, try a few non-controversial postings. The response will likely be a pleasant surprise.

1.2 Support Services

Support services provide functions used by other services. This could include almost any system-level service running on the same machine as (or available via the net to) an application service.

1.2.1 DNS

A four-byte hexadecimal Internet Protocol (IP) address identifies each computer on the Internet. Each byte of an IP address is typically referred to by its decimal equivalent. For example, 192.207.117.2 is the IP address for Addison-Wesley Publishing Group's World Wide Web server. Whatever interest this site may hold, 192.207.117.2 is nearly impossible to guess and certainly hard to remember. The name www.aw.com is far easier to deal with. A service is obviously required to translate mnemonic names to IP addresses, and this is why the Domain Name System (DNS) exists.

DNS names are hierarchical, starting from the right, with periods separating each level. DNS servers, which perform the actual name-to-IP-address translation, are similarly hierarchical.

Each country is responsible for defining its own hierarchy. The United States uses organizational top-level domains, and the rest of the world uses geographical ones, as Tables 1.2 and 1.3 illustrate.

The .us geographical code is rare; when used, it's usually preceded by the two-letter state postal abbreviation. Many other countries precede the country code with an organization code; some use two-byte codes such as .co for commercial and .ac for academic. Table 1.4 gives examples of some DNS names.

Table 1.2 United States Top-Level Domains

Domain	Description
com	Commercial
edu	Educational
gov	Government
mil	Military
net	Network support
org	Other, such as professional and nonprofit

Table 1.3   Selected International Top-Level Domains

Domain	Description
au	Australia
ca	Canada
de	Germany (Deutschland)
jp	Japan
nl	Netherlands
uk	United Kingdom
us	United States

Each country is responsible for establishing its own domain registration entity. In the United States, this is the Internet Network Information Center (InterNIC) at http://ds.internic.net/.

When you apply for a domain name, you must provide the address of two DNS servers that will support it. InterNIC provides pointers to your DNS servers, and your DNS servers provide pointers to your computers. In the simplest case, InterNIC's .com DNS server would identify the DNS server for aw.com, and the DNS server for aw.com would supply the specific address for www.aw.com.

If you expect to have only a few computers in your domain, it'll probably be cheapest and easiest to pay a commercial provider to handle your listings. Sites with more than a few listings usually prefer to run their own DNS. The same is true of private networks since they are beyond the reach of public DNS providers and, in any case, don't want their computers identified to the world.

1.2.2 Network Security

Every element of society uses the Internet. So, just as in society, there are lots of good, honest people on the Internet, a few who like making trouble, and a few

Table 1.4   Selected International DNS Computer Names

Location	Host and Domain Name	Description
Australia	toolshed.artschool.utas.edu.au	Tasmanian School of Art, Hobart, Tasmania
Canada	www.corel.ca	Corel Corporation
China	www.bta.net.cn	ChinaNet
England	www.nmsi.ac.uk	Science Museum, London
Jamaica	www.uwimona.edu.jm	University of the West Indies, Mona
Japan	www.hitachi.co.jp	Hitachi Group
Russia	sunsite.cs.msu.su	SunSITE Multimedia Information Service, Moscow State University
Scotland	www.arts.gla.ac.uk	University of Glasgow, Faculty of Arts
USA	www.odci.gov	Central Intelligence Agency
USA	www.state.az.us	State of Arizona

more willing to rob you for their own gain or someone else's. Some have activities or beliefs that may revolt you, and your mission may not appeal to them.

Given these divisions, no matter what the mission of your site, you'll probably wish to keep some people out. Network security is your first line of defense. If intruders can't get to your network, they can't get to your computers.

Many sites achieve network security simply by not connecting to any outside networks. It's easy to develop a false sense of security in such an environment, ignoring the fact that information going to and from the Internet may simply be traveling the first few miles on diskette. Nevertheless, if you have no external network connections and no internal network security concerns, you don't need network security devices.

The first level of network security is typically encryption. Sometimes, only passwords and other highly secure data are encrypted; sometimes, whole packets. The objective is to prevent snoopers with network analyzers from "wiretapping" network traffic and learning something they shouldn't. Encryption can also verify that transmissions are originating from the proper source; anyone else would lack the proper encryption keys and produce packets that decode to garbage.

Another common security precaution is router configuration. If a router controls entry to your network, you can configure it to block certain kinds of traffic. You may decide, for example, that only SMTP mail traffic may pass or that only connections to certain hosts will be allowed.

Unfortunately, a simple router can't implement some kinds of network security. A common requirement, for example, is to allow internal users access to outside FTP sites but not allow outside FTP users to access internal machines. Unfortunately, FTP involves two sessions: one from the client to the server and one from the server back to the client. If the router blocks connections from the server back to the client, FTP doesn't work. If the router passes such connections, it passes connections from outside FTP clients as well. A *firewall* is the solution to this dilemma.

A firewall is typically a computer with physical connections to both an outside (untrusted) network and an internal (trusted) one. The firewall computer acts as an agent (or "proxy") of the authorized internal computer so that outside machines need only interact with the firewall.

The security you require depends on the nature of your site and the information it contains. This is a value judgment only you or your site management can make, but once security decisions are made, you must be sure they're implemented properly and tested regularly.

1.2.3 User Login Security

Another important security measure is requiring user names and passwords to access secured systems. Your operating systems should provide secure password systems, meaning ones that can't be broken into, and should support minimum password length, forced password changes, and passwords known only to the user.

Passwords usable on more than one system are popular with users because multiple passwords are hard to remember and troublesome to enter. Then again, having one key to everything can lead to a major intrusion if that key is broken. The number of password challenges your users should encounter is another value judgment you'll have to make.

1.2.4 File System Security

The innermost level of security is typically at the file system level. One user should certainly not be capable of accessing files belonging to another—at least not without special permission. File areas owned by a small group of people should be accessible only by that group. System areas should be off limits to everyone but system administrators. These requirements virtually mandate an operating system that provides robust user- and group-level security built into the file system.

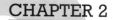

CHAPTER 2

Why Use Windows NT?

For computer operating systems to arouse passion once seemed absurd. Now, it's commonplace. Whether this is progress, a reflection of our society, or a product of human nature, no one can say. The fact remains that choice of O/S has become a deeply ingrained personal value.

This chapter reviews predominant operating systems for suitability in providing Internet services. This isn't a personal attack on anyone; the Internet is based on open systems, and there's enough room for everyone. However, as you might surmise from the title of this book, Windows NT is going to fare rather well.

2.1 Weaknesses of Other Operating Systems

2.1.1 UNIX

UNIX is the predominant operating system currently used to provide Internet services. In fact, virtually all of today's Internet services were developed with UNIX servers exclusively in mind. UNIX-based services are full-featured, mature, stable, and often free. UNIX has excellent multitasking, acceptable file system security, and full remote administration.

Unfortunately, much of UNIX is arcane, character based, and difficult to learn. UNIX demands for hardware are considerable, and that hardware tends to cost much more than comparable PC equipment. Depending on whose numbers you consult, unit sales of UNIX machines hover around 1 or 2 percent of PC unit sales.

Although many kinds of PC-to-UNIX integration are possible, none are as seamless and easy to use as a PC-LAN file server.

2.1.2 OS/2

OS/2 is a powerful 32-bit operating system with an advanced file system and excellent multitasking. Sadly, IBM has shackled it with poor marketing and positioning throughout its life. OS/2's poor market share and lack of application software are now a well-known vicious circle.

Despite assurances from IBM, OS/2's future seems uncertain. The combination of low unit sales and low prices cannot have produced large profits for IBM, if any. Even if IBM succeeds in a timely port of OS/2 to PowerPC, it isn't clear this combination will yield compelling price/performance compared to either Windows 95 or Windows NT. Application vendors are more likely to port to Windows NT on PowerPC than to OS/2 on the same platform.

Many observers predict that the Next Big Thing on the Web will involve much more intelligence on the server. Whether this involves advanced presentation of documents, object distribution, animation, database processing, or multiuser interactive games makes no difference; any one of them requires specialized server software that, like all other software, is less likely to be available on OS/2 than on other platforms.

2.1.3 Netware

Novell Netware, as an Internet server, is operating far from its traditional strength in file and print services. Novell's support for TCP/IP has been mixed and its ownership of UNIX unworkable.

Netware is generally viewed as a weak application server. Internet services require strong application server support and almost nothing in the way of file and print services.

The thought of a Netware server running half a dozen or more NLMs (Netware Loadable Modules) for HTTP, FTP, Mail, News, DNS, Gopher, and so on, isn't particularly attractive. Neither is the image of the same machine also running a database server and various user-written CGI and SSI processes.

Netware supporters may strongly disagree, but Novell apparently sold its strategic Internet service platform when it sold UNIX.

2.1.4 Client Operating Systems (Windows 3.1, Windows 95, Macintosh)

Many users wishing to join the Web, rather than just watch it, start out trying to use their existing PC and operating system as a server. After all, this is the platform they already have and (presumably) understand. It's already networked—at least well enough to function as a client.

Setting up one or two services on a single-user computer can be an excellent and enjoyable learning experience, but these platforms simply don't scale well. Multitasking and security features are limited. Management of background services is weak. If service is to be continuous, the user can never turn off or reboot the machine. Every time a network user requests services, the local user may experience a performance hit.

In short, the typical Mac or PC user attempting to provide Internet services will almost certainly run into performance bottlenecks before long. The solution is to migrate toward a more robust server.

2.1.5 Mainframe and Minicomputer O/Ss

Mainframe and minicomputer operating systems such as MVS, VM, OS/400, and VMS are unlikely platforms for general-purpose Internet servers because of cost. They are also quite difficult to use; becoming a system administrator requires years of education and experience.

An interesting counter theory is that Web browsers signify a return to relatively unintelligent, low-bandwidth clients—terminals—and more powerful hosts.

2.2 Strengths of Windows NT

UNIX has considerable head start and momentum as an Internet server. However, UNIX is unfamiliar and hard to learn for the majority of computer users, hobbyists, and local network specialists. In going from Windows 3.1 or Windows 95 to Windows NT, there is simply less to learn than in going to UNIX. As construction of Internet application servers expands beyond the existing milieu of UNIX expertise, an increasing percentage of implementors is likely to choose Windows NT.

2.2.1 Microkernel Architecture

An operating system *microkernel* is a very small, highly tuned core module that provides elementary services such as setting and releasing locks; responding to timer events, device events, and lock changes; and scheduling threads. Functions provided by a microkernel are rather abstract, being decomposed from higher-level functions more apparent to the user.

A well-designed microkernel provides its operating system with outstanding stability and multitasking. Designing one requires extensive experience designing and tuning high-capacity operating systems—experience that Dave Cutler, Windows NT's chief designer, gained by designing the VMS operating system used on Digital Equipment Corporation's VAX.

2.2.2 Multitasking

Windows NT's microkernel architecture, 32-bit addressing, and task isolation provide robust multitasking. It can keep literally thousands of threads moving smoothly. Since Windows NT multitasks preemptively, a stuck application or task does not lock the system. Complete task isolation means that Windows NT can terminate stuck applications cleanly—that is, with all resources accounted for and reclaimed.

2.2.3 Portability

Only the Windows NT microkernel and a Hardware Abstraction Layer (HAL) use machine-dependent code; the remainder is portable C. This greatly facilitates porting Windows NT to many different platforms and processors. In fact, Windows NT runs on more CPU types than any other brand of operating system.

2.2.4 Scalability

Windows NT supports a virtual address space of 4 gigabytes of memory per process. Total available memory is this size times the number of current processes—a huge number indeed. Windows NT also supports physical RAM up to 4 gigabytes. Overcommitted memory is paged to disk, but not to worry: Windows NT accommodates drives up to 17 billion gigabytes in size. The Windows NT File System (NTFS) supports these huge volumes without the overhead of large cluster sizes.

In a multi-CPU system, symmetric multiprocessing allows any part of Windows NT (or any application) to run on any or all processors, sharing memory. This, plus Windows NT's portability, means Windows NT virtually never hits a brick wall with regard to performance; there's always a way to add more hardware and have it effectively used.

2.2.5 Reliability

Microkernel architecture, a large memory space, and full process isolation all ensure Windows NT's reliability. There is no ridiculous 640K memory limitation, no garbage left over from failed or terminated processes, no brick wall preventing more processes from being created.

The Windows NT File System is transaction oriented, meaning updates occur either completely or not at all. This eliminates file system errors such as the lost or cross-linked clusters incurred by the FAT (File Allocation Table) file system. NTFS also supports fault-tolerant disk with software disk mirroring and RAID level 5.

2.2.6 Security

Windows NT has achieved a U.S. Department of Defense C2 security rating, which is the highest security rating an operating system by itself can receive. Higher ratings involve physical access to the system, key-lock devices, and so on.[1] Secure access to files, secure logon, and comprehensive audit facilities are built intrinsically into Windows NT without back doors.

2.2.7 Familiarity

The Windows look and feel, general organization of functions, and Application Programming Interfaces (APIs) are remarkably consistent among all forms of Windows. For the tens of millions of people with Windows desktop experience, this simply makes Windows NT the easiest server operating system to learn.

Another major strength is that programmers can create Windows NT functions using widely known tools like Visual Basic and Visual C++. The millions of programmers proficient in these tools will find their skills directly transferable to Windows NT, which is again much easier than learning to write UNIX daemons, NMLs, or native OS/2 applications. If, as seems likely, the Web progresses beyond simple transmissions of HTML pages and toward presenting a unified, front-end interface to back-end processes of many kinds, ease of back-end programming will be a major concern.

Windows 95 will accelerate interest in running Windows NT at Internet access sites. The new operating system includes an outstanding dial-up networking component destined for widespread use in connecting to the Internet. Full functionality of this feature requires a Windows NT server at the dial-in site.

Make no mistake: Windows NT is a completely different operating system from Windows 3.1 or Windows 95. Given Windows NT's unique underpinnings—the microkernel, the multitasking, the security, the advanced file system, the task protection, the memory management—it shouldn't be surprising that

---

[1]Configuring Windows NT for C2 compliance requires a number of very specific settings, some of which are not in place by default. Also, because of the difficulty in achieving network security on any system, a C2-compliant Windows NT system cannot have a network adapter installed.

Windows NT's system management tools differ from those in other forms of Windows. Nevertheless, the interface, the look and feel, and the APIs remain the same.

2.3 Why Use Windows NT at an Internet Site?

Windows NT is a powerful and attractive Internet server platform. It features a robust and full-featured TCP/IP stack, powerful 32-bit multitasking, broad scalability, wide portability, certified file and logon security, high system reliability, and remote management. Furthermore, it's much easier to learn and administer than UNIX. In sites with many PCs, Windows NT can provide both Internet services and local file and print sharing.

The principal disadvantage in using Windows NT to provide Internet services is lack of mature and full-featured software. Internet services were invented on UNIX and extensively refined over the years. The same services are new to Windows NT, occasionally incomplete, harder to find, and, if recently ported from UNIX, no easier to administer. However, given the tremendous growth of the Internet and widespread desire to provide services, Windows NT products are likely to emerge and improve quickly.

2.4 What about Microsoft Windows Networking?

Microsoft designed Windows NT long before the World Wide Web's rapid ascent in popularity. HTTP didn't exist, and there was no inkling of future demand for "UNIX-style" mail, newsgroups, and so on. Windows NT was designed to be

- A PC-LAN file and print server.
- A network application server.
- A high-end user workstation.

Microsoft decided to call Windows NT's approach to networking the *Microsoft Windows Network*. That the Windows Network also works with DOS and OS/2 machines was apparently not an issue.

2.4.1 Microsoft Windows Networking

Windows Networking evolved from a high-level networking approach invented by IBM for its original PC-LAN offering. In those early days, the Network Basic Input Output System (NETBIOS) incorporated both the operating system

About Microsoft Windows Networking

Windows NT provides six means to access the network (Custer 1993):

1. **NETBIOS API.** This provides naming and name lookup service for all APIs listed here except Windows Sockets. It also provides compatibility for existing applications that directly pass streams of data over the network as NETBIOS datagrams.

2. **Win 32 Network (Wnet) API.** These routines support browsing and connections to other Microsoft Windows Network machines.

3. **Win I/O API.** Standard I/O routines support open, read, write, close, and other operations on files. These operate over the network when a Universal Naming Convention (UNC) file name (\\<server>\<sharename>\...) is used or when the file's drive letter refers to a remote machine.

4. **Win 32 named pipe and mailslot APIs.** Named pipes support one-to-one interchange of data between two processes, which may be local or remote. *Mailslots* are similar but support one-to-many and many-to-one exchanges.

5. **Remote Procedure Call (RPC) facility.** This permits subroutines and modules calling them to run, fairly transparently, on different machines. Named pipes are used for communication.

6. **Windows Sockets (Winsock) API.** Windows Sockets is based on Berkeley sockets, a standard UNIX API. Because of its compatibility with UNIX, this is a very popular API for Internet applications and services. Winsock uses the Internet-style Domain Name System for computer names and Domain Name Service (or a HOSTS file) for name lookup.

Winsock uses different computer names and a different means of name resolution than the first five approaches, and it demands the use of TCP/IP. The first five can use other protocols such as NetBEUI, IPX/SPX, and DECnet.

The disparity in standards used by Winsock and the other APIs is an unfortunate but necessary consequence of Windows NT's strong ability to function in disparate environments.

For clarity, this book will use the terms *Windows Networking, Windows Computername,* and *Windows NT Domain Name* for the first five approaches listed here. The terms *Winsock Networking, DNS Host Name,* and *DNS Domain* will be used in a socket context.

interface and a network protocol. Later, the network protocol was separated, enhanced, and given the name NETBIOS Extended User Interface (NetBEUI). The same enhancement allowed NETBIOS to work with other network protocols such as 3Com's XNS, Novell's IPX/SPX, Digital's DECnet, and the Internet's TCP/IP.

Windows NT still uses many NETBIOS functions, particularly those for naming and finding computers. These don't have much in common with Internet applications. For example,

- They don't necessarily use TCP/IP.
- They don't use the Domain Name System to name computers.
- They don't use Domain Name Service to find them.

Fortunately, Internet applications running on Windows NT use a Windows Sockets API for which the preceding statements are precisely negated. For a further explanation, see the sidebar titled "About Microsoft Windows Networking."

Microsoft Windows Networking, even running over TCP/IP, isn't generally considered an Internet protocol. However, the most focused Internet Service Providers (ISPs) will likely still find uses for Windows Networking on the site's local network, and administrators with no plans for using it should at least know what it is since Windows NT's features and documentation are laced with it.

2.4.2 Windows NT File and Print Sharing

Any site with more than one Windows computer will likely be interested in sharing files and printers among them. Windows Networking provides the best and most natural way of doing this.

To make a file area or printer available on the network, the administrator of the machine owning the resource must "share" it. File Manager is generally used for sharing file areas; Print Manager, for sharing printers. Other Windows Networking users can then locate the Windows Computername in a browse list, view a list of shared file areas or printers on that machine, select, and connect.

2.4.3 Windows NT Distributed Administration

Most Windows NT administration tools are client-server applications that communicate using named pipes. In each case, the client is a front-end GUI program that displays data and accepts commands; the server is a background process on the same or another machine. Event Viewer, Performance Monitor, Server Manager, and User Manager are programs that work this way.

Internal processes use Windows Networking as well, as when several Windows NT servers in one Windows NT domain synchronize user account updates and other changes among themselves.

2.4.4 NETBIOS versus Internet Names and Name Resolution

Windows Computernames are 1 to 15 characters in length. Letters are all upper-case, and the names can't contain spaces; there are no subfields or hierarchical aspects. There are four NETBIOS name resolution methods: b-node, p-node, m-node, and h-node. For a further description, see the sidebar titled "Windows Networking NETBIOS Name Resolution Methods."

Windows Networking NETBIOS Name Resolution Methods

The four NETBIOS name resolution methods are as follows:

1. **b-node.** This name resolution method works by *broadcasting*. When booting up or otherwise starting the network, each computer broadcasts the name it plans to use. If no other computer hears the broadcasts and transmits an objection, the name is considered valid. Computers locate one another on the network by broadcasting a query for the desired name; if a computer of that name is listening, it responds and supplies its network address so that the conversation can continue without further broadcasting.

    Broadcasting was an acceptable scheme when PC-LANs were small and physically isolated, but it scales poorly. Each broadcast requires attention from each computer on the network, and, as the number of broadcasts rises, overhead becomes unacceptable. A more serious problem occurs when broadcasts aren't transmitted to all parts of the network, as typically occurs in TCP/IP networks with more than one subnet. Machines on remote subnets don't hear the broadcasts, and name resolutions fail. Conversely, duplicate name registrations may improperly succeed.

    Windows Networking uses a modified b-node scheme involving a file named LMHOSTS. This is a simple ASCII file containing a list of IP addresses and computer names. If a name to be resolved has an entry in the LMHOSTS file, the corresponding IP address from LMHOSTS is used, and broadcasting is avoided. This reduces broadcasting, but keeping LMHOSTS files updated on many computers is a daunting task.

2. **p-node.** This name resolution method operates more like Domain Name Service. Each computer is configured with the IP address of one or more NETBIOS Name Servers (NBNSs). Computers register their names with the NBNS during start-up; the NBNS then remembers the name and associated network address. Other computers can get the network address of any registered computer by sending a name query to the NBNS.

continued

Windows Internet Name Service (WINS) is an NBNS provided by Windows NT. WINS actually builds its database of computer names and IP addresses from three sources: start-up name registrations (as just described), static (preconfigured) entries loaded by an administrator, and notifications from the Dynamic Host Configuration Protocol (DHCP) service (which automatically assigns IP addresses to computers).

Note that p-node name resolution eliminates broadcasting and the problems that go with it, but the network fails if the NBNS can't be found.

3. **m-node.** This name resolution method is a mixture of b-node and p-node. Computers attempt both b-node and p-node name registration (in that order) on start-up, and both must succeed. When resolving names, computers try broadcasting first; only if that method fails do they query the NBNS. This approach has the advantage of two ways to succeed, but, like b-node, it may create too many broadcasts for a large network.

4. **h-node.** This method is the reverse of m-node. Clients contact the NBNS first and then, if necessary, revert to broadcasting.

The name resolution method used by a particular Windows Networking client depends on whether DHCP assigned its IP address and whether WINS servers appear in its TCP/IP configuration. If DHCP assigned the IP address, DHCP may have assigned a specific name resolution method as well. If no specific method is assigned, the next paragraph applies.

If DHCP didn't assign the computer's IP address (or did but didn't also assign a name resolution method), the computer will use modified b-node (LMHOSTS, then broadcasting) if no WINS server addresses are specified. If any WINS server addresses are specified, the computer will use the easy six-step procedure described in the sidebar titled "Name Resolution by WINS Clients."

By now, it should be obvious that the Windows Computername and DNS Host Name have nothing in common (unless the administrator assigns them to be the same). Furthermore, Windows NETBIOS name resolution and Domain Name Service are two very different processes. Either process can fail or succeed independent of the other; in event of failure, problem resolution for each service will be independent.

Remember: Winsock applications use Domain Name Service, and all others use NETBIOS name resolution.

Name Resolution by WINS Clients

By default, systems configured as WINS clients use h-node for name registration and a modified h-node for name resolution. The modification consists of trying the following methods in sequence until one succeeds:

1. Determine whether the desired name is the name of the local machine.
2. Review a cache of previously resolved names. Such names remain cached for 10 minutes.
3. Query the identified WINS servers.
4. Attempt to resolve the name by broadcasting.
5. Look up the name in the LMHOSTS file (if the "Use LMHOSTS" TCP/IP configuration option is checked).
6. Look up the name in the HOSTS file and then query any identified DNS servers (if "Use DNS for NETBIOS Name Resolution" is checked).

2.4.5 Workgroups and Windows NT Domains

As noted, NETBIOS doesn't have a structure or hierarchy as DNS names do. This is inconvenient in large networks; a list of active computer names simply becomes cumbersome. Microsoft therefore introduced the concept of workgroups. A Microsoft Networking *workgroup* is simply a group of computers configured with the same workgroup name. Its only purpose is grouping related computers in a list.

A Windows NT *domain* shares some aspects of a workgroup: Each computer in the domain is configured as a member, and the members are sorted and displayed together. However, computers in a Windows NT domain also share a common security system controlled by a Windows NT *server*.

2.4.6 Obtaining Windows Networking Browse Lists

The point-and-shoot concept is a key element of Graphical User Interfaces (GUIs); users expect to choose items from a list and not to type them from memory. A WINS server may appear to be an excellent source for such a list, but WINS is only present in TCP/IP environments and sometimes not even then. Therefore, Windows Networking obtains computer lists from a completely different service called a *BrowseMaster*.

When a Windows Networking computer starts its network software, it sends out a broadcast asking any local BrowseMasters to identify themselves. There should be one master BrowseMaster per workgroup or domain plus one backup BrowseMaster for every 32 computers. Workgroups or Windows NT domains having 2 to 32 computers will thus have two machines acting as BrowseMasters, those with 33 to 64 will have three, and so forth. If a computer can't locate a BrowseMaster, it will start providing the service itself. In any event, once a BrowseMaster is present, the computer starting up will register with it. That BrowseMaster then propagates information about the newly registered computer to other BrowseMasters in the same workgroup or Windows NT domain.

Since locating and registering with the BrowseMaster depend on broadcasting, there are separate BrowseMasters for each protocol having Windows Networking computers on the network. Computers running more than one protocol use the BrowseMaster for their default protocol.

A pecking order exists for determining which computer is the master BrowseMaster. Among Windows for Workgroups and Windows 95 machines, selection of the master BrowseMaster is random. However, if a Windows NT workstation discovers the existing BrowseMaster isn't running Windows NT, the Windows NT workstation will insist on becoming the BrowseMaster. This is called *forcing an election.* The computers in the workgroup are, in effect, electing a new BrowseMaster; the election is rigged so that a Windows NT machine, if present, will always win. Similarly, a Windows NT workstation can't be the BrowseMaster if a Windows NT server is present; the Windows NT server will force an election and become the master BrowseMaster.

Since locating the BrowseMaster and registering computer names are accomplished by broadcasting, problems occur when computers in the same workgroup or Windows NT domain exist on multiple TCP/IP subnets. The reason is that broadcasts on one subnet do not appear on the others. These problems are eliminated if the BrowseMaster is running Windows NT since Windows NT BrowseMasters will exchange browsing information with one another across subnets (assuming they can communicate at all—that is, via an LMHOSTS file, WINS, and so on). Windows for Workgroups and Windows 95 machines can also browse across subnets if WINS or an LMHOSTS file allows them to find a Windows NT browser on another subnet.

Amazingly, this entire scheme exists solely to produce "browse lists" of computers in dialog boxes. The BrowseMaster doesn't remember the network address of computers in its list and thus can't perform NETBIOS name resolution; this continues to operate as described in the previous section. Thus, situations occur where a user selects a computer name from a browse list and then gets a message like, "The computer name can't be found on the network." The BrowseMaster is working, but NETBIOS name resolution isn't; these are two completely different services, which also explains why computers not listed in the browse list can sometimes be contacted by hand typing their computer names.

The Windows Networking BrowseMaster service doesn't apply to Winsock applications. Domain Name Service is used instead.

2.5 Windows NT Server versus Windows NT Workstation

Two versions of Windows NT are available: Workstation and Server. Which to buy is a frequent question; Table 2.1 should provide the answer.

Both versions support 255 Windows Sockets connections and thus support an equal number of connections for HTTP, FTP, Gopher, Mail, News, and other Internet services.

Remote Access Service (RAS) which supports dial-in using modems connected directly to a Windows NT computer, supports only one user at a time on Windows NT Workstation. On Windows NT Server, RAS supports up to 255 simultaneous users. Realistically, most servers will encounter hardware bottlenecks before reaching the 255-user RAS limitation, but at least the gating factor will be hardware, not Windows NT. Note that client licenses (discussed shortly) are required for each RAS user or port.

In accordance with their intended roles, Windows NT Workstation is optimized for foreground application performance, and Windows NT Server is optimized for background task performance. However, changing Control Panel settings can largely reverse this optimization.

Table 2.1 Windows NT Workstation versus Windows NT Server

Feature	Windows NT Workstation	Windows NT Server
Sockets	255	255
Remote access users	1	255*
Process optimization	Foreground	Background
Windows Networking clients	10	Unlimited*
Provide single UADB for multiple systems	No	Yes
Membership	Workgroup or domain	Domain only

*Must purchase client license for each seat or session.

Windows NT Workstation supports up to 10 other computers at a time for LAN file and print sharing. Client licenses aren't required. Windows NT Server supports an unlimited number of such users but requires the purchase of client licenses.

Finally, if you want one set of user names and passwords used on more than one Windows NT computer, you'll need at least one Windows NT server. You can install any number of Windows NT workstations on the same network, but they'll be only a workgroup, not a Windows NT domain. Each Windows NT workstation in a workgroup has its own user database, one not shared with any of the others. A Windows NT server, by contrast, can belong only to a domain. When you install it, the only choices are to "Join an existing domain" or to "Create a new domain." An administrator can add any number of Windows NT workstations to the Windows NT server's domain and thereby permit them to use the Windows NT server's User Account Database (UADB).

There are two ways of counting the number of client licenses required: by seat or by session. For example, suppose you have 400 PCs and 5 Windows NT servers in your enterprise. If you choose to count required client licenses by seat, you need 400 licenses. If you choose to count required licenses by session, you need to set maximum sessions per server and add them up. An example follows:

Server	Maximum Sessions
1	50
2	200
3	75
4	100
5	160
Total	585

The total exceeds the number of computers on the network because some users connect to more than one server at a time. In this example, you're obviously better off buying 400 licenses than 585, so you'll probably want to license clients by seat.

Contrarily, if you have 200 subscribed dial-in users accessing 2 Windows NT servers with 16 serial ports each, you'll save money buying licenses for 32 sessions rather than 200 seats.

CHAPTER 3

Planning Your Site

Building an Internet site is much like any other endeavor. You begin by identifying customers with a need and then designing a product that meets that need. You finish by building the product, promoting it, and running it. Equipment and services for each site will differ drastically; what's successful at one site will fail miserably at others. The objective of this chapter is to provide guidance in identifying the mission and critical success factors for your site. One thing's for sure: Just knowing how to create Web pages won't be enough.

3.1 Provider Segments

The amazing growth of the Web is proof that Internet services appeal to the needs of many different customer types. Operators of Internet sites fall into one of five general categories:

1. **Internet Service Providers (ISPs).** Many small, new companies (and a few large ones) have sprung up to buy large pipes into the Internet and sell small pieces to individuals and other businesses. Providing basic connectivity is currently profitable, but this may decrease as large competitors gain market share. However, entrepreneurs frequently derive considerable income from related services such as creating Web pages, renting out Web page space, and providing services such as E-Mail, News, FTP, and DNS. These services were designed to be distributed, not concentrated in a few large national sites, and are thus likely to remain viable as locally provided services.

2. **Hobbyist sites.** The individuals who run these sites want a presence on the Web—one they operate themselves. Internet services have so many advantages that many dial-up Bulletin Board Systems (BBSs) will close or become Web sites within the next few years. As with dial-up BBSs, these

Web site operators will try to collect enough fees to pay for their hobby but will keep operating at a loss if necessary. Availability of cheap high-speed digital communication such as the Integrated Services Digital Network (ISDN) or Community Antenna Television (CATV) "cable modem" will govern growth of this segment.

3. **Public information sites.** Businesses, government agencies, educational institutions, and other organizations frequently create sites to promote their image, distribute public information, advertise, solicit job applicants, and so forth.

4. **Commercial sites.** These sites transact commerce directly on the Web. For example, various publishers and booksellers have established Web sites that allow users to search for books by title, author, subject, date, and so on, and order them on-line. This market has huge potential for growth; any industry or business that uses direct marketing is a candidate.

5. **Internal sites.** Many Internet-type sites are actually restricted to users on a private network. Organizations find this very useful for disseminating company news, policies and procedures, organization charts, project write-ups, hints and tips for computer users, and so forth. Increasingly, organizations view Internet technology as an easier and more cost-effective approach to document distribution and groupware than products like Lotus Notes.

Each type of Internet site provides a different combination of Internet services. ISPs need the most complete set of services and features because they must provide one-stop shopping for their customers. Hobbyists are the most price sensitive and have the lowest volume, so they're most likely to run everything on a single computer. Public information, commercial, and internal sites are unlikely to support dial-up and may already have E-Mail and News in place. These sites usually want security firewalls, whereas entrepreneurs and hobbyists will probably have little interest in them.

Measures of success differ by site as well. Hobbyists want their sites to be popular and self-sustaining. For ISPs, success may simply mean profits; however, these profits result from a complex mix of products, resources, operating procedures, and marketing approaches. Perceived success of public information and internal sites will probably depend on whether the project finishes on time and within budget and accomplishes the original objectives. Owners of commercial sites also gauge success by profit—in their case, profit derived by subtracting the Internet site's installation and operating costs from sales revenues.

3.2 Service Provider Roles

Another way to categorize Internet sites is by application role. It isn't unusual for the same site to fulfill two of the following roles or even all three, but a better point is that many sites *don't* provide all three (don't assume your site must):

1. **Communications provider.** A provider acting in this role provides basic connectivity services, typically by aggregating relatively slow local connections onto a higher-speed uplink. The local circuits may be analog phone lines using dial-up modems, ISDN lines, or dedicated circuits leased from the telephone company or some other local circuit provider.

2. **Application service provider.** A provider in this role supplies applications such as E-Mail, News, Web page delivery (but not authoring), data storage and management, and FAX gateways. At first, it might seem odd for a site to provide such services without also providing communications, but this occurs frequently with internal sites; an existing enterprise network provides connectivity.

3. **Content provider.** A content provider is concerned with information itself rather than the means used to deliver it. The content may consist of almost anything—a software archive, a hierarchical collection of Web pages, a database of articles accessed through a search engine, a stock photo collection, or a book.

The astronomical growth of the World Wide Web is a testament to the value of content providers. Web pages provide a simple way to display and navigate content in a way that earlier Internet applications never approached, and the desire to present and urge to consume such content both appear boundless. Some of the most active sites on the Web have abstracted the desire to publish and consume content to a higher level; these are the giant search engines whose only purpose is to index the content of other sites.

3.3 Applications

A third way to characterize providers is by range of services provided. There are three general categories:

1. **Full Service.** See Section 3.3.1.

2. **Limited Service.** See Section 3.3.2.

3. **Specialized Service.** See Section 3.3.3.

3.3.1 Full Service

A full-service Internet provider isn't necessarily a site that provides every conceivable service; it's simply one that provides a full range of popular communication and application services. Such providers usually serve as a concentration point for dial-in and local leased-line circuits, and they provide host support for services such as HTTP, E-Mail, News, and FTP. These "core" services require additional support services such as DNS, user account management, usage metering, and billing.

Full-service providers typically don't create or manage much content except for user documentation, operating procedures, and a bit of site publicity. The aesthetic skills of creating and organizing content usually involve a much different mindset from the technical skills of networking and system administration.

Providing basic services is very competitive because differentiation is limited. All providers must conform to the same technical standards, or their sites won't work. Sites must compete on price, marketing, and customer service—factors that technicians looking to start a new business may not understand.

3.3.2 Limited Service

Some of the most heavily used sites in the Internet provide considerably less than full service, possibly even a single service. Corporate home sites are perfect examples of this; they frequently consist of just a few machines running HTTP, a router, and a high-speed uplink. These sites specifically avoid further connectivity for security reasons. A major scandal would result if hackers or disgruntled employees broke into a major corporation's home site and modified Web pages, infected download files with viruses, posted objectionable material for distribution, or leaked proprietary information.

Sites limited to Mail, News, DNS, and other services are less obvious but not uncommon. Many sites start out with E-Mail as their only Internet application, for example. Large Internet providers such as Sprint and PSI operate "backbone" sites that concentrate News, DNS queries, and traffic of all kinds from smaller providers.

The larger the limited site, and the more limited, the greater the likelihood of being part of an even larger enterprise. Small, entrepreneurial sites generally require a wider range of services to survive. However, this shouldn't dissuade anyone from building a limited site if this meets local needs.

3.3.3 Specialized Service

Higher differentiation, and hence higher margins, may be available providing specialized Internet services. Specialized services also make it harder for customers, once established, to switch to another provider. On the downside, providing specialized services—especially custom programming—can be labor intensive, costly, and hard to sell. The more specialized the product, the narrower the market and the fewer the number of prospective customers.

3.3.3.1 Secure Transactions This service may at first seem simple—a matter of selecting an HTTP server that supports a Secure Sockets Layer (SSL) or another secure HTTP protocol. Secure HTTP (HTTPS) requires extra administration, though, and secure applications tend to be complex. Such applications tend to use multiple HTML forms with complex database interfaces. Typical functions are catalog lookup, order entry, account creation, account verification, order number assignment, and order status lookup.

Reliability, data security, and physical security are all likely to be much more important at a site that handles secure transactions. Every minute of downtime represents lost transactions, meaning lost money. Lack of proper guardianship over customer account information could expose the provider, the client, or both to extreme embarrassment or lawsuits if the information leaked into the wrong hands.

Finally, the provider of secure transactions will need to become a security watchdog, watching security bulletins to build awareness of recent break-ins at other sites, how they occurred, and how to prevent similar break-ins locally. The provider must also maintain a certain proficiency and eloquence to assure customers their data is secure initially and to reassure them from time to time.

3.3.3.2 Credit Card Numbers Most people are actually rather careless with their credit card numbers; they don't collect and destroy their charge-slip carbons, they leave signed credit card slips on restaurant tables where anyone could steal them, and they disregard the fact that dozens of store clerks and banking personnel can easily take note of numbers. Nevertheless, sensitivity about transmitting credit card numbers over the Internet runs high.

Computer security vendors constantly tweak encryption algorithms. Code crackers, whether operating with criminal, professional, or hobbyist intent, take such attention as a challenge and merely intensify their efforts. The U.S. government erects legal obstacles against codes that are too hard to crack, lest the government be impeded in cracking codes used by criminals, diplomats, and foreign agents. Each public security breach seems to gather major attention in the press and major embarrassment for everyone but the code cracker (who is generally perceived as some kind of antihero). If all this seems intensely exciting and challenging, Internet commerce is for you.

3.3.3.3 Partitioned Data (Pay-Per-View)   Most Internet data is free (or at least available for the cost of the connection). Some providers, however, have tried the alternative of requiring a paid subscription to obtain access. In many cases, the information provider is already in the publish-for-profit business with, for example, an encyclopedia, a newspaper, or a newsletter.

If there are any major successes or money-makers of this type on the Internet, they haven't been reported. Trends may change, but, to date, most Web browsing is just that—casual browsing—not repeated visits to the same site for the same category of information. Users are reluctant to enter their credit card numbers, and they quickly forget account numbers required to access a specific site.

Someone needs to develop a means for a user to log in once (preferably at the point of entry to the Internet), for that identity to be available in a secure and verifiable way (with the user's permission) to other sites the user connects to, and for other sites to charge the user's account (again with permission) for services received.

3.4 Developing a Business Plan

Every successful venture or project involves products people are willing to buy in sufficient quantity and price that the producer recovers costs and has something left for his or her effort. This is clearly true not only in an independent business or profit center but also in organizational settings where cost benefit, budget adherence, and contribution to the bottom line are important.

Building a successful Internet site involves much more than just buying computers, software, and communication lines. It involves devising service packages (products), attracting customers, and having revenues exceed costs. This section provides an overview of one approach to that process.

3.4.1 Customer Identification

The type of site you build must be useful to the type of customers you can attract—and useful enough to retain customers and make them pay enough to keep you in business. This relationship may require rethinking the type of site to build, the type of customers to seek, or both.

Customers, in this context, are those who will pay your bills. If the site is an independent business or profit center, your customers are the people who mail you checks or allow you to charge their accounts. Generally, you'll need to find these customers yourself. In an organizational setting, your customers are the users who justify your budget. If someone else initiated the project and it was assigned to you for implementation, the customers will likely be identified as part of the project scope. If you are the one proposing the project, however, then it's you who must foster interest, identify customers, demonstrate return on investment, and get the project funded.

3.4.2 Customer Needs

Regardless of application, the purpose of the Internet is communication. Your customers may benefit, not so much from what your site provides directly, but more from what other people and places on the Internet provide. This is a common characteristic of communication companies. There's no intrinsic value in making phone calls; it's the information exchanged during the call that has value.

In a sense, Internet providers can't sell their own services as a benefit; they can only sell the benefits of using the site to reach others. This requires a certain empathy with the potential customer's customers, suppliers, and other contacts.

3.4.3 Customer Profiles and Numbers

Some of the easiest customers to find are the ones you already have. If you've been operating a dial-up BBS, you probably have lists of current and past subscribers and callers. If you're expanding an existing site into a new city or district, you can identify existing customers better served by the new site. If you're adding an Internet gateway to an existing LAN, some or all of the LAN users will be your Internet users.

Identifying potential customers may also be very complex. If you're starting a totally new business, for example, potential customers, customer behaviors, and expectations are much less known.

Most Internet sites have several types of customers, and you should develop a customer profile for each type of customer you will address. Customer profiles describe groups of users sharing the same needs, usage pattern, required marketing approach, billing method, and other elements that require separate treatment. For each profile, you should gather as much relevant information as possible: what they want from the Internet, how much of it they want, what days or hours they want it, how they'll connect, how much they're willing to pay, what method of payment they prefer, what restrictions apply, and so forth.

As will shortly become evident, it's critical to know how many customers within each profile to expect at start-up and how fast growth will be.

3.4.4 Services Required

Once you have a preliminary list of customer profiles, the next step is defining the applications, services, and equipment each customer profile requires. Optimally, this will include, for each profile, everything in the site that costs money and is necessary to support that profile.

Services, in this context, include not only end-user applications such as Mail, News, and Web service but also background applications like DNS and backup, plus administrative functions like billing and account management.

As a completeness check, you should also review every planned expense and make sure it's accounted for in one or more customer profiles.

3.4.5 Support Plan

Support is an extremely broad service category and includes presales planning support, installation support, ongoing support, upgrade support, problem support, billing support, and account termination support—just to name a few types. Support is critical in attracting and retaining customers because if customers can't use the site's services effectively, they won't remain customers for long.

Despite the importance of support, network administrators and site operators frequently overlook it. Services delivered by computers, software, and other network devices may get far more attention than personal support, which is considered a nuisance. Equipment and software provide very little opportunity for differentiation, however, and customers appreciate personal and professional contact when they have a problem or question.

To ensure proper service, a support profile should be part of each customer profile. Different customer types will expect different types of support. You should consolidate support plans by customer profile into a site support plan and then review it for feasibility and refine it.

If possible, you should go beyond what will satisfy each customer and look for ways to astound and delight them. The cost of delivering astonishment and delight is frequently low, and the rewards are typically great.

3.4.6 Cost Model

Tabulating application, service, and support quantities required for each customer profile will result in a total demand forecast for the site. You can use this data to develop plans for site equipment, software, phone lines, data lines, electricity, floor space, staff, and so on. Planned costs of these items are then grouped into categories called *cost centers*.

Costs that belong in the same cost center are those that vary together and vary in proportion to natural measures of site activity. Dial-in expense might be a cost center, for example, and include such items as dial-in phone lines, modem banks, and dial-in routers. All these items require coordinated increase or decrease as dial-in usage rises and falls.

Optimally, you should assign every cost in the site to a cost center that relates directly to customer activity. If not, whatever costs remain typically get lumped into an *overhead* cost center. Overhead is recovered either by inflating other cost centers or by prorating it over time (that is, as a flat charge per month).

3.4.7 Product and Pricing Strategy

Given your customer profiles, your list of required services, your support plan, and your cost center analysis, you can now assemble service packages that will appeal to each customer profile, calculate the cost per customer of each package, and establish prices.

3.4.8 Marketing Plan

People frequently confuse marketing with sales. *Marketing* involves detecting opportunity for new products, designing the products, promoting them to the constituencies where the opportunity exists, and then repeating the cycle. *Sales* involves contacting individual customers, taking orders, and providing warranty and other follow-up services.

The preceding sections concerning customer identification, needs analysis, and product design in fact described marketing functions. Marketing and business planning are highly related; the question of how the business will be doing three to five years out is highly dependent on what (and to whom) the business will be selling. In any event, identification of potential customers and site promotion are essential activities.

Cost-effective promotion involves maximum use of free opportunities and careful targeting. You can advertise your site on the Web, of course, and you can get it listed on public search services such as Lycos, WebCrawler, and Yahoo. You can post frequently on newsgroups where your target customers hang out and advertise your site in your signature block. Speaking at user-group meetings, schools, and local trade shows provides additional exposure. Word of mouth is an exceptional way to grow new customers from existing ones; you can encourage this by offering current customers a finder's fee or other incentive. Perhaps you can get local employers (or social clubs at those employers) to post a book of free sign-up coupons on their activity board.

If you decide to try more expensive options, such as advertising in publications or by mail, it's important to remained focused. Advertising to poor prospects is generally no less expensive than advertising to good ones, but it's far less effective.

The larger the potential customer, the less effective local advertising is likely to be. These accounts generally require personal contact. Finding the right audience within the corporate monolith, however, can be a difficult exercise.

A bit of marketing is useful even in assigned, organizational projects. The success of any project tends to depend on a few key people—frequently, the power users or local power brokers rather than the managers or project sponsors. Gaining the participation and support of these key people will almost certainly expedite development and ease rollout. Further marketing may involve the department down the hall, across the street, or elsewhere in the company. If you can convince them of the value of your current project, you may enhance your job security by building demand for additional, similar projects.

3.4.9 Business and Capacity Plans

Most likely, several iterations of this entire planning process will be necessary. A given site design may produce too high a cost—hence, unattractive prices and lack of customers. With too small a site, you may be unable to recover overhead and may have to review the original customer profiles; perhaps you can expand or add some profiles to produce additional volume. Some customer profiles originally included may be unprofitable on paper; you can exclude these.

In practice, the first few iterations of a business plan are relatively informal and undocumented. Later iterations, after change becomes less rapid, are more formal. If you plan to fund start-up costs with a business loan, an accountant will help you prepare pro forma balance sheets, income statements, and statements of cash flow. These are hypothetical financial statements based on your estimates of sales volumes, revenues, and costs.

In the end, it all comes down to this: Make sure your numbers line up before you start spending money.

CHAPTER 4

Selecting Equipment

When it comes to selecting equipment for an Internet site, the trade-offs among performance, reliability, compatibility, expandability, brand preference, and price certainly involve subjective judgments. Service mix, service load, physical setting, criticality, and budget will vary from site to site as well. Be that as it may, this chapter discusses choices of equipment and provides suggestions.

Overall, the best advice is to spend your money where your bottlenecks are or will be. Upgrading a component that's already underused gains nothing. Communication lines and equipment are discussed in a later chapter, but these items (or RAM) are generally the gating performance factors.

4.1 CPU Type and Speed

Serving up Web pages isn't a particularly resource-intensive process. Figure 4.1 illustrates the CPU load involved in delivering two specific pages.

The left side of the trace illustrates delivery of a 1,722-byte HTML page containing two icons: one of 1,373 bytes and one of 1,036 bytes. The server software was EMWAC HTTPS, a common freeware HTTP server. Another computer on the same local Ethernet as the server requested the pages using Netscape Navigator. The Netscape cache was disabled, and the maximum number of simultaneous connections was 20. This resulted in peaks of about 12 percent CPU usage, almost all occurring in the HTTPS server.

The right side of the trace illustrates CPU usage for a more complex page: one of 2,144 bytes referencing 14 GIF (Graphic Interchange Format) images with a total size of 15,487 bytes. The browser and server conceivably had 15 connections open during these transfers. Server CPU usage peaked at 20 to 30 percent.

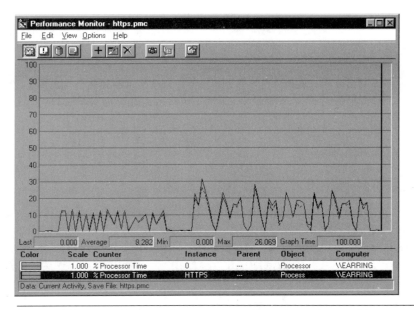

Figure 4.1 CPU Utilization of an HTTP Server (One-Second Intervals)

The server used for these tests had a 100MHz Pentium CPU and 32MB RAM; it was running Windows NT Server 3.51. For more details, see the sidebar titled "Lab Setup Used for This Book."

The point of this demonstration is that delivering Web pages by HTTP isn't particularly CPU intensive. The process simply involves receiving an incoming page request, transmitting a text file of a few thousand bytes out to the network, and then supplying any requested GIF files. Since none of this is CPU intensive, there's usually no point in paying a premium price for the latest and speediest CPU chip.

FTP is similarly easy on CPU power. Transfer of a 100K file over Ethernet typically produces a 5 percent CPU blip lasting less than a second. Transmitting the same file over a modem link would spread the same usage over more time (because of communication speed), and the CPU percentage would hardly be noticeable. Services like DNS and Gopher are similarly efficient. Mail and News handle larger volumes of data, especially when exchanging mail with higher-level servers, taking newsfeeds, expiring old news articles, and so on. However, these activities occur in the background where speed isn't essential, and they can be scheduled at times when other demands for system resources are low.

CGI processing, especially database activity and text searching, is far more likely than other services to exhaust CPU power. Implementing high-volume CGI functions warrants careful advance testing and benchmarking to ensure performance will be acceptable.

Lab Setup Used for This Book

The following lab equipment was used for many of the experiments, demonstrations, and examples in this book:

	Server	Client
Name	EARRING	CHOKER
Manufacturer	Gateway 2000	Gateway 2000
Model	P5-100	4DX2-50V
CPU type	Pentium	486DX2
CPU speed	100MHz	50MHz
RAM	32MB	12MB
Disk	1.6GB EIDE	384MB IDE, 260MB IDE
CD reader	Mitsumi, Quad speed, ATAPI	Laser Magnetics, CM250, proprietary
Video adapter	ATI Graphics, Pro Turbo PCI (mach 64)	ATI Graphics, Ultra Pro VESA (mach 32)
Network adapter	3Com Etherlink III, ISA bus	3Com Etherlink III, ISA bus
Network media	Thin Ethernet	Thin Ethernet
Operating system	Microsoft Windows NT Server 3.51 (preliminary Windows 95 shell)	Microsoft Windows 95

This is the author's lab setup, not an actual Internet service site. The author neither endorses nor discourages purchase of any equipment listed. Your choices, or the author's, would probably differ for any specific site.

4.2 Sizing RAM

Virtual memory paging is the most common cause of poor performance under Windows NT. Watching "Memory Pages/sec" in Performance Monitor can prove this, but, in most cases, watching the hard-disk access light is just as convincing. When the light flashes (and the disk rattles) in response to trivial actions such as opening windows or switching among applications, the system is surely memory constrained. Systems with 16MB or less RAM are almost always memory constrained, while those having 32MB or more aren't. Having 48 or 64MB of RAM is reasonable for a busy system running many processes. Assuming basic needs are met, money spent on RAM will usually provide greater benefit than money spent on CPU power.

4.3 Choosing the I/O Bus, Disks, and Peripherals

Input/output devices and buses are seldom an Internet server bottleneck; the server's connection to the Internet and the clients' connections to the server are almost always slower than the server itself. Fast personal computers are cheap; fast wide-area communication lines are expensive. However, unduly slow I/O can affect virtual memory paging with serious effects on overall system performance. Stability and expandability are also considerations, and some approaches are notably superior to others.

SCSI I/O devices and Windows NT are an excellent match. This contrasts sharply with DOS and Windows 95, whose single-tasking I/O systems preclude taking full advantage of SCSI. For one such example, see the sidebar titled "Multitasking and Elevator Seeking."

Multitasking and Elevator Seeking

After a SCSI (Small Computer System Interface) adapter receives a command from the operating system, it can accept subsequent commands before completing the first. When the adapter has several commands pending, it's free to execute them in any order. As it completes each command, it signals the operating system so that the task waiting for that I/O can proceed.

When several commands are pending for the same disk, most SCSI adapters will schedule them so that the access arm makes only one pass across the disk's surface. This is called *elevator seeking* by analogy to passengers on an elevator. In the order they arrive, the passengers may be headed for floors 2, 17, 5, 8, 12, and 5. It's obviously inefficient to service the customers in first-come, first-served order, though; having the elevator stop at floors 2, 5, 8, 12, and 17 (in that order) is much more efficient.

The MS-DOS code that handles disk access isn't reentrant; once a thread issues an I/O request, no other thread can issue a request until the prior one completes. Returning to the elevator analogy, first-come, first-served is the only available option. Unfortunately, this MS-DOS logic seems to be present in Windows 95 as well.

MS-DOS and Windows 95 reduce the single-threading I/O bottleneck through the use of disk caching in the operating system. The problem is also limited because users of desktop operating systems want task switching more than true multiprocessing; they want foreground performance and don't care much about the speed of what's happening in background. A server, by contrast, needs to keep dozens or hundreds of background tasks moving smoothly.

IDE (Integrated Drive Electronics) controllers don't support elevator seeking and other performance enhancements provided by SCSI. IDE was designed for desktop computers running MS-DOS, and it would have been a waste of money to provide such enhancements in an environment unable to use them.

Also, servers tend to accumulate a greater number and larger variety of I/O devices than single-user workstations. SCSI's ability to accommodate many such devices is a valuable feature.

Windows NT requires three or more physical disks to support disk striping with parity (RAID level 5). Adding a CD-ROM reader and SCSI tape drive results in five I/O devices and exceeds the capacity of both IDE and EIDE. It isn't unusual for a server to have four, five, six, or more hard drives after it has been growing for a while.

With excellent high-speed disks selling for less than $.25 a megabyte, there's no reason to start small. Less than 2 gigabytes of usable disk (after any duplexing or RAID is applied) is almost certainly false economy. The best advice is to calculate your needs for 6 or 12 months of operation and provide for expansion.

SCSI CD-ROM drives are fast, reliable, and almost universally supported by the Windows NT Setup and Emergency Repair procedures. IDE ATAPI (AT Attachment Packet Interface) CD drives are also fully supported, but most other IDE and proprietary drives aren't. Having a CD reader not supported by Emergency Repair means you'll need a set of Windows NT Setup floppy disks to complete the repair; else, you'll have to reinstall Windows NT from the unsupported drive. For more informaton, see the sidebar titled "Unsupported CD-ROM Support."

A server can support many SCSI CD-ROM drives. A handy way to distribute CD-ROM data to a large user base is to install a second SCSI adapter and an external array of CD-ROM drives (seven is typical because that's the number one adapter can usually support). The array is nothing more than seven ordinary SCSI CD-ROM drives, a power supply, and a plain metal box. The seven drives show up in Windows NT as seven drive letters you can share using Microsoft Windows Networking, FTP, or NFS (Network File System). Be sure to honor license restrictions applicable to each compact disk, however.

Comprehensive data backup on user workstations is frequently a wink and a shrug rather than a real process. This simply isn't acceptable when a commercial (or at least professional) site is the repository for its customers' critical data—data the customers may have entrusted to the server because they trust its backups more than their own.

Not only is backup itself necessary, so are speed and capacity. Ten megabytes per minute seems fast until the volume to be backed up reaches a few gigabytes; at that speed, a 5-gigabyte server requires 8 hours and 20 minutes to back up. Running such a backup overnight is a possibility, but it's also a nuisance if the data won't fit on one tape.

The two leading tape formats for high-speed, high-capacity server backups are 8mm helical scan and 4mm DAT. Internal drives, external drives, autoloaders,

Unsupported CD-ROM Support

Windows NT can be installed from a CD-ROM drive which NT Setup doesn't support, provided either DOS or Windows 95 supports it. The procedure is simple: Insert the Windows NT CD, switch to that drive, and run the WINNT.EXE program from DOS or Windows 95. WINNT.EXE copies all required files from the CD to the computer's hard disk and then installs from one area of the disk to another.

Support for CD drives not supported by Windows NT Setup may be available after Windows NT installation is complete. There's no trick here; it's simply a case of the required driver not being present on the Windows NT CD but provided elsewhere. Windows NT can add such drivers after initial installation.

Unfortunately, neither of these procedures may be of use if Windows NT files become corrupted and the system becomes unbootable—an Emergency Repair is then necessary. Emergency Repair compares system files on the hard disk to signatures saved on an Emergency Repair diskette created during initial installation and updated after each system change. When Emergency Repair finds a corrupted file, it replaces it with a fresh copy from the installation media. If the only installation files you have are on CD-ROM, Emergency Repair needs access to the appropriate CD-ROM and controller drivers.

Emergency Repair goes through the same hardware detection phase as Windows NT Setup and may be capable of loading an unsupported driver from a vendor's driver disk. This, however, can be difficult to verify ahead of time. When in doubt, stick to the Windows NT Hardware Compatibility List.

and automatic tape libraries are available for both formats, but all these devices have SCSI interfaces. In the case of tape devices, you should check not only the Windows NT Hardware Compatibility List but also the compatibility list for the backup software you plan to use.

4.4 Choosing a System Bus

ISA, EISA, MCA, VESA, PCI, and PC Card are the predominant PC expansion card buses. Of these, EISA has remained the preferred bus for servers; PCI is gaining ground but took a long time gaining maturity.

IBM invented the ISA (Industry Standard Architecture) bus for the original 1981 PC and expanded it to 16 bits in 1984 for the PC-AT. Oddly, Compaq invented the name ISA years later. Very few personal computer technologies have remained the same so long, but the ISA bus is a compatibility standard that remains adequate for many slow-to-medium-speed expansion cards. It's too slow for today's RAM, video, and disk controllers, but it remains adequate for serial and parallel ports, sound cards, most network adapters, and many special devices like telephony interfaces. However, this bus can address only 16MB of memory, and it has a reputation for occasionally missing interrupts.

IBM invented MCA (MicroChannel Architecture) as a technical advance but also as a roadblock to clone builders. IBM hoped MCA's technical superiority would entice buyers into buying high-margin IBM PCs, but, in retrospect, it accelerated the shift to low-cost ISA clones. IBM was simply unable to demonstrate any applications that ran better on MCA machines than on ISA computers. MCA is no longer being manufactured, but it spurred development of the next bus—namely, EISA.

To combat IBM's MCA, Compaq and eight other PC makers united in a "Gang of Nine" to invent EISA (Extended Industry Standard Architecture). EISA is a full 32-bit bus that doesn't drop interrupts and that also supports 8-bit and 16-bit ISA cards. The Gang of Nine was no more successful than IBM in finding user applications that ran worse on ISA. Compaq, however, was able to demonstrate considerable benefits to servers built with EISA buses. As a result, EISA has become the standard bus for PC-based servers.

The Video Electronics Standards Association developed VESA as a high-speed local bus for video cards. Unlike ISA, MCA, and EISA, a local bus theoretically connects pins on the expansion card sockets directly to pins on the system's CPU chip. This addressed video bottlenecks that appeared when running Windows on 486-class machines.

Although VESA is a 32-bit bus, 16-bit ISA bus controllers are limited to 24-bit addressing. Huh? The 16-bit ISA was designed for the 16-bit 80286 CPU, which can address 16MB of RAM. 16MB (OK, minus 1) is a 24-bit binary number. The 286 accomplishes 24-bit addressing by adding two 16-bit values, one of which is shifted right 8 bits.

The VESA bus, which is partly hot-wired to the CPU, supports only three slots. More slots would lead to too many expansion cards, leading to excessive current drawn through the CPU, leading to overheating and failure. Therefore, virtually all VESA-equipped computers have ISA buses as well. Unfortunately, the ISA address controller prevents more than 24 of VESA's 32 bits from being accessed; system RAM, the VESA bus, and the ISA bus are all limited to 16MB of addressability.

Just in case you or someone you knew had a VESA system with more than 16MB of RAM, here's how the manufacturers did it. The 80486 CPU didn't have an on-board cache, so virtually all VESA-equipped 486 systems had external static RAM caches. The pathway from the CPU to the SRAM cache was 32 bits. The ISA bus controller moved data between the SRAM cache and main memory below

16MB. The bus controller couldn't transfer data to main memory above 16MB, so the DMA controller chip was used instead. This meant that access to memory above 16MB was 5 to 10 percent slower than access to memory below that address.

If this 16-bit, 24-bit, 32-bit business on VESA bus systems seems a bit kludgey, you're right. If it seems as though it would create a performance penalty for systems that run in 32-bit memory, you're right again. ISA/VESA machines don't make good servers.

Intel developed the PCI bus (Personal Computer Interconnect), which has essentially displaced VESA on Pentium-class motherboards. PCI is 32 bits from the CPU to SRAM, to main RAM, and on to any PCI expansion cards. However, PCI has been slow in attaining compatibility, and early PCI cards frequently interfered with one another. Windows NT drivers for these cards have been slow to appear and even slower to stabilize. Lack of maturity and stability are abhorrent to network administrators, and adoption of the PCI bus in servers has been slow. Some EISA/PCI systems have been successful, with PCI being used for video only.

The PC Card bus is mentioned for completeness, but this is a 16-bit bus for portable computers, not a 32-bit industrial-strength bus for servers. However, if you do have need for a portable server, Windows NT 3.51 supports PC Cards.

4.5 Network Adapter(s)

As with storage devices, network adapters are seldom bottlenecks in an Internet server. ISA cards costing less than $100 can saturate a 10-megabit Ethernet. How much more do you want?

Early PCI network cards, especially 100-megabit versions, had a reputation for consuming inordinate amounts of system CPU. This is something to check before proceeding. Given PCI's past problems with card conflicts, thoroughly test any server containing more than one PCI expansion card before proclaiming it ready for prime time.

EISA-based network cards generally have excellent reputations with none of the problems of PCI. Nevertheless, any card capable of pumping 100 megabits per second in and out of a PC is going to require a fast PC.

Maturity, stability, and compatibility with Windows NT remain major issues. Be sure to obtain network adapters listed on the Hardware Compatibility List; avoid cards with new or unproven driver software; and, if possible, stick to brands you know.

4.6 Fault Tolerance and Reliability

The cost of downtime is frequently difficult to assess. The cost of adding fault tolerance to an installation, however, is quite evident; it appears plainly on the equipment vendor's invoice. Unfortunately, no one can predict the specific amount of downtime this expense will avoid. Despite these uncertainties, fault-tolerant hardware is an option to consider in planning for the required degree of reliability.

An Uninterruptible Power Supply (UPS) is one of the simplest and most effective fault-tolerant devices. A good UPS filters and regulates voltage supplied by the electric company and uses rechargeable batteries to continue delivering power if power lines fail. UPS systems designed for computer use also connect to the computer's serial port, keeping a software service on the computer apprised of the UPS's condition. When the UPS tells the service that AC power has been lost, the service typically sends out a warning message to all current users. If power returns, the service sends an "all clear" message; else, when the batteries are about to fail, the service sends out a last warning and then shuts the server down. Once the server is down, the UPS cuts power to the system unit and enters a standby mode until reliable AC power returns. It then automatically powers the server back up. UPS systems aren't terribly expensive, so there's good reason to protect every device that, if down, would affect service to customers.

RAID technology is a series of approaches for using redundancy to improve the speed or reliability of disks. RAID stands for Redundant Array of Inexpensive Disks. For an explanation of the RAID system, see the sidebar titled "RAID Concepts."

Windows NT provides two kinds of fault tolerance for disks: mirroring (RAID level 1) and stripe sets with parity (RAID level 5). Mirroring requires two physical disks to be available; Windows NT then writes all data for the mirrored logical drive(s) to both disks. If one disk fails, the system continues to operate normally on the remaining disk. This can even protect the boot disk, although if the disk that fails is the first physical disk in the system, booting from the secondary disk requires a specially prepared boot diskette. A mirrored disk uses twice as much physical space as logical space. Writing to a mirrored disk is slower than writing to a normal volume, but reading back is faster because two routes to the desired data are available. Windows NT will take the faster route.

Using stripe sets with parity requires at least three physical disks. When Windows NT writes data to the logical drive, it spreads the data plus calculated redundancy bits across all disks in the set. If one disk fails, Windows NT can always infer its contents from the remaining disks; the system continues running.

RAID Concepts

The computer industry has defined seven general approaches to RAID, as listed below:

- **RAID 0, data striping.** The RAID system divides data into blocks and spreads it uniformly across all the disks in the array. There is no redundancy and therefore no fault tolerance, but RAID 0 is very fast; if there are three disks in the array, each disk has only 1/3 the data to write, and the operation may therefore complete in 1/3 the time. Some people call this strategy *disk striping* and the data areas *stripe sets*.

- **RAID 1, disk mirroring.** The RAID system duplicates all data on one or more disks to a second disk or set. Duplexing adds even more redundancy by using a second host adapter for the duplicated drives.

- **RAID 0+1, data striping on multiple mirrored drives.** This approach combines elements of both RAID 0 and 1. Basically, one stripe set mirrors another.

- **RAID 2, bit interleaving with multiple check disks.** There are currently no commercial products supporting this technique for file server or desktop systems. RAID systems that use bit or byte interleaving are inefficient with PC-type disks, which operative natively at the block (sector) level.

- **RAID 3, bit interleaving with single check disk.** A single check disk stores parity, and the remaining drives contain data striped at the byte level. The host system views each array of drives as a single volume.

- **RAID 4, block interleaving with single check disk.** This approach is identical to RAID 3, except that striping is at the block level.

- **RAID 5, block and parity interleaving with no check disks**. The RAID system stripes data and parity at the block level across all drives in the array. Usable capacity equals the amount of space allocated per drive times the number of drives minus 1.

Windows NT supports RAID levels 0, 1, and 5 in software. No special hardware is necessary; conventional disk drives and controllers will suffice.

If n disks comprise the stripe set with parity, the logical volume size will be $(n - 1)$ times the space allocated on each drive. A stripe set with 500MB on each of three drives will appear as a 1,000MB logical drive; a stripe set with 600MB on each of four drives will appear as an 1,800MB logical drive. Both writing and reading stripe sets with parity are slower than for "native" drives, and parity striping can't protect boot drives.

Mirrored or stripe-set-with-parity disks that experience "soft" failures can be regenerated, although these operations require a reboot of the server. Disks that fail completely can be replaced and then regenerated.

Hardware RAID 5 uses firmware on the disk controller to spread the data and parity information across multiple disks. These disks don't appear as separate drives to Windows NT, but rather as one large physical volume. Sophisticated caching and predictive read-ahead negate any performance penalties, and, since the array appears as a single drive to Windows NT, it can protect the boot partition. Some hardware RAID 5 controllers are simply that—controllers—and use conventionally mounted drives inside the system unit. Compaq, Hewlett-Packard, and other vendors additionally provide system units with "hot-swappable" drives that can be removed or replaced without tools while the system is running. Stand-alone RAID 5 systems look and respond as single external disks but in fact are a redundant array. Some of these systems can lose a disk, sound an alarm, accept a replacement, and regenerate its contents without interrupting system operation.

ECC (Error Correcting Code) memory circuitry makes RAM fault tolerant. ECC typically uses parity-checking SIMMs (Single Inline Memory Modules) but applies checking to more than one byte at a time; four bytes is typical. The algorithm that calculates the four bits of parity for each four bytes of data allows not only detection but also correction of one-bit errors. One-bit memory errors are the most common type, and for ECC memory to correct these eliminates one cause of random system crashes.

In addition to disk and memory fault tolerance, advanced servers have integrated monitoring and diagnostic features. These systems detect both hard (system-crashing) and soft (recoverable) errors and write them to a log. Repeated soft failures, whether in RAM, on a disk drive, or in some other part of the system, frequently qualify a server component for warranty replacement before the component actually fails. Some of these systems are also capable of beeping an administrator when certain errors occur, of supporting hardware diagnostics by modem while the system is down, and of accepting "hardware reset" commands by modem. Another handy feature is hardware capability to detect an operating system crash, record the cause, and automatically reboot the system.

4.7 Specific Recommendations

"Exactly what equipment should I buy?" is among the most frequent questions new system managers ask. Unfortunately, there is no single answer.

At minimum, most Internet services require at least a mid-range Pentium CPU, 32MB RAM, and 1GB disk. If budget concerns are an extreme priority, a mail-order system unit with an IDE disk subsystem will do. Expect to pay less than $3,000.

For the most active and critical sites, consider a system truly designed to be a server, such as the Compaq Proliant or Hewlett-Packard NetServer. Purchase the fastest processor available, and make sure the system has expansion capability for multiple processors and/or faster CPUs available in the future. Look for fast wide SCSI I/O systems, at least 64MB RAM, and capability for 256MB RAM. Consider fault-tolerant subsystems such as Error Correcting Memory and hardware RAID. Expect to pay $25,000 to $50,000 for such a system and never buy just one; it's silly to spend this much on high-capacity, high-reliability equipment and not have a fallback capability. To avoid finger pointing when problems occur, configure the entire server with parts from one system-unit vendor.

Your needs will probably fall somewhere between these extremes. In general, you should upgrade RAM (to 64MB) and I/O (to fast wide SCSI) before upgrading CPU speed. Given today's low disk prices, buy in large increments, such as 4GB drives. The false economy of buying small drives becomes apparent when CPU and RAM resources remain adequate but all your drive bays are full.

CHAPTER 5

TCP/IP Fundamentals

The networking scheme used to identify and connect Internet computers is TCP/IP (Transmission Control Protocol/Internet Protocol).

5.1 Origin of TCP/IP

The U.S. Department of Defense sponsored development of TCP/IP with the objectives of interconnecting separate existing networks, interconnecting different kinds of computers, and surviving destruction by nuclear war. The department adopted TCP/IP as a Military Standard in 1983 and required all computers it purchased to have TCP/IP capability. It also funded incorporation of TCP/IP into Berkeley UNIX.

Defense requirements provided tremendous incentives for computer makers to provide TCP/IP support. The market consisting of the Department of Defense, its contractors, and its research institutions was simply too large to ignore.

Table 5.1 provides a list of Internet milestones.

The ability to readily exchange information among computers of different types and different locations proved to have tremendous benefits. TCP/IP's use in networking UNIX workstations led to construction of TCP/IP networks at thousands of nondefense-related sites. As IBM's dominance of the computer industry decreased, organizations realized the need for any-to-any connectivity, and TCP/IP fulfilled that need better than any other approach. As a result, TCP/IP has become the lingua franca of connectivity.

5.2 Advantages of TCP/IP

The primary advantages of TCP/IP are interoperability, reliability, and scalability.

TCP/IP networking and applications are available for virtually every kind of general-purpose computer. This is critical in today's heterogeneous, multivendor

Table 5.1 Internet Milestones

Year	Event
1969	Defense Advanced Research Projects Agency (DARPA) funds development of an experimental, packet-switched network (ARPANET). Four nodes begin operating on this network.
1973	E-Mail becomes the most popular application on the ARPANET.
1973	DARPA begins research to interconnect various packet networks.
1975	ARPANET status is upgraded from experimental to fully operational.
1977	DARPA demonstrates the first workable internetwork.
1983	Department of Defense adopts TCP/IP as a Military Standard. All computers on the ARPANET must convert.
1983	Military traffic moves to a second network (MILNET). The term *Internet* comes into use to denote the combination of MILNET and ARPANET.
1984	National Science Foundation begins construction of NSFNET, a high-speed backbone connecting six supercomputer centers, MILNET, ARPANET, and other regional networks.
1986	Domain Name System is deployed.
1986	NSFNET is implemented at 56 kilobits per second.
1988	NSFNET is upgraded to T1 speed (1.544 megabits per second).
1990	ARPANET ceases to exist as a separate entity.
1990	NSFNET is upgraded to T3 speed (45 megabits per second).
Early 1990s	Department of Defense begins using MILNET for classified purposes.
Mid 1990s	Internet opens to commercial use, and government drops funding for NSFNET backbone. Commercial providers assume backbone responsibility.

environments. Proprietary gateways can generally provide connectivity between any two environments, but the number of such gateways becomes unmanageably large in many-to-many situations. TCP/IP's ability to provide a common technology on each computing platform is unparalleled.

TCP/IP is reliable in several respects. Extensive error checking and correction assure reliable transmission. Multiple pathways and automatic routing assure that connections remain stable even if parts of the network fail. Finally, TCP/IP is a mature protocol—well known, readily tested, and widely supported.

Scalability is evident in several ways. First and most obviously, the Internet itself provides evidence that fairly large TCP/IP networks are possible. Second, TCP/IP is designed for distributed administration. Administrators can make local changes quickly and easily without requiring changes at other sites. Finally, TCP/IP is both a wide-area and local-area protocol. Local protocols such as NetBEUI and IPX/SPX operate poorly over wide-area links, and wide-area protocols such as X.25 are awkward locally. TCP/IP's suitability in both environments provides a seamless path from the user's desktop to the world.

5.3 How TCP/IP Stacks Up

Like most network protocols, TCP/IP has a layered design. This means the path from the software application to the transmission medium (and back) consists of several logically independent components having well-defined interfaces. These components occur logically in a vertical "stack" with the physical medium at the bottom and applications at the top. Data flows from the application down through each component in the stack, across the transmission medium, and then back up through the other computer's stack.

Figure 5.1 illustrates the OSI Reference Model, a theoretically complete stack. OSI is the acronym for Open Systems Interconnection, an undertaking of ISO, the International Standards Organization.

Starting from the bottom, the seven OSI layers provide the following services:

1. **Physical.** Provides the physical connection and hardware used to transmit data from one point in the network to another. Concerns at this level include wiring specifications, voltages, connector type, and so forth.

2. **Data link.** Delivers data reliably across the underlying physical network. Ethernet, Token Ring, FDDI (Fiber Distributed Data Inteface), and ATM (Asynchronous Transfer Mode) are data link specifications.

Figure 5.1 Layers in the OSI Reference Model

3. **Network.** Manages connections across the network and isolates higher-level services from the underlying network.

4. **Transport.** Guarantees that the destination computer receives exactly what the originating one sent.

5. **Session.** Manages sessions between cooperating applications on two different computers. A *session* is a connection that remains in effect through multiple transactions, with state information being remembered from transaction to transaction.

6. **Presentation.** Handles inconsistencies in the way different computers represent data. The presentation layer would typically handle translations from ASCII to EBCDIC, from big-endian to little-endian, and so on.

7. **Application.** Runs network processes accessed by the end user. However, if the user application is itself layered or built on layered operating system services, processes in the application layer may appear to the user as background services.

Figure 5.2 shows the relationship between the protocol stacks on two computers. Within a given machine, services at each layer interact only with services directly above and below themselves. These interactions occur through *interfaces*.

On a network, services on one computer can interact with services on another only if both services occupy the same layer. These interactions obey rules called *protocols*.

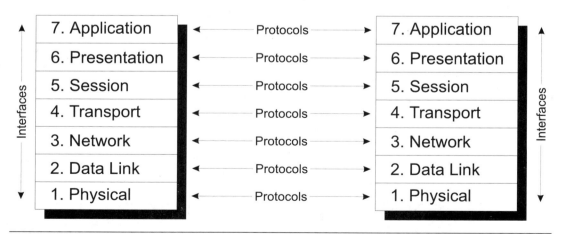

Figure 5.2 Protocols and Interfaces in the OSI Reference Model

In plain language, a protocol is a way of acting. Diplomatic protocols are rules that govern interaction and foster understanding between international negotiators. Network protocols are rules that govern interaction of devices and services on the network; they specify what commands and signals can be sent, what responses are expected, and what to do in case of unexpected or no response.

Referring again to Figure 5.2, only the physical layer is capable of transmitting data between the computers. The data link services on each computer can communicate only through their respective physical layers. The network layers communicate by requesting services from their data link layers, which then request services from the physical layers. Communication between applications requires traversing the entire stack on both machines.

Ideally, all interfaces in the stack would be protocol independent. Components at any layer could be replaced at will without requiring changes in any other layer. In practice, there are limits to this independence. Ethernet, for example, is a layer 2 protocol; you can run Ethernet over a variety of layer 1 media but not over every type of wire ever manufactured.

Adherence to the OSI Reference Model is more in spirit than in letter. Most network software is in fact layered; this is what allows you to run the same network over different Ethernet cards merely by changing one software module. Even so, most real-world stacks contain some number of layers other than seven, and the interfaces typically occur at different boundaries. Figure 5.3 shows how the TCP/IP stack compares to the OSI Reference Model.

The five TCP/IP layers provide the following services:

1. **Physical layer.** Provides the physical connection and hardware—just as in the OSI Reference Model.

2. **Network interface layer.** Provides the network card or other device that physically connects the computer to the network, plus the associated software interface. This layer handles details such as physical network addressing and physical minimum and maximum data lengths. A *frame* is the basic unit of data.

3. **Internet layer.** Provides the basic packet delivery service used by TCP/IP networks. The Internet layer uses IP addresses rather than physical addresses, and the basic unit of data is the *datagram*.

4. **Transport layer.** Within this layer, Transmission Control Protocol (TCP) provides reliable data delivery with end-to-end error detection and correction. TCP handles data in terms of segments. User Datagram Protocol (UDP) provides unreliable, connectionless delivery with low overhead. UDP deals with data as *packets*.

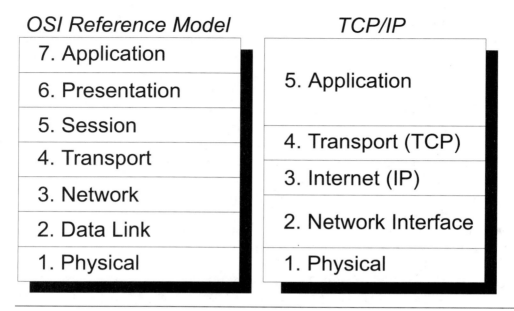

Figure 5.3 TCP/IP Layers versus the OSI Reference Model

   5. **Application layer.** Provides functionality to the end user. Programs such
       as FTP, Telnet, E-Mail, and Web browsers belong to this layer.

   Notice there are two transport protocols: TCP and UDP. Applications send
data into TCP as a continuous stream and have no concern over how the data
divides into packets, how the lower layers transmit it, or what the destination
address might be. TCP breaks the application stream into numbered and check-
summed packets, sends them out, and awaits acknowledgment that the destination host has accurately received each packet. (For historical reasons, TCP/IP calls
all computers, even PCs, *hosts*.) If TCP receives negative acknowledgment or if
the acknowledgment times out, TCP tries sending the packet again.
   LAN protocols such as NetBEUI perform acknowledgment one packet at a
time. The loop is: Send packet 1; wait for acknowledgment 1; send packet 2; wait
for acknowledgment 2; and so on. This is fine on local Ethernets, but transmission delays render it unacceptable for wide-area use; the protocol spends much
more time waiting for acknowledgments than transmitting data. Throughput
degrades terribly. TCP therefore uses a "sliding window" concept and transmits
several outbound packets without waiting for acknowledgment. Copies of
transmitted packets stay in the outbound buffer until the destination host
acknowledges them—that is, until it's certain they won't have to be retrans-
mitted. If the outbound buffer gets full, transmission stops until some positive

acknowledgments arrive or the process times out. The source host also knows the size of the destination host's inbound buffer and will not exceed it. Timeouts return an error status to the application.

UDP receives application data as packets of discrete length. It transmits each packet and then immediately forgets about it; there is no acknowledgment and retransmission. This makes UDP quick, easy, and unreliable.

A frequent question is why anyone in his or her right mind would use an unreliable protocol. However, if you're running a five-layer or seven-layer stack, there's simply no need for acknowledgment and retransmission at each and every level. UDP simply requires the application or user to perform error detection and recovery, while TCP performs this function itself. Simple query-and-response applications often employ UDP.

Both TCP and UDP surround the application data with control information. This is called *encapsulation* or *providing an envelope*. TCP, given its extra functionality, generates more data than UDP, but neither protocol includes the source or destination network address. The Internet Protocol, which resides, logically enough, in the Internet layer, manages these addresses.

The Internet Protocol (IP) manages transmission of segments or packets between hosts. This requires both the source and destination hosts to have an address the Internet Protocol can deal with—an IP address.

The data link (or network access) layer also requires each host to have an address, but these are local network addresses that get replaced as the packet travels from local network to local network toward its final destination. The IP address is a logical address that remains unchanged as the packet crosses networks of any type, as Figure 5.4 illustrates.

Net1 and Net3 are Ethernet networks; Net2 is X.25. When Host1 sends data to Host2, the source and destination IP addresses are IP1 and IP2, but the data link addresses are E1 and E2. E2 isn't the Ethernet address of Host2, but the local

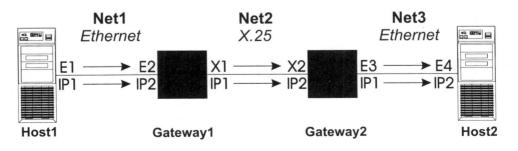

Figure 5.4 Local Data Link Addresses versus IP Addresses

data link address of a gateway to Net2. Gateway1 transmits the data to Gateway2, but the data link source and destination addresses are now X1 and X2—X.25 addresses. The gateway has dropped the original Ethernet addresses but has preserved the IP addresses. On Net3, the source and destination data link addresses change again, this time to those of Gateway2 and Host2, but the source and destination IP addresses again remain unchanged.

The preceding paragraph raises a number of issues. How did the source host know that Gateway1 needed to receive the data and not a host on the same local network? How did the gateways know where to send the data next? What do IP addresses look like? The following sections will answer these questions.

Having seen the OSI Reference Model stack and the TCP/IP stack, all that remains is the Windows NT stack. It is illustrated in Figure 5.5.

Windows NT uses the Network Device Interface Specification (NDIS), so the data link layer consists of two kinds of modules: a MAC (Media Access Control) driver for each network adapter and a Protocol Manager. The MAC drivers forward all packets they receive to the Protocol Manager, which then offers each packet to each network layer protocol that is loaded. The figure shows TCP/IP, IPX/SPX, and NetBEUI, but others are certainly possible. The IP networking software will pick up any TCP/IP packets the Protocol Manager offers and forward

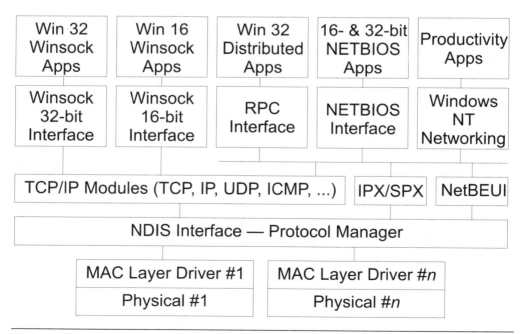

Figure 5.5 Windows NT Protocol Architecture

them to TCP, UDP, ICM, (Internet Control Message Protocol), or other transport layer protocol modules as necessary. Winsock interfaces are present in the application layer, as are NETBIOS and Microsoft Windows Networking. Note that IPX/SPX and NetBEUI, as well as TCP/IP, support NETBIOS and Microsoft Windows Networking, but only TCP/IP supports Winsock.

As an exercise, you may wish to open Control Panel... Network... Bindings on your Windows NT system and try relating the displayed information to Figure 5.5.

5.4 Address Structure

IP addresses consist of 32 bits divided into four groups of eight—that is, into four octets. Dotted-decimal notation states the value of each octet in decimal, with periods indicating the octet boundaries. 192.207.117.2 is a typical IP address; this would be C0-CF-75-02 in hexadecimal or 11000000-11001111-01110101-00000010 in binary. 192.207.117.2 is better. For an explanation of *byte* versus *octet*, see the sidebar titled "Byte or Octet: What's the Difference?"

Of the 32 bits, some indicate a network number and the rest indicate the number of a host on that network. Table 5.2 illustrates the division between network numbers and host numbers.

In theory, a 32-bit network address should allow for 4,294,967,296 hosts—just about enough for everyone on Earth to have one. However, Class A networks, Class B networks, and reserved addresses consume 7/8 of all available addresses. Early TCP/IP sites have snapped up virtually all the Class A and B networks, leading to a problem called *address depletion*.

Just as the United States is running out of telephone numbers, the Internet is running out of IP addresses. Various schemes have provided additional addresses,

Byte or Octet: What's the Difference?

If a byte and an octet are both eight bits, why have two terms? The answer is probably lost in antiquity, but network people usually speak in terms of octets when data is flowing serially and bitwise through a network. Data at rest within a host is measured in bytes.

Think of it this way: If you call the 117 in 192.207.117.2 the third octet, network people will think you're an expert and less socially challenged people will think you're a nerd. If you call the 117 a byte, network people will consider you a user and users will consider you a geek.

Table 5.2 Internet Protocol Address Structure

First n bits	First Octet	Class	Octets in Net	Octets in Host	Number of Networks	Hosts per Network	% of Total
0000	0	Reserved					
0	1–126	A	1	3	126	16,387,064	48.1
0111	127	Loopback					
10	128–191	B	2	2	16,256	64,516	24.4
110	192–223	C	3	1	2,064,512	254	12.2
1110	224–239	Multicast					
1111	240–255	Experimental					

Notes: 1. Calculated totals of networks and hosts exclude octet values of 0 and 255.
2. The "% of Total" column is relative to 4,294,967,296, the theoretical number of 32-bit addresses.

but eventually longer addresses will be required. The Internet Engineering Task Force (IETF) decided in 1995 that IP addresses will increase from 4 to 16 octets, but many details remained unanswered. One thing's certain: IP addresses like 192.207.117.2.102.57.203.6.157.189.71.204.199.93.11.133 will be difficult to remember.

5.5 Routable versus Nonroutable Protocols

A major advantage of the Internet Protocol address structure is that the network number is readily available. This means that just by looking at a packet's destination IP address, you can tell not only if this packet is for a host on the local network but also, if not, which network it should be routed to. This makes IP a *routable* protocol. You can route the packet just by looking at the packet's address.

Protocols such as NetBEUI are *nonroutable* because they only use data link addresses—typically, Ethernet addresses. Assignment of Ethernet addresses to networks is random, so, given a host's Ethernet address, there's no way to determine which remote network the host is on. This makes large, wide-area NetBEUI networks very hard to build and manage.

A further example may help. Telephone numbers are routable because the area code denotes a geographic location; given the 10-digit telephone number, the telephone system knows where to route the call. If someone had decided to use Social Security numbers as telephone numbers, there would be no way to route calls based only on the number. Social Security numbers would be nonroutable telephone numbers.

5.6 Overview of TCP/IP Routing

5.6.1 Address Resolution and Routing

Figure 5.6 illustrates an environment combining three networks into one internet. For simplicity, the figure shows IP network and host numbers as one octet each. E1 through E10 denote Ethernet addresses, which would normally be 12 hexadecimal digits.

Suppose a user on Host1 needs to contact Host2. The user's application will provide Host2's IP address but not Host2's data link address; finding the data link address is IP's problem.

The source and destination IP addresses are 10.21 and 10.31, respectively. Network 10 equals Network 10, so IP knows both addresses are on the same network.

The Address Resolution Protocol (ARP) handles the job of getting Host2's data link address. ARP maintains a cache of recently used IP addresses, and, if 10.31 is in that cache, the data link address will be present also. Else, ARP must transmit a broadcast packet asking each and every machine on the network to respond if its IP address is 10.31. When Host2 receives this broadcast, it responds to Host1, and the ARP service on Host1 adds Host2's IP and data link addresses to its cache. To learn how to display the ARP cache, see the sidebar titled "Examining the Windows NT ARP Cache."

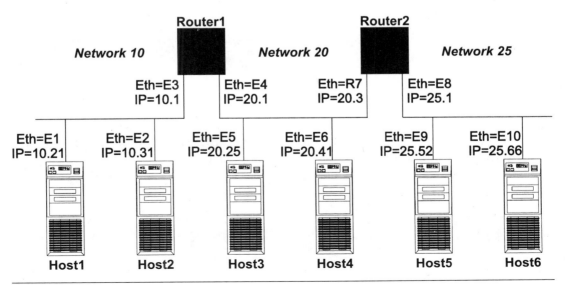

Figure 5.6 Internet Combining Three Networks

Examining the Windows NT ARP Cache

You can display the ARP cache on any Windows NT machine running TCP/IP with the command "arp -a."

The same ARP scheme won't work if Host1 needs to contact Host3, because Host3 is on a different network and broadcasts won't pass between them. However, Host1 knows from comparing the two IP addresses that Host3 is on a remote network; Network 20 doesn't equal Network 10. Part of Host1's configuration is the address of a default gateway—that is, an address where Host1 will send all outside traffic. The default gateway in this case is Router1, so that's where Host1 will send the packet destined for Host3.

To achieve local delivery, the packet from Host1 to Router1 must contain data link addresses of E1 and E3 (Host1's and Router1's). ARP determines E3, Router1's data link address, if necessary. However, to achieve final delivery, the packet will contain IP addresses 10.21 and 20.25 (Host1's and Host3's).

Notice that Router1 has two IP addresses—one for each network port. When the packet from Host1 to Host3 arrives on Router1's 10.1 port, Router1 notices that the destination IP address is for a host on Network 20 and says, "Aha! I know where Network 20 is; it's on my other port." Router1 therefore determines Host3's data link address (by ARP) and sends the packet to Host3. This packet will have data link source and destination E4 and E5, respectively, but the source and destination IP addresses will still be 10.21 and 20.25:

```
                         Data Link
      Transmission        Address          IP Address

Host1    →  Router1     E1  →  E3      10.21  →  20.25

Router1  →  Host3       E4  →  E5      10.21  →  20.25
```

The name for this process is *routing*. It becomes slightly more complex when Host1 communicates with Host6:

```
                         Data Link
      Transmission        Address          IP Address

Host1    →  Router1     E1  →  E3      10.21  →  25.66

Router1  →  Router2     E4  →  E7      10.21  →  25.66

Router2  →  Host6       E8  →  E10     10.21  →  25.66
```

Host1 sends the packet to Router1 simply because Network 10 doesn't equal Network 10 and Router1 is the configured default gateway. However, Router1 doesn't use the same logic when deciding to send the packet to Router2. To see why this is so, consider Figure 5.7.

If a host on Network 10 wanted to contact one on Network 47, how would Router1 know where to forward the packet? Router1 has two choices: Router2 and Router4. Router2 would forward the packet to Router6, and Router6 would then forward it to Network 47; Router4 would forward the packet to Router5, and Router5 would similarly forward it to Network 47:

```
Network 10 → Router1 → Router2 → Router6 → Network 47
Network 10 → Router1 → Router4 → Router5 → Network 47
```

Both of these routings will work, and, since both pass through the same number of routers, the router is equally likely to use either one (unless an administrator has configured a preferred route). If one route had involved fewer hops than the other (that is, passed through fewer routers), the route with fewer hops would have taken precedence.

Having multiple routes provides great fault tolerance. If one route stops working or is busy, packets simply take another route. However, since different routes may operate at different speeds and since the source host may send several packets before receiving an acknowledgment, packets may not arrive in the order the source host sent them. TCP/IP handles this automatically.

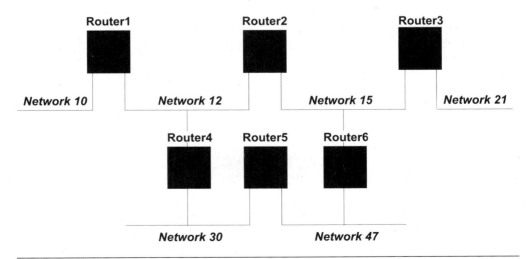

Figure 5.7 Internet Combining Six Networks

Returning to the example of transmitting packets from Network 10 to Network 47, consider the role of Router2 in the first route. Router2 has a choice of forwarding packets either to Router3 or to Router6. How does it know that forwarding the packet to Router6 will work and that forwarding to Router3 won't? The answer is yet another protocol, the Router Information Protocol (RIP).

When a router powers up or resets, it builds a list of routers on each directly connected network. This list may be preconfigured by an administrator, discovered through a broadcast-based process called *router discovery*, or both. The router then contacts each known router, asks what routes it can support, and adds those routes to its own routing table.

So, referring again to Figure 5.7, when Router2 powers up, it will discover and contact Router1, Router4, Router6, and Router3. Router1 will state it can reach Network 10 in one hop. Router4 will state it can reach Network 30 in one hop, Network 47 in two hops, Network 15 in three hops, and Network 21 in four hops. After collecting similar information from Router3 and Router6, Router2's routing table looks like this:

```
Network      Hops      Router

   10          1        Router1
   10          4        Router6
   12          0        Router2
   12          3        Router6
   15          0        Router2
   15          3        Router4
   21          1        Router3
   21          4        Router4
   30          1        Router4
   30          2        Router6
   47          1        Router6
   47          2        Router4
```

This is how Router2 knows that forwarding packets destined for Network 47 to Router6 will work and that forwarding such packets to Router3 won't. Packets going to Network 47 will get routed only to Router6 or Router4.

As it turns out, RIP operates all the time, not just when routers initialize. If someone hangs another router onto Network 21, any networks available to the new router will quickly become known to Router3. Router3 will then inform Router2 and Router6; those routers will then inform Router1, Router4, and Router6. Routers on the far side of the new router will also learn they can reach Networks 10, 12, 15, 21, 30, and 47 via the new router. As long as RIP is operating freely, no manual configuration is necessary.

Routers don't have to run RIP; an administrator can also configure them manually. Such configuration may involve setting all routes by hand, blocking certain routes, or enabling only a few blocks of routes. Manual configuration generally applies when RIP isn't available, or for security reasons, or for performance tuning. For instructions on how to display the current route table, see the sidebar titled "Examining the Windows NT Route Table."

5.6.2 Subnetting

Class A and B networks, with 16,387,064 and 64,516 hosts, respectively, are very difficult to manage as single, large networks. In practice, administrators almost always break these networks into smaller ones called *subnets*. This involves dedicating some host bits as subnet bits. A common scheme for Class B networks is eight bits for subnet number and eight bits for host number, but other divisions are certainly possible and completely valid.

Routers handle subnets just as they do networks, but they need to know which host bits denote the subnet number and which really indicate the host number. A value called a *subnet mask* conveys this information. The subnet mask is simply an IP address having 1-bits in the locations used for network and subnet numbers and 0-bits where the host number resides.

The IP address of www.compaq.com, Compaq's World Wide Web site, is a Class B address: 131.168.249.230. If they use eight bits for subnet number and eight bits for host number, the subnet mask would be 255.255.255.0. Note that 255 is the decimal equivalent of FF hexadecimal, which is eight 1-bits. Obtaining the subnet number is then a matter of ANDing the IP address and the subnet mask:

Examining the Windows NT Route Table

You can display the current route table on any Windows NT machine running TCP/IP with the command "route print."

Binary	Hexadecimal	Decimal
10000011.10101000.11111001.11100110	83-A8-F9-E6	131.168.249.230
11111111.11111111.11111111.00000000	FF-FF-FF-00	255.255.255.0
10000011.10101000.11111001.00000000	83-A8-F9-00	131.168.249.0

The procedure to decide whether two IP addresses are on the same subnet, then, is to AND the subnet mask with both addresses (effectively zeroing out the host bits) and compare the results.

A subnet mask of 255.255.255.0 is very common on Class A and B networks because it's so evident that addresses beginning with the same three octets are on the same subnet. A subnet mask of 255.255.192.0, or FF-FF-FA-00, reserves six bits for subnet and ten for host. 131.168.249.230 and 131.168.251.47 would then be on the same subnet (the 131.168.248.0 subnet!):

Binary	Hexadecimal	Decimal
10000011.10101000.11111001.11100110	83-A8-F9-E6	131.168.249.230
11111111.11111111.11111100.00000000	FF-FF-FA-00	255.255.252.0
10000011.10101000.11111000.00000000	83-A8-F8-00	131.168.248.0
10000011.10101000.11111011.00111111	83-A8-FB-2F	131.168.251.47
11111111.11111111.11111100.00000000	FF-FF-FA-00	255.255.252.0
10000011.10101000.11111000.00000000	83-A8-F8-00	131.168.248.0

By the way, it's technically possible to have subnet masks in which all the 1-bits aren't contiguous from the left, such as 255.255.3.0. This would indicate that the two rightmost bits of the third octet indicate the subnet number and that the six leftmost bits of the third octet plus the whole fourth octet constitute the host number. If you're thinking of doing this, please stop. It will surely cause you more grief than it saves.

5.7 Port Numbers and Connections

Once a computer receives an IP datagram, it must internally route it to the correct process or application. Two fields in the IP header make this possible: the protocol number and the port number. Table 5.3 lists common protocol numbers. For a complete list, view the file <systemroot>\system32\drivers\etc\protocol on any Windows NT system.

Table 5.3 Common Protocol Numbers

Protocol	Protocol Number	Description
IP	0	Internet Protocol
ICMP	1	Internet Control Message Protocol
TCP	6	Transmission Control Protocol
UDP	17	User Datagram Protocol

The IP layer examines the protocol number on incoming datagrams and forwards them to the correct transport protocol handler. The transport protocol forwards segments (in the case of TCP) or packets (for UDP) to the correct application based on a port number. Port numbers fall into three assigned ranges:

1. **Well-known ports.** Internet server applications ready themselves for work by listening on a standardized port number. That is, on start-up they call a TCP or UDP API that says, "If anything arrives on this port number, pass it to me." This requires that clients know what port server applications are listening on, so servers always listen on standard, "well-known" ports. Table 5.4 lists some of these well-known ports. For a complete list, inspect the file <systemroot>\system32\drivers\etc\services on any Windows NT system. Well-known ports are always less than 256.

2. **UNIX-specific services.** Ports numbered 256 through 1024 belong to a variety of UNIX applications such as LPR, the UNIX time service, and UUCP. These services now appear on many operating systems other than UNIX but continue to use ports 256 through 1024.

3. **Dynamically allocated ports.** A client opening a connection needs a port for itself as well as a port on the server. By convention, the operating system assigns these ports randomly or sequentially in the range 1025 through 65535, avoiding ports already in use. Windows NT assigns these ports sequentially.

Five IP header fields identify each connection:

1. Protocol (usually TCP or UDP)
2. Source address
3. Source port number
4. Destination address
5. Destination port number

Table 5.4 Common and Well-Known Port Numbers

Application	Port Number	Protocol	Description
ftp-data	20	TCP	FTP data connection
ftp	21	TCP	FTP control connection
telnet	23	TCP	Telnet (virtual terminal)
smtp	25	TCP	Simple Mail Transfer Protocol
time	37	TCP	Time server
time	37	UDP	Time server
name	42	TCP	Name server
name	42	UDP	Name server
whois	43	TCP	NIC name (usually to sri-nic)
domain	53	TCP	Domain Name Server
domain	53	UDP	Domain Name Server
bootp	67	UDP	Boot program server
tftp	69	UDP	Trivial File Transfer Protocol
gopher	70	TCP	Gopher
finger	79	TCP	Finger
http	80	TCP	HyperText Transfer Protocol
pop2	109	TCP	Post Office Protocol 2
pop3	110	TCP	Post Office Protocol 3
nntp	119	TCP	USENET News
ntp	123	UDP	Network Time Protocol
nbname	137	UDP	NETBIOS name
nbdatagram	138	UDP	NETBIOS datagram
nbsession	139	TCP	NETBIOS session
snmp	161	UDP	Simple Network Management Protocol
snmp-trap	162	UDP	SNMP traps
printer	515	TCP	Line Printer (LPR) spooler
timed	525	UDP	Time server
uucp	540	TCP	UNIX-to-UNIX Communication Protocol

It takes all five fields, in combination, to identify a connection. This is what allows a single client to establish, say, multiple Telnet sessions to the same server. The protocol, source address, destination address, and destination port (23) will be the same for each session, but the client source port number will be different.

To see the IP connections currently active on a Windows NT or Windows 95 computer, use the "netstat" command:

```
C:\>netstat -n

Active Connections

   Proto   Local Address          Foreign Address          State
   TCP     130.131.90.67:1033     130.131.90.111:21        ESTABLISHED
   TCP     130.131.90.67:1035     130.131.90.111:20        ESTABLISHED
```

Note the dynamically assigned port numbers (1033 and 1035) on the client machine and the well-known port numbers (21 and 20) on the server. An FTP file transfer is in progress.

5.8 Typical Configuration Settings

Most TCP/IP stacks for hosts require just three configuration settings, all of which should now be familiar:

1. **IP address.** The Internet Protocol address assigned to this host.
2. **Subnet mask.** The pattern of 1-bits that, when ANDed to the IP address, produces the subnet number. The defaults, which indicate subnetting isn't in effect, are 255.0.0.0 for Class A networks, 255.255.0.0 for Class B networks, and 255.255.255.0 for Class C networks. If subnetting is in effect, the octets that default to zero will have 1-bits inserted, generally starting from the left. All hosts and routers on the same subnet must use the same subnet mask.
3. **Default gateway.** The IP address of the router to which this host will send traffic leaving the local subnet.

Figure 5.8 shows the Windows NT TCP/IP Configuration dialog. The path to this window is Control Panel, Network, Installed Network Software: TCP/IP Protocol, Configure. Later chapters will cover the WINS, DNS, and Advanced settings.

5.9 Domain Name System

Section 1.2.1 briefly discussed DNS; Chapter 9 will discuss it in much greater detail and explain a sample installation. However, the following information is necessary here to provide continuity.

Names are easier to remember than numbers, especially random numbers. This is why the Domain Name System exists—to publish names that equate to IP addresses in a public, distributed database. When a user specifies a DNS name rather than an IP address, the application must ask DNS to translate the name to the corresponding IP address. The application then carries out the requested operation using the IP address.

To configure a host as a DNS client, you must generally provide the name of the domain the host belongs to, the host name the host will use, the address of the DNS servers to query, and the default domain names to search. You might

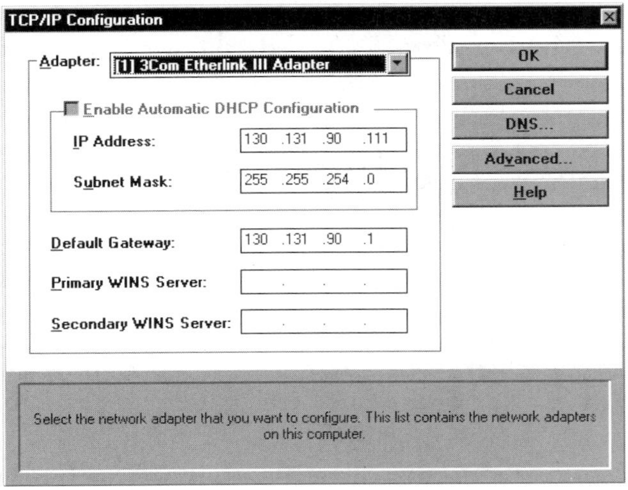

Figure 5.8 Windows NT TCP/IP Configuration Dialog

think this would register the specified host name with the specified Domain Name Server, but it doesn't; the network administrators who maintain the DNSs must perform all registrations.

At the simplest level of understanding, each period in a DNS name represents a server. Looking up a multipart name like www.windows.microsoft.com involves first locating the server that stores all .com entries. That server will give you the address of the server that stores all microsoft.com entries. The server that controls microsoft.com names will tell you what server knows about windows.microsoft.com names. Finally, the server for windows.microsoft.com will give you the IP address of host www.windows.microsoft.com.

Of course, nothing in real life is ever so simple. Consider these points:

- You may have noticed you don't have to configure each host with the IP addresses of the DNS servers for .com, .mil, .gov, .edu, and so on. Instead, this is part of the configuration on local DNS servers.

- If a DNS server cannot resolve a name, it can query a configured list of other DNS servers. This means not all DNS servers need the list of "core" servers; many servers resolve such requests through a number of "fall-back" servers instead.

- Both hosts and DNS servers cache recent DNS lookup results. Once your host has externally resolved the name www.windows.microsoft.com, it won't need to do so again until its name cache gets flushed. Furthermore, the local DNS server that resolved www.windows.microsoft.com won't have to query other servers to resolve that name again; it'll use information cached from the first lookup to answer future ones.

Although both are hierarchical, there's no relationship between DNS names and IP networks and subnets. IP addresses are just random numbers to DNS. Also, there's no reason for every DNS name to point to a different IP address; any number of aliases can exist.

5.10 Registering Your Site

Preventing duplicate use of IP addresses and domain names requires centralized assignment. The organization that provides this service is the Internet Network Information Center (InterNIC). A company named Network Solutions handles day-to-day operations.

To obtain a registered network number or domain name, browse http://rs.internic.net/rs-internic.html. From that page, you can choose to obtain text templates of the application forms or jump directly to HTML forms. You can also jump to InterNIC's whois service, where you can check registration information for existing names.

The text versions of the registration forms are as follows:

- To request an IP network number
  ftp://rs.internic.net/templates/internet-number-template.txt
- To request a domain name
  ftp://rs.internic.net/templates/domain-template.txt

Each form includes instructions at the bottom. When you've completed the form(s) you require, e-mail them to hostmaster@internic.net. If you prefer to use the HTML forms, just fill them out and click the "submit" button.

There is no charge for obtaining an IP network number, but if you want a Class B address or a block of Class Cs, you'll have to submit network diagrams and growth projections to justify the request.

Domain names cost $50 a year, with two years service billable in advance. InterNIC will send you a hard-copy bill for this amount. To get a domain name, you must also supply the addresses of two DNS servers, preferably in different physical and network locations, that are already up and running.

You may wish to have your Internet Service Provider complete these applications for you and provide DNS service, at least initially. Fees are usually small, and they know how to get it right the first time. This is true even if you're an

Internet Service Provider yourself; after all, except for the really big guys, everybody buys their uplink from somebody. If you're one of those really big guys, you probably don't need this advice.

5.11 Locating Standards Documents

Requests For Comment (RFCs) are the standards that define TCP/IP, the Internet, and related services. These standards seem to be invented, approved, and implemented faster than in almost any other technology. Internet standards committees tend to be groups of technicians facing immediate problems, not corporate representatives attempting to gain advantage for their own products and to crowd out competitors.

The term *request for comment* stems from the concept of someone posting an idea for comment, receiving collaboration and assistance from other interested persons, and beating the concept into shape. The process has become much more formal that that, involving committee meetings and formal review, but an approved standard is still an RFC. To locate a particular RFC, browse http://www.internic.net/ds/dspg1intdoc.html.

CHAPTER 6

Selecting Communications

Communication requirements vary widely from one Internet services site to another. Fortunately, there are many options to choose from. Unfortunately, choosing from among so many options can be difficult.

Communications are also a major expense. It isn't unusual to spend more on communications equipment than on servers, nor for communications to be the site's largest single operating expense. Costs are dropping and bandwidth is increasing, but neither trend is occurring fast enough to suit most operators.

Most Internet sites use different approaches for connecting local users to the site, connecting various pieces of equipment at the site, and connecting the site to the Internet. Seldom are these technologies combined into a single computer. More often, an Ethernet LAN connects dial-in equipment, a number of site hosts, and routers providing wide-area connectivity. This general model is the basis for most of this chapter.

There are many choices for categorizing communication issues: client-to-server versus server-to-Internet, local area versus wide area, dial-up versus dedicated, switched versus leased, and many more. This chapter first discusses circuit types, then Internet site configuration, and finally client software.

6.1 Introduction to Circuit Types

Table 6.1 lists the most common circuit types used for Internet connections. No one circuit type is best for everyone; the type you choose will depend on your operating environment, the number of users, and the amount of performance the enterprise or customers are willing to pay for.

Table 6.1 Circuit Types

Common Name	Min. bps	Max. bps	Connection	Latency	Local Equipment
Dial-up	1200	28.8K	Switched	Low	Modem
ISDN	56K	128K	Switched	Low	NT-1
56Kb	56K	56K	Dedicated	Low	CSU/DSU
Switched 56	56K	56K	Switched	Low	CSU/DSU
X.25	1.2K	256K	Packet	High	PAD
Frame Relay	56K	140M	Packet	Medium	CSU/DSU
T1	1.544M	1.544M	Dedicated	Low	CSU/DSU
Token Ring	4M	16M	Local	Low	MAU
Ethernet	10M	100M	Local	Low	Wiring hub
T3	45M	45M	Dedicated	Low	CSU/DSU
ATM	155M	660M	Packet	Low	LAN emulation hub or ATM switch

6.1.1 Switched Circuits

Individual users typically use switched circuits because it saves money to pay only for minutes connected. Sites with many users usually buy dedicated circuits because they need continuous service; the odds of having significant periods of no activity are very low. Local Area Networks (LANs) connect groups of users in the same office, building, or campus.

6.1.2 Packet Services

Individual users tend to consume bandwidth in bursts. Most of the time they demand no bandwidth at all, but every minute or so they want thousands or millions of bytes transferred very rapidly. They care how long their transactions take, not how much bandwidth they waste between transactions. The perfect circuit for this type of activity would be very high speed and would charge only by the byte—nothing for connect time. No such service is currently available, but packet networks approach it. This explains their popularity despite latency.

Latency is a measure of network delay beyond that caused by line speed. Put another way, it's the delay between sending a given bit and receiving it at the destination. Latency is greatest in packet networks that receive and completely validate each packet before sending it to the next station. The effect is like an inchworm crawling along or a taxi working its way through traffic. When either moves, it moves at a certain rate; however, neither moves continuously. Time spent not moving is latency.

Despite their latency, packet networks have the advantage that a given user occupies a circuit only for the duration of each packet delivery. Providers can sell gaps between packets to other users, reducing the cost to each user. Of course, this introduces even more latency, as one user may need to wait for another user's packet to clear the network.

6.1.3 Dedicated Circuits

Dedicated circuits are just that—permanently in place, consistently available 24 hours a day, 7 days a week. For intermittent use, dedicated circuits are more expensive than switched circuits of the same speed. However, a full month of switched service kept up 24 hours a day is more expensive than a dedicated circuit.

Each type of circuit requires its own specialized equipment at each end of the line. The following sections describing each circuit type will cover these.

6.2 Dial-Up Circuits

Voice telephone circuits are relatively inadequate for today's digital communication needs. They have only one strong point, but it's an important one: ubiquity. Whether at home, at your office or someone else's, or in a hotel, an airport, an airplane, or a convention center, you can always find a telephone.[1]

Analog modems have evolved into a confusing array of speeds and standards. Table 6.2 lists the most common current types.

The CCITT, known in English as the International Consultative Committee on Telegraphy and Telephony, sets all "V-dot" standards. Before its breakup, the Bell Telephone Company set Bell standards. The Microcom Network Protocol (MNP) is a set of proprietary techniques that Microcom released into the public domain.

Table 6.2 Modem Types and Standards

Carrier Speed	Carrier Standard	Typical Compression, Error Correction and Detection
1200	Bell 212A, V.22	None
2400	V.22bis	V.42, MNP4, MNP5
9600	V.32	V.42, MNP4, MNP5
14,400	V.32bis	V.42bis
28,800	V.34	V.42bis

---

[1]Finding an RJ-11 jack and a nearby power outlet is another matter entirely. Someone should devise a single outlet that provides a phone line and operating power for portable computers and then blanket airports, airplanes, hotel lobbies, hotel rooms, and convention centers with them.

Analog modems operating above 2400 bits per second (bps) are virtually certain to encounter frequent transmission errors, so error detection and correction are practical necessities. Error detection necessarily involves packetizing transmitted data, computing checksums, and withholding packets from the receiving computer until the checksum is verified and any necessary retransmissions are complete. This implies that high-speed modems introduce a certain amount of latency but total throughput still improves. An added bonus is that, as the modem packetizes the data, it can also compress it. Compression ratios up to 4:1 are possible but seldom achieved. 2:1 is more typical for general work, and 1:1 (no compression) is likely for data in compressed formats like GIF (Graphic Interchange Format), JPEG (Joint Photographic Experts Group), and Zip.

Non-error-detecting, noncompressing modems such as older 1200bps and 2400bps models were strictly bitwise devices. The carrier speed, the modem's serial port speed, and the computer's serial port speed necessarily had to be the same. Error-detecting modems, however, are packet-oriented, buffered devices with no relationship between carrier speed and serial port speed. Best practice is to fix the serial port speed at four times the fastest supported carrier speed or whatever your hardware will support.

Serial ports for high-speed modems should use 16550A serial port chips and hardware (RTS/CTS) handshake. Older serial port chips are too slow and lack on-chip buffering. The 16550A has a 16-byte on-chip buffer that provides two advantages. First, if data is arriving faster than the computer can receive it, the serial port can accommodate a backlog up to 16 bytes before having to discard data. Hopefully, during the time it takes 16 bytes to arrive, the serial port can signal the local modem that it can't receive more data, and the local modem can signal the remote modem to stop sending. Second, having a buffer on the serial port chip means it needn't trigger an interrupt for every arriving character. Otherwise, data from a 28.8Kbps modem achieving 4:1 compression would trigger 115,200 interrupts a second—enough to disrupt smooth operation of almost any system.

Handshake (or flow control) is the way a modem informs a computer whether it's capable of accepting more data to be transmitted. The computer uses the same mechanism to inform the modem whether it's capable of accepting incoming data. Most setup dialogs for modems have three handshake options:

1. **None.** This choice specifies that the computer and the modem won't exchange readiness to send and receive data. This is acceptable only with very slow modems and nonmultitasking operating systems.

2. **XON/XOFF.** This option states that when the modem is unable to accept more data from the computer, it will transmit an XOFF character (Ctrl-Q) to the computer. When the modem is again ready to accept data, it

will transmit an XON character (Ctrl-S). The computer will transmit its status to the modem using the same two characters. Use of the XON and XOFF characters is somewhat acceptable when transmitting text data but not when transmitting binary files that may contain these characters. Transmitting an entire character to convey status is also a relatively time-consuming operation.

3. **Hardware or RTS/CTS.** CTS is the acronym for Clear To Send, a pin on the serial port connector. The modem's CTS pin connects to the computer's RTS (Request To Send) pin, and the computer's CTS connects to the modem's RTS. Each device puts voltage on its respective CTS pin when it's capable of accepting data and withdraws voltage when it's not. Because this scheme uses different pins from the ones that transmit actual data, it never gets confused by the data's content. Also, it's very fast—much faster than transmitting a control character. RTS/CTS is the preferred handshake for high-speed modems.

One caution with respect to using RTS/CTS handshake is that the modem cable must have these pins wired. Some cables omit these wires or apply constant voltage from another pin. If you encounter repeated problems using RTS/CTS handshake with an external modem, try purchasing another cable that has all the necessary pins connected.

6.2.1 Modem Management and Modem Banks

Managing a bank of modems involves several problems that users with a single modem don't have to worry about—at least not until they call your site. Whether you're running 8, 12, 16, or hundreds of modems, you need to get them all configured alike, securely mounted, and properly wired to the telephone system. After installation, you need to know how many are in use by time of day and day of week and whether any phone lines or modems are consistently failing. Not having enough modems means you're turning away customers or internal users, but how many are enough?

Managed modem banks provide solutions to these issues. Such systems consist of a chassis, a control module, and a series of slots for plugging in modems. The modems conform to industry standards for modulation, compression, error correction, serial port use, and so forth, but the rest of the system is proprietary. That is, you can't mix components from several vendors. The chassis generally fits in a standard 19-inch equipment rack.

The control module keeps activity logs for each modem so that for each call you can determine whether the modems connected and how long the call lasted.

Modems that repeatedly fail to connect or show a pattern of very short calls are those that require further investigation. The control module may also provide security features such as prompting for user IDs and passwords and using passwords configured into both modems (remote and central). The control module may also let you "break in" to the modem's serial port for diagnostics and configuration without physically disconnecting the modem cable.

Mounting modems, or any other equipment, in racks and chassis provides efficient use of space, convenient access to the front and back of all equipment, and secure physical connections. In the case of modems, a tangle of dozens or hundreds of power bricks plugged into a loose collection of power strips at one end and an equal number of slide-in/slide-out power connectors at the other is almost certain to be troublesome. Leading manufacturers of managed, rack-mount modem systems include Codex, Microcom, and US Robotics.

Smaller sites may wish to consider modem banks integrated with dial-in routers. This eliminates serial port throughput problems and gives you fewer boxes to manage, but it also requires using the same vendor for modems and the dial-in router. Some of these systems achieve compactness and modem independence by using PCMCIA modems, but you should be suspicious of phone line connections to such modems. Many PCMCIA modems have flimsy external connections and heavy dongles. (PCMCIA stands for the Personal Computer Memory Card Industry Association.)

When you order several phone lines that callers will access through a single inbound number, each line nevertheless has its own number. You should carefully tag and record each such line so that if it stops working, you can dial into it specifically for testing or report it to the phone company. Also, you should order a "rotary group" rather than a "hunt group."

In a hunt group, the telephone switch always searches for an available line starting with the same number and using the same search sequence. If, say, modem 3 isn't answering, almost every caller will get modem 3 and no answer. (Modems 1 and 2, of course, will be chronically busy.) The only way to get to modem 4 and beyond is to call while someone else is timing out on modem 3.

A rotary group will advance to the next number in the group after every call. This means, in the example just described, that once somebody calls modem 3, the switch will start its next search from modem 4, not from modem 1. The next search will start at modem 5, and so on.

Load balancing is another factor to consider when connecting telephone lines. If you have 16 incoming lines and 2 eight-port routers, you should probably connect the lines so that the first call goes to router 1, port 1; the second call to router 2, port 1; the third call to router 1, port 2; and so on. This minimizes redialing when a router is down and equalizes the load on both routers.

6.2.2 Introduction to SLIP and PPP

Rick Adams invented the Serial Line Internet Protocol (SLIP) in 1984 for use on Sun workstations (Gilster 1995). Like so many ideas that meet a pressing need, SLIP quickly gained popularity for dialing into UNIX and is now an integral part of that operating system.

SLIP doesn't provide a complete protocol stack on the remote computer. It provides most of the Application Programming Interfaces (APIs) a full stack would provide, but then it uses a serial port to transmit the data to another computer for networking. There is no compression or error checking.

Certain things about SLIP make sense. There's no need to include source addresses in packets sent by the remote computer, for example; there's only one computer at the far end of a SLIP connection, and its addresses are constant. There's also no need to clog up modem bandwidth with acknowledgments, retries, and other overhead.

Still, SLIP has its limits. It only supports TCP/IP—and a subset of TCP/IP at that. Microsoft Networking can't operate over SLIP as it can over local TCP/IP because of incomplete broadcast support. CSLIP adds compression to SLIP, but support isn't universal. Neither SLIP nor CSLIP has full, officially published standards that completely describe it.

The Point-to-Point Protocol (PPP) provides a more complex but more complete solution. PPP first appeared in 1989 with implementations by Russ Hobby at the University of California at San Diego and Drew Perkins at Carnegie-Mellon University. A Point-to-Point Working Group exists within the Internet Engineering Task Force (Gilster 1995).

Unlike SLIP, PPP provides (and in fact requires) a complete protocol stack on the remote computer. On PCs, PPP software typically consists of a MAC layer (data link) driver that fits neatly into the structure of Figure 5.5. As a data link protocol, PPP supports many higher-level protocols, such as NetBEUI, DLC, IPX/SPX, and DECnet, as well as TCP/IP.

PPP automatically supports error checking and data compression based on connect-time negotiation between PPP client and server. This negotiation first establishes compatible framing rules (compression, error detection, and encryption methods to be used) and then authenticates the remote used using PAP, CHAP, or SPAP depending on client and server security configurations (see the sidebar titled "PPP Authentication Protocols" for more details). Finally, Network Control Protocols (NCPs) establish the transport protocols and related settings (such as the IP address) the client and server will use.

PPP Authentication Protocols

The Point-to-Point Protocol authenticates remote connections using one of the following protocols (a negotiation prior to login determines the most secure protocol available on both client and server):

Protocol	Description	Encryption	Security
MD5	MD5	DES and RSA Security	High
CHAP	Challenge Handshake Authentication Protocol	One-way	High
SPAP	Shiva Password Authentication Protocol	Two-way	Medium
PAP	Password Authentication Protocol	Clear-text	Low

SLIP has been in use longer than PPP, is simpler to configure, and is more widely used and understood. Microsoft, however, has established a preference for PPP and included an excellent, easy-to-configure PPP client with every copy of Windows 95.

6.2.3 Dial–In Routers

In a simplistic view, a dial-in router is a device with several serial ports and one network interface. Software running inside the box manages SLIP and PPP sessions, putting inbound data onto the network and transmitting outbound data back to the SLIP and PPP clients. Having software run inside the box means it must also have a CPU, RAM, and some kind of console interface.

Actually, such a box could be a repeater, bridge, router, or gateway, but for handling TCP/IP it's usually a router. Dial-up connections are very slow compared to other types, and dial-in servers normally take every precaution to keep unneeded traffic off the modem link. A device that can filter traffic by IP address is, by definition, a router.

The choice of dial-in routers is plentiful; 3Com, Bay, Cisco, Microcom, Shiva, and Xyplex are a few of the many vendors. No one vendor's box is best for all sites, but here are some features to consider:

■ **Supported client types.** Whether you need to support a single client type or a long list of clients, make sure in advance the dial-in router you select will support them all.

- **Serial port speed.** Make sure the serial ports support speeds equal to at least twice (and preferably four times) the maximum carrier speed of your modems.

- **User name and password management.** If there's any possibility you may be running two or more dial-in routers, you should look for equipment that supports a single user name/password database. That is, if you're operating five dial-in routers, you don't want to enter new users, make password changes, and delete old users five times each (once on each box).

- **Statistics and logging.** This issue is critical if you plan to bill or charge back by connect minute. However, even if you don't need these statistics for billing, you'll appreciate them for demand analysis and capacity planning. Lack of usage on a particular router port is also an indicator of hardware problems that warrant investigation. SNMP (Simple Network Management Protocol) features permit collecting and recording statistics from a network management console.

- **IP address and parameter assignment.** The router should support whatever mode of IP address assignment you wish to use. Possibilities include fixed IP addresses assigned to each remote user, fixed IP addresses assigned to each dial-in port, and IP addresses assigned by another network service like BOOTP (Bootstrap Protocol) or DHCP. If you want remote clients to obtain other parameters such as the default gateway, subnet mask, host name, domain name, and DNS addresses, you should make sure the router supports configuration protocols the intended clients can use.

- **Protocols.** An Internet services site will undoubtedly want to support TCP/IP, but if it needs to support other protocols, you should ensure that the dial-in routers are compatible. For example, you may need to support IPX/SPX, DECnet, or NetBEUI clients over the same equipment.

6.2.4 Windows NT Remote Access Service

Microsoft's Remote Access Service (RAS) is a software solution that supports network dial-in and dial-out using Windows NT Workstation or Windows NT Server. RAS supports both SLIP and PPP for dial-out, but only PPP for dial-in.

Windows NT Workstation supports only one simultaneous dial-in connection, but Windows NT Server supports up to 255. Connections may be via serial port (modem), ISDN, X.25, or null modem cable. Supporting modem banks requires a multi-serial-port card such as a Digiboard. As always, consult the Windows NT Hardware Compatibility List to locate supported hardware for the connection types you require.

RAS uses Windows NT user names and passwords for login validation. This means if you have several RAS servers on the same domain, the same Windows NT user names and passwords will be valid on each of them.

Note that, by default, Windows NT user names and passwords aren't valid for use with RAS. An administrator must use the RAS Administrator program to grant RAS privileges to each authorized dial-in user. Chapter 7 will present details on how to install RAS.

6.3 Switched Digital Connections

6.3.1 ISDN

Virtually the entire United States telephone system is digital except for the local circuits that extend to each home, store, or office. Data communications would improve markedly if telephone companies (telcos) could convert such local circuits to digital as well. This is the "last-mile" problem. If the last mile or so of wiring could be converted from analog to digital, ordinary telephone circuits would become 64Kbps digital lines and modems would be unnecessary.

One technology that solves the last-mile problem has been available for years; it's the Integrated Services Digital Network (ISDN). Unfortunately, several factors have slowed adoption of ISDN:

- At most, ISDN can traverse only about two miles of copper wire. This means ISDN subscribers must be within two miles of a central office or remote switching unit. In most cities and virtually all rural areas, this results in very spotty ISDN availability.

- Supporting ISDN requires major, expensive changes in the telco's central office switch.

- Availability of ISDN might reduce demand for other profitable services such as Switched 56, Leased 56, and Frame Relay.

- Several emerging technologies offer much more bandwidth than ISDN and are much cheaper for the telco or other provider to install.

- Many telcos have concluded additional revenues from selling ISDN would not recover the cost of supplying it.

- ISDN is notoriously difficult to configure.

■ Even if you can obtain ISDN service for your home, store, or office, chances are the services you wish to call can't or won't support ISDN.

The cost of ISDN varies widely by location. In some areas, it costs little more than conventional analog service and is easy to get installed. Elsewhere, it may cost three or four times the local analog rate plus per-minute charges even for local calls. Despite the difficulty of obtaining and configuring ISDN, it remains a far superior technology to analog modems and is certainly worth considering if available in your area.

There are two common ISDN classes of service: Basic Rate Interface (BRI) and Primary Rate Interface (PRI). BRI supplies two B-channels of 64Kbps each plus one D-channel of 16Kbps for control—hence, the name 2B+D. The two B-channels are independent; you can make separate voice calls on each B-channel, one data call and one voice call, or two data calls to the same or different locations.

B-channels are nominally 64Kbps, but, in many implementations, framing reduces this to 56Kbps. Framing refers to control bits interspersed with data. These control bits aren't visible to the user, but they do soak up bandwidth.

PRI provides 23 subscriber B-channels plus a D-channel for control—hence, the name 23B+D. This adds up to 1.544Mbps, which is the same as T1. BRI circuits are generally appropriate for end users and PRI circuits for central sites with many incoming lines.

A telco delivers BRI circuits using a two-wire circuit called a U interface. An "NT-1" device converts this to a four-wire S/T interface. The S/T interface can support several ISDN devices, each of which is individually addressable. This eliminates the problem of discriminating incoming FAX, voice, and data calls.

The ISDN data equipment market is young and evolving; vendors are producing and scrapping new kinds of products rapidly. Three general categories, however, have emerged:

1. **ISDN modems.** These devices aren't really modems, but modem emulators. They connect to a computer's serial port and obey a modified AT command set. Such devices have only recently come to market; they're an attempt to make ISDN comprehensible to those who don't understand network adapters, bridges, and routers. ISDN modems typically use the same software a modem would use: SLIP, PPP, and dial-up communication programs such as Procomm and Crosstalk.

2. **ISDN network adapters.** Devices of this type function in place of an Ethernet or a Token Ring adapter. They may originate and answer data calls automatically, based on demand, or in response to manual commands.

3. **ISDN bridges and routers.** This class of devices essentially converts ISDN to Ethernet or Token Ring. This permits any number of devices on the same LAN to use the same ISDN circuit. Like ISDN network adapters, ISDN bridges and routers may originate and answer calls either on demand or based on specific commands.

Cost of this equipment varies widely, but, in general, ISDN modems are the cheapest and ISDN routers the most expensive. Note, however, that only the bridges and routers support multiple devices.

ISDN call setup times are typically a fraction of a second. A connect-on-demand router or network adapter therefore introduces very little delay even if it's not connected when data is ready for transmission.

You'll need to do extra investigation if you plan to get the full 112Kbps or 128Kbps out of two B-channels; this requires a technique called *inverse multiplexing*. An Internet standard, the Multilink Point-to-Point Control, defines use of inverse multiplexing, but current ISDN products use proprietary methods or fail to support inverse multiplexing at all. Use of proprietary methods means you must have matching ISDN adapters at both ends of the circuit. You must also use a network protocol that can break large packets into smaller ones, deliver them independently, and reassemble them upon delivery. Fortunately, TCP/IP has this capability.

Compression over ISDN is another area lacking standards. Again, the only current solution is to buy matching equipment.

ISDN modems, network adapters, bridges, and routers are available with and without the NT-1 device built in. Having a built-in NT-1 device is generally cheaper, but it usually prevents you from connecting several devices to the same ISDN circuit. Pick your poison, but be sure your NT-1, internal or external, is compatible with the telco switch that will provide your service. ISDN equipment is available from vendors such as 3Com, Ascend, Cisco, Digiboard, Gandalf, and Intel.

6.3.2 Switched 56

This service combines features of ISDN (discussed in the preceding section) and DS0 (discussed in the next section). Switched 56 provides a single 56Kbps circuit that subscribers can activate or terminate at will.

Switched 56 is generally more expensive and less flexible than ISDN, which has twice the bandwidth. If connect hours per month are high enough, it can also be more expensive than Dedicated 56 (DS0). Frame Relay (also discussed later) tends to be less expensive than Switched 56 if sites are far apart.

Unlike ISDN, call setup time for Switched 56 may be 20 seconds or more. This may be an unacceptable delay when, for example, a remote Internet user requests a page from your site and the circuit isn't active.

Despite its limitations, Switched 56 may nevertheless be desirable in situations where demand is intermittent and alternatives such as ISDN and Frame Relay aren't available.

6.4 Dedicated Digital Circuits

Also called *point-to-point*, *private*, and *leased* lines, these circuits provide fixed bandwidth between fixed points 24 hours a day, 7 days a week. Dedicated lines have been available longer, are better supported, and are more prevalent than any other type of circuit. Table 6.3 lists the most common classes of service.

The cost of T1 service has been falling faster than that of DS0, so T1, which provides 24 times the bandwidth of DS0, frequently costs only two to four times as much. Multi-DS0 is frequently not much cheaper than T1 because the provider generally must install a T1 and then throttle it back.

Dedicated digital lines require a bridge or router at each end plus a Data Service Unit/Channel Service Unit (DSU/CSU) at each end. Figure 6.1 illustrates this configuration.

In theory, DSU/CSUs of any brand should work together because they conform to the same standards. In practice, installation is much simpler with identical equipment at each end. The same tends to be true for routers. If you control both ends of the circuit, you can pick whatever equipment you're comfortable with. If someone else—perhaps your uplink provider—controls one end, it's likely they'll offer to equip and configure your end as well. This service usually isn't expensive, and it can eliminate major interoperability headaches for both parties.

Table 6.3 Dedicated Digital Circuit Classes

Class of Service	Total Bandwidth Kbps	Effective Bandwidth Kbps
DS0	64	56
Multi-DS0	128–1,480	112–1,288
T1	1,544	1,344
T3	44,736	37,632

Figure 6.1 Dedicated Digital Line Schematic

6.5 Packet-Switched Networks

The nature of data communications is such that when someone requests service from an interactive application, providing quick response requires high momentary bandwidth. Between transactions, a dedicated circuit does nothing but run up charges.

Aggregating many users onto a few circuits is typically much cheaper than providing dedicated circuits for everyone, and it usually results in very little degradation. Unless the network is overcrowded, random bursts of activity seldom occur at exactly the same time; even if they do, delays waiting for an empty time slice are usually very brief. This is the principle behind shared-media LANs such as Ethernet and Token Ring.

Circuit providers can also decrease costs and prices by aggregating users. However, no aggregation is possible if all users expect full bandwidth 100 percent of the time. Packet-switched services provide cheaper but somewhat inconsistent service compared to dedicated circuits, and are therefore sold as separate products.

Packet switching implies that the service provider understands the supplied traffic as network packets and routes them through the network based on individual packet addresses. The alternative, circuit switching, supplies a fixed bandwidth for the duration of the connection. Even permanent circuits are switched; provider technicians simply "nail" the switch connections so that the circuit never disconnects.

6.5.1 X.25 Circuits

Figure 6.2 illustrates some typical X.25 components. The X.25 network appears as a cloud because the exact arrangement of circuits and switches isn't externally apparent. Connected computers simply push addressed packets into the cloud, and the X.25 network pops them back out at the specified location.

A Packet Assembler/Disassembler (PAD) provides entry to the X.25 cloud. Figure 6.2 shows three PADs: one with a serial port, one with a direct host

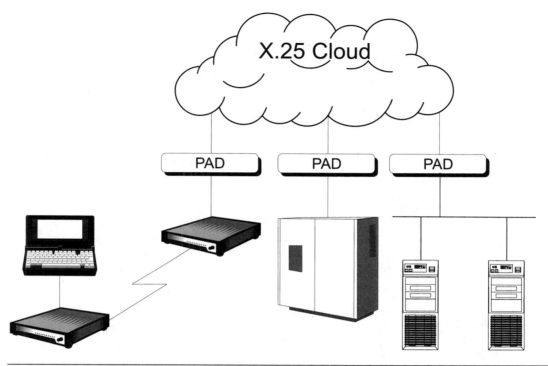

Figure 6.2 X.25 Network Components

connection, and one with an Ethernet port. PADs usually function as gateways by translating addresses, repacketizing, and encapsulating as required. They may also function as IP routers.

IP routers on an X.25 network don't discover each other with protocols like RIP. Instead, an administrator must configure each pair of routers with static routes. In Figure 6.3, for example, Router1 wouldn't automatically learn of Router2's existence; an administrator would have to manually identify Router2's X.25 address to Router1. Once the connection between Router1 and Router2 existed, however, RIP from Router2 would inform Router1 of all other routers on Network2; RIP from Router1 would inform Router2 of all other routers on Network1; and so on.

X.25 circuits are virtual, and a single physical connection can support up to 255 virtual circuits. If Figure 6.3 illustrated three or more networks, each would need only one PAD and one router. That is, connections from each router to two, three, or more others would coexist on the same X.25 line.

Latency is X.25's greatest disadvantage. Inside the cloud lies a complex mesh of circuits and switches. Each packet typically passes through several hops on its

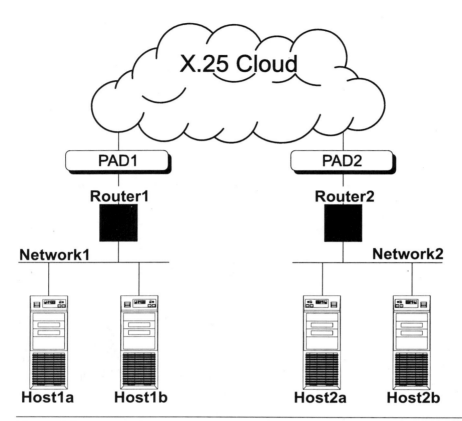

Figure 6.3 IP Routing through X.25

way through the network, and error detection and correction occur at each hop. That is, an X.25 switch won't start transmitting a packet until it receives the packet's last incoming bit and checks the entire packet for errors. The more hops, the more latency.

Using small packet sizes reduces latency but increases encapsulation overhead. As a result, most X.25 networks are unable to support speeds in excess of 56Kbps.

X.25's latency and limited bandwidth have recently retarded growth of X.25 networking. Nevertheless, several worldwide X.25 networks have existed for years and will undoubtedly continue to do so. These include the CompuServe network, Genie, SprintNet (formerly called Telenet), and Tymnet. Widely used applications include time-sharing on-line services, credit card verification, and international commerce. You are more likely to encounter X.25 as a facility your company or customer already has in place than as an attractive option for new installations.

6.5.2 Frame Relay Circuits

Frame Relay is a new packet-switching technology that, unlike X.25, is growing rapidly. It combines the best features of packet-based services with the speed of dedicated circuits. Frame Relay can attain speeds up to 140Mbps but has much less error checking and control than X.25. Fortunately, errors are typically rare on today's fiber optic national backbones.

As with X.25, a cloud usually depicts Frame Relay. Unlike X.25, however, all Frame Relay connections must currently be permanent virtual circuits. That is, if you buy Frame Relay connections for five sites, that doesn't mean any site can open a connection at will to any of the other four. Instead, you must order each connection in each direction you want.

Figure 6.4 illustrates a Frame Relay network. A router, a CSU/DSU, and a dedicated point-to-point circuit connect each site to the Frame Relay cloud. Frame Relay providers typically don't charge for distance, but providers of local, dedicated point-to-point circuits do, which is a good reason to select a Frame Relay provider with nearby points of presence.

Permanent Virtual Circuit (PVC) Plan #1 illustrates full interconnection of all four sites. Twelve virtual circuits are required. PVC Plan #2 accomplishes the same connectivity using only four circuits. True, transmissions from Network1 to Network4 must pass through sites 2 and 3, but perhaps four high-bandwidth circuits are cheaper than twelve low-bandwidth ones. PVC Plan #3 provides one-hop connectivity between all sites and site 3, plus two-hop connectivity among sites 1, 2, and 4. This arrangement might be appropriate if site 3 were a headquarters or main network control site.

Note that all three PVC plans, plus many others that are equally possible, follow the same physical schematic. Whether one, two, four, six, or some other number of virtual circuits are being used at a site, only one router and one CSU/DSU are necessary. This can significantly reduce equipment costs. The router must physically have ports compatible with the local network and with the CSU/DSU, and it must have the necessary Frame Relay features in its software.

As with X.25, reducing latency requires shortening packets, but shortening packets increases their quantity, and the overhead of additional packet headers eventually offsets any further gain. One way that Frame Relay reduces header overhead is by using Data Link Connection Identifiers (DLCIs) instead of source and destination addresses. A DLCI is basically an abbreviation for a given source and destination address pair. The DLCI is shorter than the original address pair, reducing overhead.

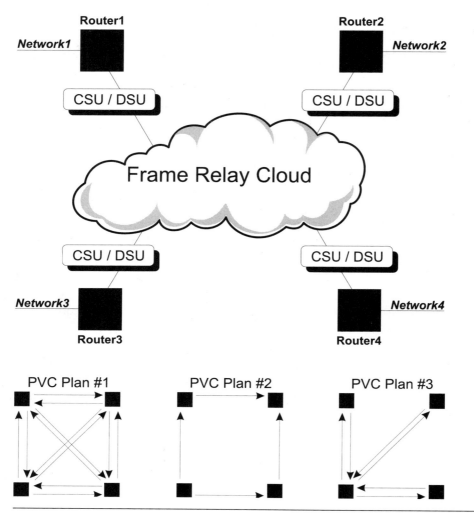

Figure 6.4 Frame Relay Configuration

Each Frame Relay PVC has a Committed Information Rate (CIR). This is the average bandwidth the provider guarantees to provide over a stated time period. The data rate received at any given moment may vary from the CIR, but it is usually faster rather than slower. The upper bound is the Excess Information Rate (EIR). The CIR isn't bound to the speed of the line connecting a site to the Frame Relay network. You may buy a 128Kbps or 256Kbps line to connect to a PVC with CIR of 56Kbps for several reasons. For one, you may wish to take advantage of bandwidth beyond the CIR when it's available. For another, you may plan to run four CIR 56Kbps lines over the single 256Kbps connection.

Note that buying a T1 to connect to 24 CIR 56Kbps lines is probably a bad idea. If the router at the T1 site transmits data at full T1 speed to a 56Kbps site for very long, the buffers in the Frame Relay network will overflow and lose packets. Frame Relay returns no error indication in such cases but depends on TCP or some other layer to detect lack of acknowledgment and initiate retransmission. Perhaps someone will invent a router that paces data sent to remote sites with slower PVCs than its own.

Use of multiple PVCs can reserve bandwidth for specific services. You may prefer to support newsfeeds and FTP over a separate PVC from the one that supports HTTP, for example. This would ensure that HTTP service doesn't degrade when heavy newsfeeds or FTP transfers are in progress.

Since Frame Relay requires dedicated circuits from each site to the Frame Relay service provider, connecting nearby sites may be uneconomical. That is, it may be cheaper to buy a dedicated circuit connecting two nearby sites than to buy circuits from each site to a Frame Relay provider.

Availability of Frame Relay is growing rapidly but is still far from universal. Expect service from different providers to vary widely in features, price, and availability. In the future, providers may offer Frame Relay Switched Virtual Circuits (SVCs). This would further reduce costs and increase flexibility by allowing routers to open and close sessions based on demand.

6.5.3 Asynchronous Transfer Mode

ATM technology promises to become the common worldwide standard for voice, data, video, and other multimedia communication.

6.5.3.1 ATM Concepts ATM handles data in 53-byte cells, of which 48 are data and 5 are header. The 48-byte length was a compromise between the United States (which favored a 64-byte payload as better for data communication) and Europe and Japan (which felt a 32-byte payload was better for telephony). The committee chose a 5-byte header length because more than 10 percent overhead seemed unreasonable.

ATM supports Switched Virtual Circuits (SVCs), which clients can set up or terminate on demand, and Permanent Virtual Circuits (PVCs), which deliver a fixed bandwidth between two fixed points. A 3-byte Virtual Path Identifier/Virtual Circuit Identifier (VPI/VCI) provides addressing in much the same way as the DLCI in Frame Relay.

The bandwidth of ATM is impressive. Most ATM equipment sold today supports OC-3, a signaling standard that provides 155Mbps. An OC-12 standard provides 622Mbps, but not much equipment of this type is available yet. OC-48 will provide bandwidth in the gigabit range.

The most appealing aspect of ATM, however, is the prospect of a universal high-bandwidth network. The small, high-speed, fixed-length cells are very easy for packet switches to handle. Unlike Frame Relay, ATM switched virtual circuits provide any-to-any connectivity on demand.

6.5.3.2 Use of ATM for Data Applications Little if any ATM service is currently available from public carriers. Most data communication installations have therefore involved high-speed LANs for large organizations. These installations highlight a lack of standards in two areas: congestion management and LAN emulation.

ATM relies on cells arriving in the exact order sent with no cells dropped. This is especially critical when handling data originated using LAN protocols since TCP/IP packets, for example, may be considerably longer than ATM's 48-byte per cell payload. To handle these longer packets ATM has a process called *segmentation* that breaks them into cells. If a single cell is lost or received out of sequence, reassembly (which is the opposite of segmentation) will fail or the packet will fail cyclic redundancy checking (CRC) in the TCP/IP stack.

6.5.3.3 Congestion Management The most common cause of lost or out-of-sequence cells is congestion—that is, too many cells arriving in the same place at the same time. ATM has no congestion management system, no XON/XOFF, no ACK/NACK, no "Please stop the bubble machine!" signal. It depends on proper pacing by the sender. The faster the sender sends, the more potential throughput but also the more likelihood of cells lost to congestion. Statistical methods predict the sending speed that, if either raised or lowered, would result in less throughput. This is tricky business, though, because the effect of dropped cells varies by application. For telephone or video, a dropped cell creates a tiny bit of static that the end user probably won't even notice. For data communication, it may cause a noticeable timeout and retransmission of hundreds of cells. Lack of a congestion management system is a serious problem that requires resolution for ATM to reach full potential.

Congestion occurs much less frequently with PVCs than with SVCs, so most work to date has been with PVCs.

6.5.3.4 LAN Emulation LAN backbones are an attractive application for ATM. One or more 155Mbps backbones can easily connect several 10Mbps LAN segments. If several ATM backbones exist, a relatively economical ATM switch can connect them. Communication that involves two or more LAN segments gets segmented into ATM cells, transmitted through the ATM network, and then reassembled into images of the original LAN packets. Figure 6.5 presents a simple example.

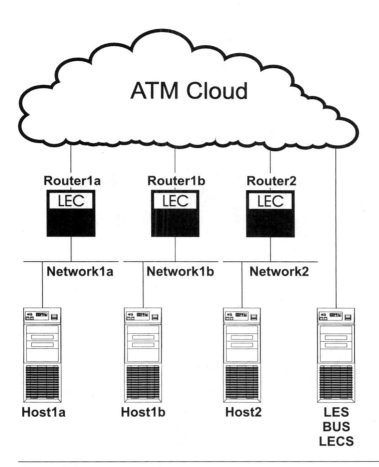

Figure 6.5 ATM LAN Emulation

There are three LAN segments and one ATM cloud. Network1a and Nework1b comprise a single LAN—a single IP subnet—but connect only through ATM. Network2 is a different subnet. Four problems arise:

1. **Multicast/broadcast support.** Almost all LAN protocols use broadcast or multicast packet delivery for some functions. Two TCP/IP functions that depend on broadcasting are ARP and router discovery, for example. Unfortunately, ATM has only a very limited broadcast facility. The router on Network1a must somehow detect broadcasts and multicasts and specially send them to Router1b. Router1b must then retransmit each broadcast and multicast on Network1b. No standards exist for this process, nor for the procedure whereby Router1a detects the presence of Router1b and like devices.

2. **MAC address to ATM address resolution.** LAN emulation needs a way to discover MAC layer (data link) addresses and map them to VPI/CPI addresses. No standards exist for this process either.

3. **SVC management.** There is currently no standard means to automatically set up virtual circuits for hosts that open sessions through the ATM network.

4. **MAC definition.** For performance reasons, it's attractive to hook up file servers and other high-volume devices directly to the ATM network. However, such a connection would have no LAN MAC layer address at all. There is no standard way to provide MAC addressability to devices connected in this way.

Given the lack of LAN emulation standards, vendors currently shipping product use proprietary techniques. These products have four main components:

1. **LAN Emulation Client (LEC).** This component resides on each ATM-attached device that participates in LAN emulation. These would typically include all hosts, routers, and gateways that translate between ATM and protocols like Ethernet and Token Ring. The LEC translates 6-byte LAN addresses to and from 20-byte ATM addresses and opens ATM sessions based on demand. (Note that ATM is session oriented, whereas LAN protocols are connectionless.)

2. **LAN Emulation Server (LES).** Each emulated LAN requires one LES, which maintains a database of LAN and ATM addresses. Each LEC registers the addresses it controls with the LES and queries the LES for address translation.

3. **Broadcast and Unknown Server (BUS).** ATM supports only a limited form of broadcasting: a one-way point-to-multipoint mechanism with one station as the root. The BUS supports LAN broadcasting by acting as that root and maintaining a destination tree consisting of all stations on the emulated LAN. It also maintains two-way virtual circuits with each LEC. LECs emulate LAN broadcasts by sending them to the BUS, which, in turn, broadcasts them in an ATM point-to-multipoint sense.

4. **LAN Emulation Configuration Server (LECS).** The LECS maintains the configuration of each emulated LAN.

An emulated LAN (ELAN), is a collection of devices sharing LAN connectivity. Consider a collection of 10 Ethernet-to-ATM wiring hubs. An administrator could use the LECS to configure hubs 1, 3, 5, 7, and 9 as a different ELAN from hubs 2, 4, 6, 8, and 10, even though all 10 hubs connect to the same ATM network. This would allow devices on hubs 1, 3, 5, 7, and 9 (ELAN-1) to communicate among themselves but not with devices connected to hubs 2, 4, 6, 8, and 10 (ELAN-2). This is analogous to ELAN-1 and ELAN-2 being physically separate networks. A bridge or router connected to one port on each ELAN could provide communication between ELANs if necessary.

Note that administrators can move any hub onto any ELAN, regardless of physical location, simply by issuing software commands at the LECS. This is an immensely powerful network management feature. Some hubs support ELAN configuration at the individual port level.

ATM is an exciting technology that's likely to grow rapidly. The prospect for cheap, seamless integration of distant corporate backbones is enticing. Several years may transpire before ATM becomes commonplace, but when it comes, you should be ready.

6.6 Future Options—Cable TV and Telco

An interesting thing happened while telcos were agonizing over the economic impossibility of rewiring the United States for ISDN. Somebody else rewired the United States with enough bandwidth for 40 to 75 television channels. The cable television industry, through numerous consolidations, is developing into a small number of very large providers nearly equal to telcos in size and influence.

Table 6.4 summarizes some key attributes of existing and future telephone and cable television networks.

Both telephone and cable television companies see tremendous profits in providing Video On Demand (VOD) services, but neither currently has a network capable of supporting it. Consider that to offer a popular two-hour movie on demand, showings on scrambled channels would have to start once every 15

Table 6.4 Attributes of Telephone and Cable Television Networks

Attribute	Telephone	Cable Television	Future
Mode	Switched	Broadcast	Mixed
Direction	Two-way	One-way	Two-way
Bandwidth	Low	Moderate	High
Signal			
Backbone	Digital fiber	Satellite	Digital
Metro	Digital fiber and twisted pair	Analog coax	Digital fiber
Subscriber	Twisted pair	Analog coax	Undetermined

minutes. Each movie would thus consume eight one-way channels. Subscribers would order the movie and receive unscrambling codes through an additional two-way channel. Current broadcast television channels are 6MHz (or about 6Mbps) in bandwidth. So, offering 10 movies on demand might involve providing 80 channels (or 480Mbps) of bandwidth into each subscriber's home.

Frankly, it seems pretty silly to keep using a 28.8Kbps modem for data communication when you have a 480Mbps (or more) circuit for video in the same home or office. The video market is much larger and more lucrative than the data communications arena, but even 1 or 2Mbps of data bandwidth would be heaven compared to 28.8.

The advent of cheap, universal, high-bandwidth digital service will have severe implications for Internet Access Providers (IAPs). The business of providing dial-in access to high-speed Internet circuits will become obsolete when everyone can get cheap, direct, high-speed service to their home or office. However, the better the connectivity, the more users will participate, and the greater the demand for content and services will be.

Here are some technologies worth watching as determinants of future Internet growth and direction:

- **Cable modem.** This device would have a digital connection for a computer—probably RS-232 or twisted pair Ethernet—and an analog connection to the cable television network. It would allow cable television providers to enter the data communications market without rewiring the city, but would still require new electronics at each distribution point. There is some question on how cable modems would handle collisions and therefore how well such a solution would scale. Also, if cable operators are going to buy new electronics, they may prefer jumping to a more advanced technology with greater revenue possibilities.

- **Fiber To The Loop (FTTL).** Most planners and observers see no alternative to fiber optics for the most centralized, highly used circuits. However, there is controversy, as the network fans out, on how far to keep using fiber and when to switch to something else. FTTL proposes installing fiber out to local distribution units hanging on poles, housed in roadside pillboxes, or enclosed by sidewalk utility cabinets. From there, existing coax (in the case of cable television companies) or twisted pair (in the case of telcos) would connect subscribers. Cable operators are in a better position to use this alternative because their coax has more bandwidth than a telco's twisted pair.

- **Fiber To The Curb (FTTC).** Providers choosing this approach would bury fiber near curbs or string it on existing utility poles. This would move the fiber point of presence close enough to the subscriber that twisted pair would provide enough bandwidth for several digitized television channels or high-bandwidth data. Telephone companies tend to favor this approach.

- **Hybrid Fiber Coaxial (HFC).** This technology would merge 550 to 750MHz of digital capacity with 50 to 75 channels of existing analog service. The digital capacity would transmit digitized (MPEG-2) video over ATM. This would require ATM switches at the fiber end points and MPEG-2 decompression chips in set-top boxes. Cable operators favor this technology because it leverages existing wiring, equipment, and set-top boxes (for subscribers who don't upgrade).

- **Asynchronous Digital Subscriber Loop (ADSL).** A candidate for use with FTTC, ADSL provides up to 6Mbps of bandwidth over relatively short lengths of telephone wiring. This is enough for one broadcast-quality television signal pulled from many available on the fiber. There is some controversy whether 6Mbps is enough bandwidth to be worth delivering.

If 6Mbps isn't enough bandwidth to be worth delivering, what about ISDN's two 56Kbps channels? Long-term prospects appear bleak. Another point: With all the bandwidth being planned for video, bandwidth for telephony and data networking represent a very small part of the picture. Whoever ends up supplying the interactive video will probably end up providing telephone and data service as a sideline.

6.7 Local Area Networks

You may completely avoid the complexities of wide-area networking if you're simply adding services to an existing LAN. In this case, you just connect the Internet service hosts to the same LAN as the clients and pat yourself on the back. You've just created an Intranet!

The process may be considerably more complex if the LAN is large and didn't previously use TCP/IP. In this case, you'll need to obtain network numbers from InterNIC, plan out IP subnets, configure and install routers, and install TCP/IP network software and applications on each client computer. Many users can install applications like Web browsers and E-Mail clients themselves, but it's best if network specialists install network software. Minor errors made by users can have serious effects on the network and are frequently difficult to locate.

TCP/IP software that supports remote or centralized configuration can eliminate many installation errors. The following are several approaches:

- If you're using Microsoft's TCP/IP-32 stack for Windows for Workgroups 3.11, the Windows 95 TCP/IP stack, or the Windows NT TCP/IP stack, the Dynamic Host Configuration Protocol (DHCP) service can configure most parameters remotely. DHCP is a full Internet standard defined by RFCs. As such, vendors other than Microsoft have begun supporting it as well.

- Novell shops can remotely configure TCP/IP on client computers having Novell's LAN WorkGroup product installed. This is basically a version of LAN WorkPlace for DOS and Windows with remote configuration added.

- Many other stacks support BOOTP configuration. BOOTP is a protocol that returns configuration information to a workstation based on its data link (Ethernet) address.

For some non-TCP/IP networks, it may be preferable not to install TCP/IP on each workstation, but instead to use existing protocols to reach a TCP/IP gateway. This most often occurs on Netware networks, as many large Microsoft networks are trending away from NetBEUI and toward TCP/IP anyway. Banyan Vines networks can use TCP/IP natively.

Here are two IPX/SPX-to-TCP/IP gateways (CyberJunction runs on Windows NT; IWareConnect runs on a Netware server):

- CyberJunction

  Frontier Technologies, Mequon, Wisconsin
  http://www.frontiertech.com/products/cyjunctn.htm

- IWareConnect

  Quarterdeck Corporation, Marina Del Rey, California
  http://www.qdeck.com/qdeck/products/iware_connect/

Security is a major concern if you're connecting the Internet to an internal LAN for the first time. A firewall is a computer with two network ports: one on the internal LAN and one on the Internet. Software on the firewall allows transactions initiated internally to reach the Internet but prevents unsolicited Internet traffic from entering the internal LAN. Chapter 18 will cover firewalls in much greater detail.

6.8 Internet Site Configuration

All but the tiniest Internet sites will probably have a LAN with several hosts and routers on it. The most common LANs are thin Ethernet (10Base-2) and twisted pair Ethernet (10Base-T).

Thin Ethernet has become almost the cheapest LAN on the planet. Network adapters are available for less than $50 and connecting them requires only wiring—no electronic components. Wiring consists of coaxial cable terminated with BNC (Bayonet Neill-Concelman) connectors; each node has a BNC T-connector for connecting two lengths of cable or one length of cable and a terminating resistor. The main problem with thin Ethernet is that any cable break causes the entire LAN to fail.

Twisted pair Ethernet uses telephone-type twisted pair terminated with RJ-45 (eight-contact telephone) jacks. The minimum acceptable cable grade is Category 3, a jacketed cable containing two twisted pairs. Category 5 is better; this is also a jacketed cable, but it contains four pairs having a very precise twist. Category 5 supports both 10Mbps and 100Mbps Ethernet. You can purchase premade 10Base-T cables and patch cords at most computer and electronics stores, or you may choose to buy a spool of wire, a bag of RJ-45 connectors, and a crimping tool.

10Base-T networks use a star architecture; wiring extends from each node to an active hub. Unmanaged hubs supporting 8 or 10 devices cost less than $300, but rack-mounted "stackable" hubs with management cost considerably more. Stackable hubs typically have 24 or 36 ports plus connectors that permit operating several such hubs as one. Management features support remote activation or deactivation of ports, collection of activity and error statistics, and generation of alerts and automatic port shutdown when error counts or other statistics exceed configured limits.

The advantage of 10Base-T Ethernet is that if one circuit fails, the rest keep operating. The active hub automatically isolates ports that have no circuit attached or that generate excessive errors.

It's possible with Windows NT to build a site-in-a-box. You could support dial-in with the Windows NT Remote Access Service and use an ISDN or V.35 card for your Internet uplink. If you ran services like HTTP, FTP, News, Mail, and DNS on the same machine, you wouldn't need a local network at all. Don't do this unless you're the type of person who likes to pack college students into phone booths or small cars. Even then, only do it for fun. Here's why:

- A site-in-a-box has very little expansion capability. Without major reconfiguration, all you can do is upgrade the one and only machine.

- Such a site has little or no redundancy. If the one machine fails, the whole site is down.

- With all functions concentrated in one device, failure analysis may be more difficult than usual. Failure analysis of several devices having discrete functions is generally easier than analysis of a single complex device.

- A site-in-a-box has no separate facility for testing or administrative functions.

Finally, be sure to physically configure your site so that you can work on and check out equipment without bumping into other equipment or cables. Some 19-inch equipment racks are great for this purpose; shelves and tables are bad because they don't permit easy access to the backs of things. Keep cabling and wiring neat, but don't bundle it up so tightly that you can't trace individual cables later. Purchase adhesive cable tags and identify both ends of each cable with a unique number. Buy quality cables and connectors. In no time at all, your site will have hundreds of wires and connections, and life's too short to spend it wiggling wires to keep your Internet site alive.

6.9 Client Software

The world seems overpopulated with books explaining how to connect client computers to the Internet and run a browser; only books on HTML are more prevalent. Nevertheless, a brief discussion of TCP/IP client software seems appropriate here.

In most cases, supporting clients on internal LANs is simpler than supporting commercial dial-in customers because, on an internal LAN, organizational standards limit the number of hardware and software types supported. Commercial providers face a much more difficult problem in that any client type they don't support represents lost business.

6.9.1 Sources of Client Software

This section is neither a software evaluation nor a comprehensive list; trade papers and magazines provide those functions very well and are more current than any book can hope to be. Consider the following only a starting point biased by the author's preferences and random experiences.

6.9.1.1 DOS Most DOS-based TCP/IP stacks are plagued by high base memory usage, proprietary APIs, and poor performance under Microsoft Windows. Memory consumption is a consequence of these products being TSR-based (Terminate and Stay Resident); all traditional tricks of DOS memory management apply. There is no standard TCP/IP application interface for DOS as there is for Windows, so every vendor has implemented its own. As to performance, some degradation is caused by small network buffers (due to DOS memory constraints) and some by the necessity of switching the CPU out of Windows 386 Enhanced Mode every time the TSR needs processor cycles.

Here are some further points to consider:

- The oldest and most mature TCP/IP stack for DOS is probably PC/TCP from FTP Software. PC/TCP also includes a variety of character-mode applications such as Telnet, TN3270, and FTP.

- Microsoft still distributes the DOS-based TCP/IP stack 3Com and Hewlett-Packard developed for 3+Open, which became Microsoft LAN Manager. This stack exists primarily to support Microsoft Networking with TCP/IP but without Windows. Few Internet applications work with it.

- Novell's LAN WorkPlace for DOS and Windows adds TCP/IP (as a second protocol) to the standard Netware shell. It also includes a suite of DOS and Windows-based applications and a Winsock API for third-party Windows-based Internet clients.

- Novell's LAN WorkGroup is essentially the same as LAN WorkPlace for DOS and Windows, except that LAN WorkGroup supports centralized configuration.

6.9.1.2 Windows 3.1 Several TCP/IP stacks implemented as Dynamic Link Libraries (DLLs) appeared for Windows 3.1. These had the advantage of not using any DOS memory, and they signaled the arrival of Winsock as a standard application interface. NetManage Chameleon and Frontier Super TCP/IP are the primary commercial-vendor products in this arena.

The most popular TCP/IP stack for Windows 3.1, however, has been the shareware product Trumpet Winsock. It has a reputation for being hard to configure but very stable once working. Many Internet providers preconfigure copies of Trumpet Winsock for distribution to customers or at least provide detailed setup instructions. Providers can freely distribute Trumpet Winsock as shareware, but end users should pay $25 to the following address:

■ Trumpet Software International Pty Ltd.

GPO Box 1649, Hobart Tasmania 7001, Australia

You can obtain Trumpet Winsock from almost any FTP archive on the planet (see the sidebar titled "Obtaining Trumpet Winsock" for further details). The file name is twsk*xxx*.zip, with a version number replacing the *xxx*. In October 1995, the current version was twsk21f.zip.

6.9.1.3 Windows for Workgroups 3.11 With Windows for Workgroups 3.11, Microsoft introduced network drivers implemented as Virtual Device Drivers (VXDs). VXD drivers operate entirely in 386 Enhanced Mode where memory is plentiful and there's no need to switch the processor back to 8086 mode. Microsoft also introduced Network Device Interface Specification (NDIS) 3.0, which provided a VXD-based Protocol Manager and some VXD-based network card drivers. The result was excellent performance, zero DOS memory consumption, and control of the network card right down to the bare metal in 386 Enhanced Mode.

Unfortunately, Microsoft supplied Windows for Workgroups 3.11 with VXD-based network drivers only for NetBEUI and IPX/SPX. Fortunately, they later released TCP/IP-32, a VXD version of TCP/IP. This has become a very popular TCP/IP stack for use on LANs, but Microsoft hasn't provided SLIP or PPP drivers for TCP/IP-32. RAS for Windows 3.1 and Windows for Workgroups 3.11 only supports NetBEUI. Shiva developed a PPP driver for TCP/IP-32 but only for use with Shiva dial-in routers.

Most DOS-based stacks also work with Windows and provide Winsock application interfaces. This is true for all stacks mentioned in Section 6.9.1.1. FTP has enhanced its PC/TCP to provide a VXD-based stack as well as a DOS stack. Frontier Super TCP/IP is also now VXD based.

6.9.1.4 Windows 95 Microsoft has enhanced TCP/IP-32, added 32-bit PPP support, and bundled it with every copy of Windows 95. A 32-bit SLIP driver is available as well. This stack is so stable and easy to configure that it will likely become the predominating, de facto standard for Windows 95.

6.9.1.5 Windows NT Like everything else in Windows NT, the Microsoft TCP/IP stack is fully 32-bit and multitasking. Users have found it both robust and well performing. Given the difficulty of developing a superior competing product, it's likely that Windows NT's bundled stack will remain the common choice.

Windows NT Remote Access Service provides client software for SLIP and PPP dial-out, plus server software for PPP dial-in.

Obtaining Trumpet Winsock

The World Wide Web site for Trumpet Winsock is http://www.trumpet.com.au/. The following are official archive and mirror sites:

- USA

  Carl Hayden Community High School in Phoenix, Arizona
  ftp://www.hayden.edu/winsock/

  IEEE Student Group at the University of Cincinnati's College of Applied Science
  ftp://ieee.cas.uc.edu/pub/winsock/TRUMPET/

  Missouri Research and Education Network
  ftp://ftp.more.net/pub/mirrors/winsock/

  SimTel Archive
  http://www.coast.net/SimTel/vendors/trumpet/

  Synapse Internet
  ftp://ftp.synapse.net/contrib/trumpet/

  The Ultimate Collection of Winsock Software
  http://www.tucows.com/softtcp.html#trumpet

- Australia

  INIAccess in NSW, Australia
  ftp://ftp.laa.com.au/pub/trumpet/

  Trumpet Software International
  ftp://jazz.trumpet.com.au/

- Greece

  Association of Hellenic Internet Users in Athens, Greece
  ftp://ftp.eexi.gr/pub/systems/windows/win31/sockets/winsock

  ONNED Internet Access Provider in Greece
  http://www.onned.gr/toolchest.htm

- Germany

  MMS Communication GmbH
  ftp://ftp.mms-gmbh.de/pub/trumpet

6.9.1.6 Macintosh Running TCP/IP on a Macintosh generally requires software called, logically enough, MacTCP. Apple bundles MacTCP with System 7.5 and above; Apple Programmers and Developers Association (APDA) and software resellers also provide copies for people who need to run earlier versions of the Macintosh system.

MacTCP supports TCP/IP over LocalTalk, Ethernet, and Token Ring but doesn't provide SLIP or PPP. A free SLIP dialer is available from

- InterCon Systems Corporation

  ftp://ftp.intercon.com/pub/sales/InterSLIP/

A free PPP dialer is available from

- Merit Network, Inc.

  ftp://ftp.merit.edu/internet.tools/ppp/mac/

Commercial products are available from Attachmate, CompuServe, InterCon, Novell, and Ventana.

6.9.1.7 OS/2 IBM's OS/2 3.0 Warp operating system provides bundled TCP/IP support for dial-up connections using SLIP and PPP and for LAN connections using Ethernet and Token Ring.

6.9.1.8 UNIX SLIP and PPP both originated on UNIX, and SLIP, at least, is a component of almost every UNIX version. Users of UNIX are generally quite competent and need only general assistance connecting.

6.9.2 Supporting Client Software

Support procedures on internal LANs are usually well defined. Support for Internet services should parallel support procedures for other networked or client-server systems. If you have users dialing in, you should provide them with supported software and complete, step-by-step installation instructions for supported configurations.

Employees using their own computer for dialing into organizational LANs present a particular problem. At the office, the organization pays for the computer and software and thus has great leverage in limiting the number of types purchased and supported. The resulting lack of diversity reduces support costs. At home, the employees pay for their own computers and buy whatever they want. Supporting a wide variety of home systems raises support costs, but asking employees to spend their own money in accordance with an MIS-approved list smacks of big brother. As a solution, you might set a policy for "unsupported platform support" stating exactly what level of services you *are* willing to provide. For example, you might document the exact dialing and command sequence required to dial into the organization's equipment but only provide software and write scripts for supported platforms. Users who purchase other platforms or software would have to write their own scripts based on generic specifications you provide.

Commercial sites usually provide new users with start-up kits that include software and instructions for the user's platform. A single automated installation includes the provider's host names, IP addresses, and other codes. Providers should also have a test machine of each type to develop, test, and document installation procedures and reproduce reported problems. In reality, the platforms with the most existing and potential customers will probably get the best support, and the least common may simply be unsupported or considered "best effort."

## CHAPTER 7

Installing and Administering Windows NT

Exhaustive, step-by-step instructions on how to install Windows NT are beyond the scope of this book. For one thing, clear documentation ships with the product; for another, the installation is likely to vary somewhat depending on your hardware.

This chapter provides various hints, tips, and techniques for setting up Windows NT in general and for setting those options most relevant to providing Internet services.

7.1 Preparing and Certifying the Hardware

Assume you've sized your site and selected equipment as described in Chapters 3 and 4. Also assume you've ordered the parts for at least one server, and they've arrived. The next steps are physical site preparation, assembly, and test.

7.1.1 Physical Assembly and Location

The room and floor space you provide for your equipment can have a major impact on support efficiency and reliability. The following factors are all important:

- Provide adequate physical security. You don't want unauthorized people poking around your equipment.

- Make sure you have access to both the building and the room 7 days a week, 24 hours a day.

- Install adequate electricity and lighting. It's far easier to wire additional telephone wiring, electrical circuits, wall outlets, and lighting fixtures before a room fills up with equipment than after. With respect to electrical wiring, it's better to install more than you need up front than to add more later.

- Guarantee 7-day, 24-hour climate control. Manufacturers design computers and communications equipment to run in dry, 72-degree Fahrenheit rooms.

- Avoid rooms containing steam pipes, plumbing pipes, and so on. Sooner or later these will leak.

- If possible, locate the telco point-of-presence inside the server room. This is the set of punch-down blocks where the telco lines end and your wiring begins. Otherwise, attach a piece of plywood to the wall, fasten an initial supply of punch-down blocks[1] to the plywood, and, if possible, wire the punch-down blocks to the telco point-of-presence with continuous runs.

- Try, at least, to arrange equipment in a logical progression across the room. Starting from your punch-down blocks, for example, you might arrange your modem banks, CSU/DSUs, routers, servers, and printers in sequence around the room.

- Provide space to walk behind equipment as well as in front of it.

- Consider rack-mounting as much equipment as possible. This saves floor space, keeps equipment off the floor, and prevents accidental disconnections.

- Run wiring through overhead cable troughs, not across the floor.

- Avoid congestion around the door.

- Make sure monitors and keyboards are in comfortable positions. When the site is running well, you should spend very little time at the server consoles, but, in case of failure, you may need to spend long hours there.

- If possible, have a desk or workbench.

- Don't forget shelves or a bookcase for manuals.

Of course, you'll be anxious to assemble and power up your servers once they start arriving. Read and follow manufacturer's instructions carefully. An excellent approach is to assemble a minimal system first, boot it up, and run diagnostics. If diagnostics pass, you can add more components and then run diagnostics again.

---

[1]This is particularly important if you're planning to install very many dial-in lines, either now or in the future. Telephone wiring for more than a few lines typically uses 25-pair jacketed cables wired to a block of 50 slotted connectors. To make connections from the block, position a wire at the edge of the slotted connector and then punch it into the slot with a punch-down tool. The slot is narrow enough that it tears away the insulation on the wire and makes contact. Some punch-down blocks require punching down all the wires in the incoming 25-pair cable, and others require wiring the 25-pair cable to a 50-pin telco jack. A 50-pin telco jack resembles a Centronics parallel port or SCSI connector.

This not only provides familiarity with each component but also aids tremendously in identifying components that are defective out of the box.

If something doesn't fit or doesn't work as expected, now is the time to replace it. Despite any anxiousness to get your site running, the time to make changes is before you go into production, not after.

7.1.2 Pre-Installing MS-DOS

Programs such as diagnostics and utilities for EISA configuration, network cards, SCSI adapters, and video cards usually run from DOS and not under Windows NT. Such programs directly manipulate the hardware, and this is something Windows NT specifically prohibits. In addition, it's generally much easier to diagnose and repair hardware problems under DOS than under NT. DOS simply has fewer levels of software to mask symptoms.

For these reasons, you should seriously consider installing MS-DOS on every Windows NT machine before you install Windows NT. A 50MB partition is usually more than sufficient. Once you get the server booting to this partition, install copies of whatever utilities came with the system unit, peripherals, or expansion cards. Get the CD and network card working as well; for example, you might install a CD driver and Microsoft CD-ROM Extensions (MSCDEX) for the CD and Microsoft's DOS-based TCP/IP stack for the network card. This will provide a sanity check if something doesn't work under Windows NT; if the same component worked under DOS, the problem is likely with your Windows NT drivers or settings for that device. Installing all the correct utilities on each server's hard disk also helps in finding them months or years down the road.

Some machines, such as Compaq servers, come with bootable CDs that contain all required diagnostics and configuration programs. In such cases, an MS-DOS partition may be unnecessary. The CD will usually contain diagnostics only for components sold by the system vendor, but this isn't much of a disadvantage. To assure matched components and prevent vendors from pointing fingers at one another, administrators usually configure high-end servers as single-vendor systems anyway.

7.1.3 Diagnostic Shakedown

Figure 7.1 illustrates the famous bathtub curve. It shows a relatively high probability of failure for new components, low probability during normal life, and rising chance of failure as components age.

Don't make the mistake of assuming new components can't fail. As shown by the bathtub curve, components are more likely to fail when new than at any other

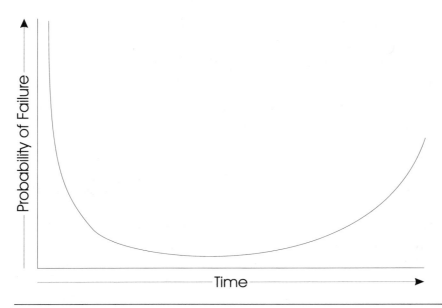

Figure 7.1 Probability of Component Failure over Time

time. The solution is simple: You should exercise all new equipment for at least a week before placing it in production. At minimum, leave the equipment powered up and check it once or twice a day; at best, use a diagnostic program to continuously exercise RAM, hard disks, video, and removable media drives.

Another common mistake is "babying" new equipment. No, don't throw it on the floor to expose subtle defects, but do give it a tough workout within rated parameters. If it breaks, you'll have an easy time returning it within 30 days of purchase, and you'll have avoided a production outage.

Above all, don't take comfort in long mean times between failures quoted by manufacturers. Any component can fail at any time.

7.2 Initial Setup Options

If you're creating a new Windows NT domain, be sure to install the Primary Domain Controller (PDC) before any other Windows NT server or Windows NT workstations. The PDC must validate computer accounts for each Windows NT machine joining its domain. For the same reason, you must install network adapters and wiring to the PDC before installing other Windows NT servers in the same domain. For more details, see the sidebar titled "Windows NT Computer Accounts."

Windows NT Computer Accounts

A Windows NT domain is a collection of Windows NT machines that share a common User Account Database (UADB). Once in the domain, a Windows NT machine can access the UADB and other security information from the PDC even when the current user isn't a domain member or when no one is logged on. This could be a large security problem if hacked, impostor, or unknown machines got onto the network. Such machines could bypass the normal Windows NT software that prevents users from breaking into security internals.

To guard against abnormally configured machines, Windows NT requires each Windows NT machine in a domain to have a computer account established by an administrator. There are three ways to set up and activate such accounts:

1. Create the account using the Server Manager application on an existing Windows NT computer in the domain. Then, with the new computer on the network, give it the expected name during setup. The new computer will contact the domain, complete the first computer account login, and exchange all necessary security identifiers to fully activate the computer account.

2. If an administrator is performing the installation, he or she can create the computer account as part of the setup process. This also requires the new computer to be on the network at the time of installation, and it requires an administrator to enter his or her ID and password when creating the account.

3. An alternate procedure (for Windows NT Workstation only) is to take the machine out of the domain by placing it into a workgroup and then adding it back in with a new name.

New computer accounts created with Server Manager are initially available to any computer that knows what name to ask for. However, when the named computer logs on for the first time, it exchanges additional security IDs with the UADB, and thereafter no other computer can log on with the given name.

Renaming a computer account isn't possible. If you find it necessary to rename a Windows NT computer, you'll have to create a new Windows NT computer account for the new name. You can create the computer account for the new name using procedure 1 or 3 (listed herein).

Starting the Windows NT Setup program is relatively easy; either boot from Windows NT Setup Disk #1 or start the WINNT program from the CD:

■ If you purchased Windows NT on CD and boot from Windows NT Setup Disk #1, Setup will try to detect your CD and adapter, load the necessary Windows NT drivers, and install directly from the CD to the hard disk.

■ If you purchased Windows NT on CD and run the WINNT program from DOS, WINNT will copy all the files needed for the install to your hard disk and create Setup disks #3, #2, and #1 (in that order). Then, WINNT will reboot the system. Windows NT Setup will then install Windows NT from one area of the hard disk to another, deleting installation files behind itself to conserve space.[2]

■ If you purchased Windows NT on diskettes, simply insert Setup Disk #1 and reboot. Windows NT Setup will prompt you for additional diskettes as required.

Regardless of the setup media you choose, select "Custom Setup" when prompted. Even if you don't change any default settings, at least you'll have a chance to see what they are.

You can install Windows NT entirely from CD or over a network (without creating and reading back the three floppy disks) by specifying the "/b" switch when you start WINNT. However, the three floppy disks do serve a purpose. If your Windows NT installation becomes damaged and won't boot, you'll need the three setup disks to run the Emergency Repair process. If you already have a set of setup disks that correspond to your CD, go ahead and use "/b." Otherwise, create the diskettes and file them with your Emergency Repair disk.

7.2.1 Disk Partitioning

Resist all temptation to partition your disks as one large drive. For one thing, Windows NT has no disk quota system other than setting the size of drives. If you want anonymous FTP space limited to 250MB, for example, setting up a 250MB drive letter is the only way to do it. For another, you absolutely positively don't want users or hackers poking around your system drive. The best way to prevent this is by locating all user space and sharenames on a different drive.

Drives formatted with NTFS (NT File System) are much easier to manage than FAT (File Allocation Table) or VFAT (Virtual FAT) drives. If an NTFS volume other than the system drive fills up, an administrator can enlarge the drive without backing up, reallocating, reformatting, and restoring. Even if you do have to back up and restore, this should be easy using the backup hardware and software you use for regular backups.

Table 7.1 shows a recommended drive arrangement. The Windows NT system drive is D:, and a second drive, E:, contains application software such as

---

[2]This "unsupported CD-ROM support" allows you to install CD-ROM editions of Windows NT using CD-ROM drives Windows NT doesn't support. The same process allows Windows NT to be installed over a DOS-based network connection. WINNT won't run under Windows 3.x, but there's a WINNT32 version that runs under Windows NT.

Table 7.1 Recommended Windows NT Drive Arrangement

Drive	File System	Size (MB)	Description
A:	FAT	1.4	Floppy disk
B:	FAT	1.2	Floppy disk (if desired)
C:	FAT	50	DOS utilities and diagnostics partition
D:	NTFS	300	Windows NT system partition
E:	NTFS	200	Windows NT utilities drive
F:	CDFS	CD	System CD
G:–Z:	NTFS	?	User and application volumes

backup/restore. The system drive can't be extended later, so it's best to start large. Backup/restore software tends to fill surprising amounts of disk space with logs and catalogs, so it's best to keep these off the system drive. A Windows NT system with no space on the system drive isn't a happy system: It can't create more virtual memory swap space when it needs to, it can't spool print jobs, and it may crash. Anything that eats disk space doesn't belong on the system drive.

The size and number of user and application volumes will obviously depend on the specific users and applications. You can create and modify volumes with the Windows NT Disk Administrator utility.

Note that Windows NT allows only four partitions per physical drive. Once you've created four partitions, any remaining space on the physical drive is unusable. Furthermore, only one partition per drive can be an extended partition. Only an extended partition can contain multiple drive letters.

Based on the preceding paragraph, you should almost always make the second, third, or fourth partition you create an extended partition that consumes all remaining space on the physical drive. Then, you can create additional drive letters within the extended partition.

By default, Windows NT Setup will create a system drive that entirely occupies the first physical disk in the system. You can avoid this in two ways:

1. Use the MS-DOS FDISK program to create the drive that will be your Windows NT system drive. Then, select that drive during setup. There's no need to format the drive after creating it with FDISK; NT Setup will do that for you.

2. Use Windows NT Setup to create the Windows NT system drive. When prompted where to install Windows NT, select "Unformatted space." Then, press "C" for "Create Partition" and specify the partition size you want. Finally, select that partition as the location for Windows NT.

7.2.2 File System

The Windows NT File System (NTFS) has so many advantages over MS-DOS's FAT that using FAT should be unthinkable. NTFS accommodates much larger physical and logical disks than FAT, and it operates much more reliably and efficiently. NTFS supports long file names. Most important, NTFS supports security at every point in the file system, down to the individual file. For information on repairing the Windows NT system, see the sidebar titled "Repairing a Windows NT System Partition."

Repairing a Windows NT System Partition

Some new Windows NT users develop considerable anxiety over the belief that if their system resides on NTFS and becomes unbootable, they can't boot off a floppy disk and fix it. However, this isn't true. The three-disk set of Windows NT Setup diskettes actually loads the Windows NT kernel, any required disk controller drivers, and any required CD-ROM drivers. If you choose "Repair" instead of "Setup," the Repair process will prompt you for your Emergency Repair disk and reset the registry and all system files to their state as recorded on the Emergency Repair disk.

Note that to work perfectly, the Emergency Repair process needs the following items:

1. A set of setup disks that correspond to the version of Windows NT installed on the unbootable system.

2. An up-to-date Emergency Repair disk.

3. A readable copy of the Windows NT installation disks (CD or floppy).

4. A readable copy of the most recently installed Windows NT service pack.

5. A readable copy of any other applications installed in the Windows NT directory.

Briefly, item 1 provides the Emergency Repair software, and item 2 recalls the state of the system when it was working. If the repair process finds any differences between what's recorded on the Emergency Repair disk and what's actually on the hard disk, it will replace the bad or missing hard-disk files using items 3, 4, and 5.

Using an old Emergency Repair disk may restore the Windows NT system to an outdated state. If so, you'll need to reapply fixes or reinstall software to get the system fully working again. A program called RDISK can create an Emergency Repair disk at any time; it's a good policy to run this program on all servers from time to time and carefully file the resulting diskettes.

If you're missing any installation disks or if your only copy resides on the network, you can bypass repairing those files. However, this obviously compromises the quality of the repair.

7.2.3 Computer and Domain Names

You should choose Windows NT computer names and domain names with some care. Computer names can be a real nuisance to change, not so much because changing the name is difficult, but because other machines on the network may expect to reconnect automatically to the old name when they log on.

Windows NT domain names are very difficult to change. To move a Windows NT server to another domain, you must reinstall Windows NT. You can rename a domain, but this involves visiting and reconfiguring every NT server and workstation.

There's no relationship between the Windows Networking computer name and the DNS name of a Windows NT computer—that is, unless you choose to make them the same. Making them the same is a good choice, however. Computer names like www and ftp are usually DNS aliases for a "real" computer name.

There's also no relationship between the Windows NT domain and the DNS domain of a computer. These are two different name spaces with different features, uses, and syntaxes; and the computers that comprise a Windows NT domain are usually a different group from those in a DNS domain. Except in the simplest cases, it probably won't be possible to keep the two domain names the same.

7.2.4 Network Settings

You can change any network settings after initial installation, so there's no need for great anxiety during setup. Nevertheless, to avoid more work later, here are some suggestions.

First, don't install protocols other than TCP/IP unless you're sure to need them. Second, when you see the Windows NT TCP/IP Installation Options dialog (pictured later in Figure 10.5), you can just check all the options ON or be selective using the following list:

- **Connectivity Utilities.** If checked, this option installs the utilities listed in Table 7.2. At least one of these programs is likely to be useful sometime, so check the option ON.
- **SNMP Service.** Checking this option installs the Simple Network Management Protocol. Network management consoles such as HP Open View, Sun Net Manager, and Compaq Insight Manager use this protocol to gather statistics about devices on a TCP/IP network; so does Windows NT Performance Monitor. Check this box ON.

Table 7.2 Windows NT Connectivity Utilities

Utility	Description
arp	Displays and modifies tables used by the Address Resolution Protocol (ARP). These tables relate LAN addresses to IP addresses.
finger client	Displays information about users on a remote system running the Finger service.
ftp client	Transfers files to and from a remote system running an FTP Server service.
hostname	Displays the name of the current host.
ipconfig	Displays all TCP/IP configuration values currently in effect.
lpq	Obtains and displays the status of a local or remote LPD print queue.
lpr	Copies a file into a print queue on a host running LPD.
nbtstat	Displays statistics and status for NETBIOS running over TCP/IP.
netstat	Displays statistics and status for TCP/IP network connections.
ping	Verifies connectivity to other TCP/IP hosts by sending a simple query and waiting for a response.
rcp	Copies files either between the local Windows NT computer and a system running a remote shell server (rshd) or between two remote systems running rshd.
rexec	Executes commands on a remote host that is running the rexecd service.
route	Displays and modifies network routing tables.
rsh	Executes commands on a remote host that is running the rsh service.
telnet client	Provides simple terminal emulation to remote hosts running a Telnet service.
tftp client	Transfers files to and from a remote system running a TFTP Server service.
tracert	Determines the route taken to a destination.

- **TCP/IP Network Printing Support.** This options specifies whether the computer will be able to send jobs to LPD print queues on other machines and to receive LPD jobs on this machine. LPD (Line Printer Daemon) is a print spooling service often used on UNIX and other TCP/IP-based hosts. Network printers from manufacturers like Hewlett-Packard and QMS can also use the LPD protocol.

- **FTP Server Service.** If checked, this option installs the Windows NT FTP Server service. Check this option if this computer will act as a server for anonymous or user FTP file transfers. Don't select it if you plan to install the FTP service that comes with Microsoft Internet Information Server.

- **Simple TCP/IP Services.** This option provides client software for the Character Generator, Daytime, Discard, Echo, and Quote of the Day services.

- **DHCP Server Service.** This choice only appears for Windows NT Server. If checked, it installs server software to automatically configure remote Windows NT, Windows 95, and Windows for Workgroups 3.11 TCP/IP stacks using Dynamic Host Configuration Protocol. Chapter 8 discusses DHCP in some detail.

■ **WINS Server Service.** This is another choice that only appears for Windows NT Server. It installs the Windows Internet Name Service, a name resolution service for Microsoft Networking. Chapter 8 discusses WINS in some detail.

■ **Enable Automatic DHCP Configuration.** Check this box if you've already installed a DHCP server elsewhere on your local network and you want it to control this computer's TCP/IP settings.

Third, depending on which TCP/IP installation options you checked, you may get additional configuration dialogs after you press the Continue button. Unless you're already familiar with the settings for these services, just press OK and accept the defaults.

7.2.5 TCP/IP Settings

After you've specified all the network software you want installed, Windows NT Setup will perform a "binding analysis" and then prompt you with the TCP/IP Configuration dialog shown in Figure 7.2.

The configurable fields in this dialog are as follows:

■ **Adapter.** Many people don't notice it, but this field is a dropdown list box. If you have more than one network adapter in the machine, use this

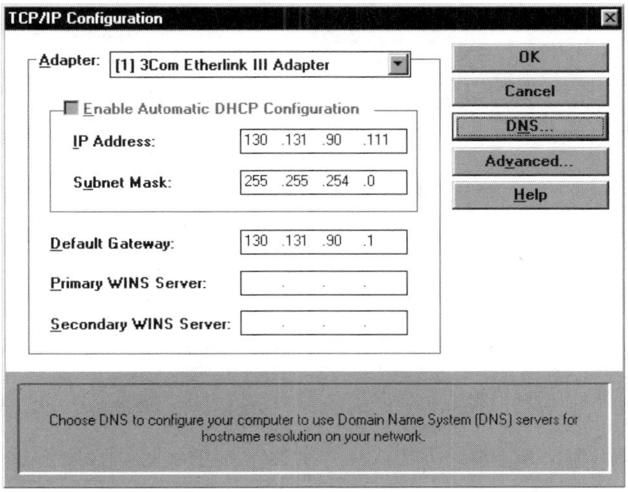

Figure 7.2 Windows NT TCP/IP Configuration Dialog

list box to select the adapter you want to inspect or configure. There will be one dropdown list entry for each network adapter bound[3] to TCP/IP.

- **Enable Automatic DHCP Configuration.** If your site uses DHCP, you may be able to simply check "Enable Automatic DHCP Configuration," leave everything else blank, and click OK. However, this depends on conventions used at your site. If DHCP doesn't supply a necessary parameter at your site or on the computer's subnet or if the DHCP setting isn't appropriate for this computer, you'll still have to enter that parameter by hand. Most Internet servers use hard-coded (as opposed to DHCP-assigned) IP addresses. This keeps the IP address from changing to a value other than what's registered in the Domain Name System.

- **IP Address.** This is the network adapter's primary IP address.

- **Subnet Mask.** This is the subnet mask used within the network.

- **Default Gateway.** This specifies the address of a router to which IP, in the absence of other information, will send packets not addressed to the local subnet.

- **Primary WINS Server/Secondary WINS Server.** If your site uses Windows Internet Name Service for Windows Networking name registration, enter the IP address of one or two WINS servers.

Figure 7.3 shows the dialog produced by pressing the DNS... button shown in Figure 7.2.

The fields in this dialog are as follows:

- **Host Name.** This is the name of the computer as used with TCP/IP applications. It will default to the same name used for Microsoft Networking, translated to lowercase. This is an excellent choice.

- **Domain Name.** This is the name of the Internet domain the computer is registered to, and not the Windows NT Domain Name.

- **Domain Name Service (DNS) Search Order.** This frame contains a list of DNS servers the TCP/IP stack will query to translate Internet computer names to IP addresses. To add a DNS server, type its IP address in the text box at the left and then click the Add→ button. To remove a DNS server, select it in the list box to the right and then click the ←Remove button.

---

[3]Binding is essentially the process of drawing the connecting lines as in Figure 5.5.

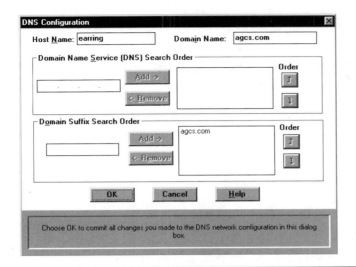

Figure 7.3 Windows NT DNS Configuration Dialog

To change the order of DNS servers in the list box, select the IP address of the server you want to move and then move it with the up and down Order buttons.

- **Domain Suffix Search Order.** This frame contains a list of Internet domains Windows NT will append to host names during DNS queries. If the list contained butcher.com, baker.com, and candlestick.com and if you requested a TCP/IP connection to host name "jobs," Windows NT would ask the listed DNS servers to look up the names jobs.butcher.com, jobs.baker.com, and jobs.candlestick.com until a match resulted.

Figure 7.4 shows the dialog produced by pressing the Advanced... button shown in Figure 7.2.

The fields in this dialog are as follows:

- **Adapter.** Note that, again, the adapter identification is a dropdown list box. Instances of the settings in this frame exist for each network adapter that has TCP/IP bound to it. To review or modify settings for a particular adapter, select that adapter from the dropdown list.

- **IP Addresses/Subnet Masks.** This is another list like the ones for DNS Server and DNS Search Order, but each row has two fields: IP Address and Subnet Mask. To add a row to the list, enter an IP address and a subnet mask in the two text boxes at the left of the frame and then click the Add→ button. To remove a row, select the row and then click the

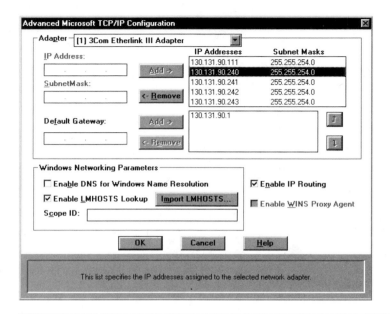

Figure 7.4   Advanced Microsoft TCP/IP Configuration Dialog

←Remove button. For a further explanation, see the sidebar titled "Why Have Mutliple Addresses on One Network Adapter?"

- **Default Gateway.** This list specifies additional gateways the computer can query for routes. That is, if the Windows NT computer attempts to send a packet to a network the first default gateway doesn't know of, Windows NT will try sending the packet to the second gateway in this list, then the third, and so on, until a router provides positive acknowledgment.

- **Enable DNS for Windows Name Resolution.** If this option is ON, Windows NT will attempt to resolve Windows Networking names by querying the configured list of DNS servers for the Windows Networking name plus any configured DNS suffixes.

- **Enable LMHOSTS Lookup.** Checking this box will instruct Windows NT to resolve Windows Networking names by looking them up in a file named \<systemroot>\system32\drivers\etc\lmhosts. This is useful in cases where name resolution by broadcast or WINS fails.

- **Scope ID.** This is a rarely used field. Assigning a scope ID to a group of computers using NETBIOS over TCP/IP allows computers in that group to locate one another but excludes computers configured with a different scope ID. Normally, you should leave this field blank.

Why Have Multiple Addresses on One Network Adapter?

Microsoft provided the ability for one network adapter to have several IP addresses because it's possible to have several IP networks on one Ethernet. In such a case, it's advisable to give the Ethernet adapter an IP address on each network.

More recently, providers have found that customers will pay more for Web space if the provider can name their home page www.custname.com rather than www.provider.com/custname. It's not economical to set up an additional server for each additional customer, but setting up an additional domain name and IP address are well worth the while. The Web server, in such cases, must have a feature whereby it displays a different default page depending on which of the server's IP addresses received the page request.

Assigning 5, 16, or more IP addresses to a single host seems extravagant in view of the address depletion problem. In addition, the Domain Name System assumes a hierarchical name space, not a flat one like www.custname.com. Nevertheless, this is the convention millions of World Wide Web users have come to expect.

- **Enable IP Routing.** Checking this box will activate static IP routing. There's no such thing as a one-ported router, so this option is unavailable on computers having one network adapter and one IP address. Even with routing on, Windows NT will only honor routes among local network adapters or those you enter by hand with the "route" command-line utility.

- **Enable WINS Proxy Agent.** This box is available only if a primary WINS server is present in the main TCP/IP Configuration dialog. If checked, it means this computer will "listen" for broadcast name resolution queries from other computers, resolve them via WINS, and respond to the computer that attempted the broadcast name resolution. Use of this facility is uncommon; it's generally much better to configure the clients to access WINS directly.

7.2.6 Completing Initial Installation

The remaining questions asked by Windows NT Setup are unlikely to be confusing. You may as well install all the Windows NT accessories and applets, but there's usually no reason to install printers or applications already existing on the hard disk. Don't leave the Administrator password blank, don't make it something obvious like "password" or "none," and don't make it overly original or difficult to remember. Leave passwords like "eucalyptus" and "rhododendron" to spelling champs. A good practice is to avoid using any dictionary word as a password.

7.3 Testing and Refining the Installation

If you haven't done so already, you should now make a detailed list of everything you want the new server to do. This list might include items such as the following:

- Log on as Administrator at console.
- Execute clean shutdown and bootup.
- Ping other machines on the local network.
- FTP to other machines on the local network.
- Telnet to other machines on the local network.
- Connect to sharenames on other NT machines in the domain.
- Read files in connected sharenames.
- Connect to sharenames on this machine from other computers in the same domain.
- Replicate scripts to and from other computers (as required) in the same domain.
- Take backups.
- Perform restores.
- Respond to UPS signals (send out broadcast messages, shut down system automatically depending on UPS status).

After adding whatever applications the server will support, such a list will usually contain 30 to 50 items. You won't be able to test all items immediately after initial installation because you won't have installed them all yet. However, you should initially test as many as you can and then install and test the remaining items in logical order. It's much easier to debug one new service at a time, always starting from a known good configuration, than it is to diagnose a number of services added together.

7.4 Allocating Disk Space

After Windows NT Setup completes, you'll have only the DOS utilities and diagnostics drive (if you created one) and the Windows NT system drive. You must create any remaining drives with Disk Administrator. Figure 7.5 illustrates the main Disk Administrator window.

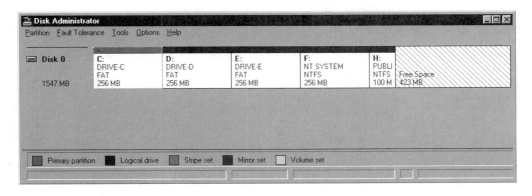

Figure 7.5 Windows NT Disk Administrator

The Partition and Fault Tolerance menu items create, modify, and delete partitions and logical drives. The Tools menu supports formatting, labeling, and assigning drive letters, while the Options menu controls display settings. The text that follows here discusses commands within the first three menus, where the actual work gets done. Disk Administrator uses the familiar Windows "select-action" paradigm; that is, you must use the mouse to select the drive or free space area you wish to affect before you pull down the required menu.

The Partition menu items are as follows:

- **Create.** This option is available only after selecting an area of free disk space. If the free space is in an existing extended partition, the command will create a logical drive. If the free space is unpartitioned space, the command will create a partition containing a single drive. After selecting this command, Disk Administrator will prompt you for the number of megabytes the drive should contain.

- **Created Extended.** This command is available after selecting unpartitioned space on a drive that contains three or fewer partitions. The command will prompt you for the number of megabytes the extended partition should contain.

- **Delete.** This command deletes a selected logical drive or empty extended partition. Any data contained in the drive is irrevocably lost.

- **Create Volume Set.** This command creates a single large drive from two or more free space areas on 1 to 32 physical disks. Once created, a volume set is logically indistinguishable from a drive occupying contiguous space on a single drive. This command is available only after you've Ctrl-clicked two or more areas of free space.

- **Extend Volume Set.** After selecting an existing drive and then Ctrl-clicking additional areas of free space, you can enlarge the existing drive with this command. The free space can be on the same drive as the original volume or on one or more additional drives. Data on the existing drive remains in place. After extending an existing volume or volume set, you must allow Windows NT to reboot. Disk Administrator will schedule a CHKDSK command to run during the boot process; this formats the free space Disk Administrator appended to the extended volume set without disturbing the previously used portion.

- **Create Stripe Set.** The procedure for creating a stripe set is very similar to that for creating an extended volume set: Ctrl-click two or more free space areas and then select the command. However, creating a stripe set requires selecting free space on more than one disk. Furthermore, the amount of space actually used on each drive must be equal. An extended volume set is a "flat" area of disk much like ordinary drive space. A stripe set spreads the data in each file across all physical disks in the set so that, on retrieval, all disks in the stripe set can transfer data simultaneously.

- **Mark Active.** Selecting this command marks the currently selected drive as the boot drive.

- **Configuration.** This submenu allows you to save, restore, or search for disk configurations. The Save option saves the current drive letter, volume set, stripe set, stripe set with parity, and mirror set configurations to a floppy disk. The Restore command restores this information from floppy disk. Search searches for and optionally restores disk configuration information from a previously installed version of Windows NT.

- **Commit Changes Now.** Normally, Disk Administrator changes don't take effect until you quit Disk Administrator. However, you can apply changes made during the current session immediately by using this command.

The Fault Tolerance menu items include the following:

- **Establish Mirror.** To use this command, you must first select an existing partition and then Ctrl-click an equal or larger amount of free space on another drive. Selecting this command then creates a redundant copy of the existing drive—a copy that Windows NT will keep continuously updated. If one disk in the mirror set fails, Windows NT will keep running by using the remaining copy.

- **Break Mirror.** This command breaks the relationship between the two partitions in a mirror. If both drives are working, the original partition retains the original drive letter, and Disk Administrator assigns the redundant partition a new drive letter. If one drive has failed, Disk Administrator assigns the original drive letter to the working partition. If you wish, you can then remirror the good partition onto free space on another drive.

- **Create Stripe Set with Parity.** A stripe set with parity is software RAID 5. Windows NT spreads the data, plus parity information, across 3 to 32 physical drives in such a way that if one drive fails, NTFS can infer its contents from data on the remaining drives. To establish such a set, select free space on three or more physical disks and then select this command.

- **Regenerate.** If a stripe set with parity experiences temporary failure, such as a power loss or momentary disconnection of one drive, you can recreate the contents of the temporarily failed drive by selecting the entire stripe set with parity and then choosing this command. If the drive has failed permanently, select the recoverable stripe set with parity and then Ctrl-click an area of free space on a drive not yet participating in the stripe set with parity. This free space must be at least as large as the spaces used on every other drive in the stripe set with parity. Finally, choose the Fault Tolerance...Regenerate command.

The Tools menu items are as follows:

- **Format.** This command formats logical drives. All existing data on the drive is lost. Available file system types are NTFS and FAT. You cannot format the system partition or unpartitioned space.

- **Label.** The Label command assigns and modifies volume labels. It's a good practice to label each drive with a brief designation of its intended use, such as NT SYSTEM, ANON FTP, and so on.

- **Drive Letter.** This command changes the drive letter assigned to a drive. Windows NT will assign drive letters in alphabetical sequence as you create drives, but you can change these assignments if convenient. For example, suppose you want to move drive E: from physical disk 0 to physical disk 1. You could create a new drive called G: on disk 1, back up the data on E:, restore it to G:, delete drive E:, and rename G: to E:[4]

---

[4] For unknown reasons, Windows NT has no "file copy" command that copies permissions along with data. Instead, you must use NT Backup to back up and restore with permissions. However, the Windows NT Resource Kit does contain a utility called SCOPY that copies permissions as well as files.

- **CD-ROM Drive Letters.** This command allows you to change the drive letter assigned to CD-ROM drives. There's usually no reason to change the drive letter of the system CD-ROM drive, but you may wish to reassign drive letters for shared CDs.[5]

7.5 Creating User Accounts

The need for Windows NT user accounts varies widely depending on the services your site will provide. Remote Access Service, user FTP, and local file and print sharing all require NT user accounts. Some other services like Mail can use either NT user names and passwords or their own. Secure HTTP servers may use Windows NT user names and passwords as well, although many don't because they wish to keep their code platform independent. A server that provides only simple HTTP and anonymous FTP probably doesn't need NT user names and passwords at all, except to differentiate ordinary users from site administrators.

You can circumvent the need for user accounts by giving all necessary permissions to the Guest account and by giving Guest a blank password that never expires and users can't change. However, this results in complete lack of accountability when things go wrong. Don't do this, even if you're a professional and you're not at home.

7.5.1 Windows NT Domain Account Structure

Windows NT stores user account information in a User Account Database (UADB). Each Windows NT workstation has its own UADB, which is usable only on that Windows NT workstation.

A Windows NT server acting as a Primary Domain Controller (PDC) provides a single UADB for all computers in the domain. This makes the same user names and passwords available on all computers in the domain.

Workgroups are collections of Windows NT workstations that aren't in a domain and therefore have no shared user accounts. Instead, each user who needs access to a given machine must have an account on that machine. This quickly becomes unwieldy as the number of Windows NT workstations grows.

---

[5]A nice addition to many sites is an external array of CD-ROM drives connected to an additional SCSI adapter in the server. One SCSI adapter can usually support 7 or 14 drives, so this is the number usually ordered. Once added, these drives will show up in Windows NT as the next 7 or 14 drive letters. You may wish to give the CDs high drive letters such as S: through Y:, however, to keep future hard-disk drive letters contiguous with existing ones.

Windows NT servers must belong to a domain. They must either be a PDC and have their own UADB or belong to an existing domain and use that domain PDC's UADB. If you want two Windows NT servers to have different UADBs, you have to put them in different domains.

When a Windows NT workstation belongs to a domain, a user may elect to log on either to the workstation or to the domain:

- A session logged on with a workstation account will have privileges granted to that account on that workstation and will have Guest privileges elsewhere on the domain. If the account has Administrator privilege, it will only be an Administrator on that workstation.

- A session logged on with a domain account will have whatever privileges exist for that account anywhere on the domain. If the account has Administrator privilege, it will be an Administrator on every workstation and server in the domain.

Even if an organization has several Windows NT domains, each user should have a single account valid in all domains. Windows NT provides this facility through *trust relationships*. That is, for example, if Payroll and Accounting are separate domains but Payroll trusts Accounting, a Payroll administrator can code a rule that says, "Ann from Accounting can read this file (which resides on my server)." Ann can then access the file on Payroll's server, even though Ann has no account on the Payroll domain. Ann must log on to her account in the Accounting domain, though.

Microsoft recommends four schemes for combining domains into an enterprise structure. They are listed in Table 7.3. As a rule of thumb, Microsoft also recommends that domains be limited to 10,000 users each. Single domain and master domain are therefore suitable for organizations up to 10,000 users. Organizations needing more than 10,000 accounts should choose the multiple master model.

Table 7.3 Windows NT Domain Models

Domain Mode	Description
Single domain	There is one domain, with no trust relationships.
Master domain	All user accounts reside in one master domain. All other domains trust the master, but the master doesn't trust any of the others.
Multiple master domain	There are several master domains that trust one another. All other domains trust all the masters, but no master trusts any nonmaster.
Multiple trust	All domains trust all other domains.

The multiple trust scheme seems simple at first but can get out of hand. If there are n domains, each domain has $(n-1)$ trust relationships, and the total number of trust relationships is $n(n-1)$, or $(n^2 - n)$. This can quickly become an unmanageable number.

7.5.2 Setting User Account Policies

User Manager is the Windows NT application that manages user accounts. Figure 7.6 illustrates the main User Manager window.

The View, Options, and Help menus require no additional explanation; the User and Policies menus do all the work. Pulling down the Policies menu and selecting "Account..." brings up the dialog shown in Figure 7.7.

Most of these settings are fairly obvious. As shown, passwords expire 31 days after being set; passwords must be at least 6 characters long; once set, passwords are changeable immediately; and a new password must be different from the last one. Five failed logon attempts in a 30-minute period lock out an account, but these lockouts last only 20 minutes.

These aren't the Windows NT defaults. By default, passwords expire after 42 days, blank passwords are permissible, new passwords can be the same as old passwords, and repeated failed logon attempts never lock out an account. You should almost certainly tighten these policies.

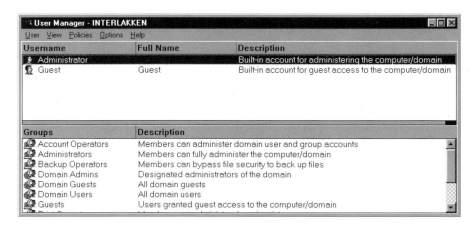

Figure 7.6 Windows NT User Manager

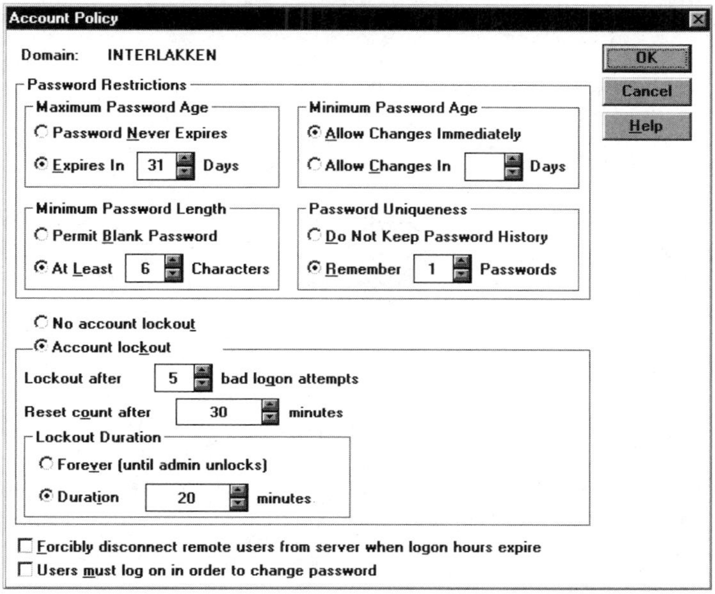

Figure 7.7 Account Policy Dialog

7.5.3 Managing User Rights

Figure 7.8 shows the User Rights Policy dialog. Pulling down the Policies menu and selecting "User Rights" invokes this dialog.

These settings seldom require change. The dropdown list selects a specific user right, and the list box below it specifies the users or groups having that right. An administrator can add or remove users or groups from the list using the

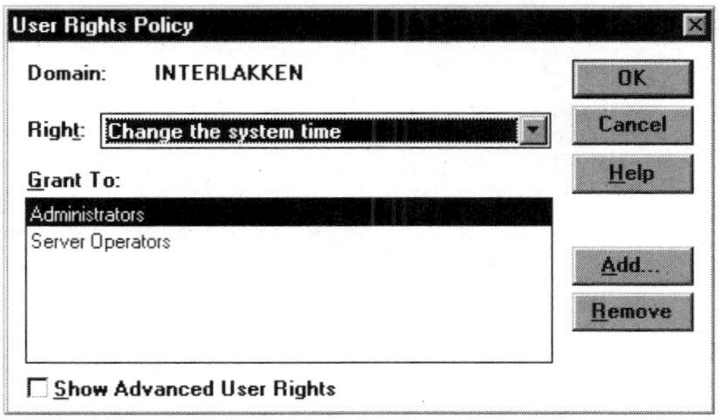

Figure 7.8 User Rights Policy Dialog

Add... and Remove buttons. Clicking the "Show Advanced User Rights" checkbox adds additional items to the dropdown list. Note that user rights are administrative capabilities, not file-access permissions.

7.5.4 Managing Audit Tracking

Pulling down User Manager's Policies menu and selecting "Audit..." results in the dialog shown in Figure 7.9.

Selecting "Audit These Events" and checking any box causes Windows NT to record the specified events in the Windows NT Security Log. To view the Security Log or manage its size, use Event Viewer.

7.5.5 Managing Trust Relationships

Establishing a trust relationship between Windows NT domains is a two-step process that requires collaboration between administrators of each domain. Figure 7.10 shows the dialog for managing trust relationships; to bring it up, pull down Policies and select "Trust Relationships...."

The process begins when an administrator of the domain to be trusted (the INTERLAKKEN domain, in this case) clicks the lower Add... button. This brings up the Permit Domain to Trust dialog shown in Figure 7.11. The INTERLAKKEN administrator types MOON, the name of the domain that will be permitted to trust INTERLAKKEN, enters a password twice (for confirmation), and then clicks OK.

Later, to complete the process, an administrator of the MOON domain starts his or her User Manager, pulls up the Trust Relationships dialog, and clicks the upper Add... button. The dialog shown in Figure 7.12 results. The MOON

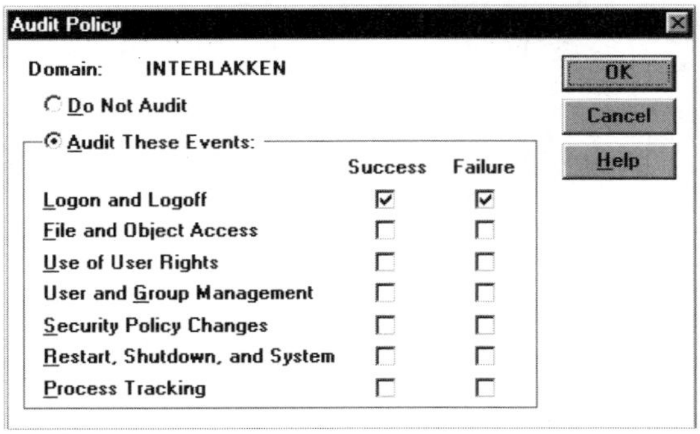

Figure 7.9 Audit Policy Dialog

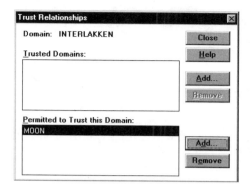

Figure 7.10 Trust Relationships Dialog

administrator enters the password that the INTERLAKKEN administrator specified and then clicks OK. The MOON PDC confirms the password with the INTERLAKKEN PDC, and the relationship is established. Users in the MOON domain can now include users and global groups from the INTERLAKKEN domain in MOON domain security rules.

7.5.6 Creating User Accounts

To create a Windows NT user account, pull down User Manager's User menu and select "New User...." The dialog in Figure 7.13 results.

In this dialog, Username is the name of the account—the name the user will log on with. Windows NT will remember Username's alphabetic case for readability, but the user name isn't case sensitive at logon time. Full Name is the user's given and family name. Description is anything you wish to record. Password and Confirm Password will become the user's password; both entries must match, and they must satisfy the length restrictions set in Policies...Account. Passwords are case sensitive.

The three checkboxes titled "User Must Change Password at Next Logon", "User Cannot Change Password," and "Password Never Expires" are self-explanatory. Administrators can turn the "Account Disabled" checkbox ON or OFF to prevent or allow use of the account.

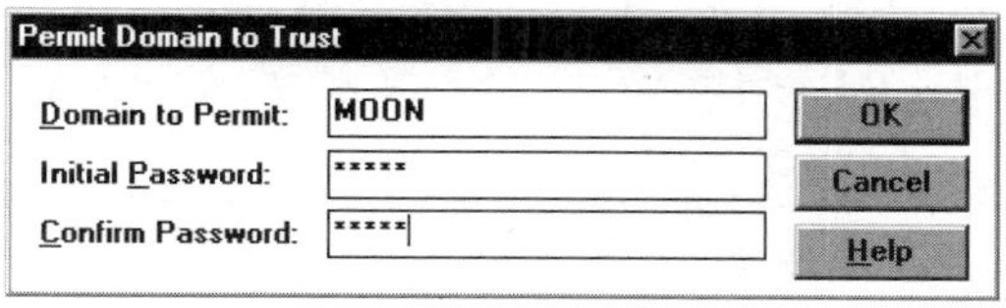

Figure 7.11 Permit Domain to Trust Dialog

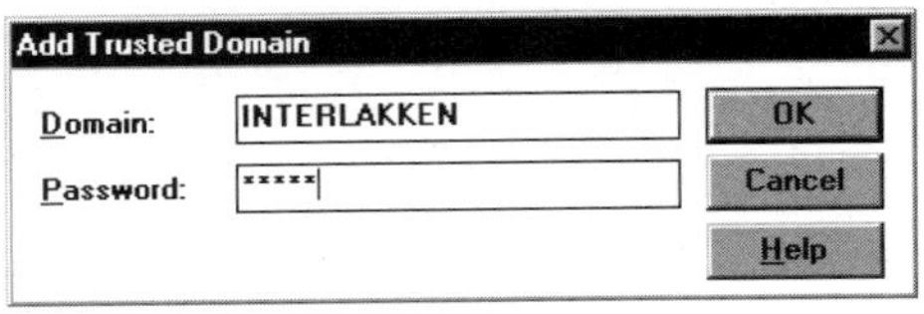

Figure 7.12 Add Trusted Domain Dialog

The five buttons at the bottom of the New User dialog have the following functions:

- **Groups.** This button brings up a dialog box for adding the user to one or more groups. Groups are the topic of the next section.

- **Profile.** This button controls several settings that affect Windows NT domain logins but have no relevance to other kinds of login, such as FTP. User Profile Path specifies the location of a user's Windows NT User Profile, a collection of settings that follow a Windows NT user from machine to machine. Logon Script Name is the name of a batch file Windows NT will run each time a user logs in to the domain; the batch file runs on the machine the user logs in from. Home Directory is the user's personal sharename on a Windows Networking server.

- **Hours.** This dialog specifies days of the week and hours of the day a user may log in. The default is 7 days a week, 24 hours a day. This facility would be useful if, for example, some users are eligible for prime-shift (or non-prime-shift) usage only.

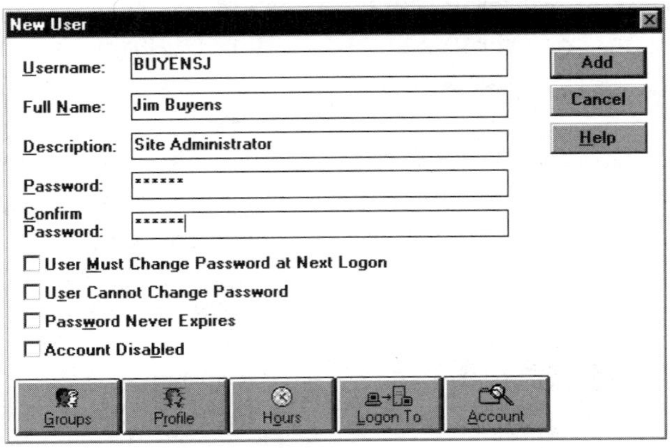

Figure 7.13 New User Dialog

- **Logon To.** After pressing this button, you can restrict this user to logging in at specific workstations only.

- **Account.** You can use this button to set a future expiration date for an account or to flag an account as a local account. Use of local accounts is rare; this is an awkward facility designed to provide access to users of other, untrusted domains.

7.5.7 Creating Groups

Windows NT *groups* are a convenient way to manage user accounts with similar security privileges. A group might encompass all employees of a certain client, all users who've rented space for Web authoring, or all people authorized to review anonymous FTP uploads. Once you've established such a group, you can set file and other permissions based on group membership rather than individual account. This greatly simplifies administration as users gain and lose privileges; the administrator simply modifies membership in the appropriate group. A group may contain any number of users, and users may belong to any number of groups.

There are two kinds of groups: local and global. Unless you have multiple domains with trust relationships, the type of group you use doesn't make a difference. With a trust relationship in effect, the trusting domain can "see" the trusted domain's users and global groups, but not the trusted domain's local groups. So, if there's a chance that a group might be useful to another domain that trusts the current domain, you should create a global group.

In general, groups can't be nested; one group can't contain another. There is, however, one exception: A local group can contain a global group. Suppose the FRISCO, WINDY, and BEANTOWN domains each contains a global group called MGRS, and the HEADCUE domain wants to form a group called ALLMGRS consisting of FRISCO\MGRS, WINDY\MGRS, and BEANTOWN\MGRS. HEAD-CUE\ALLMGRS would have to be a local group because only a local group can contain a global group.

To create a global group, pull down User Manager's User menu and select "New Global Group...." To create a local group, select "New Local Group...."

Figure 7.14 illustrates the New Global Group dialog. In the two text boxes at the top of the dialog, enter a group name and a text description. Then, double-click each user name in the Not Members list that should become a member (or select the user name and click the ←Add button). Click OK when done.

The New Local Group dialog appears in Figure 7.15. Again, you should enter a group name and a text description in the two text boxes at the top. To add users

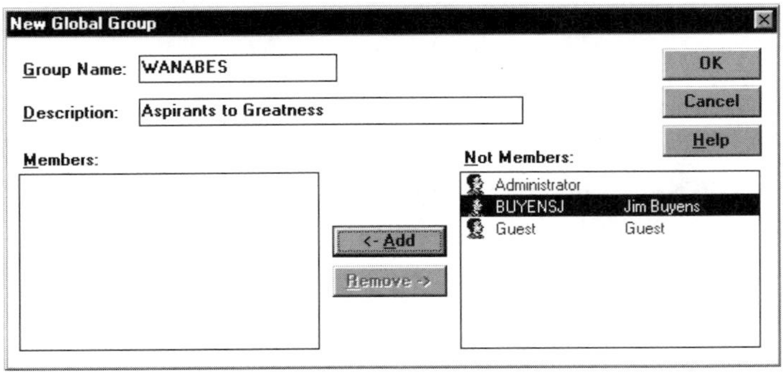

Figure 7.14 New Global Group Dialog

or groups, however, you must click the Add... button and bring up the dialog shown in Figure 7.16.

At the top of the Add Users and Groups dialog is a dropdown list of domains. This will contain the local domain and every trusted domain. The Names list contains user accounts and global groups from the selected domain. To add one of these to the new local group, select it and click the Add button. You can select user accounts and global groups from as many domains as you like. Then press OK to update the Members list in the New Local Group dialog (Figure 7.15). Continue adding and potentially removing members until the composition of the new local group is correct. Then click OK.

7.5.8 Other User and Group Operations

Changing user accounts and groups is very much like adding them. Simply double-click the object that needs changing, update the dialog box, and click OK.

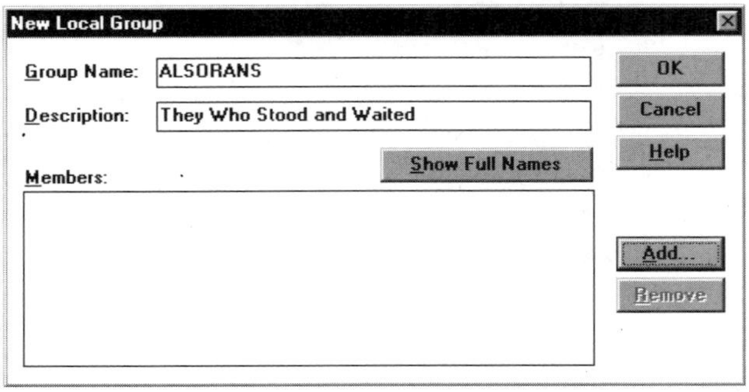

Figure 7.15 New Local Group Dialog

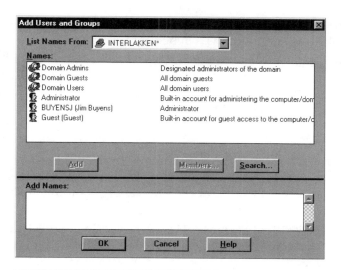

Figure 7.16 Add Users and Groups Dialog

To copy a user account or group, select it and then pull down User and select "Copy." Copying a user account initializes the new account with the copied account's group memberships, profiles, hours, and so on. Copying a group initializes the new group with the copied group's members.

Figure 7.17 illustrates a special warning that appears when you attempt to delete a user account or group. This occurs because the real identity of a user account or group isn't the displayed name, such as BUYENSJ, but a long binary string called a Security Identifier (SID). When you build an access rule granting permission to BUYENSJ, the rule actually contains the SID, not the string BUYENSJ.

If you delete the BUYENSJ account and create a new one with the same name, the new account will have a different SID. Any permissions or group memberships that applied to the deleted SID won't apply. So, if someone is going on leave of absence or fails to pay his or her bill, you should probably disable the

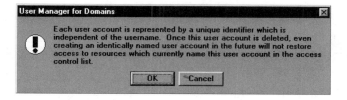

Figure 7.17 User Account Deletion Warning

account rather than delete it. When the member returns or pays up, you can then enable the account, and the old permissions will be back.

If someone wants the name of his or her account changed, you should select it and apply the User...Rename... command. Renaming an account leaves the SID (and hence the permissions) unchanged. The result of deleting the old account and creating a new one is a new SID and the loss of all permissions associated with the old SID.

7.5.9 Setting File Permissions

Figure 7.18 illustrates how to select a directory in File Manager and invoke the Security...Permissions... command. In the future, finding the directory (folder) in Explorer, right-clicking it, selecting Properties, and clicking Permissions will probably have the same effect.

Figure 7.19 shows the resulting dialog. \<systemroot>\system32\Repl\Export \Scripts is the directory that the Replicator service normally copies to \<system-root>\system32\Repl\Import\Scripts on other servers. This is the NETLOGON sharename from which Windows Networking clients obtain their logon scripts. Administrators, the CREATOR OWNER, and the SYSTEM account have full control, meaning they can do anything. Everyone can read files in this directory, and

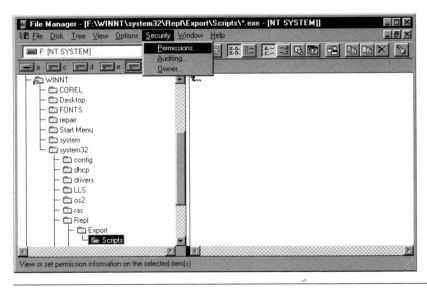

Figure 7.18 Setting Permissions on a Directory

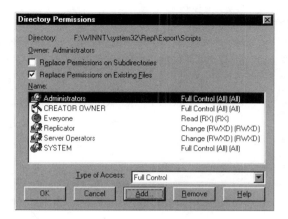

Figure 7.19 Directory Permissions Dialog

accounts in the Replicator and Server Operator groups can read, write, execute, and delete files.

Note that two sets of permissions appear, as in "(RWXD) (RWXD)." The first permissions are those that apply by default to new files, and the second permissions apply to files already in the directory that have no specific permissions set. You can manipulate these permissions separately by pulling down the Type of Access list and selecting "Special Directory Access..." or "Special File Access...."

To modify permissions for an existing entry in the Name list, select the entry and then select a new setting in the Type of Access dropdown list.

To add a user or group to the Name list, click the Add... button. A dialog like the one in Figure 7.20 will result.

Select the domain that contains the group or user you want to add permissions for, then select the specific group or user, and then click Add to complete the addition. Select the type of access you wish to grant and then click OK. The new entry should appear in the Directory Permissions dialog.

Before clicking the OK button, note the two checkboxes labeled "Replace Permissions on Subdirectories" and "Replace Permissions on Existing Files." If you check the first box ON, the dialog will replace all permissions in the directory tree starting at the selected directory. If you leave the second box checked ON, the dialog will also replace all permissions for existing files.

The set of permissions for a given file or directory is an Access Control List (ACL). You can set permissions only for files and directories on NTFS volumes because the FAT file system and HPFS (High-Performance File System) have no provision for storing ACLs.

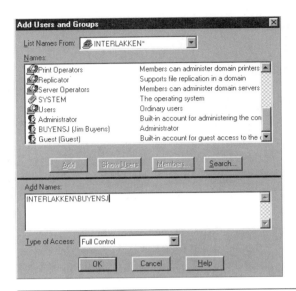

Figure 7.20 Add Users and Groups Dialog

7.5.10 How Many Passwords?

A common user request is for one password to work for everything. Currently, Windows NT supports this only to the extent that you can use Windows NT services for everything. If you use Microsoft Remote Access Service (described later in this chapter) for dial-in, the Windows NT FTP service for user FTP, and a Windows-NT-based mail system, keeping passwords down to one may be a real possibility.

If you run various kinds of dial-in routers and servers, keeping passwords synchronized will be more difficult. Your users will have to cope with different passwords for different services, you'll have to coordinate password changes manually, or you'll have to develop a homegrown solution.

Perhaps, in the future, manufacturers of third-party equipment will develop interfaces to control their devices with Windows NT passwords, or perhaps Microsoft will support a more open security scheme such as Kerberos.

7.6 Advanced TCP/IP Configuration

You can change a Windows NT machine's Network configuration at any time.[6] To begin, open Control Panel and double-click the Network icon. The Network Settings dialog shown in Figure 7.21 will appear.

---

[6]However, most changes to network software don't take effect until the computer reboots. For this reason, it's generally best to change (and test) network settings during a scheduled outage.

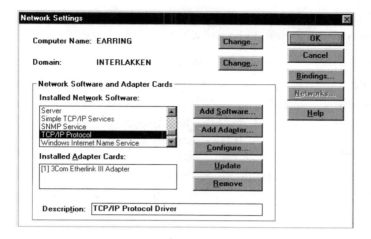

Figure 7.21 Network Settings Dialog

The Installed Network Software list box lists each component currently installed:

- To configure a component, double-click its entry or select it and click the Configure... button.
- To add a component, click the Add Software... button.
- To refresh the software for a component, select its entry and then click the Update button.
- To remove a component, select its entry and then click the Remove button.

For example, to change TCP/IP settings, select "TCP/IP Protocol" in the Installed Network Software list and then click the Configure... button. This will invoke the TCP/IP Configuration dialog shown earlier in Figure 7.2. The dialog continues to work as described in Section 7.2.5.

Some components, such as "Simple TCP/IP Services," have no configurable options. In such cases, clicking the Configure... button results in the message "Cannot configure the software component."

7.6.1 Multiple Network Adapters per System

The Network Settings dialog (Figure 7.21) also contains an Installed Adapter Cards list. To add physically installed adapters to the list, click the Add Adapter... button, select the type of adapter card, indicate the I/O port address, interrupt number, and other settings, and keep clicking OK. Figure 7.22 again shows the Network Settings dialog—this time with two 3Com Etherlink III adapters installed.

Both adapters have the name "3Com Etherlink III Adapter," but they have different prefixes—"(1)" or "(4)." To configure the TCP/IP settings for either card, select the Installed Network Software entry "TCP/IP Protocol," click the Configure... button, and select "(1) 3Com Etherlink III Adapter" or "(4) 3Com Etherlink III Adapter" in the "Adapter:" dropdown list at the top of the dialog. A similar dropdown appears at the top of the "Advanced" dialog.

As always, be sure you've configured all adapters physically and in software with nonconflicting I/O port addresses, interrupt numbers, upper memory addresses, and DMA channels.

7.6.2 Multiple IP Addresses per Network Adapter

Section 7.2.5 describes how "Advanced" settings in the TCP/IP Configuration dialog can specify up to five IP addresses per network adapter. Once you've entered the fifth address, however, Windows NT disables the data entry text boxes and the Add→ button so that you can't add a sixth IP address to the list.

This isn't acceptable to some administrators for a simple reason: money. Table 7.4 shows the fees one provider charges to set up two different home page URLs. In each case, the client has already paid for the domain name.

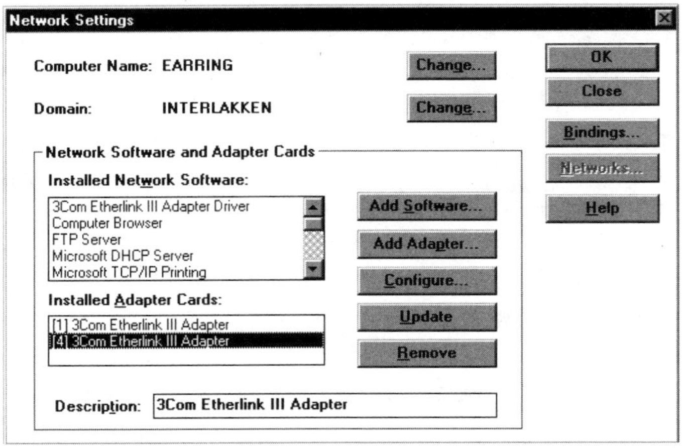

Figure 7.22 Network Settings Dialog with Two Network Adapters Installed

Table 7.4 Home Page Addressing Fees (One Provider)

Home Page URL	Setup Charge	Monthly Fee
http://www.client.com/client	$50	$0
http://www.client.com	$250	$50

Clients pay $200 more up front plus $600 a year for the URL without the /client suffix because that's the format most Web users expect. Also, if the client chooses the form that requires the suffix, Web surfers who type the URL without the alias get the provider's home page, not the client's.

Of course, even with the extra fees, the provider can't afford to build a new server for every client. The provider satisfies the request by

1. Adding an extra IP address to an existing Web server.

2. Configuring DNS so that looking up www.client.com returns the IP address defined in step 1.

3. Configuring the HTTP service to respond with the client's home page when someone transmits a default page request to the IP address defined in step 1.

This is good business; 5 or 10 minutes of pointing and clicking yields happier customers plus $200 up front and $600 a year. Why stop at five IP Addresses per adapter just because Microsoft decided Windows NT would disable a dialog box at that point?

No one outside Microsoft seems to know why Windows NT imposes a limit of five IP addresses per adapter. If you want to manage your site for maximum stability, stick with the supported limit of five IP addresses. If you want to take a chance and make a buck, keep reading.

Windows NT stores the IP addresses bound to each adapter in the registry. To locate them, take the following steps:

1. Start Regedt32.

2. Open the HKEY_LOCAL_MACHINE hive.

3. Open the tree to SYSTEM\CurrentControlSet\Services\Tcpip\Linkage, as show in Figures 7.23 and 7.24.

4. Note the identity of the network adapter. In the example (Figure 7.24), it's Elnk31.

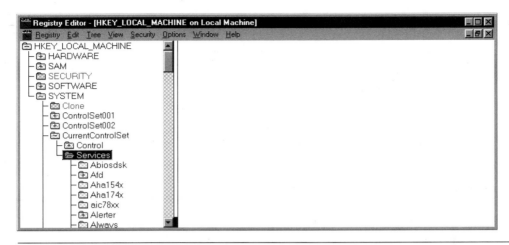

Figure 7.23 Finding SYSTEM\CurrentControlSet\Services in HKEY_LOCAL_MACHINE

5. As shown in Figure 7.25, open the tree to SYSTEM\CurrentControlSet\Services\<adapter>\Parameters\Tcpip, where <adapter> is the identity from step 4.

6. Double-click on the value titled "IP Address: REG_MULTI_SZ." A Multi-String Editor box, as shown in Figure 7.26, will appear.

7. Enter the additional IP addresses, being careful not to add any spaces at the end of a line. To start a new line, press Enter. When done, click OK.

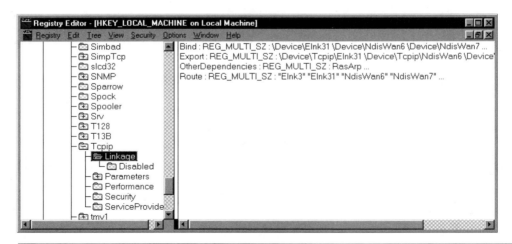

Figure 7.24 Finding SYSTEM\CurrentControlSet\Services\Tcpip\Linkage in HKEY_LOCAL_MACHINE

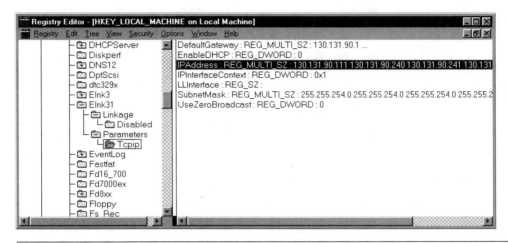

Figure 7.25 Adding a Sixth IP Address to a Network Adapter

8. Double-click on the value titled "SubnetMask: REG_MULTI_SZ." Another Multi-String Editor box will appear.

9. Enter the additional subnet masks, being careful not to add any spaces at the end of a line. To start a new line, press Enter. Be sure the number of subnet masks is the same as the number of IP addresses from step 7. Click OK when done.

10. Quit Regedt32.

Just for curiosity, you may wish to return to the Control Panel...Network... TCP/IP Protocol...Configure...Advanced dialog. The additional address should appear in the expected list box, and Windows NT even supplies a scroll bar to examine them.

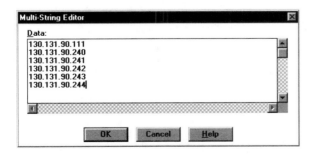

Figure 7.26 Entering IP Addresses with Regedt32 Multi-String Editor

Windows NT 3.5 reportedly supports up to 16 IP addresses per adapter. If 17 or more are present, Windows NT reportedly honors only the first 16. Windows NT 3.51 reportedly honors more than 16, perhaps 255. If you decide to try this, good luck! You're on your own.

7.6.3 Static IP Routing

Figure 7.27 pictures a Windows NT computer with two network adapters on different subnets. Table 7.5 the displays IP addresses, subnet masks, and default gateways for Server1 and Router1.

The IP service in Server1 has three possible sources of traffic: the first network adapter, the second network adapter, and the computer itself:

1. When IP gets a packet from the computer, IP transmits the packet on the network adapter whose subnet matches that of the packet. That is, in Figure 7.27, it exits via route A or B. If no network adapter has the same subnet as an outgoing packet, IP forwards the packet to the default gateway.

2. When IP gets a packet from one of the network adapters and the packet's IP address matches the computer's (or is a broadcast or multicast), IP forwards the packet up the stack. In the figure, it enters via route A or B.

3. When IP gets a packet from one of the network adapters that doesn't match the computer's IP address and that isn't a broadcast or multicast, IP will do one of two things: either ignore the packet or retransmit the packet on the other adapter so that the packet, in effect, follows route C.

In order for the last case to occur, routing must be turned ON and Windows NT must know that forwarding the packet will be useful. Turning routing ON is

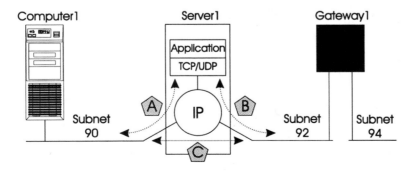

Figure 7.27 Two Network Adapters on Different Subnets

easy; it's a checkbox in the Advanced TCP/IP Configuration dialog. Informing Windows NT what routes are useful is more complex. The rest of this section will discuss how to define such routes.

With a Windows NT server configured according to Table 7.5, entering the command "route print" results in the following output:

```
Active Routes:

Network Address          Netmask  Gateway Address      Interface  Metric
        0.0.0.0          0.0.0.0    130.131.92.1  130.131.92.122       1
        0.0.0.0          0.0.0.0    130.131.90.1  130.131.90.111       1
      127.0.0.0        255.0.0.0      127.0.0.1       127.0.0.1       1
   130.131.90.0  255.255.254.0  130.131.90.111  130.131.90.111       1
 130.131.90.111  255.255.255.255      127.0.0.1       127.0.0.1       1
   130.131.92.0  255.255.254.0  130.131.92.122  130.131.92.122       1
 130.131.92.122  255.255.255.255      127.0.0.1       127.0.0.1       1
130.131.255.255  255.255.255.255  130.131.90.111  130.131.90.111       1
      224.0.0.0        224.0.0.0  130.131.92.122  130.131.92.122       1
      224.0.0.0        224.0.0.0  130.131.90.111  130.131.90.111       1
255.255.255.255  255.255.255.255  130.131.90.111  130.131.90.111       1
```

Determining how to route a given IP address involves testing it against each displayed route entry. To determine whether a given entry is applicable, take these steps:

1. AND the "Netmask" value to the given IP address.

2. Compare the result to "Network Address."

3. If equal, the routing entry applies. Route the packet to the stated "Gateway Address" using the network adapter whose address is "Interface."

Table 7.5 Sample Configuration for Two Adapters in One Computer

Host	Parameter	Network Adapter 1	Network Adapter 2
Server1	IP address	130.131.90.111	130.131.92.122
	Subnet mask	255.255.254.0	255.255.254.0
	Default gateway	130.131.90.1	130.131.92.1
Router1	IP address	130.131.92.1	130.131.94.1
	Subnet mask	255.255.254.0	255.255.254.0

4. If not equal, repeat steps 1 through 3 using values from the next routing table entry.

Because the preceding output is difficult to read, the following version contains the same lines of output in a more logical sequence:

```
Active Routes:
```

Network Address	Netmask	Gateway Address	Interface	Metric
127.0.0.0	255.0.0.0	127.0.0.1	127.0.0.1	1
130.131.90.111	255.255.255.255	127.0.0.1	127.0.0.1	1
130.131.92.122	255.255.255.255	127.0.0.1	127.0.0.1	1
130.131.255.255	255.255.255.255	130.131.90.111	130.131.90.111	1
255.255.255.255	255.255.255.255	130.131.90.111	130.131.90.111	1
130.131.90.0	255.255.254.0	130.131.90.111	130.131.90.111	1
224.0.0.0	224.0.0.0	130.131.90.111	130.131.90.111	1
0.0.0.0	0.0.0.0	130.131.90.1	130.131.90.111	1
130.131.92.0	255.255.254.0	130.131.92.122	130.131.92.122	1
224.0.0.0	224.0.0.0	130.131.92.122	130.131.92.122	1
0.0.0.0	0.0.0.0	130.131.92.1	130.131.92.122	1

127.0.0.0 is the loopback address—the internal address of the local host. The first three lines (after the headings) show IP addresses 127.0.0.0, 130.131.90.111, and 130.131.92.122 routed to the computer itself. These are the host computer's own addresses, and it's logical that they would route upward through the stack for processing.

The next two lines show the routes for 130.131.255.255, the Class B network broadcast address, and 255.255.255.255, the wide-area broadcast address. The table routes these to 130.131.90.111, the first network interface card.

The next three lines show the subnet entry, the multicast entry, and default gateway entry for the first network adapter. Anything on this adapter not addressed to the local subnet and not a multicast will go to the default gateway. The last three lines are similar to the previous three, but they are for the second network adapter.

Windows NT knows where the 130.131.90.0 and 130.131.92.0 subnets are; after all, it has adapters on these subnets. If routing is ON and Windows NT detects subnet 130.131.92.0 traffic on the 130.131.90.0 adapter, Windows NT will retransmit the traffic on its 130.131.92.0 adapter. This is the essence of routing: If a router (Windows NT in this case) hears traffic in the "wrong" place, it retransmits it in the "right" place (or at least one hop closer to the right place).

Returning to Figure 7.27, Computer1 can gain access to hosts on Subnet 92 by configuring Server1 as its default gateway. However, this won't provide Computer1 with access to Subnet 94 because Server1 doesn't have a route to Subnet 94. Windows NT only supports static routing—routing hand-configured by an administrator—and can't automatically learn routes using protocols like RIP.

The following command, issued on Server1, adds a route to Subnet 94:

```
route  add  130.131.94.0  mask  255.255.254.0  130.131.92.1
```

This says, "If you see any packets whose destination IP address is 130.131.94.0 (after zeroing the nine low-order bits), send them to the gateway located at 130.131.92.1." The following listing shows the effect of this command:

```
C:\>route print

Active Routes:

Network Address          Netmask  Gateway Address      Interface  Metric
      0.0.0.0            0.0.0.0     130.131.92.1   130.131.92.122       1
      0.0.0.0            0.0.0.0     130.131.90.1   130.131.90.111       1
    127.0.0.0          255.0.0.0        127.0.0.1        127.0.0.1       1
 130.131.90.0      255.255.254.0   130.131.90.111   130.131.90.111       1
 130.131.90.111  255.255.255.255        127.0.0.1        127.0.0.1       1
 130.131.92.0      255.255.254.0   130.131.92.122   130.131.92.122       1
 130.131.92.122  255.255.255.255        127.0.0.1        127.0.0.1       1
 130.131.255.255 255.255.255.255   130.131.90.111   130.131.90.111       1
    224.0.0.0          224.0.0.0   130.131.92.122   130.131.92.122       1
    224.0.0.0          224.0.0.0   130.131.90.111   130.131.90.111       1
255.255.255.255  255.255.255.255   130.131.90.111   130.131.90.111       1

C:\>route add 30.131.94.0 mask 255.255.254.0 130.131.92.1

C:\>route print
```

```
Active Routes:

Network Address          Netmask  Gateway Address       Interface  Metric
        0.0.0.0          0.0.0.0     130.131.92.1   130.131.92.122       1
        0.0.0.0          0.0.0.0     130.131.90.1   130.131.90.111       1
      127.0.0.0        255.0.0.0        127.0.0.1        127.0.0.1       1
   130.131.90.0    255.255.254.0   130.131.90.111   130.131.90.111       1
 130.131.90.111  255.255.255.255        127.0.0.1        127.0.0.1       1
   130.131.92.0    255.255.254.0   130.131.92.122   130.131.92.122       1
 130.131.92.122  255.255.255.255        127.0.0.1        127.0.0.1       1
   130.131.94.0    255.255.254.0     130.131.92.1   130.131.92.122       1
130.131.255.255  255.255.255.255   130.131.90.111   130.131.90.111       1
        224.0.0.0        224.0.0.0   130.131.92.122   130.131.92.122       1
        224.0.0.0        224.0.0.0   130.131.90.111   130.131.90.111       1
255.255.255.255  255.255.255.255   130.131.90.111   130.131.90.111       1

C:\>
```

Note the added line, emphasized with bold type, for the 130.131.94.0 subnet. Windows NT itself has determined it should transmit subnet 130.131.94.0 traffic on the 130.131.92.122 adapter; this is the only adapter on the same subnet as the specified gateway.

The "route" command can only specify gateways on subnets for which Windows NT has a local adapter. This means, in our example, that the last address on the command line must be in subnet 130.131.90.0 or 130.131.92.0. To configure a multihop route through a number of Windows NT computers, you must configure each hop on each computer.

The "route change" command updates a route, and "route delete" deletes one. Specifying the "-f" switch erases all gateway entries before processing the add, change, delete, or print command (if any).

To permanently establish a route (that is, to make it persistent across reboots), specify the "-p" switch when adding or changing that route. By default, Windows NT discards manually configured routes every time it shuts down.

As you may have surmised by now, Windows NT routing is a limited facility suited only for small, stable environments.

7.7 Installing Remote Access Service

Remote Access Service (RAS) provides network dial-out and dial-in services for Windows NT computers. Table 7.6 summarizes these capabilities with respect to TCP/IP.

7.7.1 Equipment for Remote Access Service

RAS supports communication over dial-up modem, X.25, and ISDN. Serial ports in the system unit can support one or two modems; for more, you'll need to purchase a multiport serial adapter from Digiboard or another supported vendor. Check the Windows NT Hardware Compatibility List for X.25 and ISDN adapters. If you expect heavy dial-in usage, such as 16 or 32 ports supporting a 28.8Kbps modem bank, it's best to run RAS on a dedicated server.

You should install modems and other equipment before installing the RAS software and should run diagnostics and other simple tests to make sure the hardware is working. Try connecting to each modem and verifying it responds to the ATZ command, for example. It's always best to eliminate as many problem variables as possible before trying something new.

7.7.2 Installing the RAS Software

To start the RAS installation process, start Control Panel and double-click the Network icon. This will display the Network Settings dialog shown in Figure 7.28.

Click the Add Software... button to bring up the Add Network Software dialog pictured in Figure 7.29. Select "Remote Access Service" and click the Continue button.

A Windows NT Setup dialog will appear, prompting you for the location of your Windows NT installation files. In the example (Figure 7.30), G: is the local CD drive letter, and \I386 is the CD directory for the Intel version of Windows NT. After entering the correct path for your system, click the Continue button.

RAS Setup will next display a list of all ports available to RAS. Figure 7.31 illustrates this. Select the port you'd like to configure first and then click OK.

Table 7.6 Remote Access TCP/IP Capabilities

Product	Dial-Out Protocols	Dial-In Protocols	Number of Dial-In Clients
Windows NT Workstation	PPP	SLIP, PPP	1
Windows NT Server	PPP	SLIP, PPP	255

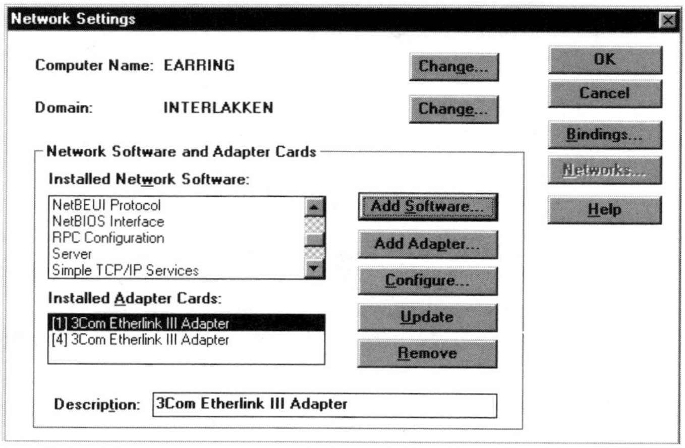

Figure 7.28 Network Settings Dialog

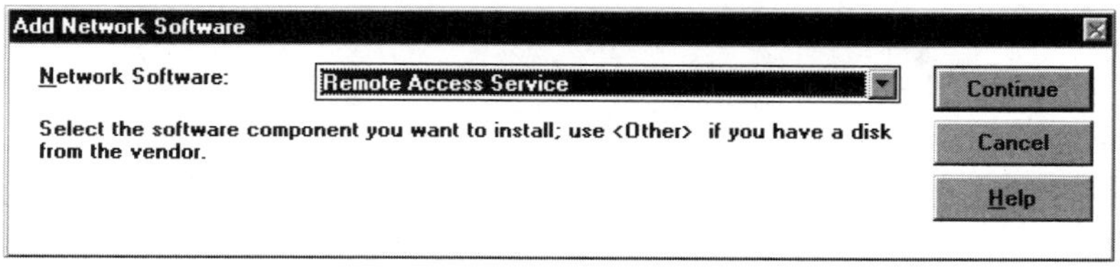

Figure 7.29 Add Network Software Dialog

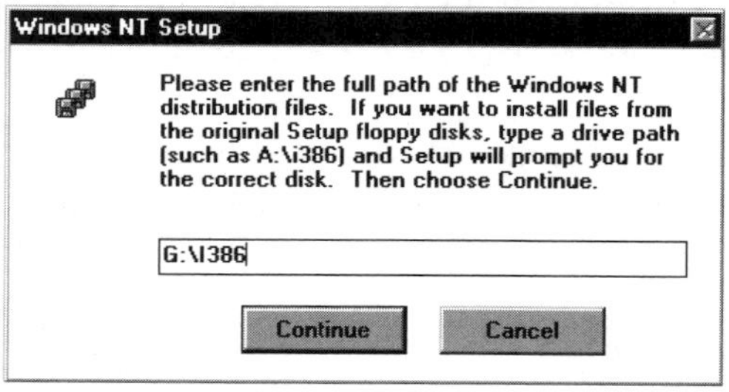

Figure 7.30 Windows NT Setup Dialog

The prompt in Figure 7.32 will appear next, offering to automatically detect the type of modem or other device connected to the port you selected. It's generally best to click OK.

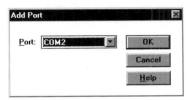

Figure 7.31 RAS Add Port Dialog

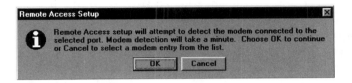

Figure 7.32 RAS Modem Detection Prompt

If RAS Setup believes it has detected your modem correctly, it will display the Configure Port dialog with that modem selected. Figure 7.33 shows this dialog. If RAS Setup can't identify the modem, it will ask you to select from a list of possibilities. If the exact model of your modem doesn't appear on the list, choose the most similar model from the same manufacturer.

In the Port Usage frame, indicate whether this modem on this port should dial out only, receive calls only, or do both. You should also click the Settings... button and verify choices on the resulting dialog, shown in Figure 7.34. "Enable Hardware Flow Control (RTS/CTS)" and "Enable Error Control" should almost certainly be checked ON.

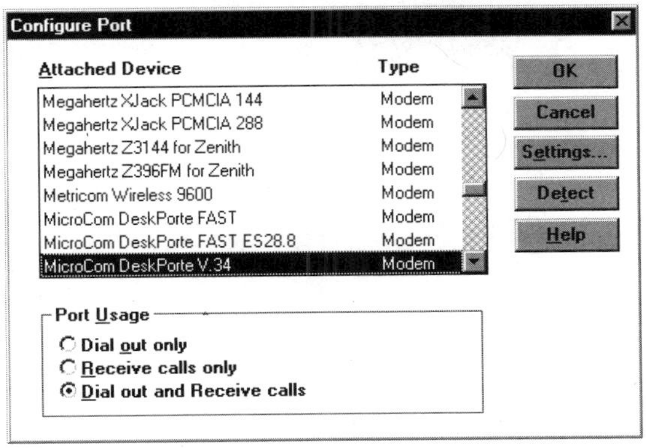

Figure 7.33 RAS Configure Port Dialog

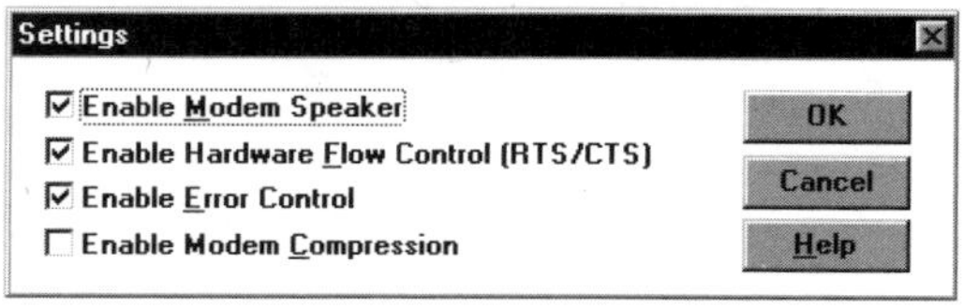

Figure 7.34 RAS Configure Port Settings Dialog

Exiting the Settings and Configure Port dialogs will cause the Remote Access Setup dialog shown in Figure 7.35 to appear. You can add additional ports at this time by clicking the Add... or Clone buttons; you can also remove ports with the Remove button and modify them after clicking Configure....

After you're done adding ports, click the Network... button to display the Network Configuration dialog illustrated in Figure 7.36.

Select the protocols you wish to support for dial-in and for dial-out. However, the dial-out choices will be disabled if you have no ports configured for dial-out, and the server settings will be disabled if you have no ports configured to receive calls.

Internet use obviously requires TCP/IP. You can also support NetBEUI and IPX if you want. RAS uses a highly optimized[7] version of NetBEUI for NETBIOS communication, so you may decide to support dial-up NetBEUI just to speed up remote administration tasks.

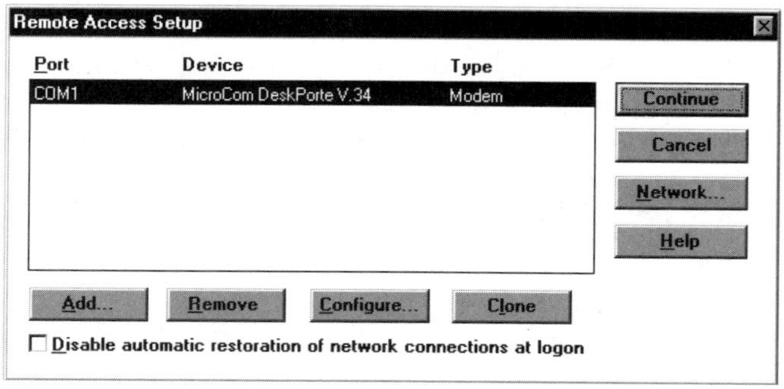

Figure 7.35 Remote Access Setup Dialog

---

[7]A serious problem with running NETBIOS over modem links involves broadcasts. A quantity of broadcasts considered trivial on Ethernet can overwhelm even a high-speed modem connection. RAS's modified NetBEUI protocol suppresses broadcasts to the remote client by distributing functions that depend on broadcasting to the RAS server.

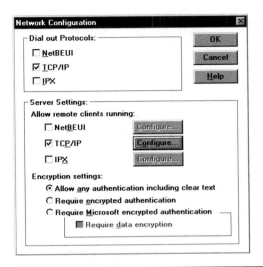

Figure 7.36 RAS Network Configuration Dialog

For NETBIOS or Windows Networking functions, RAS can convert NetBEUI traffic between the RAS server and the modem user to TCP/IP before it leaves the RAS server. Users still can't use NetBEUI for Internet applications, though; for that, they need to run TCP/IP over the modem link.

Encryption settings refer primarily to password protection. Clear-text authentication would allow a wiretapper to discern the user's password by sending a live or recorded copy of the modem tones to another modem. Despite the security risk, enabling clear-text authentication supports the widest variety of dial-in clients. RAS will still negotiate encrypted login if the remote client is capable of it. The choice "Require data encryption" means RAS and the remote client will encrypt not only the logon password but also all subsequent data packets.

If you're supporting RAS dial-in, you should review the network configuration of each protocol you check ON. Figure 7.37 illustrates the dialog you get after pressing the TCP/IP Configure... button.

For most Internet sites, you'll want to specify "Allow remote TCP/IP clients to access: Entire network." This permits RAS to route traffic from dial-in clients through the server and onto whatever networks the server is connected to. If you choose "This computer only," clients can't access network resources beyond the RAS server itself.

RAS needs a block of IP addresses to assign clients. Two methods are available:

1. If you choose "Use DHCP to assign remote TCP/IP client addresses," you must set up and configure a DHCP server somewhere within listening

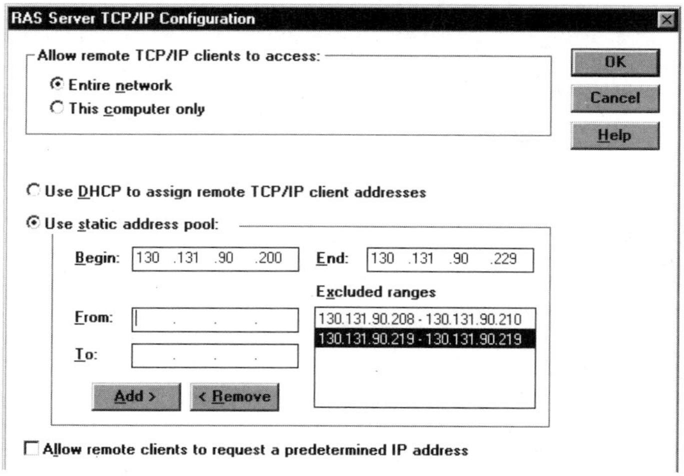

Figure 7.37 RAS Server TCP/IP Configuration Dialog

range of the RAS server. Also, your dial-in clients will have to use DHCP-capable client software. DHCP has two major advantages. First, it can automatically configure many TCP/IP settings in addition to the IP Address—settings like default gateway, subnet mask, and DNS servers. Second, if you're willing to run Microsoft's DNS server, remote hosts can resolve dial-in host names to IP addresses. The primary disadvantage is that clients whose software doesn't support DHCP won't be able to connect.

2. If you choose "Use static address pool," RAS assigns client addresses using a block of IP addresses assigned specifically to RAS. This method supports the widest range of dial-in client software, but the remote users must configure all other TCP/IP parameters by hand.

If you choose to use a static address pool, the addresses must be a sequential range. However, you can exclude certain addresses within that range.

The last option in this dialog controls whether clients can "hard-code" their IP address. It's generally best not to allow this practice.

When you're satisfied with your initial configuration, click the Continue button in the Remote Access Setup dialog. If you chose not to install NetBEUI, you'll get the informational message shown in Figure 7.38. RAS services will be available after you allow the computer to reboot.

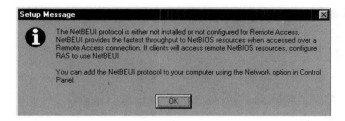

Figure 7.38 RAS NetBEUI Setup Message

7.7.3 RAS Configuration and Administration

Once you've installed RAS, there are three entry points to RAS services:

1. You can return to the RAS Setup dialog (Figure 7.35) by starting Control Panel, double-clicking the Network icon, selecting "Installed Network Software: Remote Access Service," and clicking the Configure... button. This dialog will continue to work as it did during setup.

2. Setup will have created a "Remote Access Service" program group or Start menu folder. This will contain a Remote Access icon, which, if double-clicked, opens the window used for dialing out from Windows NT.

3. In the same program group or Start menu folder is a program called RAS Administration. Double-clicking this icon produces a dialog for managing the RAS dial-in service.

7.7.4 Dialing Out with RAS

The first time you start the Remote Access icon, RAS will detect that your phone book is empty and prompt you to create an entry. Figure 7.39 illustrates this dialog.

Give the entry a name, enter its phone number, and, if desired, describe it in some way. The option "Authenticate using current user name and password" means RAS will log you into the remote system using the ID and password of your current Windows NT session; you probably want this OFF. You can also choose a specific modem port, or you can agree to take any port.

Clicking the Modem button invokes the Modem Settings dialog shown in Figure 7.40. The settings shown in the figure are usually correct. Click OK when finished with this dialog.

The Network button in the Add Phone Book Entry dialog brings up the window pictured in Figure 7.41.

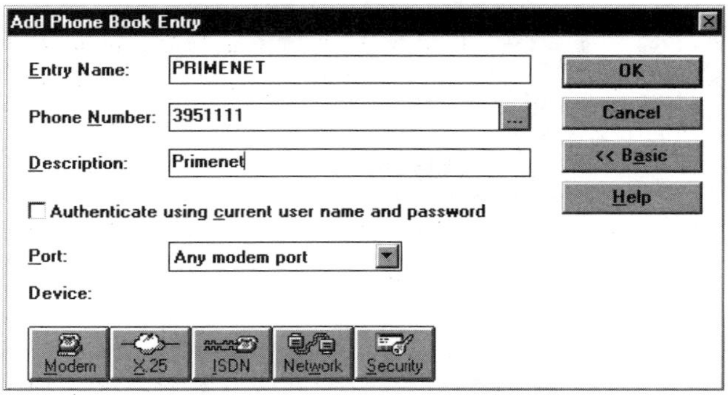

Figure 7.39 RAS Add Phone Book Entry Dialog

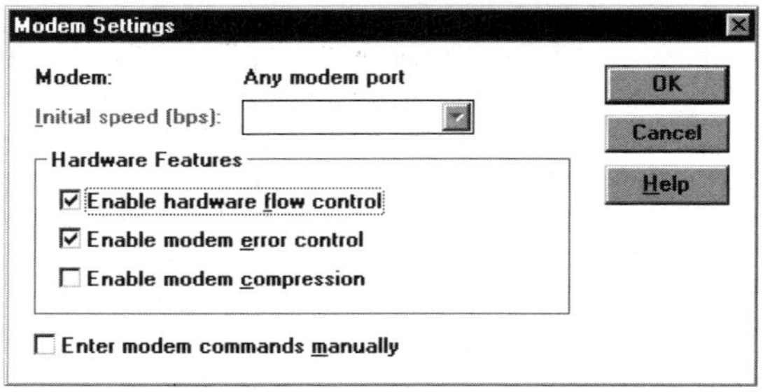

Figure 7.40 RAS Outbound Modem Settings Dialog

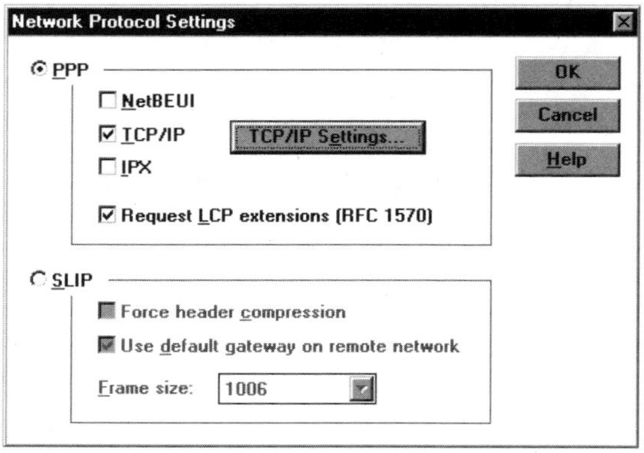

Figure 7.41 RAS Outbound Network Protocol Settings Dialog

Choose PPP or SLIP; PPP is preferable if the remote system supports it. For Internet connectivity, you will need to select TCP/IP. RFC 1570 refers to certain extensions to PPP involving LCP (Link Control Protocol) negotiation. Try running with RFC 1570 ON and turn it OFF only if consistent problems result.

If you selected the TCP/IP protocol, you should review TCP/IP settings by clicking on the TCP/IP Settings button. This will invoke the PPP TCP/IP Settings dialog illustrated in Figure 7.42.

Normally, you should let the remote server assign your IP address. If the server you're connecting to supports remote configuration of DNS (and WINS) addresses, select "Server assigned name server addresses." If not, choose "Use specific name server addresses" and enter DNS and WINS server addresses as required.

"Use VJ header compression" refers to Van Jacobson IP header compression. Setting this option ON improves performance, so you should try checking the box and back off only in the event of problems. Most newer PPP servers support VJ compression.

"Use default gateway on remote network" applies only when the computer dialing out also has a local network connection. If you check this box ON and your LAN software can't locate a given IP address, RAS will send the packet to the default gateway of the remote PPP server.

Clicking the Add Phone Book Entry's Security button requests the Security Settings dialog shown in Figure 7.43. Here, you can specify what level of password or data encryption you're willing to accept as a remote client, as well as the name of any dialing or logon scripts.

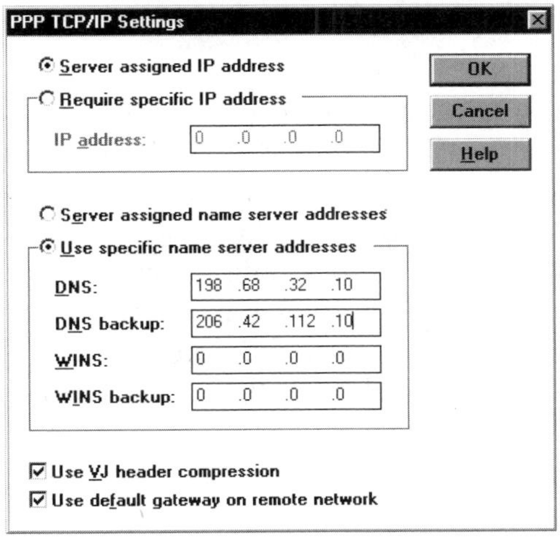

Figure 7.42 RAS PPP TCP/IP Settings Dialog

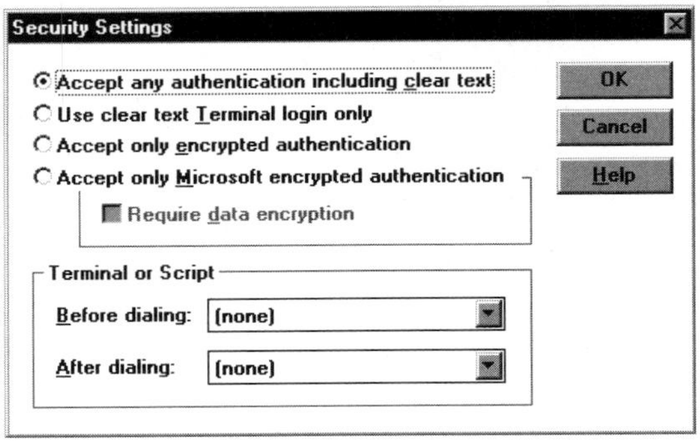

Figure 7.43 RAS Security Settings Dialog

RAS scripts reside in a file in \<systemroot>\system32\ras called SWITCH.INF. Each script occupies a block of lines delimited by a section header named in square brackets. For example, here are the significant statements in the generic logon script that Windows NT uses:

```
[Generic login]
   COMMAND=
   OK=<match>"ogin:"
   LOOP=<ignore>
   COMMAND=<username><cr>
   OK=<match>"assword:"
   LOOP=<ignore>
   COMMAND=<password><cr>
   OK=<ignore>
```

The on-line Remote Access Help provides adequate guidance on using the scripting language. Scripts added to SWITCH.INF show up in the RAS Security Settings dialog (Figure 7.43) identified by their header names.

To actually dial a remote host, select an entry name in the Remote Access window (Figure 7.44) and then click the Dial button. Remote Access will display the Authentication dialog pictured in Figure 7.45. If the remote system is a RAS server, enter your Windows NT user name, password, and domain name. If the remote system is UNIX or a third-party terminal server, leave the Domain field blank.

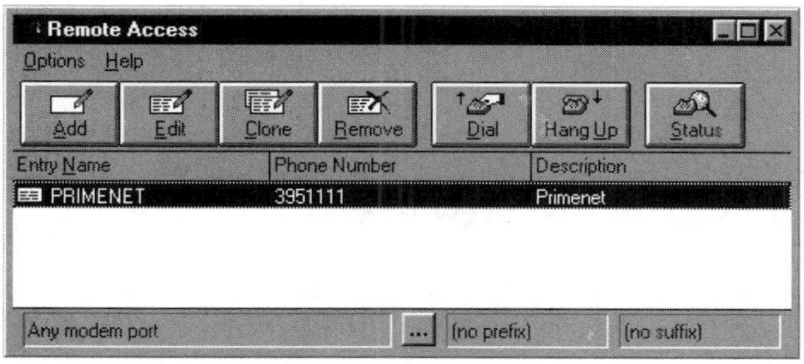

Figure 7.44 Remote Access Dialog

After specifying your user name and password, click OK, and RAS will connect you. If it doesn't, check your modem and phone number configurations, your TCP/IP settings, and the SWITCH.INF script you're using.

To log in to the remote host interactively (by hand), edit your phone book entry, click the Security button, and choose "After Dialing: Terminal." After you get manual logon working, you can create or revise an appropriate SWITCH.INF script.

To adjust redial and automatic reconnect settings, pull down the Remote Access dialog's Options menu and select "Redial Settings...." To apply a prefix or suffix to all telephone numbers dialed, pull down Options and select "Phone Number Settings...."

The "Rasdial" command initiates dial-out connections from the command line. This can be useful in batch files invoked by the Windows NT Schedule service to make connections, transfer files, and disconnect at specified times. The syntax is

```
rasdial entryname [username [password|*]] [/DOMAIN:domain]
    [/PHONE:phonenumber] [/CALLBACK:callbacknumber]
    [/PHONEBOOK:phonebookfile] [/PREFIXSUFFIX]
```

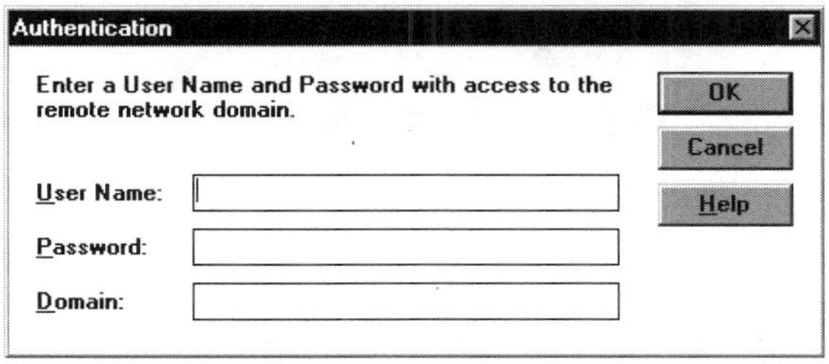

Figure 7.45 RAS Dial-Out Authentication Dialog

The entry name is the name of the phone book entry, as seen in the Remote Access GUI application. The user name, password, and /DOMAIN:domain work the same as in Figure 7.45.

7.7.5 Managing RAS Dial-In Services

Double-clicking the RAS Administration icon in the Remote Access Service group or folder brings up the dialog shown in Figure 7.46.

The dialog will display a line for each server in the domain running RAS. To add a server, pull down the Server menu and select "Select Domain or Server." Notice also that commands under the Server menu can display the status of communication ports on any selected RAS server and also start, stop, pause, and continue the RAS server service.

Pulling down the User menu and selecting "Permissions..." invokes the dialog appearing in Figure 7.47. This displays a list of Windows NT users in the domain (or local UADB in the case of Windows NT Workstation). No one can dial into RAS unless they have an account and their "Grant dialin permission to user" box is checked ON. Use the User Manager application (described previously) to create accounts. Use Remote Access Admin...User...Permissions to grant such accounts dial-in permissions.

7.8 Installing Internet Information Server

As of this writing, Microsoft Internet Information Server (IIS) was available only as a beta product installable on Windows NT Server 3.51 with Service Pack 2. However, Microsoft had announced plans to integrate and bundle IIS with the next version of Windows NT Server, possibly numbered 4.0.

For the beta, a single setup program installed FTP, Gopher, and HTTP server software, database interfaces, and a comprehensive management application. NT

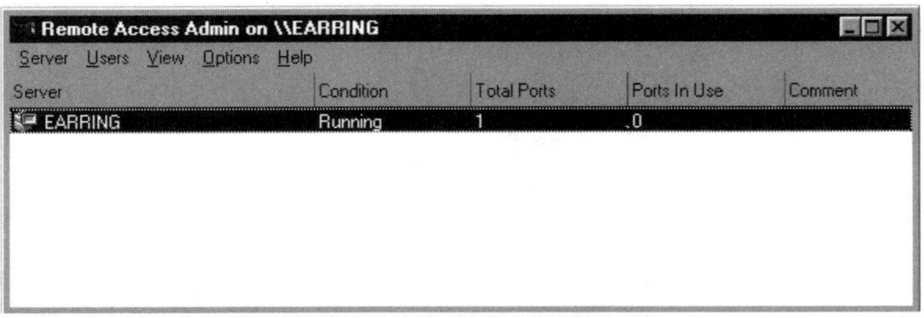

Figure 7.46 Remote Access Admin Dialog

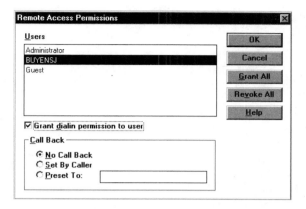

Figure 7.47 Remote Access Permissions Dialog

Server 4.0 may continue to use this setup program; it may add these services to the dialog shown in Figure 10.5, or it may adopt Add/Remove wizards like those used in Windows 95. This section will describe installation using the beta version's setup program because this was the only version available at the time of writing. Also, if Microsoft does change the installation process, it will probably be a question of "same questions, different dialogs."

To begin the installation, locate the I386 directory on the setup CD and double-click the SETUP.EXE program. Setup will display an introductory screen warning you to close any other applications you're running. Do so and then click the Continue button.

The next dialog, pictured in Figure 7.48, asks whether you are installing or removing components. Click Add/Remove to continue.

The next dialog asks you to confirm the location of the setup files. Do so and then click OK to display the dialog shown in Figure 7.49.

Select the services you want to install and then click the OK button to continue. If the Install Directory specified (Figure 7.49) doesn't already exist, Setup will prompt you whether to create it. Click Yes to continue and receive the dialog shown in Figure 7.50.

This dialog establishes the "home" directories for the HTTP, FTP, and Gopher services. The default locations on drive C: aren't usually a good choice—you don't want users browsing around your boot drive. Specify the actual locations you want and then click OK. Setup will copy all the necessary files to your computer and start the associated services. If you choose to install ODBC drivers, you'll receive a dialog box like the one in Figure 7.51 asking which drivers IIS will use. Select the appropriate drivers and then click OK to continue.

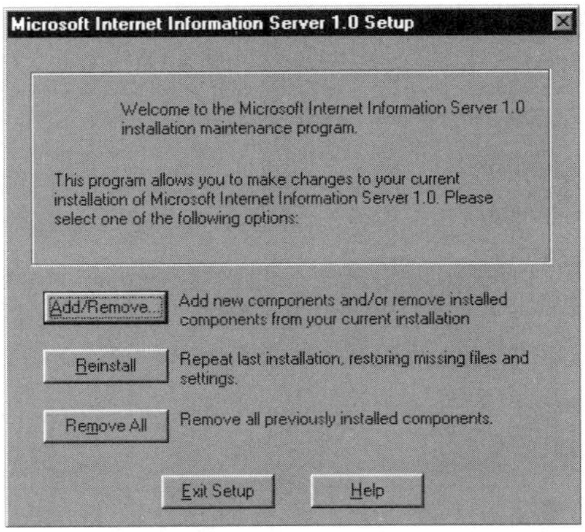

Figure 7.48 IIS Setup Dialog

When Setup completes, you'll receive a dialog stating, "Microsoft Internet Information Server 1.0 setup was completed successfully." Click OK. If you check the Control Panel Services dialog, you should see "FTP Publishing Service," "Gopher Publishing Service," and "World Wide Web Publishing Service" displayed as in Figure 7.52. If any services aren't started, start them. Once started, services should be accessible from client machines on the network. If you don't want one or more services to start automatically (the default), select them and click the

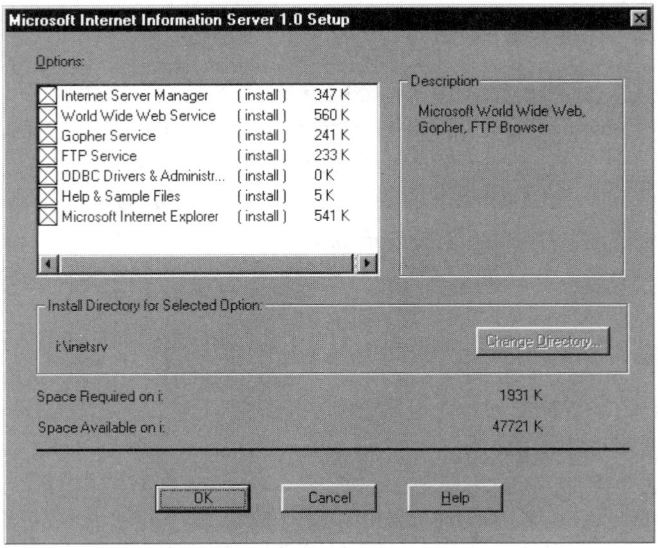

Figure 7.49 IIS Service Selection Dialog

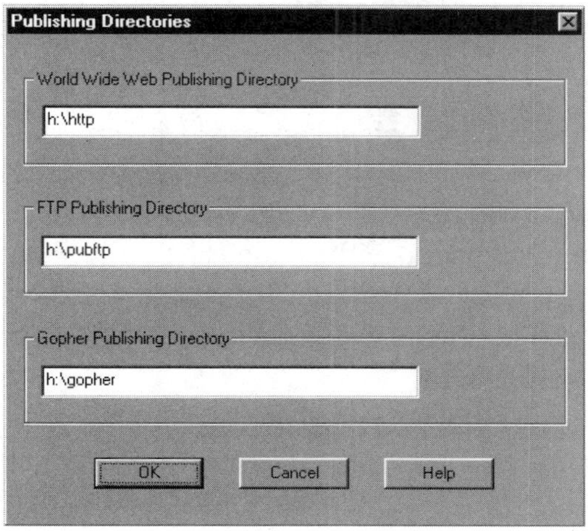

Figure 7.50 IIS Publishing Directories Dialog

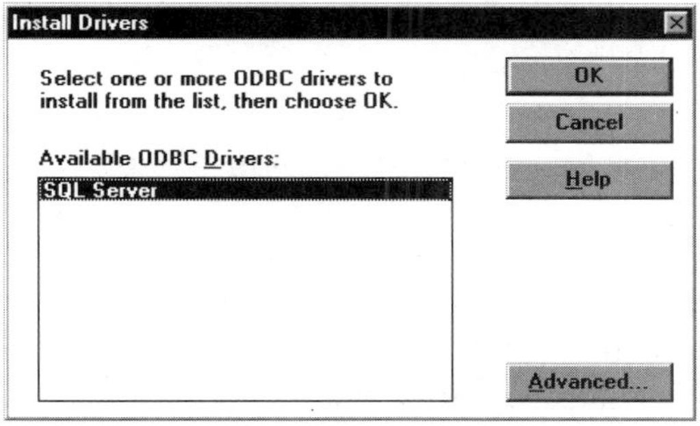

Figure 7.51 IIS ODBC Drivers Dialog

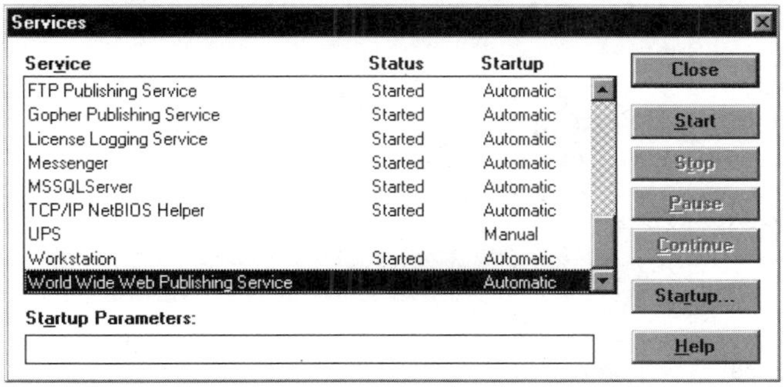

Figure 7.52 IIS Services in Control Panel Services Dialog

or more services to start automatically (the default), select them and click the Startup… button to reconfigure.

As shown in Figure 7.53, Setup will also install a new Start Programs menu, the "Microsoft Internet Server." Internet Server Manager provides local and remote administration of IIS, FTP, Gopher, and HTTP servers. Microsoft Internet Explorer is Microsoft's Web browser.

Starting Internet Server Manager will produce the dialog shown in Figure 7.54. To learn more about managing and configuring FTP, Gopher, and World Wide Web services, consult Chapters 10, 11, and 15, respectively.

7.9 Applying System Maintenance

Microsoft distributes minor Windows NT updates and fixes as *service packs*. These are specific to a given version of Windows NT; for example, you shouldn't try to apply Service Pack 2 for Windows NT 3.5 to a Windows NT 3.1 or 3.51 machine. By the way, service packs won't upgrade your system from one version of Windows NT to another. Service packs are available free, but you have to pay for upgrades.

Service packs are cumulative. This means Service Pack 3 for a given version of Windows NT contains all fixes included in Service Packs 1 and 2. There's no need to install Service Packs 1, 2, and 3 in sequence.

In general, service packs contain beneficial fixes and are worth installing on your systems. Nevertheless, don't install a service pack on the first day or week of release; if there's a problem, it's better to let someone else discover it. Also, if you have several systems, apply the service pack to one of them and then wait a week or two to see what happens.

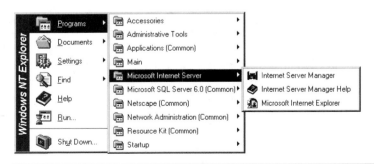

Figure 7.53 Microsoft Internet Server Start Programs Menu

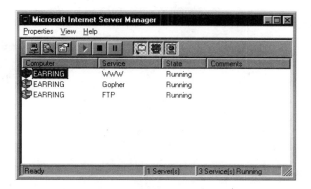

Figure 7.54 Microsoft Internet Server Manager

To check for the latest service pack for your version of Windows NT, browse http://www.microsoft.com/kb/softlib/BackOffice/winnt.htm.

CHAPTER 8

Installing and Configuring DHCP and WINS

DHCP (Dynamic Host Configuration Protocol) is a standards-based method for assigning IP addresses and other operating parameters centrally and automatically. Microsoft has promoted DHCP as a way to enjoy the world-wide connectivity of TCP/IP with low administrative overhead.

WINS (Windows Internet Name Service) provides a way to resolve NETBIOS names by means of a central directory service rather than by broadcasting. NET-BIOS broadcasting previously constrained the growth of large Microsoft Windows networks, and it leads to serious complications on TCP/IP networks subdivided by routers.

Together, DHCP and WINS permit construction of large Microsoft Windows networks that use TCP/IP as their only protocol, don't require broadcasting, and provide automatic configuration of client hosts. Such networks also interoperate readily with other hosts and networks supporting TCP/IP, and they operate transparently over wide-area and local links.

Sites typically install DHCP and WINS for use on local networks, not over the Internet. Your interest in DHCP and WINS will probably vary directly with the number of local Windows clients you need to configure with TCP/IP.

8.1 Operating Concepts and Standards

8.1.1 DHCP Principles

DHCP is an evolution of the older BOOTP protocol. When a workstation configured with BOOTP starts, it transmits a broadcast packet containing, of course, its data link address. A BOOTP server hears the broadcast, looks up the data link address in a database, and transmits an assigned IP address and other settings back to the originating workstation. This becomes the workstation's configuration until it boots again.

DHCP enhances BOOTP in several ways. First, no database of preconfigured data link addresses is necessary. If a DHCP server gets a TCP/IP address request from a previously unseen workstation, the DHCP server simply takes the next entry from a pool of available addresses. Second, DHCP can configure more parameter fields than BOOTP. Finally, DHCP introduces the concept of *leases*. A lease means that once a machine gets an IP address, it may continue using that IP address for the duration of the lease.

Short leases in the range of 8 to 24 hours permit oversubscription of IP addresses—that is, for perhaps 125 machines to share 100 IP addresses. This assumes that at least 25 machines will be powered off on any given day. Although this is possible, it's not popular. For one thing, if everyone comes into the office or if many people leave their machines powered up, the system may run out of addresses. For another, keeping DNS updated with rapidly changing IP addresses is nearly impossible.

More popular are DHCP leases in the range of 2 to 8 weeks. A DHCP client renews its lease after half the lease period expires or, if that fails, at shorter and shorter intervals until the lease expires. In practice, this means that a workstation with a one-month lease on an IP address will lose that address only if the computer stays off the network for a month or more. As long as it stays on the network and keeps renewing its lease, it will have the same IP address forever.

Using DHCP in a routed environment requires the router to support RFC 1542. This is the RFC that defines the current version of BOOTP—the version that includes DHCP. Routers that support BOOTP as described in RFC 951, the prior BOOTP standard, won't work.

RFC 1542 requires two things of the router. First, when the router hears a DHCP broadcast on a subnet that has no DHCP server, it must forward the packet to a predefined server. Second, when forwarding the packet, the router must indicate on which network or subnet the broadcast occurred. (The originating computer won't know its own network or subnet because it doesn't have an IP address or subnet mask yet.)

The DHCP server looks at various fields in the DHCP broadcast and searches its database to see whether a lease for the computer already exists. If so, DHCP renews the lease; if not, DHCP creates a new lease. DHCP then forwards all required configuration data back to the router for broadcast to the originating workstation. (DHCP can't transmit this information with a directed send because the originating workstation still doesn't know its IP address.)

On the DHCP server, each block of available IP addresses is called a *scope*. Defining a scope requires starting and ending IP addresses plus a subnet mask; the DHCP server then counts out IP addresses using whatever bits of the mask are zeros. If necessary, an administrator can exclude certain addresses within a scope. Also, there can be several scopes within a single network or subnet. These two facilities simplify the use of DHCP when large, contiguous blocks of IP addresses aren't available.

Administrators can assign settings other than the IP address and subnet mask at the scope level, globally, or not at all. Scope settings override global settings. If neither scope nor global settings specify a particular option, someone must configure that setting at each workstation. Settings configured at individual workstations override settings established in DHCP.

A secondary DHCP server can guard against one DHCP server being down when a new workstation requests its first lease. If the DHCP server and the workstation are on the same subnet, the first DHCP server to respond will handle the transaction. If a router is forwarding a remote DHCP broadcast, it will try the DHCP servers in a configured sequence.

If you relocate a computer to a different network or subnet, DHCP will detect that the machine's old lease is invalid, cancel the lease, and establish a new lease on the new network or subnet.

To see the TCP/IP parameters configured by DHCP, use the IPCONFIG /ALL command unless the machine is running Windows 95. Under Windows 95, use the WINIPCFG command.

8.1.2 WINS Principles

Windows Internet Name Service resembles Domain Name Service in that its primary purpose is to look up computer names and return the corresponding IP addresses. Beyond this, however, the services are quite different.

NETBIOS names are 16 bytes long. The first 15 bytes are left justified, and all letters are uppercase. As Table 8.1 illustrates, the sixteenth byte is a hexadecimal service code. For an example of these codes in use, see Figure 8.11.

WINS clients register themselves at boot time with the WINS server. This is the purpose of the primary and secondary WINS addresses you may have noticed in various TCP/IP configuration dialogs. If you're running WINS and not DHCP, you should enter the IP address of two servers running WINS in these fields. If you're running DHCP, you can leave the WINS addresses blank and have DHCP configure them automatically. Once a computer registers itself with WINS, other computers can query WINS and get the computer's IP address. WINS resolves NETBIOS names, even through routers, without broadcasting.

If you have several WINS servers in your network, you'll probably want all your computers registered in all the WINS servers. (If they're not, you'll have

Table 8.1 NETBIOS Names Registered in WINS

Bytes 1–15	Byte 16	Description
COMPUTER_NAME	00h	Workstation service on the WINS client.
COMPUTER_NAME	03h	Messenger service on the WINS client.
COMPUTER_NAME	BEh	Network Monitoring Agent service. This will appear only if the service is running. Plus signs replace spaces at the right of the name.
COMPUTER_NAME	1Fh	Network Dynamic Data Exchange service. This will appear only if NetDDE services are started.
COMPUTER_NAME	20h	Server service on the WINS client.
DOMAIN_NAME	00h	The Workstation service registers this instance of the domain name so that it can receive LAN Manager browser broadcasts.
DOMAIN_NAME	1Bh	Windows NT Server domain controllers register this instance of the domain name.
DOMAIN_NAME	1Ch	Contains the IP address of the Primary Domain Controller (PDC) and up to 24 backup domain controllers.
DOMAIN_NAME	1Dh	Contains the IP address of the BrowseMaster for the domain. Backup BrowseMasters use this name to communicate with the BrowseMaster.
DOMAIN_NAME	1Eh	Supports browsing and BrowseMaster elections.
__MSBROWSE__	01h	A special name used by the Windows NT Browser service.
USERNAME	03h	User names of currently logged on users. "net send" messages use this.

users in one part of the network complaining they can't contact machines located in another part.) WINS supports this through "push" and "pull" replication methods. A WINS push server transmits database changes to other designated WINS servers whenever a specified number of database updates have occurred. A WINS pull server requests database updates from other WINS servers based on time intervals. WINS servers that participate in either push or pull replication with each other are called *replication partners*.

8.2 Installing DHCP and WINS

Microsoft includes the DHCP and WINS server software with every copy of Windows NT Server. If you installed them during initial setup, you'll see entries under Control Panel Services titled "Microsoft DHCP Server" and "Windows Internet Name Service." Also, in a Program Manager group or Start folder titled "Network Administration," you'll have applications called "DHCP Manager" and "WINS Manager."

If DHCP and WINS don't seem to be installed, proceed as follows:

1. Go to Control Panel and double-click the Network icon, bringing up the dialog shown in Figure 7.21.

2. Click the Add Software... button, bringing up the Add Network Software window shown in Figure 7.29.

3. Select "TCP/IP Protocol and related components" and click the Continue button. The dialog pictured in Figure 10.5 will result.

4. Check the boxes "DHCP Server Service" and "WINS Server Service" ON and then click Continue.

5. Windows NT will prompt for the location of your Windows NT Server setup files with a dialog like the one in Figure 7.30. Enter the location and press Continue.

6. Windows NT will copy all necessary files to the server, build the corresponding Program Manager groups or Start folders, and prompt you to restart the server.

8.3 Administering DHCP

To control the DHCP service, start DHCP Manager from the Network Administration Program Manager group or Start folder. A dialog similar to the one in Figure 8.1 will appear.[1]

In the figure, five scopes appear in the left pane of the dialog. Configuration parameters appear on the right. An icon showing three computers precedes parameters defined at the scope level; global parameters have a globe icon.

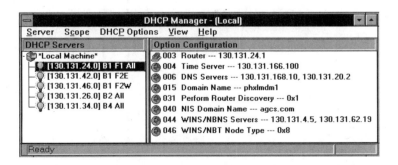

Figure 8.1 Windows NT DHCP Manager Main Dialog

---

[1]To provide useful examples, servers with several months' DHCP and WINS history provided screenshots for this chapter. This accounts for the Windows NT 3.5 appearance of the DHCP dialogs.

"B1 F1 All" is the currently selected scope. Double-clicking on this line (or selecting it, pulling down Scope, and selecting "Properties...") will bring up the dialog shown in Figure 8.2.

IP addresses in the range 130.131.24.101 through 130.131.24.254 belong to this scope. The subnet mask is 255.255.254.0, so DHCP will increment the nine low-order bits of the IP address. No addresses are excluded; all host numbers between 101 and 254 are available. Lease durations will be 14 days, the name of the scope is "B1 F1 All," and someone has commented, "Building 1, 1st floor." To create a new scope from the main window, pull down Scope, select "Create...," and supply the same sort of information (using IP addresses that are yours). When finished, click OK.

Once the scope has been in use for a while, you can view active leases by pulling down the Scope menu and selecting "Active Leases...." Figure 8.3 illustrates a typical display.

This dialog reports that of 154 addresses in the scope, 67 are in use and 87 are available. The list box labeled "Client" displays the IP addresses and computer names currently leased. Selecting a lease and clicking "Delete" will cancel that lease. Double-clicking on the entry for "130.131.24.167 (WIN95)" (or selecting that entry and clicking "Properties...") produces the dialog shown in Figure 8.4.

The IP address is the address assigned by DHCP at the start of the lease. The client computer supplied the Unique Identifier and Client Name when it first

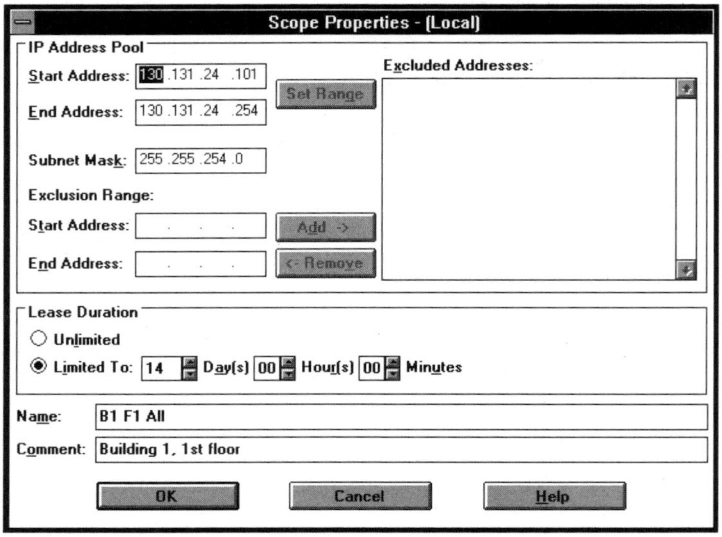

Figure 8.2 DHCP Scope Properties Dialog

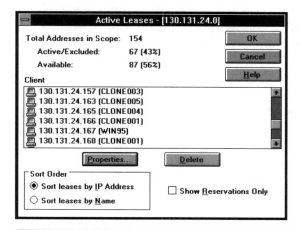

Figure 8.3 DHCP Active Leases Dialog

requested the lease; the Unique Identifier, as you may have recognized, is the client's Ethernet address. There is no comment. The lease expires 11/15/95 at 2:16:06 PM; DHCP most likely created or renewed it exactly 14 days before then. (Recall the 14-day lease duration shown in Figure 8.2.) You can modify the Unique Identifier, the Client Name, or the Client Comment, but there's usually no reason to do so. The Cancel button cancels the dialog, not the lease.

Returning to the DHCP Manager main dialog (Figure 8.1), seven properties are global and one is scope-specific. The scope-specific parameter is "003 Router," the default gateway. Defining this parameter at the scope level assigns different default gateways, as required, to clients in different subnets.

The remaining parameters are constant for all computers using this DHCP server. "015 Domain Name" is the Windows NT domain name, while "040 NIS Domain Name" is the DNS domain.

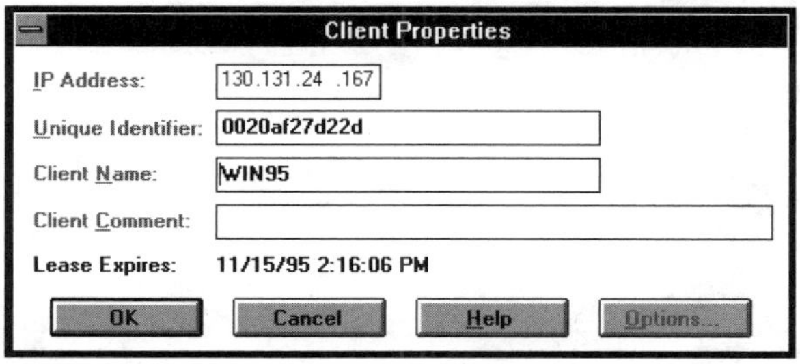

Figure 8.4 DHCP Client Properties Dialog

Briefly, adding a new computer to the 130.131.24.0 subnet involves plugging the machine into the network and configuring only one parameter—namely, "Obtain an IP address automatically." Figure 8.5 illustrates the Windows 95 dialog for this; you can bring it up with Control Panel, Network, TCP/IP, Properties. DHCP will configure the new computer with an IP address, a subnet mask, and all the parameters listed on the right side of Figure 8.1.

To add, change, or delete client configuration options, pull down the DHCP Options menu and select "Global," "Scope," or "Defaults." Figure 8.6 illustrates the DHCP Options: Global dialog.

This dialog lists unused options in a list box at the left and active options at the right. To activate an unused option, select it and click the Add→ button. To remove an active option, select it and click ←Remove. (To change the default value assigned to newly activated options, use the DHCP Options...Default... command from the main menu.)

Each option has its own format: an array of IP addresses, a single integer, a string, whatever. To expose the value, click the Value>>> button. You can edit some value types directly, but, for others, such as the array of IP addresses shown in Figure 8.6, you must click an Edit button to invoke another dialog.

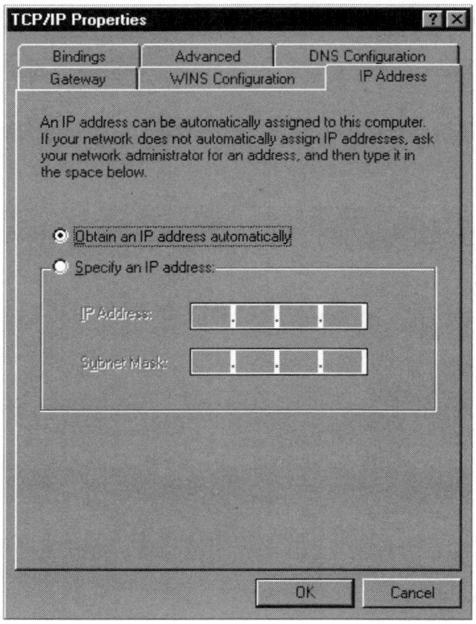

Figure 8.5 Windows 95 TCP/IP Properties Dialog

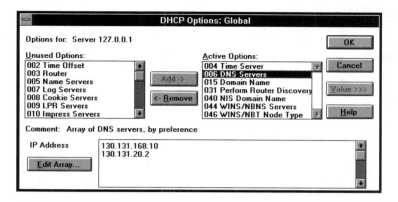

Figure 8.6 DHCP Options: Global Dialog

If you have two or more DHCP servers (to guard against one being down), be sure not to assign overlapping scopes. If you assign the primary server host numbers 100 through 179, for example, you might want to assign the secondary server 180 through 199. If one server runs out of addresses, the other will take over. If the scopes overlap, though, you may get duplicate IP addresses on the network.

A word may be in order regarding "046 WINS/NBT Node Type." This option is configurable only by DHCP, and it specifies what kind of name registration and name resolution a Windows Networking computer will use. Table 8.2 lists the available options and their effect. The h-node type, which does no broadcasting as long as either the primary or secondary WINS server is working, is the best choice for large networks and for situations where broadcasts fail to pass through routers.

8.4 Administering WINS

WINS Manager is the program that manages WINS servers. Setup installs its icon in the Network Administration Program Manager group or Start folder. Figure 8.7 shows the WINS Manager main dialog.

Table 8.2 WINS/NBT Node Types

DHCP Value	Node Type	Name Resolution	Name Registration
0x1	b-node	Broadcast	Broadcast
0x2	p-node	WINS	WINS
0x4	m-node	Broadcast WINS (if broadcast fails)	Broadcast WINS (always both)
0x8	h-node	WINS Broadcast (if WINS fails)	WINS Broadcast (if WINS fails)

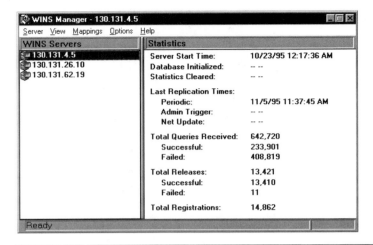

Figure 8.7 WINS Manager Main Dialog

The left pane shows three active WINS servers. In fact, this network has more than three WINS servers, but the administrator hasn't added them to the display using Server...Add WINS Server.... At the right are statistics for the highlighted WINS server—the one at 130.131.4.5. The fact that about 2/3 of all queries failed isn't necessarily a problem; processes on the network frequently search for names by sequential query until one succeeds.

Pulling down the Server menu and selecting "Replication Partners..." produces the Replication Partners dialog shown in Figure 8.8.

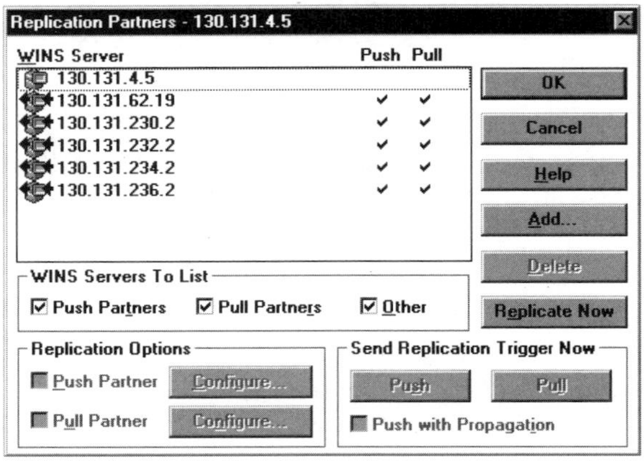

Figure 8.8 WINS Replication Partners Dialog

The WINS Server list box shows that this server is a push and pull replication partner with five other WINS servers. Selecting the 130.131.62.19 server and clicking the Push Partner Configure button produces the dialog depicted in Figure 8.9.

Server 130.131.62.19 will push updates to server 130.131.4.5 every time one update occurs to server 130.131.62.19's database. This is an extremely aggressive schedule, but one that a fast local Ethernet can easily support. If the servers were separated by a slow, busy, wide-area link, it would be advisable to wait for more updates before starting replication.

Selecting the 130.131.62.19 server in Figure 8.8 and clicking the Pull Partner Configure button produces the dialog shown in Figure 8.10.

Server 130.131.4.5 will pull updates from server 130.131.62.19 every three minutes. Again, this is an extremely aggressive schedule and is only appropriate on fast local Ethernets.

The question of WINS replication frequency has no single answer. The more frequent the updates, the fewer times users will call with questions like, "Hey, I just logged on to the network, but the guy in Accounting says my computer isn't found. What gives?" The more frequent the updates, the more network traffic and server overhead will result.

Returning to the WINS Manager dialog, pulling down Mappings, and selecting "Show Database..." will produce a dialog like the one in Figure 8.11.

WINS database entries are "owned" by the server where the original copy resides. The Show Database dialog can display a merged view of all databases or a view of entries owned by one server in particular. Figure 8.11 is displaying entries for server 130.131.4.5 only. The "Highest ID" column shows the sequence number of the last change replicated from the selected owner to the local machine.

The Mappings list box displays the WINS database entries. Note the appending of hex codes in compliance with Table 8.1. The "A" column indicates active entries, and the "S" column indicates static entries. There is no direct correlation between WINS expiration dates and DHCP lease expirations; WINS entries are more transitory, and WINS deletes them fairly quickly when computers remain inactive.

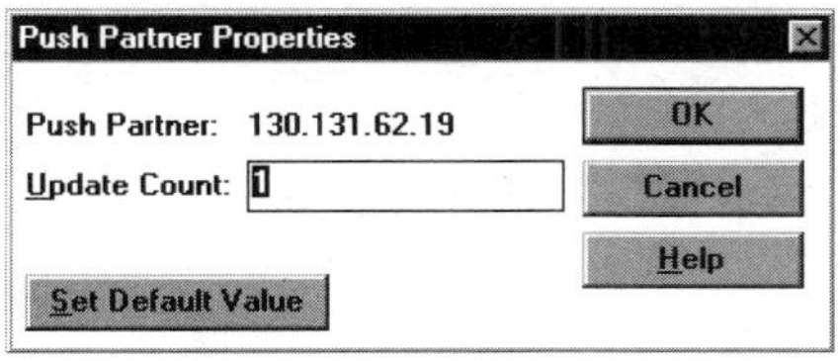

Figure 8.9 WINS Push Replication Partners Dialog

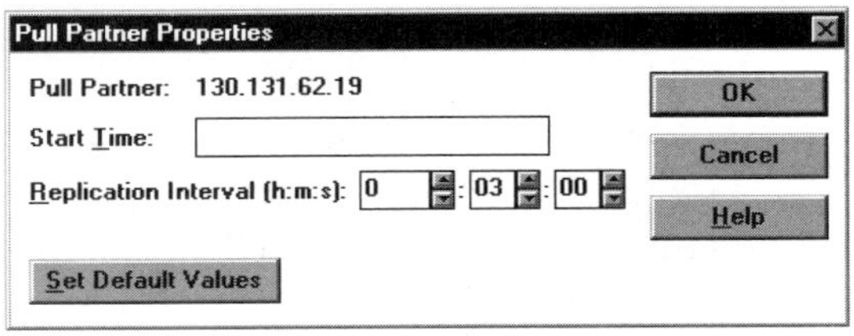

Figure 8.10 WINS Pull Replication Partners Dialog

Static WINS mappings are those an administrator has configured by hand. Administrators do this because static mappings never expire and the administrator wants to ensure another computer can't take over the computer name or IP address. Entering static mappings can be tricky, however. Not only must you get the host name and IP address right; you must also create an array of names with the correct hex suffixes from Table 8.1. To create static entries, pull down the Mappings menu and select "Static Mappings...."

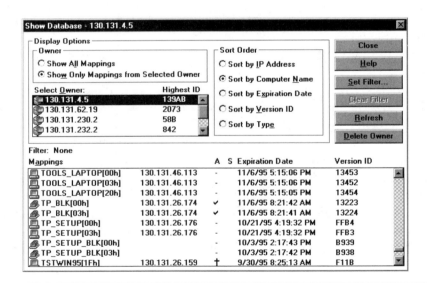

Figure 8.11 WINS Show Database Dialog

CHAPTER 9

Installing and Configuring Domain Name Service

D omain Name Service is a hierarchical, highly distributed, network database that translates mnemonic computer names to IP addresses. Without DNS, you'd have to remember 198.105.232.6 rather than www.microsoft.com.

Although users think they connect to names like www.microsoft.com, they really don't. Instead, their application calls a *resolver*—software that runs on their own computer and translates the mnemonic name to an IP address—and then connects using the IP address. The resolver works by sending the requested name over the network to a DNS server that hopefully responds with the corresponding IP address. If the first DNS server can't supply the address, the resolver will try the next one in its list.

Every modern TCP/IP stack includes a built-in resolver; it's usually so tightly integrated that it doesn't appear as a separate component. Configuring a resolver usually involves nothing more than entering the IP address of the DNS servers you want the resolver to query.

You don't need a DNS server at your site to look up hosts at other sites; each site arranges lookup facilities for its own hosts. You need a DNS server only if you operate hosts that local or remote users need to find by name.

The primary alternative to using DNS is using a HOSTS file. This is simply an ASCII file with an IP address and a host name on each line. The resolver reads through the file until it finds a record containing the requested host name; then it returns that line's IP address to the application. This is fine for small networks, but it becomes very troublesome on large ones. On a large network, changes occur too frequently, and distribution of updated HOSTS files is too time-consuming. Centralized mapping of host names to IP addresses is so much easier than administering HOSTS files that most large sites run DNS even if they aren't connected to the Internet.

Chapter 1, Section 1.2.1 briefly introduced DNS; Chapter 5, Section 5.9 provided additional detail. If you're new to DNS, you may wish to review those sections before proceeding.

9.1 Operating Concepts and Standards

DNS names are hierarchical, with periods indicating the levels. The name www.aw.com, therefore, has three levels. The order of levels is from right to left, so that .com is the highest, most global level and .www is the lowest. There are millions of computers at the .com level, far fewer at aw.com, and only one at www.aw.com.[1]

A different DNS server typically stores the database for each level in a DNS name. To resolve a name like www.aw.com, DNS first asks the server that handles .com for the IP address of the server that handles aw.com. DNS then asks aw.com's server for the IP address of www.aw.com.

Root servers index entries within the top-level domains: .com, .edu, .gov, .mil, .net, .org, .au, .uk, and so forth. Finding these servers involves a trick because they're at the top of the hierarchy; there's no higher server to query. Instead, DNS administrators must obtain a list of top-level servers by FTP and preload it into their DNS server's cache. Table 9.1 lists two anonymous FTP sources for this information.

The word *domain* is subject to some confusion, both with itself and with the word *zone*. Some people are careful to call domains like .com "root domains," those with one intervening period (like aw.com) "domains," and anything with more than two periods (like demon.co.uk) "subdomains." Others simply refer to all three entities as "domains." Making matters worse, *domain* sometimes means a single level and sometimes means an entire tree.

The difference between a domain and a zone is equally obscure. In one sense, a zone is that portion of the entire Domain Name System that a particular organization controls. In another, a zone simply consists of the names defined in a given zone database file.

Table 9.1 Root Name Server Cache File Locations

Site	Directory	File
ftp.rs.internic.net	/domain/	named.root
nic.ddn.mil	/netinfo/	root-servers.txt

---

[1]A few large sites distribute load among several identically configured hosts by selecting and returning one IP address from the set. The selection may be random or based on current utilization.

A zone database usually contains all the entries for exactly one domain level. In such a case, the zone and the domain become identical. It's then customary to call the domain a "zone" if you're talking about maintaining it and to call it a "domain" in any other context.

Another common term is the word *authoritative*. A given DNS server is authoritative for a zone if it loads all entries for that zone on start-up and never discards them. Primary DNS servers load zone databases from local files, while secondary servers load them over the network from primary servers. Both primary and secondary servers are authoritative. Other servers may build up significant zone history in their caches, but since an administrator can't directly update such caches when changes occur, they aren't authoritative for the given zone.

9.1.1 Configuring a DNS Server

To set up your own DNS server, you'll need the following information:

- The name of your domain.
- Your IP network number.
- The names and IP addresses of two machines that will be DNS servers.
- The names and IP addresses of the other computers you want to register with DNS.

You must register the name of your domain and the addresses of its servers with the authority one level higher. If you want the domain name eng.enterprise.mil, for example, you'll need to work with the administrator of the enterprise.mil domain. Note that a DNS server for eng.enterprise.mil will be almost useless unless it's registered with the enterprise.mil DNS server.

If you want a domain name containing only one dot, such as enterprise.mil, you or your provider will have to obtain it from InterNIC. Section 5.10, "Registering Your Site," describes this procedure. InterNIC administers the top-level domains like .com, .edu, .gov, and .mil. InterNIC requires that you supply the IP address of two DNS servers, and they verify these servers are active. You'll need to get your communication lines and network number first, get your DNS servers up and running, and only then register the domain name with InterNIC.

If you want, the provider that supplies your Internet connection will usually supply your DNS service as well. The fee for this isn't usually large, but paying additional fees for each host added, changed, or deleted can, over time, become a real nuisance. A compromise is to run a primary server yourself and pay the provider to run a secondary server. The secondary server will update itself automatically from the primary, so there are no transaction charges for routine changes. This is also attractive if bandwidth between your site and your provider is limited; hosts on each side of the limited-bandwidth link can avoid unnecessary traffic by using the local DNS server.

Configuring a DNS server requires editing arcane control statements in plain ASCII files. The details and syntax are primitive compared to most Windows NT configuration dialogs, but it keeps DNS administrators employed. Also, these administrators claim they're more productive because they can copy the ASCII files among systems with little rework. Perhaps someone will eventually write a GUI utility to do this job.

There are six types of DNS configuration files:

1. **Boot.** This mandatory file contains the commands that control initialization of the DNS server. These commands establish the server's operating mode and load the remaining files.

2. **Forward zone database.** Appearing in this file are settings for the domain (zone), plus a database that translates names to IP addresses. A given DNS server may use zero, one, or several forward zone database files.

3. **Reverse zone database.** This database is similar to the forward zone database, but it translates IP addresses to host names. There should be one reverse zone database for each forward zone database.

4. **Local database.** Curiously, this file is a database that translates the name "localhost" to the address 127.0.0.0. This file is mandatory.

5. **Reverse local database.** This file is a database that translates the address 127.0.0.0 to the name "localhost." Administrators frequently omit this file.

6. **Cache.** This file preloads the server's name cache with the IP addresses of the DNS root servers. For an Internet DNS server, this is the file downloaded per Table 9.1. Except in rare circumstances, this is a mandatory file.

9.1.2 The DNS Server Boot File

A fully implemented DNS service honors seven commands within the boot file:

1. **directory.** This command is usually the first one in the boot file. It specifies the directory where files on the remaining statements reside. Its syntax is

```
directory <directory>
```

2. **primary.** This command declares this server as a primary server for the specified zone (domain). DNS servers always load primary zones from a local file, so the third and final parameter specifies the name of that file:

```
primary <domain name> <database file name>
```

The database file must be a forward or reverse zone database.

3. **secondary.** This command instructs the server to function as a secondary server for the zone specified. A secondary server loads its database over the network from a primary server, so the third parameter specifies the IP address of a primary server. The fourth parameter specifies the name of a local file in which the server will store a copy of the downloaded database. If the secondary server can't contact the primary (or if it detects that the primary server's database hasn't changed), it will reload the zone from the local file instead. The syntax is

```
secondary <domain name> <primary IP Address> <local database file name>
```

4. **cache.** The cache statement loads the database of root servers downloaded per Table 9.1:

```
cache <root server file>
```

5. **forwarders.** The forwarders statement supplies a list of DNS servers that this server will consult if it can't resolve a query itself:

```
forwarders <server IP Address> <server IP Address> ...
```

6. **slave.** This statement causes the local server to resolve queries only by consulting forwarders (DNS servers used on the Internet typically wouldn't use this command):

```
slave
```

7. **sortlist.** This command supplies a list of preferred networks. If a query results in more than one IP address for a given name, the server will present addresses on sortlist networks first:

```
sortlist <network> <network> ...
```

Note that a single DNS server may encompass zero, one, or many primary and secondary zones. A cache server is one with no primary or secondary zones; it merely caches entries to reduce that number of queries that must travel over some part of the network. The same server would never be the primary and secondary server for the same zone; this would defeat the purpose of having two servers. However, a single server can support any number of primary or secondary zones; just keep adding "primary" or "secondary" statements in the boot file and supplying appropriate zone databases.

9.1.3 The DNS Zone Database Files

Database files contain two kinds of records: control statements and standard resource records. Control statements begin with a dollar sign. Semicolons denote comments (the DNS server will ignore the semicolon and anything following it on the same line).

9.1.3.1 DNS Zone Database Control Statements
There are two control statements:

1. **$INCLUDE.** This statement logically includes another file into the current file. When the DNS server encounters the $INCLUDE statement, it suspends reading records from the current file and starts reading records from the included file instead. When the included file is at end, the DNS server resumes reading records from the original file. This can be useful if it's convenient to maintain sections of a database file independently. The syntax is

```
$INCLUDE <file name>
```

2. **$ORIGIN.** This command changes the default domain name used by subsequent records:

```
$ORIGIN <domain name>
```

The DNS software appends the current $ORIGIN string to any name that doesn't end in a period. In addition, the $ORIGIN value replaces the "@" character wherever it appears.

9.1.3.2 DNS Zone Database Standard Resource Record Format
Standard resource records, which comprise the bulk of most database files, all have the following general format:

```
<name> <time-to-live> <class> <type> <data>
```

- **<name>.** This parameter names the object affected by the record. DNS actually supports several kinds of names, with host names being only one. The DNS server will append the current $ORIGIN setting to this name unless it ends in a period. A space or any other white-space character in column 1 indicates a blank name, causing the name from the previous record to remain in effect. A single dot refers to the root domain. "@" in a name refers to the current origin. "*" indicates any string, as in "*.whatever.com."

- **<time-to-live>.** If present, this optional field specifies the number of seconds that information in this record should remain in the cache of other DNS servers. Any value up to eight decimal digits is valid. If not specified, time-to-live defaults to the <minimum> value in the SOA record (described in Table 9.2).

- **<class>.** On the Internet, this field is always "IN." Other networks may use other classes.

- **<type>.** This field indicates the type of data this record contains.

- **<data>.** This field contains data appropriate to the type of record.

Table 9.2 summarizes the valid standard resource record types and the data expected on each type. A further explanation of each record type follows.

9.1.3.3 DNS Zone Database Standard Resource Record Types The eight standard resource record types are as follows:

1. **Start Of Authority record.** The SOA record is usually the first standard resource record in a zone file. It marks the beginning of a zone (domain)

Table 9.2 DNS Standard Resource Record Types

Description	Name	TTL	Class	Type	Data
Start Of Authority	<origin>	<ttl>	IN	SOA	<pri dns> <contact> (<serial> <refresh> <retry> <expire> <minimum>)
Name Server	<domain>	<ttl>	IN	NS	<dns>
Address	<host>	<ttl>	IN	A	<address>
Mail Exchanger	<name>	<ttl>	IN	MX	<preference> <host>
Canonical Name	<alias>	<ttl>	IN	CNAME	<host>
Name Pointer	<name>	<ttl>	IN	PTR	<host>
Host Information	<host>	<ttl>	IN	HINFO	<hardware> <software>
Well Known Services	<host>	<ttl>	IN	WKS	<address> <prot> <svc>

and specifies global and default parameters. The SOA record is the most complex in the database and is usually the only record that requires continuation. To continue a record, end the line with a left parentheses. To end the continuation, enter a right parentheses.

- **<origin>** indicates the name of the zone. If an $ORIGIN statement precedes the SOA record, you can usually specify <origin> as "@."

- **<pri dns>** specifies the name of the primary DNS server for the zone.

- **<contact>** supplies the E-Mail address of the zone's administrator. However, you must replace the "@" in the E-Mail address with a period; otherwise, the current $ORIGIN value replaces the "@." Specify admin.voyager.mil, not admin@voyager.mil.

- **<serial>** is a number you must increment each time you update the database. If you forget to increment the serial number, secondary servers won't reload their copy of the database.

- **<refresh>** denotes the interval, in seconds, at which secondary servers should check for zone updates. A value of 86400 causes secondary servers to check the primary server's database version once a day.

- **<retry>** indicates how often, also in seconds, secondary servers should try to contact a primary server after the initial attempt fails. A value of 3600 specifies hourly retries. Don't set this value to a short interval like once a minute. This accomplishes nothing and may result in a retry loop; nth retry starts before $(n-1)$th retry completes.

- **<expire>** specifies how many seconds a secondary server should keep supplying data about a zone without contacting that zone's primary server. After the <expire> period has elapsed, the secondary server will stop supplying data about the zone. A common value is 3600000; this is roughly 42 days.

- **<minimum>** indicates how many seconds, by default, records from this zone may remain in the cache of remote servers. A value of 604800 seconds is a week. If you seldom change the IP address of a machine, you can set this parameter to a large value. The longer the time-to-live, the fewer hits your DNS server will take. If, on the other hand, you set <minimum> to a month and then change a host's IP address, remote systems may keep resolving the name to the old IP address. This will continue for up to a month even though your DNS servers are supplying the new address.

2. **Name Server record.** The <name> field of the NS record contains a domain name, and the <data> field contains the fully qualified host name of a primary or secondary server for that domain. The fully qualified host name need not be in the domain it supports. It's very common, for example, to find a client's domain name supported by a provider's DNS server.

3. **Address record.** This is the most common type of record in a forward zone database. The <name> field contains a host name, and the <data> field contains its IP address. The DNS server will append the current $ORIGIN value to the host name unless the host name ends in a period. If $ORIGIN is "blob.com,"

glob	would become	glob.blob.com
slob.blob.com	would become	slob.blob.com
kbob.blob.com	would become	kbob.blob.com.blob.com

Note that, in the last case, lack of a trailing period causes appendage of an extra blob.com.

4. **Mail Exchanger record.** When you send mail to an address like billg@microsoft.com, microsoft.com obviously isn't the name of a computer. Everyone knows microsoft.com is the name of a domain. This trick is the work of an MX record in Microsoft's DNS server. That MX record equates the E-Mail destination microsoft.com to the host name of an E-Mail server. The <name> field of the MX record contains the name the E-Mail sender will specify, and the <data> field specifies a preference number and a host name. If one E-Mail destination matches several MX records, the sender's E-Mail program will try using all the MX host names, lowest preference number first, until one responds successfully.

5. **Canonical Name record.** The CNAME record establishes an alias for a real host name. Names like www.defiant.mil and ftp.yorktown.mil are usually CNAMEs that can point to another machine if necessary. The <name> field is the alias, and the <data> field is the real host name. Be careful not to specify a CNAME in other records that require a real host name. For example,

Wrong:
```
$ORIGIN   titanic.co.uk
dinghy   IN   A      63.254.250.1
lifeboat IN   CNAME  dinghy
         IN   MX     scuba
```

```
Right:   $ORIGIN   titanic.co.uk
         dinghy   IN   A      63.254.250.1
                  IN   MX     scuba
         lifeboat IN   CNAME  dinghy
```

The first example is wrong because the MX record for scuba inherits the CNAME lifeboat and CNAMEs aren't valid on MX records. The second example is correct because the MX record inherits the true host name dinghy.

6. **Name Pointer record.** This record, identified by the type code PTR, is the inverse of an address record. A reverse zone database file generally should contain a PTR record for each address record in the corresponding forward zone database file. If the forward zone database contained the lines

```
$ORIGIN costeau.fr
calypso IN A 223.30.20.10
```

the reverse zone database should contain

```
$ORIGIN 20.30.223.in-addr.arpa
10 IN PTR calypso.costeau.fr.
```

Note that IP addresses in the reverse zone database are reversed. It's supposed to make sense that, for reverse lookup, the least significant part of the address appears first, just as the least significant part of the fully qualified domain name appears first.

7. **Host Information record.** Very seldom used, this record supplies any desired information about a computer's hardware and software. A typical record might be

```
www IN HINFO proliant-1500 nt-server-351
```

8. **Well Known Services record.** This is another seldom-used record. It contains a host name, that host's IP address, TCP or UDP, and then any services on this host you wish to advertise. (For a list of valid service

names, consult the SERVICES file in \<systemroot>\system32
\drivers\etc.) Here is an example:

```
www IN WKS 223.250.240.5 tcp ftp telnet smtp domain
```

In the sample installation of Section 9.3, a complete set of DNS files will be
constructed for a hypothetical domain.

9.2 Relationship to WINS

DNS resembles WINS in that both services look up computer names and return
corresponding IP addresses. However, as previous chapters have shown, there is
no direct relationship between a computer's NETBIOS name and its DNS host
name. There is also no relationship between a Windows NT domain and an
Internet domain; they have different syntaxes and don't interoperate. Windows
computers register themselves into WINS, whereas a central administrator enters
host names into DNS.

DHCP and WINS present a problem for DNS administrators in that computers appear spontaneously on the network with user-selected names and automatically assigned IP addresses. These computers may or may not need to be in DNS,
but if they do, there's nothing to inform the administrator of their identities or
subsequent changes.

Largely for this reason, Microsoft has distributed a beta DNS server for
Windows NT. This first appeared with the Windows NT 3.5 Resource Kit. Adding
a "$WINS <computername>" statement to a zone database file instructs the
Microsoft DNS server to query the WINS service on <computername> when it
can't resolve a host name using the zone database.

9.3 Sample Installation

This section discusses installation and configuration of a popular DNS server for
Windows NT. The example chosen is MetaInfo DNS. Contact information for
MetaInfo appears in Appendix A.

Chapter 7 discusses installation of Windows NT, but this is the first chapter
that considers third-party software products. The author neither recommends,
discourages, nor supports use of these products. There was no comprehensive
review of available products and no formal attempt to choose best of breed. In
most cases, they are products that seemed popular, based on Internet newsgroup

postings, that granted releases for free use of sample files and screenshots, and for which installation and configuration seemed most instructive. In short, this book mentions third-party products as examples, not as endorsements.

9.3.1 Obtaining and Installing MetaInfo DNS

You can obtain a demo copy of MetaInfo DNS from the CD accompanying this book or from MetaInfo's Web site, http://www.metainfo.com/. The software comes with a demo serial number good for 30 days.

If you download the software from the Web, create a temporary directory, make it the current directory, and decompress the downloaded file into it. If you install from the CD, make \METAINFO on the CD the current directory. Either way, continue by running SETUP.EXE.

After the opening banners and copyright statements, MetaInfo DNS Setup will display the dialog shown in Figure 9.1. Enter your name and company and then click Next→.

Click Yes at the registration confirmation (or No if you need to make a correction) and then review the proposed installation directory. The default, an \etc directory on the Windows NT system drive, is usually a good choice. Click Next→ to proceed.

MetaInfo DNS Setup will copy a number of files to the \etc directory and to your \<systemroot>\system32 directory and then display the dialog shown in Figure 9.2. Click OK: MetaInfo DNS Setup will then inform you that setup is complete.

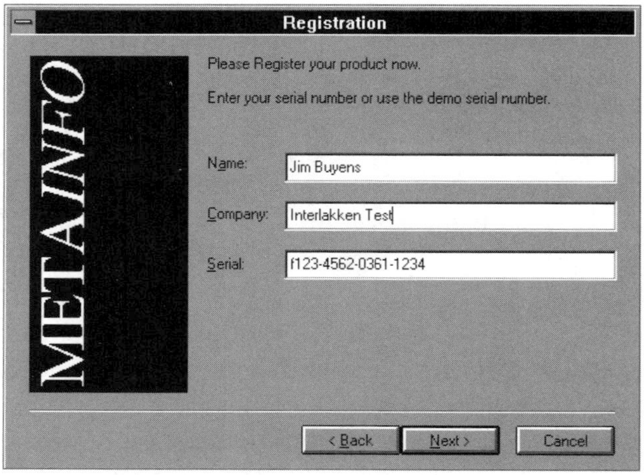

Figure 9.1 MetaInfo DNS Registration Dialog

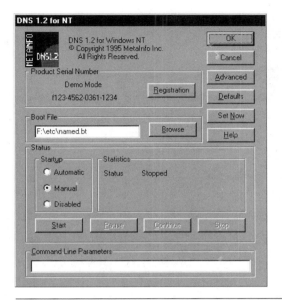

Figure 9.2 MetaInfo DNS Control Panel

9.3.2 Configuring MetaInfo DNS

MetaInfo supplies five sample DNS configuration files, as shown in Table 9.3. This is typical; most DNS software comes with sample files you can modify. The sample files describe the hypothetical domain prado.org. The example will convert these to another hypothetical domain, sandwich.com.

MetaInfo DNS Setup installs Program Manager or Start folder icons useful for examining and modifying these files. Figure 9.3 illustrates these icons.

9.3.2.1 Reviewing Sample Configuration Files The essential content of the MetaInfo sample files appears next. Minor editing was necessary to improve readability.

Table 9.3 Sample MetaInfo DNS Configuration Files

Configuration File	Sample File
Boot	named.bt
Forward zone database	prado.db
Reverse zone database	reverse.db
Local database	n/a
Reverse local database	local.db
Cache	cache.db

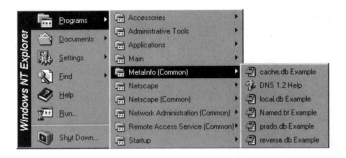

Figure 9.3 MetaInfo Default Configuration File Icons

named.bt:

```
directory /etc/examples
; type         domain                    source file or host
;********************* primary servers ************************
primary     prado.org               prado.db
primary     28.29.204.in-addr.arpa  reverse.db
;******************** secondary servers **********************
;secondary   prado.org               204.29.28.13   backup/prado.db.bak
;secondary   28.29.204.in-addr.arpa  204.29.28.13   backup/reverse.db.bak
;******************** common entries ************************
primary     0.0.127.in-addr.arpa    local.db
cache       .                       cache.db
```

prado.db:

```
prado.org. IN      SOA     elgreco.prado.org. raphael.prado.org. (
                                1        ; serial
                                10800    ; refresh
                                3600     ; retry
                                604800   ; expire
                                86400 )  ; minimum
; name servers
prado.org.                      IN      NS      elgreco.prado.org.
; mail server(s)
prado.org.                      IN      MX 10   rubens.prado.org.
```

```
; host addresses
localhost.prado.org          IN      A       127.0.0.1
elgreco.prado.org.           IN      A       204.29.28.3
valesquez.prado.org          IN      A       204.29.28.10
goya.prado.org               IN      A       204.29.28.11
rubens.prado.org.            IN      A       204.29.28.12
; aliases
www.prado.org.               IN      CNAME   goya.prado.org.
ftp.prado.org.               IN      CNAME   goya.prado.org.
```

reverse.db:

```
28.29.204.in-addr.arpa.  IN   SOA elgreco.prado.org. raphael.prado.org. (
                              1       ; serial
                              10800   ; refresh
                              3600    ; retry
                              604800  ; expire
                              86400 ); minimum
; name servers
28.29.204.in-addr.arpa.      IN      NS      elgreco.prado.org.
; addresses to names
3.28.29.204.in-addr.arpa.    IN      PTR     elgreco.prado.org.
10.28.29.204.in-addr.arpa.   IN      PTR     valesquez.prado.org.
11.28.29.204.in-addr.arpa.   IN      PTR     goya.prado.org.
12.28.29.204.in-addr.arpa.   IN      PTR     rubens.prado.org.
```

local.db:

```
0.0.127.in-addr.arpa.    IN   SOA elgreco.prado.org. raphael.prado.org. (
                              1       ; serial
                              10800   ; refresh
                              3600    ; retry
                              604800  ; expire
                              86400 ) ; minimum
; name servers
0.0.127.in-addr.arpa.        IN      NS      elgreco.prado.org.
; addresses to names
1.0.0.127.in-addr.arpa.      IN      PTR     localhost.
```

`cache.db:`

.	99999999 IN	NS	ns.nic.ddn.mil.
.	99999999 IN	NS	aos.brl.mil.
.	99999999 IN	NS	a.isi.edu.
.	99999999 IN	NS	gunter-adam.af.mil.
.	99999999 IN	NS	ns.nasa.gov.
.	99999999 IN	NS	c.nyser.net.
.	99999999 IN	NS	terp.umd.edu.
.	99999999 IN	NS	sitka.wsipc.wednet.edu.
ns.nic.ddn.mil.	99999999 IN	A	192.112.36.4
aos.brl.mil.	99999999 IN	A	128.20.1.2
aos.brl.mil.	99999999 IN	A	192.5.25.82
gunter-adam.af.mil.	99999999 IN	A	26.1.0.13
a.isi.edu.	99999999 IN	A	128.9.0.107
a.isi.edu.	99999999 IN	A	26.3.0.103
ns.nasa.gov.	99999999 IN	A	128.102.16.10
ns.nasa.gov.	99999999 IN	A	192.52.195.10
c.nyser.net.	99999999 IN	A	192.33.4.12
terp.umd.edu.	99999999 IN	A	128.8.10.90

These files contain quite a bit of information about the prado.org domain. Trace through the file listings and relate them to the following facts:

named.bt

1. The name of the domain is prado.org.

2. The named.bt file makes this computer a primary server for the prado.org domain. It's also a primary server for the reverse domain 28.29.204.in-addr.arpa. The forward and reverse zone databases are prado.db and reverse.db, respectively.

3. Based on the reverse domain name, prado.org apparently exists within the class C network 204.29.28.

4. This server isn't a secondary server for any domains. Two comment statements illustrate the statements needed to make another DNS server act as the secondary server for prado.org.

5. The primary prado.org DNS is apparently at 204.29.28.13 since this is the location from which a secondary prado.org DNS would obtain its databases.

6. The loopback forward zone database is local.db.

7. The loopback reverse zone database is absent.

8. The server will preload its cache from the cache.db file.

prado.db

1. The SOA record indicates
   - The domain name is prado.org.
   - The primary name server is elgreco.prado.org.
   - The administrator's E-Mail address is raphael@prado.org.
   - This is the first version of this zone's database.
   - Secondary servers will check in with the primary server every 10,800 seconds (every 3 hours) to see whether a new copy of the database is available.
   - Secondary servers that can't contact the primary should retry every 3,600 seconds (once an hour).
   - If, despite trying once an hour, a secondary server hasn't been able to contact the primary for 604,800 seconds (7 days), it should consider its last downloaded databases invalid and stop using them to resolve queries.
   - Servers that aren't primary or secondary servers of prado.org may cache prado.org name entries for up to 86,400 seconds (24 hours).

2. The NS record indicates that elgreco.prado.org is a name server for prado.org. For us, this is old news, but name servers frequently contain the same information in several different contexts because remote computers may ask the same question in several different ways.

3. The MX record states that rubens.prado.org is a mail exchanger for mail addressed to prado.org. The preference number of 10 is irrelevant because there's only one mail exchanger, but a value of 10 makes it easy to add higher or lower values in the future.

4. Four computers are registered in prado.org: elgreco, valesquez, goya, and rubens. They have host numbers 3, 10, 11, and 12 in network 204.29.28.

5. The computer goya.prado.org apparently runs the HTTP and FTP services. Remote computers attempting to reach www.prado.org or ftp.prado.org will actually get goya's IP address.

reverse.db

This file is exactly as expected.

1. The SOA record is the inverse of the forward zone database's SOA.
2. The reverse zone's name server is the same as the primary zone's.
3. There are four reverse lookup pointers corresponding to the four host entries in the forward zone database.

local.db

Again, this file is as expected.

1. The SOA resembles that of the reverse zone database.
2. The name server is the same as in the reverse zone database.
3. A PTR record defines the loopback address.

cache.db

There isn't much to say about the cache database.

1. Both aos.brl.mil and a.isi.edu have two IP addresses each, but this isn't an error.
2. Hosts terp.umd.edu and sitka.wsipc.wednet.edu have no "A" records, so the name server will have to locate them using the six servers listed above them.

9.3.2.2 Modifying Sample Configuration Files As an example, assume an actual site differs from prado.org in the following ways:

- The actual domain name is sandwich.com.
- The actual network number is 223.99.88.
- Hosts club, meatball, pastrami, and rueben have host numbers 21, 25, 30, and 34, respectively.
- HTTP runs on club.
- FTP runs on meatball.
- The administrator is dagwood.
- E-Mail services run on the host beasley. Its host number is 5.
- DNS servers are lunch and menu. They have host numbers 9 and 10, respecitvely. Lunch is the primary.
- ftp.rs.internic.net will supply a new version of the cache file.

Making these changes, in almost every case, is simply a matter of opening the files with a text editor and using Edit...Replace... commands. Here are the results. As an exercise, compare these listings to the originals in Section 9.3.2.1 and account for all differences using the assumptions just given.

named.bt:

```
directory /etc/sandwich
; type         domain                    source file or host
;********************* primary servers ************************
primary       sandwich.com              sandwich.db
primary       88.99.223.in-addr.arpa    reverse.db
;********************** secondary servers **********************
;secondary    sandwich.com              223.99.88.13  backup/sandwich.db.bak
;secondary    88.99.223.in-addr.arpa    223.99.88.13  backup/reverse.db.bak
;******************** common entries ************************
primary       0.0.127.in-addr.arpa      local.db
cache         .                         cache.db
```

sandwich.db:

```
sandwich.com.  IN       SOA      lunch.sandwich.com. dagwood.sandwich.com. (
                                 1        ; serial
                                 10800    ; refresh
                                 3600     ; retry
                                 604800   ; expire
                                 86400 )  ; minimum
; name servers
sandwich.com.                    IN      NS      lunch.sandwich.com.
sandwich.com.                    IN      NS      menu.sandwich.com.
; mail server(s)
sandwich.com.                    IN      MX 10   beasley.sandwich.com.
; host addresses
localhost.sandwich.com.          IN      A       127.0.0.1
beasley.sandwich.com.            IN      A       223.99.88.5
lunch.sandwich.com.              IN      A       223.99.88.9
```

```
menu.sandwich.com.              IN      A       223.99.88.10
club.sandwich.com.              IN      A       223.99.88.21
meatball.sandwich.com.          IN      A       223.99.88.25
pastrami.sandwich.com.          IN      A       223.99.88.30
rueben.sandwich.com.            IN      A       223.99.88.34
; aliases
www.sandwich.com.               IN      CNAME   club.sandwich.com.
ftp.sandwich.com.               IN      CNAME   meatball.sandwich.com.
```

reverse.db:

```
88.99.223.in-addr.arpa. IN SOA lunch.sandwich.com. dagwood.sandwich.com. (
                            1        ; serial
                            10800    ; refresh
                            3600     ; retry
                            604800   ; expire
                            86400 )  ; minimum
; name servers
88.99.223.in-addr.arpa.     IN      NS      lunch.sandwich.com.
88.99.223.in-addr.arpa.     IN      NS      menu.sandwich.com.
; addresses to names
5.88.99.223.in-addr.arpa.   IN      PTR     beasley.sandwich.com.
9.88.99.223.in-addr.arpa.   IN      PTR     lunch.sandwich.com.
10.88.99.223.in-addr.arpa.  IN      PTR     menu.sandwich.com.
21.88.99.223.in-addr.arpa.  IN      PTR     club.sandwich.com.
25.88.99.223.in-addr.arpa.  IN      PTR     meatball.sandwich.com.
30.88.99.223.in-addr.arpa.  IN      PTR     pastrami.sandwich.com.
34.88.99.223.in-addr.arpa.  IN      PTR     rueben.sandwich.com.
```

local.db:

```
0.0.127.in-addr.arpa. IN SOA  lunch.sandwich.com.   dagwood.sandwich.com. (
                            1        ; serial
                            10800    ; refresh
```

```
                             3600     ; retry
                             604800   ; expire
                             86400 )  ; minimum
; name servers
0.0.127.in-addr.arpa.        IN       NS       lunch.sandwich.com.
; addresses to names
1.0.0.127.in-addr.arpa.      IN       PTR      localhost.
```

cache.db:

```
.                            3600000  IN  NS   a.root-servers.net.
a.root-servers.net.          3600000      A    198.41.0.4
.                            3600000      NS   b.root-servers.net.
b.root-servers.net.          3600000      A    128.9.0.107
.                            3600000      NS   c.root-servers.net.
c.root-servers.net.          3600000      A    192.33.4.12
.                            3600000      NS   d.root-servers.net.
d.root-servers.net.          3600000      A    128.8.10.90
.                            3600000      NS   e.root-servers.net.
e.root-servers.net.          3600000      A    192.203.230.10
.                            3600000      NS   f.root-servers.net.
f.root-servers.net.          3600000      A    39.13.229.241
.                            3600000      NS   g.root-servers.net.
g.root-servers.net.          3600000      A    192.112.36.4
.                            3600000      NS   h.root-servers.net.
h.root-servers.net.          3600000      A    128.63.2.53
.                            3600000      NS   i.root-servers.net.
i.root-servers.net.          3600000      A    192.36.148.17
```

As a final example, the following version of sandwich.db specifies the domain name with an $ORIGIN statement. This permits removal of sandwich.com from most places it occurs. In addition, the NS and MX records are left blank, allowing them to default to the prior record's name. That prior record is the SOA record, whose name field contains "sandwich.com" (after substitution of the "@").

sandwich.db:

```
$ORIGIN sandwich.com.
@              IN      SOA     lunch.sandwich.com. dagwood.sandwich.com. (
                               1       ; serial
                               10800   ; refresh
                               3600    ; retry
                               604800  ; expire
                               86400 ) ; minimum
; name servers
                       IN      NS      lunch.sandwich.com.
                       IN      NS      menu.sandwich.com.
; mail server(s)
                       IN      MX 10   beasley.sandwich.com.
; host addresses
localhost              IN      A       127.0.0.1
beasley                IN      A       223.99.88.5
lunch                  IN      A       223.99.88.9
menu                   IN      A       223.99.88.10
club                   IN      A       223.99.88.21
meatball               IN      A       223.99.88.25
pastrami               IN      A       223.99.88.30
rueben                 IN      A       223.99.88.34
; aliases
www                    IN      CNAME   club.sandwich.com.
ftp                    IN      CNAME   meatball.sandwich.com.
```

9.4 Testing and Problem Resolution

To test the DNS files modified in the preceding section,

1. Save them to a new directory (such as F:\etc\sandwich).

2. Bring up the MetaInfo Control Panel applet. (The applet's main screen appears in Figure 9.2.)

3. If the name server is running (as shown in the Statistics frame), click the Stop button to stop it.

4. Change the Boot File text box to F:\etc\sandwich\named.bt.

5. Click the Set Now button and confirm that you wish to update registry settings.

6. Click the Start button to start the name server.

Record any messages you receive after you press the Start button, and check the Windows NT Application Log as well. Most errors are likely to be mistyped commands and other syntax problems.

If starting the name server produces no error messages, go to the command prompt, issue the "cd" command to get to the location where you installed the DNS software, and look for a program called NSLOOKUP. This is a standard test tool for DNS servers. The results of running NSLOOKUP on EARRING, the author's Windows NT test server, are as follows (boldface indicates hand-typed input):

```
F:\etc>nlslookup
Default Server:  earring
Address:  0.0.0.0
server 130.131.90.111
> res_mkquery(0, 111.90.131.130.in-addr.arpa, 1, 12)
———

SendRequest(), len 45
    HEADER:
        opcode = QUERY, id = 1, rcode = NOERROR
        header flags:  query, want recursion
        questions = 1, answers = 0, authority records = 0, additional = 0

    QUESTIONS:
        111.90.131.130.in-addr.arpa, type = PTR, class = IN

———

timeout (5 secs)
timeout (10 secs)
SendRequest failed
Default Server:  [130.131.90.111]
Address:  130.131.90.111
```

```
> Server:  [130.131.90.111]
Address:  130.131.90.111
```

club.sandwich.com

```
res_mkquery(0, club.sandwich.com, 1, 1)
_____

SendRequest(), len 35
    HEADER:
        opcode = QUERY, id = 2, rcode = NOERROR
        header flags:  query, want recursion
        questions = 1, answers = 0, authority records = 0, additional = 0

    QUESTIONS:
        club.sandwich.com, type = A, class = IN


_____

_____

Got answer (205 bytes):
    HEADER:
        opcode = QUERY, id = 2, rcode = NOERROR
        header flags:  response, auth. answer, want recursion, recursion
avail.
        questions = 1, answers = 1, authority records = 2, additional = 2

    QUESTIONS:
        club.sandwich.com, type = A, class = IN
    ANSWERS:
    ->  club.sandwich.com
        type = A, class = IN, dlen = 4
        internet address = 223.99.88.21
        ttl = 86400 (1 day)
    AUTHORITY RECORDS:
    ->  sandwich.com
```

```
        type = NS, class = IN, dlen = 20
        nameserver = lunch.sandwich.com
        ttl = 86400 (1 day)
->  sandwich.com
        type = NS, class = IN, dlen = 19
        nameserver = menu.sandwich.com
        ttl = 86400 (1 day)
ADDITIONAL RECORDS:
->  lunch.sandwich.com
        type = A, class = IN, dlen = 4
        internet address = 223.99.88.9
        ttl = 86400 (1 day)
->  menu.sandwich.com
        type = A, class = IN, dlen = 4
        internet address = 223.99.88.10
        ttl = 86400 (1 day)
```

```
Name:    club.sandwich.com
Address:  223.99.88.21
exit
F:\etc>
```

The command "server 130.131.90.111" results in an error because
sandwich.com isn't a real domain and EARRING isn't a member of it. However,
that command does accomplish its purpose: The default server address changes
from 0.0.0.0 to 130.131.90.111. Entering "club.sandwich.com." then results in a
plethora of familiar information. This is a good result. Timeouts are bad results.

Figure 9.4 illustrates a GUI version of NSLOOKUP provided by Ashmount
Research Ltd. and found on many anonymous FTP archives. This is a 16-bit
Windows program shown running under Windows 95.

Another test—a more practical one—is to configure a workstation to use the
new server as its DNS and test for proper name resolution. Figure 9.5 shows the
Windows 95 dialog for configuring DNS servers.

To access this dialog, start Control Panel, double-click Network, and then
double-click the line "TCP/IP → Adapter," where Adapter is the network interface
that connects the workstation to the DNS server. Enter the IP address of the DNS
server and then exit by clicking OK. Allow the computer to reboot.

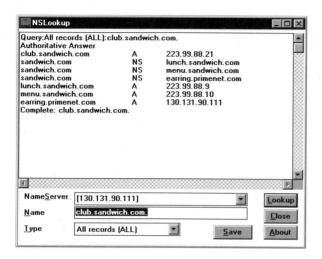

Figure 9.4 Ashmount Research NSLOOKUP

Once the workstation is pointing to the DNS server under test, try pinging a host you know is configured in the DNS:

```
C:\>ping club.sandwich.com
```

```
Pinging club.sandwich.com [223.99.88.21] with 32 bytes of data:
```

```
Request timed out.
```

The request times out because, again, sandwich.com is a fictitious domain and there's no such machine as club.sandwich.com. This test is a success, however, because specifying club.sandwich.com on the command line did result in the expected IP address being pinged: 223.99.88.21. This proves that the resolver contacted the DNS server and obtained the configured address.

Another source of diagnostic information is a trace that MetaInfo DNS can produce. To activate the trace,

1. Start the MetaInfo DNS Control Panel applet.
2. Stop the DNS service.
3. Click the Advanced button to bring up the dialog shown in Figure 9.6.
4. Choose a debug mode level other than "LEVEL 0—Debug Off."
5. Note the suggested debug mode file location and modify it if necessary.
6. Click OK.
7. Start the DNS service.

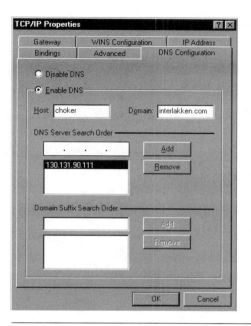

Figure 9.5 Windows 95 TCP/IP Properties Dialog for DNS Configuration

Depending on the debug mode you select, the debug file can grow quite large with amazing speed. It's best to leave the log turned ON only for running short tests in isolated environments. Finding a specific error in a large trace can be time-consuming.

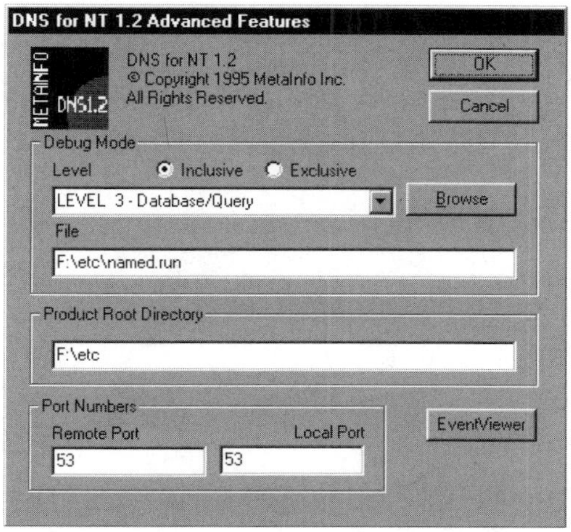

Figure 9.6 MetaInfo DNS Advanced Features Dialog

9.5 Ongoing Management

To add, change, or delete a DNS entry, you must update the appropriate configuration file and then stop and restart the primary DNS server. Stopping and restarting the server is normally a fast operation, and having the primary server down for a few minutes doesn't create a service outage. The secondary server will function in the primary's absence.

Be sure to test all changes, including routine maintenance, and to verify that the name server comes up properly after making any changes. Also be sure that you have adequate backup of DNS configuration files. Never replace an existing, known, good configuration file with an updated version unless you're sure you have a backup.

DNS isn't usually a resource-intensive service, but if you encounter capacity constraints, first consider increasing the cache period (allowing other servers on the Internet to resolve more queries for you). Other possibilities include relocating existing servers around your network and redistributing load among existing servers.

CHAPTER 10

Installing and Configuring FTP

There's not much glamour in simply copying files from one computer to another; nevertheless, this is one of the most common Internet applications. The application and the protocol it uses are both called FTP (File Transfer Protocol).

Two programs are involved in running FTP: a client and a server. The client responds to interactive commands on the user's computer, and the server runs in the background on a remote machine. The roles of client and server have no relation to the direction of the file transfer, which may occur in either direction.

FTP has achieved an honored "least common denominator" status on the Internet. HTTP can perform server-to-client transfers with great simplicity and efficiency, and platform-specific LAN protocols such as NFS, NETBIOS, and AppleTalk provide more convenient "transparent" file sharing. Nevertheless, FTP provides more kinds of file transfer in more kinds of environments than any other approach. If the Web is the Internet's BMW, FTP is its eighteen-wheeler.

FTP is so ubiquitous that most Web users expect it as a matter of course. They want their Web pages to support FTP URLs, and they probably need FTP themselves to update their Web pages and other content. They may want remote users to post certain types of files as well. In short, most Web sites will want to run an FTP server. Fortunately, a full implementation ships with each version of Windows NT.

10.1 Operating Concepts and Standards

Unlike HTTP, FTP is a *connection-oriented* protocol. A client FTP program always initiates the connection, and an FTP server program maintains it.

FTP is also session-oriented and state-oriented. Being *session-oriented* means the user logs on and the FTP server remembers facts about that logon session, such as the user name, until it ends. Being *state-oriented* means the FTP server preserves status, such as the current directory location, from one command to another. The FTP session consumes resources on the server (such as sockets and memory) even when the session is idle from a user point of view.

Actually, FTP uses two sessions: a control session and a data session. The control session is the one that the user logs into, that accepts and processes user commands, and that persists until the user logs off. An additional session is opened for each actual file transfer. FTP servers listen for control sessions on port 21 and initiate data sessions from port 20.

Consider the following transcript of a short, character-mode FTP session:

```
1.   D:\>ftp
2.   ftp> open primenet.com
3.   ftp> Connected to primenet.com.
4.   220 usr3.primenet.com FTP server (Version wu-2.4(3) Mon Nov 28
         13:38:26 MST 1994) ready.
5.   User (primenet.com:(none)): buyensj
6.   331 Password required for buyensj.
7.   xxxxxx
8.   230 User buyensj logged in.
9.   ftp> lcd d:\winword\primenet
10.  Local directory now D:\winword\PRIMENET
11.  ftp> cd public_html
12.  250 CWD command successful.
13.  ftp> ls nt*.*
14.  200 PORT command successful.
15.  150 Opening ASCII mode data connection for file list.
16.  ntwebsrv.html
17.  226 Transfer complete.
18.  15 bytes received in 0.00 seconds (15000.00 Kbytes/sec
19.  ftp> put NTWEBSRV.HTM ntwebsrv.html
20.  200 PORT command successful.
21.  150 Opening ASCII mode data connection for ntwebsrv.html.
22.  226 Transfer complete.
23.  16997 bytes sent in 2.96 seconds (5.74 Kbytes/sec)
24.  ftp> bye
25.  221 Goodbye.
```

The control connection (port 21) remains open from line 5 through line 25. The server remembers state information, such as the user name, during this interval. After processing the "cd" command on line 11, the FTP server remembers the current directory and uses it later on line 13. To return the output of the "ls" command to the user, the server opens a data connection (port 20) on line 14 and closes it on line 17. To process the "put" command on line 19, the server opens a second data connection on line 20 and closes it on line 22.

Dialogs such as the preceding are becoming less common as developers build more attractive front-end interfaces. Nevertheless, the FTP protocol and associated processing remain the same. Anything that worked differently couldn't be called FTP.

RFCs 959 and 1123 formally describe the File Transfer Protocol.

10.1.1 Security Concerns

FTP servers typically provide two types of access: anonymous and user. User access requires a Windows NT user name and password when the control session starts. Anonymous access allows anyone to start an FTP session by specifying "anonymous" as the user name and their E-Mail address as the password. Most FTP servers, including Windows NT's, accept a user name of "ftp" as synonymous with anonymous.

Users logged in with a Windows NT user name and password have the same file system privileges they would enjoy if logged in at the server console or at a workstation on the local network. All anonymous users are logged in with a single user name specified by the Windows NT system administrator—typically, the Guest account—and have whatever privileges that account would normally have.

Security provided directly by the Windows NT FTP Server service is broad. When you configure the service, you can specify

- A home directory that will be the current directory whenever an FTP user logs in. There is no provision to assign different home directories to different users. The home directory assigned in User Manager to a Windows NT user name has no effect here.

- Whether to allow anonymous logons.

- The Windows NT user name and password to use for FTP users who log on anonymously.

- Whether to allow only anonymous logons.

- For each drive letter on the system, whether "Read" access is allowed.

- For each drive letter on the system, whether "Write" access is allowed.

FTP transmits passwords over the network as clear text. This presents a significant security risk because anyone with a network analyzer can look for FTP logon packets and easily extract the user names and passwords. Current-day designers would undoubtedly require password encryption, but clear text apparently seemed good enough to FTP's actual designers in 1985. If you don't want clear-text passwords transmitted over the net, you should allow anonymous logons only.

The clear-text problem is less serious if user FTP logons will occur only on the local network or via local dial-in equipment. However, there's no way to configure a single machine so that FTP sessions from the Internet must be anonymous while local sessions may be user.

Drive-letter control of Read and Write permissions is simple-minded at best—perhaps crude would be a better word. You can't protect part of a drive using FTP service parameters alone. This argues strongly for using NTFS on any drive to which the FTP service will have access.

The FTP protocol doesn't include a "change current drive" command, so the Windows NT FTP service combines this function with the "change directory" command. For example, the FTP command "cd H:\USERS" changes both the current drive to H: and the current directory to \USERS on H:. This means an FTP user, even an anonymous one, can move about to any part of any drive the service can access. This is another reason to use NTFS on drives that will support FTP.

Obviously, all users should have Read access to the FTP home directory. Less obvious is that all users should also have Read access to all directories between the FTP home directory and the root directory of the drive on which it resides. The reason for this is illustrated by the following command sequence:

```
1.   ftp> pwd
2.   Current directory is H:\FTP\ANON
3.   ftp> cd ..
4.   250 CWD command successful.
5.   ftp> ls
6.   Access denied.
7.   ftp>
```

This can be quite confusing to a user. After cd'ing from H:\FTP\ANON to its parent directory, you expect to see the \ANON directory listed as a member. Users can solve this dilemma by issuing the command "cd ANON," but most don't; they assume if they can't "ls" a directory, they can't "cd" to it either.

10.1.2 Disk Organization and Management

FTP sites have a bad reputation for supporting pornography, pirated software, and other materials with which the site operator may not wish to be involved. Typically, someone logs on anonymously and uploads several megabytes or giga-bytes of files to a public directory, and then announces the site's existence by means of a "listserv." The list's subscribers then pummel the site with download activity. The result is degraded performance and lack of disk space for legitimate users until the site administrator discovers what's happened and deletes the unwanted material.

There are three primary defenses against unwanted FTP activity:

1. Preventing upload by anonymous FTP users.
2. Setting directory permissions so that newly uploaded files can't immediately be downloaded.
3. Confining anonymous FTP uploads to a single drive of limited size.

Option 1 solves the problem, but it also prevents users outside your site from sending desirable, legitimate files to you and your users. With option 2, anony-mous users can upload only to a specific directory, typically called INCOMING. Permissions on the INCOMING directory grant the Guest account Write and List permissions, but not Read. Someone else, either an authorized user or adminis-trator, then checks the file and moves it to a more accessible location. This pro-vides an excellent opportunity for virus checking as well. You may wish to develop a scheduled process to periodically check the size of the INCOMING directory, check all new files with a batch virus checker, and then move every-thing to an OUTGOING directory if the volume was reasonable and no viruses were found.

Options 3 is good practice for many reasons beyond security. Even registered users tend to consume large amounts of disk from time to time, and confining such uploads to a single drive prevents other services from being affected.

10.1.3 Internet Conventions

Most sites register a public anonymous FTP server with a name of the form ftp.domain.name. "ftp" usually isn't the real name of this computer; it's just an alias defined by adding a line to the DNS database file for the machine's zone:

```
ftp   IN   CNAME   domain.name.
```

FTP home directories frequently contain several common directory names such as those shown in Table 10.1. These are simply conventions and are by no means required.

On UNIX systems, you'll typically find "bin" and "etc" directories as well. These aren't required by Windows NT.

10.2 Installing the Windows NT FTP Service

This chapter discusses installation of two Windows NT FTP servers:

1. The standard FTP server supplied with versions of Windows NT up to and including 3.51.

2. The FTP server supplied with Internet Information Server, a component of Windows NT Server 4.0. This discussion appears in Section 10.3.

In this section, we'll add the FTP service to an existing computer with Windows NT, Microsoft TCP/IP, and Microsoft SNMP already installed. Only anonymous logins will be allowed. Anonymous FTP activity will be confined to a single 100MB drive. Anonymous uploads will be permitted only to a write-only directory called INCOMING.

10.2.1 Installing a Basic FTP Server

Here are the steps for installing the server:

1. Log on with a user name in the Administrators group.

2. Use Disk Administrator to create a 100MB logical drive. We'll assume this becomes drive H:. See Figure 10.1.

Table 10.1 Commonly Defined FTP Directories

Directory	Typical Use
dist	Contains files your site distributes in an official capacity. For example, you may be the official home site for some piece of software or documentation.
incoming	Is a holding area for anonymous file uploads.
outgoing	Contains anonymous file uploads that have been checked. Also used to store private files such as password-protected ZIP files intended for a specific anonymous user.
pub	Contains additional directories and files your site wishes to disseminate.
user	Contains file areas owned by specific users with a need to manage their own incoming/outgoing FTP activity.

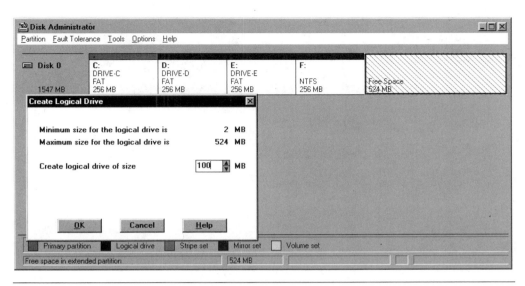

Figure 10.1 Creating a 100MB Drive with Disk Administrator

3. Open a command window and format the new drive for NTFS. The command to do this is

```
format h: /fs:ntfs
```

When prompted for a volume label, enter something descriptive (such as "PUBLIC_FTP").

4. Start User Manager and double-click the Guest account. This will bring up the User Properties screen displayed in Figure 10.2. Specify the values shown in Table 10.2.

5. Go to Control Panel...Network and verify that the TCP/IP protocol and SNMP are present in the Installed Network Software list box. If not, install them as described in an earlier chapter.

Table 10.2 Anonymous FTP User Account Policies for Guest

Field	Value
Password	Blank
Confirm Password	Blank
User Must Change Password at Next Logon	Checked OFF
User Cannot Change Password	Checked ON
Password Never Expires	Checked ON
Account Disabled	Checked OFF
Account Locked Out	Checked OFF

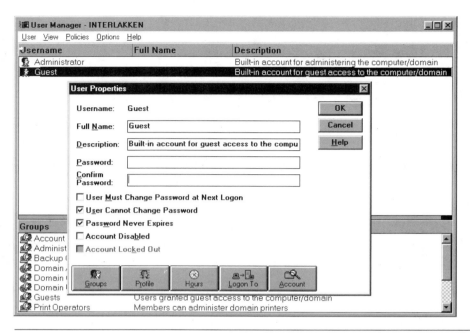

Figure 10.2 Setting Guest Account Properties for Anonymous FTP

6. Verify that the FTP Server service isn't already installed. See Figure 10.3. If installed, a line titled "FTP Server" will be present in the Installed Network Software list box. If so, exit the Network Settings dialog, double-click on Control Panel's FTP Server icon, and skip to step 12. If not installed, continue with step 7.

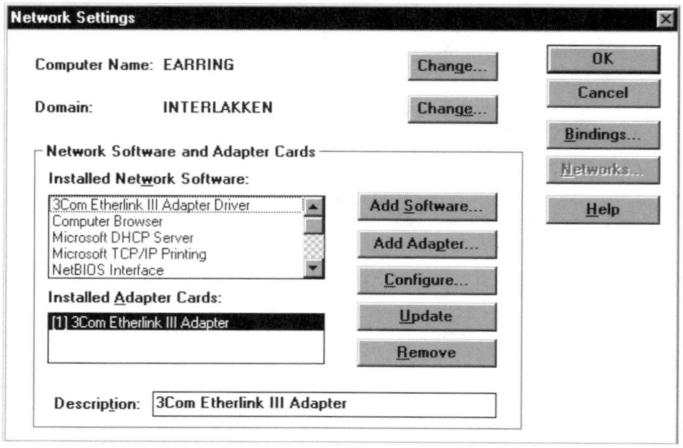

Figure 10.3 Starting FTP Server Installation from Control Panel

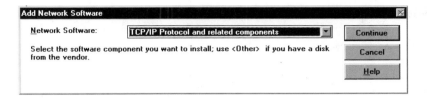

Figure 10.4 Add Network Software Dialog

7. Click the Add Software... button.

8. When the Add Network Software dialog box appears, select "TCP/IP Protocol and related components" and then click the Continue button. See Figure 10.4.

9. The next dialog box should be titled "Windows NT TCP/IP Installation Options." Make sure the checkbox labeled "FTP Server Service" is checked ON and then click the Continue button. See Figure 10.5.

10. Specify the full path to the Windows NT installation files when prompted. If you're installing from a CD in drive G:, this would be G:\I386. See Figure 10.6.

11. A message box will appear warning you about FTP's use of unencrypted passwords. Click Yes to proceed. See Figure 10.7.

12. The installation process will copy the necessary files to your computer and then present the FTP Service's Control Panel dialog shown in Figure 10.8. Enter the settings listed in Table 10.3.

13. Click OK to close the FTP Service dialog box.

14. Click OK to close the Network Settings dialog box.

15. If you're prompted to restart Windows NT, click the Restart Now button and allow the computer to reboot. See Figure 10.9.

Table 10.3 Typical Windows NT FTP Settings

Field	Value
Maximum Connections	20 (the default)
Idle Timeout (min)	10 (the default)
Home Directory	H:\
Allow Anonymous Connections	Checked ON
Username	Guest
Password	Blank
Allow Only Anonymous Connections	Checked ON

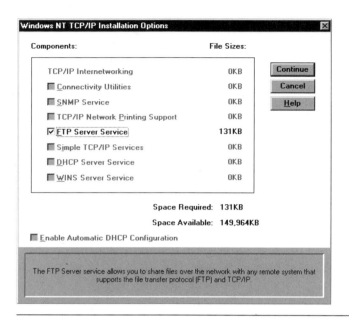

Figure 10.5 Windows NT TCP/IP Installation Options Dialog

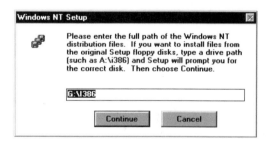

Figure 10.6 Specifying the Path to Windows NT Distribution Files

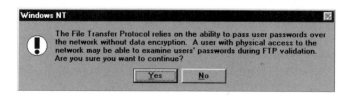

Figure 10.7 File Transfer Protocol Password Warning

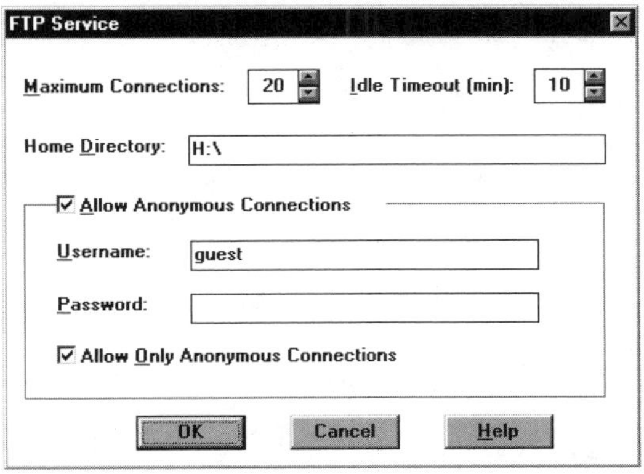

Figure 10.8 Setting FTP Service Properties

If not prompted to reboot, check Control Panel to see whether the FTP Server icon is displayed. If so, continue with step 17. If not, close Control Panel and continue with step 16.

16. Open Control Panel.

17. Locate and double-click the FTP Server icon. See Figure 10.10.

If you're prompted whether to start the FTP Server service, answer "Yes."

18. The FTP User Sessions dialog box will appear. Click the Security... button. See Figure 10.11.

19. The FTP Server Security dialog box will appear next. Locate the dropdown list titled "Partition:" and review the Allow Read and Allow Write settings for each drive. Ensure both settings are checked ON for drive H: and OFF for all other drives. See Figure 10.12.

20. Click OK to close the FTP Server Security dialog. Then press Close to close the FTP User Sessions dialog.

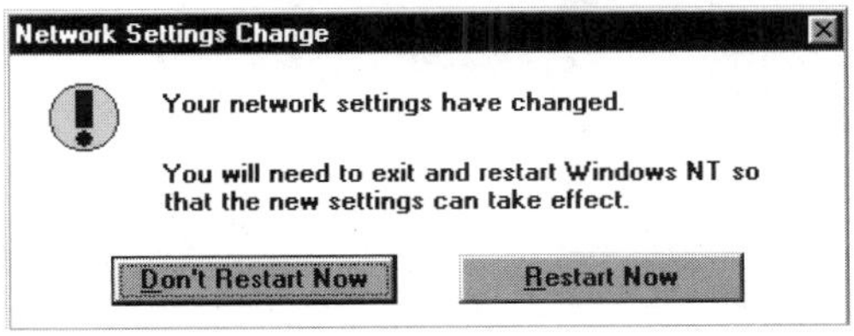

Figure 10.9 Network Settings Change Dialog

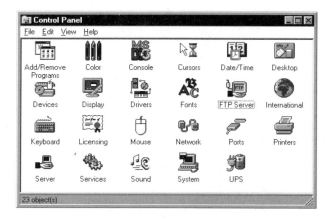

Figure 10.10 Control Panel FTP Server Icon

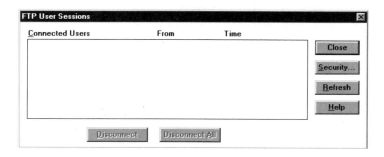

Figure 10.11 FTP User Sessions Dialog

21. Double-click Control Panel's Services dialog and verify that FTP Server is configured for automatic start-up. See Figure 10.13.

   If not, select the FTP Server line, click Startup..., and select "Automatic" as the start-up type. The Log On As box should be "System Account." Click OK when finished. See Figure 10.14.

Figure 10.12 FTP Server Security Dialog

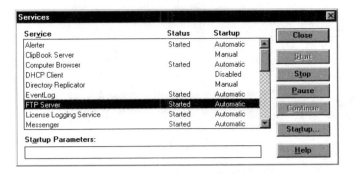

Figure 10.13 Control Panel Services Dialog

22. Close Control Panel.

23. Go to File Manager, open a window for drive H:, and create directories named INCOMING, PUB, and OUTGOING.

24. Select the root directory (H:\) and then pull down the Security menu and select "Permissions...." Grant "Full Control" to administrators and the system. Grant "Read" permission to everyone else and domain guests. Click to apply to all subdirectories and then click OK. See Figure 10.15.

25. Select the INCOMING directory and then pull down the Security menu and again select "Permissions...." Change permissions for domain guests and everyone else to "Add (WX)(Not Specified)." Click to apply to all subdirectories and then click OK.

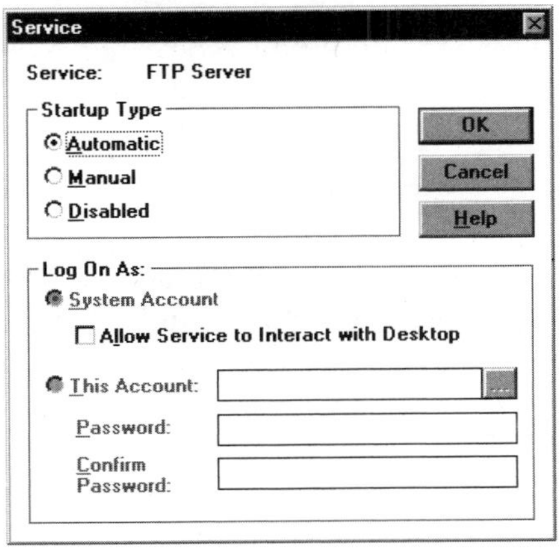

Figure 10.14 Service Startup Dialog

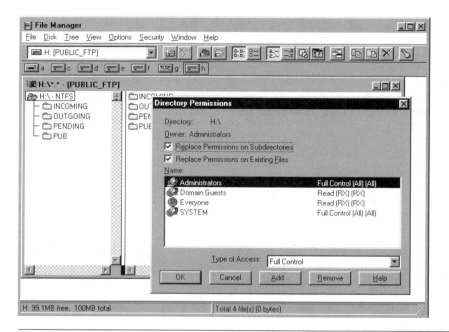

Figure 10.15 Setting Directory Permissions for the FTP Drive

10.2.2 Enhancing Security

Running a public FTP server always entails the risk that someone will post large amounts of objectionable or illegal material for retrieval by others. One approach to minimizing this risk is to insert a waiting period during which uploaded files can't be downloaded. The administrator can use this period to inspect the new files.

In this example, files received in INCOMING will be moved once a day to a holding area called PENDING. Files in PENDING will be moved to an OUTGOING directory 24 hours later.

Continuing from the previous example, create a directory called PENDING in the root of drive H:. Set permissions so that administrators have full control and no one else has access. Use File Manager's File...Properties dialog to make this directory "Hidden." Finally, create the following batch file in the \users\default\ directory on the Windows NT system drive:

incoming.bat

```
1.   xcopy h:\pending\*.* h:\outgoing /s
2.   md h:\pending\newpend
```

```
3.    move h:\pending\newpend h:\newpend
4.    rd /s/q h:\pending
5.    ren h:\newpend pending
6.    attrib +h h:\pending
7.    xcopy h:\incoming\*.* h:\pending /s
8.    md h:\incoming\newincom
9.    move h:\incoming\newincom h:\newincom
10.   rd /s/q h:\incoming
11.   ren h:\newincom incoming
```

Statement 1 copies any \PENDING files to \OUTGOING. Using "xcopy" ensures that copied files will inherit new default permissions from the target location. Note that using "move" would preserve permissions previously inherited from \INCOMING.

Deleting and recreating the \PENDING directory would cause the new \PENDING directory to inherit permissions from the root directory. This isn't what we want, so statement 2 creates a new directory with the same permissions as \PENDING; statement 3 moves that directory (preserving permissions) to the root. This sets the stage for statement 4 to delete the old \PENDING directory and statement 5 to rename the new one to its proper name. Statement 6 ensures the new \PENDING directory is hidden as before.

Statements 7 through 11 repeat the logic of statements 1 through 6, this time transferring \INCOMING to \PENDING.

To run this command automatically, issue the following command at the Windows NT command prompt. In this example, F: is the Windows NT system drive. If prompted whether to start the Schedule service, respond "Yes":

```
at 05:00 /every:mo,tu,we,th,fr "f:\users\default\incoming.bat"
```

To make sure this command always executes, go to Control Panel, double-click Services, locate the entry for the Schedule service, and make sure it's configured for automatic start-up.

10.2.3 Configuring Advanced FTP Parameters

The Windows NT FTP service has nine parameters not configurable through the standard dialogs described so far; these settings must be configured using the system registry editor. They appear in Table 10.4.

Table 10.4 Windows NT FTP Registry Settings

Parameter	Type	Specifies
MsdosDirOutput	REG_DWORD	Whether the "ls" command will produce DOS-like or UNIX-like output.
MaxClientsMessage	REG_SZ	The message sent to an FTP user when the maximum number of clients has been reached or exceeded.
Greeting Message	REG_MULTI_SZ	The message sent to an FTP user upon successful login.
ExitMessage	REG_SZ	The message sent to an FTP user who has entered the "quit" command.
AnnotateDirectories	REG_DWORD	Whether, if a directory contains a file named ~FTPSVC~.CKM, that file will be displayed whenever users cd to that directory.
LogAnonymous	REG_DWORD	Whether anonymous logins are to be recorded in the System Event Log.
LogNonAnonymous	REG_DWORD	Whether user logins are to be recorded in the System Event Log.
LogFileAccess	REG_DWORD	Whether file accesses are to be recorded in a text file named FTPSVC.LOG.
LowercaseFiles	REG_DWORD	Whether file names in noncase-preserving file systems will be displayed in lowercase.

Contrary to popular belief, editing the registry isn't particularly difficult. It's true that screwing up the registry can make a system unbootable, but this can be done with dialog boxes almost as easily. In any event, double-check your entries before clicking OK.

Editing the registry requires a program called Regedt32.exe. This program is installed by Windows NT Setup but is not referenced in Program Manager or the Start menu. However, you can run Regedt32 from Program Manager's File...Run dialog, from the Start button's Run dialog, or by adding an icon or menu option in the usual way. Regedt32 is installed in the \<systemroot>\system32 directory and therefore doesn't require a path specification to execute.

The parameters listed in Table 10.4 won't be present following a new installation of the FTP service; you'll have to add them yourself using Regedt32's Edit...AddValue... dialog. Step-by-step instructions for adding FTP registry values appear in the next section.

10.2.3.1 MsdosDirOutput This setting controls whether directory listings sent to an FTP client are presented in DOS-like or UNIX-like format. A user can toggle this state using the "quote site dirstyle" command, as shown next:

```
ftp> dir
200 PORT command successful.
150 Opening ASCII mode data connection for /bin/ls.
09-16-95  09:22PM        <DIR>          INCOMING
09-16-95  03:05PM        <DIR>          OUTGOING
09-16-95  03:04PM        <DIR>          PUB
```

```
226 Transfer complete.
142 bytes received in 0.06 seconds (2.37 Kbytes/sec)
ftp> quote site dirstyle
200 MSDOS-like directory output is off
ftp> dir
200 PORT command successful.
150 Opening ASCII mode data connection for /bin/ls.
d-wx-wx-wx   1 owner     group              0 Sep 16 21:22 INCOMING
dr-xr-xr-x   1 owner     group              0 Sep 16 15:05 OUTGOING
dr-xr-xr-x   1 owner     group              0 Sep 16 15:04 PUB
226 Transfer complete.
202 bytes received in 0.05 seconds (4.04 Kbytes/sec)
ftp>
```

DOS-like listings are the default, but Web browsers such as Netscape Navigator and Internet Explorer expect the UNIX-like format. If accessing your FTP server with a Web browser produces a listing of file dates rather than file names, you need to correct the MsdosDirOutput value.

After starting Regedt32, locate the MDI window titled "HKEY_LOCAL_ MACHINE on Local Machine" and expand the following icons by double-clicking:

```
SYSTEM
   CurrentControlSet
      Services
         FTPSVC
            Parameters
```

If MsdosDirOutput isn't listed in the right side of the HKEY_LOCAL_MACHINE on Local Machine window, it defaults to 1 (DOS-like output). To change it to 0 (UNIX-like output), proceed as follows:

1. With the Parameters line (under SYSTEM\CurrentControlSet\Services\ FTPSVC\Parameters) selected, pull down the Edit menu and select "Add Value..."

2. Specify MsdosDirOutput as the value name and select a data type of REG_DWORD. Note: If you're following this procedure to add a value other than MsdosDirOutput, be sure to specify the data type listed in Table 10.4.

3. Click the OK button and then enter "0" in the Data field of the resulting dialog box. See Figure 10.16. The Radix setting makes no difference in this instance because a zero is a zero in any radix listed.

4. Click the OK button again and then verify that

```
MsdosDirOutput: REG_DWORD: 0
```

appears in the right side of the window. You can make further changes to MsdosDirOutput by double-clicking on its entry on the right side of the window, or you can delete it using the Edit...Delete menu and responding "Yes" to the confirmation prompt.

5. To allow your change to take effect, quit Regedt32, go to Control Panel...Services, stop the FTP service, and then restart it. Note: It's good practice to check for active users before stopping the FTP service. You can view a list of active FTP users by double-clicking the FTP Service icon in Control Panel.

10.2.3.2 MaxClientsMessage By default, clients receive the message "Maximum clients reached, service unavailable" when they attempt to log in and the maximum number of connections specified in the FTP Service dialog box (Figure 10.8) has been reached. You may wish to change this message to suggest a mirror site, if one exists.

Unfortunately, this value is only a REG_SZ—that is, a single line. Be brief.

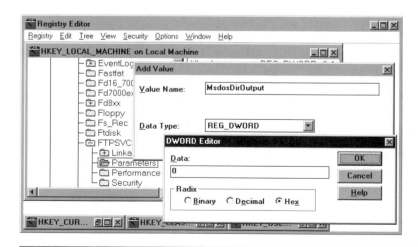

Figure 10.16 Adding the MsdosDirOutput Value to the Registry

10.2.3.3 Greeting Message The FTP service has no default greeting message. You can use a greeting message to confirm the name of your site and briefly state operating policies. An example follows:

```
Welcome to the Redd Inc. Anonymous FTP Site.
We support free speech and the law.
All logons and file accesses will be logged.
No pornographic or pirated materials allowed.
Uploads permitted to \incoming directory only.
```

Anonymous users can bypass the greeting message by prefixing a minus sign to their E-Mail address when they enter it at the login password prompt.

10.2.3.4 ExitMessage This message defaults to "Goodbye." Perhaps you prefer, "Thanks for your patronage," "Have a nice day," or "Visualize Whirled Peas." There's no accounting for taste.

10.2.3.5 AnnotateDirectories If set to 1, this value activates the Directory Annotation feature. This feature displays a client message each time the user switches to a directory containing a file named ~FTPSVC~.CKM; the message is simply the contents of that file. This is useful for displaying messages such as

```
You are positioned at the \incoming directory.
You may add files to this directory, but they won't
be visible or available to you or anyone else until
an administrator has reviewed them. Reviewed files
will appear in the \outgoing directory within 48 hours.
```

Generally, ~FTPSVC~.CKM should have the hidden file attribute turned ON so that it doesn't appear in directory listings.

Users can toggle Directory Annotation ON and OFF for their session by issuing the following command:

```
ftp> quote site ckm
```

10.2.3.6 LogAnonymous, LogNonAnonymous, and LogFileAccess These three parameters all default to zero (no logging). Adding value entries of "1" causes logging to occur. The log entries for LogAnonymous and LogNonAnonymous appear in the System Event Log, which you can view or dump using the Windows NT Event Viewer application. The FTP service writes LogFileAccess entries to an ASCII file named \<systemroot>\SYSTEM32\FTPSVC.LOG.

10.2.3.7 LowercaseFiles Setting this value to 1 will cause file names in noncase-preserving file systems to be listed in lowercase. Currently, FAT is the only such file system Windows NT supports. For other file systems, such as HPFS and NTFS, this value has no effect.

10.2.4 ResKit 3.51 FTP Configure

To eliminate the tedium of setting advanced FTP parameters with Regedt32, the Windows NT 3.51 Resource Kit contains a program called FTPCONF.EXE. Resource Kit setup creates an icon called "FTP Configure" for this program. Starting this program displays the dialog shown in Figure 10.17.

This dialog provides no new features, just a more convenient interface:

■ The Maximum User Count, Allow Anonymous Connections, and Allow Only Anonymous Connections fields control the same parameters as the corresponding fields in the FTP Service Properties dialog.

■ The Log Anonymous Connections and Log NonAnonymous Connections settings record logons in the Windows NT System Event Log. These correspond to the LogAnonymous and LogNonAnonymous settings described in Section 10.2.3.6.

Figure 10.17 Setting Directory Permissions for the FTP Drive

- The MS-DOS Directory Output setting should be OFF if users with Web browsers will be obtaining directory listings. This corresponds to the MsdosDirOutput setting described in Section 10.2.3.1.

- The Annotate Directories setting is equivalent to the AnnotateDirectories setting of Section 10.2.3.5. If ON, FTP will display a file named ~FTPSVC~.CKM, if one exists, whenever an FTP user changes directories.

- The Greeting, Goodbye, and Maximum Users messages correspond to the Greeting Message of Section 10.2.3.3, ExitMessage of Section 10.2.3.4, and MaxClientsMessage of Section 10.2.3.2, respectively.

10.2.5 Performance Management

The counters listed in Table 10.5 are available for display in Windows NT Performance Monitor. You must be running the SNMP service as well as the Windows NT FTP Server, however.

To display any of these counters, start Performance Monitor, click the "+" button (or pull down Edit and select "Add to Chart"), and select the "FTP Server" object. Select the counter you wish to monitor and then click the Add button. See Figure 10.18.

Table 10.5 FTP Counters Available in Performance Monitor

Type/Counter Name	Explanation
Instantaneous	
Current Anonymous Users	Number of current anonymous FTP sessions.
Current NonAnonymous Users	Number of current user FTP sessions.
Current Connections	Total of current anonymous users and current nonanonymous users.
Bytes Received/Second	Rate at which the FTP service is receiving data.
Bytes Sent/Second	Rate at which the FTP service is sending data.
Bytes Total/Second	Total of bytes received/second and bytes sent/second.
Total Since FTP Service Was Started	
Logon Attempts	Number of incoming FTP logins attempted.
Connection Attempts	Number of incoming connections attempted.
Total Anonymous Users	Cumulative number of simultaneous anonymous FTP sessions.
Total NonAnonymous Users	Cumulative number of simultaneous user FTP sessions.
Files Received	Number of files the FTP service has received.
Files Sent	Number of files the FTP service has sent.
Files Total	Files received plus files sent.
Maximum Since FTP Service Was Started	
Maximum Anonymous Users	Largest observed number of simultaneous anonymous FTP sessions.
Maximum NonAnonymous Users	Largest observed number of simultaneous user FTP sessions.
Maximum Connections	Largest observed number of simultaneous FTP connections.

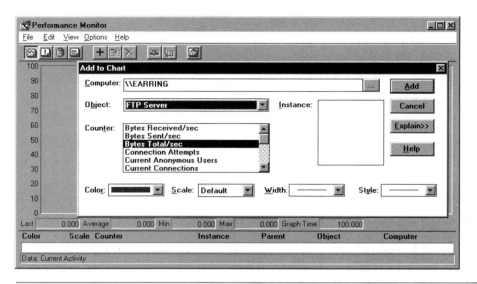

Figure 10.18 Managing FTP Counters in Performance Monitor

10.2.6 Remote Management

Several dialogs used in managing the Windows NT FTP service can be used remotely. Table 10.6 lists these dialogs and the procedures for accessing them remotely.

10.3 Internet Information Server FTP Service

An integrated setup program installs all Internet Information Server components—FTP, Gopher, and WWW—with standard defaults. Refer to Section 7.8 for information about installing IIS.

To configure IIS FTP, start Internet Server Manager (Figure 7.54), locate the line for the desired computer and FTP service, and double-click it. If the computer you wish to configure isn't listed, try pulling down the Properties menu and selecting "Find All Servers."

Table 10.6 Administering Windows NT FTP Remotely

Dialog	Figure	Procedure for Accessing Remotely
FTP User Sessions	10.11	Select computer in "Server Manager," pull down the FTP menu, and then select "FTP Service...."
FTP Server Security	10.12	Click the Security... button in the FTP User Sessions dialog.
Services (Control Panel)	10.13	Select computer in "Server Manager," pull down the Computer menu, and then select "Services...."
Performance Monitor	10.18	Specify computer in Performance Monitor's Add to Chart dialog.

10.3.1 IIS Service Configuration for FTP

There are five tabs to the IIS FTP Service Properties sheet: Service, Messages, Directories, Logging, and Advanced. Figure 10.19 shows the Service tab. "Connection Timeout" is the number of seconds an FTP session may remain idle without being dropped; 900 seconds (15 minutes) is the default. "Default Maximum Connections" is 1,000—an ambitious goal for most hardware.

Controls over anonymous FTP are much the same as for the standard FTP server; one checkbox permits or denies anonymous connections, while another controls whether all connections must be anonymous. Since FTP doesn't encrypt passwords as they pass over the network, some sites insist that all FTP be anonymous.

IIS setup creates the InternetGuest account and sets it as the default Windows NT account for anonymous logins. Whether you continue using InternetGuest or decide to use another account, make sure you set NTFS permissions so that anonymous users can do what's allowed and no more. Any entry in the Comment box will appear in Internet Server Manager server listings.

10.3.2 IIS Messages Configuration for FTP

The Messages tab permits entry of customized welcome, exit, and maximum connections messages. If you desire, the welcome message can include several lines.

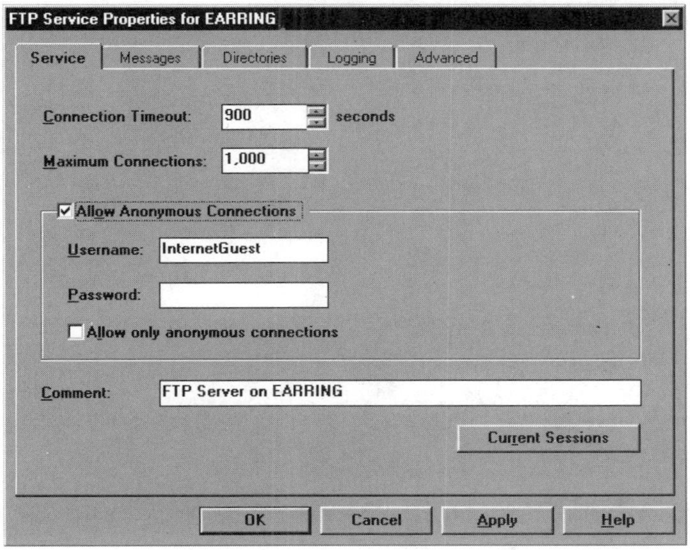

Figure 10.19 IIS FTP Properties—Service

10.3.3 IIS Directories Configuration for FTP

Figure 10.21 illustrates the Directories tab. "Directory Listing Style," near the bottom of the dialog, should be UNIX to accommodate Web browsers that connect with FTP URLs. The list box at the top shows currently configured virtual directories.

A virtual directory appears to the FTP client as an ordinary subdirectory of the FTP home directory. However, when a client changes to a virtual directory, the server actually switches to a completely different part of the server or network.

Figure 10.22 illustrates configuration of a virtual directory. The "Directory" entry, at the top of the dialog, contains the "real" location—a local drive:directory combination or a \\<server>\<sharename> (UNC) directory path. Specifying a UNC name allows files on other computers (perhaps running other operating systems or protocols) to appear as local to the FTP client.

Choose "Home Directory" if you're defining the FTP server's default starting directory; else, choose "Virtual Directory." If you specify a virtual directory, use the Alias box to specify the directory name that users will see.

The Account Information frame will be grayed unless you entered a UNC directory path. If you did enter a UNC path, you should enter the user name and password required to access the UNC resource. You can control read and write permissions using the checkboxes provided.

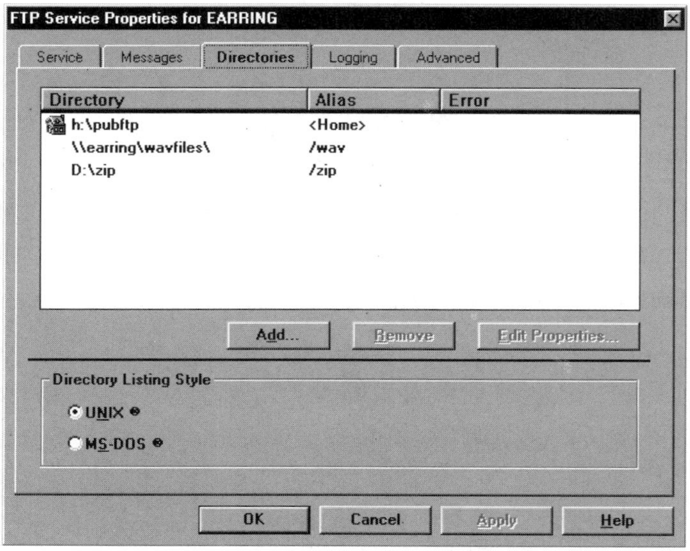

Figure 10.21 IIS FTP Properties—Directories

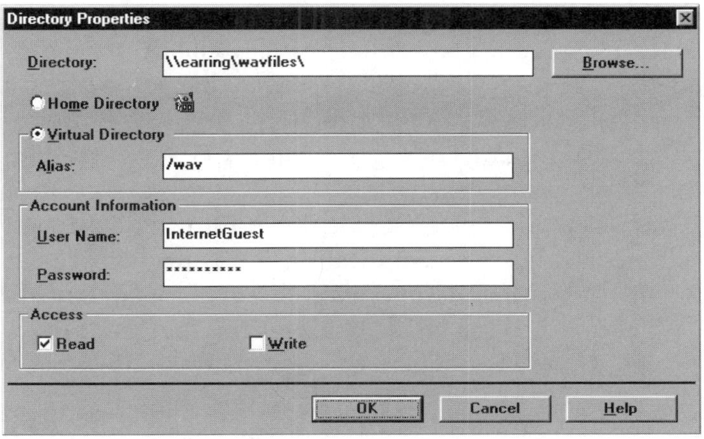

Figure 10.22 IIS FTP Virtual Directory Properties

10.3.4 IIS Logging Configuration for FTP

The IIS Logging dialog appears in Figure 10.23.

The Enable Logging checkbox activates or bypasses logging. If this is ON, you can log activity to an ASCII file or directly to a database. If you choose "Log to File," you can also choose whether to advance automatically to a new file and,

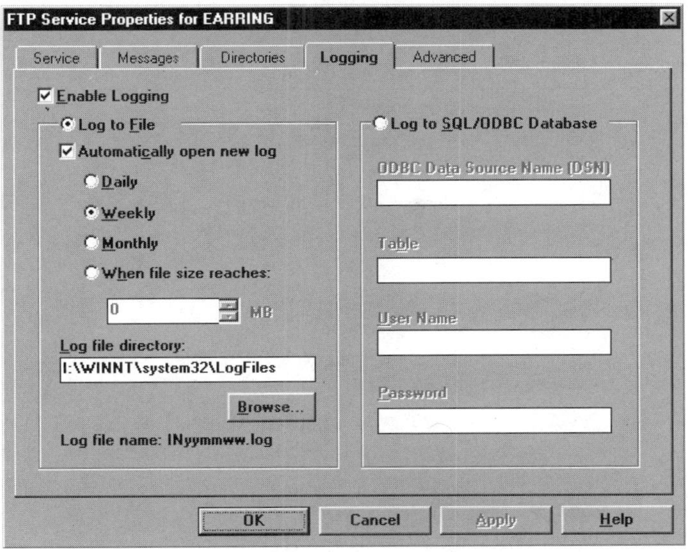

Figure 10.23 IIS FTP Properties—Logging

if so, how often. The "Log file directory" entry controls where these logs will appear. Note that the log file naming convention changes slightly depending on the log advance frequency; the "Log file name" comment changes to reflect this.

By default, all three IIS services log to the same directory: <systemroot> \system32\LogFiles. This means that FTP, Gopher, and HTTP log entries will all appear in the same file. If you want separate files, specify different directories.

Each log record contains the 15 fields listed in Table 10.7. In ASCII logs, these fields are comma-delimited, with hyphens indicating empty fields.

If you installed ODBC 2.5 with IIS, you can also log activity directly to a database. Microsoft SQL Server 6.0 is a good choice for this, but you can also use Microsoft Access. For the required log-database field structure, skip ahead to Figure 16.14.

Use the ODBC-32 applet (in Control Panel) to set up a data source name for the database. For SQL Server databases, this is the SQL database name. For Access databases, it's the Access database file name. (See Section 16.5.4.1.)

Once you've identified the log database to ODBC, return to Internet Server Manager, select the FTP service, go to the service's Logging tab (Figure 10.23), and choose "Log to SQL/ODBC Database." Also supply the following entries:

- **ODBC Data Source Name.** Enter the data source name you defined to ODBC.

- **Table.** Enter the name (not the Access file name) of the table.

- **User Name.** Enter a user name valid for accessing the log database.

Table 10.7 Field Definitions for Logging IIS to a Database

Field	Type	Length	Description
ClientHost	char	50	Client IP address
username	char	50	User name
LogTime	datetime	8	Date and time of log entry
service	char	20	Service name (i.e., "MSFTPSVC")
machine	char	20	Server computer name
serverip	char	50	Server IP address (usually "-")
processingtime	int		Processing time
bytesrecvd	int		Bytes received
bytessent	int		Bytes sent
servicestatus	int		Status code from service
win32status	int		Status code from Win32
operation	char	200	Type of request
target	char	200	Operation-specific
parameters	char	200	Operation-specific

- **Password.** Enter the password corresponding to the specified user name.

Note that database accounts and network accounts aren't necessarily the same. For network access, logging services use the "Anonymous Connections" user name and password from the Service dialog.

10.3.5 IIS Advanced Configuration for FTP

Clicking the IIS FTP Advanced tab brings up the dialog in Figure 10.24. The upper portion controls access permissions by incoming IP address. If you choose the "Granted Access" option, the server will accept connections from any IP address except those listed in the center of the dialog. If you choose "Denied Access," the server will accept connections from listed IP addresses only.

At the bottom of the dialog, you can limit total IIS network output from the Windows NT server. This may be useful in balancing workload and not overwhelming your Wide Area Network (WAN) links. To activate this feature, click "Limit Network Use by all Internet Services on this computer" ON. Then set the desired maximum number of kilobytes per second the server should transmit.

Figure 10.25 illustrates the dialog used for adding or editing access list entries. Selecting "Group of Computers" enables the subnet mask field; 1-bits in the mask

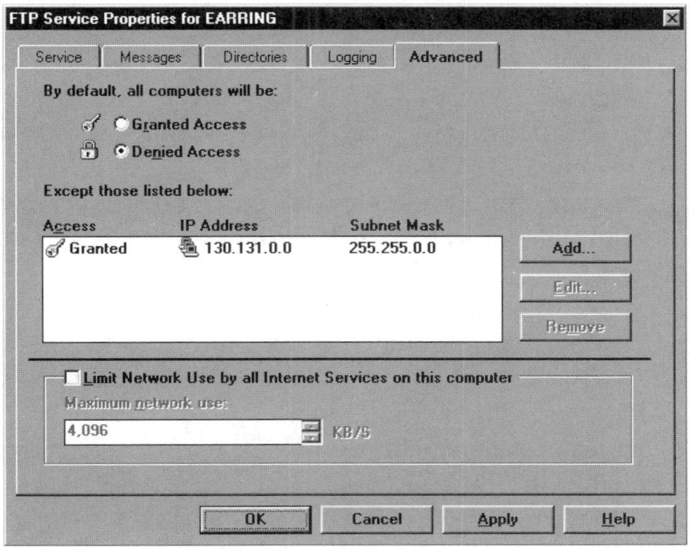

Figure 10.24 IIS FTP Properties—Advanced

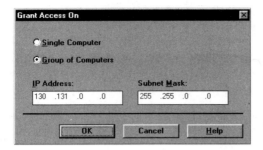

Figure 10.25 IIS FTP Properties—IP Access List Maintenance

then indicate which portions of the IP address the FTP server should check. Thus, in the example shown, only those computers in the 130.131 network will have access to the FTP service.

10.4 Testing and Problem Resolution

By far, the best way to test an FTP server is to fire up an FTP client and attempt a connection. A character-mode client is best for debugging, as GUI clients may ignore or mask unusual server messages.

If the client can't connect, test for proper client operation by connecting to a few other, known good sites. Test basic connectivity by pinging the machine running the FTP server; if you can't ping, you can't FTP either.

If connections to other FTP servers and pinging to the new FTP server both work but FTP to the new server doesn't, use Control Panel...Services to verify the FTP Server service is running. If not, start it and verify the service is set to auto-start whenever the system boots.

If the FTP Server service is running, double-click the Control Panel...FTP Server icon to see how many users are connected. Perhaps the maximum number of users has been exceeded.

You can also check to see whether the logon mode you're attempting (user or anonymous) is permitted. This dialog is hidden under Control Panel...Network... FTP Server...Configure.... Remember that changes made to this dialog box don't take effect until the FTP Server is stopped and restarted.

As always in cases of curious behavior, it may also be useful to start Event Viewer and review the System and Application Logs.

10.5 Ongoing Management

The types of management required for an FTP server depend greatly on the server's role. If the FTP server is primarily used as a primary or mirror site for software distribution, problems generally relate to servicing as many simultaneous users as possible. As usage warrants, you may need to add processing power, RAM, or faster I/O devices; alternatively, you may need to limit connections to what your hardware can support. Making decisions of this type requires collecting and comparing data from good times and bad.

If, on the other hand, your site is a general archive for registered and anonymous users, problems are more likely to involve sudden or gradually developing out-of-disk conditions. If the problem develops suddenly, you need to know who recently uploaded what and why. If the problem develops slowly, you need a way to identify old, obsolete, and duplicate files for archival.

Finally, if you charge users for disk space or file activity, you need a way to collect the necessary usage statistics for billing.

10.5.1 Space Management

The easiest way to control disk space is simply to limit file additions. If only one person (or a small group of administrators) can add files, not much unexpected should occur. This is practical for relatively static archive sites, less so for general user space and public archives.

A staged addition procedure, such as that described in the example in Section 10.2.2, at least gives the administrator a chance to detect sudden increases. If logging is active, the log may reveal the person responsible for large or suspicious uploads.

General-purpose disk space managers for Windows NT are surprisingly scarce. One homegrown approach would be a Visual Basic program that walks a directory tree, calculates the number of files and bytes per directory, and stores this information in a database. This would permit "delta" analysis of changes in utilization between runs.

Disk space management changes dramatically if you're selling disk space for a monthly profit. In this case, unbridled growth is a wonderful thing, and your biggest problem is to keep adding disk drives fast enough to accommodate growth.

10.5.2 Content Management

Controlling the content of an FTP site can be a tricky business. At some level, you undoubtedly wish to encourage the proliferation of valuable files while eliminating inappropriate, obsolete, or virus-ridden material. The extent of such responsibility varies widely with the role of your site, however. A corporate site added to the Web for public relations obviously will be much more sensitive to content than a public Internet provider selling bulk space.

Only you can decide how often to scan your FTP volumes for useless, inappropriate, or damaging material; only you can decide what falls into such categories. The important thing is to review the mission of your site, to develop a content policy that makes sense, and to make that policy known to users.

CHAPTER 11

Installing and Configuring Gopher

Somewhere along the evolutionary trail from FTP to the World Wide Web lies Gopher. Gopher replaces FTP's cryptic file names with text descriptions, displays straightforward menus, and provides transparent jumps from one computer to another. Gopher also provides a way to start programs on the user's computer based on the type of file downloaded.

Be that as it may, Gopher menus have proven no match to the Web's hypertext document links and graphic displays. As a result, most Gopher sites are converting themselves to Web sites. Still, some applications require no more functionality than Gopher provides, and these sites remain active and growing. Knowledge of Gopher server management is useful if you are part of such a site, wish to integrate with one, or wish to convert an existing Gopher site to HTTP.

11.1 Operating Concepts and Standards

A Gopher server is a background process (a Windows NT service) that listens on TCP/IP port 70. A single Gopher data directory contains all files, menus, and subdirectories the Gopher server can access. If the Gopher administrator hasn't set up any menu definitions, clients connecting to the Gopher server will simply receive a directory listing of the Gopher data directory. Selecting a file downloads that file; selecting a directory name displays the contents of that directory.

Even at this level, Gopher has some advantages over anonymous FTP. File transfers occur over a single, client-initiated connection. Compared to FTP's separate control and transfer sessions, this is simpler from a network security point of view and somewhat less resource-intensive. The Gopher server also supplies default file types—either set by an administrator or defaulted based on Windows NT file name extensions—that allow programs on the client's computer to start automatically.

237

Gopher is an extremely simple protocol. To see Gopher in action, Telnet to any Gopher server on port 70 and press Return. Pressing Return is the simplest possible query; it requests the server's default menu. Output such as the following should result:

```
gNavigation Icon          g\NAVIGAT.GIF    earring.interlakken.com 70
0Welcome to the Interlakken Gopher Server        0\README.TXT
    earring.interlak
ken.com 70
1Zipped Archive Files    1\ZipFiles        earring.interlakken.com 70
5EMWAC Gopher Server for Intel CPU's        5\zipfiles\gsi386.zip
    earring.interlak
ken.com 70
1University of Minnesota Gopher Server  1/      gopher.tc.umn.edu
    70
.
```

Gopher is a stateless, non-session-oriented protocol. This means that after delivering results such as the preceding, the Gopher server immediately drops the connection. If the client wants more information from the same server, it must open a new connection each time.

Adding some carriage returns and other formatting makes the Gopher server's output easier to read and discuss. The result of this editing follows:

```
gNavigation Icon
    g\NAVIGAT.GIF
        earring.interlakken.com 70
0Welcome to the Interlakken Gopher Server
    0\README.TXT
        earring.interlakken.com 70
1Zipped Archive Files
    1\ZipFiles
        earring.interlakken.com 70
5EMWAC Gopher Server for Intel CPU's
    5\zipfiles\gsi386.zip
```

```
        earring.interlakken.com 70
1University of Minnesota Gopher Server
    1/
        gopher.tc.umn.edu          70
```

There are five fields for each line that will appear on the Gopher menu:

1. A one-byte Gopher type code.
2. Menu text
3. A Gopher selector consisting of a type code, a backslash, and a server-dependent location.
4. A computer name.
5. A connection port.

The opening type code instructs the Gopher client which icon to display, and the menu text specifies the text to display. Clicking on the displayed menu text causes the Gopher client to request the associated Gopher selector from the named computer on the named port. (To try this by hand, Telnet to the named computer and port, type the selector, and press Return.) Table 11.1 lists common Gopher types and typical file name extensions.

Gopher has no dependency on a server's file system naming conventions or structure; it deals with Gopher selectors as arbitrary text strings. Most Gopher servers run on file systems with a hierarchical directory structure, though, and they treat a designated directory tree as a tree of Gopher menus. (Use of a designated tree denies Gopher users free run of the entire server.) In Windows NT terms, this means the contents of a designated directory become the main Gopher menu for that server, and any subdirectories become submenus. A Windows NT Gopher server typically supplies a default type code of "1" for each directory and, for individual files, type codes derived from file name extensions. The default menu text is simply the name of each file or directory.

To make full use of Gopher, administrators usually modify default menu handling by

- Presenting descriptive menu text in place of system file and directory names.
- Adding menu items for objects other than local files and directories.
- Suppressing display of menu items for certain files.

Table 11.1 Gopher Types and File Name Extensions

GopherType	Meaning	Typical File Name Extensions
0	Text file	ps, txt
1	Directory	
2	CSO name server	
3	Error	
4	Macintosh binhex	hqx
5	Binary archive	arc, lzh, exe, zip, zoo
6	UUencoded	uue
7	WAIS index	src, mindex
8	Telnet session	
9	Binary	dll, tar, exe
c	Calendar	
g	GIF image	gif
h	HTML	html, htm
I	In-line text (not an item)	
I	Image	bmp, gif, jpg, pict, pcx, tiff
m	BSD mbox	
M	MIME file	
P	PDF (Adobe Acrobat)	pdf
s	Sound	au
T	TN3270 session	
:	Bitmap image*	
;	Movie*	
<	Sound file	
+	Redundant server	

* Use Gopher+ information for type.

The method for maintaining this information varies by operating system and by server. The Gopher specification standardizes only the interaction of client and server, not the interaction of server and file system.

11.2 Installing and Configuring EMWAC Gopher

This section discusses installation of the freeware Gopher server distributed by EMWAC, the European Microsoft Windows NT Academic Centre located at The University of Edinburgh, Scotland.

11.2.1 Installing EMWAC Gopher

The \GSI386 directory on the CD accompanying this book contains a set of EMWAC Gopher distribution files. To check for version upgrades or obtain software for non-Intel processors, point your Web browser to http://www.emwac.ed.uk.

If you install EMWAC Gopher from the accompanying CD, start installation by positioning to your CD drive letter and making \GSI386 the current directory.

If you download a new copy of the software, create a utility directory on your hard disk, make that the current directory, and decompress the downloaded archive file into it.

Either way, continue as follows:

1. Print or review the contents of the documentation files. The same information appears in two files of different formats: GOPHERS.DOC and GOPHERS.WRI.

2. Copy the following files to your \<systemroot>\system32 directory: GOPHERS.EXE, GOPHERS.CPL, and GOPHERS.HLP.

3. Open a command window, position to the \<systemroot>\system32 directory, run the following commands, and verify correct output:

```
gophers -version
gophers -ipaddress
```

   The first command should display the expected GOPHERS version, and the second should display the local machine's host name and IP address. If not, obtain the correct version or correct the computer's TCP/IP configuration.

4. Run the following command to register GOPHERS as a Windows NT service and identify it to Event Logger:

```
gophers -install
```

5. Create a directory that will be the Gopher data directory. For illustration, assume this is H:\GOPHER. Copy a few files into this location.

6. Close the command window, go to Control Panel, and double-click the Gopher Server icon. The dialog in Figure 11.1 should appear.

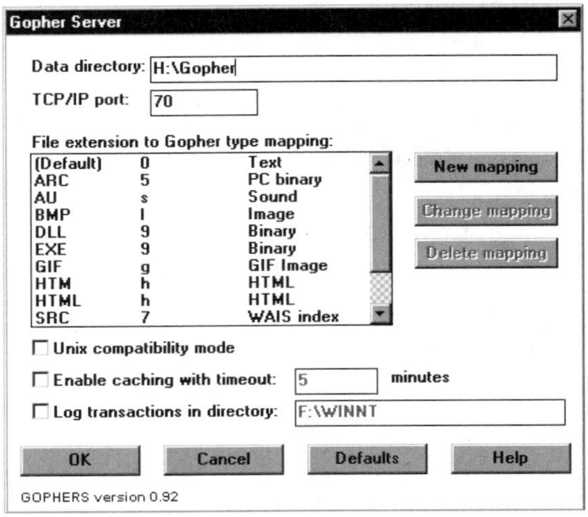

Figure 11.1 EMWAC Gopher Server Control Panel

7. Update the "Data directory" text box to indicate the Gopher data directory you just created.

8. Click OK.

9. Double-click the Control Panel Services icon, select the "Gopher Server" service, and click the Start button. See Figure 11.2.

10. Start a Gopher client or Web browser and point it at the machine where you just installed Gopher. Figure 11.3 illustrates use of a Web browser; note use of the URL gopher://earring.interlakken.com.

11. If Netscape Navigator is familiar with the type of file you click on, Netscape Navigator will display the file. Figure 11.4 shows the result of clicking on the README.TXT file in Figure 11.3.

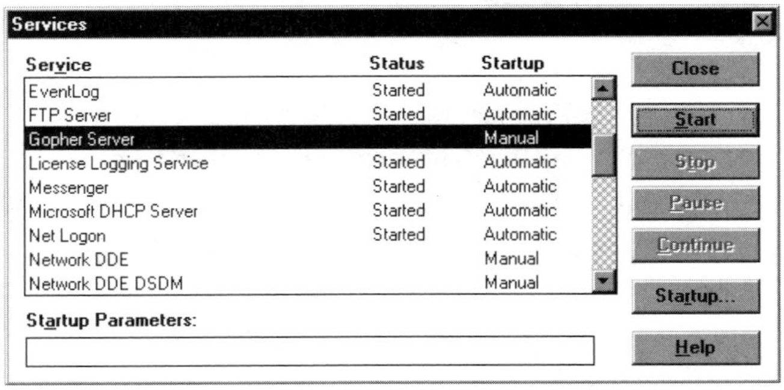

Figure 11.2 Starting the Gopher Service

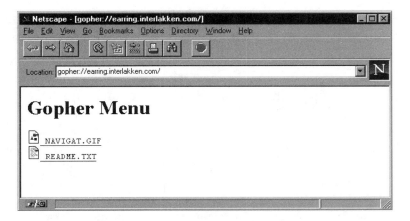

Figure 11.3 Retrieving a Gopher Menu with Netscape Navigator

11.2.2 Configuring Alias Files for EMWAC Gopher

The Gopher protocol allows great flexibility in the design of servers; the protocol itself is quite simple, and the format of selectors is arbitrary. The normal approach, however, is for selectors to consist of file and directory names in the server's file system.

Alias files assign menu text to O/S-specific file names. To locate the alias file for any given file,

■ Look for a special alias directory within the directory where the given file resides. (In UNIX, .cap is the name of this directory. Under EMWAC Gopher, alias directories usually have the name ALIAS.GFR.)

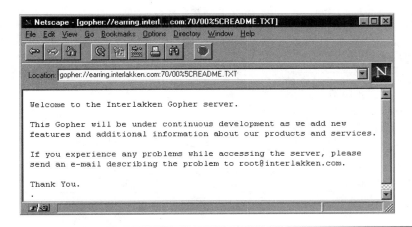

Figure 11.4 Displaying a Gopher Text File with Netscape Navigator

■ Within the alias directory, look for a file with the same name as the given file. To find alias information for the file SAMPLE.TXT, look for another file named SAMPLE.TXT in the .cap or ALIAS.GFR directory.

Alias files contain several lines of plain text with a keyword at the beginning of each line. Lines beginning with a pound sign ("#") are comments. Table 11.2 lists common alias file keywords.

The simplest alias file consists of a single line with the Name keyword and its associated value. EMWAC Gopher will supply a Gopher type based on the file name extension and a file location based on the actual value. Administrators can also set the Gopher type specifically by adding such a line to the alias file. Specifying a blank Name field suppresses the menu entry for the associated file or directory. Numb entries, if used, simply change the order of menu items.

Normally, Gopher menus list items in a single directory. Each directory in the Gopher tree is therefore a menu. Link files provide a way to add menu items not in a menu's default directory. The UNIX convention is that any file name beginning with a dot (".") is a link file; under EMWAC Gopher, link files usually have the GFR extension. Like alias files, link files are plain text, and each line begins with a keyword from Table 11.2. A single link file can contain several menu items separated by comment ("#") lines.

Figure 11.5 shows another display of the same two files from Figure 11.3. As you can see, text descriptions appear in place of system file names. An administrator—the author, actually—accomplished this by placing two text files in a directory called ALIAS.GFR. Figure 11.6 illustrates this relationship.

The Gopher server has located the alias files NAVIGAT.GIF and README.TXT based on their presence in a directory called ALIAS.GFR. It uses instructions in the alias file NAVIGAT.GIF to describe the actual file NAVIGAT.GIF; likewise, for README.TXT. Here are the contents of the two alias files:

Table 11.2 Common Alias and Link File Keywords

Keyword	Description
Name	The menu text the client will display.
Host	The name of the host to contact.
Port	The port number on which to contact the host.
Type	The Gopher type of the file (see Table 11.1).
Path	The Gopher selector—typically, a repetition of the Gopher type followed by a backslash and then an operating system file location.
Numb	A sequence number that controls the order of the menu items. Menu items appear in ascending Numb sequence followed by any menu items that have no Numb value assigned.

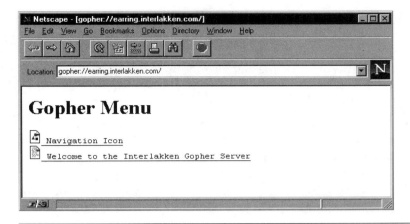

Figure 11.5 A Gopher Menu with Aliases Applied

```
navigat.gif
Name=Navigation Icon
Path=g\NAVIGAT.GIF
Type=g
Numb=100
#


readme.txt
Name=Welcome to the Interlakken Gopher Server
Numb=200
#
```

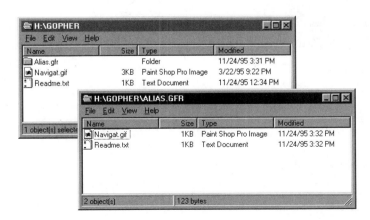

Figure 11.6 Gopher Alias Directory Structure

For NAVIGAT.GIF to be a plain text file clearly flies in the face of all convention. Nevertheless, that's how Gopher works. The alias file and the "real" file both have the same name, even though all alias files are plain text.

In the case of NAVIGAT.GIF, the Name= line specifies the text that will replace the real NAVIGAT.GIF's file name on the Gopher menu. The Path= statement specifies a Gopher descriptor of "g," which means a GIF file, and the real file's name. Type=g again states the original file is a GIF file, and Numb=100 supplies a sequence number. Sequence numbers are optional, but, if present, they cause Gopher to list menu lines in sequence-number order.

The README.TXT alias file also contains a Name= line but doesn't bother to specify Path or Type. Path will default to the file's known location, and Type will default based on the file name extension. The Gopher Control Panel applet (Figure 11.1) controls mapping of file name extensions to Gopher types. Refer to Table 11.1 for a list of common type codes and associated extensions.

In Figure 11.7 the Gopher menu includes a pointer to another directory; this item is titled "Zipped Archive Files."

The actual name of the directory is ZIPFILES, so that's the name of its alias file as well. Here's the alias file:

```
zipfiles:
Name=Zipped Archive Files
Numb=300
#
```

Figure 11.7 Gopher Menu with Pointer to Another Menu

Within the ZIPFILES directory are some files with the ZIP extension, plus another ALIAS.GFR directory. The ZIPFILES\ALIAS.GFR directory contains just as many files as the ZIPFILES directory, and these Files have the same names as those in the ZIPFILES directory. Of course, despite its ZIP extension, each alias file contains plain text describing the parent directory file with the same name.

To point to a Gopher menu or file on another computer, save a text file with the GFR extension in any Gopher data directory (but not in an ALIAS.GFR directory). The file name can be whatever you want, but the content must resemble the following:

```
outside.gfr:
Name=University of Minnesota Gopher Server
Host=gopher.tc.umn.edu
Port=70
Type=1
Path=1/
#
Name=EMWAC Gopher Server for Intel CPU's
Host=+
Port=+
Type=5
Path=5\zipfiles\gsi386.zip
#
```

Note that in the first group of lines, Name=, Type=, and Path= have the same meaning as for local descriptors. The Host= and Port= lines direct the user's browser to contact server gopher.tc.umn.edu on port 70, however.

In the second group of lines, Host=+ and Port=+ refer to the settings for the local machine. This menu item directly references a file in another directory. Adding this file to the Gopher data directory on EARRING produces the menu in Figure 11.8.

The two new items—"EMWAC Gopher Server for Intel CPUs" and "University of Minnesota Gopher Server"—appear at the end of the list because their descriptors have no Numb= lines; lines having assigned Numb values appear before any lines that don't.

A final caution: Don't save files like OUTSIDE.GFR with blank lines or extra carriage returns at the end. You'll get spurious menu lines consisting of the underline character only.

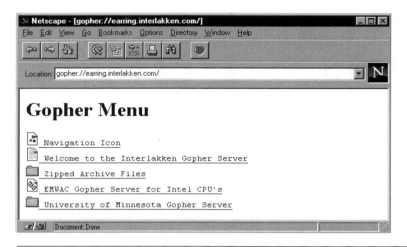

Figure 11.8 Gopher Menu with OUTSIDE.GFR File Present

11.2.3 Automating EMWAC Alias File Maintenance

Adding new files to Gopher directories is quick, easy, and pleasant; in fact, many sites assign the same directory tree for Gopher and anonymous FTP. Keeping alias files updated isn't nearly so pleasant. No matter how well organized and readable a set of Gopher menus starts out to be, it quickly becomes sprinkled with raw file names.

To deal with this problem, the author wrote a program some time ago called GO4MAINT. Within certain limitations, this program can greatly ease the creation and maintenance of Gopher alias files. Figure 11.9 displays the opening screen.

To install GO4MAINT, copy all the files from the \GO4MAINT directory on the CD to your \WINDOWS directory. Then create an icon in Program Manager or Start Programs in the usual way.

To use GO4MAINT, you must first establish the location of the Gopher data directory—the location you specified in the dialog of Figure 11.1. To allow for administration of both local and remote Gopher directories, GO4MAINT can use local drives, mapped network drives, or UNC file names:

- To use local or mapped network drives, click the Drive option button and select a drive from the list box at its right.

- To use a UNC file name, click the UNC option button, type a \\<server>\<sharename> combination in the associated text box, and then press Enter or tab to another control.

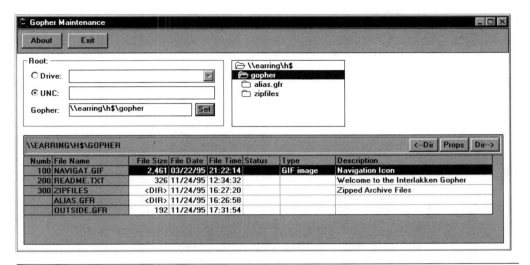

Figure 11.9 GO4MAINT Opening Dialog

After either procedure, use the directory list at the right to locate the Gopher data directory and then click the Set button in the "Root:" frame. GO4MAINT will then consider the directory appearing in the "Gopher:" box as the Gopher data directory and will construct all locators relative to that point.

Having learned the location of the Gopher data directory, GO4MAINT will display the current files in that directory, plus any corresponding alias information from the ALIAS.GFR subdirectory. The files appear in the order they will assume on a Gopher menu:

- To modify an item, select it by single-clicking and then click the Props button. Alternatively, right-click the line containing the item.

- To move to a subdirectory, select it by single-clicking and then click the Dir→ button. Alternatively, double-click the line containing the sub-directory name.

- To move back to a higher directory, click the ←Dir button.

If you choose to modify an item, the dialog box shown in Figure 11.10 will appear.

As usual, the Numb field controls the order of items on the Gopher menu. The Alias field controls the menu text. The Hide checkbox causes the alias file to contain a null value for Name=; this prevents even the file name from appearing as a menu entry. Type specifies a Gopher type that will override the server-assigned default.

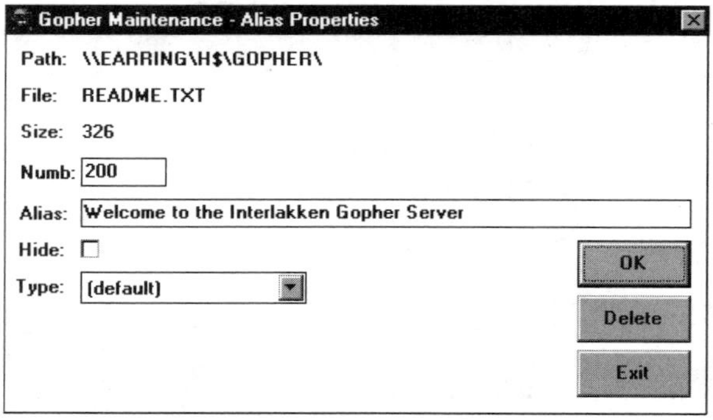

Figure 11.10 GO4MAINT Alias Properties Dialog

11.3 Configuring and Managing IIS Gopher

The Microsoft Internet Information Server setup process installs the IIS Gopher server with standard defaults. Refer to Section 7.8, "Installing Internet Information Server," if you need to perform this step.

To configure IIS Gopher, start Internet Server Manager (Figure 7.54), locate the line for the desired computer and Gopher service, and double-click it. If Internet Server Manager doesn't list the computer you wish to configure, try pulling down the Properties menu and selecting "Find All Servers."

There are four tabbed choices within the IIS Gopher Service Properties dialog: Service, Directories, Logging, and Advanced.

11.3.1 IIS Service Configuration for Gopher

Figure 11.11 illustrates the IIS Gopher Service Properties dialog. The stateless nature of Gopher means the Connection Timeout setting will seldom be used. Since Gopher closes connections immediately after servicing each client request, connections should never remain open more than a few seconds. Sixty seconds is probably a better value than the default 900. The transient nature of Gopher sessions also makes reaching the default limit of 1,000 simultaneous connections very unlikely. If excessive Gopher activity ever becomes a problem, however, you can respond by decreasing this value.

The fields in the Service Administrator frame support features of Gopher+ whereby clients can obtain the name and E-Mail address of the person responsible for any menu item. Values you enter here serve as the default for all menu items on the given server.

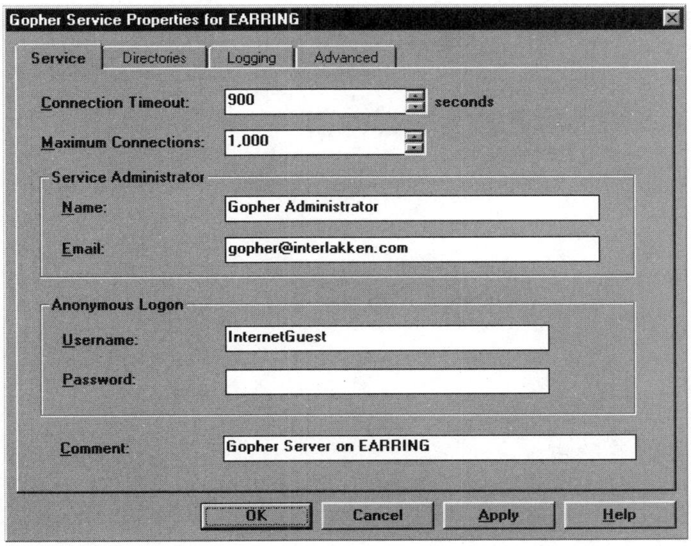

Figure 11.11   IIS Gopher Service Dialog

The Anonymous Logon Username and Password values specify the account IIS Gopher will use in accessing files. The account you specify here will need permission to access all Gopher resources users may request.

The Comment line is for display in the main Internet Server Manager window.

11.3.2 IIS Directories Configuration for Gopher

Normally, Gopher users can only access files and directories on the local system that reside within the Gopher home directory. If users are to access files on any other servers, those servers need to run their own Gopher service. Gopher virtual directories provide a way around these restrictions.

To configure a Gopher virtual directory, click on the Directories tab of the IIS Gopher Service Properties dialog. A display like that of Figure 11.12 will result.

In this display, h:\gopher is the Gopher home directory on the local server. Any files and subdirectories in the h:\pubftp local directory will appear to Gopher users as if they actually resided in a directory named "ftp" in the Gopher home directory. Files at the network location \\earring\wavfiles\ will appear to Gopher users as if they were located in a directory named "wav" in the Gopher home directory. (This example is a bit trivial because files in \\earring\wavfiles\ are actually local. In practice, networked virtual directories would be on remote machines.)

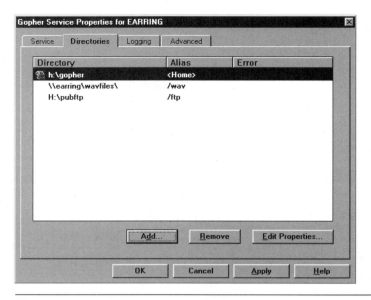

Figure 11.12 IIS Gopher Directories Dialog

The three command buttons at the bottom of the dialog support adding, removing, and editing virtual directory definitions. Figure 11.13 illustrates the dialog for adding or editing these entries. The Directory text box contains the actual local or network location you're mapping. Choose the "HomeDirectory" option to make the Directory text box location the Gopher home, or choose "Virtual Directory" to define that location as a virtual directory. In the latter case, you must also specify a virtual directory alias, which is the directory name Gopher clients and selectors will use.

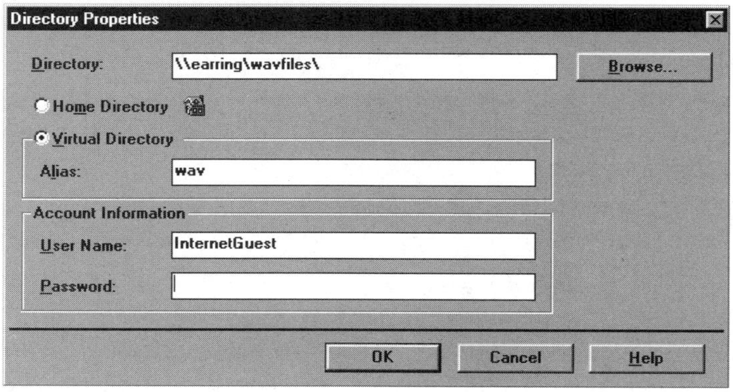

Figure 11.13 IIS Gopher Directory Properties Dialog

The Account Information frame will become accessible whenever the Directory text box contains a UNC file name. In this case, you must provide the user name and password the Gopher server will use in accessing the networked information.

Note that virtual directories using UNC file names allow a Windows NT server to provide Gopher access to files residing on other machines not running their own Gopher service. Furthermore, such other machines can be running any operating system that supports UNC access.

11.3.3 IIS Logging and Advanced Configuration for Gopher

These two dialogs are essentially identical in function and appearance to those for the IIS FTP service. If you have questions about their operation, review Sections 10.3.4 and 10.3.5.

11.3.4 IIS Gopher Alias Configuration

Creating alias files for the IIS Gopher server is both easier and harder than under the EMWAC software. It's easier because Microsoft supplies a utility to do the job, but harder because the utility runs on the command line. The command syntax is

```
gdsset [-crl]
    -G debuGflags
    -g<GopherItemType>
    -f <FriendlyName>
    -s<Selector>
    -h<HostName>
    -p<PortNumber>
    -D<Directory>
    -d
    <filename>
    -a <AdminName>
    -e <AdminEmail>
```

The first parameter ("-c," "-r," or "-l") is a command code that indicates whether to create new tag information, read an existing tag, or create a Gopher link. "-c" is the default. The remaining arguments are optional, prohibited, or required depending on the command code. Table 11.3 summarizes this information.

Table 11.3 GDSSET Command Arguments (for IIS Gopher)

Argument	Description
-c	Command code to change existing tag information. The default is to create new tag information.
-r	Command code to read tag information and display it on the console.
-G	Specifies debug flags.
-g\<Type\>	Specifies the Gopher object type (per Table 11.1). This argument is invalid with the -r command code.
-f\<FriendlyName\>	Defines a friendly menu name for an object. This is invalid with the -r command code.
-D\<DirName\>	The directory where the given file resides.
-d	Indicates that the given file name refers to a directory.
\<FileName\>	The file to which this tag applies.
-l	Command code to build a Gopher link. This is invalid with the -r command code.
-s\<Selector\>	Specifies the selector for a link. This is only valid in combination with the -l command code.
-h\<HostName\>	Specifies the DNS computer name for a link. This is only valid in combination with the -l command code.
-p\<PortNumber\>	Specifies the port number for a link. This is only valid in combination with the -l command code.
-a \<AdminName\>	Optional. Specifies the administrator name for an item.
-e \<AdminEmail\>	Optional. Specifies the administrator E-Mail address for an item.

Internet Information Server setup installs the gdsset program in the \inetsrv \server directory. To make using gdsset more convenient, you may wish to move or copy gdsset.exe and gdspace.dll to a directory (such as \<systemroot\>\system32) that is on the system path.

11.3.4.1 Defining Menu Names for Local Files The following is a typical gdsset command to supply tag information for a local file:

```
gdsset -c -g0 -f "Read Me documentation file" readme.txt
```

This creates a tag stating that the readme.txt file not only is plain text—Gopher type 0—but also should appear as "Read Me documentation file" on the Gopher menu seen by the user. If you want the user to know the actual file name, you must include it in the friendly text.

To indicate a specific administrator name and E-Mail address for readme.txt, supply the following additional parameters:

```
-a "J. T. Kirk" -e captain@enterprise.mil
```

11.3.4.2 Defining Menu Names for Local Directories To supply a friendly menu name for a directory, you must add the "-d" switch to inform gdsset you are supplying information for a directory rather than a file; in addition, you must specify Gopher type 1 (directory):

```
gdsset -c -g1 -f "ZIP Archive Files" -d ZipFiles
```

11.3.4.3 Defining Links to Other Gopher Servers To define a menu item that links to a Gopher menu on another computer, use a gdsset command of the following form:

```
gdsset -l -gn -f "Friendly Name" -s/dirname -hhostname -p70 -dlinkname
```

- ■ -l indicates this command will create a new link.
- ■ -gn supplies a Gopher type code as listed in Table 11.1. The default is 9 (binary).
- ■ -f supplies friendly text that will appear in the Gopher menu.
- ■ -s/dirname specifies the directory path relative to the Gopher home directory on the remote system.
- ■ -hhostname names the computer where the linked data resides.
- ■ -p70 supplies the port number required for connecting to the remote computer. Port 70 is the default.
- ■ -dlinkname specifies the name of the link file. This will actually be a directory.

11.3.4.4 Viewing Existing Gopher Tag Information To view existing tag information, use the "-r" command code as shown next (the second command displays tag information for all files in the current directory):

```
gdsset -r readme.txt
for %i in (*.*) do gdsset -r %i
```

11.3.5 IIS Gopher Type Assignments

As of this writing, Microsoft had not revealed the location of IIS Gopher tag information, nor had they exposed the table that translates file name extensions to Gopher types when no tag is present.

On FAT partitions, tag information seems to reside in a hidden file named *filename*.gtg, where *filename* is the original file name (including extension). No such files appear on NTFS partitions, however. This gives rise to suspicion that NTFS stores Gopher tags in extended attributes.

Translation of file name extensions to Gopher type may use the table shown in Figure 11.14. Entries in this location appear to contain MIME type, file name extension, icon name, and Gopher type code.

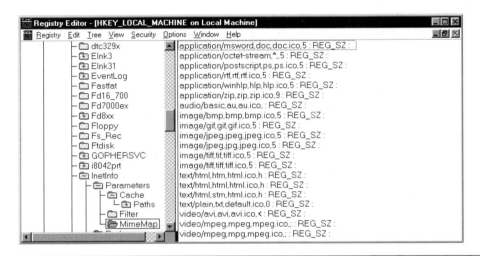

Figure 11.14 HKEY_LOCAL_MACHINE\SYSTEM\CurrentControlSet\Services\InetInfo \Parameters\MimeMap

## CHAPTER 12

Installing and Configuring POP/SMTP Mail Service

Electronic Mail was one of the first Internet applications and remains among the most popular. E-Mail closely follows the universally known paradigm of paper mail; it's fast; it's easy; it avoids time-consuming telephone tag. Acceptance of E-Mail has become so universal that for a large or medium enterprise not to have it is a sign of backwardness.

The primary E-Mail protocol of the Internet is the Simple Mail Transport Protocol (SMTP). UNIX systems in general and the Internet in particular have used SMTP as their primary mail transport for years, resulting in great maturity, stability, and acceptance. Given corporate acceptance of the Internet and the fragility of shared-file E-Mail systems such as Microsoft Mail and cc:Mail, it's surprising that more enterprises haven't switched to SMTP ("Internet-style") mail systems for internal users as well.

12.1 Operating Concepts and Standards

12.1.1 SMTP Message Forwarding

The fundamental E-Mail transaction is the message. Two kinds of software process these messages:

1. A User Agent (UA) is any program that interactively sends and receives messages. Common UAs include Air Mail, Eudora Light,[1] Pegasus, and Z-Mail.

2. A Message Transfer Agent (MTA) is any software that supports temporary storing and forwarding of messages. The most common MTA for SMTP

---

[1]Eudora Light is a trademark of QUALCOMM Incorporated.

is the UNIX sendmail program. Straight ports of sendmail are now available for Windows NT, as are other programs that support the same standards but provide vastly more intuitive interfaces for the administrator.

When someone sends a message to another user on the same machine, the MTA simply appends the message to the recipient's "in-box." If the recipient's in-box isn't on the same computer as the sender's MTA, the sender's MTA opens a connection to another MTA and forwards the message. Each MTA in the chain must provide temporary storage for messages it has received but not yet delivered. The basic architecture of E-Mail is therefore "store and forward." Note that each MTA must have rules prescribing where to send a given message.

When a site has several mail servers, it's common to designate one of them as a single gateway to the Internet. Internal mail servers then send all Internet mail to the gateway machine for forwarding to the prescribed destination. Of course, that destination may also be a gateway—one that routes messages to several other machines at its site. A message may pass through any number of servers before reaching the recipient's computer and getting appended to the recipient's in-box.

An SMTP address consists of two parts separated by an "@," such as the address president@whitehouse.gov. The portion after the "@" (whitehouse.gov) is the *domain part* and points to the computer that should receive the message. The portion before the "@" is the *local part* and identifies the specific recipient.

MTAs usually have rules for transforming both parts of any address they process. The term for this is *aliasing*. Normally, MTAs first apply domain part aliases and then apply local part aliases only if the domain part points to the local machine. Suppose someone addressed a message to postmaster@hq and sent it to branch.gov:

■ If branch.gov's alias for hq is central.gov, branch.gov wouldn't apply local aliases.

■ If branch.gov's alias for hq is branch.gov, local aliases would then apply.

The simplest local aliases are those that substitute one local user for another. For example, branch.gov might translate postmaster@branch.gov to bfranklin@branch.gov if bfranklin is branch.gov's current E-Mail administrator.

Local part aliases can also supply a new domain part, causing delivery of mail to another computer. For example, branch.gov might alias postmaster@branch.gov to bfranklin@central.gov. At central.gov, another alias could forward bfranklin@central.gov to postmaster@email.usps.gov. As Figure 12.1 illustrates, though, there's more to the name email.usps.gov than might first appear.

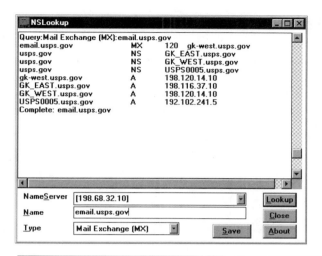

Figure 12.1 NSLOOKUP Results for email.usps.gov

Recall from Chapter 9 that DNS record type A indicates an address and type MX indicates a mail exchanger. E-Mail programs look for an MX record first, so looking up the domain part "email.usps.gov" returns the host name GK_WEST.usps.gov. A subsequent address lookup translates GK_WEST.usps.gov to the IP address 198.120.14.10; this is where the MTA will actually send the message.

An interesting problem (interesting, that is, if you like watching disasters) occurs if GK_WEST.usps.gov aliases postmaster back to postmaster@branch.gov. This is a *circular definition*. To prevent the resulting loops from continuing end-lessly, SMTP servers discard messages that have bounced between servers beyond a certain limit, such as 17 times.

Figure 12.2 illustrates NSLOOKUP results for the name "microsoft.com." At the time of this inquiry, Microsoft was advertising three mail servers on the Internet: tide03.microsoft.com, tide10.microsoft.com, and netmail.microsoft.com. Machines sending mail to microsoft.com sequentially tried connecting to each of these MTAs until a connection succeeded. The hosts tide03 and tide10 have a lower preference number (10) than netmail (20), so the sending computer would try tide03 and tide10 first.

Domain part rules can also instruct an MTA to

- Replace all occurrences of one domain with another.

- Forward all mail addressed to a particular domain to a specific host instead (not necessarily in that domain).

- Forward all nonlocal mail to a specific host.

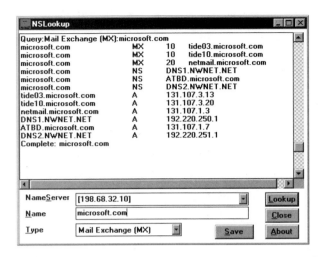

Figure 12.2 NSLOOKUP Results for microsoft.com

Figure 12.3 illustrates a typical situation involving Internet mail and gateway MTAs. Suppose a user at d.tla.org sends a message to someone at z.sch.edu. The sender would address the message to someone@sch.edu and send it to b.tla.org, the sender's normal mail server. The tla.org mail administrator has configured b.tla.org to send all nonlocal mail to a.tla.org, tla's Internet mail gateway. Upon receiving the message, a.tla.org performs a DNS lookup on sch.edu and discovers, based on MX records, that u.sch.edu is sch.edu's preferred mail server.

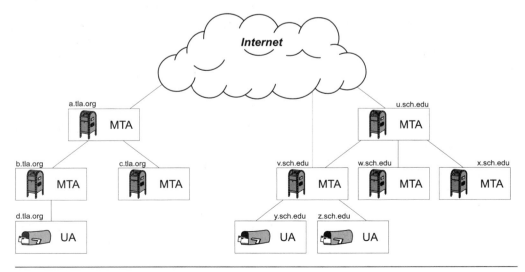

Figure 12.3 SMTP Message Delivery Using Gateway MTAs

At the next opportunity, a.tla.org will open a connection to u.sch.edu and transmit the message. An alias table on u.sch.edu will translate "someone" to "someone@v.sch.edu," causing u.sch.edu to forward the message. There will be no further aliasing on v.sch.edu, so that machine will append the message to someone's mailbox.

The dotted line at v.sch.edu indicates a possible second gateway connection to the Internet. If this connection were in place, the administrator of the authoritative DNS server for sch.edu could define a second MX record for sch.edu—one that identified v.sch.edu with a greater preference number than u.sch.edu. Since other systems try lower preference numbers first, u.sch.edu would still handle most incoming mail, but v.sch.edu would continue providing service if u.sch.edu stopped responding. Note that, in this case, v.sch.edu would need either of the following:

1. An alias table redirecting mail for users on w.sch.edu and x.sch.edu to those machines.

2. A rule stating that all messages not local to v.sch.edu should be forwarded to u.sch.edu.

Simple Mail Transport Protocol sessions are, as you might expect, simple. The following listing illustrates a basic session, opened with the Windows 95 Telnet program on port 25 (boldface indicates text entered via the keyboard). All SMTP transfers work by automating the same essential keystrokes:

```
220 usr5.primenet.com ESMTP Sendmail 8.7.1/8.7.1; Sat, 18 Nov 1995
   14:02:30 -0700 (MST)
HELO usr5.primenet.com
250 usr5.primenet.com Hello ip106.phx.primenet.com [198.68.46.106],
   pleased to meet you
MAIL FROM: <buyensj@primenet.com>
250 <buyensj@primenet.com>... Sender ok
RCPT TO: <buyensj@primenet.com>
250 Recipient ok
DATA
354 Enter mail, end with "." on a line by itself
Most aspects of life are grim.


The only ray of hope lies in widening acceptance
```

```
of Electronic Mail.
.
250 OAA07043 Message accepted for delivery
QUIT
221 usr5.primenet.com closing connection
```

12.1.2 POP (Post Office Protocol)

SMTP is a "push" protocol; when a UA or an MTA has something to send, it connects to the receiving system or another MTA one step closer to the receiving system. This presumes the receiving system is always ready to receive. If it isn't, the sending system must keep retrying. This quickly becomes impractical when users dial in occasionally or turn off their PCs overnight; the MTA spends most of its resources attempting connections that seldom succeed.

The Post Office Protocol (POP) solves this problem by providing a "pull" protocol for mail delivery. POP clients have an in-box on the MTA, but, instead of reading new messages interactively, POP users download them to their own computer. POP UAs download new mail based on user commands or a timed interval, but, in either event, the UA is obviously running at the time of the download.

Two versions of POP are in common use: POP2 and POP3. They aren't compatible, so you must match your POP client to what your MTA can support. POP2 operates on port 109 and POP3 on port 110, so, in theory, a single MTA can support both protocols simultaneously.

POP clients can either delete downloaded messages from the MTA or allow them to remain on the MTA. Leaving mail on the server generally incurs extra charges, but it's very convenient for the person who uses two or more computers. If only one computer deletes messages from the server, that computer will contain a complete record of all messages received.

12.1.3 SMTP Message Structure

An SMTP message consists of two parts: a mail envelope and mail contents. The contents portion also consists of two parts: the header and the body. Finally, the body may include several parts: separate components of a single message. Figure 12.4 illustrates these divisions.

Neither the sender nor the recipient sees the envelope; this information is for the MTA. Sender and recipient do, however, see the header. Header lines convey the sender's address, all recipient addresses, the subject line, and other identifiers.

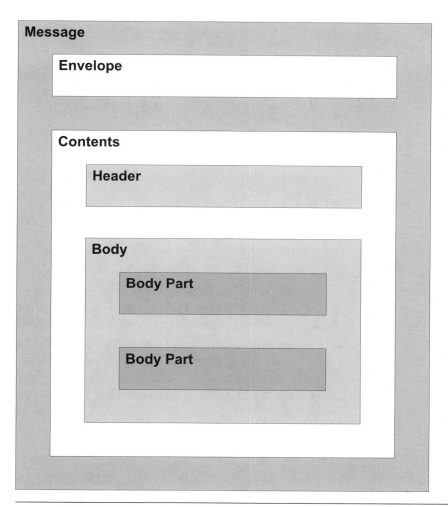

Figure 12.4 SMTP Message Components

The first blank line in the contents indicates the division between header and body. The body contains whatever the sender specified. A delimiter string specified in the header separates body parts.

Receiving the simple, hand-typed message from the example in the previous section results in the text shown in the following listing. Most of the content is familiar, but some header lines added by the MTA also appear. Note particularly that the "Received:" and "Message-Id:" lines are new. Also, the MTA supplied the sender's full name on the "From:" line (this wasn't entered on the "MAIL FROM:" line shown in the preceding listing):

```
From ???@??? Sat Nov 18 14:09:14 1995
>From buyensj  Sat Nov 18 14:04:34 1995
Received: from usr5.primenet.com (ip106.phx.primenet.com [198.68.46.106])
    by usr5.primenet.com (8.7.1/8.7.1) with SMTP id OAA07043 for
    ,H__<buyensj@primenet.com>; Sat, 18 Nov 1995 14:03:09 -0700 (MST)
Date: Sat, 18 Nov 1995 14:03:09 -0700 (MST)
From: Jim Buyens <buyensj@primenet.com>
Message-Id: <199511182103.OAA07043@usr5.primenet.com>


Most aspects of life are grim.


The only ray of hope lies in widening acceptance
of Electronic Mail.
```

Two factors make transferring attached files difficult. First, there's no standard separation of body parts; the entire header and body arrive as a single, arbitrary stream of characters. Second, many SMTP servers can only handle 7-bit ASCII characters. This isn't a problem if you're transmitting simple text, but it's a big problem if you want to mail binary files with formats like zip, exe, and wav.

The Multipurpose Internet Mail Extensions (MIME) specification separates body parts and indicates their file types. MIME works like this:

- A header line denoted "MIME-Version" specifies what version of MIME is in effect. This is usually "1.0."
- The following header line indicates the encoding scheme for the first body part ("7bit" means the data consists of ASCII characters 32 through 127 plus control characters such as tab, carriage return, and line feed):

```
Content-Transfer-Encoding: 7bit
```

- Another header field called "Content-Type" specifies the format of the message body. Simple text messages usually have

```
Content-Type: text/plain; charset=us-ascii
```

UAs that handle 8-bit characters may specify a "Content-Transfer-Encoding" of "8bit" and a "charset=iso-8859-1." However, not all UAs and MTAs can handle this.

■ Messages containing several body parts have a "Content-Type" line such as the following:

```
Content-Type: multipart/mixed; boundary="=================_809327416==_"
```

Note the change from "text/plain" to "multipart/mixed" and specification of a boundary string. Any line containing the specified boundary line will indicate the beginning of a new body part.

■ Attachments begin with a series of lines like this:

```
=================_809327416==_
Content-Type: application/octet-stream; name="JBCH10.ZIP";
 x-mac-type="42494E41"; x-mac-creator="6D646F73"
Content-Transfer-Encoding: base64
Content-Disposition: attachment; filename="JBCH10.ZIP"
```

Line 1 matches the boundary string and thus indicates the beginning of a new body part. Line 2 states the body part has a MIME type of "application/octet-stream" and the name JBCH10.ZIP. Line 3 continues line 2 and indicates Macintosh type and creator "BINA" and "mdos," respectively. (Note that hex 42=B, hex 49=I, hex 4E=N, and so on.) Line 4 indicates that base64 encoding is in effect (see the sidebar for an explanation of this technique). Line 5 indicates that the body part is an attachment having file name JBCH10.ZIP.

Several other encoding schemes are in common use. Binhex encoding is popular in the Macintosh arena, and UUencode has a long history in UNIX (see the sidebar titled "UUencode Encoding" for an explanation). It's the sender's responsibility to encode attachments using a scheme the recipient can decode. Fortunately, most UAs support several types.

MIME types denote file formats in a way that's independent of any operating system. File name extensions can't do this because some operating systems don't use them, and those that do have extensions of different length. The MIME type allows each O/S to assign a suitable file name extension, type and creator code, or other designation. Knowing a file's MIME type also permits launching an appropriate processing program if the user so desires. Table 12.1 lists some common MIME types; however, there seems to be no limit to the number of types spontaneously appearing.

Base64 Encoding

Base64 is a technique that translates arbitrary binary files to plain text characters that can pass through any mail system. It works by

- Regrouping the 24 bits from each three input bytes into four 6-bit characters.
- Prefixing each 6-bit character with the binary value "01."
- Outputting four ASCII characters in the decimal range 64 through 127.

The following diagram illustrates this process:

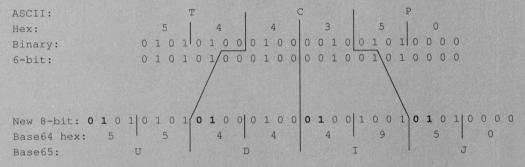

Note that the total amount of transmitted data increases by 1/3.

UUencode Encoding

The UUencode format consists of a header line, a number of body lines, and a trailer line. The decode program will ignore any lines preceding the header or following the trailer.

The header line consists of the word "begin," a space, a mode (in octal), another space, and the name of the remote file.

Body lines consist of a length code, encoded characters, and a carriage return. The length code is a single printing character derived by adding 32 (the value of an ASCII space) to the number of unencoded characters the line represents. The encoded characters consist of the original data taken 6 bits at a time and then also incremented by 32. The maximum length of a body line is 62 characters: the length code, 60 encoded characters, and a carriage return. The 60 encoded characters represent 45 unencoded characters, so the length code is "M" (32 plus 45). Unless the original file size was a multiple of 45, the last encoded line will be shorter than 62 characters. Unless the original file size was a multiple of 3, the last four encoded characters will contain some garbage characters the decode program discards based on the length code. A line consisting of one space (that is, with a length code indicating zero unencoded characters) terminates the body.

The trailer line consists of the word "end" on a line by itself.

Table 12.1 Common MIME Attachment Types

Content Type	Subtype	Description
text	/plain	Ordinary text.
	/html	HyperText Markup Language text.
application	/octet-stream	Arbitrary binary data.
	/mac-binhex40	Compressed Macintosh files.
	/postscript	PostScript and Encapsulated PostScript (EPS) files.
	/x-zip-compressed	Compressed ZIP files.
audio	/basic	Pulse Code Modulation (PCM) sound files.
	/x-wav	Microsoft sound files (wav files).
image	/gif	CompuServe Graphic Interchange Format.
	/jpeg	Joint Photographic Experts Group images.
	/tiff	Tagged Image File Format files.
	/x-MS-bmp	Microsoft bitmaps (bmp files).
video	/mpeg	Motion Picture Experts Group video.
	/x-msvideo	Microsoft video (avi files).
	/quicktime	Apple Quicktime movies.
multipart	/mixed	Body parts may be various types.
	/alternative	Body parts contain the same data in different formats.
	/parallel	Separate body parts should be viewed simultaneously.
	/digest	Each body part is a message.
message	/rfc822	Body is a complete RFC 822 message.
	/partial	Body is one part of data broken into several messages.
	/external-body	Body is a pointer to data that exists elsewhere (such as an FTP archive).

12.2 POP/SMTP Alternatives

12.2.1 Internet Message Access Protocol

IMAP is an emerging superset of POP. IMAP supports three modes of operation:

1. **Offline.** The UA downloads messages from the server, which then deletes them. All further handling occurs on the client machine.

2. **Online.** The UA remotely manipulates messages on the mail server and leaves them there. Several users can update a shared mail folder at the same time or at different times.

3. **Disconnected.** The UA connects to the MTA, makes cached copies of selected messages, and then disconnects. Later, the UA reconnects and synchronizes the cache with the server. The primary copy of each message remains on the server.

POP clients, by contrast, support offline mode only. Offline mode can't support shared folders because the server deletes each message after the first user reads it. IMAP users can alternate freely between online and disconnected mode because, with these, the primary version of any messages remains in the server.

The concept of several people using one folder may seem confusing at first—almost a throwback to the days of party lines. Shared folders are very useful, though, for cases where any one of several people could work on incoming requests or need access to message history.

At the time of this writing, only a few IMAP clients were available for Windows, and no IMAP servers. This is likely to change over time, however, as IMAP catches on. An excellent reference for IMAP information is available at http://andrew2.andrew.cmu.edu/cyrus/email/standards-IMAP.html.

12.2.2 Gateways from Other Systems

Many organizations, when they start considering use of the Internet for external mail, already have commitments to existing, internal E-Mail systems. An E-Mail gateway can be an attractive choice in such situations.

The gateway is essentially a single MTA for two or more incompatible mail systems. If the gateway is from cc:Mail to SMTP, it's capable not only of receiving SMTP messages and requeuing them as cc:Mail but also of receiving cc:Mail messages and resending them as SMTP.

SMTP is such a well-known, simple, and popular protocol that gateways exist for almost every other E-Mail system in existence. Discussion of particular gateways is beyond the scope of this book, but the issues are almost always the same: address translation and directory maintenance.

Each mail system tends to have its own addressing scheme. At best, this means addresses that are simple and natural on one system require complex representation on the other. At worst, the address formats are incompatible, and an administrator must maintain address translation directories.

Administration for internal, non-SMTP users is usually straightforward, using features of the existing mail system. The gateway will generally have its own domain part SMTP address, and the local part of the SMTP address will generally be the user's name on the existing mail system. A handy feature is the ability to write out alias lists an SMTP system can use to redirect appropriate mail to the gateway system.

If the non-SMTP mail system can't accommodate an SMTP address, exchange of Internet mail may be impossible unless an administrator establishes an internal account for each desired Internet user. Receiving mail from unregistered outside users may otherwise be impossible because, without translation of the "From:" line, the recipient wouldn't know who sent the message and certainly wouldn't be able to answer it. If you have an internal mail system this inflexible, you may wish to consider running parallel mail systems instead of installing a gateway.

12.2.3 X.400

X.400 is the Open System Interconnection (OSI) approach to Electronic Mail. It's very reliable and full-featured, and it ties together commercial E-Mail systems like AT&T Mail, MCI Mail, SprintMail, and others. X.400 is much less likely than SMTP to drop a message without notification.

Two factors have combined to make X.400 much less popular than SMTP. First, X.400 addresses are long and complex. For example, the author once had the following X.400 address:

```
(C:USA,ADMD:TELEMAIL,PRMD:AGCS.PHO.VAX,OU:981,SN:BUYENSJ,FN:JIM)
```

Given a choice between addresses such as the preceding and Internet addresses like billg@microsoft.com, most people choose the Internet form.

The second factor inhibiting the growth of X.400 has been its association with X.25. The Internet and TCP/IP have grown to provide far more connectivity than X.25 networks. Of course, commercial E-Mail providers use X.25 networks they constructed long ago and wish to preserve.

RFC 1506, available at ftp://ds.internic.net/rfc/rfc1506.txt, discusses gateway and address translation issues involving X.400 and Internet mail.

12.3 Sample Installation

The sample installation for this chapter uses NTMail 3.0 from Internet Shopper Ltd., London, England, as the MTA. The UA is PC Eudora Light[2] 1.5.2 from QUALCOMM, San Diego, California. As always, choosing these products as examples is neither an endorsement nor a promise of suitability. NTMail has an attractive GUI configuration interface, and Eudora Light is simply a program the author started using long ago.

---

[2]Eudora Light is unsupported, copyrighted freeware. The name Eurdora Light is a trademark of QUALCOMM Incorporated, which also sells a fully supported commercial version.

12.3.1 SMTP Software Installation

You can install NTMail in either of two ways:

1. Download the current ZIP file from http://www.net-shopper.co.uk. Unzip it to a temporary directory, and change to that directory.

2. Change to the \NTMAIL directory on the CD that accompanies this book. You'll also need a validation key from http://www.net-shopper.co.uk to unlock the software. Once you have the software and key, run SETUP.EXE. The NTMail Setup dialog shown in Figure 12.5 will result.

Enter the validation key you obtained from the www.net-shopper.co.uk Web site and confirm the target directory and domain name. After entering the validation key, you can verify it by clicking the Check button. Choose a target drive with an NTFS file system, but don't choose the Windows NT system drive. The target directory tree will contain the user mailboxes as well as the software, and you don't want users filling up the system drive with undelivered mail. When satisfied with your entries, click OK and keep clicking OK through the rest of the installation.

After setup completes, start Control Panel and double-click the new NTMail icon.[3] The dialog pictured in Figure 12.6 will result.

This dialog contains 15 index tabs that perform all common configuration tasks for NTMail. By default, it configures the local machine; to configure remote machines, click the Remote button and type the remote machine's name.

12.3.2 DNS Configuration

Internet mail and Domain Name Service are inexorably linked. Without DNS, the various clients and servers involved in delivering a message simply couldn't find one another.

The example here will use the fictional domain interlakken.com[4] configured with two nodes: EARRING and CHOKER. The SNMP MTA will run on EARRING, a Windows NT server; Eudora Light[5] will run on CHOKER, a Windows 95 node. The following DNS databases are adequate for this task:

---

[3]To readers in the United States, NTMail's icon will look more like a fire hydrant than a mailbox. One can only wonder what American mailboxes look like to Brits.

[4]Interlakken is a street near the author's home.

[5]Eudora Light is a trademark of QUALCOMM Incorporated.

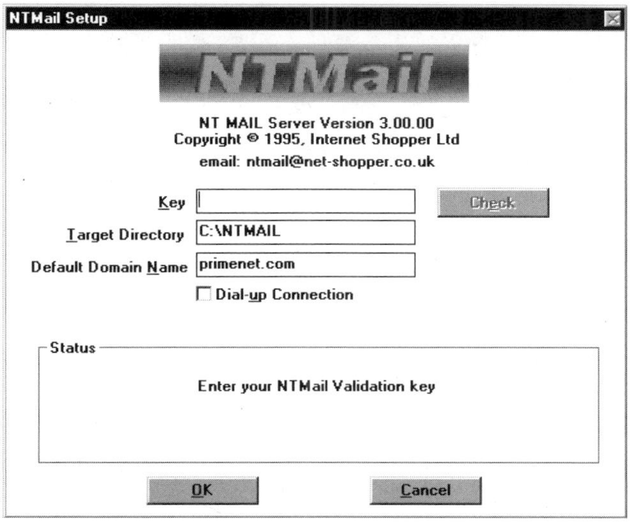

Figure 12.5 NTMail Setup Dialog

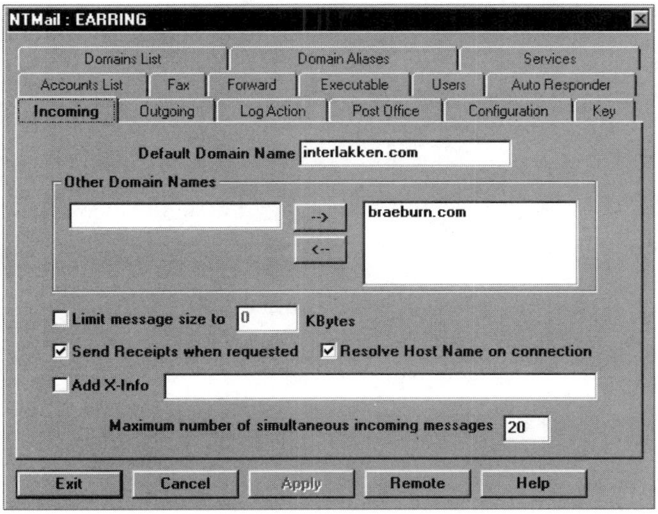

Figure 12.6 NTMail Control Panel Dialog

named.bt

```
directory /etc/interlak
; type       domain                    source file or host
;********************* primary servers ************************
```

```
primary        interlakken.com          interlak.db
primary        90.131.130.in-addr.arpa  reverse.db
;********************** secondary servers **********************
;secondary  interlakken.com          223.99.88.13  backup/interlak.db.bak
;secondary  90.131.130.in-addr.arpa  223.99.88.13  backup/reverse.db.bak
;********************** common entries **********************
primary        0.0.127.in-addr.arpa     local.db
cache          .                        cache.db
```

interlak.db
```
$ORIGIN interlakken.com.
@              IN      SOA  earring.interlakken.com. root.interlakken.com. (
                            1        ; serial
                            10800    ; refresh
                            3600     ; retry
                            604800   ; expire
                            86400 )  ; minimum
; name servers
                            IN       NS       earring.interlakken.com.
                            IN       MX 10    earring.interlakken.com.
; host addresses
localhost                   IN       A        127.0.0.1
earring                     IN       A        130.131.90.111
choker                      IN       A        130.131.90.67
```

reverse.db
```
90.131.130.in-addr.arpa. IN SOA earring.interlakken.com.
root.interlakken.com. (
                            1        ; serial
                            10800    ; refresh
                            3600     ; retry
                            604800   ; expire
                            86400 )  ; minimum
; name servers
                            IN       NS       earring.interlakken.com.
```

```
; addresses to names
111                            IN      PTR       earring.interlakken.com.
67                             IN      PTR       choker.interlakken.com.
```

The content of these files should be familiar; if not, refer back to Chapter 9. The nodes EARRING and CHOKER have IP addresses 130.131.90.111 and 130.131.90.67, respectively, and the database lists EARRING as a mail exchanger and name server.

Figure 12.7 illustrates NSLOOKUP results obtained from the databases just listed. Running such NSLOOKUP queries provides excellent diagnostic feedback.

Figures 12.8 and 12.9 display the DNS configurations required on earring and choker. Pinging each host name from each machine provides further diagnostic confirmation.

12.3.3 SMTP Software Configuration

Exhaustive discussion of each feature in NTMail is beyond the purpose of the book; consult the on-line product documentation for such information. However, to complete the example, the following two subsections first discuss settings that affect mail routing and then examine user account setup.

12.3.3.1 Environmental and Routing Settings Double-clicking the NTMail Control Panel applet produces the display shown previously in Figure 12.6. Note

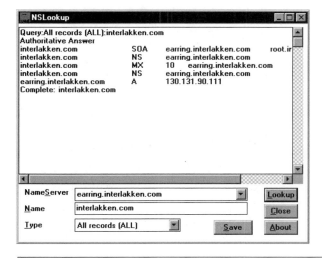

Figure 12.7 NSLOOKUP Query Results—interlakken.com

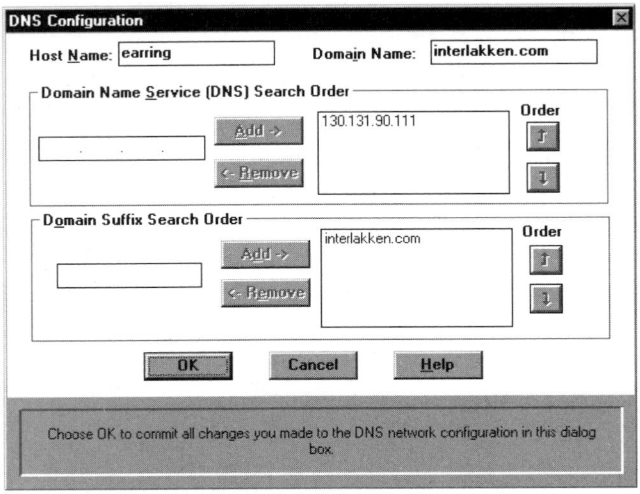

Figure 12.8 Windows NT TCP/IP Configuration—DNS Configuration (on EARRING)

that the Incoming tab is current; clicking on another tab will bring up the corresponding dialog page in typical Windows fashion.

The Default Domain Name field contains the name NTMail will append to any mail address that arrives without a domain part. This is also the only domain that NTMail will accept for delivery. If you want NTMail to accept incoming mail for other domains, you must add them to the Other Domain Names list. Wildcard characters support other-domain pattern matching. If the Add X-Info field isn't blank, NTMail will add the specified text to the header of each message it handles. The option box "Resolve Host Name on connection," if ON, causes NTMail to perform a reverse DNS lookup on incoming IP addresses, which simply makes headers easier to read.

Figure 12.10 illustrates NTMail's Outgoing tab. The Remote Mail Server frame specifies which MTAs NTMail will contact when delivering nonlocal mail. An asterisk entry indicates that NTMail should send mail directly to the machine specified by an addressee's domain part. If there are multiple entries, NTMail will try them in order until one succeeds. If NTMail runs on an internal network and delivers internal mail through a gateway machine, this frame is the place to specify the name of that gateway. Another use pertains to dial-up; in this case, you might want NTMail to try direct delivery to the addressed host first but, if that fails, to forward the message to your provider's MTA. The provider's MTA can continue retrying after the dial-up connection ends.

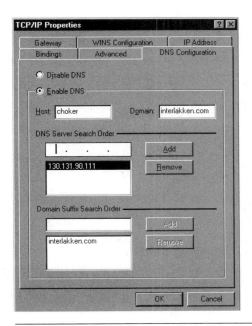

Figure 12.9 Windows 95 TCP/IP Properties—DNS Configuration (on CHOKER)

The lower half of the Outgoing dialog controls how often NTMail will try to deliver mail. The options to send outgoing mail immediately or every few minutes are more appropriate in a "direct connect" situation than for dial-up. For

Figure 12.10 NTMail Control Panel—Outgoing Tab

Running a Dial-Out E-Mail Gateway

If your MTA connects to the Internet via a dial-out or other intermittent connection, you probably shouldn't use immediate or timed delivery. Instead, periodically invoke a batch file such as the following:

```
@H:
@cd \ntmail
@rasdial "Provider Name" >> mail.log
@MAIL -k >> mail.log
@MAIL -w >> mail.log
@rasdial "Provider Name" /disconnect >> mail.log
@echo ─────────────────────────────────────────── >> mail.log
```

The "rasdial" command comes with Windows NT Remote Access Server. The two rasdial commands tell RAS to dial and disconnect using the "Provider Name" phone book entry. The "MAIL -k" command "kicks" NTMail; that is, it tells NTMail to send whatever mail is currently pending. The "MAIL -w" command pauses until NTMail is idle.

You can use a series of Windows NT "at" commands to run this batch file on a scheduled basis. The more often it runs, the more timely e-mail will get delivered. However, runs must be spaced far enough apart that only one at a time is running.

Assuming the batch file has the name getmail.cmd, a typical "at" command might be

```
at 06:00 /every:M,T,W,Th,F,S,Su "cmd /c h:\ntmail\getmail.cmd"
```

You would need one of these commands for each time of day you want NTMail to connect and exchange mail. The "winat" program Microsoft provides as part of the Windows NT Resource Kit accomplishes the same thing more attractively, as Figure 12.11 illustrates. Either way, remember to use the Control Panel Services applet to configure the Schedule service for automatic start-up at boot time.

dial-up, you should probably uncheck both options and consult the sidebar titled "Running a Dial-Out E-Mail Gateway."

The contents of the Configuration tab appear in Figure 12.12. This is a catch-all dialog that addresses several areas. You should configure the Time Zone fields to reflect the time used on the server's date-and-time clock. The Password fields, if activated, require entry of a password when getting statistics or starting the Control Panel applet, respectively.

If NTMail receives a message for a user that doesn't exist, it can take one of three actions:

1. It can bounce the mail back to the sender.
2. It can send all such mail to a single account.

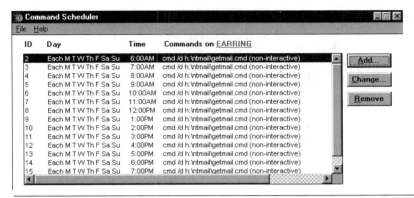

Figure 12.11 Windows NT Resource Kit Command Scheduler Used for RAS Dial-Out

3. It can redirect the mail to another MTA. This might be useful if there are several MTAs in one domain and another MTA might recognize the recipient.

The Domains List tab, shown in Figure 12.13, displays domain aliases currently in effect. NTMail will check outgoing addresses for domain parts listed on the left and, if it finds a match, replace the domain part with the corresponding alias. This can be useful to

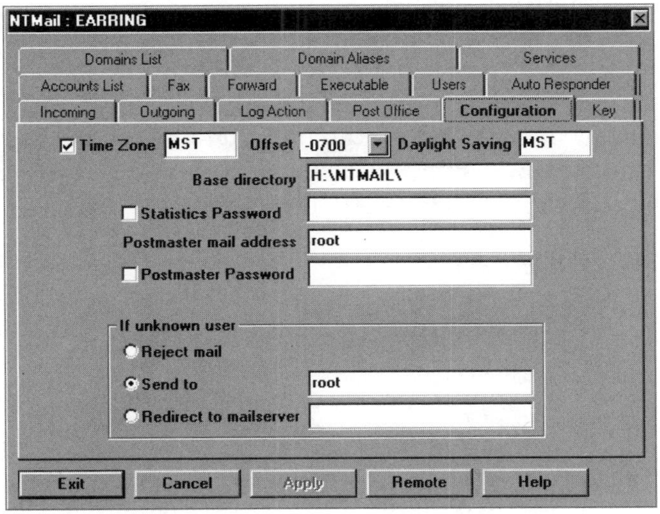

Figure 12.12 NTMail Control Panel—Configuration Tab

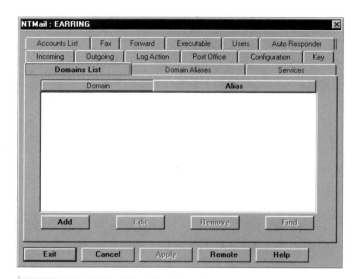

Figure 12.13 NTMail Control Panel—Domains List Tab

- Provide a shorthand name for long or frequently mistyped domain names.

- Specify a local gateway for a standard service. If you have internal gateways to certain other domains or sites, you can use this feature to route mail specifically to those gateways.

- Have NTMail send messages to a specific host. This would override the destination domain's MX record.

Note that aliases must be host names you can ping and not domain or MX names. Also note that using the Add, Edit, and Remove buttons only updates the displayed list. To save the edited list, click the Apply button.

12.3.3.2 Setting Up User Accounts Figure 12.14 illustrates NTMail's Accounts List tab. Note that aliases appear in the first column; actual user IDs, in the third column. If a user has several aliases, the dialog will contain a line for each one. To sort on the user (or any other) column, click on its heading.

As shown in Table 12.2, six account types are possible. To add a user, click the Add button in the Accounts List tab or click the Users tab directly. Either way, the Users dialog shown in Figure 12.15 will result.

To add a user, type the desired account name in the Username box. Then click the Password option box if you want to assign a specific password. If the Password option box isn't checked, the user's Windows NT password will be their mail password as well. If you buy the unlimited version of NTMail, you can globally specify that every user in the Windows NT UADB will also be a mail user.

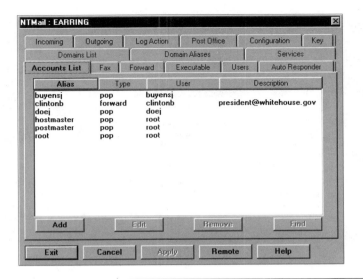

Figure 12.14 NT Mail Control Panel—Accounts List Tab

The lower part of the User tab's dialog specifies aliases for the account and the current holiday message (if any).

12.3.3.3 Preparing to Run NTMail If you're running "Simple TCP/IP Services," run the Control Panel Services applet and stop them. It's also a good idea to stop and restart the three services that make up NTMail: POP Server, POST Server, and SMTP Server. You can stop and start these services from Control Panel Services or from the NTMail Services tab. The Services tab can also update NTMail's services, causing them to reload their configurations.

As shown earlier in this chapter, you can Telnet to an SMTP MTA on port 25 and send typed messages. This is a useful test. A sample NTMail session appears next (keyboard text is again indicated by boldface):

Table 12.2 NT Mail User Account Types

Account Type	Configuration Tab	Description
pop	Users	An ordinary POP mail account user.
holiday	Users	A POP user that has a holiday (vacation) message in effect.
forward	Forward	An account for which NTMail will reject or redirect all incoming mail.
fax	FAX	An account whose incoming mail NTMail will fax to a fixed or sender-specified number. Security rules control which users can send to which FAX numbers.
info	Auto Responder	NTMail will respond with a fixed message and discard the original. (To save originals, use a holiday account.)
robot	Executable	NTMail will start a specified program whenever this account receives a message. NTMail will pipe the message contents into the program's standard input.

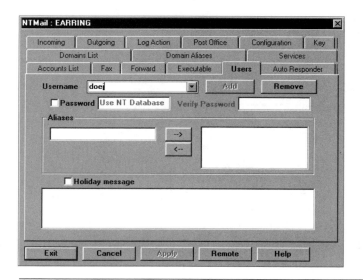

Figure 12.15 NTMail Control Panel—Users Tab

```
220-Evaluation version of Internet Shopper's NT Mail Server
220 earring.interlakken.com NT SMTP Server v3.00.06 ready at Tue, 21 Nov
    95 05:3
9:09 +0000 (GMT)
HELO choker.interlakken.com
250 earring.interlakken.com choker.interlakken.com
MAIL From: <buyensj@interlakken.com>
250 Ok.
RCPT To: <buyensj@interlakken.com>
250 Ok.
DATA
354 Start mail input, end with <CRLF>.<CRLF>.
This is a test of NTMail.
It's a Telnet session on port 25.
.
250 Requested mail action Ok.
QUIT
221 Goodbye choker.interlakken.com
```

If you can't Telnet to port 25, check again to see if "Simple TCP/IP Services" is running. If NTMail and Simple TCP/IP Services were ever running at the same time, configure Simple TCP/IP Services not to start automatically, verify that NTMail's services do start automatically, and then reboot the server.

If you seem to be having host name problems, retest using IP addresses. If this solves the problem, your DNS configuration probably needs correction. Remember to update the version numbers in the DNS database files, and don't forget to stop and restart the DNS service so that changes can take effect.

12.3.4 POP Client Configuration

The acid test, of course, is to send and receive mail using a known good UA—a version you know works with other MTAs. To eliminate as many variables as possible, this should be a program you know well and trust.

To configure Eudora Light,[6] start the program, pull down the Special menu, and select "Settings." The dialog shown in Figure 12.16 should result. This dialog displays different controls on the right depending on which icon you select at the left.

Under "Getting Started," specify the POP account as the user name followed by "@" and the full host name of the MTA. Note that the example shows the host name address buyensj@earring.interlakken.com, not the MX address buyensj@interlakken.com. "Real Name" is whatever you want to appear on mail you send.

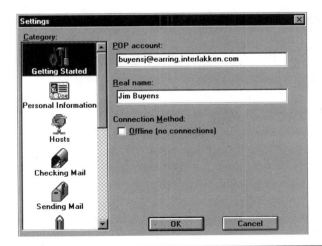

Figure 12.16 Eudora Light Settings Dialog—Getting Started

---

[6]Eudora Light is a trademark of QUALCOMM Incorporated.

Figure 12.17 shows the Settings dialog again, but with "Personal Information" selected. Note that the return address is the MX name buyensj@interlakken.com. The POP account should automatically appear as entered under "Getting Started."

Clicking the Hosts, Checking Mail, and Sending Mail icons will reveal additional instances of the POP account, return address, and SMTP server. All configured POP accounts and SMTP servers should contain the full host name, and only return addresses should contain the MX name.

Click the OK button to save settings and then pull down the Message menu and select "New Message...." Compose a message to an account you know exists, as shown in Figure 12.18, and then click the Send button.

If you don't get any obvious error messages while sending, pull down the File menu, select "Check Mail," and enter your mail password when prompted. This is the password you specified on the Users tab in NTMail Control Panel. Eudora Light should download the message you just sent yourself and display the results seen in Figure 12.19. If so, life is good. Congratulate yourself.

12.4 Testing and Problem Resolution

Most problems getting mail to work will probably involve the following areas:

- **Network failure.** Make sure you can ping the server from the client and vice versa. If no traffic is passing, mail traffic isn't passing.

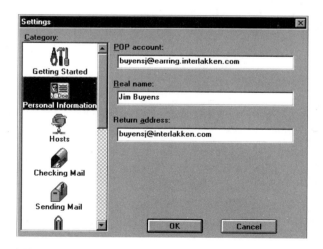

Figure 12.17 Eudora Light Settings Dialog—Personal Information

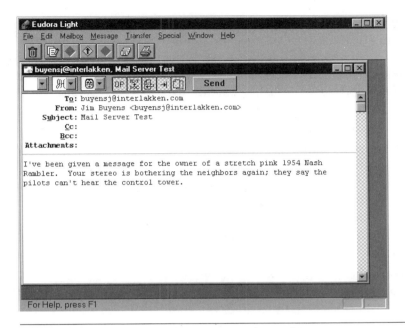

Figure 12.18 Creating a New Message in Eudora Light

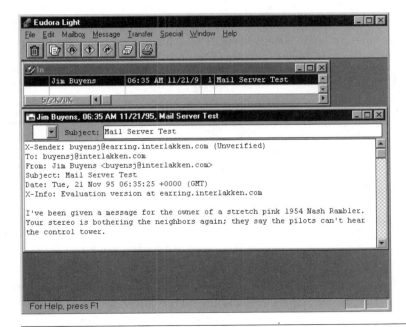

Figure 12.19 Receiving a Message in Eudora Light

- **Faulty DNS configuration.** Run NSLOOKUP and make sure the domain name and host name of your server are resolving properly. Review Figures 12.1, 12.2, and 12.7. Check the local DNS configuration on both the mail client and the server. If you've made DNS changes recently, make sure the mail client and server are using an authoritative DNS server. Outdated information may remain in the cache of other DNS servers. If you can ping IP addresses but not host names, the problem is likely in DNS.

- **TCP/IP port conflicts.** NTMail and Windows NT Simple TCP/IP Services both provide Finger service using the well-known port 79. You can't run two fingers at the same time, so you must either stop running Windows NT Simple TCP/IP Services or use NTMail's Post Office tab to disable the NTMail Finger server. In at least one case, correcting the port conflict wasn't enough to solve the problem; the server also required a reboot.

- **Incorrect client configuration.** Telnet to the server on port 25 and hand-enter a message as shown in Section 12.3.3.3. If this produces no errors, the problem is likely in the mail client. Carefully check usage and spelling of the mail server name, the domain name, and the mail user ID.

- **Incorrect server configuration.** Check spelling and usage of all gateways. Verify status and spelling of user accounts; reset passwords on accounts that aren't working. Activate all logging functions, retry the failing condition, and review the logs. Try running a UA on the mail server; if this works, the error is probably in the network or client.

If you aren't receiving mail from one or more other sites, make sure those sites aren't sending to another server or gateway. MTAs exchange mail using the same mechanism as UAs, so if local clients work fine, problems with external sites usually lie in the network or the remote server. If local mail isn't getting through to other sites, check gateway connections and aliases.

12.5 Ongoing Management

Adding and changing user accounts is the most common E-Mail administration task. This is clearly a job for an administrator; you wouldn't want users setting up their own unauthorized accounts, adding aliases that conflict with other accounts, or changing gateway connections.

Routine changes to passwords, holiday messages, autoresponders, and so on, are more appropriate for users to make themselves, assuming they supply the account's existing password first. However, this is not a feature most POP mail clients provide. Some MTAs provide utilities for remote users to modify their own accounts; if important in your environment, this is definitely a feature to look for. Be sure, too, to check what operating systems the remote administration utility supports: Windows 3.1, Windows 95, Windows NT, Macintosh, UNIX (many flavors), and so forth.

Setting up mail addresses that contain the client's domain name is a fairly simple process: Just add an MX record for the client's domain name and configure your MTA to accept mail sent to that domain. For example, if the normal MX record for your site is

```
interlakken.com   IN   MX 10    earring.interlakken.com.
```

you can add MX records such as the following for additional domains:

```
sine.com            IN   MX 10     earring.interlakken.com.
cosine.com          IN   MX 10     earring.interlakken.com.
tangent.com         IN   MX 10     earring.interlakken.com.
```

You'd then configure earring.interlakken.com not to reject messages sent to sine.com, cosine.com, and tangent.com.

Disk space for E-Mail messages is something that can sneak up on you. Most users establish a fairly consistent pattern in the amount of mail they send and receive and in how often they retrieve mail. This doesn't preclude peaks and valleys, however, as when incoming mail piles up during company or school vacations. Outgoing mail may pile up if your network connection or a popular remote site goes down. If your E-Mail system shares a logical drive with other services, there's also the possibility those other services may fill up the drive and interfere with E-Mail. FTP and News are two applications that can chew up a lot of disk space rapidly.

You may want to find or develop a utility to summarize the amount of disk space each E-Mail user is currently consuming. This can be used for billing or merely for locating stagnant accounts. Writing such programs is usually easy because most MTAs create a separate directory for each user.

If you're in a chargeback situation, be sure the activity logs from your MTA collect the statistics you need for billing. Typical charges are by message or kilobyte sent or received and by megabyte of disk. Frequently, though, billing is by flat rate until some threshold is exceeded. It's common to charge a premium for unread messages beyond a certain age; this encourages people to read their mail and get value from your service.

CHAPTER 13

Installing and Configuring a List Server

list servers are robots that receive mail and automatically send it to each recipient in a database. Some people call list servers "mail exploders," a more colorful term that suggests creating many messages from one.

Most lists are specific to a particular area of interest; interested people join the list by sending a specially formatted mail message to a list manager. A *list manager* is a background process that adds and removes addresses from the list. For example, you can sign up to receive E-Mail copies of the Microsoft WinNT News Electronic Newsletter by sending the following message to winntnews-admin@microsoft.bhs.com:

```
subscribe winntnews
```

People frequently confuse list servers with *mailing lists.* Table 13.1 compares these two mechanisms.

Table 13.1 List Servers versus Mailing Lists

Feature	List Server	Mailing List
Process	Dedicated process resends each incoming message to each list member.	UA or MTA replaces single address with multiple addresses in the same message.
Message header	Final recipients see only themselves in To: and cc: fields.	Final recipients see all other recipients in To: and cc: fields.
Membership	Recipients join and leave the list by sending commands in formatted messages.	Administrator maintains server-based lists. Users maintain UA based lists.

13.1 Operating Concepts and Standards

The concept of standards is relatively foreign to list servers. All Internet list servers use standard E-Mail protocols such as SMTP, but software structure, command syntax, security, and other list server features vary widely. The one unchanging concept is that of a software robot receiving one message and replicating it once per designated recipient.

Each list typically uses two E-Mail addresses: a list address and a list manager address:

1. The list address is the one that explodes received messages into one message per member of the list.

2. The list manager address accepts commands such as "join" and "leave," "subscribe" and "unsubscribe," or whatever commands the designers choose. Some list managers look for commands in the "Subject:" line of the header, while others accept multiple commands in the body. A common convention treats all body lines prior to the first blank lines as commands. List manager commands include the name of the list they modify, so a single list manager can manage several lists.

A common error occurs when users send command messages such as "unsubscribe sewage" to a list address such as sewage@landfill.com. Instead of removing the sender's name from the list, such messages get sent to every member of the sewage list. The user should have sent the command message to the list server's list manager address.

Some list servers support a feature called *digests*. Users who sign up for digests get one message per day—a message containing all messages posted in the last 24 hours.

Another feature of some list servers is the ability to distribute libraries of files. Users send the list manager a command to list or retrieve available files, and they receive the requested item by return mail. This used to be the poor man's alternative to FTP but, in today's world of clogged FTP servers and high-speed mail, it's looking better and better.

13.2 Sample Installation

NTMail, the example from Chapter 12, contains a built-in list server. Unfortunately, there are no Windows dialogs for creating list managers and lists.

To manage lists, you must use the Windows NT Registry Editor, an ASCII editor such as Notepad, and the NT command prompt.

13.2.1 Creating a List Manager Address

A list manager processes commands for lists it controls. One list server can have many list managers, and each list manager can control many lists.

Figure 13.1 illustrates creation of a list manager called "list."

Here are the steps to do the complete job:

1. Start the Windows NT Registry Editor Regedt32.exe.
2. Select the hive "HKEY_LOCAL_MACHINE on Local Machine."
3. Expand the keys SOFTWARE, InternetShopper, Mail, Users.
4. With Users selected, pull down the Edit menu and select "Add Value...."
5. Type the value name "<manager name>.manager," where <manager name> is the name you want the list manager to have.
6. Verify that the data type is "REG_SZ."
7. Click OK.
8. In the String Editor dialog, enter an "X," <manager name>, a space, and then the name of a Help file. (Step 12 will explain how to create this Help file.)
9. Click OK.

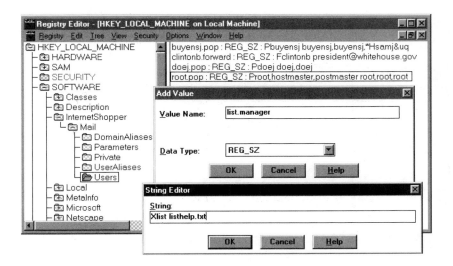

Figure 13.1 Creating an NTMail List Manager Called "list"

10. Close Registry Editor.

11. Go to the \Ntmail directory and make sure there's a directory called <manager name>. If there isn't, create one.

12. Using Notepad, Winpad, or any other editor capable of saving plain ASCII files, create a Help message and save it in the \Ntmail\<manager name> directory.

Figure 13.2 shows the required directory structure and Help file location. A sample Help file follows.

listhelp.txt

```
Hello from list@interlakken.com. This is an automated list server.

The following lists are available:


    None


The following actions are supported for each list (although some
lists may password-protect certain actions.) To perform an action,
send mail to

    list@interlakken.com


and place the commands in the body of your message.
```

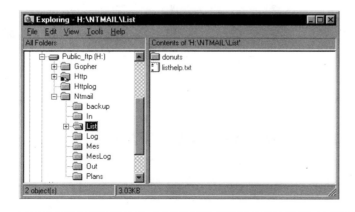

Figure 13.2 NTMail List Manager Directory and Help File Structure

<> Arguments enclosed in angle brackets are required.

[] Arguments in square brackets are optional.

Actions	Arguments	Description
JOIN	<list> [address]	Adds the sender's [or another] address to the list. The address will receive a copy of each message posted.
DIGEST	<list> [address]	Like JOIN, but the sender's [or other] address will receive one message per day containing all posts for that day.
LEAVE	<list> [address]	Removes the sender's [or another] address from the list. UNSUBSCRIBE is a synonym.
HELP	[list]	Responds with the HELP file for the designated list. If you don't specify a list, you get this HELP message.
LIST	<list> [order]	Responds with a list of <list>'s members. [order] may be: ALPHA - By local part. DOMAIN - By domain part. blank - In order of joining
PASSWORD	<password>	Supplies a password for password-protected functions. If you don't want the password printed in the response, the PASSWORD command must be the first line in the message.

```
PARAMETERS <list>                          Responds with complete
                                           configuration details of the
                                           specified list.


RESEND      <list> [day month year]  Resends the current [or specified]
                                     digest file to everyone who
                                     signed up for DIGEST service.


DIR         <list> [address]            Mails a listing of files available
                                        from <list> to the sender's [or
                                        another] address.


GET         <list> <file> [address]  Mails the named <file> to the
                                     sender's [or another] address.
                                     Binary files will be sent as
                                     MIME attachments.
```

NTMail will send the contents of listhelp.txt to anyone who sends a message containing the single word "help" to the address list@interlakken.com. The message simply describes the 10 commands NTMail supports. So far, however, there are no lists.

To test the list manager, stop and restart NTMail (the surest way to make your changes take effect). Then send a "help" message to the list manager (list@inter-lakken.com in this case). Figure 13.3 illustrates the expected response to this message.

The list manager actually returned two messages: one containing a transaction log and one containing the requested Help file. If the original message had contained several commands, the transaction log message would have listed each one along with its success or failure.

13.2.2 Creating a List

To create a list, you must again use Registry Editor. Figure 13.4 illustrates this process.

Here are the steps to do the complete job:

1. Once again, start the Windows NT Registry Editor Regedt32.exe.

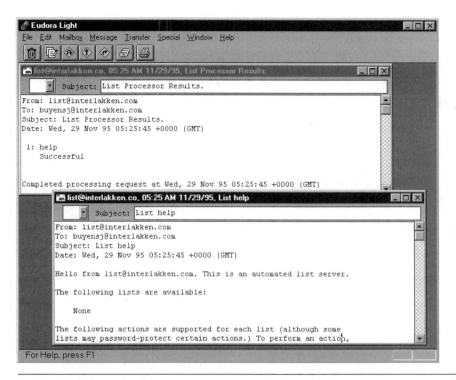

Figure 13.3 Response from List Manager to "Help" Message

2. Select the hive "HKEY_LOCAL_MACHINE on Local Machine."

3. Expand the keys SOFTWARE, InternetShopper, Mail, Users.

4. With Users selected, pull down the Edit menu and select "Add Value...."

5. Type the value name "<listname>.list," where <listname> is the name of the list.

6. Verify that the data type is "REG_SZ."

7. Click OK.

8. In the String Editor dialog, enter the parameters for the list. For guidance, see the sidebar titled "NTMail List Definition Parameters."

9. Click OK.

10. Close Registry Editor.

11. Go to the \Ntmail\<manager name> directory and make sure there's a directory called <listname>. If there isn't, create one.

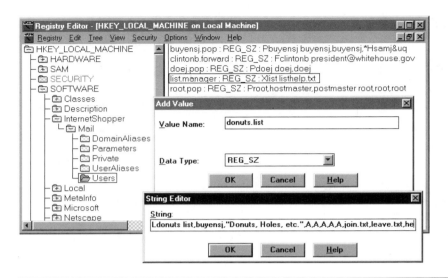

Figure 13.4 Creating an NTMail List Called "donuts"

12. Using any editor that can create plain ASCII files, create the Join message, Leave message, and Help message files specified in step 8. Save these in the \Ntmail\<manager name>\<listname> directory.

13. If you want NTMail to keep activity logs for this list, create a Log subdirectory within \Ntmail\<manager name>\<listname>.

14. If you want NTMail to distribute files through this list, create a Files subdirectory within \Ntmail\<manager name>\<listname>.

The complete parameter string entered in Figure 13.4 is

```
Ldonuts list,buyensj,"Donuts, Holes, etc.",A,A,A,A,A,
   join.txt,leave.txt,help.txt,donuts.mbr
```

NTMail expects to find the three message files and the member file in a directory named after the list. This directory must also contain a subdirectory called Log if NTMail should record activity for the list and a subdirectory called Files if the list will distribute files. The Log subdirectory (and accompanying log) are necessary to support the digest feature.

Figure 13.5 illustrates the required list directory structure.

Sample contents for each message file (Join, Leave, and Help) appear next (in practice, the Help message should explain the list's purpose, rules, and operating procedures):

```
join.txt:
```
Welcome to the donuts@interlakken.com list.

You will receive a copy of all mail posted
to the address donuts@interlakken.com.

For more information about this list, send the message:
    help donuts
to list@interlakken.com.

To leave the list, send
    leave donuts
to list@interlakken.com

To post a message, send it to donuts@interlakken.com.
```
leave.txt:
```
You have been removed from the
donuts@interlakken.com list.

You will no longer receive copies of mail
posted to the address donuts@interlakken.com.
```
help.txt:
```
This is the HELP file for the donuts@interlakken.com list.

If you run into problems, please ask one
of the other policemen for assistance.

Table 13.2 NTMail Permission Codes for Join, Post, List, Get, and Put

Code	Who May Perform the Operation
A	Anyone.
W<address>	Only users whose E-Mail addresses match <address>. The <address> value may contain "?" (indicating any single character) or "*" (indicating any sequence of characters). Any number of "?" and "*" characters may appear.
P<password>	Only users who include the line "Password <password>." NTMail will remove this line from messages replicated to members, but only if it's the first line of the message.
R<password>	This is the same as "P," except that NTMail will deliver messages lacking the specified password to the "Human Name" address.
M	Only list members.
F<filename>	Only addresses appearing on a line in <filename>.
N	No one.

NTMail List Definition Parameters

A value name in the Windows NT registry defines each NTMail list. The value associated with this name consists of the list name, a space, and 14 parameters separated by commas.

The value name consists of the list name, a period, and the word "list." Enter this value in the Value Name box of Registry Editor's Add Value dialog. In Figure 13.4, the value name is donuts.list. See step 5 in the step-by-step instructions.

After clicking the OK button in step 7, enter an "L," then the list name, and then a space. Continue the parameter string by entering the following 14 parameters, separated by commas, into the String Editor text box:

1. **Manager Name.** The name of the list manager that will control this list. This will be the local part of the address to which users must send "join <list>," " leave <list>," and other commands. See Section 13.2.1.

2. **Human Name.** The E-Mail address of the person who is responsible for the list—the moderator.

3. **Message.** A message, up to 60 characters, that NTMail will add to the header of each message processed through this list. This is usually the name of the list or a Help message such as

    ```
    To leave, send
    leave donuts
    to list@interlakken.com
    ```

    To send no message, specify "-" as the message string.

4. **Join Allow.** A code that specifies who can join this list. See Table 13.2 for a list of codes valid for this and the next four parameters.

5. **Post Allow.** A code that specifies who can post to this list.

6. **List Allow.** A code that specifies who can obtain a list of current members.

7. **Get Allow.** A code that specifies who can request files available through this list.

8. **Put Allow.** A code that specifies who can make files available through this list.

9. **Join Message.** The name of a file that NTMail will send to each person who joins the list.

10. **Leave Message.** The name of a file that NTMail will send to each person who leaves the list.

11. **Help Message.** The name of a file that NTMail will send to anyone who sends the list manager a message containing the line "help <list>."

12. **Member File.** The name of a file that NTMail will use to store member addresses in the list.

13. Message Size. The maximum permissible size of a message. This field is optional, and a value of zero indicates unlimited size.

14. Header File. The name of a file containing a list of header fields to change during reposting. For example, if this file contained the record

```
-ErrorTo: root@interlakken.com
```

then NTMail would force the "ErrorTo:" header field of every message to contain "root@interlakken.com."

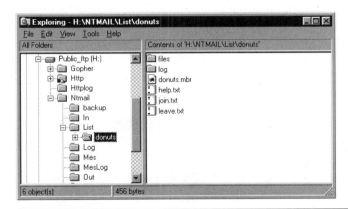

Figure 13.5 Directory Structure for donuts@interlakken.com List

To test the list, stop and restart NTMail to be make sure your maintenance takes effect. Then send a "join" message to the list manager. NTMail should respond with two messages such as those shown in Figure 13.6.

Continue testing by sending a test message to the new list; you should receive the same message in return. Figure 13.7 displays a typical outgoing message and the same message received from the list server. Note the extra fields in the message header.

If the list manager Help file contains a list of available lists, now is the time to update it with the name of the newly created list.

13.3 Problem Resolution and Ongoing Management

Assuming your MTA was working properly when you started and that all your definitions have the correct syntax, you shouldn't have many problems getting a list server to work. If you choose to run separate MTA and list server products on the same machine, make sure the list server doesn't take over the SMTP port for itself.

You can minimize ongoing maintenance by having the requester of each list, or some other designated person, be its moderator (the "list human").

Sudden increases in activity or file space may indicate someone is using a list for questionable activities. Persons with such interest have learned they get shut down quickly after starting to use a system and therefore adopt a "Quick, before somebody notices!" attitude. You can restrain distribution of photographic and compressed software files by imposing a maximum permissible message size, but

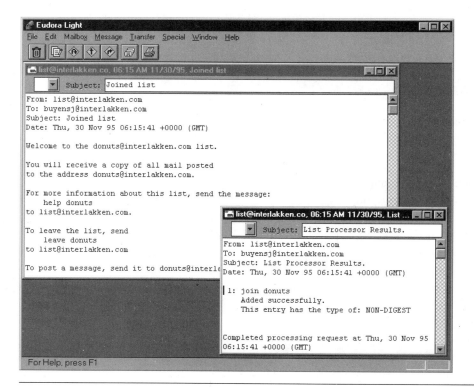

Figure 13.6 Successful Result of Joining donuts@interlakken.com

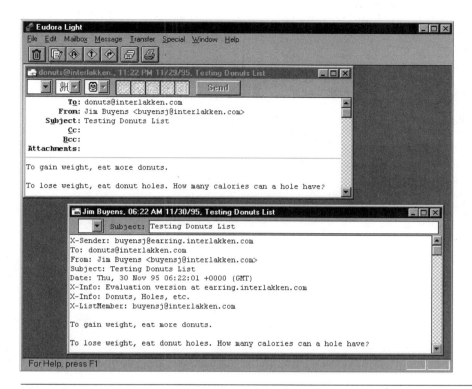

Figure 13.7 Receiving a Message Sent to donuts@interlakken.com

this is only temporary. There are several well-known techniques to automatically split large files into as many messages as required.

It was surprising that, at press time, no list servers with GUI configuration dialogs were available for Windows NT. Administrators with a passion for arcane command-line syntax usually gravitate toward UNIX, while those who value ease-of-use prefer Windows. Perhaps easier-to-configure list servers will appear as the Windows NT Internet market grows.

CHAPTER 14

Installing and Configuring USENET News Service

A funny thing happened during the evolution of USENET News. In its current state, it's neither USENET nor News.

USENET was, and in fact still is, a large network of primarily UNIX machines that periodically connect via dial-up modem. During these connections, each machine transfers batches of files for various applications until it exhausts all queues and the connection terminates. Given enough time and connections, any traffic can go anywhere. Today, high-speed WAN links have replaced most multi-hop, 1200bps, dial-up transmissions, but some of the original applications developed on USENET continue to carry its name.

Outside the Internet, news generally involves one person or organization sending information to many passive recipients—passive in the sense that recipients don't have access to the same audience the original publisher had. USENET News generally allows anyone to post anything and have it replicated to every News server on Earth. One recent estimate counted 90,000 USENET News servers in the world, but that number has surely risen.

News, as the remainder of this chapter will call it, is the soapbox, the open forum, the grapevine, the meeting place, the bull session of the Internet. It's open; it's far reaching; it's vibrant; it's diverse. It's praised; it's abused; its freedom of speech revolts some people. It's eminently useful; where else can you search the world for someone to answer your question or respond to your opinion?

14.1 Operating Concepts and Standards

Articles are the fundamental units of News. Articles consist of plain ASCII text and have headers and bodies much like those of SMTP mail messages. News authors don't mail articles to specific individuals, though. Instead, they post them to a *newsgroup*, where thousands of people can read them and respond.[1]

Newsgroup names are hierarchical, with the highest order at the left. Three newsgroups of almost certain interest to readers of this book are

```
comp.infosystems.www.servers.ms-windows
comp.os.ms-windows.nt.admin.misc
comp.os.ms-windows.nt.admin.networking
```

Note that, like military nomenclature, each qualifier narrows the topic defined by the preceding one. Table 14.1 lists a few of the many first-level qualifiers.

News follows the familiar Internet client-server architecture. End users run client programs called *newsreaders* that not only read News but also post it. Newsreaders communicate only with their local News server, but that News server exchanges new articles with other News servers. An informal hierarchy of News servers collects—with some exceptions—all postings on Earth and replicates them to all News servers on Earth.

Table 14.1 First-Level Newsgroup Qualifiers

Qualifier	Full Name	Description
alt	Alternative	A large, eclectic group of newsgroups with fewer controls than groups in other areas.
biz	Business	Groups with commercial uses.
comp	Computers	Computers and computer science.
fedreg	Federal regulations	Federal regulations.
k12	Kindergarten—12th grade	Elementary and high school education.
linux	Linux	The Linux operating system. (Apparently, someone doesn't consider this "real" computing.)
misc	Miscellaneous	Topics that don't fit elsewhere, such as misc.forsale.misc.
news	News	The News system itself.
rec	Recreation	Recreational activities.
sci	Science	The sciences: biology, chemistry, cryptography, engineering, mathematics, medicine, physics, and so on.
soc	Sociology	Sociology
talk	Talk	A place for "hot air" enthusiasts.

---

[1]Some newsreaders can post News articles and mail them at the same time, but these are two separate transactions: one to post News and another to send mail.

14.1.1 NNTP (Network News Transfer Protocol)

NNTP is the means used to replicate News articles across the Internet. NNTP is a TCP application that operates on port 119, so you can experience it first hand by Telnetting to any News server on that port. A simple session appears next (hand-typed commands are in boldface):

```
200 nnrp3.news.primenet.com greets ???@ip019.phx.primenet.com for NNRP
   (posting ok).
```
help
```
100 Legal commands
   authinfo user Name|pass Password
   article [MessageID|Number]
   body [MessageID|Number]
   date
   group newsgroup
   head [MessageID|Number]
   help
   ihave
   last
   list [active|newsgroups|distributions|schema]
   listgroup newsgroup
   mode reader
   newgroups yymmdd hhmmss ["GMT"] [<distributions>]
   newnews newsgroups yymmdd hhmmss ["GMT"] [<distributions>]
   next
   post
   slave
   stat [MessageID|Number]
   xgtitle [group_pattern]
   xhdr header [range|MessageID]
   xover [range]
   xpat header range|MessageID pat [morepat...]
   xpath xpath MessageID
Report problems to <usenet@primenet.com>
```

group comp.infosystems.www.servers.ms-windows

211 141 5049 5191 comp.infosystems.www.servers.ms-windows

article

220 5049 <DIJ3MJ.Fs6@ez0.ezlink.com> article

Newsgroups: comp.os.linux.networking,comp.infosystems.www.servers.unix,
    comp.infosystems.www.servers.ms-windows

Path: nnrp3.news.primenet.com!nntpdist.primenet.com!nntp.primenet.com!
    news.asu.edu!news.eas.asu.edu!cs.utexas.edu!howland.reston.ans.net!
    swrinde!newsfeed.internetmci.com!in1.uu.net!ez0!cwayne

From: cwayne@ez0.ezlink.com (Clark Wayne)

Subject: Re: http server possible with 4MB RAM ?

Message-ID: <DIJ3MJ.Fs6@ez0.ezlink.com>

Organization: EZLink Internet Access

Date: Fri, 24 Nov 1995 03:42:15 GMT

References: <48t4bm$939@yama.mcc.ac.uk>

X-Newsreader: TIN [version 1.2 PL2]

Followup-To: comp.os.linux.networking,comp.infosystems.www.servers.unix,
    comp.infosystems.www.servers.ms-windows

Lines: 12

Xref: nntpdist.primenet.com comp.os.linux.networking:25480
    comp.infosystems.www.servers.unix:7640
    comp.infosystems.www.servers.ms-windows:5049

Xref: nnrp3.news.primenet.com comp.os.linux.networking: 25480
    comp.infosystems.www.servers.unix: 7640
    comp.infosystems.www.servers.ms-windows:5049

Bruce Kent (brucek@wiau.mb.man.ac.uk) wrote:
: Does anyone know whether one will get acceptable performance using a
: cable-TV set-top box with a 486 DX/33, 4MB RAM, no disk, and running
: Linux as an Internet view station? Or, would one be better off using
: another (non multi-tasking) OS (with e.g. a winsock-compatible server)
: for the task?
: The machine will not be required to do anything else except for
: watching low-budget Science Fiction movies.

: Any ideas?

I run one here on a 486SLC2/66, 4mb ram, but I get snow on certain episodes of Flash Gordon.

Clark

.

next

223 5050 <493hor$7r2@suba01.suba.com> Article retrieved; request text
   separately

.

article

220 5050 <493hor$7r2@suba01.suba.com> article

Path: nnrp3.news.primenet.com!nntpdist.primenet.com!nntp.primenet.com!
   news.asu.edu!news.eas.asu.edu!cs.utexas.edu!usc!chi-news.cic.net!
   news.suba.com!news

From: madmax@thunder.com (Mad Max)

Newsgroups: comp.infosystems.www.servers.ms-windows

Subject: Web Appliances

Date: 24 Nov 1995 04:30:19 GMT

Organization: T-Dome Recycling

Lines: 12

Message-ID: <493hor$7r2@suba01.suba.com>

NNTP-Posting-Host: s25.thunder.com

Mime-Version: 1.0

Content-Type: Text/Plain; charset=US-ASCII

Xref: nntpdist.primenet.com comp.infosystems.www.servers.ms-windows:5050

Xref: nnrp3.news.primenet.com comp.infosystems.www.servers.ms-windows:5050

Recently I bought a new toaster and now am greatly disappointed as it
seems to lack a network port. It seems a shame to buy a new machine and
not have it on the net. Does anyone know how to do this? Please either
reply or send email to madmax@thunder.com.

Thank you,

```
Mad Max
madmax@thunder.com

.
```

```
quit
205
```

The News server automatically responded with a banner upon connection. Typing the command "help" produces a list of available commands; this is a diagnostic aid and is not intended to promote interactive use via Telnet. The "group" command selects the comp.infosystems.www.servers.ms-windows group; the four numbers in the response are a result code, an approximate count of available articles, the starting article number, and the ending article number.

The "article" command tells the server to transmit the current article. On the next line, "220" is a result code, 5049 is the article number, and the string in angle brackets is a message ID assigned by the originating system. A given article will have a different article number on each News server but the same message ID.

The format of a News article strongly resembles that of an E-Mail message. The first blank line separates the body from the header, and many of the header fields are familiar: From, Subject, Date, and so on. The "Newsgroups :"line identifies the newsgroups containing the article, and the "Path:" line shows which systems this article passed through on its way to this server. On USENET, the path information was useful in returning mail and response postings to the originator; on the Internet, this information reduces duplicate transmissions and loops.

Note the "References:" header line referring to message ID <48t4bm$939@yama.mcc.ac.uk>. This is the information used to identify threads: The current article <DIJ3MJ.Fs6@ez0.ezlink.com> is a response to the article <48t4bm$939@yama.mcc.ac.uk>.

The "next" command advances the current article number from 5049 to 5050, as the line following the command shows. The "article" command retrieves article 5050. Then the "quit" command ends the session.

A much condensed version of a more typical newsreader session follows. The author captured this session with a protocol analyzer; the client software was WinVN 99.6:

```
XOVER
412 Primenet News error: must open database before overviewing records
LIST
```

```
215 You asked for it.....
a.bsu.programming 0000000676 0000000596 y
a.bsu.religion 0000002098 0000001909 y
a.bsu.talk 0000000295 0000000284 y
aaa.inu-chan 0000000000 0000000001 m


   (...17,314 more records...)
```

GROUP comp.infosystems.www.servers.ms-windows
```
211 455 6700 7160 comp.infosystems.www.servers.ms-windows y
```
XOVER 6700-7160
```
224.Primenet.News.query.results.follow.for.6700.to.7160
6700 NT,Perl, & Netscape.Server
   Alex Mook <amook@west.net>
   Sat, 13 Jan 1996 00:27:34 GMT
   <DL3Fy0.IJ3@news.zippo.com>
   1203
   10
   Xref: news.primenet.com.comp.infosystems.www.servers.ms-windows:6700
6701 Re: Images on NetscapeB4a
   suedenyc@earthcom.net
   Fri, 12 Jan 1996 02:20:07 -0800
   <30F635D7.5C4E@earthcom.net>
   <30dc0ead.1746979@news.interport.net>
   <4btfnj$qa@news.nstn.ca>
   <4c2s3s$hc8@dns.tcel.com>
   <30E5D5FE.77CA@rs6000.cmp.ilstu.edu>
   <30ea282d.357042432@news.got.net>
   <4cn4hr$n0p@status.gen.nz>
   <4cvdbc$33l@news1.deltanet.com>
   2581
   11
   Xref: news.primenet.com.comp.os.ms-windows.win95.misc:90553
   comp.os.ms-windows.apps.winsock.misc:2924
   comp.os.ms-windows.win95.setup:44121
```

```
alt.winsock:76379

comp.os.ms-windows.apps.winsock.mail:2490

comp.os.ms-windows.apps.winsock.news:2348

alt.internet.services:68480

comp.protocols.tcp-ip.ibmpc:40977

comp.infosystems.www.browsers.misc:4772

comp.infosystems.www.browsers.ms-windows:19092

comp.infosystems.www.servers.ms-windows:6701

comp.infosystems.www.authoring.html:44244

comp.os.ms-windows.misc:97623

comp.os.ms-windows.nt.misc:106302

comp.os.ms-windows.nt.setup:595

comp.windows.misc:18877

comp.os.ms-windows.apps.misc:15908

comp.os.ms-windows.apps.utilities:18656

alt.winsock.trumpet:13412
```

ARTICLE 6795

```
220 6795 <4dhl72$5p6@nnrp1.news.primenet.com> article

Path: news.primenet.com!news.primenet.com!not-for-mail

From: buyensj@primenet.com. (Jim.Buyens)

Newsgroups: comp.infosystems.www.servers.ms-windows

Subject: Re: Virtual Domains on Windows NT

Date: 16 Jan 1996 19:00:02 -0700

Organization: People Of Earth

Lines: 53

Sender: root@primenet.com

Message-ID: <4dhl72$5p6@nnrp1.news.primenet.com>

References: <4df30g$sdi@news.imssys.com>

X-Posted-By: ip186.phx.primenet.com

X-Newsreader: WinVN.0.99.7

MIME-Version: 1.0

Content-Type: Text/Plain; charset=US-ASCII

Xref: news.primenet.com.comp.infosystems.www.servers.ms-windows:6795


In article <4df30g$sdi@news.imssys.com> on Mon, 15 Jan 1996 02:28:06 GMT
```

```
madmonk@imssys.imssys.com said
>
>OK, Here's the scoop.  My service provider has just taken me on as his
>web master and he wants to set up a new webserver.  We're leaning
>towards NT at the moment, but I need to solidify something.
>Many https' say they support virutal domains (listening for several
>internet address as long as your system is set up to listen for
>them. What he wants to do is start a web space and design capability
>for interested businesses.  Virtual domains are critical here as they
>will almost all want their own domain name  In my recent research I
>have seen how to assign up to five domains to NT, but I want to be

    (...remainder of body...)


quit
```

The newsreader opens the connection on port 119 and then issues an XOVER command. XOVER is a very useful but nonstandard command; the newsreader issues it here just to determine whether the News server supports it. The 412 error response indicates that the newsreader issued XOVER without first positioning to a newsgroup, but the newsreader takes this as evidence of XOVER support. If the News server didn't support XOVER, it would have responded, "500 Command not recognized."

Next, the newsreader uses the LIST command to download a list of all current newsgroups. Most newsreaders detect new newsgroups at this point by checking each returned newsgroup against a local file of previously seen groups—a file called "newsrc."

The newsreader issues the GROUP command when the user selects a newsgroup. Response from this command includes the 215 status code, the number of articles in the group, the starting and ending article numbers, the name of the group, and a "y" or an "m" (meaning "posting allowed" or "moderated," respectively).

Knowing the starting and ending article numbers, the newsreader issues the XOVER command for that range. The GROUP command positions the session to a newsgroup, so this time the XOVER command succeeds. For each article in the requested range, XOVER returns one record containing the article number, subject, author, date, message ID, references, byte count, line count, and any other fields the News server is configured to supply. Note that the references themselves are message IDs; if the user configured the newsreader to display a threaded list of articles, the newsreader will try to display articles with references directly under the article whose original message ID matches.

XOVER is the fastest, most efficient way for an on-line newsreader to get the data to build a threaded article list. Without XOVER, the newsreader must either use the HEAD command to download all the headers for each article or use the XHDR command to download specific headers. Both XOVER and XHDR are nonstandard commands and are not universally supported.

After viewing the article list, the user downloads an article—number 6795—and then disconnects.

Posting articles is equally simple. The newsreader issues the POST command and then examines the News server's response. Response 340 indicates that the News server is ready to receive the article and that the client should transmit the headers, a blank line, the body, and a terminating line consisting of a single period. Response 440 indicates the newsgroup prohibits posting.

Section 14.1.2 presents a summary of common NNTP commands. Section 14.1.4 describes common header types.

14.1.2 Standard NNTP Commands

Listed in this section are the major commands that Network News Transfer Protocol supports. For more detailed information, consult RFC 977 (Network News Transfer Protocol) and RFC 1036 (Standard for Interchange of USENET Messages, obsoletes RFC 850).

- **HELP.** Displays a list of supported commands.
- **LIST.** Displays a complete list of available newsgroups.
- **NEWGROUPS Date [Dist].** Displays a list of newsgroups added since the specified date and time. If they appear, distributions restrict the list.
- **NEWNEWS Group Date [Dist].** Displays a list of new articles added since the specified date and time. Distributions may restrict the list.
- **GROUP Group.** Establishes the named group as the current group and positions a pointer at the first article.
- **ARTICLE.** Displays a status response, the current article's header, a blank line, and then the article's body.
- **ARTICLE Message-ID.** Creates the same display as ARTICLE but for the specified message ID. The current-article pointer doesn't change.
- **ARTICLE Number.** Creates the same display as ARTICLE but for the specified article number. This becomes the current article.

- **BODY/BODY Message-ID/BODY Number.** These three commands work like the ARTICLE commands but return only the status response and the article's body.

- **HEAD/HEAD Message-ID/HEAD Number.** These three commands work like the ARTICLE commands but return only the status response and the article's header.

- **STAT/STAT Message-ID/STAT Number.** These three commands work like the ARTICLE commands but return only the status response.

- **NEXT.** Advances the current-article pointer to the next article and displays a status response.

- **LAST.** Backs the current-article pointer to the preceding article and displays a status response.

- **IHAVE Message-ID.** Informs the server that the client has an article with the given message ID. The server will give response code 335 to retrieve the article or 435 if it already has a copy.

- **POST.** Informs the server that the client wants to post an article. The server returns 340 stating it's ready to receive the article or 440 if it isn't. If the response is 340, the client transmits the headers, a blank line, the body, and a line containing only a period.

- **QUIT.** Terminates the NNTP session.

- **SLAVE.** Informs the server that the client is actually another server. The server may use this fact to adjust task priorities or other settings.

14.1.3 Selected Nonstandard News Commands

Over time, News servers have tended to support new commands without waiting for new standards. This tends to make understanding NNTP a black art. For more complete information, look for an Internet Draft called "Common NNTP Extensions."

Descriptions of several very useful, nonstandard, and commonly implemented commands appear next.

- **AUTHINFO USER Username/AUTHINFO PASS Password.** If, at any time, a server returns the 480 response code, the client should return the AUTHINFO USER Username command, replacing the user name with the current user's identity code. A 381 response from the server requests the password. If the user name/password is valid, the server returns 281, and the client can retry the original command. If the user name/password isn't valid, the server returns 502. The entire exchange takes place in clear text.

■ **AUTHINFO SIMPLE/Username Password.** The server initiates this exchange by returning the 450 response code. The client responds by sending the AUTHINFO SIMPLE command, which the server acknowledges with a 350 if this is acceptable. Upon receiving the 350, the client transmits the user's identity code, one or more spaces, and then the password on a single line. If the user name/password is valid, the server returns 250, and the client can retry the original command. If the user name/password isn't valid, the server returns 452. The entire exchange takes place in clear text.

The response codes used by AUTHINFO SIMPLE conflict with those specified in RFC 977. This means of authentication is therefore a good one to avoid.

■ **AUTHINFO GENERIC Arguments.** The server initiates this exchange by returning the 380 response code. The client responds by sending AUTHINFO GENERIC followed by the name of the authenticator services and whatever additional parameters it requires.

The client and server complete authentication using the named service. This may involve any number of transmissions and responses. When completed, the process returns 380 if authentication succeeded, 501 if the invocation was incorrect, 502 if authentication failed, and 503 for other errors.

■ **LIST OVERVIEW.FMT.** If the server supports this command, it returns a list of the fields the XOVER command will provide. Output consists of a line containing a 215 response code, the list of XOVER fields (each followed by a colon and each on its own line), and then a line containing only a period.

■ **LISTGROUP Group.** If the server supports this command, it returns a list of article numbers in the specified newsgroup. Each article number appears on a separate line.

■ **XHDR Header Range/Message-ID.** If the server supports this command, it returns specific headers from specific articles. Output consists of a 215 status code line, the matched headers, and then a period on a line by itself.

- **XOVER Range.** If the server supports this command, it returns information from an "overview database" for the range of article numbers requested. The range may consist of a single article number, starting and ending article numbers separated by a hyphen, or a starting article number, a hyphen, and no ending article number (indicating "all following").

    Overview database information consists of the article number, subject, author, date, message ID, references, byte count, line count, and then possibly other fields. The server sends all fields on a single line delimited by tab characters (hex "09").

14.1.4 NNTP News Article Header Types

The following header codes must be present in the header of every News article. Header lines consist of a keyword, a colon, one space, and the relevant data. The first blank line in an article signifies the end of the header and the beginning of the body.

- **Date.** The article's original posting date. Several formats are acceptable, but the RFC suggests

    Weekday, DD-Mon-YY HH:MM:SS TIMEZONE

    as in

    Saturday, 02-Dec-95 11:31:10 MST

- **From.** The E-Mail address of the user who posted the article. Three formats are acceptable:

    johnd@absentia.com
    johnd@absentia.com (John Doe)
    John Doe <johnd@absentia.com>

- **Message-ID.** An identifier, unique in the world, assigned by the article's original site, and consisting of an angle bracket, a site-unique string, the "@" character, the original server's fully qualified host name, and a closing angle bracket. <493hor$7r2@suba01.suba.com> is one example.

- **Newsgroups.** Specifies in which newsgroups the article belongs. Commas separate multiple newsgroups.

- **Path.** A list of all machines a particular copy of an article has traversed; each machine adds itself to the front of the list. News servers use this information to prevent sending the same article to the same machine more than once.

- **Subject.** Conveys the article's topic. It should permit readers to decide whether a particular article is interesting.

The following header lines are optional:

- **Approved.** Identifies the newsgroup moderator who posted an article. Certain control messages also require this field.

- **Control.** Identifies this article as a server-to-server message rather than an article intended for users. The remainder of the line contains a command the receiving system should process. See the sidebar titled "Control Message Commands."

- **Date-Received.** The date on which the local server received an article.

- **Distribution.** A series of codes, separated by commas, that restrict distribution of an article. News servers reject articles with distribution codes that are not of interest. See the sidebar titled "USENET News Distributions."

- **Expires.** The date on which all servers should purge an article. If absent, each site's local expiration policy applies.

- **Followup-To:** A list of newsgroups where responses should appear. If absent, the "Newsgroups:" list applies.

- **Keywords.** One or more single-word content identifiers. They should help potential readers decide whether the article is interesting.

- **Lines.** The number of lines in the body of the article.

- **Organization.** The full name of the sender's or sending machine's organization. This should be more descriptive than the sender's domain name.

- **References.** A list of message IDs that prompted this article—an article's parents in a thread.

- **Reply-To.** Specifies an E-Mail address for replies to this article. If absent, replies go to the "From:" address.

- **Sender.** Reports a "From:" address the sender overrode manually.

- **Summary.** A one-line synopsis of the article, generally in response to another article. (In such cases, the "Subject:" field generally contains "Re:" followed by the original subject.)

- **Xref.** This line contains the local host name (minus the domain) and a list of newsgroup names and message numbers. If the same article exists in several newsgroups (a result of cross-posting), this field provides the article-number pointer applicable to each one. This has no value to remote systems, and outgoing newsfeeds should suppress it.

The standard News article format permits additional header fields. Usually, these correspond to E-Mail headers or begin with the letter "X." Multipart MIME attachments are perfectly feasible, for example.

Control Message Commands

RFC 1036 defines the following control messages. Most apply to USENET connections rather than to interactive NNTP links, but several—including CANCEL, NEWGROUP, and RMGROUP—apply to NNTP as well.

Control messages arrive intermixed with regular news articles but contain the "Control:" header. Control messages don't get posted to the newsgroups they pertain to, but they do get forwarded like any other article.

- **CANCEL Message-ID.** Delete the article with the stated message ID.

- **CHECKGROUPS.** Check the newsgroup list on the local system against newsgroups listed in the body of the control message.

- **IHAVE Message-ID... RemoteSys.** The sending system announces available article numbers. If it wants them, the receiving system will return SENDME messages.

- **NEWGROUP Groupname Moderated.** Creates a new newsgroup with the given name. If the keyword "Moderated" is present, ignore future articles having no "Approved:" header.

- **RMGROUP Groupname.** Removes the newsgroup with the given name. This control message requires the "Approved:" header to be present.

- **SENDME Message-ID... RemoteSys.** This is the receiving system's response to incoming IHAVE control messages.

- **SENDSYS.** Mail a copy of the "sys" file, which lists all newsfeeds and the newsgroups sent on each, to the author of the control message.

- **VERSION.** Mail the name and version number of the News server's software to the author of the control message.

USENET News Distributions

Codes called *distributions* control the extent of newsgroup replication; a few of these appear here. The control mechanism is simply that News servers bypass newsgroup activity for unwanted distributions.

Distribution	Description
ba	San Francisco Bay Area
ca	California
can	Canada
ga	Georgia
inet	The Internet
na	North America
ne	New England
uenet	Uenet (Europe)
usa	United States
world	Everywhere

14.1.5 NNTP Server Operation

All the commands described in Section 14.1.2 are available to both end-user newsreaders and to servers exchanging news in the background. However, the normal pattern of commands used by these two applications usually differs considerably.

On-line newsreaders usually retrieve a list of newsgroups, then retrieve article lists, and then select a few listed articles for reading. Occasionally, the user may post an article to the News server (using the POST command).

Off-line newsreaders usually retrieve an article list and then download all new articles. Although it takes some time to download all these articles, total dial-in connect time may be less than reading articles from the same group interactively. This presents a dilemma for the site operator; people using off-line newsreaders typically consume more News server capacity than interactive users, yet pay for less connect time. If this becomes a serious problem, the operator may have to revise billing policies—perhaps charging by the megabyte (above some threshold) for newsgroup usage.

Traditionally, News servers get News from other sites by signing up for a feed. Feeds can originate from other News servers inside the organization, from outside local sources such as universities, or from large Internet Service Providers (ISPs) such as Sprint or MCI. A server may accept or originate any number of feeds.

The remote system initiates the feed. Thus, to get News fed to a server you control, you must contact the administrator of the other News server and ask them to send you a feed at scheduled intervals. Here's a typical (though unusually short) newsfeed session (the server doing the feeding is the client, and its activity appears in boldface; responses by the server receiving the feed appear in normal text):

```
(server providing newsfeed connects to port 119)
201 Pressroom NNTP server ready (no posting)
IHAVE <4105@ucbvax.ARPA>
435 Been there, done that.
IHAVE <4106@ucbvax.ARPA>
335 News to me!  <CRLF.CRLF> to end.
(sends article)
.
235 Article transferred successfully.  Thanks.
QUIT
205 Pressroom NNTP server bids you farewell.
```

The News server originating the feed sends an IHAVE command for each article it believes may be new to the server it's feeding. This normally includes all articles the newsfeed server has received from any source since it last fed the local server. The newsfeeder may suppress some articles, however, such as those containing the local server's name in the "Path:" header field. The local server may download the IHAVE article by returning result code 335 or skip it by sending code 435. Normally, the local server will accept all articles except those already received from another source. The message ID allows detection of duplicates. Feeds occur in one direction only. Full synchronization of two News servers requires scheduling independent feeds in both directions.

The newsfeeds described in the previous paragraph are "push" feeds because the originator of the connection pushes the news to the receiving server. Another scenario is possible, however; the receiving server could simply behave like a user newsreader getting lists of articles and downloading them. This is a "pull" (or "sucking") feed; the server originating the connection pulls (or sucks) the news from the remote server.

News server operators are frequently not amused when someone signs up for ordinary user access and then starts sucking a full newsfeed. For one thing, the charge for a full feed may be more than the charge for casual user access. For another, feeding a thousand articles via IHAVE consumes far fewer resources than feeding a thousand articles requested by article number or message ID. Pulling articles one at a time forces the newsfeed machine to perform a database lookup, directory lookup, or both for each article. Push feeds deliver articles in whatever sequence is most efficient for the pusher.

Pull feeds are popular with small operators for three reasons:

1. The sites don't have to negotiate feeds with larger sites.

2. The local site schedules the feed. This is particularly advantageous if the local site has dial-out connectivity only—that is, if the newsfeeder site can't initiate its own connection when it's ready to deliver a feed.

3. Some pull servers can effectively function as new article caches. When a user requests a newsgroup list, the pull server instantly downloads new article headers from the feed source and then delivers an updated list to the user. If the user requests an article the pull server hasn't downloaded yet, the server instantly downloads the article, saves it, and delivers it to the user. If the pull server has already downloaded the article, it delivers the saved article locally.

In all three cases, advantages for the local site come at the cost of heavier system demands at the newsfeed site. In the third case, for example, the newsfeed site may incur almost as much utilization as if the pull server weren't even present and the end users accessed the newsfeed server directly. The newsfeed site also loses scheduling control and the ability to do resource leveling.

In late 1995, there were over 18,000 newsgroups on the Internet. Taking a full feed and storing the articles for a reasonable length of time requires several gigabytes of disk space. Scanning this volume of files, detecting and deleting expired articles, and updating the associated databases is a resource-intensive activity, as is receiving and cataloging 100MB a day (or more) of new articles. Buying a server large and powerful enough to handle News can be a problem, but obtaining the necessary bandwidth for a full push feed can be a larger one. Pull feeds may provide an answer, but not if your ISP disconnects you for policy violations. If you plan to pull a feed, discuss it in advance with the site you'd like to pull from.

14.2 Sample Installations

As of this writing, News servers were undoubtedly the least developed of the major Internet applications available for Windows NT. There were two choices:

1. **DNEWS**
   Provider: NetWin World
   Address: PO Box 27574, Mt. Roskill, Auckland, New Zealand
   E-Mail: netwin@world.std.com

Web site:	http://world.std.com/~netwin/default.htm
FTP site:	ftp://ftp.std.com/ftp/vendors/netwin/dnews/
Reseller:	Internet Shopper
Address:	Internet Shopper Ltd., PO Box 6064, London, SW12 9XG, UK
E-Mail:	webmaster@net-shopper.co.uk
Web site:	http://www.net-shopper.co.uk/software/dnews/index.htm
FAX:	+44 181 673 2149

2. **NNS**

Author:	Jeff Coffler
E-Mail:	nns@jeck.seattle.wa.com
Reseller:	NetManage, Inc.
Address:	10725 North De Anza Blvd., Cupertino, CA 95014
E-Mail:	sales@netmanage.com
Web site:	http://www.netmanage.com/
Voice:	(408) 973-7171
FAX:	(408) 257-6405

Both programs are protected by copyright. See the Web pages just listed for more licensing and pricing information. You can use DNEWS for four weeks, and then you must either delete it or pay for it; support is available separately. The CD that accompanies this book contains a copy of DNEWS, but you may wish to download a newer version.

NetManage acquired NNS just as this book reached deadline. To get current information about this product, send mail to nns@jeck.seattle.wa.com or look around NetManage's Web site at http://www.netmanage.com. A freeware version will always be available, plus a commercial version with more features. These versions, unlike the beta version described later in this chapter, will have 100 percent GUI administration.

Several other vendors have also announced intentions to produce, by the time you read this, full commercial News servers with all the ease of use and amenities administrators expect from a licensed Windows NT product. It's reasonable to expect newsreaders with groupware features using NNTP for transport and replication.

News servers are deceptively complex programs. The server must accept feeds, deliver feeds, delete expired articles, and maintain several large databases while servicing any number of client newsreader sessions. In addition, the world market for News servers isn't large and the technology isn't changing rapidly. As result, both of these News servers emphasize core functions over usability. There are no setup programs here, no GUI configuration screens, no standardized syntax. Each product has multiple plain ASCII configuration, each file having its own syntax.[2] Documentation consists of Microsoft Word files shipped with the programs.

Because the News server market is so likely to change and because both DNEWS and NNS are likely to undergo significant change, this book will provide only an overview of the installation process. This should be enough to impart a sense of what's involved in setting up News and provide a basis for installing new or enhanced products in the future.

One general caution for installing any News server is to use the NTFS file system on all drives. News is a disk-intensive service, and you'll need NTFS's performance, expandability, reliability, and long file name support.

14.2.1 Installing DNEWS

DNEWS is a product from New Zealand that makes much of its ability to pull newsfeeds. However, it can also take push newsfeeds if you or your provider prefer them.

To install DNEWS, take the following steps:

1. Switch to the drive where you want DNEWS installed.
2. Create a temporary directory with a name other than DNEWS.
3. CD to that directory.
4. If you decide to install the version of DNEWS that accompanies this book, copy all the files from the CD's \DNEWS directory to the temporary directory.
5. If you download a newer version of DNEWS, decompress the archive files to the temporary directory.
6. Run the resulting INSTALL.CMD file. This will rename a number of files from 8.3 syntax to long file names and create a \dnews directory on the current drive. It will also copy a number of configuration files there, copy other files to the <systemroot>\system32 directory, and register DNEWS as a system service.

---

[2]Actually, both programs borrow command file structure and syntax from UNIX. However, the UNIX standard is apparently for every command file for every program to be different.

Table 14.2 lists the DNEWS configuration files.

Edit the \winnt\system32\dnews.conf file, review the following fields, and update as necessary:

- nntp_feeder
- myname
- diskspace
- manager
- confirm
- config, logdir, workarea, history, and spool (the five drive/directory specifications)

Further instructions appear in the dnews.conf file itself:

```
dsnews.conf:
# Windows NT config file.  DNEWS.CONF
# ----------------THINGS YOU MUST CHANGE --------------------------------
# The main up-stream server that DNEWS should get groups from
nntp_feeder your.feeder.ohio.edu
# the IP name of your own machine, e.g. mypc.here.com Use a number if
# you don't have a working DNS system.
myname  my.ipname.ohio.edu
# Total diskspace available, in MEGABYTES, recommended 10-100 for
# dynamic, 500-2000 for full feed
diskspace 100
# Person to email log files and control messages etc to.
manager you@this.domain
```

Table 14.2 DNEWS Configuration Files

File Name	Directory	Description
dnews.conf	\winnt\system32	Main configuration file.
access.conf	\dnews	Controls NNTP access.
newsfeeds.conf	\dnews	Controls newsfeeds the local system initiates.
expire.conf	\dnews	Controls article expiration.
control.conf	\dnews	Controls automatic creation and deletion of newsgroups (based on control messages).
moderators.conf	\dnews	Specifies E-Mail location for moderated newsgroups.

```
# Send email confirms for any message successfully sent up stream from a
    post.
# put your domain in here.  You might want to change this to  *my.domain
confirm *.this.domain


# If dnews is not running on the C drive, then you MUST change the section
# lower down which defines all the DNEWS disk and directories.
# --------------OPTIONAL THINGS TO CHANGE BELOW HERE --------------------
# Refuse news articles with a 'date' more than this old, this is just to
    avoid
# accepting news from a restored news disk.
too_old 35
# Send daily reports, default is 'yes'
# report no
# Logging and debug settings, error,warn,info,debug
# debug item:group:feed:chan:  Selective debugging output Default is all
loglvl info
# Number of days to keep each news group for after it's uploaded.
life 15
# expire_at mins hours
#
# this example would only do updates at night
# update_at *5 17-7
#
# Update every 10 minutes and do one expire at 2 in the morning
update_at *5 *
expire_at 5 2
# The DISK DIRECTORIES we will use, everything except this file.
# which MUST be stored as %systemroot%/system32/dnews.conf
config   c:/dnews
logdir   c:/dnews
workarea c:/dnews/spool
history  c:/dnews/spool
spool    c:/dnews/spool
```

```
# If less than 'n' megabytes are free on any partition/volume/disk then
# news will stop  sucking and accepting feeds, posts still work.
workarea_min 5
# for a full feed increase history_min to about 50
history_min 5
spool_min 5
```

DNEWS will use the ntp_feeder value for pulling a newsfeed from another News server. If that server stamps "Path:" headers with a host name different from the required nntp_feeder string, edit the newsfeeds.conf file and add an exclude field for the host name string used. You can normally accomplish this by replacing feeder.other.name with the host name the other server inserts in "Path:" headers.

Whether or not you need to change feeder.other.name, you should open newsfeeds.conf and change mailgateway.site.name (near the bottom) to the name of an SMTP mail server, thus allowing DNEWS to send mail:

newsfeeds.conf:

```
# You must get the EXCLUDE parameter correct, to do this:
# Use a reader or telnet to get a message from the site you feed from,
# look at the PATH header record and see what name that site is stamping
# its messages with,  then put that name in place of 'FEEDER.OTHER.NAME'
# if it is different from the feeder's ip name as defined in news.conf
#
# File format:
# BUILTIN means the internal nntp feed is used
# POSTING means to use 'POST' instead of IHAVE to send messages up stream.
# EXCLUDE sitename Stops items from going to that site again.
# POSTING is best for LEAF sites (where you don't feed to any other sites)
# a POSTING site can have leaf sites but it can't accept IHAVE messages
   from
# them, only POST messages.
#
# Two special site names,  me   and   $NNTP_FEEDER (from news.conf)
#
site me
  groups *,!to.*,!*.binaries.*
```

```
site $NNTP_FEEDER
 groups *
 builtin
 posting
 exclude feeder.other.name

# This is really the mail gateway, but it works a bit like a feed, you
  MUST
# change the gateway name and remove the '#' characters from the next two
  lines

#site mailgateway.site.name
# smtp
```

The access.conf file controls access to the News server. As usual, records beginning with a pound sign ("#") are comments. Other records have the format

```
<host>:<perm>:<user>:<pass>:<groups>
```

<host> is the remote computer name or IP address, with wild cards permitted. <perm> indicates the type of permission this record controls: R to read, P to post, or I to allow IHAVE. <user> and <pass> are null or the user name and password required to perform the operation. <groups> indicates the newsgroups this record controls.

DNEWS checks permissions by reading all rules, so the last rule that matches the incoming host name or IP address and also matches the operation is the one that applies. A start is to

1. Keep the rule "*::::!*" so that, by default, no one can do anything.
2. Change the "161.29.23" in "161.29.23.*:Read,Post:::*" to your network number, allowing all users from your network to read and post all newsgroups.
3. Change the "my.domain.name" in "*.my.domain.name:Read,Post:::*" to your domain name, allowing all users from your domain to read and post all newsgroups.
4. If you plan to receive a full IHAVE newsfeed from an upstream site, uncomment the "# upstream.feeder.edu:ihave:::*" line and change "upstream.feeder.edu" to the name of the machine that will provide the feed.

Here is the access.conf file:

```
access.conf
##   Format:
## <host>:<perm>:<user>:<pass>:<groups>
##  Connecting host must be found in this file; the last match found is
##  used, so put defaults first.
## <host>    Wildcard name or IP address
## <perm>    R to read; P to post; I to allow Ihave xfer's
## <user>    Username for authentication before posting
## <pass>    Password, for same reason
## <groups> Newsgroup patterns that can be read or not read
##
## Default is no access, no way to authentication, and no groups.
## If user is trying to post, then only P records are tested
## if user is trying to read, only R records are tested.
## In this way you can specify a user can read lots of groups but only
## post to local groups and thus not embarass your company world wide.
## The groups list is not checked for IHAVE feeds.
##
## This file processed when connection is made, and then again if authinfo
## command is sent.
## Don't let anyone in by default
*:::::!*
## Except people from my site, put in your ip number or use names
## if you have reverse name translation working.
# (REQUIRED: CHANGE NEXT TWO LINES and remove the #'s)
# 161.29.23.*:Read,Post:::*
# *.my.domain.name:Read,Post:::*
## Give any nntp-send feeding site IHAVE access, not needed for a
## sucking only feed.
# (OPTIONAL: CHANGE NEXT LINE)
# upstream.feeder.edu:ihave:::*
```

Assuming you're willing to accept the defaults for article expiration and handling of control messages, you can use Control Panel Services to start the DNEWS service. The control applet is a Windows NT console program called tellnews. Use the "status" subcommand to get a quick status check, as shown next:

```
C:\>tellnews status
200 earring.interlakken.com DNEWS Version 2.1i, posting OK
483 Temporary License expires after 31-1-1996, (2 users allowed)
483 Please read LICENSE.TXT for registration information
Feed[0]: me *,!to.*,!*.binaries.*
Feed[1]: news.primenet.com Posting Builtin *
Chan[0:108] (0:0) 130.131.90.111 earring.interlakken.com C_CMD
Expire started at  Done, start 0% end 0%
   Processed 0 removed 0 deleting 0/0/0 speed 0
Expire finished at: , Elapsed 0 hours, 0 minutes

Nothing is being sucked at present, all groups are now up to date.
NNTP open of {news.primenet.com} failed, check dnews.log
History: disk 0k memory 0k/80k, Str 1k/2k/500k Malloc 659k/659k/520k
Used 0MB=0%, Free work 92Mb, hist 92Mb, spool 92Mb, log 92Mb
Groups Cached 0 of 0,  Uptime 0 day(s) 0 hour(s)
.

281 Manager command processed OK
205 closing connection - goodbye!
C:\>
```

You may also wish to check the \dnews\dnews.log file for errors as well. If all is well, try taking a feed and posting some articles. Enjoy.

14.2.2 Installing NNS

The version of NNS described here is a beta version produced before NetManage acquired the product. By the time you read this, NNS will likely have a standard Windows setup program and 100 percent GUI administration.[3] Although the mechanics of installation and configuration will change, the collection of parameters virtually cannot. News, after all, is News.

For this example, the author downloaded a beta version of NNS and decompressed the archived files into F:\NNS. If you are still working with this version, copy NNSPERF.DLL, MSVCRT20.DLL, and MFC30.DLL from F:\NNS to the <systemroot>\system32 directory and copy NEWSCTL.EXE to any directory on the path (probably <systemroot>/system32).

NNS uses the configuration files listed in Table 14.3. These files and nns.exe can be in whatever directory you want, but they must all be in the same directory.

Edit the nns.ini file and update the fields that appear next in bold. For the various directories, you'll probably need to update the drive letters; note that, as in the defaults, it's best to place incoming, outgoing, and storage directories on different drives. It's also a good idea to keep volatile file areas (such as news files) off the <systemroot> drive:

nns.ini

```
; NetNews configuration file
;
[General]


Host Name=<enter-your-host-name-here>
CommBuffers=20
ExpireTimes=12:30 AM
```

Table 14.3 NNS Configuration Files

File Name	Description
nns.ini	Main configuration file.
newsfeeds	Controls newsfeeds the local system initiates.
expire.ctl	Controls article expiration.
control.ctl	Controls automatic creation and deletion of newsgroups (based on control messages).
moderators	Specifies E-Mail location for moderated newsgroups.

---

[3]To look for a new version of NNS, send mail to nns@jeck.seattle.wa.com or check NetManage's Web site at http://www.netmanage.com. A freeware version will always be available.

```
Mail Type=SMTP
Mail Account=<enter-your-admin-mail-account - like foo@bar.com>
MAPI Username=
MAPI Password=
SMTP Host=<enter-your-SMTP-host-name-here>
DirControlPath=e:\news\config
DirLogPath=e:\news\log


[Performance]

;WorkingSetMin=0
;WorkingSetMax=0


[Batcher]

BatchFrequency=60
ImmediateFrequency=5
OutgoingDir=e:\news\outgoing


[Unbatcher]

IncomingDir=i:\news\incoming
BadBatchDir=i:\news\incoming\bad
BadPostFilename=i:\news\badPosts.txt


[Network]

NNTP Pipes=0
NNTP Sockets=1
CONTROL Pipes=1
CONTROL Sockets=0
Client Pipe Timeout=60
Client Socket Timeout=60
Server Pipe Timeout=5
Server Socket Timeout=5
```

```
Control Account=Administrators

[Storage]

UseHardLinks=1
DeviceTranslation=_%s
DirSpoolPath=h:\news\spool
```

After updating nns.ini, you must create by hand all the directories mentioned in that file. If the files "active" and "active.times" aren't present in the configuration directory, create two empty files with the commands

```
copy nul: active
copy nul: active.times
```

If you're installing NNS for the first time or wish to erase and initialize your history database, run the command

```
nns -makehistory
```

Start NNS with the command "nns -c." The command's output should look like this:

```
F:\nns>nns -c
Dec  5  9:35 PM: Performance monitor initialization failed - statistics
   disabled

Dec  5  9:35 PM: Newsgroup 'control' not found, automatically created
Dec  5  9:35 PM: Newsgroup 'junk' not found, automatically created
Dec  5  9:35 PM: News daemon has been started
```

With the NNS command window left open, open another command window and try the command "newsctl help." This is a simple command that communicates with the NNS task and proves that NNS is communicating:

```
F:\nns>newsctl help
Legal news X2.06 control commands are:
```

```
CANCEL            Cancel an article from the news system
CHANGEGROUP       Change group moderation flag for a group
                  Syntax: "changegroup <group> <flag:y/n/m>"
CHECKFILE         Validate syntax of one or more control files
                  Syntax: "checkfile <file-to-check>" or "checkfile" for all
EXPIRE            Expire news from the news spool
                  Syntax: "expire [<fudge-hours>]"
FEED              Feed news to the specified site
FLUSHCACHE        Flush in-memory structures to disk
GETNEWS           Get news from a remote NNS server
                  Syntax: "getnews <site-name> [wait] [<transport>]"
HELP              List available control commands
IMPORT            Import new active file
MAILTEST          Send test MAIL message to administrator
NEWGROUP          Add a new newsgroup to the news system
                  Syntax: "newgroup <group-name> <flag> <creator>"
RELOAD            Reload one or more control files (see CHECKFILE for
                  syntax)
RENUMBER          Update low water mark for specified group;
                  Updates all groups if no group specified
RMGROUP           Remove a newsgroup from the news system
STATUS            Display current status of the news server
TRACE             Set/reset TRACE (debug) flags

[End of help]
```

Terminate NNS by giving its window the focus and pressing Ctrl-C.

If you have an SMTP mail system, check the nns.ini file to ensure that the mail type equals SMTP, the mail account is your user name and MX domain, and the SMTP host is the name of your mail server. If you need to send mail via MAPI or UUCP, consult the NNS documentation.

To install NNS as a Windows NT service and identify its performance counters to the registry, issue the following commands:

```
nns -install autostart
lodctr nnsperf.ini
```

Start the NNS service using Control Panel Services or the command

```
net start nns
```

Test mail with the command

```
newsctl mailtest
```

A mail message like that displayed in Figure 14.1 should result.

If this works, try creating a newsgroup and posting an article. To create a newsgroup, use the command

```
newsctl newgroup <newsgroup>
```

where <newsgroup> is the name of the group you want to create. To create a large set of groups, take these steps:

1. Obtain the active file from your feed site.

2. Edit your copy of the active file to omit any groups you don't want to receive.

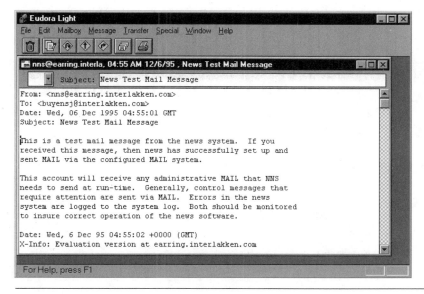

Figure 14.1 NNS News Test Mail Message

3. Save the edited file with the name ACTIVE.IMPORT.

4. Run the command

```
newsctl import
```

Note that until you add a newsgroup to NNS, NNS will ignore incoming articles for that group.

Figure 14.2 shows a sample article posted to the fictional newsgroup alt.interlakken.news.

NNS stores articles in directories with names derived from newsgroups. Each period in the newsgroup name becomes a backslash in the article's path, and the article number becomes the file name. Figure 14.3 illustrates this structure.

The fact that newsgroup name qualifiers can exceed eight characters is a strong argument for always using NTFS volumes for News. NTFS's ability to enlarge drives is also a valuable feature for running News. Finally, note that Figure 14.3 shows the same drive being used for incoming, outgoing, and spooled news; in practice, these areas should be on separate drives dedicated to these purposes.

14.3 Ongoing Management

The primary ongoing activities for managing News are maintaining the list of newsgroups and watching disk space.

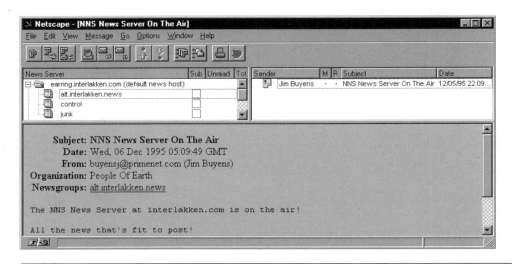

Figure 14.2 NNS Test News Article Successfully Posted and Retrieved

Figure 14.3 NNS Article Spool Directory Structure

You can automate the addition and deletion of newsgroups somewhat by honoring the pertinent control messages. This assumes, however, that you wish to start taking new groups without inspecting their content. You can exert some control over automated additions and deletions by using DNEWS's control.conf file or NNS's control.ctl file. For example, you can allow control messages to remove any newsgroup but allow them only to add new groups having the comp, linux, and sci qualifiers.

A full newsfeed can consume considerable disk space and bandwidth. Using a pull feed saves resources on your server but increases demand on the server sending the feed. Check with your newsfeed site before deciding on this solution. Else, your choices are to

- Get your newsfeed site to be more selective at its end.
- Reject more newsgroups at your end.
- Review article expiration periods.
- Buy more disk (gigabytes are very cheap these days).

Expiring of articles refers to the process of scanning all articles on the server and deleting those beyond a certain age. Shortening expiration periods is an obvious way to reclaim disk space. Expiration periods may vary by newsgroup.

When reclaiming disk space, it's important to have a sense of which are the largest newsgroup areas and which are the least used. This requires a directory profiler that reports disk usage within each branch of a directory tree and News server log summaries, respectively. However, only you can decide how much effort is worthwhile to avoid buying another gigabyte or two of disk.

From time to time, the News server's databases may get out of sync with the actual spool files. Things like this should never happen, but they do; software is never completely bug-free, and systems do crash for odd reasons (hardware failure, power failure, sunspots, phases of the moon). Newsreaders typically have utilities that rebuild the databases by scanning the spool area, but running these over a large spool can take 12 hours or more even on a powerful system.

News server performance is usually more disk-bound than CPU-bound. This argues for high-speed I/O buses—certainly not ISA buses—and plenty of RAM. The more RAM you have, the more I/O Windows NT can cache.

Be sure to have a plan for handling a disk failure. Perhaps you need to take daily backups of the entire News server, perhaps your feed site will commit to refeeding a week or more of activity, or perhaps you'll simply tell your users they're starting from scratch. Whatever your decision, you should make it in advance.

Given widespread interest in replication engines as groupware, it's surprising that no solutions based on USENET News have arisen. Consider the following USENET News features:

- Distributions can control the scope of replication.

- The "Keywords:" header could be used for newsgroup (that is, for database or shared folder) scanning and selection.

- MIME encoding supports multiple binary attachments.

- PEM (Privacy Enhanced Mail) and other security schemes support encryption and authentication.

- Together, the CANCEL control message plus a new posting allow existing articles to be replaced.

- Integration with E-Mail is excellent.

- The design has proven scalability.

This is not to claim USENET News as a complete replacement for commercial groupware packages. However, the possibilities are intriguing.

## CHAPTER 15

Installing and Configuring HTTP

What more is there to say about the World Wide Web? It was January 1993 when the National Center for Supercomputing Applications released the first version of Mosaic, a version that ran only on UNIX workstations. In the next 18 months, Web servers on the Internet increased from 50 to 10,000, and Web browsing became a worldwide phenomenon: a new, true killer app.

No one wonders anymore when "The Year of the LAN" is coming. It arrived in January 1993, and the world is its village. A computer without a network connection, not even a modem, has become a pitiful, dysfunctional machine. Proposals to eliminate everything but the network connection, screen, mouse, and keyboard receive serious attention.

And everything that's happened up to now is only the tip of the iceberg. It remains only for someone to deliver the bandwidth.

15.1 Operating Concepts and Standards

As is so often the case, simplicity has been a key to the Web's astounding growth. Complex, expensive technologies can't foster such rapid, widespread adoption.

HTTP clients, called *browsers*, actually do most of the work on the Web. This is as it should be. Clients outnumber servers by several hundred to one, so it makes sense for clients to do as much of the work as possible.

Web browsers act seamlessly as clients for a number of services. A list of these applications appeared back in Table 1.1. Server applications like FTP, Gopher, E-Mail, and News, however, remain quite separate and distinct. Most sites don't even run them all on a single computer.

The service that gives the Web its unique interface and personality is HyperText Transfer Protocol (HTTP). From a server point of view, HTTP is one of the simplest services on the Internet. One sentence explains most of what an HTTP server does: *The client sends the server a file name, and the server sends back the file.*

For the most part, HTTP servers treat all file types alike. The client can request a Web page, an image file, a text file, a ZIP file, or any other type of file, but the server cares little; in all cases, it simply transmits the file "as is" to the requesting client.[1]

HTTP is a stateless protocol. The browser can ask for whatever file it wants, but the server completely forgets about the browser once it delivers that file. Even if the browser asks for several files at once (that is, it asks for a second file while transmission of another is still in progress), the server senses no relationship between the requests.

15.1.1 HyperText Markup Language

Hypertext files—those that contain Web pages—use a coding scheme called HyperText Markup Language (HTML). HTML files contain plain ASCII text, formatting instructions, and references to additional files. The Web browser interprets the HTML coding, asks the HTTP server for copies of any additional files mentioned within the HTML code, and formats the pages for display.

HTML coding depends on tags identified by angle brackets (< >). The first (and frequently only) parameter within the brackets is a tag identifier. Most tags occur in pairs, with appearance of the tag turning on some effect and appearance of the same tag (with a slash preceding the identifier) ending the effect. The tag identifier for bold is "B," so inserting a <B> turns bolding on and </B> turns it off.

An elementary HTML file appears next; Figure 15.1 shows how Netscape Navigator displays this page:

```
element.html
<HTML>
  <HEAD>
    <TITLE>Figure 15.1</TITLE>
  </HEAD>
```

---

[1]In addition to asking an HTTP server for files, browsers can also ask them to run programs on the server, look up image maps, and perform various other services. The next chapter will focus on these topics.

Figure 15.1 An Elementary HTML File Displayed by Netscape Navigator

```
<BODY>
    <H1>An Elementary HTML File</H1>
  <HR>
    <IMG SRC="windows.gif">
    <A HREF="http://www.microsoft.com">Microsoft</A>
  </BODY>
</HTML>
```

Consider the following points:

- The page begins with <HTML> and ends with </HTML>. All HTML files contain these statements.

- There are two major sections, delimited <HEAD> and </HEAD>, <BODY> and </BODY>. These four statements appear in almost all HTML files.

- The <HEAD> section contains the text "Figure 15.1" set off by <TITLE> and </TITLE>. Note in Figure 15.1 that the <TITLE> text appears in the browser's menu bar and not in the main display. Most automated Web indexers also use the title string as the human-readable name of the page. Best practice, therefore, is to give every page a title.

- Within the <BODY>, <H1> and </H1> tags set off the text "An Elementary HTML File." The browser displays this text using the largest available heading style; styles <H2> through <H6> are progressively smaller.

- The <HR> tag produces a horizontal rule—the heavy line extending across the page just below the heading.

- The tag <IMG SRC="windows.gif"> has no corresponding end tag, but it does contain a file name. The <IMG> tag tells the browser to retrieve the specified file and display it where the <IMG> tag would otherwise appear on the page. The server doesn't send the windows.gif file on its own; the server doesn't even "know" windows.gif is part of the element.html page. The browser must get windows.gif from the server as a completely separate transaction from asking for element.html.

- The tag <A HREF="http://www.microsoft.com"> is an anchor. Everything between the <A...> and </A> tags becomes hypertext that, if clicked, causes the browser to retrieve the data specified in the anchor tag's HREF argument. In other words, if the user clicks on the "Microsoft" text, the browser will retrieve the page at "http://www.microsoft.com."

Consult Appendix B for additional information on HTML and for Web pointers to various resources. A complete discussion of HTML, however, is beyond the scope of this book.

15.1.2 Uniform Resource Locators

Browsers act as HTTP clients and retrieve files based on Uniform Resource Locators (URLs). The first part of a URL indicates the application protocol, and the rest contains identifiers specific to that application. Here's a sampling of URLs:

```
mailto:buyensj@interlakken.com
news:comp.infosystems.www.servers.ms_windows
ftp://ftp.interlakken.com/pub/blat14.zip
http://www.interlakken.com:80/fiction/index.html
```

Note there's no computer name in the mailto and news URLs. Instead, Mail server and News server computer names are part of the browser's local configuration.

URLs for HTTP and FTP consist of

- The application protocol identifier, ended by a colon.

- A double slash, indicating that a computer name follows.

- A computer name.

- An optional colon, indicating that a port number follows.
- An optional port number. If absent, the application's well-known port will apply.
- A slash.
- Optionally, one or more directory names separated by slashes.
- A file name.

For FTP URLs, it's generally best to always specify the complete computer name, path, and file name.

In the case of HTTP, everything but the "http" is optional, except that blank URLs are invalid. If the computer name is absent, the browser uses the computer name that provided the currently displayed page. Port number defaults to 80. Directories are optional if the desired file resides in the HTTP server's starting directory. If no file name appears, the HTTP server looks for a default file name; if that fails, it may display a list of available file names.

Responsibility for defaulting HTTP URL fields falls to the browser. It's the browser that parses the URL, extracts or defaults the computer name, translates the computer name to an IP address, and connects using the specified or default port. The browser must also parse or default the directory path. The only default resolved by the server is the default file name.

As already described, the browser sends the server a file name, and the server returns the named file. The server never remembers the state of the client. Sessions last only for the duration of a single file transfer; obtaining multiple files involves opening several sessions.

15.1.3 HyperText Transfer Protocol

At the time of this writing, no official standards existed for HTTP. The rate of change and enhancement simply outstripped the speed of the standard-setting process. Several Internet Drafts describe the versions of HTTP, but the IETF can withdraw, update, or supersede Internet Drafts at any time.

To locate Internet Drafts describing the HyperText Transfer Protocol, point your browser at http://www.ietf.cnri.reston.va.us/ids.by.wg/http.html.

Three versions of HTTP are in common use: HTTP/0.9, HTTP/1.0, and HTTP/1.1. A good way to see the difference between versions is to Telnet to a server on the appropriate port (usually port 80) and manually invoke methods. Such a session appears next:

```
get /element.html
<HTML>
  <HEAD>
    <TITLE>Figure 15.1</TITLE>
  </HEAD>

  <BODY>
    <H1>An Elementary HTML File</H1>
  <HR>
    <IMG SRC="windows.gif">
    <A HREF="http://www.microsoft.com">Microsoft</A>
  </BODY>
</HTML>
```

A browser would run this session in response to the URL http://www.inter-lakken.com/element.html. The protocol identifier http is a browser command and is not passed to the server. Likewise, the browser removes the computer name and port number from the URL and uses them to open a TCP connection to the named computer.

The session just shown is an HTTP/0.9 session. The only method available in that version was "get." The server responds by transmitting the identified file and then closes the connection.

HTTP/1.0 had two major additions: first, a number of additional methods and second, header fields. Header fields follow the format of SMTP Mail messages: a keyword, a colon, a space, and a value. As with Mail, a blank line signifies the end of the headers and the start of the body. Some methods and some responses don't have bodies, but the blank line is still necessary.

HTTP/1.0 servers must support HTTP/0.9 browsers by responding to HTTP/0.9 methods in an HTTP/0.9 way. This can lead to ambiguity when the same method syntax persists from version to version, so a version string such as "http/1.0" must appear at the end of each line invoking a method greater than HTTP/0.9.

Compare the following HTTP/1.0 session to the previous HTTP/0.9 session:

```
get /element.html http/1.0

HTTP/1.0 200 OK
Server: Netscape-Communications/1.12
```

```
Date: Thursday, 14-Dec-95 05:08:15 GMT
Last-modified: Thursday, 14-Dec-95 04:42:02 GMT
Content-length: 223
Content-type: text/html

<HTML>
  <HEAD>
    <TITLE>Figure 15.1</TITLE>
  </HEAD>

  <BODY>
    <H1>An Elementary HTML File</H1>
  <HR>
    <IMG SRC="windows.gif">
    <A HREF="http://www.microsoft.com">Microsoft</A>
  </BODY>
</HTML>
```

As before, the session starts by opening a TCP connection to port 80 on www.interlakken.com. The "get" method has almost the same syntax as before, but "http/1.0" appears at the end. The server doesn't respond until it receives a blank line.

The server's response begins with a status line containing the HTTP version, a status code, and a verbal status description. The server follows this with header lines indicating the name and version of the server software, the current date and time, the requested object's last modification date and time, its length, and its type. A blank line indicates the end of the headers and the start the of body.

Table 15.1 lists the methods supported under HTTP/1.1 and provides an interesting glimpse of what the Web may someday provide. Methods like POST, PUT, PATCH, COPY, and DELETE at first seem frightening: We don't want users doing these things to our Web pages! Header fields can provide authentication, though, so administrators can control who does what to whom.

Although most current Web usage consists of GETting HTML pages, the new update methods (combined with authentication) might provide the means for users of diskless "Internet terminals" to save and retrieve personal data on remote file servers. This data wouldn't have to be HTML files, or even files; it could be database records, images, word-processing documents, sounds, or any other electronic format.

Table 15.1 HyperText Transfer Protocol 1.1 Methods

Method	Description
OPTIONS	Requests information about available communication options.
GET	Retrieves whatever information the resource identifier implies.
HEAD	Returns the same headers the GET method would return, but no body.
POST	Asks the server to accept the entity in the method's body as a new subordinate of the identified resource. This could involve adding a record to a file, an article to a newsgroup, etc.
PUT	Requests that the entity in the method's body be stored under the given identity. If an entity with the given name already exists, the server should replace it.
PATCH	Supplies a list of changes the server should apply to the named entity.
COPY	Copies an object on the server to a new object with a specified name.
MOVE	Copies an object and then deletes the original.
DELETE	Removes an object from the server.
LINK	Establishes a link name (alias) for an existing object.
UNLINK	Deletes a link name (alias) for an existing object.
TRACE	Asks the server to reflect whatever it receives back to the client. This is useful in complex environments to determine exactly what the server is receiving.
WRAPPED	Asks the server to interpret the request body as one or more (possibly encrypted) requests. Header fields indicate the request and encryption types.

The communication path between an HTTP client and server may involve one or more intermediary computers. There are three types of intermediaries:

1. A *proxy* is a forwarding agent; it receives requests, reformats all or parts of the message, and forwards the results toward the server identified by the URL. Note that, unlike requests sent to a local server, requests sent to a proxy must include the destination computer name. Proxies often serve as security firewalls; in such a role, they forward "inside" requests to the "outside" but not the reverse.

2. A *gateway* is a receiving agent that runs on top of another server. If necessary, the gateway translates requests to the underlying server's protocol.

3. A *tunnel* relays requests and responses between two connections without changing them. Tunnels allow communication to pass through an intermediary (such as a firewall) even when the intermediary doesn't understand the message's contents.

Some of these intermediaries may additionally cache activity. This means the intermediary observes the response to a given request and then supplies the same response if it notices the same request again. Certain header fields (described shortly) can control such caching in cases where it might be inappropriate.

Table 15.2 summarizes the well-defined HTTP/1.1 header types. Some of these are in wide use today, such as the "If-Modified-Since" header, which allows browsers to locally cache and redisplay remote entries that haven't changed. Other header types, like the newer methods listed in Table 15.1, seem more like science fiction than today's Web, and no software may ever implement them. Then again,

- Why shouldn't users configure their browsers once with the natural language, character set, and file types (by class) they prefer and have the server automatically supply the most preferred available type?

- What configuration on the server would associate multiple versions of the same object and automatically deliver, say, the French "au" file rather than the Portuguese "wav"?

- Could providers of potentially offensive material stem opposition by adding category headers so that browsers and proxy servers can, if desired, filter it?

Table 15.2 HyperText Transfer Protocol 1.1 Header Types

Header	Description
Accept	Indicates a list of media types (file formats) the client will accept. This can include preferences like "I'd prefer a wav file but I'll take au if that's all you have."
Accept-Charset	Indicates what character sets are acceptable (and, optionally, preferable) for the response.
Accept-Encoding	Resembles "Accept" but identifies acceptable encoding schemes: zip, gzip, lzh, base64, etc.
Accept-Language	Provides a list of acceptable natural languages.
Allow	Lists the methods supported by whatever resource by the request specified.
Authorization	Supplies client credentials to perform a method on a secured resource.
Base	Specifies a base location the server should prefix to relative resource locators.
Cache-Control	Governs caching mechanisms along the transmission route to avoid interference with the request.
Connection	Lists keywords and identifies headers applicable only to the current connection. If an end-to-end connection involves proxies or gateways, this information pertains only to a single "hop."
Connection: Keep-Alive	Requests a connection that lasts beyond the current request/response interaction. This allows a client to submit several requests without setting up a new connection for each one.
Content-Encoding	Indicates the content encoding scheme used for the current entity.
Content-Language	Identifies the natural language(s) of the current entity.
Content-Length	States the size of the body-entity sent to the recipient (or, in the case of the HEAD method, that the server would send).
Content-Type	States the media type of the body-entity being sent (or, in the case of the HEAD method, that the server would send).
Content-Version	States the version of a particular rendition of an entity.
Date	Records the date and time the message originated.

Table 15.2 HyperText Transfer Protocol 1.1 Header Types *(continued)*

Header	Description
Derived-From	Indicates the starting version of an entity now being returned with modifications. This allows the server to detect if other changes to the entity have occurred.
Expires	Specifies a date and time an entity will become stale. This allows an information provider to delete, archive, or take other appropriate action.
Forwarded	Records intermediate transmission points between client and server. This is useful for tracing and for avoiding request loops.
From	Specifies the E-Mail address of the client person.
Host	Specifies, for the server's benefit, the host name in the original URL.
If-Modified-Since	Makes the GET method conditional on the date last modified. If no one has modified the requested resource since the given date and time, the server returns a 304 (not modified) response rather than a new copy of the entity.
Keep-Alive	Includes diagnostic information and other optional parameters associated with the "Connection" header "Keep-Alive" keyword.
Last-Modified	Indicates the date and time someone modified the resource (as apparent to the sender).
Link	Describes a relationship between the entity and some other resource.
Location	Defines the exact location of the resource identified by the request. For response codes in the 200s, this is the actual URL after content negotiation. For responses in the 300s, this is the URL the client should use instead of the original.
MIME-Version	Indicates what version of MIME the sender used to construct the message.
Proxy-Authenticate	Contains a challenge indicating the authentication scheme and parameters required to access the requested entity. Any 407 response (proxy authentication required) must include this header.
Proxy-Authorization	Supplies user agent credentials to a proxy that requires authentication.
Public	Lists nonstandard methods supported by the server. This informs the recipient of unusual methods and other capabilities the server may support.
Referrer	Specifies where the client found the requested URL. This allows a server to accumulate a list of links to itself.
Retry-After	Indicates how long a service may be unavailable to the requesting client. This can accompany a 503 (service unavailable) response.
Server	Contains information about the server software that handled the request. Typical information includes the name and version.
Title	Indicates the title of the entity.
Transfer Encoding	Indicates any transformation applied to safely transmit the message body. This is a property of the message, while "Content-Encoding" is a property of the original resource.
Unless	Makes a method conditional on any entity-header field of the requested resource.
Upgrade	Specifies what additional communication protocols a client supports and would like to use if the server is agreeable. When a server supplies a 101 (switching protocols) response, it must use the "Upgrade" header to indicate which protocol(s) it's switching.
URI	Informs the recipient of other Uniform Resource Identifiers that identify the resource and all negotiable variants corresponding to the Request-URI.
User-Agent	Describes the user agent originating the request (name and version).
WWW-Authenticate	Contains at least one challenge that indicates the authentication scheme(s) and parameters applicable to the Request-URI. This header must appear in all 401 (unauthorized) response messages.

The remainder of this section consists of Table 15.3, a list of common HTTP/1.1 response codes. If you've ever received a "404 Not Found" message in your browser window, here's the list it came from.

The specification neither requires a server to issue all these responses nor prohibits it from sending others. In addition, there's no standardization of message text; each server can use whatever text (in whatever language) it wants. The table shows five groups of response codes that are grouped by first digit.

Table 15.3 HTTP/1.1 Response Codes

Response Code	Description
1xx	*Informational*
	Request received; continuing process.
100	Continue
101	Switching Protocols
2xx	*Success*
	The action was successfully received, understood, and accepted.
200	OK
201	Created
202	Accepted
203	Non-Authoritative Information
204	No Content
205	Reset Content
206	Partial Content
3xx	*Redirection*
	Further action must be taken in order to complete the request.
300	Multiple Choices
301	Moved Permanently
302	Moved Temporarily
303	See Other
304	Not Modified
305	Use Proxy
4xx	*Client Error*
	The request contains bad syntax or cannot be fulfilled.
400	Bad Request
401	Unauthorized
402	Payment Required
403	Forbidden
404	Not Found

Table 15.3 HTTP/1.1 Response Codes *(continued)*

Response Code	Description
405	Method Not Allowed
406	None Acceptable
407	Proxy Authentication Required
408	Request Timeout
409	Conflict
410	Gone
411	Length Required
412	Unless True
5xx	*Server Error*
	The server failed to fulfill an apparently valid request.
500	Internal Server Error
501	Not Implemented
502	Bad Gateway
503	Service Unavailable
504	Gateway Timeout

15.1.4 Advanced HTTP Features

For simplicity, this chapter concentrates primarily on HTTP as a simple file delivery mechanism. Nevertheless, HTTP, like any other technology, literally begs for enhancement. Sections later in this book will discuss the following services in detail (for now, just realize they exist):

- **Image maps.** A special HTML tag specifies that clicking an associated image will immediately transmit the click's X–Y coordinates to the HTTP server. The server then delivers a specified HTML file based on the X–Y coordinates.

- **Common Gateway Interface (CGI).** A special URL causes the HTTP server to launch a program instead of delivering a file. Such programs can obtain command-line input appended to the URL or read data from HTML forms piped into Standard Input (STDIN). They return output to the user by writing HTML to Standard Output (STDOUT).

- **Server Side Include (SSI).** The server scans outgoing HTML files for a special tag that, if found, triggers a program. Output from the program replaces the tag, and then transmission of the original file resumes.

- **Access control.** User names and passwords control access to specified pages.

- **Secure HTTP.** Encryption secures transmissions between the browser and the HTTP server on a page-by-page basis.

- **WAIS and other search engines.** An input field on an HTML form supplies keywords used for index lookups.

- **Virtual domains.** On a server with multiple IP addresses, each address has a different default home page.

15.2 Sample Installations

The phenomenal popularity and relative simplicity of the Web have resulted in quite a number of Web server products. The basic HTTP protocol is so simple that the products must differentiate themselves in user interface features and advanced functions. This section presents brief case studies of four representative HTTP servers:

1. **EMWAC HTTPS.** The European Microsoft Windows NT Academic Centre at the University of Edinburgh, Scotland, distributes this software free of charge. This was one of the first HTTP servers for Windows NT and is still quite common. A fully supported commercial version also exists.

2. **Netscape Communications Server.** In addition to being the "official" companion product to the Netscape Navigator client, this server software has been a leader in security-related features. (Netscape Commerce Server provides even more security features, including encryption of data transmitted in both directions between client and server.)

3. **O'Reilly WebSite.** In the year preceding authorship of this book, WebSite was the market-leading HTTP server for Windows NT.

4. **Microsoft Internet Information Server.** This is the unified HTTP, FTP, and Gopher server Microsoft has begun shipping with every copy of Windows NT Server.

This list is by no means inclusive of the market; many other fine HTTP server products for Windows NT exist. You should compare your needs to features provided by all these products before committing your site.

The case studies in this chapter take installation only to the point of displaying simple HTML pages. The next chapter on advanced HTTP functions covers additional features.

15.2.1 Preparing for HTTP Server Installation

Before jumping into the installation process for any of these servers, you should complete the following steps:

1. Set up a "www" CNAME for the server. Generally, "www" won't be the name of the computer that runs the primary HTTP service at your site; it will be an alias you define in DNS with a CNAME record in the primary zone database. In the following example, the second line establishes www.interlakken.com as an alias for earring.interlakken.com (an earlier $ORIGIN command established interlakken.com as the default domain):

```
earring      IN      A        130.131.90.111
www          IN      CNAME    earring
```

2. Stop any other HTTP servers running on the same computer. This avoids port conflicts and other problems.

3. Choose a drive and, if you like, a directory where the server's HTML files will reside. Choose a drive that uses the NTFS file system, avoid the system drive, and avoid the drive where the HTTP server software will reside.

   Typically, many users have access to portions of the server's HTML data directory; each user may have access to a personal "home page" area, for example. It's good policy to isolate such areas as much as possible from operating system and other software areas.

4. Decide where you want the HTTP server's software to reside. Choose a drive that users never have access to.

5. Select a drive where the HTTP server's log files will reside. Don't choose the system drive—choose a drive that won't affect system operation if unexpectedly large activity (or oversight) causes the log file to consume all space on the drive.

15.2.2 Installing and Configuring EMWAC HTTPS

You can obtain the EMWAC HTTPS service from EMWAC at http://www.emwac.ac.uk, from the Microsoft Windows NT Resource Kit versions 3.5 and 3.51, or from the CD accompanying this book. To get the server up and running, proceed as follows:

1. To install EMWAC HTTPS from the CD accompanying this book, change to the \HSI386 directory on your CD drive.

2. If you download a new version, create and change to a temporary directory and then decompress the archive file, generally called HSI386.ZIP, into it.

3. If you install from the Windows NT Resource Kit, first install the Resource Kit and then position to the \RESKIT\EMWAC directory.

4. Copy the following files to the server's <systemroot>\system32 directory: HTTPS.EXE, HTTPS.CPL, HTTPS.HLP, and MSVCRT20.DLL. Be sure not to replace a newer version of MSVCRT20.DLL, if one exists.

5. Cd to the <systemroot>\system32 directory and issue the following commands:

```
https -remove
```

to remove an old version of HTTPS, if one exists;

```
https -version
```

to verify the new version number;

```
https -ipaddress
```

to verify that HTTPS sees the correct IP address.

If information from the "https -version" or "https -ipaddress" commands isn't correct, obtain the desired version or correct your TCP/IP network settings before continuing.

6. If results from the prior step are correct, issue the command

```
https -install
```

7. Return to the Windows NT GUI, start Control Panel, and double-click the icon titled "HTTP Server." A dialog like that in Figure 15.2 should result.

8. In the text box titled "Data directory," enter the drive and directory where your HTML files reside. For now, allow the other fields to default. If you haven't created a directory for HTML files yet, do it now. The data directory should be on an NTFS drive.

If the data directory resides on another server, specify a UNC (Universal Naming Convention) name rather than a drive letter. Drive letter assignments disappear when you log off the server console.

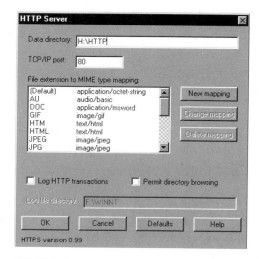

Figure 15.2 EMWAC HTTP Server Control Panel Dialog

9. Click OK to save the HTTP Server settings.

10. Double-click the Control Panel Services icon.

11. Highlight the line "EMWAC HTTPS Server" and then click the Start button. Status of the EMWAC HTTPS Server should change to "Running."

12. Ensure that there's at least one HTML file in the HTTP data directory and that you know its name.

13. From any computer on the same network as the server, start a Web browser and enter the following URL:

```
http://<server name>/<HTML file name>
```

where <server name> is the server's DNS name, host file name, or IP address and where <HTML file name> is a file name in the server's data directory.

The HTTP server resolves directory paths in URLs relative to the HTTP data directory. Also, in UNIX fashion, slashes rather than backslashes indicate directory names. Consider the following example:

■ Data directory is h:\http.

■ Local path of HTML file is h:\http\french\fries.htm.

■ URL is http://<server>/french/fries.htm.

If the HTTP server won't start, check that all required files are in the <systemroot>\system32 directory and that no other services (such as other HTTP servers) are running on port 80. As always, note any alerts that appear in dialog boxes or in the Windows NT Event Log.

Most problems you encounter are likely to be connectivity issues. If you can ping the server and the HTTP service is running, you should be able to retrieve Web pages.

Here are the functions of the remaining controls in the HTTP Server Control Panel dialog (Figure 15.2):

- **TCP/IP port.** This controls the TCP/IP port number the HTTP server will use. The HTTPS and industry defaults are port 80.

- **File extension to MIME type mapping.** The HTTP server uses MIME file type strings to inform the browser what kind of file the server is sending. The EMWAC HTTP server derives this information from the file name extension. Table 15.4 lists the default MIME type assignments.

- **Log HTTP transactions.** Checking this box ON causes the HTTP server to write a log record every time it delivers a file. The log is a plain ASCII file named HSyymmdd.LOG, where yymmdd is the current date. The log is useful for determining how often users are hitting individual pages.

- **Log file directory.** This specifies the directory where the HTTP server will write the log file. The <systemroot> directory, which is the default, isn't a good choice; write log files and other miscellaneous files to another drive less affected by running out of space.

- **Permit directory browsing.** If this box is checked, if a user submits a URL that specifies no file name, and if no default.htm file is present, then the HTTP server will present a clickable list of file names in the specified directory.

15.2.3 Installing and Configuring Netscape Communications Server

The following steps will install an evaluation copy of Netscape Communications Server:

1. Obtain a copy of the software from Netscape's Web site at www.netscape.com.

Table 15.4 EMWAC HTTP Server Default MIME Type Assignments

File Extension	MIME Type
Default	application/octet-string
AU	audio/basic
DOC	application/msword
GIF	image/gif
HTM	text/html
HTML	text/html
JPEG	image/jpeg
JPG	image/jpeg
MPEG	video/mpeg
MPG	video/mpeg
PDF	application/pdf
PS	application/postscript
RTF	application/rtf
TIF	image/tiff
TIFF	image/tiff
TXT	text/plain
WAV	audio/wav
XBM	image/x-xbitmap
ZIP	application/zip

2. Create a temporary directory, switch to it, and then expand the down-loaded archive.

3. Start SETUP.EXE.

4. Click the Continue button on the Welcome dialog.

5. Choose an installation directory for the Netscape program files. For maximum security, keep this directory off any drive that users can access. Click Continue.

6. Setup will copy quite a number of files to various directories and then ask if the server's host name already exists in DNS. Click "DNS Configured" or "No DNS Entry" as the case may be.

7. If you click "DNS Configured," Setup will prompt you for the server's DNS name. The default is the name specified in Control Panel, Network, TCP/IP Protocol, Configure, DNS. You should override this if you've created a "www" CNAME entry in DNS. Click Continue.

8. Click OK at the screen informing you that Setup is starting a temporary Web service.

At this point in the installation, the user interface switches from Windows NT dialogs to HTML forms. Setup installs a copy of Netscape Navigator for this purpose. Netscape Server software uses HTML forms exclusively for administration; this presents a more awkward interface than native Windows NT dialogs, but it does support complete remote administration. Continue as follows:

9. Click "Accept" at the Netscape License Agreement dialog.

10. The temporary Netscape server will display the HTML form shown in Figure 15.3. Note the randomly chosen port number displayed in the Net site: field. Click "Start the Installation!" to continue.

Figure 15.3 Netscape Httpd 1.1 Communications Server Installation Form

11. Netscape Navigator displays the following HTML forms without security—that is, without encrypting the data. Since the browser and the temporary HTTP server are running on the same physical machine, this shouldn't be a problem. Uncheck "Show This Alert Next Time" (Figure 15.4) and then click the Continue button.

12. The next HTML form, displayed in Figure 15.5, is a jump point for three dialogs required to configure the server: Server Config, Document Config, and Admin Config. Click the Server Config button.

13. Figures 15.6, 15.7, 15.8, and 15.9 display the Server Configuration form. The example will use the following options:

Server name:	www.interlakken.com	(the default)
Server port:	80	(the default)
Server location:	F:\NETSCAPE\ns-home	(the default)
Minimum threads:	16	(the default)
Maximum threads:	32	(the default)
Host name resolution:	Always attempt	(the default)
Access logging:	Log all accesses	(the default)

After making any changes to this form, click the button titled "Make These Changes."

14. The Document Configuration form appears in Figures 15.10, 15.11, and 15.12. The example will use the following options:

Document root:	H:\HTTP	(as before)
Index files:	index.html, home.html	(the default)
Automatic indexing:	Fancy	(the default)
Home page:	(nothing)	(the default)

After choosing your own options, click "Make These Changes."

15. Figures 15.13, 15.14, and 15.15 illustrate the Administrative Configuration form. The example will use the following options:

Admin user name:	admin	(the default)
Admin password:	thecia	(whatever)
Admin hosts:	*.interlakken.com	(our domain)
Admin addresses:	(none)	(the default)
Admin port:	8088	(sentimental)

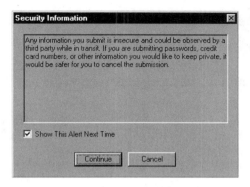

Figure 15.4 Netscape Httpd Security Information Alert

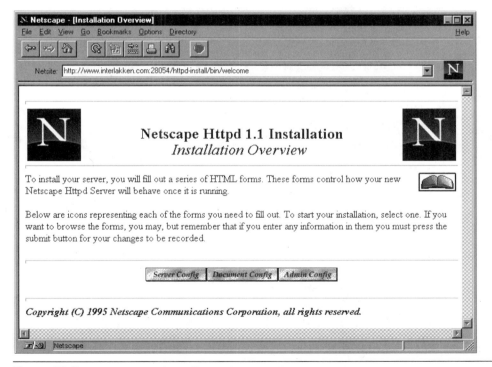

Figure 15.5 Netscape Httpd Installation Overview Form

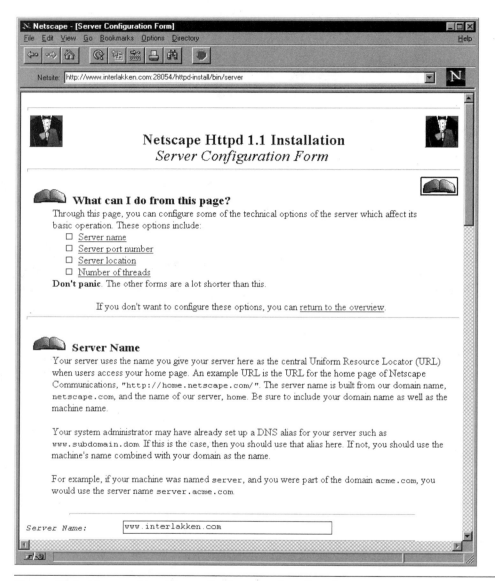

Figure 15.6 Netscape Httpd Server Configuration Form (Part 1)

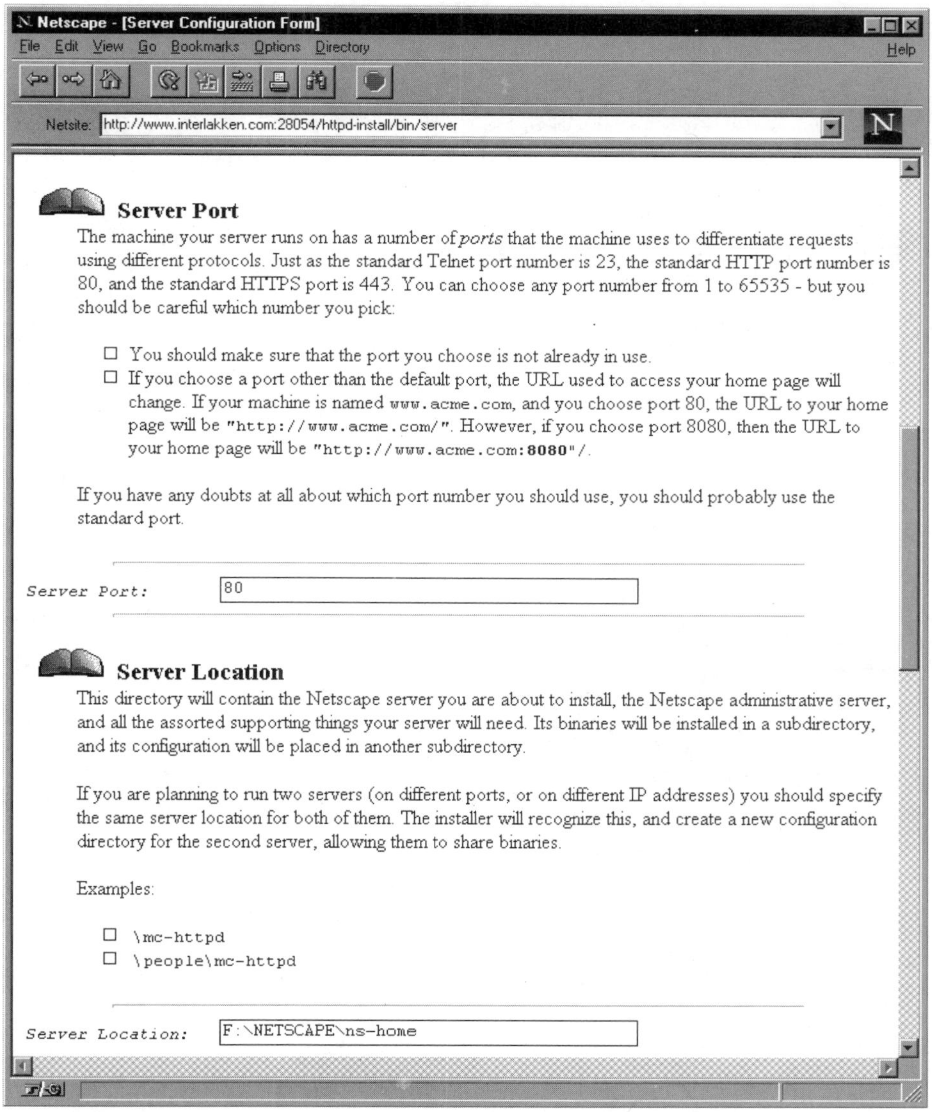

Figure 15.7 Netscape Httpd Server Configuration Form (Part 2)

```
N. Netscape - [Server Configuration Form]                                    _ □ ×
File  Edit  View  Go  Bookmarks  Options  Directory                            Help

  ⇦   ∞   🏠      🛇   🔅   🔅   🖶   🔍      ●

  Netsite: http://www.interlakken.com:28054/httpd-install/bin/server      ▾   N
```

📖 Number of Threads

The server creates a number of threads on your server machine when it starts up. These threads take turns answering requests. You can set the number of threads to achieve a balance between system load and request response time. The number should be determined by the number of requests you expect and the speed of the hardware your system runs on. On a low-demand system, the server may only need five or ten threads. On a very high demand system, you may want to use as many as thirty threads.

If you are having trouble setting this number, consult your *Server Reference Guide* for more details.

Minimum Threads: `16`

Maximum Threads: `32`

📖 Hostname resolution

When a network navigator connects to your Netsite server, the server only knows the client's IP address, e.g. `198.95.251.30`. The server does not know that this IP address is actually the host name `www1.netscape.com`. For certain operations like access control, CGI, error reporting, and access logging, the server will resolve that IP address into a host name.

If your server is very popular, and responds to many requests per day, you will want or may even need to stop this resolution from happening. Doing this can reduce the load on your DNS or NIS server, at the cost of a little convenience. Do not turn hostname resolution on if you do not have access to a DNS server or if you have not setup DNS access correctly on your machine.

◉ `Always attempt to resolve IP addresses into host names.`
○ `Never attempt to resolve IP addresses into host names.`

Figure 15.8 Netscape Httpd Server Configuration Form (Part 3)

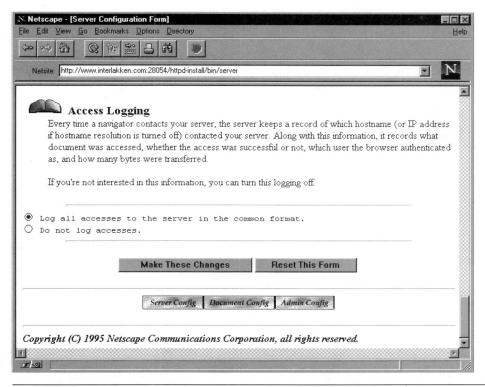

Figure 15.9 Netscape Httpd Server Configuration Form (Part 4)

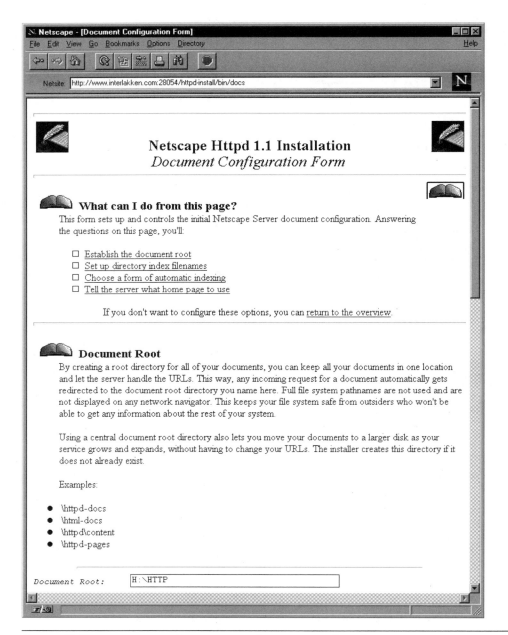

Figure 15.10 Netscape Httpd Document Configuration Form (Part 1)

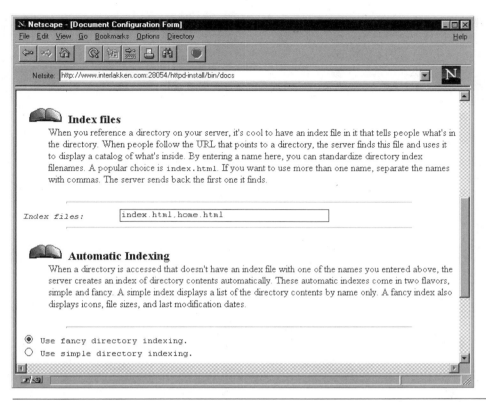

Figure 15.11 Netscape Httpd Document Configuration Form (Part 2)

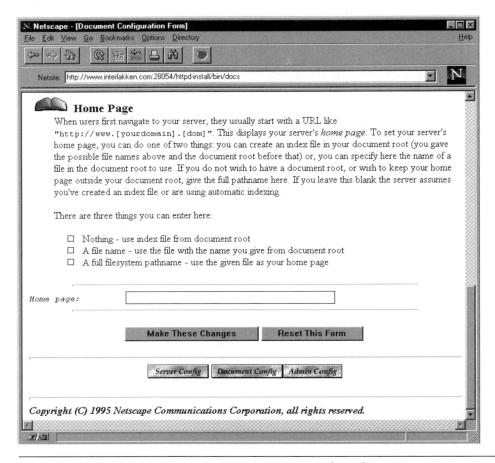

Figure 15.12 Netscape Httpd Document Configuration Form (Part 3)

Several instances of the Netscape Httpd server can run on a single computer, and, in fact, this is the norm. The simplest configuration is to run two instances: one for normal users and one for administration. Having a separate administration server helps keep users away from system functions, and it allows the administration server to perform control duties like stopping and restarting user service. Each instance of the server must, of course, run on a separate port not used by any other service on the same computer.

When you're done making changes to this form, click the "Make These Changes" button.

16. After you've completed all three forms, Netscape Httpd will display a configuration summary page like that shown in Figure 15.16. If you

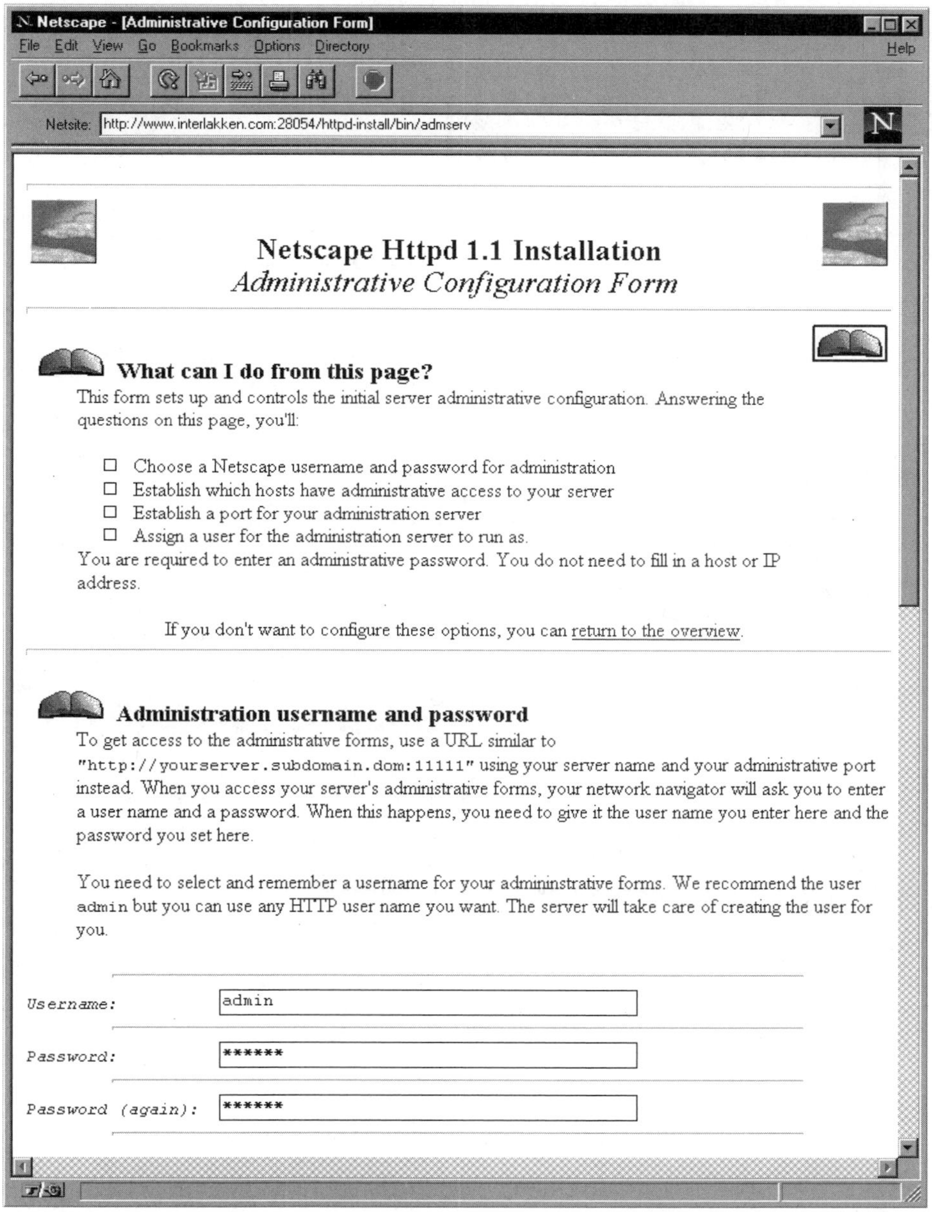

Figure 15.13 Netscape Httpd Administrative Configuration Form (Part 1)

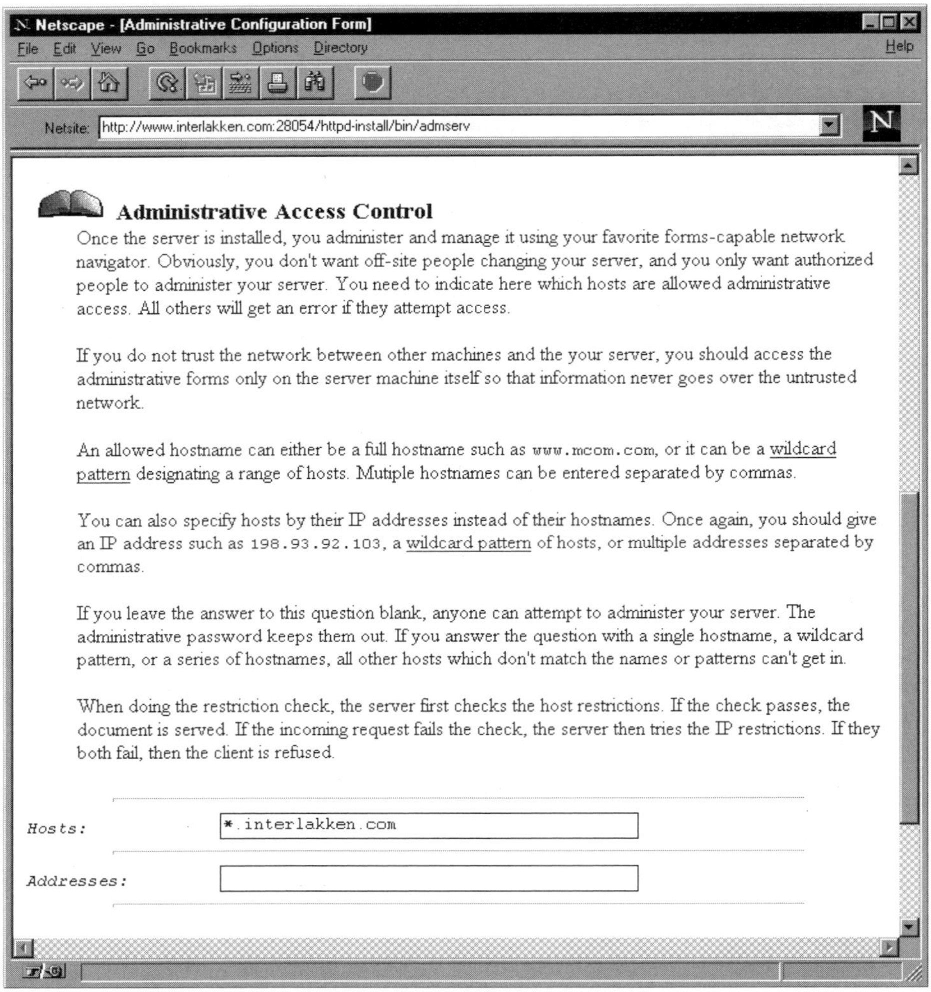

Figure 15.14 Netscape Httpd Administrative Configuration Form (Part 2)

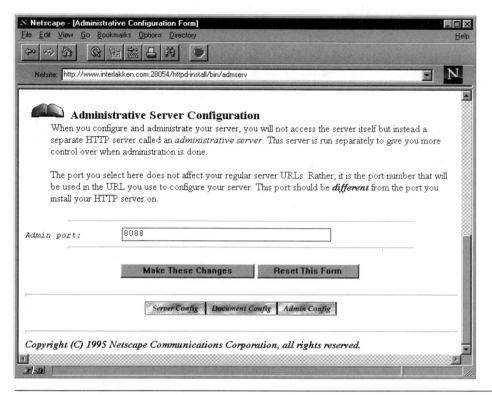

Figure 15.15 Netscape Httpd Administrative Configuration Form (Part 3)

need to make any corrections, click the Server Config, Document Config, or Admin Config button as appropriate. Once the summary page is satisfactory, click "Go for it!" to continue.

17. Setup will display a number of status messages in the browser window as it installs the user and administrative instances of Netscape Httpd. After it successfully completes, it will display a welcome page like that shown in Figure 15.17. Click the hypertext link "Administer the new server."

18. The Netscape Server Manager page shown in Figures 15.18, 15.19, and 15.20 will appear next. Note this page's URL carefully; it will be your starting point for most server administration tasks. Pull down the Bookmarks menu and select "Add Bookmark" to save it.

19. Pull down Netscape Navigator's File menu, select "New Window," and specify the URL

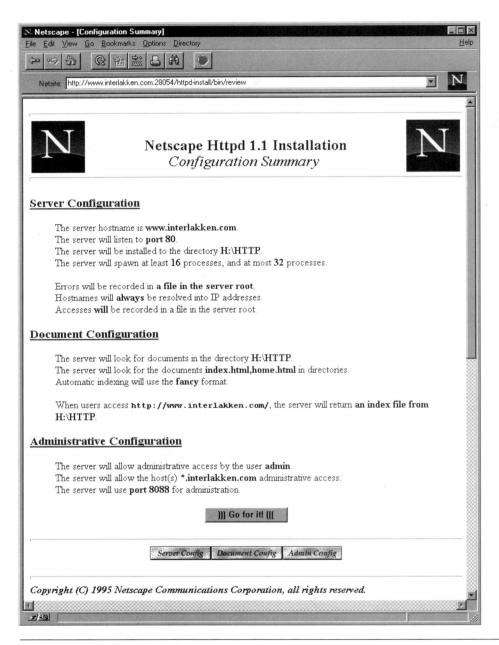

Figure 15.16 Netscape Httpd Configuration Summary Page

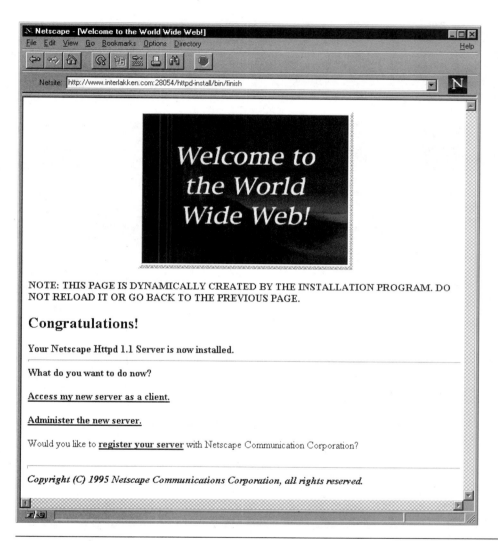

Figure 15.17 Netscape Httpd Welcome Page

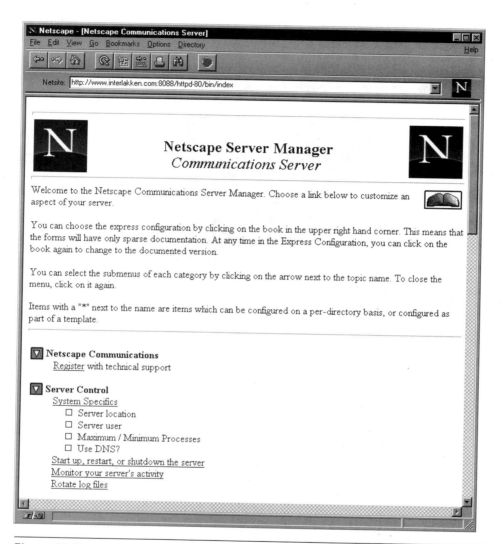

Figure 15.18 Netscape Httpd Server Manager Page (Part 1)

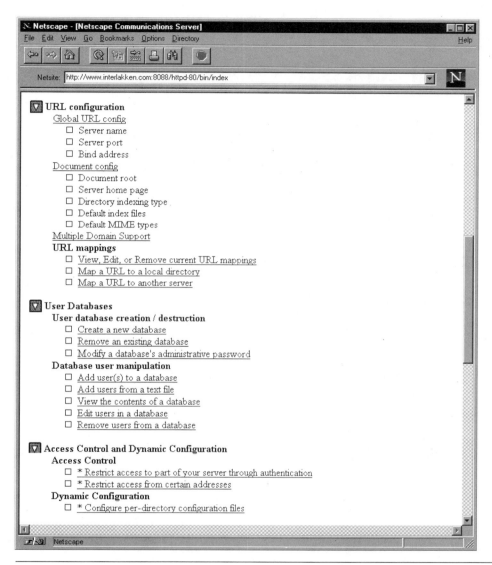

Figure 15.19 Netscape Httpd Server Manager Page (Part 2)

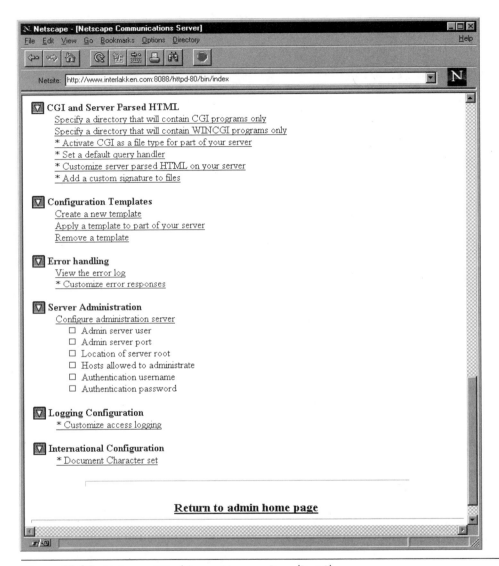

Figure 15.20 Netscape Httpd Server Manager Page (Part 3)

What appears next in the Netscape Navigator window is the current home page for the server. Setup will create a default home page as shown in Figure 15.21.

At this point, the temporary HTTP server will have ended and both instances of Netscape Httpd will be running your computer. To confirm this, go to Control Panel, double-click "Services," and find the two entries "Netscape Administration" and "Netscape Httpd-80." Both should be running as shown in Figure 15.22.

15.2.4 Installing and Configuring O'Reilly WebSite

You can install a demo copy of O'Reilly WebSite either from the \WEBSITE directory on the accompanying CD or by downloading the software from O'Reilly's Web site at http://website.ora.com.

If you download the file, unzip it into a temporary directory. If you're using the CD, change to the \WEBSITE directory on the CD drive. Either way, proceed as follows:

1.   Start the SETUP.EXE program.

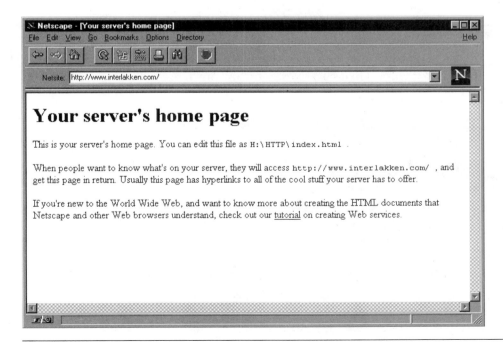

Figure 15.21 Netscape Default Home Page

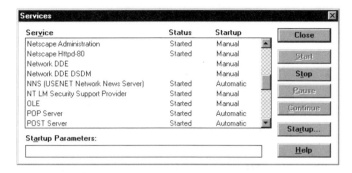

Figure 15.22 Netscape Server Services

2. Confirm that you wish to install WebSite by clicking Next> on the dialog box provided.

3. Personalize your copy of WebSite by entering your name and your company's name. Then click Next> to continue. Verify this information when prompted.

4. Choose a directory where WebSite will reside. Then click Next>.

5. The next dialog lets you select which components to install. The options, as illustrated in Figure 15.23, are WebSite server software, the Spyglass Enhanced Mosaic Browser, and the HotDog Standard HTML Editor. Choose the options you want, presumably including the WebSite server software. Then click Next> to continue.

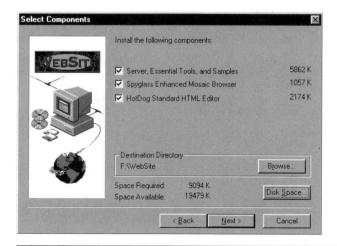

Figure 15.23 WebSite Setup: Select Components

6. In the next dialog (Figure 15.24), specify the name of your HTTP data directory (Web root) and confirm the default index document name. Locate the Web root on a drive isolated from other critical functions. "Index doc" is the file the server delivers when responding to HTTP URLs that don't specify a file name. Note that WebSite allows this to be a wild-card pattern. Click Next> to continue.

7. Figure 15.25 illustrates the next dialog, in which you specify the server's operating mode. In almost all cases, you should specify "Service (invisible)," which means WebSite will run as a Windows NT service that doesn't display a desktop icon. Running WebSite as an application means it will shut down whenever someone logs off the console, and having a Windows NT service display an icon serves no real purpose. Click Next> to continue.

8. The next dialog (Figure 15.26) prompts for the name of the server. Enter the name users will use in URLs. Then click Next>.

9. The dialog in Figure 15.27 will next prompt for the server administrator's E-Mail address. You can enter a personal address or an alias such as webmaster@interlakken.com. Click Next> when ready to proceed.

10. Setup will copy all necessary files to your server and then offer to display the README file and start the server. Check the options you prefer. Then click the Finish button.

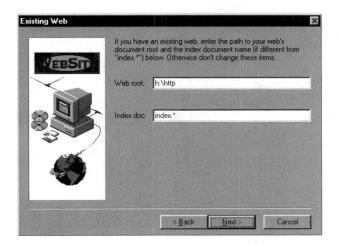

Figure 15.24 WebSite Setup: Existing Web

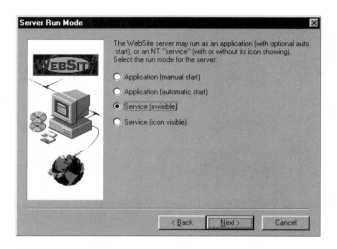

Figure 15.25 WebSite Setup: Server Run Mode

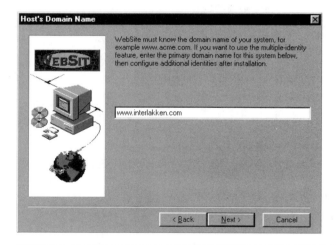

Figure 15.26 WebSite Setup: Host's Domain Name

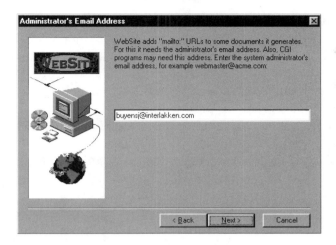

Figure 15.27 WebSite Setup: Administrator's E-Mail Address

To control WebSite, use the Server Admin program installed in the "WebSite" Program Manager group or Start Programs menu. Figure 15.28 shows the opening dialog.

The Server Admin dialog has nine tabs. Within the General dialog, the "Working Dir" and "Admin Addr" fields should be familiar from running Setup. "CGI Temp Dir" specifies a location for creating temporary files for CGI programs.

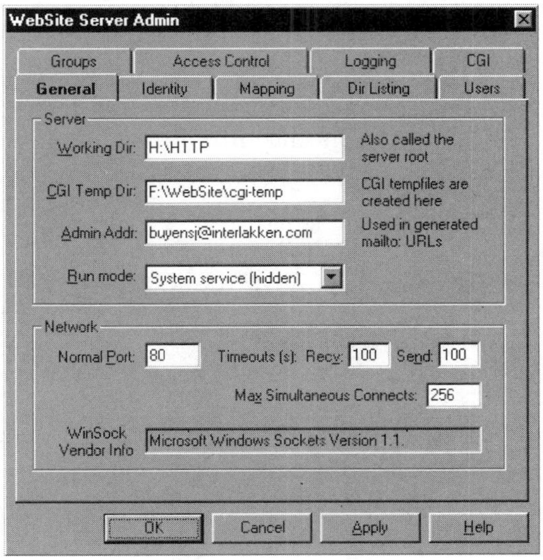

Figure 15.28 WebSite Server Admin General Dialog

The dropdown list titled "Run mode" has three possible values: "Desktop application," "System service (show icon)," and "System service (hidden)." The desktop application choice runs WebSite as a foreground application with the permissions of the current logged-on user. When the console user logs off the server, WebSite will shut itself down just like any other desktop application. This is fine for testing but is not appropriate for production.

The system service choices allow WebSite to run as a background service. The "show icon" and "hidden" options allow the WebSite service to display an icon or not on Windows NT desktop whenever someone is logged onto the console.

For brief initial testing, you may wish to run WebSite as a foreground application, but, for continuous operation, you should configure it as a Windows NT service. The reminder of this discussion assumes you've set the run mode to "System service (hidden)." With this value in effect, click WebSite Server Admin's Apply button.

To start WebSite, open the Windows NT Control Panel Services icon, check to see whether any other Web server services are running, and stop any that are. Then, highlight the service entry titled "Web Server" and click the Start button. The server should start delivering any pages you've placed in the HTTP data directory, using the same URLs described for the EMWAC server.

TCP port 80 is the well-known HTTP port, and 100 seconds is the default timeout value for sending and receiving. "Max Simultaneous Connects" is a value you can adjust if clients time out because of congested bandwidth into your site. Having too many simultaneous connections over a slow line provides too little service to each connection; turning connections away and having clients retry them may be preferable to having accepted connections time out.

Figure 15.29 shows WebSite Server Admin's Identity tab. By default, the only configurable field is the name of the server. This should initially be the name you specified during setup.

The Identity tab also supports WebSite's virtual domains feature. This allows a single server to emulate several apparent sites: www.client1.com, www.client2.com, and so on. To offer such service, follow these steps:

1. Obtain a separate IP address for each virtual site.

2. Register a domain name with InterNIC for each virtual site.

3. Configure Windows NT to respond to each of these IP addresses. Section 7.2.5, "TCP/IP Settings," describes the configuration of a single network card with up to 5 addresses; Section 7.6.2, "Multiple IP Addresses per Network Adapter," explains how to configure 6 through 16 such addresses. If you need to support more than 16 virtual sites on one NT server, you can keep adding network adapters until you run out of interrupts.

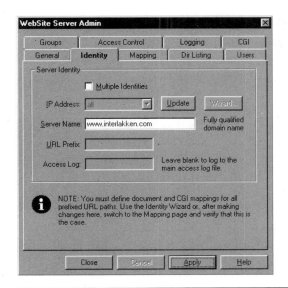

Figure 15.29 WebSite Server Admin Identity Dialog

4. Click the checkbox titled "Multiple Identities" (on the WebSite Server Identity tab) ON.

5. Select an IP address in the "IP Address" pulldown list and then click the "Wizard" button. The wizard will prompt you, in turn, for the virtual site's name, a unique internal URL prefix, CGI program-sharing options, HTTP root directory, and logging options.

The result of this configuration will be a single server that responds to two or more IP addresses and services each one from a different HTTP data directory.

The Mapping dialog shown in Figure 15.30 maintains various WebSite tables. To maintain a given table, click on its option button in the List Selector frame:

- The Documents list equates special URL paths with data located elsewhere in the server or network.

- The Redirect list defines URLs that WebSite will process by sending a "redirect" command to the requesting browser. The "redirect" command contains a corrected URL that the browser, following standard HTTP protocols, will automatically retrieve.

- The Windows CGI list specifies directories located anywhere on the server or network containing programs WebSite will invoke using the WinCGI API.

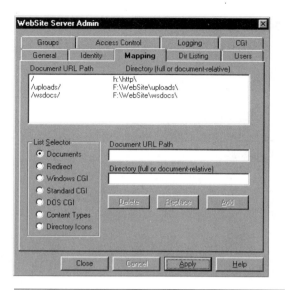

Figure 15.30 WebSite Server Admin Mapping Dialog

■ The Standard CGI list specifies directories located anywhere on the server or network containing CGI programs. Chapter 16 discusses Standard CGI and Windows CGI programs.

■ The DOS CGI list specifies locations containing batch files that will run as CGI programs.

■ The Content Types list relates file name extensions to MIME types. HTTP browsers and servers act on MIME types, not file extensions, because not all operating systems use file extensions.

■ The Directory Icons list relates file name extensions to icons. WebSite will display the corresponding icons in directory listings it sends to browsers.

As shown in Figure 15.31, the Dir Listing tab provides remarkable control over the format of directory listings WebSite sends to browsers. The "Enable directory listings" checkbox is a master switch that, if unchecked, makes most of the other fields moot. With directory listings disabled, WebSite will simply return a "Not Found" message when browsers submit URLs containing no file name and the default file name (as defined in Special Documents, Default) doesn't exit.

With directory listings enabled, the "Extended format" checkbox controls whether WebSite will add icons and other special formatting to the listing. The "Ignore Patterns" list specifies wild cards that, if matched, won't appear on directory listings.

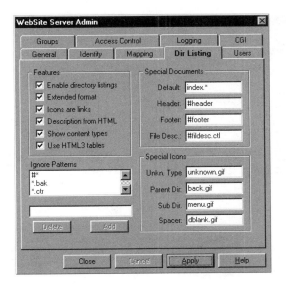

Figure 15.31 WebSite Server Admin Dir Listing Dialog

The Users, Groups, and Access Control tabs permit restriction of certain functions and Web pages to authorized users only. The Users tab allows you to set up user IDs and give them passwords; the Groups tab allows you to aggregate users into larger named entities; and the Access Control tab allows you to specify, for various resources, which users and groups WebSite should permit or deny. See Figures 15.32, 15.33, and 15.34.

The Logging tab controls the content and location of WebSite's activity logs. Figure 15.35 shows this dialog.

WebSite normally writes one record to the access log every time it delivers a file. The error log records errors such as files not found. Messages related to the WebSite internal server functions appear in the server log. You can activate additional tracing options when debugging specific features, but leaving these in effect can produce very large log files.

The default logging directory is "logs," which, since it doesn't contain a path, is relative to the \WEBSITE software directory. A better choice would be a full path entry pointing to a directory on some other drive—a drive that, if it becomes full, won't have serious impact on the entire server or any major subsystem.

The checkbox titled "Enable DNS Reverse Lookup" controls whether WebSite will translate client IP addresses to DNS names before writing log records. Analyzing logs based on DNS names is generally much more interesting than

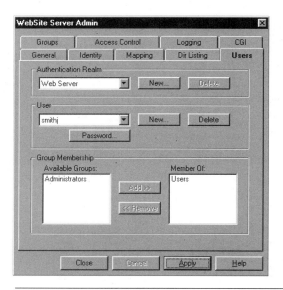

Figure 15.32 WebSite Server Admin Users Dialog

analyzing them based on IP address, but performing this translation in real time may impact overall server performance. If resource constraints force you to turn DNS reverse lookup OFF in WebSite, you may want to investigate log analysis programs that perform this activity after the fact.

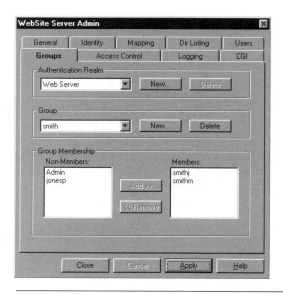

Figure 15.33 WebSite Server Admin Groups Dialog

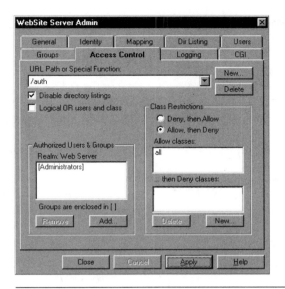

Figure 15.34 WebSite Server Admin Access Control Dialog

The last tab in WebSite Server Admin is the CGI tab. Settings in this dialog control the manner in which WebSite executes various kinds of CGI programs. These settings reflect commonly accepted APIs, and it's generally best to avoid changing them.

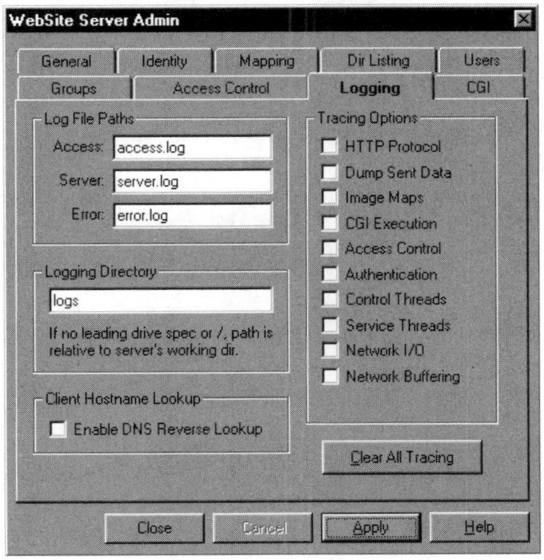

Figure 15.35 WebSite Server Admin Logging Dialog

15.2.5 Configuring Microsoft Internet Information Server

The version of Internet Information Server discussed here is a beta release dated December 1995. Some details of the final released version may vary, but the basic operating concepts and facilities should remain relatively unchanged.

The Microsoft Internet Information Server setup process installs the IIS Web server with standard defaults. Refer to Section 7.8, "Installing Internet Information Server," if you need to perform this step.

To configure the IIS Web server, start Internet Server Manager (Figure 7.54), locate the line for the desired computer and Web service, and double-click it. The first tab on the resulting dialog is the Service window displayed in Figure 15.36.

As with other IIS services, "Connection Timeout" defaults to 900 seconds, and "Maximum Connections" is 1,000. Given that HTTP is a stateless protocol, 900 seconds is a very long timeout period; 60 seconds is probably quite sufficient. Also, 1,000 simultaneous connections is a very high number; you can reduce this to avoid overwhelming other resources (such as your communication lines).

The "Anonymous Logon" user name and password specify the Windows NT account IIS will use in retrieving Web pages and other resources. Unlike most

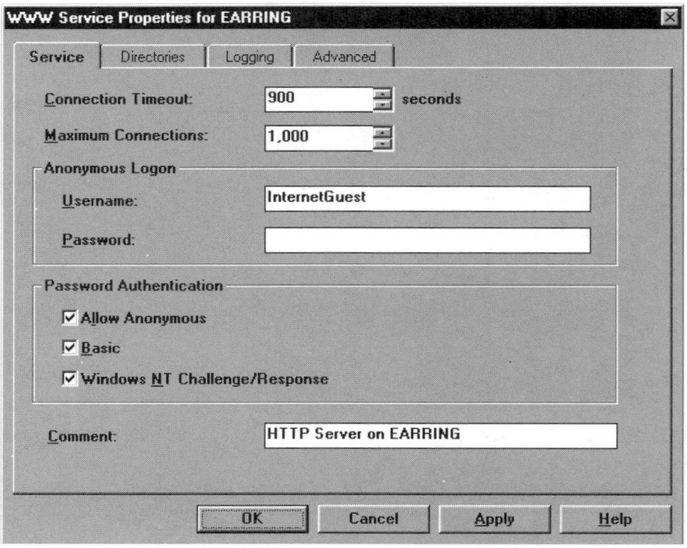

Figure 15.36 IIS WWW Properties—Service

other HTTP servers, IIS provides separate security contexts for user access and for the service itself. This means even though IIS may run under the local System account, users and CGI programs have only the privileges of the Anonymous Logon account you specify.

"Password Authentication" specifies the authentication process IIS will use if anonymous access provides insufficient privilege or if the remote client requests authentication. "Basic" authentication uses UUencoded passwords, a scheme only marginally better than clear text. "Windows NT Challenge/Response" uses securely encrypted passwords that not all browsers may support.[2]

IIS will prompt users for a user name and password if

1. Either "Basic" or "Windows NT Challenge/Response" is activated in the Password Authentication frame,

and

2. Either of the following is true:
   - ■ "Password Authentication: Allow Anonymous" isn't checked.
   - ■ The user name specified in the Anonymous Logon frame doesn't have NTFS file system permissions to access the page.

To satisfy an IIS authentication prompt, the remote user must supply the user name and password of a Windows NT account that has suitable NTFS file system permissions for the requested object.

Figure 15.37 shows the Directories tab for the IIS WWW service. As with other IIS services, this provides a way to access directories elsewhere on the server or network as if they existed within the normal HTTP data directory.

The table in the upper half of the Directories tab shows mappings currently in effect. Note there are three home directories listed, with specific IP addresses assigned to HTTP data directories h:\http2 and earring\http3. These are virtual servers operating on the given IP addresses. Note that the virtual server on 130.131.90.250 has a different home directory than the default server but the same scripts directory; the IIS WWW service neither requires nor prohibits this.

The Web server on 130.131.90.251 has no HTML or CGI files on the local server; they're all on other network locations—potentially on servers running different operating systems. (Figure 15.37 shows network locations on the local computer, but this is atypical.)

---

[2] As of this writing, only Microsoft Internet Explorer supported Windows NT Challenge/Response authentication.

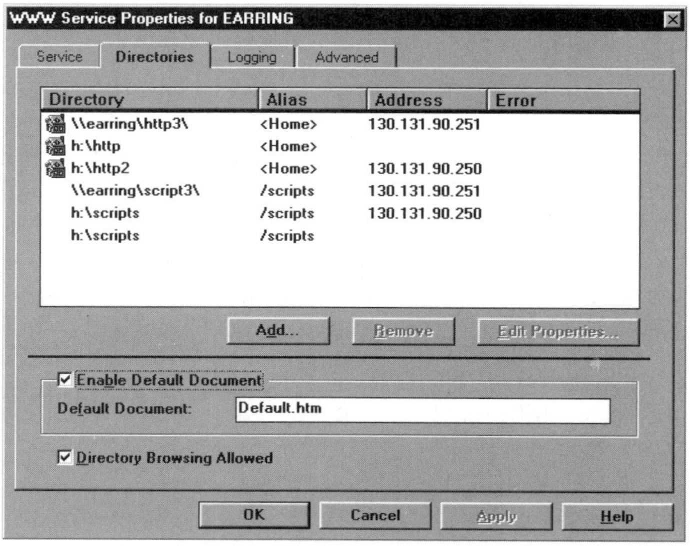

Figure 15.37 IIS WWW Properties—Directories

The Add, Remove, and Edit Properties buttons modify the list of virtual directories. The dialog of Figure 15.38 applies to both the add and edit functions.

The "Directory" text box at the top of the dialog specifies the "real" location of the files you wish to map. This can be a local drive:directory location or a

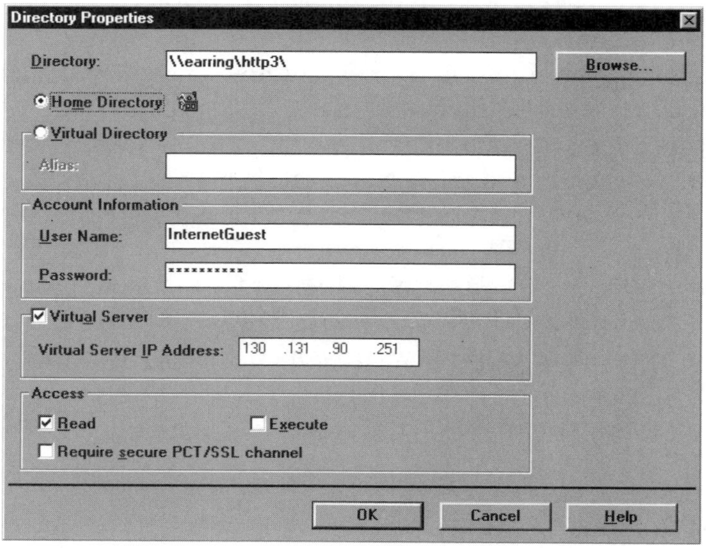

Figure 15.38 IIS WWW Properties—Directory Properties

\\<server>\<sharename> UNC name. If you specify a UNC name, the Account Information frame becomes enabled, and you must provide a user name and password that are valid for accessing the remote files.

The Home Directory and Virtual Directory buttons specify how the referenced directory will appear to HTTP users—as the HTTP server's home directory or as a subdirectory within the home directory. In the latter case, the dialog enables the Virtual Directory frame and requires that you specify a name.

Checking "Virtual Server" ON associates the home or virtual directory with a specific IP address on which the server is listening. This allows you to define different IP addresses to different DNS names and then assign different home directories to different IP addresses.

Section 7.2.5 describes the configuration of a single network card with up to 5 addresses; Section 7.6.2 explains how to configure 6 through 16 addresses.

The "Access" checkboxes at the bottom of the dialog have these meanings:

- **Read.** This allows clients to read files from the specified directory. Check this box for directories containing HTML pages but not for directories containing programs.

- **Execute.** Clients may execute programs from any directory that has this box checked. Users should never have read or write access to these directories.

- **Require secure PCT/SSL channel.** Clients may access pages or programs in this directory only in the presence of a secure (encrypted) channel between the browser and the HTTP server. If possible, the IIS WWW server will use PCT (Private Communication Technology) for this encryption. However, if the remote client doesn't support PCT, IIS will use SSL (Secure Sockets Layer) encryption.

Providing a secure PCT/SSL channel requires that you generate a private/public key pair, register it with a certification authority, and then install the keys in your server. Chapter 18 will discuss security issues further.

The Logging and Advanced tabs for the IIS WWW service are essentially identical to those for the IIS FTP service. Logging controls the activation, location, and advance frequency of IIS WWW activity logs. The Advanced tab controls access based on client IP address and regulates total IIS server throughput. If you have questions regarding these dialogs, review Sections 10.3.4 and 10.3.5.

15.3 Ongoing Management

15.3.1 Setting Up an HTTP Server User Account

Under certain circumstances, as discussed in the next chapter, HTTP servers may execute programs users place within the HTTP data directory or a special CGI (Common Gateway Interface) directory. Most HTTP servers run such programs with the same security privileges as the HTTP service itself, so it's good policy to give such services as few privileges as possible. Nevertheless, most HTTP server setup programs define the HTTP service to use the system account, that is, they give the HTTP server the same privileges as the operating system.

To set up a more appropriate account for the HTTP service to use, proceed as follows:

1. Start User Manager.

2. Pull down the User menu and select "New User...."

3. Choose a name for the account, enter a full name and description, and assign a password.

4. Uncheck "User Must Change Password at Net Logon" and check "User Cannot Change Password" and "Password Never Expires." See Figure 15.39.

5. Click "Logon To" and enter the name of the computer where the HTTP server will run. See Figure 15.40. This ensures no one can use the HTTP server's account, with its special privileges and unchanging password, on any other computer. Click OK.

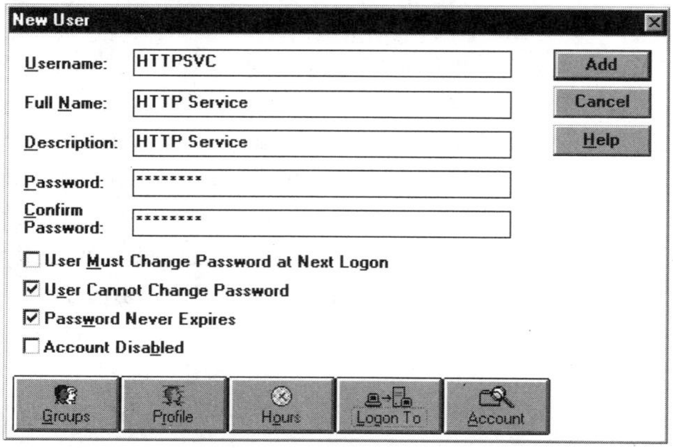

Figure 15.39 Windows NT User Manager New User Dialog

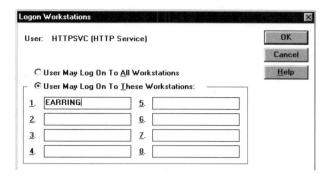

Figure 15.40 Windows NT User Manager Logon Workstations Dialog

6. Click the Add button on the New User dialog and then exit User Manager.

7. Go to Control Panel, double-click the Services icon, select the HTTP server's entry, and then click "Startup...." The Service dialog shown in Figure 15.41 will result.

8. In the "Log On As:" frame, choose "This Account," click the ellipsis ("...") button to bring up the Add User dialog, select the HTTP server account just created, and then click OK.

9. Enter the password you chose for the HTTP server's account in the "Password" and "Confirm Password" text boxes.

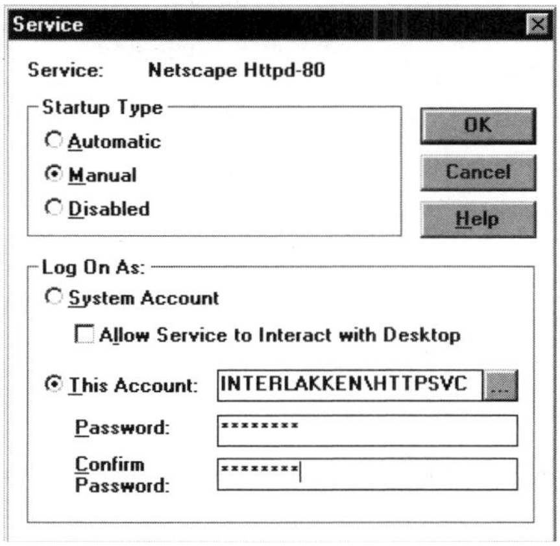

Figure 15.41 Windows NT Service Dialog

10. Click the OK button. An alert box such as that in Figure 15.42 will result. Click OK to continue.

11. Review file system security in the HTTP server's software, log, and data directories. Make sure the HTTP server will have at least read access everywhere and can create or update log files, settings files, and the like.

12. Using Control Panel Services, stop and restart the HTTP server. Then test for proper operation.

If the service won't start or won't operate properly, try adding the server's account to the Administrators group. This is a temporary expedient you shouldn't leave in place, but it may help you resolve permissions problems. If all else fails, go back to Control Panel Services Startup and revert to using the System account. Then seek outside support.

15.3.2 HTTP Service Start-Up

In almost all cases, you'll want the HTTP service to start automatically when the server boots. To see whether this will occur, go to Control Panel Services and verify that the "Startup" column for the HTTP server contains the word "Automatic." If not, select the HTTP server's entry, click "Startup...," select start-up type "Automatic," and click OK.

15.3.3 HTTP Data Directory Management

From a system administration viewpoint, ongoing HTTP administration is relatively trouble-free. Be sure to create separate directories for each user or group of users that will create content pages, and ensure you've set all permissions appropriately. From time to time, you'll need to check free-space availability on the drive. If you plan to charge for Web space, develop a means to tabulate space used by a user directory and feed it into your billing system.

Figure 15.42 Windows NT Services Alert

If ensuring the technical quality of Web pages somehow falls to you, HTML checkers and age analyzers may have appeal. HTML checkers examine individual or specified groups of pages and report syntax unacceptable to one or more browsers. Dealing with the quirks of each browser and updating the HTML checker whenever a supported browser changes are difficult tasks, and checkers are seldom 100 percent accurate. Nevertheless, they beat reviewing hundreds of HTML files by hand or displaying each of them with a collection of different browsers.

Link checkers verify that hypertext links within a set of Web pages point to valid locations. Some link checkers validate only links within a given local file system, while others test connections over the network. Most link checkers, like most HTML checkers, are perl programs with character-mode interfaces.

If you plan to charge for Web hits or bytes transferred, be sure to review the log format of any server software you're considering. A good approach is to write or find a utility that loads the log into an Access or SQL database once a day; you can then retrieve billing statistics at will.

CHAPTER 16

Advanced Web Services

L ike most software, HTTP servers beg for extensions, enhancements, and add-on services. This chapter discusses several of these commonly available on HTTP servers.

As in other chapters, discussion of each technique includes both theory and practice. Unfortunately, for a book this size, demonstrating each technique for each HTTP server in the previous chapter is impractical. Most implementations are similar, though, and discussion of each technique highlights common variations.

16.1 Clickable Image Maps

The use of bitmapped images as menus is a common Web page feature. HTML instructs the browser to retrieve and display a named image file in much the normal way, but the HTML specifies two additional parameters. One identifies the image as a clickable image map, and the other gives the name of a map file on the server.

When the user clicks on the image, the browser appends the mouse coordinates to the URL and transmits the request to the server. The server uses the map file to translate the mouse coordinates:

- If the URL is locally available, the server resolves it on the spot.

- If the URL points to another computer, the server sends the URL back to the client (via a "redirect" response), and the client gets the page from the other computer.

The first HTML servers to support clickable image maps were the CERN (European Laboratory for Particle Physics) and NCSA (National Center for

Supercomputing Applications) servers. CERN map files have a different internal format than NCSA map files, but virtually all other servers use one of these formats.

A relatively new approach, called client-side image maps, embeds mapping data in the page's HTML rather than a separate file that stays on the server. This increases the amount of data sent out with the page but eliminates the two-step process of contacting one HTTP server to translate the mouse coordinates and a second one to obtain the specified page.

Here's the HTML for a simple page with a server-side clickable image map:

scanner.htm:
```
<HTML>
<HEAD>
<TITLE>Scanner Technology at interlakken.com</TITLE>
</HEAD>
<BODY>
<H1>Scanner Technology at <I>interlakken.com</I></H1>
<HR>
<A HREF="/scn_cern.map">
<IMG SRC="scanner.gif" ISMAP></A>
<HR>
<ADDRESS>Updated by Jim Buyens</ADDRESS>
</BODY>
</HTML>
```

The ISMAP keyword identifies the scanner.gif picture as a clickable image map, and scn_cern.map is the name of the map file located on the HTTP server. Figure 16.1 shows how Netscape displays the scanner.htm page, and the listing here shows the contents of the map file:

scn_cern.map
```
default scandeft.htm
polygon (345,34) (385,34) (389,38) (384,47) (353,57) (346,49) (350,34)
    (349,34) (345,34) (345,34) scanrigt.htm
rectangle (20,228) (158,260) scanshoe.htm
circ (208,73) 30 scanleft.htm
```

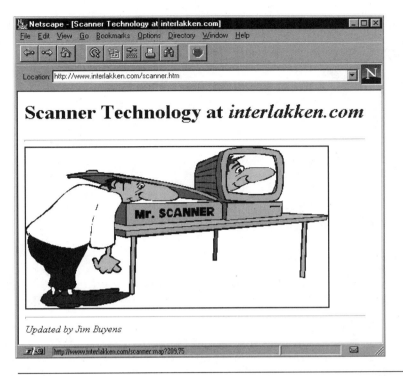

Figure 16.1 Netscape Navigator Displaying a Clickable Image Map Page

Figure 16.1 shows Netscape Navigator displaying the URL http://www.inter-lakken.com/scn_cern.map?209,75 in the status line at the bottom of the window (these are the current X–Y coordinates of the mouse pointer, which the screen-shot doesn't show):

■ Clicking the mouse at (209,75) causes the server to read the image file looking for a match.

■ (209,75) matches the last line in the file, a circle with radius 30 centered at (208,73).

■ As proven by Figure 16.2, matching the "circ (208,73) 30 scanleft.htm" line causes the server to respond with the scanleft.htm page. This is the page specified in the last line of the scn_cern.map file.

Line 2 (a single line despite the apparent continuation) specifies a polygon shape with corners at the specified X–Y coordinates, and line 3 defines a rectangle whose opposite corners are (20,228) and (158,260). The line "default scandeft.htm" specifies the action if the user clicks an area not otherwise defined. Every image map description requires a default entry.

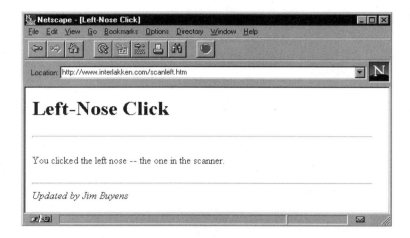

Figure 16.2 Response to Clicking scanner.gif at (209,75)

The map file scn_cern.map discussed so far is in the CERN format, which is the format EMWAC HTTPS and Microsoft IIS both require. The equivalent file in NCSA format would be

```
scn_ncsa.map
default scandeft.htm
poly scanrigt.htm 345,34 385,34 389,38 384,47 353,57 346,49 350,34 349,34
     345,34 345,34
rect scanshoe.htm 20,228 158,260
circle scanleft.htm  209,75 239,87
```

This file contains essentially the same information as the CERN file except that parentheses don't surround X–Y pairs, abbreviations replace the keywords "rectangle" and "polygon," and the URL selected in case of a match appears in the second (rather than last) position. In addition, two pairs of X–Y coordinates, rather than a center point and radius, describe the circle; this allows definition of ellipses as well as true circles.

The following code is a client-side image map equivalent to scn_cern.map and scn_ncsa.map:

```
<BODY>
<MAP NAME="scn_csim">
<AREA SHAPE=POLY COORDS="345,34,385,34,389,38,384,47,353,57,346,49,350,34,
     349,34,345,34,345,34" HREF=scanrigt.htm>
```

```
<AREA SHAPE=RECT COORDS="20,228,158,260" HREF=scanshoe.htm>
<AREA SHAPE=CIRCLE COORDS="209,75,30" HREF=scanleft.htm>
<AREA SHAPE=default HREF=scandeft.htm>
</MAP></BODY>
```

Integrating this code into the original scanner.htm file produces the following (added or changed lines appear in boldface):

scancli.htm:
```
<HTML>
<HEAD>
<TITLE>Scanner Technology at interlakken.com</TITLE>
</HEAD>
<BODY>
<H1>Scanner Technology at <I>interlakken.com</I></H1>
<HR>
<MAP NAME="scn_csim">
<AREA SHAPE=POLY COORDS="345,34,385,34,389,38,384,47,353,57,346,49,350,34,
    349,34,345,34,345,34" HREF=scanrigt.htm>
<AREA SHAPE=RECT COORDS="20,228,158,260" HREF=scanshoe.htm>
<AREA SHAPE=CIRCLE COORDS="209,75,30" HREF=scanleft.htm>
<AREA SHAPE=default HREF=scandeft.htm>
</MAP>
<IMG SRC="scanner.gif" USEMAP="#scn_csim">
<HR>
<ADDRESS>Updated by Jim Buyens</ADDRESS>
</BODY>
</HTML>
```

The block of code from <MAP> to </MAP> repeats the data seen previously in the scn_cern.map and scn_ncsa.map files. In addition,

```
<IMG SRC="scanner.gif" USEMAP="#scn_csim">
```

has replaced

```
<A HREF="/scn_cern.map">
<IMG SRC="scanner.gif" ISMAP></A>
```

The file scancli.htm contains both the page description and the client-side image map. The USEMAP parameter therefore points to a location within the same file—namely, #scn_csim. This is the same notation used for bookmarks, which also denote locations within an HTML file.

The client-side image map can also exist as a separate file on the server; in such a case, the USEMAP parameter contains a path and file name as well as the "#" map name. USEMAP can even point to the HTML file for another page, assuming the named <MAP> description exists within that file.

The job of counting pixels and constructing map files by hand quickly becomes tiresome. It cries out for an editor that displays the relevant image and lets the user define areas with mouse movements. Several such editors are available for Windows, including the freeware program called "Map This!, which appears on the accompanying CD.[1] Figure 16.3 illustrates a typical editing session using Map This!

Note from the MDI (Multiple Document Interface) document title bar that two files are open: scanner.gif and scn_cern.map. Dotted outlines with handles indicate the three now familiar clickable areas: the rectangle around the shoes, the

Figure 16.3 A Map This! Image Mapping Session

---

[1]Map This! is freeware written by Todd C. Wilson. Molly Penguin Software holds the copyright.

circle around the left nose, and the polygon outlining the right nose. Clicking the first three buttons on the toolbar would activate rectangle, circle, and polygon drawing tools, respectively; after selecting a tool, you could outline additional clickable areas with the mouse.

To assign a URL to a clickable area, select the arrow tool and double-click the outlined area. The dialog of Figure 16.4 will result. As shown, the circle area is item #3 in the list of clickable areas, and, if clicked, it will invoke the URL scan-left.htm. URLs with full paths and with computer names are also acceptable.

Pulling down Map This!'s View menu and selecting "Area List" produces the dialog box shown in Figure 16.5. This shows the currently defined clickable areas, the currently selected area's associated URL, and the order of clickable areas. The order is important because searching stops with the first match; if the user clicks an area that's part of two or more overlapping areas, the area occurring first in the list takes precedence.

Pulling down Map This!'s Edit menu and selecting "Edit Map Info" produces the dialog shown in Figure 16.6. Here, you can specify the default URL, the map file format, and other informational fields. You can also specify the map file format in the File Save As dialog.

Whenever it saves a map file, Map This! embeds comments recording the associated image file path and file name. When you reopen the same map file, Map This! uses these comments to automatically open the corresponding image file. If no comments are present or Map This! can't locate the path or file name, you'll have to locate and open the corresponding image file yourself.

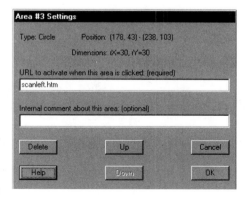

Figure 16.4 Map This! Area Settings Dialog

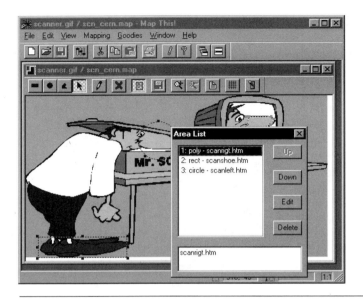

Figure 16.5 Map This! Area List

The examples in this section used the EMWAC HTTPS server. This and the Microsoft IIS Web server use image maps in CERN format. O'Reilly WebSite and the Netscape HTTP servers require NCSA-style map files. If you have trouble getting WebSite to recognize relative URLs, try specifying a full path—that is, one beginning with a slash.

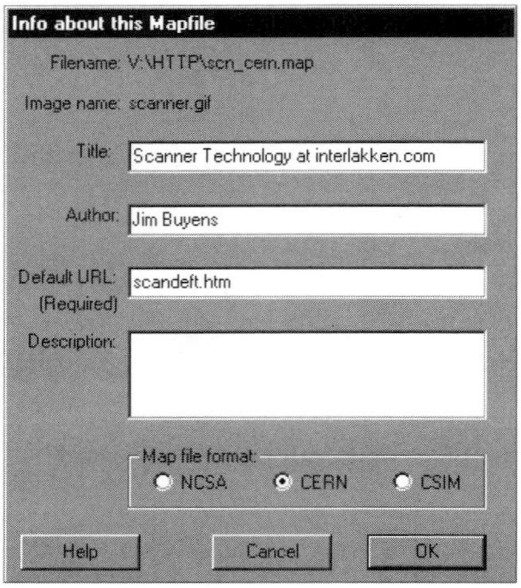

Figure 16.6 Map This! Edit Map Info Dialog

16.2 CGI—Introduction to HTML Forms and Tables

16.2.1 HTML Forms

After image maps, running specialized server-side programs is the next most common HTTP extension. However, since the input to such programs generally comes from HTML forms, a brief digression on that topic seems warranted. To set up an HTML form, proceed as follows:

1. Delimit an area of the page by using <FORM> and </FORM> tags.
2. Include one or more data entry objects by using the following tags:

    <INPUT TYPE="TEXT">
    <INPUT TYPE="PASSWORD">
    <INPUT TYPE="CHECKBOX">
    <INPUT TYPE="RADIO">
    <SELECT> and </SELECT>
    <TEXTAREA> and </TEXTAREA>

3. Include a "submit" button by using the tag <INPUT TYPE="SUBMIT">.
4. Optionally, include a "reset" button by using the tag <INPUT TYPE="RESET">.

The <FORM> tag includes three optional parameters: ACTION, METHOD, and ENCTYPE:

1. ACTION specifies the URL of the CGI process that will process the form data. If omitted, the current URL will remain in effect.
2. METHOD can be either GET or POST. The GET method appends the form data names and values to the URL using the format

```
action?name=value&name=value&name=value
```

The POST method encodes the data just as the GET method does, but it pipes the ampersand-delimited string into the CGI program's standard input. GET is the default, but POST is preferable. Among other advantages, POST avoids problems with operating system and language limits on command-line length.

3. ENCTYPE is valid only for METHOD=POST, and, in that case, the only valid setting is "application/x-www-form-urlencoded" (the default).

<INPUT>, <SELECT>, and <TEXTAREA> tags define data entry fields. As Table 16.1 illustrates, there are seven INPUT types differentiated by a TYPE= parameter; Table 16.2 lists additional parameters.

One use of the <INPUT TYPE=HIDDEN> tag is to define constants within forms rather than within programs. This may allow one program to support several different forms or simply place data that requires occasional revision in an easier-to-maintain location. The second use is for remembering data in multi-screen transactions. Because HTTP is a stateless protocol, the server remembers nothing about a particular client after processing a URL. To remember data collected on one form while processing additional forms, each CGI program in the series can write the data as one or more <INPUT TYPE=HIDDEN> tags so that the next program will receive it.

<SELECT> tags produce dropdown or scrollable selection lists. As shown here, a select list definition consists of several tags:

```
<SELECT NAME="rating">
<OPTION> Awesome
<OPTION> Mediocre
<OPTION> Off-net
</SELECT>
```

The <SELECT> tag can also include a size attribute that indicates how many items in the list are visible. SIZE=1, the default, creates a dropdown list, while SIZE=2 or more creates a scrolled list. The MULTIPLE keyword, if present, allows multiple selections and forces the display to be a scrolled list.

An <OPTION> tag can contain the SELECTED keyword; this selects the associated option by default.

Table 16.1 HTML Form <INPUT TYPE=> Options

Type	Description
TEXT	Text entry box. This is the default type.
PASSWORD	A text entry box in which typed characters appear as asterisks.
CHECKBOX	A single element that can only be ON or OFF.
RADIO	One of a group of buttons, only one of which can be ON at the same time. All buttons with the same NAME are in the same group.
HIDDEN	An input field with a NAME and VALUE but no visible display.
SUBMIT	A button that assembles the current form data into a query URL and sends it to an HTTP server.
RESET	A button that resets the elements in the form to their default values.

Table 16.2 HTML Form <INPUT> Parameters

Parameter	Description
NAME	The internal (not displayed) name of the input field. This is mandatory for all types but SUBMIT and RESET.
VALUE	For a text or password entry field, specifies the default contents of the field.
	For a checkbox or radio button, specifies the button's value when checked; the default is ON. Unchecked checkboxes don't appear on submitted queries.
	For types SUBMIT and RESET, VALUE overrides the default button label.
CHECKED	Specifies that a checkbox or radio button is checked by default.
SIZE	Specifies the field's display size in characters. This is appropriate only for text and password entry fields. The default is 20.
	Specifying both a width and height, as in SIZE=40,12, creates a multiline text entry field; however, the <TEXTAREA> tag is preferable.
MAXLENGTH	Limits the maximum number of characters accepted as input. This is valid only for single-line text entry fields. The default is unlimited.

The <TEXTAREA> tag creates a multiline text entry field. Like <SELECT>, each <TEXTAREA> tag requires a corresponding </TEXTAREA> tag:

```
<TEXTAREA NAME="question1" ROWS=5 COLS=60>
Please replace this text with a brief history of your
life, including any specific childhood incidents that
demonstrate your aptitude for nuclear reactor operation.
</TEXTAREA>
```

The area between the opening and closing <TEXTAREA> tags becomes the default contents; this can be null. The default value will retain any carriage returns.

16.2.2 HTML Tables

An HTML table arranges text and other page components in a two-dimensional grid. <TABLE> and </TABLE> tags mark the beginning and end of a table; similarly, <TR> and </TR> mark the beginning and end of a row. <TD> and </TD> bound the contents of individual cells. A simple table with two rows and three columns therefore appears like this:

```
<TABLE>
  <TR>
    <TD>Row 1, Col 1</TD>
    <TD>Row 1, Col 2</TD>
```

```
    <TD>Row 1, Col 3</TD>
  </TR>
  <TR>
    <TD>Row 2, Col 1</TD>
    <TD>Row 2, Col 2</TD>
    <TD>Row 2, Col 3</TD>
  </TR>
</TABLE>
```

The leading spaces have no significance other than enhancing readability. Any valid HTML tag or text can appear within a cell—that is, between the <TD> and </TD> tags. Table 16.3 summarizes the tags commonly used to construct tables; Table 16.4 summarizes attributes you can assign within various tags.

Tables were late additions to HTML, and various browsers handle them differently. For this reason, it's best to keep tables as simple as possible and test them with whatever browsers are important to your application.

The HTML specification has become a rapidly moving target as browser manufacturers strive to outdo their competitors by adding ever more features and tags. This argues for some compromise between producing the most standard, most boring pages on the Web and having pages so trendy and nonstandard that few users can view them. The best sources for additional documentation are generally the Web sites browser manufacturers maintain.

16.3 CGI (Common Gateway Interface)

Although its name suggests a network device of some kind, CGI is actually an Application Programming Interface (API) between an HTTP server and user-written programs. The process usually works like this:

1. The user browses an HTML page that contains a <FORM> section.

Table 16.3 HTML Table Definition Tags

Start Tag	End Tag	Description
<TABLE ...>	</TABLE>	Mark the beginning and end of a table.
<TR ...>	</TR>	Mark the beginning and end of a row.
<TH ...>	</TH>	Mark the beginning and end of a heading cell.
<TD ...>	</TD>	Mark the beginning and end of a normal cell.
<CAPTION ...>	</CAPTION>	Identifies the caption for a table. These tags should appear within the table definition but not within any rows or columns.

Table 16.4 HTML Table Tag Attributes

Attribute	Applicable Tags	Description
BORDER	<TABLE>	This keyword produces visible borders around all table cells. A numeric value, if present, controls the border width.
CELLSPACING	<TABLE>	This attribute controls spacing between individual table cells.
CELLPADDING	<TABLE>	This attribute controls space between a cell's contents and its border.
WIDTH	<TABLE>	Specified either in pixels or percentage of document width, this value controls the width of the entire table.
	<TH>, <TD>	This setting controls the width of a cell in either pixels or percentage of table width. The default allows the browser to size table elements by formula.
ALIGN	<CAPTION>	Values of TOP or BOTTOM cause the caption to appear above and below the table, respectively. TOP is the default.
	<TR>, <TH>, <TD>	Values of LEFT, CENTER, or RIGHT control horizontal alignment within a cell.
VALIGN	<TR>, <TH>, <TD>	Values of TOP, MIDDLE, or BOTTOM specify vertical alignment within a cell. BASELINE aligns all the cells in a row to the same baseline.
NOWRAP	<TH>, <TD>	This keyword prevents inserting line breaks to fit text within the default cell width.
COLSPAN	<TH>, <TD>	The current cell should horizontally span the given number of columns.
ROWSPAN	<TH>, <TD>	The current cell should vertically span the stated number of rows.

2. The form contains one or more input controls such as text boxes, drop-down lists, checkboxes, and radio buttons. Each control has an associated field name.

3. The user enters the input data and then presses a "Submit button" also defined within the form.

4. The <FORM> definition specifies an associated URL. Clicking the "submit" button transmits this URL, the field names, and all field values to the HTTP server.

5. Based on the URL, the HTTP server starts the appropriate application program. This program obtains input from environment variables (and possibly from "standard input") and writes its response to "standard output." The response normally consists of HTML statements. (Note that alternatives that don't support standard input and output exist for languages like Visual Basic.)

6. The HTTP server delivers the response HTML statements to the user's browser for display.

Standard input is the same facility that allows command-line programs to accept input from another program or file rather than from the keyboard.

Likewise, *standard output* allows redirection of output to another program or file. The following is a simple example of standard input and output:

```
dir | more
```

This command pipes (redirects) the "dir" command's standard output into the "more" command's standard input. This is exactly the means that an HTTP server uses to pipe input into a CGI program and to accept piped output.

Unfortunately, Windows programming has done away with the concept of standard input and standard output; Windows programs exchange data instead with mechanisms like DDE (Dynamic Data Exchange) and OLE (Object Linking and Embedding). In addition, because of communication problems between 16- and 32-bit programs, standard CGI programs under Windows NT must be full 32-bit applications. As a result, the most common CGI programming languages for Windows NT are

- **C or C++ console applications.** Microsoft C can produce 32-bit console applications meeting all CGI requirements. However, this obviously requires proficiency in the C programming language.

- **perl.** Much maligned but rapidly growing, perl (Practical Extraction and Report Language) is an interpreted language merging elements of C, SED, AWK, and various UNIX shell commands and conventions. Developed on UNIX and ported to Windows NT, it has almost no use in the Windows environment except writing CGI programs. For that purpose, however, it has become surprisingly popular.

The language most Windows users would prefer for writing CGI programs is Visual Basic—a 16-bit (until recently) program with no support for standard input and standard output. Windows CGI (WinCGI) has arisen to meet this demand. With this approach, the server (or a wrapper program) writes the user's data to a Windows-style INI file and launches the Visual Basic program. The VB program writes its output to a temporary file named in accordance with a value in the INI file, and then the server returns the contents of that file to the user.

From a technical perspective, WinCGI is far from a pretty picture. Nevertheless, it has achieved great popularity because more people know Visual Basic than know C or perl.

Buffered CGI describes all approaches that use temporary files rather than pipes for passing data to and from CGI programs. A server providing buffered CGI normally creates both files and passes them to the CGI program via the command line.

Microsoft and Process Software Corporation[2] have proposed another CGI-like approach, the Internet Server Application Programming Interface (ISAPI). This API has the following advantages:

- Application logic resides in DLL (Dynamic Link Library) modules that the operating system loads only once for any number of sequential transactions.

- If several transactions are using the same application code at the same time, only one copy needs to be in memory.

- DLLs can be 32-bit and multithreaded for maximum performance.

- There's no use of standard input, standard output, or environment variables.

- ISAPI passes all data in memory; there's no overhead in creating, writing, and destroying temporary files.

The disadvantages of ISAPI are as follows:

- Writing reentrant DLL modules is considerably more difficult than writing single-threaded programs that process standard input and output.

- Such applications currently aren't as portable among platforms as are other approaches such as perl. However, porting ISAPI applications to another operating system that supports loadable images is generally easy.

- If an ISAPI creates a general protection fault or other system failure, it may halt the entire HTTP service. However, well-written servers call all ISAPI entry points with try/except clauses to prevent this.

16.3.1 Writing Standard CGI Programs

This section illustrates three standard CGI programs written in perl:

1. **hello.pl.** A standard, introductory "Hello World!" program.

2. **iconlib.pl.** A program that displays all icons in a given directory and makes them available for downloading.

3. **grape.pl.** A program that accepts HTML form input and sends E-Mail.

---

[2]Process Software Corporation supplies Purveyor, the commercial (and highly enhanced) version of the freeware EMWAC server. ISAPI was originally available on Purveyor and is now available on Microsoft Information Server as well.

These programs are in increasing level of complexity, but none are difficult. Only grape.pl uses HTML forms.

You can obtain perl from the following Web sites or with the Windows NT Resource Kit 3.51:

> ftp://ftp.intergraph.com/pub/win32/perl/
>
> ftp://ntperl.hip.com/ntperl/

You can find pointers to additional perl resources at

> http://www.yahoo.com/Computers_and_Internet/Languages/Perl/

16.3.1.1 hello.pl—An Introductory Standard CGI Program The source code for hello.pl appears next, and typical output appears in Figure 16.7:

hello.pl:

```
print "Content-type: text/html\n";
print "\n";
print "<HTML>\n";
print "<HEAD>\n";
print "<TITLE>Hello World!</TITLE>";
print "</HEAD>\n";
```

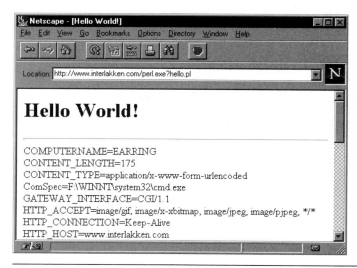

Figure 16.7 Hello World! Output

```perl
print "<BODY>\n";
print "<H1>Hello World!</H1><HR>";

for $key (sort keys %ENV) {
    print "$key=$ENV{$key}<BR>\n";
}
print "</BODY>\n";
print "</HTML>\n";
```

Since perl is an interpreted language, the URL calls up perl.exe (the perl interpreter) and follows this with a question mark and the name of the perl source code file. The URL

```
http://www.interlakken.com/perl.exe?hello.pl
```

is therefore similar to typing

```
perl hello.pl
```

at the Windows NT command prompt with the HTTP data directory as the current directory.

The program, as promised, is relatively simple. The perl "print" statement writes text to standard output—just what we need. Output begins with a one-line header telling the browser that what follows is HTML and then a blank line to separate the header and body. "\n" is the perl notation for "new line character," and perl requires a semicolon at the end of each statement. This information should make statements such as

```perl
print "<HTML>\n";
print "<HEAD>\n";
```

relatively obvious.

The only tricky statements in hello.pl are these:

```perl
for $key (sort keys %ENV) {
    print "$key=$ENV{$key}<BR>\n";
}
```

Perl loads the current environment variables into an associative array called ENV. An associative array is simply a list of values accessible by key. In the case of the ENV associative array, the keys are the names of Windows NT environment variables, and the values are the corresponding environment values. The expression $ENV("temp") therefore returns the current value of the "temp" environment variable. The expression "keys %ENV" is a list of all keys in the ENV array, and "sort keys %ENV" returns a sorted version of the same list. The "for" statement selects each entry in the sorted list, assigns it to the variable "$key," and executes the block of code in curly braces "{}" once for each key. So, the two statements say, "Take the list of all environment variable names, sort it, then for each name display the name and the corresponding value."

The list of environment variable names and values is too long for the browser screen in Figure 16.7, so here's the complete list:

```
COMPUTERNAME=EARRING
CONTENT_LENGTH=175
CONTENT_TYPE=application/x-www-form-urlencoded
ComSpec=F:\WINNT\system32\cmd.exe
GATEWAY_INTERFACE=CGI/1.1
HTTP_ACCEPT=image/gif, image/x-xbitmap, image/jpeg, image/pjpeg, */*
HTTP_CONNECTION=Keep-Alive
HTTP_HOST=www.interlakken.com
HTTP_PRAGMA=no-cache
HTTP_REFERER=http://www.interlakken.com/grape.htm
HTTP_USER_AGENT=Mozilla/2.0b3 (Win95; I)
NTResKit=F:\RESKIT\
OS=Windows_NT
Os2LibPath=F:\WINNT\system32\os2\dll;
PROCESSOR_ARCHITECTURE=x86
PROCESSOR_IDENTIFIER=x86 Family 5 Model 2 Stepping 5, GenuineIntel
PROCESSOR_LEVEL=5
PROCESSOR_REVISION=0205
Path=f:\win32app\ingr\perl\bin;F:\WINNT\system32;F:\WINNT;f:\reskit\;
QUERY_STRING=hello.pl
REMOTE_ADDR=130.131.90.67
REMOTE_HOST=choker.interlakken.com
REQUEST_METHOD=GET
```

```
SCRIPT_NAME=/perl.exe
SERVER_NAME=www.interlakken.com
SERVER_PORT=80
SERVER_PROTOCOL=HTTP/1.0
SERVER_SOFTWARE=Netscape-Communications/1.12
SERVER_URL=http://www.interlakken.com
SystemDrive=F:
SystemRoot=F:\WINNT
temp=F:\temp
windir=F:\WINNT
```

This list of variables is similar to (yet different from) the environment values displayed by issuing the SET command at the Windows NT command prompt:

- System environment variables (those listed as such under Control Panel, System, System Environment Variables) appear in both lists.
- User environment variables appear only in response to the SET command. User environment variables pertain only to foreground processes, and CGI programs run in background.
- The HTTP server supplies many process-specific environment variables such as CONTENT_LENGTH, CONTENT_TYPE, REMOTE_HOST, and HTTP_USER_AGENT. These obviously don't appear when you issue the SET command.

16.3.1.2 iconlib.pl—Passing Input Data via the Command Line The second standard CGI example is iconlib.pl, a program that reads the contents of a specified directory and displays all GIF files less than 3,076 bytes in size. This provides a handy way for users to search for and select icons. A typical URL for executing this program is

```
http://www.interlakken.com/perl.exe?iconlib.pl+mc-icons
```

The source code for iconlib.pl follows here, and Figure 16.8 illustrates typical output using the URL just given:

iconlib.pl:
```
print "Content-type: text/html\n";
print "\n";
```

Figure 16.8 Typical Output from iconlib.pl

```perl
#-------------------------------------------------------------------------
# $ARGV[0] contains the first command-line argument
# Convert this to required dir lookup parm and HTML prefix.
#-------------------------------------------------------------------------
$icopath = $ARGV[0];
if ($icopath eq "") {
    $icopath = ".";               # $icopath is dir lookup parm
    $icopfx = "/";                # $icopfx is html pfx for dir
} else {
    $icopath =~ s/\\\\/\\/g;      # converts "\\" back to "\"
    if ($icopath eq "\\") {       # dir spec is "\" only
        $icopath = ".";
        $icopfx = "/";
    } else {
        $icopfx = $icopath . "/";
        $icopfx =~ s#\\#/#g;      # convert "\" to "/"
    }
}
```

```perl
}
#--------------------------------------------------------------------
# Set up title and heading.
#--------------------------------------------------------------------
if ($icopfx eq "/") {
    $title = "Icons at $ENV{HTTP_HOST}/";
} else {
    $title = "Icons at $ENV{HTTP_HOST}/$icopfx";
}
#--------------------------------------------------------------------
# Write title and heading.
#--------------------------------------------------------------------
print "<HTML>\n";
print "<TITLE>\n";
print "$title\n";
print "</TITLE>\n";
print "<BODY>\n";
print "<H1>";
print "$title</H1>\n";
print "<HR>\n";
print "To download an icon to your computer, shift-click on its
    filename.";
print "<P>\n";
#--------------------------------------------------------------------
# Read the directory and look for gif files.
# Write HTML output for each gif file found.
#--------------------------------------------------------------------
opendir (D, $icopath) || die "Can't open directory .:$!\n";
foreach $name (sort readdir (D)){
    if (substr($name,-4,4) =~ /.gif/i) {
        if ((stat($name)) [7] < 3076){
            print "<IMG SRC=\x22";
            print "$icopfx$name";
            print "\x22><A HREF=\x22";
            print "http:$icopfx$name";
```

```
        print "\x22>";
        print "$name";
        print "</A><P>\n";

    }

}

}
closedir(D);
#─────────────────────────────────────────────────────────────────
print "</BODY>\n";
print "</HTML>\n";
```

Backslash is a reserved character in perl: "\n" means "new line character," "\t" means "tab," "\\" therefore means "single backslash." The statement

```
$icopath =~ s/\\\\/\\/g
```

near the beginning of the program performs a string substitution on the variable "$icopath" translating all double backslashes ("\\\\") to single backslashes ("\\"). The slashes are arbitrary delimiters required by the statement; you can choose whatever character you want for the first delimiter, but the second and third must match the first. The trailing "g" means that all possible replacements will occur (not just the first). If this kind of syntax seems really cool, you're going to love perl.

In the block of code

```
opendir (D, $icopath) || die "Can't open directory .:$!\n";
foreach $name (sort readdir (D)){
    if (substr($name,-4,4) =~ /.gif/i) {
        if ((stat($name)) [7] < 3076){
```

the "opendir" statement opens a directory for reading with file handle "D." The "readdir(D)" statement normally reads one directory entry at a time, but the "sort" function pulls all directory entries out of "D" and sorts them into an array. The "foreach" function assigns each entry in the "sort" array (one at a time) to the variable "$name" and executes the subsequent block of code once per entry.

"(substr($name,-4,4)" extracts the last four bytes of "$name." " =~ /.gif/i" matches these bytes to .gif in a case-insensitive way—hence, the trailing "i." "(stat($name)) [7]" retrieves parameter 7 concerning the status of the file whose name is contained in "$name." Parameter 7 is the file size.

The iconlib.pl program provides a practical example of feeding input data from HTML to a CGI program's command line. In the example repeated here for convenience, the question mark indicates the beginning of the command line, and a plus sign appears in place of a space; this is the normal URL convention. The program can retrieve the command-line data through its normal channels or via the QUERY_STRING environment variable:

```
http://www.interlakken.com/perl.exe?iconlib.pl+mc-icons
```

16.3.1.3 grape.pl—Passing Form Data to a CGI Program The third standard CGI example is a program that accepts several fields from an HTML form, checks them for validity, formats the data into an E-Mail message, and sends it. Figure 16.9 illustrates the HTML form with some input data filled in; Figures 16.10 and 16.11 illustrate the response from clicking the "Feed" button and the resulting E-Mail message, respectively.

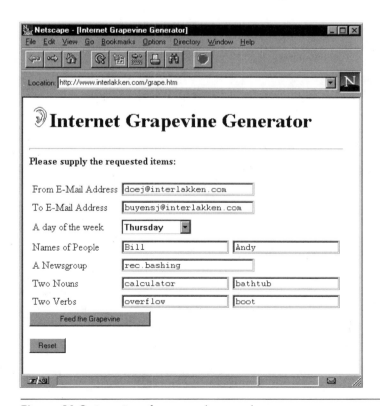

Figure 16.9 Input Form for grape.pl—grape.htm

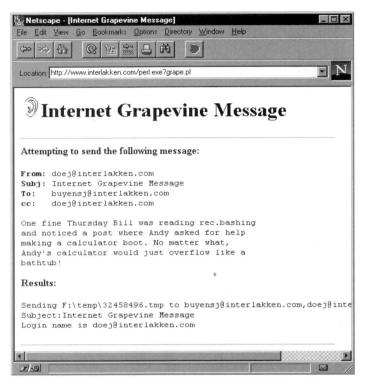

Figure 16.10 Valid Response Page from grape.pl

The HTML code for grape.htm, the page containing the input form, appears shortly. To produce a pleasing alignment, a table with seven rows and three columns contains the input fields. The table columns are most apparent in the rows "Names of People," "Two Nouns," and "Two Verbs." The text boxes for the fields "From E-Mail Address," "To E-Mail Address," and "A Newsgroup" span the second and third columns.

Note the NAME= attributes in each <INPUT> tag and the <SELECT> tag. Without these names, the receiving program would have no way to identify the incoming data fields. Note also that the <FORM> tag (and not the <INPUT TYPE="SUBMIT"> tag) defines the URL to activate the CGI program.

The attribute METHOD="POST" in the <FORM> tag specifies that the HTTP server should pipe the form data into standard input. METHOD="GET" would supply the same form data string as a command-line argument, but this tends to be limiting, and METHOD="POST" is therefore preferable. If you compare the code to the resulting display in Figure 16.9, the rest of the form should be relatively self-evident:

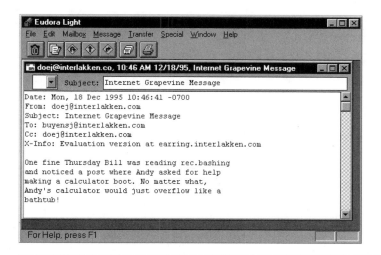

Figure 16.11 E-Mail Message Received by Eudora Light[3] from grape.pl

grape.htm:

```
<HTML>
<HEAD>
<TITLE>Internet Grapevine Generator</TITLE>
</HEAD>
<BODY>
<H1><IMG SRC="ear.gif" ALIGN="BOTTOM">Internet Grapevine Generator
</H1>
<HR>
<B>Please supply the requested items:</B>
<FORM ACTION="perl.exe?grape.pl" METHOD="POST">
<TABLE>
<TR>
  <TD>From E-Mail Address</TD>
  <TD COLSPAN=2> <INPUT NAME="fmaddr" VALUE="" SIZE=25></TD>
</TR><TR>
  <TD>To E-Mail Address</TD>
  <TD COLSPAN=2><INPUT NAME="toaddr" VALUE="" SIZE=25></TD>
</TR><TR>
```

---

[3]Eudora Light is a trademark of QUALCOMM Incorporated.

```
  <TD>A day of the week</TD>
  <TD><SELECT NAME="day" >
      <OPTION>Monday
      <OPTION>Tuesday
      <OPTION>Wednesday
      <OPTION>Thursday
      <OPTION>Friday
      <OPTION>Saturday
      <OPTION>Sunday</SELECT></TD>
</TR>
<TR>
  <TD>Names of People</TD>
  <TD><INPUT NAME="name1" VALUE="" ></TD>
  <TD><INPUT NAME="name2" VALUE="" ></TD>
</TR><TR>
  <TD>A Newsgroup</TD>
  <TD colspan=2><INPUT NAME="newsgroup" VALUE="" SIZE=25></TD>
</TR><TR>
  <TD>Two Nouns</TD>
  <TD><INPUT NAME="noun1" VALUE="" ></TD>
  <TD><INPUT NAME="noun2" VALUE="" ></TD>
</TR><TR>
  <TD>Two Verbs</TD>
  <TD><INPUT NAME="verb1" VALUE="" ></TD>
  <TD><INPUT NAME="verb2" VALUE="" ></TD>
</TABLE>
<INPUT TYPE="SUBMIT" VALUE="Feed the Grapevine">
<P>
<INPUT TYPE="RESET">
</FORM>
</BODY>
</HTML>
```

The grape.pl program itself appears next. There is some attempt to be rigorous here, and the program is therefore slightly longer than strictly necessary. However, this should be helpful if you decide to modify the Grapevine application into one that meets your own needs.

Even if you've never seen perl before, you should be able to follow the comments and read the program as pseudocode (see the sidebar titled "BLAT—A Command-Line SMTP Mailer for Windows NT" for information about BLAT):

grape.pl:

```
# _____
# grape.pl is a CGI program that receives form data from
# grape.htm, validates each field, sends mail to an intended
# recipient, and provides user feedback.
#
# Requirements:
#    1.   This program uses BLAT, a freeware command-line SMTP
#         mailer for Windows NT. You must obtain BLAT and
#         install it in your <systemroot>\system32 directory
#         before running this program.
#    2.   Before running this program, you should establish a
#         system environment variable named temp that identifies
#         a directory for temporary files. User environment
#         values named temp aren't applicable to background
#         processes such as CGI programs.
#
# Setting $debug=1 below provides extended trace information
# along with other user feedback.
# _____
$debug=0;
#
print "Content-type: text/html\n";
print "\n";
print "<HTML>\n";
print "<HEAD>\n";
print "<TITLE>Internet Grapevine Message</TITLE>\n";
print "</HEAD>\n";
print "<BODY>\n";
print qq!<H1><IMG SRC="ear.gif" ALIGN="BOTTOM">!;
print "Internet Grapevine Message</H1>\n";
print "<HR>\n";
```

```
# -------------------------------------------------------------------
# The following code reads "CONTENT_LENGTH" bytes from stdin,
# splits the resulting "&" delimited fields into an array called
# @flds, then splits each name=value pair in @flds into an
# associative array called @in. The code also translates
# hex codes received as %xx to their character equivalents.
# -------------------------------------------------------------------
read(STDIN,$fdat,$ENV{CONTENT_LENGTH});

@flds = split(/&/,$fdat);
foreach $fld (@flds) {
    ($fkey, $fval) = split(/=/,$fld);
    $fval =~ tr/+/ /;
    $fval =~ s/%([a-fA-F0-9][a-fA-F0-9])/pack("C", hex($1))/eg;
    $fkey =~ tr/+/ /;
    $fkey =~ s/%([a-fA-F0-9][a-fA-F0-9])/pack("C", hex($1))/eg;
    $in{$fkey} = $fval
}
# -------------------------------------------------------------------
# Reject transaction if any input field is blank or contains
# invalid characters.
# -------------------------------------------------------------------
$err = 0;
&ChkInFld("fmaddr","From E-Mail Address");
&ChkInFld("toaddr","To E-Mail Address");
&ChkInFld("name1","First person's name");
&ChkInFld("name2","Second person's name");
&ChkInFld("newsgroup","Newsgroup");
&ChkInFld("noun1","First noun");
&ChkInFld("noun2","Second noun");
&ChkInFld("verb1","First verb");
&ChkInFld("verb2","Second verb");
#
# Main go/nogo decision is below.
#
```

```
if ($err == 0) {
    &write_message;
} else {
    print "</UL>Please click your browser's ";
    print "<B>Back</B> button and try again.\n";
}
print "<HR>\n";
print "</BODY>\n";
print "</HTML>\n";
# ----------------------------------------------------------------
# Validate input field - non-blank and all valid chars
# ----------------------------------------------------------------
sub ChkInFld {
    if ($in{$_[0]} eq "") {
        &err_msg($_[1] . " can't be blank.");
    } else {
        if ($in{$_[0]} !~ /^[a-zA-Z0-9\._\-+ \/@%]+$/) {
            &err_msg($_[1] . " contains an invalid character.");
        }
    }
}
# ----------------------------------------------------------------
# Report errors and set $err switch
# ----------------------------------------------------------------
sub err_msg {
if ($err == 0) {
    $err = 1;
    print "There was an error in the data you entered.";
    print "<P>\n<UL>\n";
}
print "<LI>$_[0]\n";
}
# ----------------------------------------------------------------
# Format and send the output message
# ----------------------------------------------------------------
```

```perl
sub write_message {
$msg = "One fine ";
$msg = $msg . $in{"day"} . " " ;
$msg = $msg . $in{"name1"} . " was reading ";
$msg = $msg . $in{"newsgroup"} . "\nand noticed a post where ";
$msg = $msg . $in{"name2"} . " asked for help\nmaking a ";
$msg = $msg . $in{"noun1"}. " " ;
$msg = $msg . $in{"verb2"} . ". No matter what,\n";
$msg = $msg . $in{"name2"} . "'s ";
$msg = $msg . $in{"noun1"}. " would just ";
$msg = $msg . $in{"verb1"} . " like a\n";
$msg = $msg . $in{"noun2"} . "!\n";
#
# Generate a random file name <temp>\<random>.temp
# where <temp> is a system environment variable
# and <random> is a 1-8 digit random number.
#
srand;
$bodfilnm = int(rand(99999999))+1 . ".tmp";
$tempath = $ENV{"temp"};
if (substr($tempath,-1,1) eq "\x5C"){
    $bodfilnm = $tempath . $bodfilnm;
} else {
    $bodfilnm = $tempath . "\x5C" . $bodfilnm;
}
#
# Write the formatted message to the temporary file.
#
open (BODY,">".$bodfilnm);
print BODY $msg;
if ($debug == 1) {
    &mail_debug;
    }
close (BODY);
#
```

```
# Build the BLAT command line to mail the temporary file
# to the specified recipient.
#
$subj = "Internet Grapevine Message";
$sendstr = "blat.exe";
$sendstr = $sendstr . " $bodfilnm";
$sendstr = $sendstr . " -f $in{fmaddr}";
$sendstr = $sendstr . " -c $in{fmaddr}";
$sendstr = $sendstr . " -t $in{toaddr}";
$sendstr = $sendstr . qq! -s "$subj"!;
#
# Call BLAT and pipe its output to $resultstring
# (Note backticks rather than single quotes.)
#
$resultstring = `$sendstr`;
#
# Delete the temporary file name.
#
unlink $bodfilnm;
#
# Display message and results to user
#
print "<B>Attempting to send the following message:</B><PRE>";
print "<B>From:</B> $in{fmaddr}\n";
print "<B>Subj:</B> $subj\n";
print "<B>To:</B>    $in{toaddr}\n";
print "<B>cc:</B>    $in{fmaddr}\n\n";
print $msg, "</PRE>\n";
#
print "<B>Results:</B>";
print "<PRE>$resultstring</PRE>";
#
if ($debug == 1) {
    &print_debug;
    }
```

```perl
}
# ————————————————————————————————————————————————————————
# Add debug info to mail message (called if $debug=1)
# ————————————————————————————————————————————————————————
sub mail_debug {
print BODY "\n";
print BODY "Raw Form Data:\n";
print BODY "$fdat\n";
print BODY "\n";
print BODY "Form Data Array:\n";
foreach $rkey (keys(%in)){
    print BODY "$rkey = $in{$rkey}\n";
    }
print BODY "\n";
print BODY "Environment Variables:\n";
for $key (sort keys %ENV) {
    print BODY "$key=$ENV{$key}\n";
    }
}
# ————————————————————————————————————————————————————————
# Add debug info to user feedback (called if $debug=1)
# ————————————————————————————————————————————————————————
sub print_debug {
print "<HR>\n<H3>Send Mail Command:</H3>";
print "$sendstr\n";
#
print "<HR>\n<H3>Raw Form Data:</H3>\n";
print "$fdat\n";
#
print "<HR>\n<H3>Form Data Array:</H3>\n";
foreach $rkey (keys(%in)){
    print "$rkey = $in{$rkey}<BR>\n";
    }
#
print "<HR>\n<H3>Environment Variables:</H3>\n";
```

```
for $key (sort keys %ENV) {
    print "$key=$ENV{$key}<BR>\n";
    }
}
#
```

Changing the statement "$debug=0;" at the beginning of grape.pl to "$debug=1;" produces the additional debugging information shown next. Note

BLAT—A Command-Line SMTP Mailer for Windows NT

BLAT[4] is a freeware program that sends SMTP Mail messages from the Windows NT command prompt. BLAT is freely available from most Internet archive sites and is also available on the CD accompanying this book.

BLAT's strength lies not in everyday interactive use but in background processes and command files—applications where a GUI interface only gets in the way.

BLAT supports the following command-line syntax:

```
blat <filename> -t <recipient> [optional switches]
```

<filename> specifies the name of the text file BLAT should mail. To send mail from the console, specify a file name of "-" (a hyphen) and terminate input with Ctrl-Z.

Supported switches include

-t <recipient>	A list of recipients separated by commas.
-s <subj>	The subject line.
-f <sender>	A "From:" address that overrides the installed default sender address. The E-Mail server may validate the "-f" address.
-i <addr>	A "From:" address that overrides the installed default sender address. The E-Mail server won't validate the "-i" address.
-c <recipient>	A list of carbon-copy recipients separated by commas.
-b <recipient>	A list of blind-carbon-copy recipients separated by commas.
-h	Display help.
-q	Suppress all text output.
-server <addr>	Overrides the installation default SMTP server name.

To establish a default SMTP server name and sender address, issue the following command:

```
blat -install <server addr> <sender's addr>
```

---

[4]Blat was written by Pedro Mendes and Mark Neal using portions of the source code of WinVN.

how the raw form data appears with ampersands separating fieldname=value
pairs. Had the actual input data contained any ampersands or equal signs, the
strings %26 and %3D would have appeared in their places. (26 and 3D are the
hex codes for ampersand and equal sign.) Carriage returns appear as %0D, line
feeds as %0A, and so on:

```
Send Mail Command:

blat.exe F:\temp\94839477.tmp -f doej@interlakken.com
   -c doej@interlakken.com -t buyensj@interlakken.com
   -s "Internet Grapevine Message"

Raw Form Data:

fmaddr=doej@interlakken.com&toaddr=buyensj@interlakken.com&day=Thursday
    &name1=Bill&name2=Andy&newsgroup=rec.bashing&noun1=calculator
    &noun2=bathtub&verb1=overflow&verb2=boot

Form Data Array:

name1 = Bill
fmaddr = doej@interlakken.com
noun1 = calculator
verb1 = overflow
toaddr = buyensj@interlakken.com
newsgroup = rec.bashing
name2 = Andy
day = Thursday
noun2 = bathtub
verb2 = boot


Environment Variables:

COMPUTERNAME=EARRING
CONTENT_LENGTH=172
CONTENT_TYPE=application/x-www-form-urlencoded
```

```
ComSpec=F:\WINNT\system32\cmd.exe
GATEWAY_INTERFACE=CGI/1.1
HTTP_ACCEPT=image/gif, image/x-xbitmap, image/jpeg, image/pjpeg, */*
HTTP_CONNECTION=Keep-Alive
HTTP_HOST=www.interlakken.com
HTTP_REFERER=http://www.interlakken.com/grape.htm
HTTP_USER_AGENT=Mozilla/2.0b3 (Win95; I)
NTResKit=F:\RESKIT\
OS=Windows_NT
Os2LibPath=F:\WINNT\system32\os2\dll;
PROCESSOR_ARCHITECTURE=x86
PROCESSOR_IDENTIFIER=x86 Family 5 Model 2 Stepping 5, GenuineIntel
PROCESSOR_LEVEL=5
PROCESSOR_REVISION=0205
Path=f:\win32app\ingr\perl\bin;F:\WINNT\system32;F:\WINNT;f:\reskit\;
QUERY_STRING=grape.pl
REMOTE_ADDR=130.131.90.67
REMOTE_HOST=choker.interlakken.com
REQUEST_METHOD=POST
SCRIPT_NAME=/perl.exe
SERVER_NAME=www.interlakken.com
SERVER_PORT=80
SERVER_PROTOCOL=HTTP/1.0
SERVER_SOFTWARE=Netscape-Communications/1.12
SERVER_URL=http://www.interlakken.com
SystemDrive=F:
SystemRoot=F:\WINNT
temp=F:\temp
windir=F:\WINNT
```

The environment variable CONTENT_LENGTH provides the length of the raw form data. This is important because there's no carriage return, line feed, or end-of-file character terminating the raw form data; the program must read the exact number of bytes the CONTENT_LENGTH variable specifies. The rest of the environment variables are there for whatever use you make of them; perhaps you'd like to further identify the originating user by adding the REMOTE_ADDR, REMOTE_HOST, and HTTP_USER_AGENT fields to the outgoing mail message.

Finally, "Content-type: text/html" isn't the only valid header line for CGI programs. Table 16.5 lists additional possibilities.

16.3.1.4 Notes on Working with perl and Debugging Standard CGI Programs
Perl is an interpreted "load-and-go" language that reads and compiles the source code for every execution. Despite this, it runs surprisingly fast. Perl includes sophisticated array and string handling, and it interfaces very well to standard CGI.

Perl is also somewhat of a code masher's delight; it's full of little tricks, obtuse syntax, gotchas, and salvations. Everything in perl is self-defining, so if you misspell a variable name you won't get an error; you'll simply get a new variable containing a null value.

There are no interactive debuggers you can use for tracing CGI programs written in perl; instead, you should try running the perl program from the command line. This is generally the only way you can see error messages if the perl program doesn't compile. If you get correct standard output displayed at the command prompt but get system errors trying to run the CGI, you've probably forgotten the "Content-type:" header, forgotten the blank line separating header and body, or forgotten to activate CGI.

The definitive books on perl are Larry Wall and Randal L. Schwartz's *Programming perl* (1991) and Randal L. Schwartz's *Learning Perl* (1993), which appear in the bibliography at the end of this book. Larry Wall, by the way, is perl's inventor.

16.3.2 Writing Windows CGI Programs

Neither C nor perl is a language most Windows-based Web authors would choose for writing quick little programs processing small amounts of data; Visual Basic would more likely be the choice. Unfortunately, a number of issues keeps Visual Basic from being useful as a CGI development language:

- Visual Basic can't read standard input.
- Visual Basic can't write standard output.

Table 16.5 Valid CGI Response Headers

Header	Instruction to Browser
Content-type: text/html	Treat body of response as HTML.
Content-type: <MIME type>	Treat body of response as specified MIME type.
Location: <URL>	Retrieve and display the specified URL. The term for this is *redirection*.
Status: <code> <message>	Report the given status code and message to the user. The status code should comply with Table 15.3.

- Windows doesn't establish a new environment area for each Windows program executed; this prevents passing system information like CONTENT_LENGTH, CONTENT_TYPE, REMOTE_HOST, and HTTP_USER_AGENT through the normal environment variable.

- Visual Basic loads a rather large working set; that is, starting a Visual Basic program can require the operating system to load quite a few DLL, OCX, VBX, and related modules. If repeated very often, this can result in a significant performance penalty.

- Running under Windows NT, 16-bit Visual Basic programs involve a second performance penalty running inside the "Windows on Windows" box.

Despite these drawbacks, there are many people who want to write CGI programs, don't know C or perl, don't want to learn them, but do know Visual Basic. To meet this need, Bob Denny developed the Windows CGI specification.

A so-called front-end program provides the WinCGI interface and launches the user-written, typically Visual Basic back-end program that performs the application processing. The back-end program receives a command line containing five elements separated by spaces:

1. **Back-end exe name.** The name of the user-written executable program.

2. **CGI data file name.** The name of a temporary file, in INI file format, that contains what would otherwise be the normal environment variables and form data field values.

3. **Content file name.** The name of a temporary file that contains the encoded form input. This is the character string that standard CGI would normally supply through standard input (POST) or through the command line and the QUERY_STRING environment variable (GET).

4. **Output file name.** The name of a temporary file where the application should write the output returned to the user.

5. **URL args.** Anything that followed a normal "?" in the original URL.

The CGI data file conforms to the standard Windows INI file format and contains seven sections:

1. **[CGI].** This section contains a standard keyword=value pair for most standard CGI data items (CONTENT_LENGTH, REMOTE_HOST, and so on.).

2. **[Accept].** This section contains a list of data types acceptable to the client, as identified by the "Accept:" request header.

3. **[System].** Items specific to WinCGI appear here. The "Output File" keyword identifies the file name that should receive result HTML, and "Content File" gives the name of the unencoded input file.

4. **[Extra headers].** Appearing here are keyword=value pairs for any request headers not provided elsewhere.

5. **[Form literal].** If a form value contains 254 or fewer characters, all of which are legal, WinCGI stores the value in this section. The data names are those specified in the form's HTML definition, and the values are those specified by the user. (Note that certain characters, such as carriage returns and line feeds, are valid in form input but not in INI files. Furthermore, form values have unlimited length, while INI file values cannot exceed 254 bytes.)

6. **[Form external].** If a form value contains an illegal character or is 255 to 65,535 bytes long, WinCGI adds its name as a keyword in this section. The associated value is the name of a temporary file containing the value, a space, and then the length of the value.

7. **[Form huge].** If a form value exceeds 65,535 bytes in length, WinCGI creates a like-named keyword in this section and specifies the value's offset and length in the "Content File."

WinCGI starts the back-end (application) program with the command line just described. When the application ends, WinCGI transmits the temporary output file to the user and then cleans up all temporary files created for the transaction.

WinCGI programs written in Visual Basic can't be "user interface" applications; that is, their MAK file can't contain any forms, they can't use any commands like MsgBox that create GUI output, and they can't use any Windows GDI (Graphic Display Interface) functions. Execution begins with executing a Sub Main procedure rather than with loading a start-up form.

WebSite is the most common HTTP server providing WinCGI, and WinCGI seems to be one of its greatest selling features. WebSite includes several example WinCGI programs and CGI.BAS, a module that includes the required Sub Main procedure, all required start-up code, and simple interfaces for obtaining form values and writing response output.

Front-end WinCGI software is available as "glueware" for other HTTP servers as well. However, performance problems have limited the growth of WinCGI for high-volume, high-throughput applications.

16.3.3 The <ISINDEX> Tag

Simple query applications frequently make use of the HTML tag <ISINDEX>. This tag displays a horizontal rule, the prompt "This is a searchable index. Enter search keywords:", a text box, and then another horizontal rule. After the user types in the desired keywords and presses Enter, the browser appends a question mark and the keywords to the original URL and submits it using the GET method. If the original URL already had a query string, it's replaced.

Since displaying the initial form and processing it use the same URL, that URL must invoke a single CGI program capable of doing both. If the query string is blank, the program generates the initial query form; if the query string contains data, the program processes it.

Using perl to process <ISINDEX> tags presents a problem because when the browser appends the query string to a URL such as http://www.interlakken.com/perl.exe?isindex.pl, it replaces the isindex.pl part of the query string as well.

Some HTTP servers avoid this problem through system or internal file associations. When they receive a URL like http://www.interlakken.com/isindex.pl, they look in the NT Registry (or their own configuration file), determine that perl.exe is the program that processes .pl files, and internally build the requisite command line. This solution has serious security loopholes, as discussed in Section 16.3.7.

16.3.4 Netscape Server Application Programming Interface (NSAPI)

NSAPI provides a way to write your own replacements and extensions to the core services of Netscape's HTTP servers. In addition, it permits development of higher-performance user applications than are possible with standard CGI.

Netscape developed NSAPI to avoid three major limitations of standard CGI:

1. Standard CGI requires the server to load, execute, and terminate the CGI program once for each user interaction. This is expensive in terms of server resources.

2. Standard CGI programs are unable to share data and communications resources. Instead, each CGI program must acquire and release its own channel to these resources every time it executes.

3. Standard CGI is designed only for returning data to a browser. It cannot substitute its own logic for services the HTTP server normally provides.

Netscape considers processing of HTTP requests to occur in several stages:

■ Authorization translation
■ Name translation

- Path checks
- Object typing
- Response to request
- Logging the transaction

Any time one of these steps fails, another function must take over processing, report the error to the user, and take whatever recovery is necessary on the server side.

Netscape has analyzed all these steps, plus others such as server start-up and shutdown, and defined a set of *server application functions* to implement them. A configuration file controls loading of these functions and therefore replacement with others (assuming the replacements obey all the same calling conventions). User-written functions can replace Netscape functions on a global, directory, file, or group of files basis. Such modules enjoy full access to the server's internal data structures, functions, and I/O abstractions (including secure data transfer).

You can write NSAPI functions for Windows NT in Microsoft Visual C++ by compiling the function as a DLL.

The individual NSAPI functions are too lengthy and detailed to include here. For more information, connect to Netscape's Web site at http://www.netscape.com and search for NSAPI.

16.3.5 Internet Server Application Programming Interface (ISAPI)

ISAPI provides a very efficient Windows-compliant way to add functions to an HTTP server. Unlike standard CGI, there's no use of standard input and output; unlike WinCGI, there are no temporary files.

The downside of ISAPI, if it is one, is that programs must be DLLs (Dynamic Link Libraries). Thus, not only must programmers write them in C, they must write them to be reentrant.[5]

Every ISAPI DLL must have two entry points named GetExtensionVersion and HttpExtensionProc. When the HTTP server receives a request to run the ISAPI DLL, the server first checks to see whether the DLL is already in memory. If not, the server loads it and then calls GetExtensionVersion to determine whether the DLL supports a version of ISAPI the server can deal with. If not, the server unloads the DLL and ends the request with an error.

---

[5]*Reentrancy* means that a single copy of the program can handle multiple executions at the same time. That is, the code can start processing one transaction before the prior one finishes. This requires, for example, that each execution obtains its own data areas on entry and frees them on exit. It may also be necessary to use *semaphores* and *mutexes*—operating system switches that can single-thread multiple executions through a critical block of code.

If the GetExtensionVersion check passes, the server calls HttpExtensionProc and passes an *extension control block* formatted as described in Table 16.6.

Note that ISAPI supplies in-memory pointers to the essential data that standard CGI supplies through environment variables or standard input. This is much more efficient. If all the input data fits in the buffer addressed by lpbData, cbAvailable will equal cbTotalBytes. If all the data won't fit, cbAvailable will be less than cbTotalBytes; the application can access the additional data through the ReadClient call described shortly.

Once executing, the ISAPI application has access to four specialized *callback functions*:

1. **GetServerVariable.** This function copies data about the client connection or server into data areas specified as part of the call. This provides access to all the environment values normally provided for standard CGI programs.

2. **ReadClient.** Calling this function reads information from the body of the HTTP client request into a supplied buffer supplied by the caller. One possible application is reading data from an HTML form that uses the POST method.

3. **WriteClient.** Calling this function sends data to the HTTP client. This is the ISAPI equivalent of writing to standard output in standard CGI and writing to the temporary output file in WinCGI.

Table 16.6 ISAPI Extension Control Block

Variable	Type	Assigned by	Description
cbsize	DWORD	Server	Size of this structure.
dwVersion	DWORD	Server	ISAPI version (in HIWORD/LOWORD = major/minor form).
ConnID	HCONN	Server	Unique connection ID.
dwHttpStatusCode	DWORD	Application	Status of the current transaction when completed.
lpszLogData	CHAR	Application	String to be entered into the server log.
lpszMethod	LPSTR	Server	Equivalent to the CGI variable REQUEST_METHOD.
lpszQuery_string	LPSTR	Server	Equivalent to the CGI variable QUERY_STRING.
lpszPathInfo	LPSTR	Server	Equivalent to the CGI variable PATH_INFO.
lpszPathTranslated	LPSTR	Server	Equivalent to the CGI variable PATH_TRANSLATED.
cbTotalBytes	DWORD	Server	Equivalent to the CGI variable CONTENT_LENGTH. The value 4GB indicates an error.
cbAvailable	DWORD	Server	Number of bytes (out of a total of cbTotalBytes) available in the buffer pointed by lpbData.
lpbData	LPBYTE	Server	Pointer to a buffer of size cbAvailable that contains the data sent by the client.
lpszContentType	LPSTR	Server	Type of data sent by the client using POST or PUT.

4. **ServerSupportFunction.** This function supports eight different operations depending on the value of a *service request code.* Table 16.7 lists the eight operations.

The full details of writing an ISAPI application are clearly beyond the scope of this book, but the information given here should at least provide an overview and help you decide whether ISAPI is appropriate for your application. For more information, point your browser at Process Software's or Microsoft's respective ISAPI pages:

http://www.process.com/news/spec.htp

http://www.microsoft.com/intdev/TECH.HTM

16.3.6 Other CGI Approaches

Interesting developments are likely to occur with two programming languages, Java and Visual Basic, and with client-server processing.

Java is a simplified, interpreted version of C++ promoted by Sun Microsystems. Sun introduced Java as a script language for browsers, but corresponding use on servers seems a likely extension, especially to support client-server applications.

Table 16.7 ISAPI ServerSupportFunction Service Request Codes

Service Request Code	Description
HSE_REQ_SEND_URL_REDIRECT_RESP (1)	Sends a 302 (URL Redirect) message to the client.
HSE_REQ_SEND_URL (2)	Sends the contents of a local URL data to the client as if the client had requested that URL.
HSE_REQ_SEND_RESPONSE_HEADER (3)	Sends a complete HTTP server response header including the status, server version, message time, and MIME version. The application should append additional information such as the CONTENT_TYPE and CONTENT_LENGTH followed by an extra '\r\n.'
HSE_REQ_DONE_WITH_SESSION (4)	An application that holds onto the client session for extended processing uses this function to close the connection.
HSE_GET_COUNTER_FOR_GET_METHOD (1001)	Returns the number of GET requests a given server has processed since start-up.
HSE_GET_COUNTER_FOR_POST_METHOD (1002)	Returns the number of POST requests a given server has processed since start-up.
HSE_GET_COUNTER_FOR_HEAD_METHOD (1003)	Returns the number of HEAD requests a given server has processed since start-up.
HSE_GET_COUNTER_FOR_ALL_METHODS (1004)	Returns the total number of requests a given server has processed since start-up.

To compete with Java, Microsoft proposed using Visual Basic as a scripting language for both browsers and HTTP servers. Microsoft promised a lean, mean version of Visual Basic for Applications for browsers running on Windows, UNIX, and Macintosh, plus an improved API for Visual Basic on the server.

What seems certain is that none of this will slow down anytime soon.

16.3.7 Security Concerns with CGI Programs

Most HTTP servers run CGI programs with the same security privileges as the HTTP server itself. This presents a serious security risk. Consider the following scenario:

- You install the HTTP server and allow it to run under the Windows NT SYSTEM account. This is, after all, the default established by most setup programs.
- You enable *.exe as a CGI type for the entire HTTP data directory.
- A user puts an accidentally buggy (or deliberately mischievous) program in their personal Web page directory and executes it by typing the necessary URL.
- The user's program now has full operating system authority to all of Windows NT and all files local to the server.

This is probably not what you want. The alternatives are as follows:

1. Run the HTTP server under a special user account rather than the SYSTEM account. This doesn't stop user CGI programs from modifying any area the server itself can modify, however.
2. Allow CGI programs to execute only from a specified directory that only an administrator can update. This assumes the administrator can manually detect and reject all potentially damaging programs, including legitimate programs with intentional or unintended back doors.
3. Combine alternatives 1 and 2.
4. Don't run CGI programs at all.

Another potential security leak involves CGI programs that launch other programs. Intruders occasionally devise ways to embed commands within ordinary fields and get them executed. The following commands come to mind, for example:

```
net user administrator <password>
net group administrators <username> /add
```

For this reason, you should always parse the contents of any data being internally passed to a command prompt. Reject anything with suspicious characters like escape, backspace, carriage return, and line feed.

A particular problem with perl programs is that the HTTP server sees perl.exe, the perl interpreter, as the actual CGI program; the name of the perl source program is merely data in the query string. Making perl.exe generally available via the system path or through file association can be a very bad idea because, once again, anyone can run any perl program in any HTTP directory on the server and their program will run with the same security as the HTTP server itself. Various HTTP servers handle this problem differently, so read your documentation carefully and make sure the configuration you establish for your site doesn't leave you open.

The ISAPI specification fails to solve the basic problem of application code running with the same security as the HTTP server; this is exactly the security ISAPI processes enjoy. In addition, an ISAPI application that crashes (creates a general protection fault) can, unless invoked with suitable protection, bring down the entire HTTP server service.

16.4 Server Side Includes

SSI (Server Side Include) is a feature whereby an HTTP server scans all outgoing HTML and replaces specially marked portions with the contents of another file or with CGI program output. *Server parsed* HTML is another name for this feature.

The starting and ending SSI delimiters are "<!—#" and "—>." For a simple example, imagine a file named webpage.html that contains the following text:

```
Line one<P>
<!-#include file="linetwo.html" -><P>
Line three<P>
```

If linetwo.html contains

```
Line two
```

the user's browser will receive

```
Line one<P>
Line two<P>
Line three<P>
```

Even at this simple level, SSI can be useful for managing strings that occur repeatedly in pages and would benefit from centralized control. The Webmaster's E-Mail address might be such a field. Another might be an IMG tag pointing to a "New!" icon; after a certain date, an administrator could change the "included" IMG tag to a null string.

Table 16.8 provides a complete reference to SSI commands.

The "exec" command is probably the most used SSI command. The reason is that starting an SSI CGI program doesn't require a special URL as normal CGI programs do.

The ubiquitous *home page hit counter* is undoubtedly the most common SSI CGI program. Every time the server delivers a page with such an SSI exec, the exec cgi program increments a counter file and then either inserts the new count as text or inserts IMG tags to display odometer-like numbers.

There are three principal drawbacks to SSIs:

1. **Performance.** Although the amount of processing required to scan a response page for SSI tags isn't large, it's still considerably more than copying the page as is to the network port. Additionally, if the server finds an SSI tag, it must open the included file, look up the requested data in directory entries, or run the specified CGI program.

Table 16.8 Server Side Include Commands

Command	Argument	Description
config		Controls overall aspects of file parsing.
	errmsg	Controls the message the client receives if an error occurs during document parsing.
	timefmt	Alters the format of displayed dates.
	sizefmt	Determines the format used to display file sizes. Acceptable values are:
	bytes	A byte count (formatted as 1,234,567).
	abbrev	A number stated in kilobytes or megabytes.
include		Inserts a text file into the response HTML.
	virtual	A virtual path to a file.
	file	A relative path to a file. Neither back references (like "..\") nor absolute paths are acceptable.
echo		Sends the contents of a special or system environment variable.
	var	Specifies the special or system environment variable to echo.
fsize		Inserts the size of a file. This uses the same tags as the "include" command.
flastmod		Inserts the modification date of the specified file. This also uses the same tags as the "include" command.
exec		Executes a CGI script. An administrator must specially activate this feature.
	cgi	Identifies a CGI script at the given virtual path and inserts its output. There's no validation of script output, but the server will detect a "Location:" header and make it an HTML anchor.

There are two common ways of mitigating SSI performance penalties: first, by limiting SSI processing to certain directories and second, by only parsing files with a specified extension (typically shtml).

2. **Security.** The security problems with SSI CGI programs are those that exist with all other CGI programs: Most servers run them with the server's authority—authority that's inappropriate for user-written programs. This argues strongly against allowing SSI CGI programs to run from dozens or hundreds of user home directories, each of which wants a personal page counter. Control execution of all CGI programs, SSI or not, and give users access to hit counters based on daily log analysis.

3. **Limited support for user input.** SSI CGI programs can only access query strings (those following the "?" in a URL), system data, local files, and environment variables.

The environment variables an SSI CGI program can access are system (not user) environment variables, plus those in Table 16.9.

By default, most HTML servers don't parse response HTML and will thus ignore any "<--...-->" tags in your files. To enable parsing, you must issue an administrator command that specifies what directories and file extensions the server should parse. Enabling SSI CGI is usually a separate case so that security for this feature can be stricter than that for simple file inclusions and file modification date lookups. The Netscape Navigator SSI configuration pages appear in Figures 16.12 and 16.13. To call up this screen, choose "Customize server parsed HTML on your server" from the main Server Manager page.

16.5 Database and Transaction Processing

Delivering database applications via HTTP is an attractive proposition. The only client software required is the ubiquitous Web browser, and the number of

Table 16.9 CGI Environment Variables Available to SSI Programs

Variable Name	Description
DOCUMENT_NAME	The name of the current file.
DOCUMENT_URI	The virtual path to the current document.
QUERY_STRING_UNESCAPED	Any search query the client may have sent.
DATE_LOCAL	The current date and local time zone.
DATE_GMT	Same as DATE_LOCAL but stated as Greenwich Mean Time.
LAST_MODIFIED	The date of the most recent update to the current file.

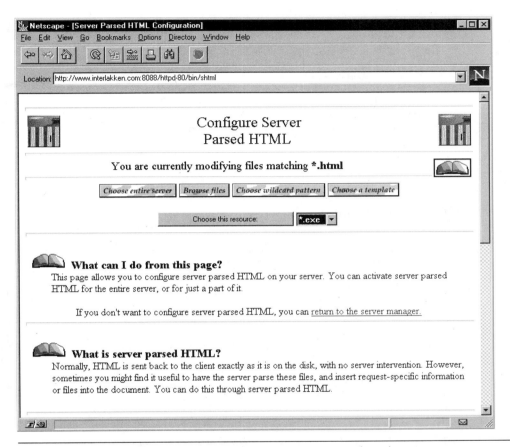

Figure 16.12 Netscape Communications Server SSI Configuration (Part 1)

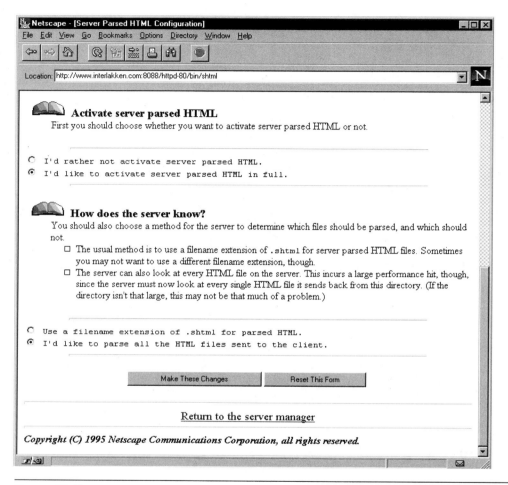

Figure 16.13 Netscape Communications Server SSI Configuration (Part 2)

potential users is huge. HTML forms provide a reasonably attractive and familiar interface. However, as the following section will discuss, the stateless nature of HTTP leads to complications.

The word *database* has fallen into such wide and varied use that it means almost anything to anybody. For purposes of this section, a database will be a formal collection of objects managed by DataBase Management System (DBMS). For the most part, DBMSs are SQL or other near-relational systems such as Microsoft Access, Microsoft SQL Server, Oracle, and Paradox.

Extended discussion of these topics is beyond the scope of this book; a full discussion could easily occupy several books or libraries. The following, therefore, is only a general introduction.

16.5.1 General Considerations

At first glance, the job of updating a database from an HTML form might seem straightforward—just another CGI program. However, the following complications arise:

- **DBMS start-up/shutdown overhead.** DBMSs typically load large amounts of code into memory when they start up. Additionally, opening a database and performing a query typically consume much more resource than performing operations on "flat" ASCII files. As a result, the DBMS should be a separate process from any application CGI program—a process that avoids start-up/shutdown overhead by running continuously in the background.

- **Stateless nature of HTTP.** In a very common scenario, the user enters one or more key fields, the application displays current database contents, the user types over fields requiring update, and then the application updates the database. This presumes that a record-locking scheme prevents two or more users from viewing and updating the same record at the same time. Being stateless, however, an HTTP server maintains no association between the request to display a record and the subsequent request to update it. This greatly increases the record-locking burden on the application.

- **Lack of transaction processing support.** *Transaction* is another word with many vague meanings. Here, it means a group of updates, all of which must occur or none of which must occur. For example, if a transaction requires updates to both Table A and Table B, the update to Table A succeeds, and the update to Table B fails, then the application or DBMS must undo the update to Table A. This implies that portions of Table A remain locked (not available for update by other transactions) until the whole transaction involving Tables A and B comes to some conclusion. This problem is particularly difficult if Tables A and B reside on different computers and use different DBMS software. Transaction-processing monitors like CICS (Customer Information Control System) and Tuxedo provide support for this kind of processing; HTTP currently does not.

- **Multithreading support.** It's perfectly acceptable and possible for two Web users to submit transactions at the same time and thus to be executing the same copy of the same code at the same time. Desktop DBMSs may lack the capability to support multiple users in this fashion and may therefore crash or malfunction.

■ **Security.** Databases and associated applications are frequently so time-consuming and expensive to set up that applications justifying the expense tend to be mission-critical. This raises the stakes considerably in ensuring that the right people have continuous access and the wrong people certainly don't. Optimally, all valid users should have continuous, unrestricted access; no impostor should ever have access; and no eavesdropper or wiretapper should ever extract information in transit.

The normal way of overcoming program start-up/shutdown overhead is to run the DBMS and possibly some of the application code as Windows NT services. This means running database services such as Microsoft SQL Server or the Oracle RDBMS (relational DBMS). Middleware that sits between the end-user application and the DBMS can also decrease the amount of code loaded and unloaded for each transaction. Applications that use monolithic single-user software, such as Visual Basic accessing Microsoft Access databases, are likely to be bulky, slow, and not suitable for moderate- or high-volume applications.

Software is available to run desktop DBMS engines under the auspices of a background process. This eliminates the overhead of constant software start-up/shutdown and database open/close processing but still doesn't provide the throughput and reliability of dedicated database management software.

16.5.2 Preserving State Information

Remote users have no continuous session and no permanent identity to an HTTP server. This presents a problem when developing applications that involve multi-step transactions, such as query-update sequences and item-at-a-time order entry. Since the server doesn't remember the identity of the user between transactions, this task falls to the application and the browser. There are two approaches to this:

1. Each program in the series must send all information about the transaction out to the browser in such a format that the browser sends it back when the user continues the transaction. HTML <INPUT> tags provide a good means to do this. If the user shouldn't see or modify the data, use <INPUT TYPE=HIDDEN>.

2. The opening program can assign the transaction a unique (possibly random) identity key and then store all pending data in a "scratch pad" database using that key. It then includes only the scratch pad key in the response HTML. Two common ways to send and receive scratch pad keys are through <INPUT TYPE=HIDDEN> tags and URL path information. Path information appears in the URL between the CGI script name and the question mark.

16.5.3 Record Locking

The statelessness of HTTP creates serious problems with regard to database record locking. Two locking schemes are in common use: pessimistic and optimistic.

Pessimistic locking holds the lock starting when the application accesses a record for update and continuing until the application explicitly frees the lock or moves to another record. Its pessimism lies in the assumption that giving any other user access to the locked record would create problems: Thus, the following scenario is possible:

1. User A retrieves record for update. OK.
2. User B retrieves same record for update. Fails.
3. User A updates record. OK.

Optimistic locking "hopes" no one else will access a record for update and doesn't bother locking it. If, when someone actually submits an update, the DBMS determines someone else has updated the record in the meantime, it fails the second update. This scenario could thus ensue:

1. User A retrieves record for update. OK.
2. User B retrieves same record for update. OK.
3. User B updates record. OK.
4. User A tries to update record. Fails.

Pessimistic locking isn't practical for HTTP database applications because HTTP transactions lack the necessary continuity. Exiting an HTTP program after one step of a transaction and leaving a lock in place is very dangerous; the user may never transact the next step, and the lock would remain in place forever. This is true regardless of whether the application or the DBMS manages the lock.

Optimistic record locking is clearly necessary, but the application, not the DBMS, must provide it. The DBMS can't manage locks from sequences of CGI programs because the HTTP server provides no association among multiple program executions that constitute a single transaction. As a result, each application must provide its own (optimistic) record locking. Two common schemes are time stamping and field comparisons.

For *time stamping*, each database record includes a "date and time last updated" field kept up-to-date by each program that updates it. The first step of a multistep transaction retrieves and saves this time stamp and then, when it's ready to update the database, checks to see whether the time stamp in the database has changed. If so, the system will require some sort of recovery action from the user.

For *field comparisons*, the approach is to save not a time stamp, but copies of all critical field values. When the process is ready to update the database, it checks to see whether any of these database values have changed. If so, the user must again perform some kind of recovery action.

Note that IP addresses aren't unique to a user and therefore can't segregate transactions from different users. Several people communicating through the same proxy server will all appear to have the same IP address—the proxy server's—rather than their own. It's also possible to have multiple browser windows open on the same computer, serving one user or several.

The REMOTE_USER environment field is also unreliable as a transaction identifier. First, this field is empty unless an administrator has password-protected the page and the user has successfully responded to a user name/password challenge. This is clearly inappropriate for transactions open to the general public. Second, even if you tell them not to, several individuals may share a single user name and password.

Perl isn't a good Windows database development language because support for all the necessary APIs is absent. Windows API calls, DLLs, and OLE are all difficult at best and awkward even if possible.

Fortunately, problems with statelessness, record locking, and transaction continuity don't arise with "inquire only" applications.

16.5.4 Microsoft IIS Database Connector

Microsoft Internet Information Server includes an Internet Database Connector (IDC) feature that greatly expedites the job of querying databases and displaying the results as a Web page. Using this feature to query a database requires three relatively simple ASCII files:

1. **HTML form.** If the query requires user input, you'll need to create an HTML form to gather it.

2. **Internet Database Connector file.** This file contains the name of the Open Data Base Connectivity (ODBC) data source, any user names and passwords required to access the data, the name of an output template, and an SQL statement. Form data replaces any tag of the form <%field-name%>.

3. **HTML extension file (output template).** This file resembles ordinary HTML but includes a special section bounded by <%begindetail%> and <%enddetail%> tags. Each record returned by the SQL statement results in one repetition of this special section. Record data replaces tags of the form <%fieldname%>.

Whenever the IIS Web service receives an HTML query with an .idc file name extension, it invokes the ISAPI module httpodbc.dll. This module examines the .idc file, substitutes form data into the SQL statement, and processes the query through ODBC. When the query results are ready, httpodbc.dll creates response HTML containing one repetition of the <%begindetail%> ... <%enddetail%> section for each record in the SQL result set.

16.5.4.1 Logging IIS Activity Directly to SQL Server IIS can log activity data directly to an SQL/ODBC database. This provides an interesting source of queries to illustrate IDCs. Any ODBC-compliant DBMS will work, including Microsoft Access, but, for maximum performance, this example will use Microsoft SQL Server 6.0.

Figure 16.14 shows the required table structure for IIS logs. The \inetsrv\ server\logtemp.sql file installed with IIS provides a basic "create table" command for performing this task.[6] You can also do this interactively using SQL Enterprise Manager.

Once you've created the logging table, you must define SQL Server to ODBC. From Windows NT Control Panel, double-click the ODBC 32 icon and then click the System DSN... button. When the System Data Sources window appears, click the Add... button and watch for a dialog like the one in Figure 16.15 to appear.

Choose the ODBC driver for the DBMS system you plan to use and then click OK. The next dialog will vary depending on the DBMS, but Figure 16.16 shows the results for SQL Server.

Give the data source a name (such as "Web SQL"), give it a description if you want, and then specify the server where SQL Server is running. If necessary, specify the server's network address and network library and then click OK. Returning to the initial ODBC 32 dialog and clicking the System DSN... button again should display the new entry as shown in Figure 16.17.

---

[6]Prior to creating this table, you must install SQL Server and create a device. A device is essentially a Windows NT file that provides bulk space to SQL Server. Once the device exists, you must create a database within it. Once the database exists, you can define tables within it. Consult the SQL Server documentation for details on performing these tasks.

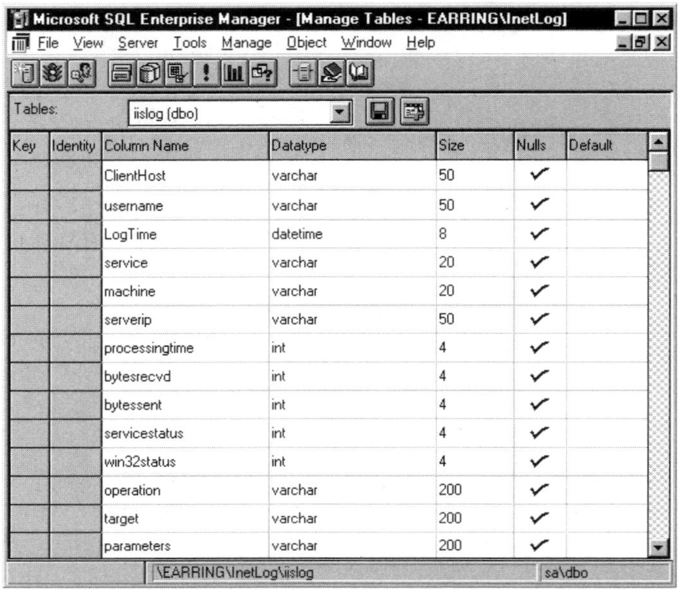

Figure 16.14 Using SQL Enterprise Manager to Create an IIS Log Database

To instruct IIS to log to this database, start Internet Server Manager, select the server's WWW service, and then select the Logging tab. Click "Log to SQL/ODBC Database," specify the ODBC data source name just created, and supply the name of the table. Figure 16.18 shows a three-part name as required by SQL Server; these are the database name, an owner code, and the table name. You can relate these values in Figure 16.18 to the same values in Figure 16.14.

The user name and password appearing in Figure 16.18 are those required to access the database. When all these entries are complete, click the OK button and then close the entire dialog window.

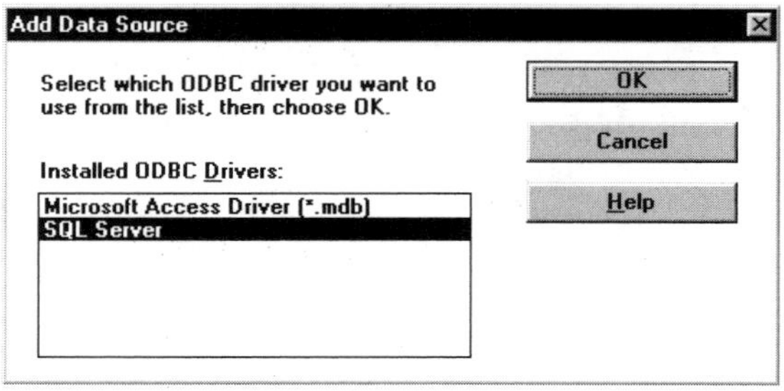

Figure 16.15 ODBC System Data Sources...Add Data Source Dialog

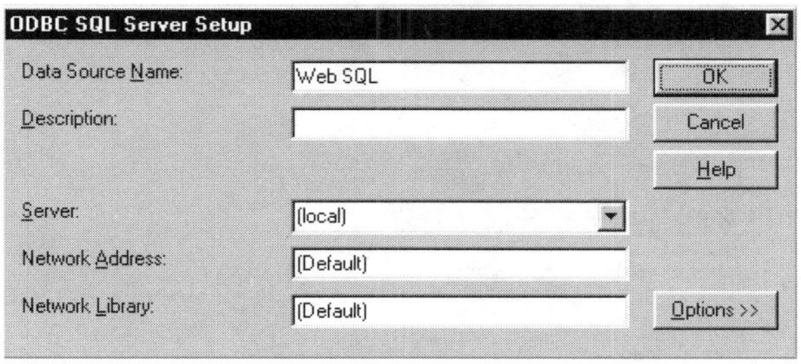

Figure 16.16 ODBC System Data Sources...SQL Server Setup

To test, browse a few Web pages on the reconfigured server and then view the database. Microsoft Access is a good tool for this—even for SQL Server databases. Start Access, create a new (blank) database, pull down the File menu, and select Get External Data...Link Tables.... Choose "Files of type: ODBC Databases" and then "Web SQL" (or whatever name you used). If prompted for a user name and password, supply one valid for the specified DBMS. Finally, specify the table you wish to view—the one you created in Figure 16.14 and specified in Figure 16.18. Opening this table should display contents such as those shown in Figure 16.19.

16.5.4.2 Using Internet Database Connectors to Summarize Log Data Providing instant, up-to-date snapshots of server activity is an interesting and easy use for IDCs. Suppose, for example, you'd like to provide a "Top Ten List" like that of Figure 16.20 in real time.

The amount of code required for this is surprisingly minimal. The topten.idc file referenced in Figure 16.20 appears next:

topten.idc:

```
Datasource: web sql
```

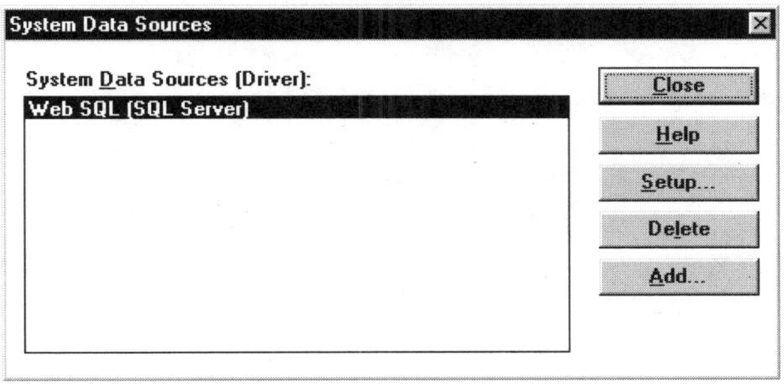

Figure 16.17 ODBC System Data Sources...Web SQL (SQL Server) Defined

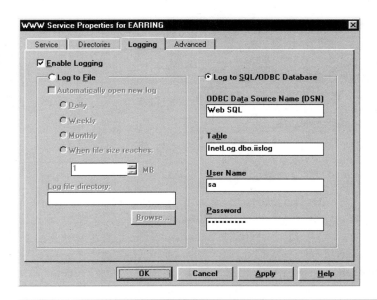

Figure 16.18 Logging IIS Activity to an SQL/ODBC Database

ClientHost	username	LogTime	service	machine	serverip	operation	target
130.131.90.111	-	1/30/96 9:43:29 PM	W3SVC	EARRING	130.131.90.111	GET	/scripts/logsum.idc
130.131.90.111	-	1/30/96 9:44:14 PM	W3SVC	EARRING	130.131.90.111	GET	/scripts/logsum.idc
130.131.90.111	-	1/30/96 9:45:00 PM	W3SVC	EARRING	130.131.90.111	GET	/index.htm
130.131.90.111	-	1/30/96 9:45:01 PM	W3SVC	EARRING	130.131.90.111	GET	/iconjjb.gif
130.131.90.111	-	1/30/96 9:45:01 PM	W3SVC	EARRING	130.131.90.111	GET	/https.gif
130.131.90.111	-	1/30/96 9:45:01 PM	W3SVC	EARRING	130.131.90.111	GET	/tools6.gif
130.131.90.111	-	1/30/96 9:45:01 PM	W3SVC	EARRING	130.131.90.111	GET	/webdocs.gif
130.131.90.111	-	1/30/96 9:45:01 PM	W3SVC	EARRING	130.131.90.111	GET	/winview.gif
130.131.90.111	-	1/30/96 9:45:01 PM	W3SVC	EARRING	130.131.90.111	GET	/windows.gif
130.131.90.111	-	1/30/96 9:45:01 PM	W3SVC	EARRING	130.131.90.111	GET	/winsock.gif
130.131.90.111	-	1/30/96 9:45:01 PM	W3SVC	EARRING	130.131.90.111	GET	/c.gif
130.131.90.111	-	1/30/96 9:45:01 PM	W3SVC	EARRING	130.131.90.111	GET	/arizona.gif
130.131.90.111	-	1/30/96 9:45:02 PM	W3SVC	EARRING	130.131.90.111	GET	/earthgls.gif
130.131.90.111	-	1/30/96 9:45:02 PM	W3SVC	EARRING	130.131.90.111	GET	/goofey.gif
130.131.90.111	-	1/30/96 9:45:02 PM	W3SVC	EARRING	130.131.90.111	GET	/theatr-h.gif
130.131.90.111	-	1/30/96 9:45:02 PM	W3SVC	EARRING	130.131.90.111	GET	/shopcart.gif
130.131.90.111	-	1/30/96 9:45:02 PM	W3SVC	EARRING	130.131.90.111	GET	/pnicon.gif
130.131.90.111	-	1/30/96 9:45:31 PM	W3SVC	EARRING	130.131.90.111	GET	/ntwebsrv.htm
130.131.90.111	-	1/30/96 9:45:48 PM	W3SVC	EARRING	130.131.90.111	GET	/scripts/logsum.idc
130.131.90.111	ftp	1/31/96 7:56:48 PM	MSFTPSVC	EARRING	-	[2] USER	ftp
130.131.90.111	buyensj@inte	1/31/96 7:57:06 PM	MSFTPSVC	EARRING	-	[2] PASS	buyensj@interlakken.com
130.131.90.111	buyensj@inte	1/31/96 7:57:17 PM	MSFTPSVC	EARRING	-	[2] sent	grape.pl
130.131.90.111	buyensj@inte	1/31/96 7:57:18 PM	MSFTPSVC	EARRING	-	[2] sent	hello.pl
130.131.90.111	buyensj@inte	1/31/96 7:57:19 PM	MSFTPSVC	EARRING	-	[2] sent	iconlib.pl
130.131.90.111	buyensj@inte	1/31/96 7:57:20 PM	MSFTPSVC	EARRING	-	[2] QUIT	-

Record: 1 of 80

Datasheet View

Figure 16.19 Viewing an IIS Log Database with Microsoft Access 7.0

```
Username: sa
Template: topten.htx
MaxRecords: 10
SQLStatement:
  +SELECT target, Sum(1) AS Hits FROM inetlog.dbo.iislog
  + GROUP BY target, service
  + HAVING (((service)='W3SVC') AND
  + ((Right(target,4)='.htm') OR
  +   (Right(target,5)='.html') OR
  +   (Right(target,4)='.idc')))
  + ORDER BY Hits DESC, target
```

The "Datasource:" statement specifies the ODBC data source name, and "Username:" specifies a valid logon identity for that data source. A "Password:"

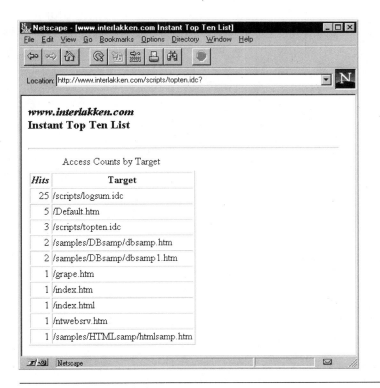

Figure 16.20 www.interlakken.com Top Ten List

line can also appear if necessary. "Template:" specifies the name of the model file that httpodbc.ddl will use for generating output to the client. "MaxRecords:" states output will end after 10 records.

The SQL statement specifies a query with two output fields: the IIS target field and a count of 1 for each record found. inetlog.dbo.iislog is the table name—actually, a database name, an owner code, and a table name. The DBMS will consolidate records by target and service and will only select records pertaining to the W3SVC ("Web") service and having an .htm, .html, or .idc file name extension. Output records will be in descending order by number of hits, then in ascending order by target.

The URL to execute the query is

```
http://www.interlakken.com/scripts/topten.idc?
```

This is simply the server's DNS name, the name of the CGI script directory, the IDC file name, and a question mark to make the URL an HTML query.

The IIS Web server associates the .idc file name extension with httpodbc.dll and passes control to that module. When httpodbc.dll gets the query results back from ODBC, it writes response HTML based on the following template:

```
topten.htx:
<HTML>
<HEAD>
<TITLE>www.interlakken.com Instant Top Ten List</TITLE>
</HEAD>
<BODY>
<H3><I>www.interlakken.com</I><BR>Instant Top Ten List</H3>
<HR>
<TABLE BORDER>
<caption>Access Counts by Target</caption>
<TR><TH><B><I>Hits</TH><TH>Target</B></I></TH></TR>
<%begindetail%>
<TR><TD align="right"><%Hits%></TD><TD><%target%></TD></TR>
<%enddetail%>
</TABLE>
</BODY>
</HTML>
```

This is conventional HTML code except for the three lines in boldface. That portion—everything between <%begindetail%> and <%enddetail%>—gets repeated once per query output record. Since the repeated portion begins with <TR> and ends with </TR>, each output record will produce one row in an HTML table. Each of these rows will contain two cells because of the two <TD>…</TD> sequences. The value of each output record's "Hits" field will replace <%Hits%>, and the value of the "target" field will replace <%target%>. Figure 16.20 displays the results.

16.5.4.3 Providing HTML Form Input to Queries Figures 16.21 and 16.22 illustrate a simple application to display log entries for a given client. An HTML form allows input of the client IP address and, optionally, the number of days' activity to display.

As shown next, the HTML form client.htm is quite conventional except that FORM ACTION submits a query URL with the .idc file name extension. The trailing question mark isn't necessary because the FORM METHOD makes the submission a query. There are two input fields: "client" and "days":

client.htm

```
<HTML>
<HEAD>
<TITLE>Client Activity Query</TITLE>
```

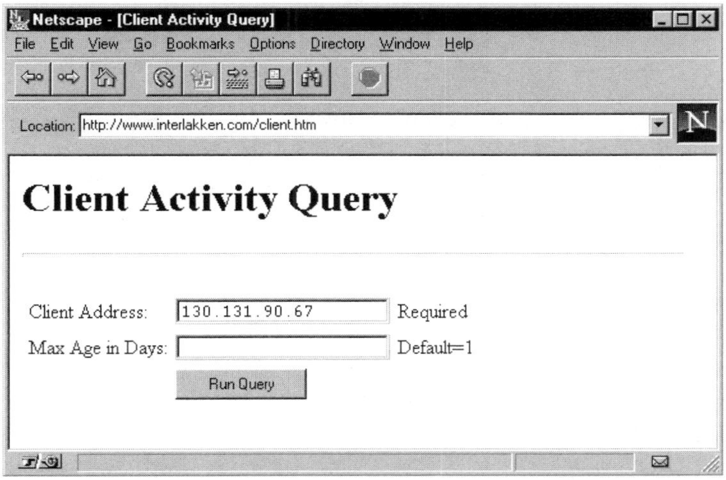

Figure 16.21 Client Activity Query Form

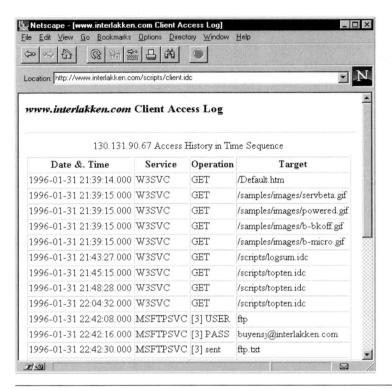

Figure 16.22 Client Activity Query Response—Client Access Log

```
</HEAD>
<H1>Client Activity Query</H1>
<HR>
<FORM METHOD="POST" ACTION="/scripts/client.idc">
<TABLE>
<TR>
  <TD>Client Address:</TD>
  <TD><INPUT NAME="client" VALUE=""></TD>
  <TD>Required</TD>
</TR><TR>
  <TD>Max Age in Days:</TD>
  <TD><INPUT NAME="days" VALUE=""></TD>
  <TD>Default=1</TD>
</TR><TR>
  <TD></TD>
```

```
    <TD><INPUT TYPE="SUBMIT" VALUE="Run Query"></TD>
</TR>
</TABLE>
</FORM>
</BODY>
</HTML>
```

As in the preceding section, submitting an .idc query URL to the IIS Web service activates httpodbc.dll, the IDC engine. The IDC engine then opens the named .idc file and runs the query. Here are the contents of client.idc:

client.idc:

```
Datasource: web sql
Username: sa
Template: client.htx
DefaultParameters: days=1
RequiredParameters: client
SQLStatement:
+ SELECT ClientHost, LogTime, service, operation, target
   + FROM inetlog.dbo.iislog
   + WHERE (((ClientHost)='%client%') AND
   + ((LogTime)>DateAdd(day, -%days%, Getdate())))
```

The first three statements (Datasource, Username, and Template) are essentially the same as before. "DefaultParameters: days=1" supplies the "days" variable with a value of "1" if the user leaves that field blank. "RequiredParameters: client" specifies that if the "client" field is blank, the user will get an error message and instructions to click their browser's Back button.

The SQL statement SELECTs five fields from the inetlog.dbo.iislog table, the same table used previously. The WHERE clause searches for ((ClientHost)='%client%'), with the HTML form value replacing "%client%."

DateAdd and Getdate are SQL Server built-in functions. Getdate obtains the current date and time, while DateAdd performs date arithmetic. The expression

```
DateAdd(day, -1, Getdate())
```

therefore computes the value of the current moment minus exactly 24 hours. In the .idc file, however, the form variable "%days%" replaces the constant "1". The

WHERE clause then selects log records whose date stamp is more recent than the cutoff time computed by DateAdd.

The HTML extension file that produces the final output appears next. IDC will repeat the <%begindetail%> … <%enddetail%> section once per output record, substituting record values for the fields LogTime, service, operation, and target; this produces the result shown in Figure 16.22:

```
client.htx:
<HTML>
<HEAD>
<TITLE>www.interlakken.com Client Access Log</TITLE>
</HEAD>
<BODY>
<H3><I>www.interlakken.com</I> Client Access Log</H3>
<HR>
<TABLE BORDER>
<caption><%ClientHost%> Access History in Time Sequence</caption>
<TR>
   <TH>Date &amp. Time</TH>
   <TH>Service</TH>
   <TH>Operation</TH>
   <TH>Target</TH>
</TR>
<%begindetail%>
<TR>
   <TD><%LogTime%></TD>
   <TD><%service%></TD>
   <TD><%operation%></TD>
   <TD><%target%></TD>
</TR>
<%enddetail%>
</TABLE>
</BODY>
</HTML>
```

16.5.4.4 Linking One IDC Query to Another Typing IP addresses into forms like that of Figure 16.21 quickly becomes boring and mundane; far more useful is a process that detects interesting addresses to query. Figure 16.23 illustrates results from such a query; clicking on any listed IP address will produce a detail report for that address—the detail report seen previoulsy as Figure 16.22.

There's no form input to this query; the user just types the URL

```
http://www.interlakken.com/scripts/topusers.idc?
```

or clicks on some hypertext with the same string as the HREF. The topusers.idc file contains

```
topusers.idc:
Datasource: web sql
Username: sa
Template: topusers.htx
MaxRecords: 10
SQLStatement:
  +SELECT ClientHost, Sum(1) AS Hits, Sum(bytesrecvd) AS "Total Bytes"
  + FROM inetlog.dbo.iislog
  + GROUP BY ClientHost
  + ORDER BY "Total Bytes" DESC, ClientHost
```

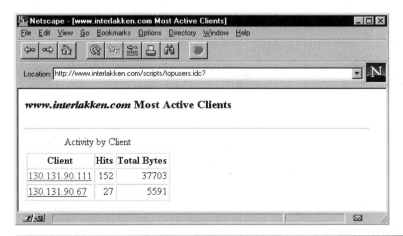

Figure 16.23 Client Activity Query Response—Most Active Clients

This query finds the 10 most frequent client addresses in the log database, summarizing number of hits and total bytes for each address. The results will appear in most-active-first order. If you understood the preceding two sections, there should be no surprises here.

The topusers.htx HTML extension file appears next:

```
topusers.htx:
<HTML>
<HEAD>
<TITLE>www.interlakken.com Most Active Clients</TITLE>
</HEAD>
<BODY>
<H3><I>www.interlakken.com</I> Most Active Clients</H3>
<HR>
<TABLE BORDER>
<CAPTION>Activity by Client</CAPTION>
<TR>
   <TH>Client</TH>
   <TH>Hits</TH>
   <TH>Total Bytes</TH>
</TR>
<%begindetail%>
<TR>
   <TD><A HREF="/scripts/client.idc?client=<%ClientHost%>">
            <%ClientHost%></A></TD>
   <TD align="right"><%Hits%></TD>
   <TD align="right"><%Total Bytes%></TD>
</TR>
<%enddetail%>
</TABLE>
</BODY>
</HTML>
```

This file should by now be unremarkable except for the first table cell. There, httpodbc.dll substitutes the "ClientHost" query output field twice: once in the HREF URL and once for display. Clicking the displayed version will submit a URL of the form

```
/scripts/client.idc?client=130.131.90.111
```

and kick off the same process that posting client.htm initiated in the preceding section.

To generate URL queries containing more than one variable, separate each name=value pair with ampersands:

```
/scripts/client.idc?client=130.131.90.111&days=2
```

16.5.4.5 Additional HTML Extension (.htx) Facilities A number of additional features exist for creating response HTML from HTML extension files. For example, the following sequence controls conditional output:

```
<%if% condition>...<%else%>...<%endif%>
```

The condition consists of two identifiers separated by one of the operators EQ, GT, LT, or CONTAINS. The identifiers can be query result variables (without enclosing percent signs), built-in variables, or literals. Here's one example:

```
<%if CurrentRecord EQ 0 %>
  <B>Sorry, no records found for <%idc.client%></B><P>
<%else%>
  <TABLE>
  <%begindetail%>
  <TR><TD><%field1%></TD><TD><%field2%></TD></TR>
  <%enddetail%>
  </TABLE>
<%endif%>
```

CurrentRecord is a built-in variable that contains the ordinal number of the current query result record. If the query returned no records, CurrentRecord will always be zero. A MaxRecords built-in variable supplies the value (if any) specified on the .idc file's MaxRecords statement. Any variable, including FORM variables, available to the .idc file is also available to the .htx file via the prefix "idc." Thus, a FORM field named "client" would be available during IDC processing as "client" and during HTX processing as "idc.client."

Finally, all values available to standard CGI programs as environment variables are also available as built-in variables for HTX processing. A few of these appear in Table 16.10.

16.6 Client Site Programming

As originally developed, Web pages had little interactivity except when replaced or updated under control of a server. This was fine for distributing scientific and scholarly papers but hardly the ultimate in mass media technology. Appealing to the large "infotainment" market will require highly interactive code running on each remote machine. There's simply not enough bandwidth or server horsepower to provide such interactivity from servers.

Vendors have proposed three approaches to providing programmability at the client workstation: Java, JavaScript, and Object Linking and Embedding (OLE). The following sections briefly discuss each of these approaches.

16.6.1 Java

Java is an interpretive form of C++ that Sun Microsystems originally designed for cableTV set-top boxes.[7] They've now adapted the technology for Web browsers.

Table 16.10 Selected HTTP Variables Available to HTML Extension Files

HTTP Variable	Description
PATH_INFO	Any URL path information received from the client. This is any part of the query URL after the script name but before the question mark.
QUERY_STRING	Any information that followed the question mark in the query URL.
REMOTE_ADDR	The current client's IP address.
REMOTE_HOST	The current client's host name.
REMOTE_USER	The current client's user name (supplied by the client and authenticated by the server).
AUTH_PASS	The password supplied by the client to validate the REMOTE_USER value.
AUTH_TYPE	The type of authorization that validated the REMOTE_USER/AUTH_PASS combination. This is typically "Basic" or absent.
SERVER_NAME	The current server's DNS name or IP address (as it should appear in self-referencing URLs).
SERVER_PORT	The TCP/IP port on which the current request arrived.

---

[7]All expectations are that set-top boxes will be a very large market. If you've ever tried to read a scrolling cable TV program listing for 50 channels and can't imagine doing so for 500, then you understand the problem. Set-top boxes will need some kind of interactive search facility and therefore some kind of remotely programmable user interface.

Programmers write Java applications using a subset of C++ and then compile them into *bytecodes*. These bytecodes aren't machine-code dependent on a particular CPU or operating system, though; they can run on any system having a suitable Java interpreter.

Applets are Java programs designed to run on a Web browser. The browser retrieves the applet based on an HTML tag such as the following:

```
<APP Class="Pinball">
```

The browser downloads the Pinball applet just as it downloads any other file; the server neither knows nor cares that the file is a Java applet rather than, say, an image file. After downloading the applet, the browser uses a local Java interpreter to execute it. Java interpreters don't deal with source code; they always expect compiled bytecode programs.

One of the first things a Java program typically does is request a portion of the browser window. Within that space, it can display text, draw shapes, and respond to whatever events it supports. Java applets cannot, in theory, extend their influence beyond the browser environment to modify or delete files. This supposedly prevents the spread of viruses and the mischievous formatting of hard disks.

As of this writing, developing a feature-rich Java app required considerable coding. No graphical development environments or interface builders were available, and prepackaged objects were low level. In short, creating a Java applet was like making a watch out of raw ore. This situation may change rapidly, however, given Java's highly object-oriented nature. Look for large, fast, prewritten function libraries and rich developments.

For more information on Java, consult Yahoo at http://www.yahoo.com/Computers_and_Internet/Languages/Java/.

16.6.2 JavaScript

Developed by Netscape, this is a simple programming language for running source code downloaded with an HTML page. A simple Web page containing JavaScript code follows:

jstest.htm:

```
<HTML>

<HEAD>

<TITLE>JavaScript Example</TITLE>
```

```
<SCRIPT LANGUAGE="JavaScript">
function compute(form) {
    if (confirm("Are you sure about this?"))
        form.result.value = eval(form.expr.value)
    else
        alert("Pfew! Close one there!")
}
</SCRIPT>
</HEAD>
<BODY>
<H1>JavaScript Example</H1>
<HR>
<FORM>
<TABLE>
<TR>
   <TD>Enter an expression:</TD>
   <TD><INPUT NAME="expr" SIZE=15 ></TD>
</TR><TR>
   <TD></TD>
   <TD ALIGN="center"><INPUT TYPE="button" VALUE="Calculate"
                    ONCLICK="compute(this.form)"></TD>
</TR><TR>
   <TD>Result:</TD>
   <TD><INPUT NAME="result" SIZE=15 ></TD>
</TR>
</TABLE>
</FORM>
</BODY>
</HTML>
```

Clicking on the "Calculate" button invokes the JavaScript function named "compute" and defined between the <SCRIPT> and </SCRIPT> tags in the <HEAD> section. That function prompts the user, "Are you sure about this?" and provides OK and Cancel buttons. If the user clicks OK, the JavaScript statement

```
form.result.value = eval(form.expr.value)
```

evaluates the value of the <INPUT NAME="expr"> control and stores the result as the value of the <INPUT NAME="result"> control. Figure 16.24 illustrates this in progress. If the user clicks Cancel, the "compute" routine displays "Pfew! Close one there!" in an alert box and doesn't update the "result" control.

For more information about JavaScript, browse Netscape's Web site at http://www.netscape.com and search for JavaScript.

16.6.3 OLE Controls and Document Objects

Microsoft's approach to browser expandability is, not surprisingly, its Object Linking and Embedding (OLE) technology. This is the same technology that allows Windows users to embed Excel spreadsheet objects in Word or PowerPoint documents. The idea is for browsers, such as Microsoft's Internet Explorer, to invoke OLE objects available locally or downloaded from the Internet. To increase ease of development and portability, Microsoft plans to make Visual Basic a suitable environment for creating OLE objects and to port the Visual Basic run-time library to various platforms.

OLE controls and document objects need not be as large and complex as Word or Excel. An OLE control can be as small as a single command button or gas gauge.

Microsoft's attempts to provide this technology will be an interesting process to watch. The vast majority of Internet users are certainly Windows based, but many content designers are not. In addition, few on-line publishers wish to

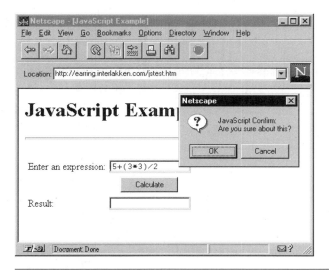

Figure 16.24 A JavaScript Program in Progreess

exclude the Macintosh and UNIX population despite Windows's 80 to 90 percent user base. Powerful interests oppose Microsoft domination of yet another phase of computing.

For current specifications and download files, browse Microsoft's Web site at http://www.microsoft.com/intdev/tech.htm.

16.7 WAIS and Other Search Engines

Much of the information available on the Internet consists, not of database records, but of text. This, plus the relatively unstructured nature of such text, has created greater interest in text searching than in traditional database processing.

Text-search databases typically work by periodically scanning a body of text files and adding each word found to an index. Users can then search these indexes and locate documents of interest.

The most common type of text-searching system operates on a local file system; that is, it searches all files in a particular directory or tree. There's usually syntax support for several kinds of files, such as HTML, newsgroups, and mail. Having syntax support means the indexer can extract document titles, for example, based on the "Subject:" header of E-Mail or News messages, or on the <TITLE> tag of HTML documents.

Text-searching systems that build indexes using network protocols such as HTTP are less common. Given the simplicity of the HTTP GET protocol and the relative ease of parsing HTML, the reasons for this are unclear. At first glance, there's no great pressing need for a plethora of services like Lycos and WebCrawler. Then again, any internal corporate or organizational Web could probably benefit from having a unified search facility that spans all servers and all operating systems.

WebSite includes a search mechanism that searches the local HTTP data directory. Various other systems are available as freeware, shareware, and commercial products. Some commercial document management systems predating invention of the World-Wide Web now have optional components that provide HTTP support through built-in, dedicated server software.

WAIS (Wide Area Information Server) is one of the most established text-indexing and text-searching systems. A company called Thinking Machines originally developed WAIS to demonstrate its Connection Machine, a massively parallel computer (Liu et al. 1994). Thinking Machines developed WAIS as a client-server system with Macintosh, UNIX character-mode, and UNIX X Windows clients. Thinking Machines also made the server code for UNIX and all the client code freely available, and the system became popular on the Internet.

Brewster Kahle, the WAIS project leader at Thinking Machines, left the company to develop a commercial version of WAIS. His company, WAIS, Inc., stayed in existence for some time and held copyright to the name WAIS. WAIS, Inc., is now part of AOL Productions, Inc.

The Clearinghouse for Networked Information Discovery and Retrieval (CNIDR) took over maintenance of the public domain WAIS software and has enhanced it over the years; the resulting software is called freeWAIS. This software is available from ftp://ftp.cnidr.org/pub/NIDR.tools/freewais/ but only for UNIX platforms.

The European Microsoft Windows NT Academic Centre (EMWAC) has ported freeWAIS 0.3 to Windows NT. The heart of this system consists of four programs:

1. **WAISINDEX.EXE.** The text-indexing program.

2. **WAISLOOK.EXE.** Accepts one or more search terms and, based on a WAIS index, displays a list of files containing those terms.

3. **WAISSERV.EXE.** Accepts WAIS requests through STDIN and sends WAIS responses through STDOUT.

4. **WAISS.EXE.** Provides WAIS services over the network via TCP/IP, usually on port 210.

The first three programs are part of the EMWAC WAIS Toolkit located in directory \WTI386 on the accompanying CD. WAISS.EXE is part of the WAIS Server software in \WSI386. This software is also available from EMWAC's Web site at http://www.emwac.ac.uk and in the \RESKIT\EMWAC directory of the Windows NT Resource Kit 3.51.

WAISS.EXE services clients such as the Macintosh and UNIX clients originally developed by Thinking Machines. The protocol for this is an ANSI standard called Z39.50 that operates on port 210. WAIS clients for Windows are now available as well, but the ubiquitous Web browser has almost completely superseded use of dedicated WAIS clients.

WAISLOOK normally operates as a *default query handler*. This is a program the server executes automatically when it receives a GET request that specifies an HTML file and that includes a search term. For the EMWAC and IIS Web servers, WAISLOOK is automatically a default query handler. For Netscape servers, the default query handler is a configurable option. WebSite includes its own text-search and lookup function.

When the server starts the default query handler, it passes the HTML file name and user-specified search terms as arguments. WAISLOOK then

- Expects the HTML file name (minus the .htm or .html extension) to specify the name of a WAIS database created by WAISINDEX.
- Looks up the specified search terms in that WAIS database.
- Creates the user response in HTML format.

The HTTP server then returns WAISLOOK's response HTML to the requesting user.

To try out the EMWAC WAIS Toolkit, proceed as follows:

1. Copy the files WAISINDEX.EXE, WAISLOOK.EXE, and WAISSERV.EXE to the <systemroot>\system32 directory. If WAISINDEX.EXE has the 8.3 file name WAISINDX.EXE, rename it.

2. Set the current drive and directory to the EMWAC HTTP server's data directory. WAISINDEX requires this to be an NTFS drive.

3. Issue the following command:

```
waisindex -d htmindex -r -t html *.htm*
```

This will create a set of seven files that constitute the WAIS index. All file names in the index will be relative to the HTTP data directory because step 2 made this current directory. In this command, "-d htmindex" means all seven files in the WAIS index will have htmindex as the base file name; "-r" states the index should recurse directories (that is, include an entire tree); "-t html" states the files being indexed are html; and "*.htm*" specifies the files WAISINDEX should index.

4. Create a simple query form such as the following (name this HTML file with the same file name base specified after "-d" in step 3):

htmindex.htm:
```
<HTML>
<HEAD>
<TITLE>WAIS Web Index - www.interlakken.com</TITLE>
</HEAD>
<BODY>
<H1>WAIS Web Index - www.interlakken.com</H1>
<ISINDEX>
</BODY>
</HTML>
```

5. If the EMWAC HTTP server isn't running, start it.

6. Start your browser and point it at the htmindex.htm file on your server. A display like that of Figure 16.25 should result.

7. Enter a search term you're sure exists in one of the Web pages on your server. Then press Enter. Figure 16.25 shows the term "winsock" entered. Within moments, you should receive a list of matching documents like that shown in Figure 16.26.

8. Clicking on any page listed in Figure 16.26 will jump to that page. Documents titled "Untitled HTML Document" have no <TITLE> tag in their <HEAD> section; this is an error to correct.

To keep WAIS indexes updated, make up a batch file that sets the current drive and directory to the HTTP server's data directory and then run WAISINDEX commands for each index you wish to support. You may wish to add an "-e <filename>" parameter to the command in step 3; this writes error messages to the named file rather than displaying them in a command window. (Command window messages are inaccessible when commands run in background.)

Then, use the AT command (or the WINAT command that comes with the Windows NT Resource Kit) to schedule execution of that batch file during off hours.

Figure 16.25 WAIS Query Page (Using <ISINDEX> Tag)

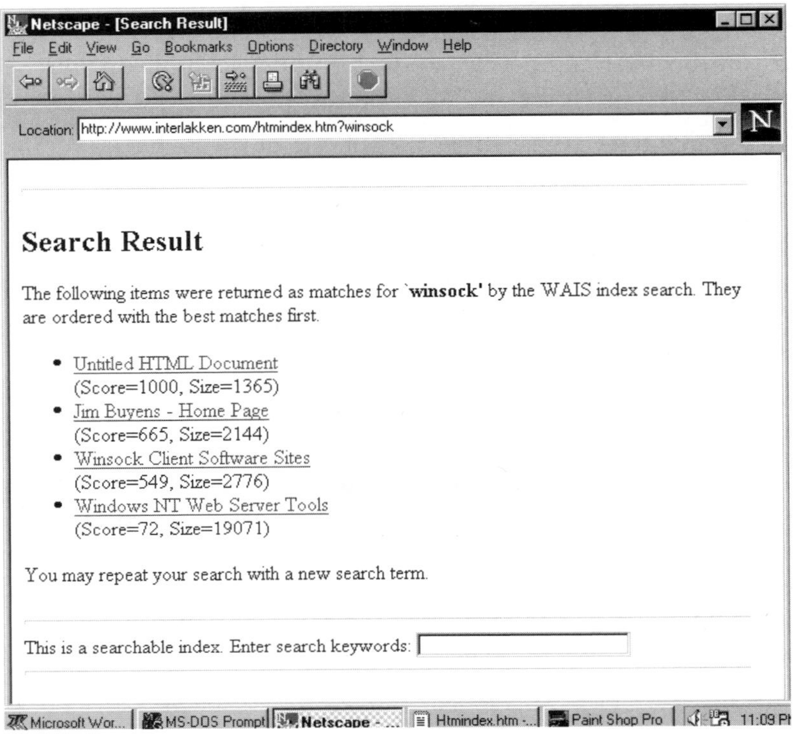

Figure 16.26 WAIS Query Response

When searching, EMWAC WAIS uses "OR" as the default operator. That is, a search for "San Francisco" returns all documents containing the word *San* or the word *Francisco*. Lengthening the search term to "San Francisco bridge" would add all documents containing the word *bridge*. To get a list of all documents containing both the word *Francisco* and the word *bridge*, enter "Francisco and bridge."

To use EMWAC WAIS with an HTTP server other than EMWAC HTTPS or Microsoft IIS, you must configure the WAISLOOK.EXE as the default query handler for that server. If this doesn't work, you may have to run both the EMWAC server and your preferred server on the same machine. There's no problem doing this if you run your preferred server on port 80 and the EMWAC server on some other unused port.

16.8 Performance Issues

Serving up Web pages is a fairly trivial task for a Windows NT server; the server merely has to locate an entry in the NTFS file system and shovel it out the network port. Windows NT is highly optimized to perform both of these tasks.

The same isn't necessarily true for server-based programs like standard CGI, WinCGI, SSI, and especially DBMS and WAIS processing. Server-based processes can easily consume several hundred times the resources of a simple Web page hit. Furthermore, identifying a lead weight on your server's performance can be difficult for processes that start and stop thousands of times a day.

The best advice is to understand the impact of each server-based process you add and to be skeptical of claims that process volumes will be low. Today's 5 hits per day could be next summer's 50,000.

## CHAPTER 17

Backup and Recovery

Once your site is up and running, even partially, the data recorded on your disks becomes your greatest asset and your customers' greatest trust. Effective backup and recovery procedures are no afterthought in such a situation. Hardware eventually fails; files get deleted, written over, or corrupted; archived data becomes useful again. For all these reasons, a backup and recovery system is arguably the most important system you run.

17.1 Backup Strategies

An effective backup strategy considers what parts of a system need backup, what backup hardware and software to use, how often to back up each part of the system, and how long and where to keep each backup. Each of these points deserves discussion.

17.1.1 What to Back Up

There's no magic formula for deciding what to back up on any particular system at a site. The nature of the site services and service commitments must play a major part in determining this.

At first glance, the most straightforward backup strategy is simply to take a full backup every day of every system you control. This is frequent enough for most purposes, and it ensures you haven't missed anything.

Full daily backups lose their appeal as the number of systems grows, as growing data volumes prolong the time required for backup, and eventually when the number of tapes grows too large. If you want timed, unattended backups, you need to avoid filling up tapes and having the backup program prompt for another volume.

Application requirements also affect the required timing and frequency of backups. For a system like USENET News, which has separate data libraries and index files, taking a backup may require stopping the service so that the various files are in sync despite being backed up minutes or hours apart.

Because of timing difficulties and the transient nature of systems like Mail and News, you may elect not to back up their spool and article files. Instead, you might spend your money on an external RAID storage array and a "hot spare" system unit. Depending on your uplink bandwidth, you may elect not to back up News at all and simply retake an initial feed from your service provider.

Backups of system "temp" areas will probably never be useful. By definition, these areas contain transitory data useful only to currently active processes.

Complete restorations of the system drive are chancy at best; you should plan to reinstall Windows NT and all your applications if you lose this drive. Do back up the system drive, however; there's always the possibility that a single file (or a small group of them) might get deleted or corrupted.

User data directories, FTP libraries, and HTTP data directories typically contain data of longer relevance and thus warrant the most frequent backup and longest retentions. Users generally expect better backup on servers than they provide on their own machines, and it's up to you, as the server operator, to provide this. Assuming updates to these directories take place somewhat continuously, you should probably back them up daily and establish a rotation schedule.

You may elect to back up all files within a given drive or directory tree, all files within selected directories, or a specific list of files. In addition, as in DOS, the NTFS file system has an "archive" bit that indicates files created or changed since the last backup:

- A *normal* backup backs up all files within a specified directory, tree, or drive. In addition, it turns off the archive bit for each file backed up.

- A *copy* backup also backs up all files within a specified part of the disk but doesn't clear their archive bits.

- An *incremental* backup only backs up files having the archive bit on, and then it turns these archive bits off.

- A *differential* backup also pertains only to files with the archive bit on, but, after backing these up, it doesn't turn their archive bits off.

A typical pattern would be to take a full, normal backup once a week and then take daily incremental or differential backups. Daily incremental backups would contain files created or changed since the previous normal or incremental backup. Daily differentials would contain cumulative additions and changes since the last normal backup. Incremental backups contain less data and therefore run faster than differentials. However, restoring a directory to Thursday using incrementals means restoring the weekend full backup and four daily incrementals. If the daily backups were differential, only the weekend full backup and the Thursday differential would be necessary.

Backing up database systems is difficult because records, files, and indexes are constantly changing. DBMSs like Microsoft SQL Server and Oracle generally have special features that permit backup while the database system is running. Generally, these work by flushing all caches and "freezing" all disk files at a point in time; the DBMS then keeps running by caching all updates until the disk backup is complete. The DBMS documentation should explain how to coordinate this.

From a business standpoint, your customer account records, billable activity logs, and billing database deserve special attention. Losing these files may result in tremendous loss of revenue or even in going out of business. This data clearly deserves the highest level of protection possible. The same is true of customer transaction data you may be accumulating. A customer receiving a steady stream of on-line orders via your site will certainly be angry to learn you've lost several thousand dollars worth of orders.

17.1.2 Backup Media and Drives

Floppy disks, magneto-optical disks, removable hard drives, WORM (Write Once Read Many) drives, and even recordable CDs are useful for occasional partial backups and data shipments. However, none of these combine the high capacity and low cost of magnetic tape.

QIC (Quarter Inch Cartridge) tapes are generally too limited in capacity for use in backing up servers. In addition, QIC tape drives generally aren't rugged enough for extended daily use. On servers, this technology is suitable for light-duty use only.

The most common tape formats used on servers are 8mm helical and 4mm DAT (Digital Audio Tape). Exabyte manufactures virtually all 8mm equipment, though many suppliers repackage and resell the drives. Archive Python drives established 4mm DAT as a viable option and continue to be popular.[1] Hewlett-Packard Jetstore drives are also well regarded and popular 4mm DAT equipment.

---

[1] After Archive introduced the Python series of drives, Archive Corporation went through a series of acquisitions and became part of Conner Peripherals. As of this writing, Conner had agreed in principle to merge with Seagate Technology.

Backup speeds typically range from 8 to 25MB per minute. High-speed internal drives are available for less than $1,000; blank tapes range from $15 to $20 each.

The 4mm and 8mm data formats are highly competitive. Although 4mm technology is newer, smaller, generally faster, and now equally proven, the choice between these media may largely depend on what already exists in your environment. If your site has an investment in blank media, storage racks, and repair expertise relative to one media, it's generally not worthwhile to switch.

DLT (Digital Linear Tape) is a new technology that provides high-speed, high-capacity, high-duty-cycle backups. Typical backup speeds are 50 to 150MB per minute, but these drives and the accompanying media are new and expensive.

Automated loaders are essentially robots that insert tapes from a specially housed collection. Small, typically 4-port loaders are convenient for taking unattended backups that exceed the capacity of a single tape (assuming, of course, that the backup software is capable of making the loader insert the proper tapes in sequence). Larger units holding 12 to several hundred tapes can accommodate days or weeks of unattended backups—a real boon for managing backups at remote sites without requiring travel.

As with any hardware you purchase for use with Windows NT, verify operating system compatibility before your buy. If you're considering a loader, be sure to verify compatibility with your backup software as well.

17.1.3 Backup Software

Every copy of Windows NT comes with an applet called Windows NT Backup that meets most simple backup needs. However, Windows NT Backup has no built-in scheduling, no support for tape loaders, and no background support for networked drives. You can use the Windows NT Schedule service to initiate unattended runs of Windows NT Backup, but the hard disk, tape drive, and backup software must all be installed on the same computer. If you need to back up data on five computers, you'll have to buy a tape drive for each one.

Windows NT Backup is really a "teaser" application supplied by Arcada, a division of Conner Peripherals. Arcada's full products have their own scheduling system, support over-the-network backup, and support a wide range of tape loaders. Operators can completely control backups on distant machines over the network. You can obtain more information from Arcada's Web site at http://www.arcada.com.

Another backup solution is ARCserve for Windows NT, by Cheyenne Software, Inc. Like Arcada Backup, ARCserve has its own scheduling system, supports network backups, and works with autoloaders. Tapes created by ARCserve for Windows NT are readable by ARCserve programs on other platforms. Cheyenne's Web site is http://www.cheyenne.com.

17.1.4 How Often to Back Up

For any given system, the frequency of backup should parallel the frequency of update. A public information Web site with tightly controlled content updated monthly obviously doesn't require daily backup. At the other extreme, a system that performs on-line data collection (such as an order entry system) might require second-by-second backup to a duplicate copy of the database located on a separate machine. Daily backups, five or seven days a week, are probably the most common pattern, but this is a decision each site must make for itself.

17.1.5 Backup Retentions

Once you've taken a backup, you must decide how long to keep it. This is another decision only you can make because only you know the useful life of the backed-up data. E-Mail messages, for example, typically have a very short useful life. If your organization has a requirement to file all correspondence for seven years, however, then you may need to retain seven years of daily backups!

A common strategy is to take at least one full backup a week and designate that backup as "the weekly." Weeklies then get longer retentions than dailies. If you retain dailies for a month, you might retain weeklies for a quarter, for example. It's also common to designate one weekly per month as a monthly and keep it even longer—perhaps a year or two. Selecting quarterlies and annuals follows a similar pattern.

Advanced tape management systems catalog each tape written and manage its retention. On demand, the tape management system prints listings of tapes whose retentions have expired since the last report. A backup operator then "pulls" these out of retention and adds them to a "scratch pile" of tapes available for use. This requires each tape to have an internal (magnetically recorded) label so that the backup program can identify the tape and place it on retention and also a corresponding external (pressure-sensitive) label the tape operator can use to pull scratches.

Lacking such an automated system, you can still manage retentions by labeling each tape with the computer name, the backup type, the backup date, and the expiration date.

17.1.6 Media Storage and Rotation

If you have a full tape management system or automated tape library, you'll probably file tapes by serial number or slot number. If not, the common approach is to designate slots for each tape. For example, if you take daily backups seven days a week and keep them for a month, you might set up 31 slots to contain each day's tape. On the fifth of the month, then, you'd pull the tape from slot 5 (last written the fifth of last month) and write over it. At the end of the month, you'd pull weeklies and replace them with blank or expired tapes. Handling of monthlies, quarterlies, and annuals would follow a similar pattern.

You should also consider rotating tapes off-site. This protects against disasters like fire, flood, earthquake, ruptured utility pipes, and theft. You can rent vault space from companies that specialize in providing off-site data backup, but much simpler alternatives will frequently suffice. For example, you may wish to place one tape a month in a bank safe-deposit vault. If your organization has sites in several cities, these sites can generally provide off-site backup for one another.

17.2 Installing a SCSI Tape Drive

Virtually all high-speed, high-capacity tape backup devices use SCSI for communication with the host computer. This is good news if your server already has a SCSI card; bad news if it doesn't. High-performance SCSI cards cost $200 to $300.

SCSI adapters differ primarily in the system bus they support (ISA, EISA, PCI, and so on), whether they are *standard* or *fast*, and whether they are *standard* or *wide*. The choice of system bus is usually easy. If your server has an available EISA or PCI slot, buy a matching SCSI adapter; else, buy ISA.

Virtually all SCSI adapters and devices today are SCSI-2; SCSI-1 is obsolete, and SCSI-3 is still a proposal, not a standard. Most SCSI-2 adapters are rated fast as well; there's no reason to buy an adapter or device not carrying this rating.

As Table 17.1 shows, narrow fast SCSI transfers 8 data bits in parallel for an effective throughput of 10MB per second. Wide fast SCSI transfers 16 data bits at a time and thus achieves twice the throughput.

Table 17.1 SCSI Interface Throughput

SCSI Speed	Million Transfers/Sec.	Narrow (8-Bit) MB/Sec.	Wide (16-Bit) MB/Sec.
Standard	5	5	10
Fast	10	10	20

Some wide SCSI adapters can function as two narrow adapters; other than this exception, each SCSI card and each connected device should be the same speed and width. Narrow SCSI requires 50-pin connectors and cables; wide requires 68-pin connections.

Each SCSI adapter requires an interrupt, a block of I/O addresses, and an upper memory ROM address.[2] In return, it provides an I/O bus that can support eight devices. Inside the computer, the SCSI bus is a 50- or 68-conductor ribbon cable daisy-chained from the adapter across each SCSI device. Internal SCSI cables can have more sockets than the computer has devices, but the unused sockets must be in the middle of the cable; that is, you must connect a device to each end.

Each device on a SCSI bus must have a unique SCSI ID numbered 0 through 7. Each device normally contains three DIP switches or jumpers, interpreted as binary digits, that assign SCSI ID 0 through 7 to the device. Most commonly, the SCSI adapter is ID 7, hard disks start at 0 and continue upward, and other devices start at 6 and continue downward. Thus, most tape drives end up as SCSI ID 6; most CD-ROM drives, as SCSI ID 5. If a SCSI disk is to be the boot drive, it must be SCSI ID 0 on the first adapter.

The physical order of devices on a SCSI bus is unimportant; there's no requirement to "line up" devices in SCSI ID order along the cable. However, the two devices at the end of the cable must each have terminating resistors installed, and those in the middle must have terminating resistors removed. These resistors are flat ceramic items about 1 inch by 1/4 inch in size, having about 10 pins, and inserted into press-fit connectors. You can remote or install them with fine-nose pliers.[3]

External SCSI devices use a separate data cable to connect each pair of devices. A cable runs from the SCSI adapter to the "IN" socket on the first device. A second cable runs from an "OUT" socket on the first device to the "IN" socket on the second device, and so on. The last device must have a terminating resistor on its "OUT" socket.

If a given SCSI bus has both internal and external devices, the terminating resistors belong on the two "end" devices—one internal and one external. You must disable the terminating resistor on the SCSI adapter in this case. If the bus contains only internal or only external devices, then the terminating resistor on the adapter must remain in place.

---

[2]SCSI adapters contain boot ROM because most built-in BIOS routines lack the ability to boot from a SCSI disk. In a system with multiple SCSI adapters, you can generally disable the boot ROM on all adapters but the one containing the boot drive.

[3]Some devices activate or deactivate built-in terminating resistors with a DIP switch or jumper, but this is uncommon.

Windows NT Setup will generally detect supported SCSI adapters and devices if they're present at setup time. If you add a SCSI adapter at a later time, identify it manually to Windows NT by starting Windows NT Setup from the Main Program Manager group or Start Programs menu. Once Setup starts, pull down the Options menu, select "Add/Remove SCSI Adapters...," then click the Add button on the resulting dialog, select the type of adapter you added, and respond to any further questions. Setup will warn that an incorrect SCSI configuration can make the system unbootable—hardly a surprise but certainly worth remembering.[4] See Figure 17.1 for an overview of this procedure.

To add a tape device, start Windows NT Setup again, pull down the Options menu, select "Add/Remove Tape Devices...," then click the Add button, and select the type of device. Figure 17.2 illustrates adding a tape device to Windows NT.

17.3 Running Windows NT Backup

The example for this chapter demonstrates how to get the most out of Windows NT Backup. This program isn't capable of meeting every need for every site, but, in some cases, it's perfectly adequate. At the very least, becoming familiar with Windows NT Backup will help you understand your needs and decide whether to purchase a more capable program.

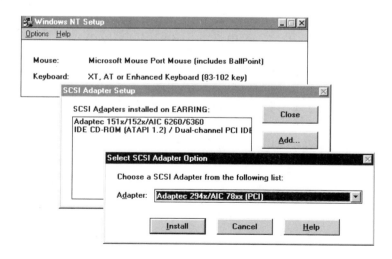

Figure 17.1 Adding a SCSI Adapter with Windows NT Setup

---

[4]If the system does become unbootable, be prepared to use "Last Known Good Menu" or your up-to-date Emergency Repair disk.

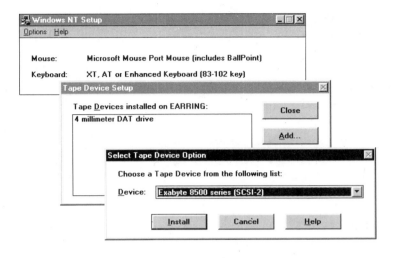

Figure 17.2 Adding a Tape Device with Windows NT Setup

Windows NT Setup normally creates an icon for Windows NT Backup called, simply, "Backup." This is in the Administrative Tools Program Manager group or Start Programs menu. When you start the program, it searches the registry for tape drives and displays an error message if none are present.

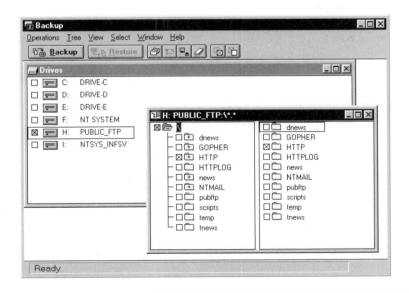

Figure 17.3 Windows NT Backup Main Window

Assuming a tape drive is present, Windows NT Backup will display a window similar to the one in Figure 17.3. Note that the user has double-clicked "H: PUBLIC_FTP" in the Drives window and selected the HTTP directory in the resulting H: PUBLIC_FTP:*.* window. This grays the checkbox in front of the "H: PUBLIC_FTP" drive because Windows NT Backup will partially back up that drive. A white checkbox indicates no backup, and a normal check indicates full backup.

Clicking the Backup button in the MDI parent form starts the backup process by prompting for further specifications. Figure 17.4 shows this dialog. Windows NT Backup supplies the default tape name and log file location shown; an operator has specified "Verify After Backup," "Hardware Compression," and the description "H:\HTTP Backup." "Operation: Append" adds the current backup behind any existing backups on the tape, while "Operation: Replace" overwrites any prior tape contents.

The remaining options are fairly self-explanatory, at least after consulting Help. Pressing the OK button starts the backup and displays the dialog shown in Figure 17.5.

The contents of the log file F:\WINNT\BACKUP.LOG appear next. This is a "Summary Only" log per the specification in Figure 17.4; a "Full Detail" log also displays the name, size, and date stamp of each backed up file. The "Verify Status" section appears because the operator specified "Verify After Backup" in the dialog of Figure 17.4. After the backup is complete, the verify option causes NT Backup

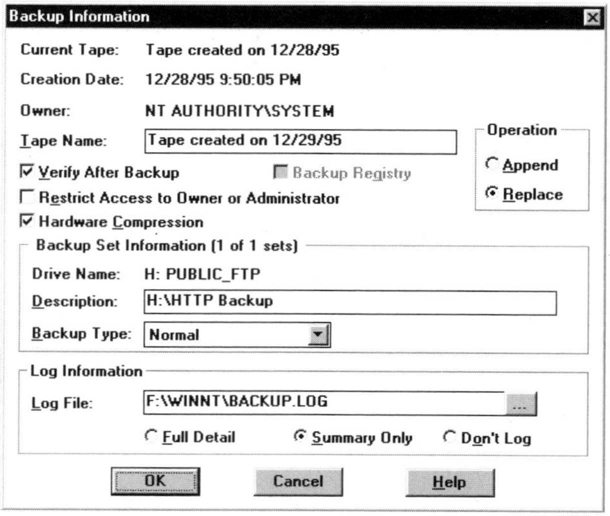

Figure 17.4 Windows NT Backup Information Dialog

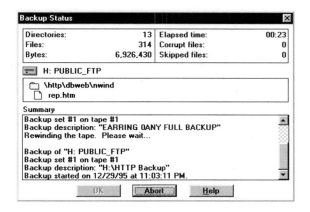

Figure 17.5 Windows NT Backup in Progress

to compare the tape contents to the disk contents and report any discrepancies. Don't be alarmed if a few such discrepancies show up; users or processes frequently modify files between the time of backup and the time of verification. Here is the log file:

```
Backup Status

Tape Name: "Tape created on 12/29/95"

Backup of "H: PUBLIC_FTP"

Backup set #1 on tape #1

Backup description: "H:\HTTP Backup"

Backup started on 12/29/95 at 11:03:11 PM.

Directory H:\

Directory H:\HTTP

Directory H:\HTTP\admserv

Directory H:\HTTP\bin

Directory H:\HTTP\bin\httpd

Directory H:\HTTP\bin\httpd\admin

Directory H:\HTTP\bin\httpd\admin\bin

Directory H:\HTTP\bin\httpd\admin\html

Directory H:\HTTP\bin\httpd\admin\icons

Directory H:\HTTP\bu

Directory H:\HTTP\cgi

Directory H:\HTTP\dbWeb
```

```
Directory H:\HTTP\dbWeb\nwind
Directory H:\HTTP\dbWeb\pubs
Directory H:\HTTP\extras
Directory H:\HTTP\extras\database
Directory H:\HTTP\extras\log_anly
Directory H:\HTTP\httpd-80
Directory H:\HTTP\httpd-80\config
Directory H:\HTTP\httpd-80\logs
Directory H:\HTTP\mc-icons
Directory H:\HTTP\nsapi
Directory H:\HTTP\nsapi\examples
Directory H:\HTTP\nsapi\include
Directory H:\HTTP\nsapi\include\base
Directory H:\HTTP\nsapi\include\base\nt
Directory H:\HTTP\nsapi\include\frame
Directory H:\HTTP\nsapi\include\frame\nt
Directory H:\HTTP\samples
Directory H:\HTTP\samples\dbsamp
Directory H:\HTTP\samples\gbook
Directory H:\HTTP\samples\htmlsamp
Directory H:\HTTP\samples\images
Directory H:\HTTP\userdb
Backup completed on 12/29/95 at 11:03:41 PM.
Backed up 413 files in 34 directories.
Processed 8,014,067 bytes in  30 seconds.

Verify Status

Verify of "H: PUBLIC_FTP"
Backup set #1 on tape #1
Backup description: "H:\HTTP Backup"
Verify started on 12/29/95 at 11:03:55 PM.
Directory H:\
Directory H:\HTTP
Directory H:\HTTP\admserv
Directory H:\HTTP\bin
```

```
Directory H:\HTTP\bin\httpd
Directory H:\HTTP\bin\httpd\admin
Directory H:\HTTP\bin\httpd\admin\bin
Directory H:\HTTP\bin\httpd\admin\html
Directory H:\HTTP\bin\httpd\admin\icons
Directory H:\HTTP\bu
Directory H:\HTTP\cgi
Directory H:\HTTP\dbWeb
Directory H:\HTTP\dbWeb\nwind
Directory H:\HTTP\dbWeb\pubs
Directory H:\HTTP\extras
Directory H:\HTTP\extras\database
Directory H:\HTTP\extras\log_anly
Directory H:\HTTP\httpd-80
Directory H:\HTTP\httpd-80\config
Directory H:\HTTP\httpd-80\logs
Directory H:\HTTP\mc-icons
Directory H:\HTTP\nsapi
Directory H:\HTTP\nsapi\examples
Directory H:\HTTP\nsapi\include
Directory H:\HTTP\nsapi\include\base
Directory H:\HTTP\nsapi\include\base\nt
Directory H:\HTTP\nsapi\include\frame
Directory H:\HTTP\nsapi\include\frame\nt
Directory H:\HTTP\samples
Directory H:\HTTP\samples\dbsamp
Directory H:\HTTP\samples\gbook
Directory H:\HTTP\samples\htmlsamp
Directory H:\HTTP\samples\images
Directory H:\HTTP\userdb
Verify completed on 12/29/95 at 11:04:20 PM.
Verified 413 files in 34 directories.
0 files were different.
Processed 8,014,067 bytes in  25 seconds.
```

Once the backup is complete, the Tapes MDI child window displays a line for the tape just used. Figure 17.6 illustrates this. The operator has double-clicked

"H: PUBLIC_FTP" in the Tapes windows, expanded the HTTP directory, and selected the "bin" directory.

Clicking the MDI parent's Restore button starts a restore operation by presenting the dialog shown in Figure 17.7. The "Restore to Drive:" and "Alternate Path:" options allow restoring data to other than its original location. "Restore File Permissions" specifies that restored files should have the same permissions they had prior to backup; if blank (the default), restored files will have default permissions. The logging and verify options work as they did for backup. A more normal scenario would be to back up whole drives, not just one directory, and possibly to back up all drives on the system.

When backing up the Windows NT system drive, you may wish to back up the Windows NT Registry as well. The registry is just a file on the boot drive, but, since the registry is always open, Windows NT Backup can't read it for backup in the normal way. Clicking "Backup Registry" in the dialog of Figure 17.4 instructs Windows NT Backup to obtain a copy of the registry through special Windows NT APIs and write it out as a special backup set. Clicking "Restore Local Registry" in Figure 17.7 similarly restores the registry. You can't back up the registry on a networked drive, however.

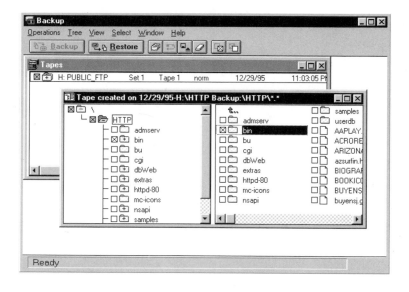

Figure 17.6 Windows NT Tape Catalog Display

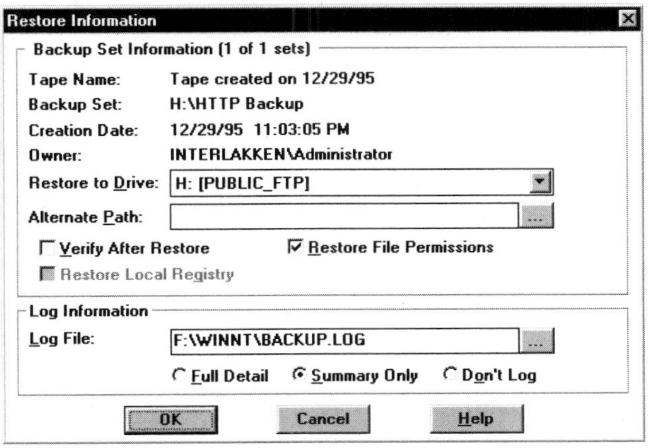

Figure 17.7   Windows NT Restore Information Dialog

Finally, although for simplicity the example used the default log location (<systemroot>), best practice is to set up a separate directory not on the system drive for this purpose.

17.4 Running Scheduled Jobs

Most system administrators prefer to take backups automatically during off hours rather than interactively at the console. To support this mode, Windows NT Backup can accept backup commands from the command line and run them in background. To completely automate such backups, you can set up command-line backups in batch files and execute the batch files using the Windows NT Schedule service. A typical batch file of this type follows:

```
fullbu.bat:
set logname=%1
if '%logname%'=='' set logname=0ANY
set logfile=h:\backups\%logname%.log
set subj="%COMPUTERNAME% %logname% Full Backup"
del %logfile%
ntbackup backup C: D: E: F: H: I: /v /d %subj% /b /hc:on /t normal /l
    "%logfile%" /e /tape:0
find <%logfile% "Directory " /v | blat - -t buyensj@interlakken.com -s
    %subj%
```

This file actually consists of seven lines rather than nine; the two indented lines are continuations. It expects one command-line parameter: a day-of-the-week code from 1MON through 7SUN.[5] Lines 1 and 2 set the environment variable %logname% to the supplied date code or to "0ANY" if no date code is present.

Line 3 builds a log file name, including path, and stores it in the environment variable %logfile%. Line 4 builds a description and stores it in %subj%. Line 5 deletes any prior log file with the same name.

Line 6 is the command that runs Windows NT Backup. A description of each element in this command follows:

- **ntbackup.** This part of the command invokes the Windows NT Backup program.
- **backup.** The first positional operator specifies the desired operation; "backup" is the only valid choice.
- **C: D: E: F: H: I:.** These drive letters specify the file areas Windows NT Backup should back up. Drive/directory specifications are also acceptable.
- **/v.** This specifies that a verify operation should follow the backup.
- **/d %subj%.** The /d setting supplies a description for the backup. The command processor will replace %subj% with the string assigned in line 4.
- **/b.** Windows NT Backup should back up the local registry.
- **/hc:on.** Hardware compression is on.
- **/t normal.** The backup type is normal.
- **/l "%logfile%".** The log file name comes from line 3 of the batch file.
- **/e.** The log file will contain summary data only.
- **/tape:0.** The backup will use tape drive 0—the first tape drive on the local system.

The last line of fullbu.bat mails a condensed version of the backup log to the administrator. Condensing is necessary because, as shown in the log file listing earlier in this section, even a summary log file contains one line per directory backed up. Scanning past these can be a real bother, so the command

```
find <%logfile% "Directory " /v
```

reads the log file looking for lines that contain the string "Directory ", and sending those that don't (because of "/v") to standard output. The pipe operator

_____

[5]This is an author's quirk; he finds log file names displayed in the sequence "1MON, 2TUE, 3WED, 4THU, 5FRI, 6SAT, 7SUN" more logical than files alphabetically sorted "FRI, MON, SAT, SUN, THU, TUE, WED."

("|") pipes this standard input into BLAT. BLAT then mails the contents of standard input (because its file name specification is a hyphen) to buyensj@interlakken.com with the value of %subj% as the message's subject. See Figure 17.8.

Once you've constructed a batch file such as fullbu.bat, test it from the command line (so that you can see any error messages) and then via the Schedule service. The command to have Schedule run the file once is

```
at 9:45 "h:\backups\fullbu.bat"
```

This assumes the current time is shortly before 9:45 A.M. The commands to schedule daily backups would be

```
at 0:05 /every:m  "h:\backups\fullbu.bat 1mon"
at 0:05 /every:t  "h:\backups\fullbu.bat 2tue"
at 0:05 /every:w  "h:\backups\fullbu.bat 3wed"
at 0:05 /every:th "h:\backups\fullbu.bat 4thu"
```

Figure 17.8 An E-Mailed Windows NT Backup Log

```
at 0:05 /every:f   "h:\backups\fullbu.bat 5fri"
at 0:05 /every:sa "h:\backups\fullbu.bat 6sat"
at 0:05 /every:su "h:\backups\fullbu.bat 7sun"
```

After entering these commands, typing the AT command with no arguments should produce the following display:

```
Status ID    Day                   Time          Command Line

         4   Each M                12:05 AM      h:\backups\fullbu.bat 1mon
         5   Each T                12:05 AM      h:\backups\fullbu.bat 2tue
         6   Each W                12:05 AM      h:\backups\fullbu.bat 3wed
         7   Each Th               12:05 AM      h:\backups\fullbu.bat 4thu
         8   Each F                12:05 AM      h:\backups\fullbu.bat 5fri
         9   Each S                12:05 AM      h:\backups\fullbu.bat 6sat
        10   Each Su               12:05 AM      h:\backups\fullbu.bat 7sun
```

17.5 Testing

Testing your backup process requires no great subtlety; simply fire up your backup program and try running a quick backup and verify. If this works, try restoring the backup you just took to another area of the disk and examine the resulting files for corruption. To test your scheduling process, schedule a job 5 or 10 minutes into the future, log off the console, and watch the tape drive lights for signs of activity. When the backup ends, log back onto the console and review the backup log.

If more than one computer has a tape drive, verify that tapes written on one drive are readable on the others. A quick check for this is to insert a tape written on one machine into the tape drive of another and see if whether second machine can catalog the tape's contents. Running a quick restore is a better test. In general, you should never own only one backup device of a given type; else, the backup device has no backup.

17.6 Ongoing Management

The read/write heads of most tape drives require occasional cleaning. This simply requires inserting a special cleaning tape into the drive. The drive recognizes the cleaning tape, runs the required amount of tape past the heads, and then ejects the cartridge. A typical cleaning cycle is one insertion of the cleaning tape per 25 hours of moving tape.

Some autoloader software can manage tape cleaning automatically. The software logs usage hours on each drive and automatically inserts a cleaning tape when required.

General cleanliness, not just head cleaning, is important to all aspects of tape handling. Keep dust away from both tapes and drives, and always store tapes in dust-resistant containers. Effective storage also requires avoiding fluctuations in temperature and humidity.

Intermittent backup failures can be difficult to diagnose. The usual causes are faulty driver software, a marginal SCSI bus, and mechanical wear on the tape drive. If you suspect bad drivers, check the Microsoft Software Library or the tape vendor's Web site for new versions. Examine the SCSI bus for missing or misplaced terminating resistors, loose connections, and frayed cables and connectors. If you suspect a bad drive, try swapping the unit with another of the same type, not forgetting to change the SCSI ID and terminating resistors if required. If the problem follows the swapped drive, the drive is almost certainly the problem. Drive manufacturers will recondition a worn drive, but the cost may be 2/3 the price of a new unit.

If you use the Windows NT Schedule service to initiate backups, be sure to configure that service to start automatically when the system boots. The dialog to do this is Control Panel, Services, Service: Schedule, Startup.

Eternal vigilance is the price of freedom—freedom, in this case, from data loss. Someone must take the time to review backup logs daily (or whatever the established frequency), or, when failure comes, you may discover the most recent valid backup is months old. Mailing yourself backup logs provides an excellent reminder.

Be sure to adjust your backup jobs after performing system maintenance that adds or removes drive letters or that moves applications to areas having different backup cycles. This is easy to forget while attempting to complete a change within a scheduled outage period.

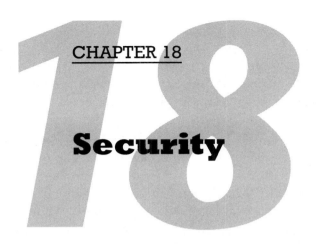

CHAPTER 18

Security

The Internet reflects every segment of society. Like our highways, our telephone system, and the U.S. mail system, the Internet supports criminals, extremists, and vandals as well as it supports good and honest citizens. Agonizing is futile, and government regulation at best accomplishes nothing; self-protection is therefore a requirement of every Internet site and user.

There has been some controversy regarding open publication of computer break-in techniques. To one point of view, it violates all reason to teach the general public all known techniques for breaking into a computer. To another, the honest public can't defend itself without knowing how the attack will come. Most computer professionals now subscribe to the latter view.

18.1 Internet Security Risks

No one would think of placing an active workstation, connected to the corporate network, in an open area such as an airport or shopping mall. Yet, the risks involved in connecting a computer to the Internet are much greater. After all, the average Internet intruder has far greater time and resources than the average traveler or shopper.

RFC 1244 classifies network security threats into the first three types listed next (the fourth item is also a growing concern):

1. **Unauthorized access.** A person gains access to (manages to log in to) a computer without permission to use it. This is tantamount to knowing someone has been walking around your house or apartment while you were away, even though they haven't damaged or stolen anything.

2. **Disclosure of information.** People obtain information they shouldn't have access to; that is, they steal something—files, passwords, whatever.

3. **Denial of service.** Someone interrupts normal services to legitimate users. This may involve deleting data, crashing systems, or destroying password files.

4. **Misuse of resources.** Someone uses a computer for purposes unacceptable to its owner. A company may prohibit use of its computing resources for noncompany activities. Most sites prefer not to become inadvertent, anonymous FTP libraries for pornography or other material they consider unacceptable. They may fear legal liability for supporting questionable activities or publicity adverse to their desired image.

At first glance, it might seem that unauthorized access is a prerequisite to the other risks. However, this isn't necessarily true. First, there are several methods by which intruders can dupe unsuspecting authorized users into doing their dirty work for them. Second, authorized users may also be security violators.

18.2 Motives for Attack

Guessing the motives of another person, especially a nameless one, is chancy at best. Nevertheless, the following agendas seem to drive intruders more often than not:

- **Intellectual challenge.** Some people consider computer security an interesting puzzle to solve—an intriguing game of cat and mouse.

- **Guarding the public trust.** These groups also consider breaking computer security a valid mental exercise, but, instead of exchanging successful techniques with other intruders, they publish them in newspapers and journals. Their stated aim is to disclose and eliminate loopholes before less honorable groups discover them.

- **Expression of grudge.** Disgruntled current and former employees are probably the most dangerous group of all. In one recent anecdote, a company fired an engineer on Friday afternoon and then, during the following week, noticed an unusual amount of activity coming from the former employee's workstation. Examination revealed this workstation had been transferring future product specifications and business plans to competitors for days.

- **Avoidance of oppression.** Groups with politically incorrect agendas frequently seek out innocent sites they can use to exchange and archive information—information such as sexually explicit images, extreme political materials, and weapons and explosives data for terrorists. Such groups may consider law enforcement agencies and security administrators valid political opponents.

- **Espionage for gain.** Break-in experts may attempt to infiltrate a site for profit. This may involve accepting "contracts" for break-ins or free-lance scrounging for information later sold with no questions asked.

- **Simple theft.** Whatever you have of value, someone else would like to have as well. Credit card numbers are a common target; one reported theft involved 20,000 numbers—an Internet Service Provider's account database. Thieves can readily sell such lists to makers of counterfeit credit cards, for example, or to providers of "discount" long-distance service.

No doubt the list goes on and on. The point is that there are capable people out there with an interest in breaking into your site and doing things you don't want. The threat is real.

18.3 Methods of Attack

The most obvious line of attack is for intruders to access your site using the same applications as authorized users. After all, these are the only applications available. (Please don't run services having no authorized users; this is just asking for trouble.)

To prepare for such an attack, the intruder needs to gather data about the site: what machines exist, what's located on each machine, what user names exist, what the passwords are, which user names have special authority (such as Administrator status), and so forth. Windows functions that provide browse lists of user names, computer names, and sharenames are particularly useful to intruders attempting to find their way around your site, as are dumps of DNS databases. Complete DNS databases profiling your site are also handy to intruders, and there's no security on who gets what from a DNS server.

Features designed for network management and diagnostics can be tremendously useful to intruders. What better way is there to poke around a network than to get control of an RMON probe (a remote monitor probe, perhaps on a router or wiring hub port) or the Windows NT Network Monitor Agent?

An intruder who gains access to your gateways, packet filters, and address spoofers can use these tools against you. Sadly, these devices are frequently difficult enough to use that administrators hesitate to "garbage them up" with tight security.

Another ploy is to discover the E-Mail address of a key user, optimally an administrator, and mail an executable file. If the user's E-Mail program executes known file types automatically, it may run the intruder's program. A common trick is to mail the administrator a program that creates another Administrator account—an account whose user name and password the intruder will know.

Chapter 16 mentioned the dangers of CGI programs on HTTP servers. If an intruder manages to upload a CGI program (say, via anonymous FTP) and get it running (by entering the proper URL), then anything is possible. The bandit program might create a number of extra Administrator accounts, for example, or function as a "rogue" file transfer server. For this reason, HTTP servers should never run under privileged accounts such as SYSTEM and Administrator.

Passwords provide far less protection than most people believe. If an intruder can get a reasonable list of user names, either directly or by getting a company phone list, it's a simple job to test each user name with a few hundred or even a few thousand of the most common passwords. Common passwords include the person's first name, last name, initials, and phone number, the 100 most common first names, the 100 most common last names, the 100 most populous cities, all 365 dates in the year, and so forth. Given a list of several hundred user names, chances are rather good that someone will have one of these passwords. Even if the intruder happens to crack the least capable password in the company, this greatly increases the ability to gather more information and pick better targets.

An excellent source of information about a site is available at

http://rs.internic.net/cgi-bin/whois

InterNIC is the organization that registers domain names. The information they provide is fairly general—the network number assigned to your domain, the names and IP addresses of your DNS servers, the E-Mail address of your network administrator, and sometimes other information (likely to contain passwords) like the full company name and street address. You may recall that DNS servers supply the administrator's E-Mail address as well. More information, such as computer names, directory names, and user names, may be available by searching Lycos, WebCrawler, or other sites for your company name.

Are you nervous yet? You should be.

18.4 Dangerous Applications

The nature of several specific applications complicates their use from a security point of view. Four of these are FTP, Telnet, X Window System, and Finger.

18.4.1 FTP

The File Transfer Protocol specification requires FTP servers to use two standard port numbers: 21 and 20. The client software opens a "control" session from an arbitrary local port to port 21 on the server. This is the connection used for sending commands to the server and receiving status messages. However, when the client initiates a GET or PUT request, the server initiates a data connection back to the client. The data connection is from port 21 on the server to an arbitrary port on the client—an arbitrary port the client specified as part of the GET or PUT request.

The following output illustrates an FTP PUT operation in progress with the client as the local machine:

```
C:\>netstat -n

Active Connections

    Proto   Local Address          Foreign Address        State
    TCP     130.131.90.67:1033     130.131.90.111:21      ESTABLISHED
    TCP     130.131.90.67:1035     130.131.90.111:20      ESTABLISHED
```

The "netstat" command doesn't show who initiated each connection, but, in compliance with the FTP protocol, the client initiated the connection from local port 1033 to server port 21. Later, the server initiated the connection from server port 20 to client local 1035. The choice of ports 1033 and 1035 was completely arbitrary. The FTP client will choose a different port number every time it starts and every time it issues a PUT or GET command.

This mode of operation poses a significant problem if a site allows internal users to access Internet FTP servers; any packet filters between the Internet and the internal users must pass connections from port 20 on any Internet machine to any port on any local machine. This presents a very serious security risk because an intruder can go anywhere on the network as long as he or she uses port 20 to initiate the connection.

If the FTP client and server both support proxy (PASV) mode, the client can initiate the data connection and avoid the return connection problem. Unfortunately, support for this mode remains uncommon. Another option is to let users Telnet to the firewall machine and perform FTP transfers from there. Some firewalls also support use of proxy FTP servers that use special application logic to accept or reject incoming connection requests.

A second problem with FTP is that passwords travel across the network as clear text. This is a problem if you wish to provide customers, remote employees, or other individuals with access to User FTP. Every time these users enter their user name and password from "outside," they risk capture by an intruder with a packet sniffer. For this reason, it may be preferable to support anonymous FTP only and protect the information through encryption.

18.4.2 TFTP

Trivial File Transfer Protocol is dangerous because it has no password security at all. If you must run TFTP for some reason, such as booting some network device, be sure it runs with an unprivileged user account and provides only read-only access to a minimal file area.

18.4.3 Telnet

The primary security risk with Telnet is that, as with FTP, passwords travel across the network as clear text and are therefore open to interception. Even if logon passwords were encrypted, the remainder of the session would still be plain text.

Telnet to Windows hosts isn't a popular application; unfortunately, one of the few common uses is allowing users or administrators to change passwords remotely without having to establish NETBIOS sessions. This allows anyone with a packet sniffer to capture passwords when users run the NET PASSWORD command.

18.4.4 X Window System

X is a client-server, graphic display system widely used in UNIX environments. To most observers, however, the roles of client and server are backwards. End users run "X servers" on their distributed computers, and central hosts run "client" applications. In essence, the remote machines provide "display services" that the actual applications use as clients.

There are at least four security risks with this approach:

1. Most X server software blindly displays transmissions from any host; a common ruse is therefore to send fake logon screens to legitimate users and capture the user name and password they enter.

2. Under certain circumstances, an unauthorized user can initiate fake keystrokes and mouse movements on another machine running an X server and get commands executed under the other user's security.

3. Like FTP, X depends on sessions initiated by another machine. For a user to run an X application beyond the firewall, the outside machine must connect inward to the user's X server.

4. X uses a block of transient port numbers beginning at 6000. This complicates the job of packet screening, as other services may use these port numbers as well.

18.4.5 Finger

The "finger" command, with no arguments, displays a list of users currently logged on to a given machine. If a user name is present as an argument, finger will display a variety of information about that user. The information displayed varies depending on the implementation and whether the user has supplied any information for finger to report.

The danger with the Finger service is the danger of giving intruders lists of active accounts ready for breaking, magnified by the risk of providing the intruder with detailed information about each user. Most sites decide they are far better off without this service.

18.5 Establishing a Security Policy and Stance

An effective security policy states what's allowed, what's not, and what happens when violations occur. If this is something your site doesn't have, you should propose at least a working draft and get consensus from all stakeholders (if the organization is participative) or the powers that be (if it's powercentric).

From an Internet point of view, the most important aspect of a security policy is the extent of connection between the Internet and the organization's internal LAN. Some organizations will decide the Internet is too dangerous to allow a wire to enter the building; others may direct-connect their entire network without restriction. Between these extremes, organizations may decide on specific services to provide to internal clients, a set of restricted functions available to Internet users, and a list of prohibited services.

A common desire is to let inside users access Internet services but prevent Internet users from accessing internal networks or services. Many organizations allow Internet users limited types of access such as sending E-Mail, browsing a designated Web server, and downloading files from a controlled, anonymous FTP server.

Corporations, government agencies, colleges, K–12 schools, and public ISPs will all have different security policies. No one policy is correct for all categories or even for all sites within a category. What's important is to think about the issues and make decisions in advance rather than under fire.

A security stance is somewhat more specific than a security policy. It addresses questions such as "Is everything permitted (barring prohibitions), or is nothing permitted (unless authorized)?" That is, do you start wide open and buckle down as needed, or start out strapped to the floor and ease up an inch at a time?

18.6 Types of Prevention

In a sense, there's no need to protect networks; they're just pieces of wire. It's the computers on the network that contain the assets and need the protection. Nevertheless, protection at the network level is generally the first line of defense. For one thing, it's easier to control one or two traffic points on a network than to control dozens or hundreds of computers. For another, as complex as router and gateway configuration can be, there's still less to go wrong than on a complex host supporting a variety of services.

18.6.1 Network-Level Security Protection

Figure 18.1 illustrates a typical network configuration for connecting a private site to the Internet. Two levels of security protect internal hosts from Internet intrusion: one in the router and another in a *firewall* (or "bastion host") machine.

Administrators generally configure routers in this configuration to block unexpected packets. Such packet screening might block packets arriving from the Internet with a source IP address on the internal network, for example. Such packets are either errors or someone on the Internet trying to masquerade as an inside user. Packet screening may also filter out connection requests for services denied to outside users.

Computers like Host1 and Host2 in Figure 18.1 might provide public services such as the organization's external Web server, an E-Mail gateway, and DNS. These hosts would share no security systems with internal hosts, so internal security information can't accidentally leak out. The DNS server would present a very small zone database—one consisting only of hosts outside the firewall. Webmaster, DNS, and other E-Mail addresses would all be aliases, not the names of actual logon accounts.

Windows NT computers outside the firewall probably shouldn't have NET-BIOS bound to TCP/IP. This prevents Internet users from obtaining browse lists, issuing commands like NET VIEW, or logging on to perform administrator functions.

The firewall is much more than a packet screener; it provides application-level services for hosts on the internal network. Internal hosts connect only to the firewall; the firewall then opens external connections on their behalf. Eliminating direct connections between internal and Internet hosts provides Internet access with a high degree of protection for internal hosts.

The architecture of Figure 18.1 is far from the only choice. Some sites will configure the router with little or no packet screening, some may replace the firewall with a router or straight piece of wire, and some may do both. However, even public ISPs whose only mission is connectivity are likely to need some protection for some hosts—those used for billing and other administrative functions, for example.

The term *firewall* is admittedly imprecise; people use it to describe almost any device or service that restricts network traffic for security reasons. In a more precise use of the term, however, a firewall is a computer with two or more network interfaces that provides application-level traffic control.

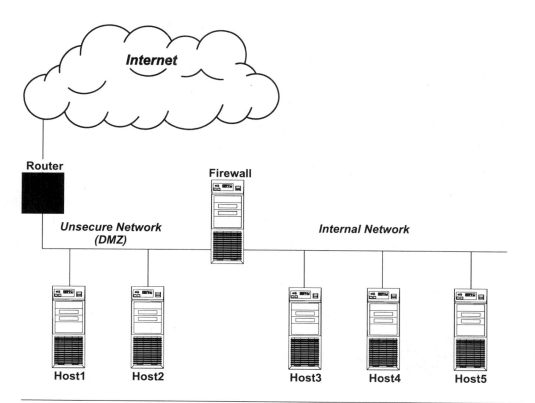

Figure 18.1 Connecting a Private Site to the Internet

A common firewall goal is not to pass any packets directly from one port to another. Instead, software on the firewall interprets applications packets, performs the desired action itself, and forwards the response back to the original requester. This provides a degree of isolation and control packet screeners can't approach.

Each application supported by a firewall generally requires its own special service and may require special configuration or commands for user applications. Supporting the World Wide Web through a firewall, for example, generally involves running an HTTP proxy server on the firewall machine. To understand how this works, consider Figure 18.2, which shows Netscape Navigator's Manual Proxy Configuration dialog.

This would be a typical configuration for a user inside the firewall. Here, wally.interlakken.com is the name of a firewall that runs a proxy server for FTP, Gopher, and HTTP on port 8888. The bottom-most text box specifies no proxy for URLs ending in "interlakken.com." The effect of configuring Netscape Navigator this way is as follows:

- The browser examines the host name in each URL the user requests. If the URL matches an entry in the "No Proxy for:" list, the browser opens a connection to the named host and submits a GET request containing only the directory and file name portion of the URL. This is the normal mode of operation.

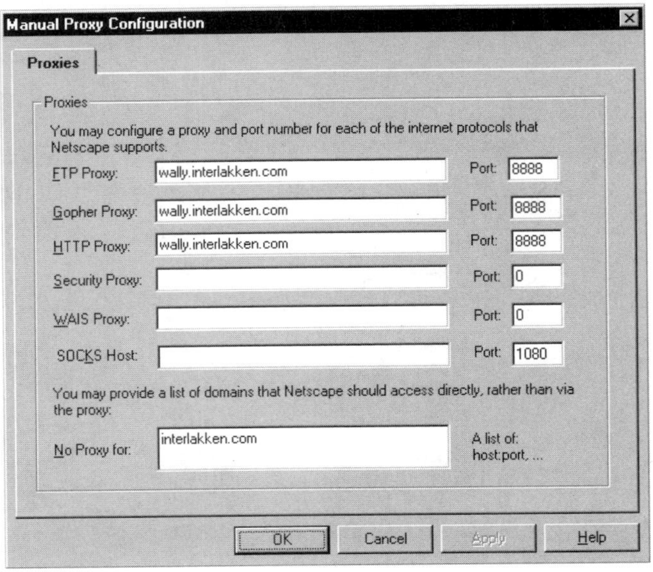

Figure 18.2 Netscape Navigator Proxy Configuration Dialog

- For any host name that doesn't match the "No Proxy for:" list, the browser opens a connection to the named proxy server and port, wally.inter-lakken.com:8888. It then submits a GET request containing the full URL (including the host name and port). The proxy server opens a connection to the host named in the URL. It then submits a GET request (sans host name) as if it were actually a browser. When the remote host responds, the proxy server relays the response back to the originating user's browser.

To understand how FTP proxies work, consider the following diagram, which shows client.interlakken.com downloading a file from ftp.microsoft.com:

Here is an explanation of the diagram:

- The user starts an FTP client and connects from local port 1050 to wally.interlakken.com's port 21.

- Using whatever syntax the FTP proxy expects, the user requests a connection to ftp.microsoft.com.

- The FTP proxy opens a connection from its port 1103 to ftp.microsoft.com's port 21.

- The user sends a GET command to wally.interlakken.com. indicating the return connection should be on port 1052.

- wally.interlakken.com sends the GET request to ftp.microsoft.com indicating the return connection should be on port 1107.

- ftp.microsoft.com opens a data connection from its port 20 to wally.interlakken.com's port 1107.

- wally.interlakken.com verifies the connection attempt on port 1107 is from an expected host, has expected source and destination port numbers, and has arrived within an expected time. If not, it rejects the attempt.

- wally.interlakken.com opens a connection from its port 20 to client.interlakken.com's port 1052.

- wally.interlakken.com relays each packet it receives from ftp.microsoft.com's port 20 to client.interlakken.com's port 1052.

Because it strictly enforces the expectations of each application protocol, the firewall

- Provides greater protection against intruders than is possible with packet screening.

- Assures no traffic passes into or out of the internal network except via approved applications.

- Assures that inside users initiate and control all sessions between inside machines and outside hosts.

SOCKS offers another firewall approach, but it requires a "socksified" TCP/IP stack or applications. SOCKS then examines each IP address and relays traffic for outside addresses to a firewall that controls connections via application-specific logic. Traffic to and from outside hosts thus tunnels from the firewall to the internal user via internal addresses.

The need to run a socksified TCP/IP stack or applications has been a limiting factor on all platforms, especially with regard to commercial software. Early SOCKS adopters were primarily on UNIX and simply recompiled their applications and stacks using freely available SOCKS source libraries. However, this expedient isn't available to users of PC and Macintosh commercial software, and vendors have been slow to add SOCKS support. A second SOCKS disadvantage is that, since it relies on IP address determinations, it requires providing internal users with access to external DNS servers. Providing such access without compromising overall security requires very careful configuration.

Firewalls are usually stripped-down systems running a bare minimum of software; the less software is running, the less room for error and the fewer bugs and loopholes there may be. Often, firewall machines have very limited UADBs and no logon capability except via the console.

To preserve the integrity of a firewall, it's very undesirable to have other machines spanning it as shown in Figure 18.3. A better solution involves using two machines with duplicate data—one inside the firewall and one outside. If you must span the firewall, ensure that NETBIOS isn't bound to TCP/IP on the "outside" network adapter and, if at all possible, use only NetBEUI or IPX (Internetwork Packet eXchange) on the "inside" adapter.

18.6.2 Host-Level Security Protection

The following suggestions pertain to security on Windows NT computers accessible by external Internet users.

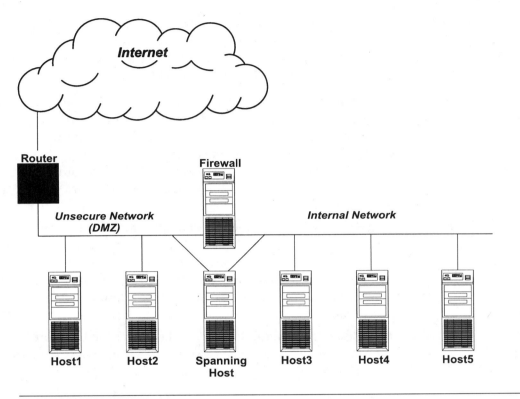

Figure 18.3 Spanning a Firewall

18.6.2.1 Avoid Risky or Unneeded Protocols and Services Internet-accessible computers of all kinds, including those running Windows NT, should run as few protocols and services as possible. Given the Winsock orientation of most Internet services, many Windows NT machines providing them may have no need to run services like NETBIOS, Server, Computer Browser, Netlogon, WINS, and DHCP.

Avoid services like User FTP and Telnet that transmit passwords unencrypted over the network.

18.6.2.2 Don't Advertise Services, Computer Names, or User Names The more information you provide about your site's configuration, the easier the intruder's job. Don't run information-providing services like Finger and Computer Browser.

18.6.2.3 Tighten User Account Security Section 7.5.2 briefly discusses setting Windows NT user account policies; nevertheless, now is an excellent time to review password lengths, expiration periods, and lockouts. Referring again to Figure 7.7, review your settings for the following fields:

- **Maximum Password Age.** The more often users change their passwords, the harder they are to guess and the shorter a compromised password remains useful. This argues strongly for setting the maximum age to a month or less. A contrary argument is that services like FTP, Telnet, HTTP, and Mail (which may also use Windows NT passwords) don't provide a way to prompt users when their old password expires. Instead, they simply start rejecting logins.

- **Minimum Password Age.** Some users circumvent requirements to occasionally change their password by first changing it and then immediately changing it back. Some users even write batch files to do the job for them. Setting a minimum age guarantees that, after a user changes a password, the user must use the new password for a certain number of days before changing it again.

- **Minimum Password Length.** In general, the longer the password, the harder it is to guess. Insisting on passwords longer than 8 or 10 characters generally excludes bad choices such as names, places, phone numbers, and dates.

- **Password Uniqueness.** Allowing users to flip-flop between two passwords is only marginally more secure than not changing passwords at all. If tight security is a concern, this value should be large enough that users forget some of the old passwords and must keep dreaming up completely new ones.

- **Account Lockout.** A common intruder tactic involves testing hundreds or thousands of possible passwords against a single account. To defend against this, you can set a limit on bad password attempts that, if exceeded, locks the account so that even the correct password stops working. For maximum security, the account can remain locked until an administrator frees it, or you can configure Windows NT to automatically unlock the account after a "cooling-off" period.

18.6.2.4 Protect Privileged Accounts Accounts with privileges such as Administrator, Server Operator, Backup Operator, and Restore Operator warrant special attention. Always rename Windows NT's built-in Administrator account, and not to an obvious name such as Admin, Root, Master, or anything based on your own name. You should also restrict use of these accounts to a few local machines.

Even if you must remotely administer a Windows NT machine on the Internet, don't allow Windows Networking logons from the net. Instead, install RAS and perform the remote administration by modem. Modem access can be fairly secure if you configure RAS for call-back to a fixed number,[1] use security modems, or purchase a device that powers the modem on and off via a completely different telephone number.

18.6.2.5 Enforce File System Security NTFS file permissions provide the finest level of access control on a Windows system. The following suggestions will all contribute to effective use of file system control:

- **Set up different drives for different uses.** Disk space and security are much easier to manage if each major system has its own drive letter. Establish different drives for the Windows NT system, logs and utility files (especially those that may grow unexpectedly), News, anonymous FTP, HTTP, and so on.

- **Use NTFS on every drive in the system.** There is no reason and great risk in having drives that lack security access control.

- **Don't permit "Everyone" in access rules.** The Everyone account permits access to anyone—even users with no logon rights at all. It's too easy for this account to show up, by default, where it shouldn't. Decide who needs access and give it specifically only to them.

- **Don't use the Guest account for anonymous FTP.** The Guest account may have default access to areas you don't want FTP users poking around in. Set up a separate user account for FTP access and grant access specifically.

- **Restrict drive access via FTP.** Use the FTP Services configuration dialogs to permit access only to legitimate drives.

18.6.2.6 Close Back Doors to System Process Authority Don't run the HTTP service under the SYSTEM account, and don't allow CGI programs to execute from user portions of the HTTP data directory. Don't allow CGI programs on the system if they may provide back-door access from HTML forms to the Windows NT command line.

---

[1] If you decide to use dial-back, install two modems and configure them to use different lines for dialing in and out. Also, get your dial-out lines configured so that they can't receive incoming calls. Otherwise, intruders may fool the dial-back system by not hanging up, waiting for the modem to go off-hook, and supplying a fake dial tone.

18.6.3 Digital Envelopes and Signatures

18.6.3.1 Encryption and Decryption *Encryption* is the process of making useful data look like random garbage—garbage no one lacking the necessary key can unscramble. Encrypting data is equivalent to sealing it in a *digital envelope.*

Some may believe that decryption is the process of turning random garbage into data, rather like recycling, but this is far from the case. *Decryption* is the process of uncoding encoded data.

Decryption requires use of a secret key—that is, a key no one knows except the intended recipient. The sender and all recipients must know the same secret key; therefore, successful decryption is no guarantee of who the sender is.

18.6.3.2 Digital Signatures Encryption and decryption solve the problem of keeping data secret while in transit. By contract a *digital signature* solves two different problems:

1. The problem of verifying the sender's identity.
2. The problem of verifying the data arrived as sent.

Physical signatures involve one person who can produce the signature (the sender) and many people who can recognize it. By definition, verifiable signatures must be somewhat public; if no one knew the appearance of a person's signature, no one could verify its authenticity. There's no special security regarding the appearance of a person's signature; signatures of corporate CEOs, government leaders, entertainers, and sports heroes appear routinely on annual reports, currency, checks, government reports, publicity photos, and trading cards.

In parallel with physical signatures, digital signatures involve two keys. The sender uses a *private key* to sign (encode) the document, and the recipient uses a *public key to* verify (decode) it. If someone modifies the data in transit or if someone uses a different private key to encode it, the public key won't work and the recipient will know the document isn't genuine.

In validating electronic signatures, the authenticity of public keys is obviously a concern. Otherwise, an impostor could send a fake public key followed by any number of fake messages, all of which would pass signature validation. The fact that public keys consist of long strings of hexadecimal digits compounds the problem; no one wants to get these by phone or registered physical mail and type them in by hand. Potential approaches include receiving a person's public key by E-Mail and confirming by voice, consulting a secure organizational directory of public keys, and consulting various national public key directories on the

Internet. In the last case, the recipient must still confirm the claimed sender, and not someone else, published the key in the national directory.

Systems that verify digitally signed documents typically keep a database of known public keys. This "key ring" database contains only public data and thus requires no special security. Protection of the private key is a more serious matter, as theft of a private key allows the thief to send whatever messages he or she likes using the victim's signature. Private keys are too long to type accurately and certainly too long to remember, so systems that use them typically store private keys on the user's hard disk protected by a passphrase.[2]

There are two general approaches to generating private/public key pairs: One is for users to do it themselves, and the other is for a certification authority to do it. When users generate their own keys, they gain immediacy and save the cost of registration, but the entire burden of key distribution also falls to the user. Presumably, a certification authority would carefully check the credentials of each applicant and distribute the public keys in a safe and reliable way. This would relieve the burden of transmitting and obtaining public keys for senders and recipients, respectively.

There is nothing to prevent using a digital envelope and a digital signature on the same block of data.

18.6.3.3 Obtaining and Using Digital Certificates If you plan to use the full encryption facilities of Netscape Commerce Server, WebSite Professional, or Internet Information Server, you must generate a public/private key pair and obtain a corresponding certificate (digital ID) from a Certification Agency (CA). A public/private key pair has two uses:

1. The holder of a private key can use it to electronically "sign" transmitted files. This encrypts the file so that only the public key can decrypt it, and then only if the encrypted file arrives intact. Recipients obtain or verify the sender's public key through reliable outside sources.

2. Anyone who knows a public key can use it to send confidential mail to the public key's owner. Decrypting such messages requires accurate delivery and possession of the private key.

A common use of public/private key encryption involves transmitting financial data over unsecured networks (such as the Internet). An HTTP server can secure these transmissions by sending the browser its public key and asking the browser to encrypt further data with it. Only the HTTP server can decrypt such data in a useful amount of time.

---

[2]The difference between a password and a passphrase is length. Some authorities recommend protecting private keys with passphrases up to 128 characters in length.

A complication arises, however, in knowing that the server and public key are genuine. Suppose, for example, that you receive E-Mail from a software vendor offering a version upgrade at an attractive price. The message includes the vendor's public key and instructions on using it to transmit your order confidentially.

Question: How do you verify that the given public key is a true public key and that it really belongs to the vendor (and not to some con artist)? Two methods are

1. To consult a recognized public directory of organizations and public keys.
2. To obtain a digital certificate that testifies to the accuracy of the given public key.

One recognized source of public keys is the Web site at http://www/verisign.com. Here, you can look up organizations and verify or obtain any public keys they have registered. Verisign is a spin-off of RSA Data Security, which retained a minority interest.

To verify public keys noninteractively, all that's required is a signed statement from the CA stating the owner's true name and true public key. If signed with the CA's private key, such a statement can pass through an unlimited number of hands without raising questions as to its authenticity. If the CA's public key decrypts it, the certificate is genuine and intact.

A *digital ID* (or "certificate") is a file, encoded with a CA's private key, that specifies a distinguished name and its corresponding public key. A *distinguished name* is one with enough qualifiers to make it unique and verifiable worldwide.

The following names aren't distinguished because they aren't unique in the world:

First National Bank

John Doe

Treasury Department

Washington School

Adding qualifiers like city, state or province, country, and parent organization names would make these names unique and therefore distinguished. In fact, this is the normal practice. Adding information difficult to verify, such as an organization's federal tax identification code, would be much less useful to end users.

It's sometimes useful to think of digital IDs as if they were drivers' licenses. Store clerks and other personnel can verify the correlation between a person's signature and identity by comparing the transaction signature to the driver's license signature.

The normal process to register a public key and obtain a digital ID is this:

- Verify the exact legal name of your organization. Typically, this will come from articles of incorporation, an agency charter, and the like. Whatever this document is, be prepared to send a copy to the CA.

- Using rules obtained from the CA, create a unique distinguished name.

- Choose a password for generating the public/private key pair. As always, choose a password that's long and has no relevance to your situation. Your company's name, address, and phone number are all bad choices.

- If required, run a utility to generate the key pair and a request file. (Discussion of the IIS utility for generating key pairs appears later.) The utility will create two files: a key pair file and a key request file. Alternatively, some CAs generate the key pair for the requestor.

- Complete payment arrangements with the CA. In early 1996, the standard Verisign fee was $290 for the first server in an organization, $95 for each additional server, and $75 per year annual renewal per server.

- Send the distinguished name and key request file to the CA. It will also want proof of your organization's official name, a statement of the webmaster's identity and E-Mail address, and a signed message, on letterhead, from an officer of the organization.

- When the CA returns your certificate, save it to a file.

- Use the certificate file, the key pair file, and the password used for generating the key pair to install the digital ID. (Discussion of this process for IIS also appears later.)

Digital IDs have expiration dates; that is, they report themselves as obsolete after some period. This is a reminder to keep changing key pairs before someone has time to break them.

A typical distinguished name for a Web server might consist of the following elements:

Common Name:	www.interlakken.com
Organizational Unit:	Operations
Organization:	Jim Buyens Computing
Location:	Phoenix
State or Province:	Arizona
Country:	US

The command to create the key pair for Microsoft Internet Information Server would be[3]

```
I:\inetsrv\server>keygen iam2curiousyellow! keypair.key request.key "C=US
    S=ARIZONA L=PHOENIX O=Jim Buyens Computing OU=OPERATIONS
    CN=www.interlakken.com"


PCT/SSL Key generation utility, Version 1.0
Copyright (c) 1995 Microsoft Corporation


Generating key pair of length 1024 bits...
Completed.


Send the request file request.key to your Certificate Authority for
    signing.
Consult the reference for more information.
```

This creates a keypair.key file of 672 bytes and a request.key file of 654. Mail the request.key file and a copy of the complete command line (minus the password) to the CA. As discussed, the agency will also need proof of official name and an authorization letter from an officer.

When the CA has approved and processed the request, it will respond by sending the digital ID. This will typically arrive by E-Mail. Select the portion bounded by "-----BEGIN CERTIFICATE-----" and "------END CERTIFICATE-----" and then copy and paste it into a file named certif.txt. Finally, add the digital ID to your server with the following command:

```
setkey iam2curiousyellow! keypair.key certif.txt
```

Procedures for Netscape Commerce Server and WebSite Professional will be similar. Note that unless you plan to obtain and install a digital ID as just described, there is little point in paying for the "secure" versions of these products.

18.6.3.4 Securing Internet Mail There are two commonly accepted means for sending secure mail over the Internet: PGP (Pretty Good Privacy) and PEM (Privacy Enhanced Mail).

---

[3] As an administrator, never use a password string that appears as an example in any public document. These are obvious additions to any intruder's list of potential break-in passwords.

Philip Zimmerman invented PGP and released it to some controversy in 1991. The controversy arose from two features: the length of PGP's encryption keys and the use of patented technology from RSA Data Security, Inc.

The issue with key length is this: By essentially a process of trial and error, computers can eventually crack any mathematically encrypted block of data. However, the longer the encryption key, the more possibilities the code-cracking computer must try and the longer the decryption must take. PGP can use such long keys that government computers can't crack them in a reasonable period of time. The government, however, feels that, in certain cases, it has the right to wiretap messages, crack codes, and use the results to fight spies and criminals.

PGP Version 2.6 apparently solves the issue with use of RSA's technology for noncommercial users because of agreements Stanford and MIT, the publishers of PGP 2.6, have with RSA Data Security, Inc. Commercial users, however, must purchase a technology license from RSA.

Philip Zimmerman implemented PGP as a UNIX command-line program; its nature is functional, not friendly. However, Ross Barkley has written a Windows front-end available from Oxford University, England. See the sidebar titled "Pretty Good Privacy—Useful Sites" for download locations.

PGP has no direct interface to any mail program—you must process the message or data with PGP and then, in a separate operation, mail the resulting file. Similarly, the recipient saves the PGP portion of the message as a file and processes it with another copy of the PGP software.

PEM is a full Internet standard described by the following RFCs:

1421   Message Encryption and Authentication Procedures

1422   Certificate-Based Key Management

1423   Algorithms, Modes, and Identifiers

1424   Key Certification and Related Services

These RFCs describe ways to embed digital envelopes and digital signatures into standard SMTP Mail messages, as well as ways to identify and distribute public and private keys. The level of detail is suitable for developers who wish to support PEM in their E-Mail systems but of only academic interest to end users. Commercial users must license PEM from Trusted Information Systems, Inc.

Neither PGP nor PEM has achieved tremendous popularity. Both approaches are complex, and complexity breeds mistrust among the general population— even among the general computer population. The difficulty of obtaining and distributing public and secret keys presents another barrier. If E-Mail isn't secure enough to transmit a secret document, then neither is it secure enough to transmit the secret key and encrypted document in separate messages. Whatever

Pretty Good Privacy—Useful Sites

- Pretty Good Privacy Workshop
  http://www.efh.org/pgp/pgpwork.html
  Electronic Frontiers Houston

- To obtain PGP for DOS
  ftp://net-dist.mit.edu/pub/pgp/
  View the file "README" for further instructions.

- To obtain the Windows front-end for PGP
  ftp://ftp.ox.ac.uk/pub/crypto/pgp/pc/windows3/
  Download file "pwf31.zip" (or a later version, if available).

- BAL's PGP public key server
  http://www-swiss.ai.mit.edu/~bal/pks-toplev.html

- Yahoo index of PGP-related pages
  http://www.yahoo.com/Computers_and_Internet/Security_and_Encryption/
  PGP____Pretty_Good_Privacy/

means is safe enough to transmit the secret key might as well transmit the secret document instead.

18.6.3.5 Securing HTTP Transactions As with secure E-Mail, there are two predominant means for transmitting HTML pages securely. Both are Internet Drafts, which means they are works in progress subject to change at any time.

Secure HTTP (HTTPS) is a proposal of Enterprise Integration Technologies that supports electronic signature, authentication, and encryption of HTTP transactions. Secure HTTP recommends the same message format as PEM and also specifies additional headers for HTTP.

If a particular secure HTTP client and server lack prearranged security keys for each other (which is almost always the case), encryption proceeds using a generated session key.

For more information on secure HTTP, point your browser at http://www.eit.com/projects/s-http/.

Netscape Communications has proposed Secure Sockets Layer (SSL) as an alternative to secure HTTP. SSL is a general-purpose security module that sits above a computer's normal socket interface and provides additional security. When SSL is active, it responds to commands initiating encryption and other features from local applications. Corresponding SSL software on the other in-session machine participates in negotiating and using compatible algorithms. SSL also uses a generated session key if no prearranged key is available between a given pair of machines.

More information about Netscape's Secure Sockets Layer is available at http://www.netscape.com/newsref/std/SSL.html.

18.7 Secure Electronic Commerce

The threat of having your credit card number intercepted and used to make unauthorized purchases has severely impeded electronic shopping on the Internet. Credit card companies, seeing this as a barrier to sales, have therefore undertaken projects to develop secure electronic commerce protocols.

In 1995, Visa and Microsoft cooperated to develop a proposal called Secure Transaction Technology (STT). Meanwhile, MasterCard, IBM, Netscape, GTE, and CyberCash produced a competing standard called Secure Electronic Payment Protocol (SEPP). Under pressure from banks, merchants, and customers, these two factions agreed in February 1996 to support a single protocol called Secure Electronic Transactions (SET).

These proposals involve encrypting transaction card data, including the credit card number, at the time of transaction to mutually assure the cardholder, the merchant, and the bank that all parties are genuine. Furthermore, they provide privacy and protection against theft, including provisions that prevent simply recording and retransmitting encrypted sessions.

Neither STT nor SEPP reached an implementation phase and, when announced in early 1996, SET had a year-end 1996 implementation target. Nevertheless, the high-level architecture of these systems isn't likely to change. The entities involved are as follows:

- **Issuer.** A financial institution that grants credit cards to cardholders.
- **Cardholder.** The authorized holder of a bank card.
- **Merchant.** A provider of goods, services, or information that accepts electronic payment.
- **Acquirer.** A financial institution that processes credit card transactions for merchants.
- **Certificate management system.** An agent of one or more bank card associations that creates and distributes electronic certificates (public/private key pairs) for merchants, acquirers, and cardholders.

■ **Banknet.** The existing, private, secure network that connects acquirers, issuers, and (now) the certificate management system.

Processing a SET transaction involves a number of steps roughly analogous to making a credit card purchase at a store. In addition, it requires that all parties have valid *electronic certificates*—that is, valid public/private encryption key pairs registered and verifiable with a secure outside source. Cardholders would obtain electronic certificates in advance of using their cards for electronic purchases; this process would likely resemble the process of obtaining a PIN number for use in an automatic teller machine. Upon receiving an electronic certificate, cardholders would add it to their browser configuration under protection of a local password.

Typical flow for making an electronic purchase would be the following:

1. The cardholder selects one or more items to order and then begins the payment transaction by sending the merchant an "Initiate" message. This corresponds to saying "I'd like to charge this" at a store.

2. The merchant's computer responds with an "Invoice" message the cardholder can use to verify the goods, services, and other transaction information. This is like presenting the customer with an itemized charge slip.

3. The cardholder sends a "purchase order request" message containing goods and services validation information and the cardholder's payment instructions (credit card number). The cardholder's computer encrypts the payment instructions so that only the acquirer can decrypt them. This corresponds to giving your credit card number or allowing the store to imprint it.

4. The merchant receives the purchase order request, formats an "authorization request," and sends it to the acquirer. Note that the merchant can't decrypt the payment information; the merchant can only send the encrypted data to the acquirer. The acquirer decrypts the payment information (and therefore validates the identity of the cardholder) using certificate information obtained through Banknet. In a store transaction, a clerk would verify your card by calling a verification center.

5. The acquirer processes the authorization request and transmits an authorization response to the merchant. This is like getting an authorization number from the call center.

6. The merchant sends a "purchase order response" to the cardholder. This is analogous to the clerk saying, "Your purchase is approved; here's your receipt."

7. Later, the cardholder can request order status by sending the merchant a "purchase order inquiry." This is like calling to ask, "It's been two days since I ordered that pizza. Where is it?" The merchant must respond with a "purchase order inquiry response."

Additional encryption assures the acquirer (and therefore the cardholder) that the merchant is genuine. Encrypted, nondecreasing transaction serial numbers—incorporated into the encryption—prevent recording a single transaction and playing it back multiple times.

Whether such a scheme can open floodgates of electronic Internet commerce remains an open question. The process is complex and highly technical, perhaps too technical for most people to trust. It also requires people to obtain electronic certificates in advance and to install them in their computer. The fact that the government requires breakable encryption keys is a further impediment; security experts will certainly break a few keys and announce the fact with much fanfare and publicity. (Never mind that it took security experts a week, using a million dollars' worth of computers, to decrypt a $25 dollar magazine subscription order.) Public trust in electronic commerce is perhaps more an issue of mind-set than technology.

Another open question is how many Web sites will provide SET support services. In addition to specialized and highly secure software, a provider of SET services will need access to Banknet. Satisfying the consequent security and auditing requirements may be a difficult proposition.

18.8 Configuring Secure Web Page Delivery

Netscape Communications and Commerce Servers, O'Reilly WebSite, and Microsoft Internet Information Server can all be configured to require a password from the user before delivering pages from all or part of the HTTP data directory. Typically, however, these passwords travel over the network with minimal UUencode encryption. The server transmits the page contents in clear text.

If your application requires strong encryption of passwords and page contents, you'll need to run Netscape Commerce Server, WebSite Professional, or IIS. Furthermore, you'll need to get a registered *digital certificate* from a certification authority and add it to the server's configuration. Finally, all URLs will need to begin with "https:" instead of "http:."

The next three sections will discuss configuring the Netscape, WebSite, and IIS servers to require simple password entry. Section 18.8.4 will then discuss how to obtain and use digital certificates.

The EMWAC HTTPS server has no security features.

18.8.1 Securing Pages with Netscape Servers

Figure 18.4 shows a part of the Netscape Server Manager main page. Activating password security requires using the following options in sequence:

1. Create a new database.
2. Add user(s) to a database.
3. Restrict access to part of your server through authentication.

First, click "Create a new database," which brings up the page shown in Figure 18.5. Give the database a name (a file name minus extension), choose "Use this administrative password for this database," and then type the password twice. Finally, click the "Make These Changes" button. If prompted whether to send the server a restart signal, for now choose to return to the server manager.

Second, after returning to the Server Manager page, click "Add user(s) to a database." The page appearing in Figure 18.6 should result. Select the database you just created from the "Select a database:" list, specify the administrative password, enter the desired user name and password, and then click "Make These

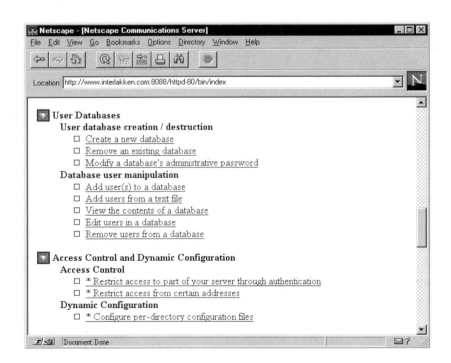

Figure 18.4 Netscape Server Manager—User Databases and Access Control

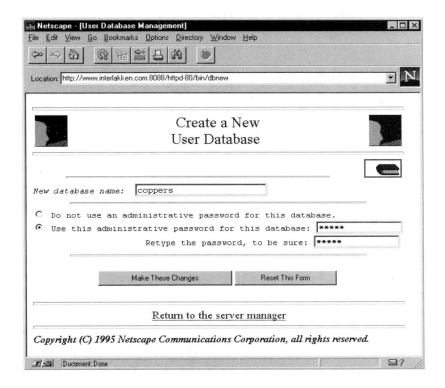

Figure 18.5   Netscape Server Manager—Create a New User Database

Changes." Repeat this process until you've defined all required users. Then return to the server manager.

Third, you'll want to restrict access to all or part of the HTTP data directory using the user database just created. Click the Server Manager option "Restrict access to part of your server through authentication." The page shown in Figure 18.7 will result.

Note the comment at the top of Figure 18.7 that states, "You are currently modifying the directory H:\HTTP/secure/*." This normally defaults to the last setting used, or to "Entire Server." To change the part of the server you'll modify, follow these steps:

1. Click the "Browse Files" button.

2. Choose the directory whose tree you want listed.

3. Specify whether to list directories only or files and directories.

Figure 18.6 Netscape Server Manager—Add Users to an Existing Database

4. Click "Make These Changes."
5. Select the directory you want to modify.
6. Click "Make These Changes."

The directory you selected should now appear at the top of the "Restrict Access Through User Authentication" page (Figure 18.7).

Use the "Select a database:" list to indicate the user name/password database that will validate access to the specified part of the server. To permit access only to some users in that database, enter their names or a wild-card pattern in the "Users to allow:" text box. Leaving this box empty means all users in the database will have access. Finally, give this part of the server a user-friendly name in the "Realm:" field. Then click "Make These Changes."

This time, when the Netscape server prompts you to send a restart signal, do so. Choose "Startup, shutdown or restart the server," as shown in Figure 18.8.

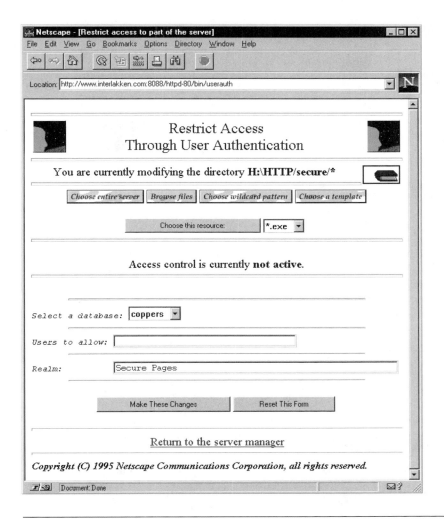

Figure 18.7 Netscape Server Manager—Restrict Access Through User Authentication

Click the Restart button when the next page appears. Restart causes the server to reload all its configuration files without forcing a complete stop and restart.

Figure 18.9 shows the result of specifying a URL in the access-controlled part of the server. Entering a valid user name and password allows the server to transmit the page as shown in Figure 18.10.

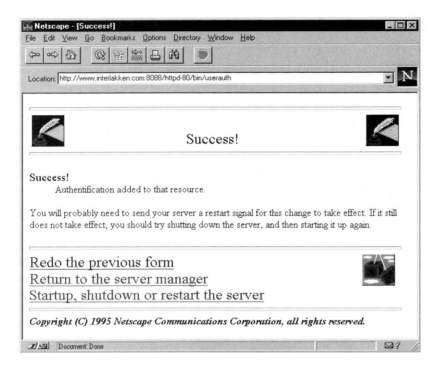

Figure 18.8 Netscape Server Manager—Success! Restart Signal

18.8.2 Securing Pages with WebSite

Chapter 15 briefly discusses WebSite's access control in its review of Server Admin dialogs.

All users requiring access to secured pages must have a WebSite user name. The WebSite Server Admin Users tab (Figure 15.32) creates these; simply choose the "Web Server" authentication realm, click the New button, and then enter the user name once and the password twice. To change a password, select the user name and then click the password button. The Delete button removes the currently selected user name from the database.

For ease in providing groups of users with the same access, you can assign users to groups under either the Users or the Groups tab. To create or delete a group, use the Groups tab (Figure 15.33).

WebSite Server Admin's Access Control tab (Figure 15.34) allows you to specify a URL path and then specify either what users and groups should have access or what users and groups the server will deny. Access restrictions defined at one

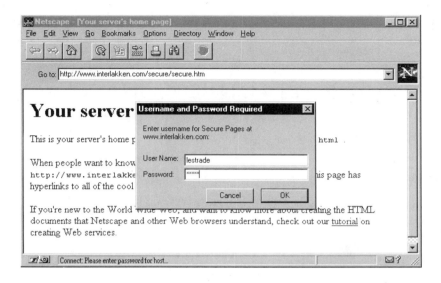

Figure 18.9   Netscape Navigator User Name and Password Prompt

point in a directory tree apply to the entire tree (unless you specifically override them).

Netscape, with its multiple user name databases, allows the same user name to have different passwords in different parts of the server. Keeping these passwords

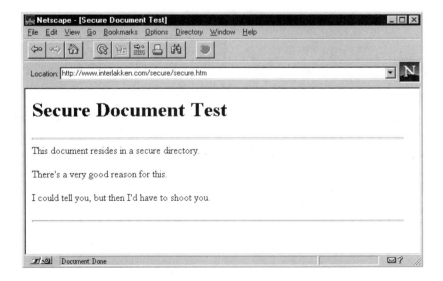

Figure 18.10   Netscape Navigator Secure Page Delivery

the same, if this is a requirement, is a manual process. WebSite, with its group structure and single-user database, ensures that the same user name has the same password everywhere.

18.8.3 Securing Pages with Internet Information Server

IIS uses NTFS file system permissions to control access to restricted parts of the server. IIS won't require a user name/password prompt as long as both of the following are true:

- The Allow Anonymous box in Internet Server Manager's WWW Services tab (Figure 15.36) is ON.

- NTFS permissions permit "Read" access for the specified HTTP Anonymous Logon user.

If either condition is false and if "Password Authentication: Basic" or "Password Authentication: Windows NT Challenge/Response" is in effect, IIS will obtain a user name and password from the browser. If the user name and password are those of a valid Windows NT account and if that account has NTFS permissions to read the file, IIS will permit access.

"Password Authentication: Basic" uses UUencode password encoding and thus works with almost any browser. "Password Authentication: Windows NT Challenge/Response" uses the same highly encrypted exchange as the Windows NT domain logon process, but, at the time of this writing, Microsoft Internet Explorer was the only browser to support it.

Figure 18.11 shows typical NTFS permissions for parts of an HTTP server open to general public browsing. Figure 18.12 shows permissions for a directory restricted to members of the PUBLISHERS group.

By default, Windows NT blocks ordinary user accounts from logging on to a server. The same restriction, if left in effect, prevents users from accessing secure Web pages. Specifically, their browser receives the message "HTTP/1.0 500 Server Error (Logon failure: the user has not been granted the requested logon type at this computer)." To avoid this problem, assign the user or group the "Logon on locally" user right as shown in Figure 18.13. To bring up this dialog, start User Manager, pull down the Policies menu, and then select "User Rights...."

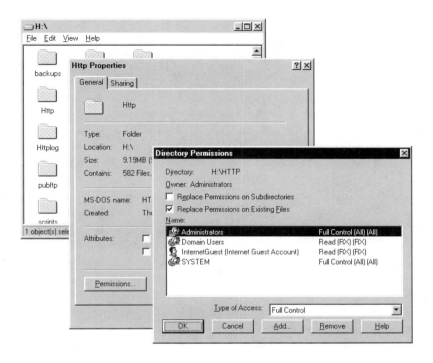

Figure 18.11 NTFS Permissions for Public HTTP Access

18.9 Log File Management

As with backups, no one has ever been sorry they had an activity log. Especially for servers located on the Internet, you should activate all available activity logs for every service you run. For example, you should record every valid or rejected logon attempt, each Web page transferred, and each FTP logon, logoff, and transfer. (Don't turn on detailed program trace logs unless you're having specific problems.)

This much logging can consume considerable disk space, so you'll need to institute a purge policy of some kind. However, you should never purge log data you haven't yet backed up to tape or some other medium.

There are several reasons for collecting and retaining all available log data:

■ In many cases, logs contain the only data available on what was going on when a given security problem or system event occurred.

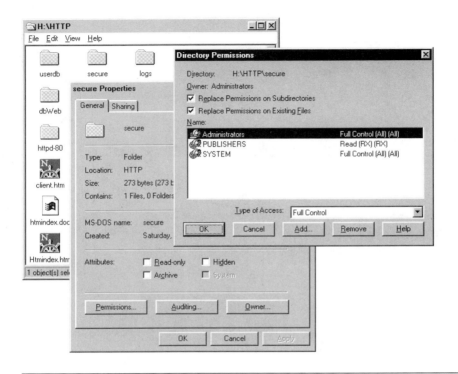

Figure 18.12 NTFS Permissions for Restricted HTTP Access

■ The significance of a given transaction or incident may not be obvious immediately. Old logs are your only resource for locating previous instances of a situation or for locating trends.

■ Logs may contain data from which you derive customer billing. This is worth retaining not only for the current billing cycle but also for a period long enough to support or refute any potential claims.

Saving all possible logs is relatively easy; reviewing them each day quickly becomes mundane and boring. Nevertheless, if after six months of normal activity your system records 1,357 refused logon attempts to the Administrator account, you should know about it. Likewise, sudden appearance of a gigabyte or two of GIF files in the anonymous FTP area may be cause for investigation. In short, you should consider some sort of automated log analysis that watches for such situations and sends an alert, possibly an E-Mail message, if one occurs. Visual Basic is a convenient language for developing these.

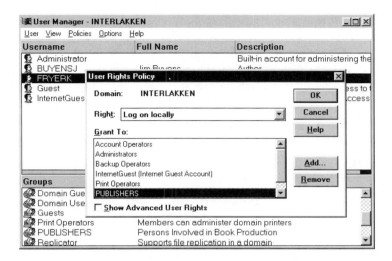

Figure 18.13 Granting the "Log on Locally" User Right

18.10 Viruses

Fortunately, as of this writing, no computer viruses affecting Windows NT had arisen, and virus activity for MS-DOS machines seemed to be declining. Nevertheless, thousands of viruses exist and virus authors continue creating more. This problem won't be going away anytime soon.

If you maintain controlled download libraries of any kind, you should take all possible measures to scan additions for viruses and periodically sweep the entire library.

If you maintain user upload file areas, you owe it to your users and their correspondents to scan these file areas also. An occasional virus showing up in the library of some cooperative user is no cause for alarm, but repeat offenders may require more serious treatment.

18.11 Backups

If an intruder manages to damage, corrupt, or infiltrate your system, restoring a backup tape may be your only recourse. This isn't the time to discover your backup job has been failing for the last five weeks.

You may need to review activity logs to determine when the attack or damage began. This is important because restoring a backup is futile if it also restores the cause of the damage, corruption, or security loophole.

Hopefully, you'll never find it necessary to reconstruct the user account database or other customer records from original documents. Nevertheless, retaining this paperwork in a format suitable for data entry remains your ultimate disaster recovery plan.

18.12 The Maginot Line

In the 1930s, France constructed an elaborate system of forts and gun sites to protect its northeastern border from another German invasion. Called the *Maginot Line* for André Maginot, one of its principal proponents, this line of defense never failed. Still, France fell to the Germans in 1940. They went around it.

The point of this little history lesson is that Internet security is only one aspect of a site's total security program. It makes little sense to enact punishing Internet security measures to prevent viruses when viruses continue to arrive via modem and floppy disk. The problem is viruses, not the Internet, and building a Maginot Line in one compass direction doesn't protect the others. The same is true for employees playing games, downloading smut, or distributing extreme political material.

This is far from saying you should leave your borders undefended or allow your employees to goof off; it merely suggests you concentrate on the total picture and not just the Internet aspect. The Internet reflects every segment of society.

CHAPTER 19

System Management Principles

Customers, users, and the people they correspond with all expect fast and reliable access to Internet services. This is the hallmark of a professionally managed site.

The primary determinants of smooth operation are the physical operating environment, the computer systems themselves, and proper operating procedures. This chapter covers these topics in turn and concludes with a few axioms that have served well over the years.

19.1 Environmental Management

No equipment can operate reliably in the absence of physical security. Else, whoever is lurking about—janitors, overtime employees, toddlers, crooks, or others—will eventually push the wrong button, kick the wrong cable, or engage in deliberate sabotage. Production computer sites belong in locked rooms accessible (barring emergencies such as fire and building structural failure) only to trained operators.

Don't locate your site in a room through which other utilities pass. Allowing water, sewage, steam, telephone, or electrical mains to pass through your site increases the risk of damage and necessitates admitting maintenance people from time to time. Avoid rooms with windows; in addition to advertising your site as a tempting target, they contribute to temperature variations.

Computers operate most reliably in conditions of proper and stable temperature and humidity. If your site's location is a basement, an odd corner of a building, or simply an area with poor circulation, you may need supplemental heating or air conditioning. Avoid buildings that don't provide the same environmental stability weekends, holidays, and evenings as they do during prime hours. Your needs are 24 hours a day, 7 days a week.

Computers also require stable electrical current and good grounding for stable operation. Verify that your UPS (Uninterruptible Power Supply) corrects both excessive and insufficient voltage; also verify that it provides adequate lightning protection. Ensure that equipment doesn't overload electrical circuits. Isolate devices such as laser printers that draw current in surges from computers and network devices by placing them on different circuits.

Bad grounding causes many erratic electrical problems. Be sure to use three-conductor outlets for all electrical sockets and to wire all three pins. Locate or install a good earth ground and connect it to your electrical ground with heavy wire or cable. To prevent static buildup, ground racks, cabinets, and metal shelving as well. To guard against lightning strikes to telephone wiring, provide suitable ground protection where telephone lines enter the building.

If you suspect or simply wish to protect against environmental problems, you should purchase recording devices for temperature, humidity, electrical voltage, and so forth. Some UPS systems log input and output electrical voltage; if so, you can search for correlation between electrical variations and system outages. If your site is frequently unattended, consider devices that can alert you (or a security monitoring company) in case of environmental extremes of any type.

Construct your site solidly and secure all cables. Minor equipment jostling or routine cleaning shouldn't cause cable breaks or system outages. Keep equipment off the floor, especially if occasional flooding or nearby dripping is a possibility.

Use quality cables and connectors and replace loose or corroded connectors immediately. Investigate and correct causes of corrosion. Avoid both sharp corners and excessive cable lengths. Route cables through troughs or loose cable guides but don't bundle them so tightly that tracing, adding, or removing a cable involves unbundling and rebundling the whole set. Label each end of all cables with numbered cable tags.

If you have a large installed base of cable (such as several floors or buildings full of users and equipment), invest in electronic cable testers and wiring hubs having built-in cable diagnostics.

19.2 Technical Management

The axiom "You cannot control what you do not measure" is not as true as advocates would have us believe; contrary examples begin with simple bodily functions. Nevertheless, managing the performance of computer systems is largely a matter of gathering and interpreting numbers.

19.2.1 Performance Monitoring

19.2.1.1 Windows NT Performance Monitor Microsoft supplies a comprehensive system-monitoring tool with every copy of Windows NT. To invoke it, start the Performance Monitor application in the Main Program Manager group or Start Programs menu. Figure 19.1 shows a typical Performance Monitor display.

In this snapshot, Performance Monitor is displaying four common indicators of overall system performance: percent processor time, percent disk time, pages per second, and total network frames received per second. These provide a general picture of CPU, disk, memory, and network utilization.

Here is an explanation of Figure 19.1:

- The first burst of activity resulted from starting the EMWAC HTTP service. This accounts for the first two spikes.

- The second burst, which contains the 100 pages-per-second spike, is the result of loading perl.exe and the perl program iconlib.pl (described in Chapter 16). This created moderate surges in disk and CPU activity as well.

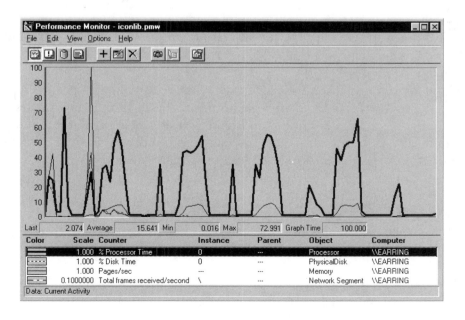

Figure 19.1 Windows NT Performance Monitor

- The third burst—the one just above the word "Counter" in the legend—represents the initial run of iconlib.pl and delivery of all the icon files. (Recall that iconlib.pl writes HTML to display all icons in a directory.)

- The fourth burst, a small spike to about 38 percent CPU, resulted from placing the cursor in the browser's "Location:" field and pressing Enter. Satisfying this request used far less capacity than the first for these reasons. First, perl.exe, iconlib.pl, and all the icon file directory entries are still in the server's disk cache. Second, the browser specifies the last-modified header on the GET request for each icon file. Third, the server responds with the "304 Not Modified" status code rather than by transmitting the file.

- The fifth burst reflects about the same CPU and memory usage as the third burst but much less disk and network usage. This is the result of clicking the Reload button.

- The sixth and eighth bursts are repeats of the fourth burst.

- The seventh and ninth bursts are repeats of the fifth burst.

Running iconlib.pl is a fairly intense activity; the server must load perl.exe, compile iconlib.pl, scan the directory, and generate the response HTML. The browser then GETs 49 GIF files. Processing a more typical URL would produce much less usage and a less instructive display. Rarely, however, will you be able to track usage attributable to a single URL. Performance Monitor shows overall system statistics.

Using Performance Monitor effectively requires searching for specific instances of high utilization, identifying bottlenecks, and eliminating constraints. This requires a good understanding of overall system operation. For example, if you notice that a constrained system has high disk utilization, the true bottleneck may be RAM. A shortage of RAM can lead to excessive memory swapping and constrained disk caching. Chronic memory shortages, in turn, may be a symptom of memory leaks in a system service or application.

Many system services register their operating statistics with Performance Monitor so that you can record or observe their operating characteristics. This is definitely a nice feature to have when analyzing system or application performance.

The Windows NT Resource Kit includes a program called datalog.exe that runs as a service and collects Performance Monitor statistics for later analysis. This is useful if you want to capture statistics over a 24-hour or 7-day period and not remain logged on to the console.

19.2.1.2 SNMP Management Systems Simple Network Management Protocol is a system whereby one network device may query another for statistics, status, and settings. A Management Information Base (MIB) is a specially formatted file that describes the values each network device can report. MIBs arrange data in a hierarchical view.

Certain standardized MIB identifiers are common to almost every network device. Additional standard identifiers exist for certain device types, such as wiring hubs, bridges, routers, and hosts. Device-specific MIBs identify parameters unique to a particular type of equipment. To obtain MIB files specific to Windows NT, install the Windows NT Resource Kit and look for files with a .mib extension.

SNMP consoles are workstations that collect, display, and store MIB values from other SNMP devices. Such consoles ship with an assortment of generic MIBs for common network device types, but they can also import and use device-specific MIBs. Once the console knows the full MIB for a device, it can retrieve and act upon any available data from that device.

Most SNMP consoles can construct network maps by pinging every IP address on every network and subnet in the facility. If the console gets a response, it sends an SNMP query, determines the device type, and adds the device to the map. An administrator or operator can then retrieve statistics by clicking on the device's map icon. In addition, SNMP consoles can periodically collect data, send E-Mail or beeper messages if readings exceed configured thresholds, and record collected data in a database for later analysis.

SNMP consoles normally take the active role in an SNMP environment, requesting, displaying, and storing values based on some frequency. However, despite their normally passive role, network devices can generate "traps" at any time. A trap is simply a message or error code the device emits under defined circumstances.

An SNMP *community* is a group of manageable devices all configured with the same community name. Most sites manage all their devices as a single community named "public."

Figure 19.2 shows the Windows NT SNMP Service Configuration dialog. The path to this window is Control Panel, Network, Installed Network Software: SNMP Service, Configure.

The frame titled "Send Trap with Community Names" specifies a list of communities to which the NT server will send any traps it generates. To add a community name, type it in the text box at the right and then click "<-Add." To remove a community name, select it in the list at the left and then click "Remove->." To configure which hosts within a community should receive

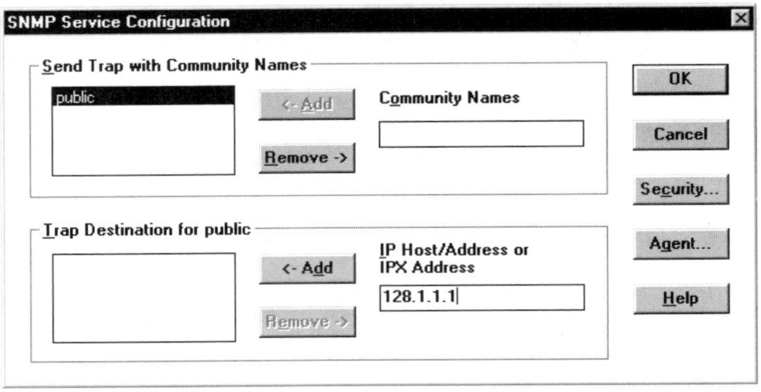

Figure 19.2 Windows NT SNMP Service Configuration Dialog

traps, select that community in the upper frame and then add or remove host IP addresses in the lower frame.

Clicking the Security and Agent buttons in Figure 19.2 produces the dialogs shown respectively in Figures 19.3 and 19.4. The Security dialog in Figure 19.3 controls which communities and hosts the Windows NT machine will respond to and whether it will generate a trap in case of a security violation. The Agent dialog in Figure 19.4 accepts identifying data the SNMP server will supply to authorized SNMP consoles.

UNIX workstation vendors such as DEC, Hewlett-Packard, IBM, and Sun are traditional suppliers of SNMP consoles. Windows NT versions of these systems

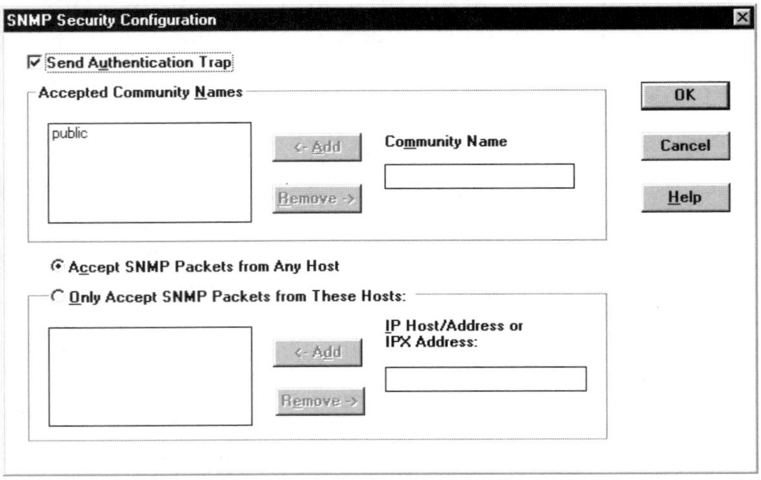

Figure 19.3 Windows NT SNMP Security Configuration Dialog

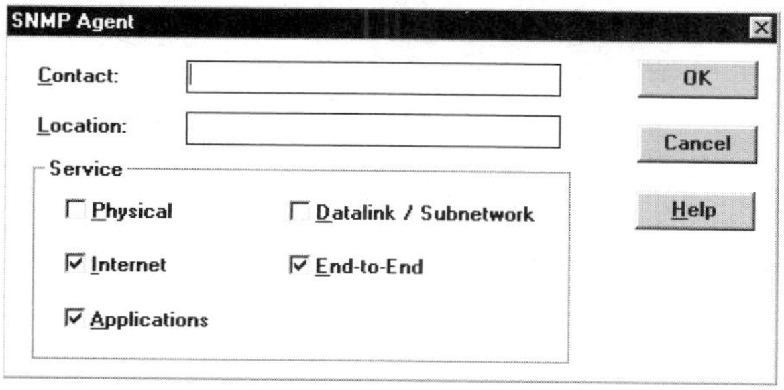

Figure 19.4 Windows NT SNMP Agent Configuration Dialog

may be available by the time you read this. Castle Rock also sells a PC-based
SNMP console called SNMPc. Figure 19.5 shows this product monitoring a
Windows NT server.

The advantages of using an SNMP console (rather than Windows NT
Performance Monitor) to gather statistics are that SNMP manages more kinds
of devices from a single station, runs on a wider range of operating systems, and
is more standards-based.

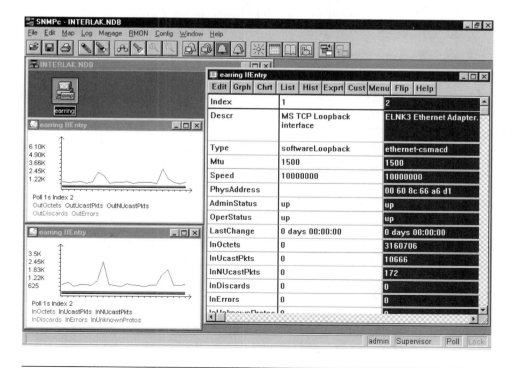

Figure 19.5 SNMPc Monitoring a Windows NT Server

19.2.1.3 Protocol Analyzers Capturing and examining packets is frequently the best way to analyze what's happening on a network. This requires a device called *a protocol analyzer* to examine all packets on a network, tabulate statistics, and retain packets in a buffer for later display.

Normally, a network adapter will only respond to broadcasts, multicasts, and packets addressed to the adapter's data link address. This prevents applications on user PCs from examining traffic intended for other users. Protocol analyzers, however, place network adapters in "promiscuous" mode and thus have access to every packet on the network.

The most capable protocol analyzers are specialized portable computers with custom, high-performance network cards having huge on-board buffers. Such features ensure that network data will never arrive faster than the analyzer can capture it. High-end analyzers also come with highly capable packet filtering and display software and with expert systems that propose possible causes based on analysis of faulty packets and traffic patterns. Dedicated analyzers can easily cost $25,000 or more. Network General and Hewlett-Packard are the best-known suppliers of such devices.

Ordinary PCs can also serve as protocol analyzers subject to certain limitations:

- The computer's network adapter must be capable of promiscuous mode.

- The computer must have suitable network and protocol analysis software.

- The computer's network card and I/O bus must be fast enough to transfer packets to the protocol analyzer application as fast as they arrive.

- The network adapter still may lose certain bad packets such as those involved in collisions, those with erroneous CRC checksums, runts (those shorter than the minimum allowable length), giants (those beyond the maximum allowable length), and those whose indicated length is different from the actual length received. The extent of loss will depend on the exact network adapter and software but will almost always be greater than achieved with dedicated analyzers.

The fact that an ordinary PC with inexpensive software can capture and examine all packets on the network is a significant security concern. Finding such software on a user PC is strong evidence of a security violation.

Microsoft System Management Server (SMS) includes protocol analyzer software called simply "Network Monitor." Network Monitor is a client-server application with two primary components. First, a background service (Network Monitor Agent) collects data and statistics. Second, a user interface program (Network Monitor) displays captured data and controls agents in various parts of the network. Thus, in an enterprise consisting of multiple networks, you can monitor any network from one central location. All that's required is to have SMS

Network Monitor installed at the central location and Network Monitor Agent installed somewhere on each subnet. Network Monitor Agent ships with every copy of Windows NT and Windows 95 but isn't installed by default.

Network Monitor Agent can provide intruders with a wonderful view of your site, including clear-text passwords for applications that don't encrypt them. Therefore, for security reasons,

1. Don't install Network Monitor Agent on any more machines than necessary.

2. Do password-protect each instance of Network Monitor Agent.

3. Don't run the Network Monitor Agent service (visible from Control Panel, Services) except when a known administrator is running Network Monitor.

4. Don't install Network Monitor Agent on Windows 95 machines. The Windows 95 version of Network Monitor Agent doesn't support recommendations 2 and 3.

To illustrate use of Network Monitor, consider the following FTP session. The client on CHOKER, a Windows 95 machine, connects to EARRING, a Windows NT server (user commands appear in boldface):

```
C:\TEMP>ftp
ftp> open earring
Connected to earring.interlakken.com.
220 earring Windows NT FTP Server (Version 3.51).
User (earring.interlakken.com:(none)): doej
331 Password required for doej.
                    (user types password but keystrokes aren't echoed)
230 User doej logged in.
ftp>ls
200 PORT command successful.
150 Opening ASCII mode data connection for file list.
.
..
ftp.txt
grape.pl
hello.pl
iconlib.pl
226 Transfer complete.
```

```
48 bytes received in 0.00 seconds (48000.00 Kbytes/sec)
ftp> get grape.pl
200 PORT command successful.
150 Opening ASCII mode data connection for grape.pl.
226 Transfer complete.
6853 bytes received in 0.06 seconds (114.22 Kbytes/sec)
ftp> bye
221 Goodbye.
```

Figure 19.6 shows the main Network Monitor screen following capture of the preceding session. Note that CHOKER sent 1,342 bytes in 21 frames to EARRING and that EARRING sent 8,856 bytes in 28 frames to CHOKER.

Network Monitor can identify entries for CHOKER and EARRING by name because it knows their data link addresses. Network Monitor can automatically learn machine names if you pull down the Capture menu and select "Find All Names" when a capture buffer is open. Find All Names scans for packets such as NETBIOS name resolutions and responses to DNS and WINS queries.

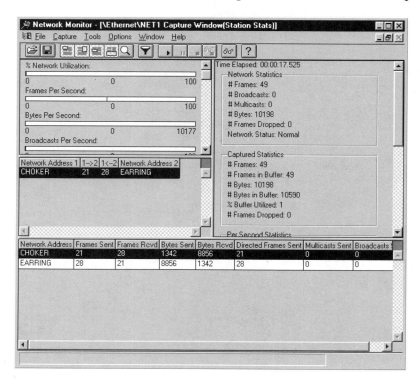

Figure 19.6 Network Monitor

Clicking the view-capture toolbar button (the one with the eyeglasses) brings up the display shown in Figure 19.7. In frame 1, CHOKER queries the DNS to get EARRING's IP address. The DNS responds in frame 2. The FTP client opens a control session from port 1045 on CHOKER to port 21 on EARRING; frame 6 is the "connect" message from the FTP server on EARRING to the client on CHOKER. The user supplies his logon ID "doej" in frame 7 and his password "johnny" in frame 9. Breaking security on applications that use clear-text passwords is just this easy.

Double-clicking the line for any frame displays a more complete view. Figure 19.8 illustrates the result of double-clicking the line for frame 14. The client requested a directory listing in frame 13, and frame 14 is the server's response that it's opening a data connection. The center pane of Figure 19.8 displays the packet's source and destination addresses (130.131.90.111 and 130.131.90.67), as well as the source and destination ports "FTP [control]" (21) and "0x0415" (1045). The bottom pane shows a hex dump of the entire packet.

Figure 19.9 shows frame 15. Here, EARRING has opened a connection from port "FTP [default data]" (20) to port "0x0416" (1046) on CHOKER.

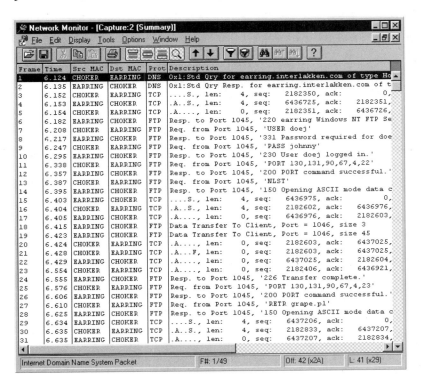

Figure 19.7 Network Monitor Capture Summary

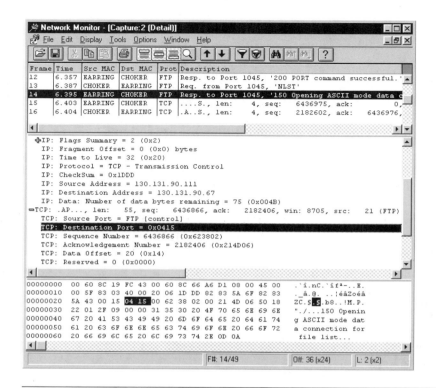

Figure 19.8 Network Monitor Capture Summary (Frame 14)

Referring back to Figure 19.7, EARRING transmits the directory listing in frames 18 and 19 and then notifies the client that the transfer is complete in frame 24. The "ack" frames (such as 3, 4, and 5) are acknowledgments wherein the recipient of a frame informs the sender that the frame has arrived and passed all consistency checks.

This example required no filtering because CHOKER and EARRING were the only two machines on the network. This level of isolation seldom occurs in real life, but you can approximate it with filters. With filters, you can include or exclude frames having any specified characteristics, either when capturing frames or when viewing them.

Detailed knowledge of all the various codes, formats, and application protocols isn't a prerequisite to using a protocol analyzer, although it helps. A general knowledge of network addressing, frame types, and protocols is often sufficient to gather information and resolve simple problems.

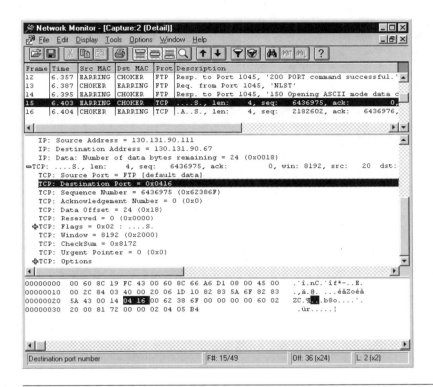

Figure 19.9 Network Monitor Capture Summary (Frame 15)

19.2.2 Event Logging

Windows NT maintains three system event logs: System, Security, and Application. These are the logs displayed by Event Viewer, an application Windows NT Setup places in the Administrative Tools Program Manager group or Start Programs menu. Figure 19.10 shows a typical Event Viewer display.

Event logs bear watching for several reasons. First, in case of system problems, there's an excellent chance one or more components involved in the failure will issue error messages. Second, many security violations and break-in attempts are apparent only in the logs. Third, detecting abnormal log contents requires knowing what normal log contents look like; you should therefore review the logs on good days as well as bad. Finally, if you plan to charge for connect time, print jobs, or other activity recorded in systems logs, the logs will probably feed your billing system.

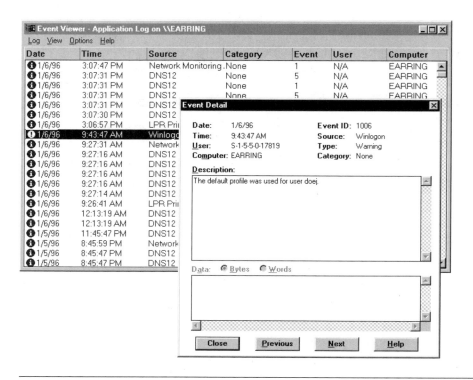

Figure 19.10 Windows NT Event Viewer

Dialogs in Event Viewer control the size of the event logs and what action to take when they fill up. The dialog of Figure 19.11 results from pulling down Event Manager's Log menu and selecting "Log Settings." Control over data added to event logs resides in the originating applications or services. Control of security auditing, for example, resides in User Manager under Policies, Audit. Control of printer auditing lies in Print Manager under Security, Auditing. Dialogs in File Manager or Explorer control file system auditing. If applications use the Application Event Log, control over what events get logged will reside in those applications.

The Windows NT Resource Kit program dumpel.exe can dump the logs (System, Security, and Application) to an ASCII file. You can run this command either from the command line or, via the AT command, on a scheduled basis. Dumping logs on a scheduled basis ensures contents get backed up and also provides the basis for any automated analysis programs you obtain or create.

Automated log analysis is a valuable tool provided you remember its limitations. Checking the Security Event Log daily quickly becomes boring, for example,

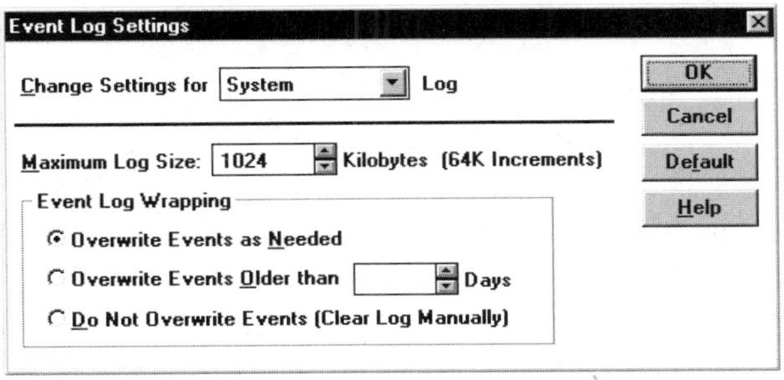

Figure 19.11 Windows NT Event Log Settings

so you might write a Visual Basic program to load each day's entries into a database, tabulate them, and mail yourself statistics. If logon violations suddenly jump from a few a day to several thousand, such a notification could be your trigger to investigate. The pitfall, of course, is unexpected activity your log-scanning program doesn't look for.

Some applications create their own log files, typically in simple ASCII format. Don't forget to examine, rotate, and back up these logs as well.

19.2.3 Capacity Planning

The twin goals of capacity planning are to add equipment in advance of capacity shortages and to avoid purchasing unnecessary equipment.

The first step in capacity planning is identifying what resources to plan. These might include network bandwidth, phone lines, modems, disk space, tape drives, tapes, tape library space, RAM, CPU capacity, threads, floor space, electrical amperage, or any other commodity that affects service. Some of these obviously require more detailed analysis and scrutiny than others, but choosing which to monitor closely should be a conscious decision.

One approach to capacity planning involves graphing periodic readings to detect trends. When a projected trend line intersects installed capacity, you should anticipate a capacity shortage and plan equipment or service upgrades accordingly.

A better approach is correlating resource usage to natural forecasting units—that is, to business- or mission-related quantities. For example, you may determine that each hundred PPP accounts requires a certain number of modems, a certain network bandwidth, and a particular amount of disk space. If so, you can plan expansion of these resources based on sales forecasts.

19.2.4 Adding Computers

Adding resources to an existing computer is usually cheaper than purchasing an additional system unit. Nevertheless, purchasing additional computers will likely be necessary from time to time. This can be a complex task if you need to split the workload of one existing machine onto several, especially if the change should be "transparent" to the user.

Creating a separate DNS CNAME (alias) for each application on a machine makes it relatively easy to redeploy the services later. Names like www.interlakken.com and ftp.interlakken.com might initially refer to the same machine, for example, but to two different machines after the site has grown. In fact, it's generally good practice never to name a machine www, ftp, gopher, mail, or any other service-specific name; always channel to services through CNAMEs.

Five approaches to subdividing an HTTP server are the following:

1. If you're supporting virtual domains on one machine, move one or more domains to a different machine.

2. Move all image files, or at least the largest and most active ones, onto a second server. This requires updating all affected <IMG> tags on the original machine.

3. Move all CGI programs, or at least the resource-intensive ones, to an additional server. This also requires updating the associated HTML files.

4. Move a subset of pages, such as one or more menu trees, to the additional server. This requires updating pointers to the moved pages and may affect external users with pointers to those pages.

5. Synchronize the content of both servers to be the same and use CGI or SSI programs to redirect browsers randomly to either machine.

Mail servers have enough aliasing flexibility that adding an additional inbound gateway or POP server can be fairly transparent. If the site is growing, existing users can stay on existing machines and new users can be accommodated on new servers. A similar strategy can apply for user FTP directories.

When modifying DNS entries,

■ Check time-to-live on the entries you plan to change. Current date plus time-to-live is the soonest you can make a transparent change.

■ Reduce time-to-live to one day; then wait the previous time-to-live. This allows cache entries in DNS servers around the world to expire.

■ Reduce time-to-live to an hour or less and wait a day; then make the change during a period of low usage.

■ Keep time-to-live at a short interval until you're sure the change is working properly; then restore it to its former value.

19.3 Procedural Management

There are two good reasons, at minimum, to establish repetitive operating procedures for a site. First, it propagates approaches that work and extinguishes those that don't. Second, users and site personnel alike appreciate consistency. Changes are easier to cope with if they follow familiar patterns.

19.3.1 Routine Procedures

"Every detail of every job documented" is a common goal of bureaucratic management, a goal less and less realized in today's high-speed business environment. Nevertheless, the more consistent your procedures, the smoother your site will run and the easier it will be to deal with. Customers and users don't appreciate erratic backup cycles, spotty technical support, random outages, and irregular billing.

If a hard-copy procedure manual is the best route to consistency, take it. Printed procedures frequently fall out-of-date, however, and the more out-of-date they become, the less your personnel will trust and consult them.

Communication among site personnel is critical to keeping operations consistent. Operators and analysts unaware of recent procedure changes are bound to make incorrect decisions.

19.3.2 Change Control

You should do everything possible to make changes in a planned and consistent manner. The alternative—making changes only in response to problems and without warning to users—is simply unacceptable.

Establish a pattern of construction, test, announcement, change during scheduled outage, and follow-up. Don't put production systems on empty, untested equipment and call them "test" until they're stable.

Never make a change without having a backout plan. Such a plan must include an estimate of how long the backout would take. The end of the outage window minus backout time then becomes the deadline for rolling in and testing the change. Preserve your ability to back out not only during the change window but also in the hours and days following. This may require a freeze on other changes, lest they complicate backing out something else.

19.4 Content Management

Content publishers and system administrators alike need feedback on usage patterns for various parts of the server. For content publishers, this provides information on what kinds of pages and topics receive attention and which don't. For administrators, understanding usage patterns suggests areas that have become obsolete and possibly ready for purge. In addition, unusual shifts in usage patterns may indicate a malfunction or security failure.

The raw data that drives such analysis comes from activity logs. As interesting as individual records in these logs may be, it's generally sorted and summarized data that provides an overall picture. You can write such tools yourself with Visual Basic or, as in Chapter 16, use database queries to tabulate statistics instantly.

Another approach involves using a utility program such as WebTrends by e.g. Software. WebTrends can read log data from a local file, an FTP location, or an HTTP URL. It then produces built-in or customized reports formatted as HTML pages. This format makes it easy to set up a library of current statistical reports on a server.

Figure 19.12 shows the main WebTrends screen. Clicking the Add button brings up a dialog where you can specify the location of additional log files; these subsequently appear in the main window's selection list. Clicking the View Log button brings up a formatted view of individual records.

Clicking the WebTrends Report button displays a dialog like the one in Figure 19.13. "Filters" and "Template" control the range of data reported and the types of reports, respectively. "SaveTo" specifies the location for the output HTML file. When you're satisfied with the output of a given report, you can save it using "Memorize," making it easy to recreate the same report with new data.

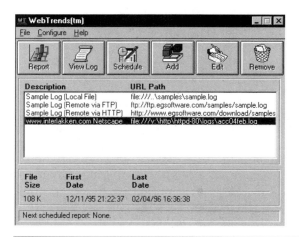

Figure 19.12 WebTrends Main Window

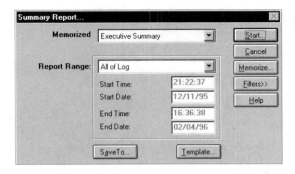

Figure 19.13 WebTrends Summary Report Dialog

Figures 19.14 and 19.15 show two sections of the WebTrends "Executive" report. Note the graphs generated as GIF files and the tabular presentation of statistics. The Schedule button in the main window can automatically recreate such pages every day, every week, whatever.

19.5 Saws and Axioms

This section presents a list of maxims the author has found to be almost universal in their applicability; they are yours for what they're worth:

- **Use the scientific method.** When confronted with a problem or failure, gather all available data, formulate possible explanations, design experiments to test the possibilities, and then refine or reject the hypotheses. This methodical approach is much more effective than making random changes until the problem goes away. If the problem becomes so repetitive the fix is obvious, apply the scientific method to determining why the problem keeps occurring.

- **Don't destroy the message.** This axiom first came to light for a server that occasionally died, displaying a message and a hex dump on the monitor. Operators learned they could "solve" the problem by pressing the system unit's Reset switch, but this, of course, destroyed the message and hex dump, making later diagnosis impossible.

  Don't reset a failed environment before gathering all possible information about it. Gather messages. Test all applications on the server, not just the failed one, to see what actually works and what doesn't. Test from the console; test over the network; test from several client workstations running different operating systems or versions.

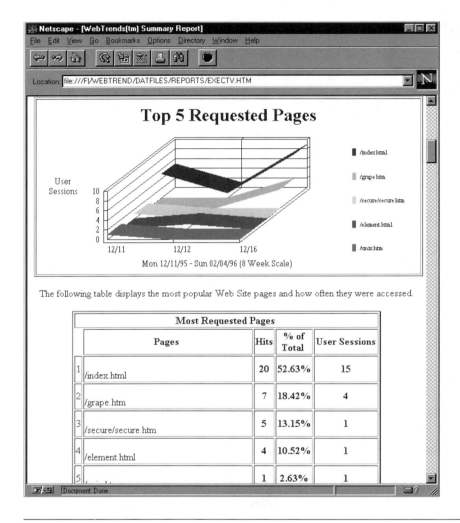

Figure 19.14 WebTrends Top Five Requested Pages

Convince yourself that time analyzing a system during failure is well spent. If you don't gather enough information to diagnose the problem, it will probably occur again.

- **Find the cause, not just the symptoms.** Reported problems are frequently only symptoms of the real problem. If users can't dial in, why not? If modems keep failing, why?

  Even seemingly clear messages can be misleading. A perfectly fine service may report it's out of memory because another service has a memory

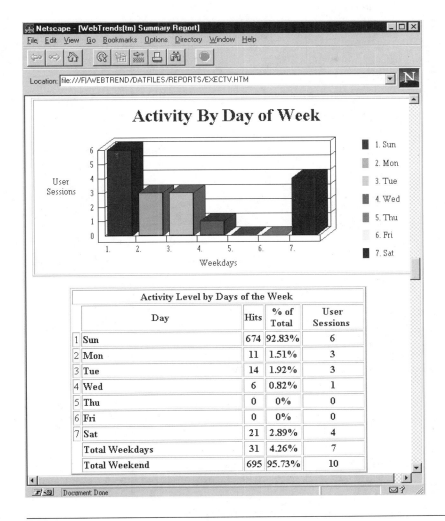

Figure 19.15 WebTrends Activity by Day of Week

leak. A tape drive may report I/O errors because a terminating resistor on hard disk zero has cracked. Read about the scientific method again.

- **Change only one thing at a time.** If you change one setting or component and get unexpected results, the cause is easy to determine. If you change two things at once, the cause of resulting problems is uncertain. Change one thing at a time.

     This advice applies to both scheduled changes and emergencies. If you resolve an emergency by making two changes at once, you won't really know what to do if the same problem occurs again.

- **Nobody changed anything—it's just different now.** A high percentage of problems are fallout from changes. If several people work on a site, you *must* develop a system for notifying everyone of every change—its nature, its timing, and who is responsible. If no one can explain how something got changed, you have an obvious procedural or security problem.

- **Testing is for babies. Not!** Test all changes before applying them to production systems and immediately after. Be sure to have a backout plan in case changes don't function as expected or cause unexpected problems.

    With a deadpan face, try reassuring people, "After all, what could possibly go wrong?" Observe their shocked expression and apply the same skepticism to your own work.

- **No one was ever sorry they had a backup (or a log).** After data gets destroyed is too late to realize your last backup is hopelessly outdated. Verify every day that scheduled backups ran as expected, and never do major work on a system without first checking backup status. Plan in advance what to do if a production disk, system unit, or network component fails.

    After a problem occurs is also too late to realize you forgot to activate logging. The result is a rather unpleasant, clueless sensation.

- **Technical elegance counts for nothing.** Customers, users, and management usually care about boring stuff like reliability, availability, and cost. Whether or not the internals of some process meet abstract technical standards matters little. Here's an interesting question: "If it's transparent to the user, why do it?"

- **You can always tell the pioneers; they've got the arrows stickin' in 'em.** Internet and personal computer technology are moving so fast that remaining behind technology to preserve stability usually isn't viable. However, installing new technology on the first day of availability is even riskier. If at all possible, wait at least two months after introduction before installing new versions of existing software and longer before installing new products. This at least gives technical support departments a chance to build up their problem databases. Meanwhile, watch the trade weeklies for reviews, problem reports, and war stories.

- **Some people aspire to greatness; others have it thrust upon them.** When new and wonderful products and technologies emerge, there will always be savage early adopters and belligerent proponents of the tried-and-true. A large, mildly skeptical, and somewhat apathetic middle group will be the largest contingent. Keep the needs of all these people in mind when considering new technology.

- **RAM is the universal antidote.** It's amazing how often adding memory solves computer-related problems. Lack of memory causes program lockups, excessive paging, timeouts, and related failures of many kinds. Recommendations change over time, but consider adding RAM to any lightly loaded Windows NT server with less than 32MB, or to any moderately loaded server with less than 64MB.

    Conversely, treat "out of memory" messages with suspicion. Lack of memory is such a common source of problems that some programmers report memory shortages whenever a specific cause isn't apparent.

- **Measure results but control inputs.** A common management technique involves setting and controlling service objectives. A common error is believing you can control outputs; you can't. You can only control inputs and processes. Excessive scrutiny and attention to outputs is counterproductive.

- **Control the activity, not the measurement.** If a voltmeter should read 115 volts but actually reads 108, one solution is to hold a magnet near the needle. If you hold the magnet in just the right place, the meter will read 115.

    Likewise, if you must reduce unscheduled outages, one approach is to categorize more outages as scheduled. Perhaps you can convert emergency reboots to scheduled outages by scheduling them 15 minutes in advance, for example. Not!

    If you find yourself or your site falling into this trap, review the immediately preceding maxim.

- **It's easier to get forgiveness than permission.** Don't agonize; make your best decision and act. Take control of the moment. When in doubt, get a second opinion.

- **You can never solve all your problems; you can only trade them for different ones.** Progress is evolutionary and never results in perfection. However, this is no reason to be discouraged. Strive to maximize benefits, limit drawbacks, and constantly adjust the operating environment to meet current requirements.

CHAPTER 20

Supporting Your Users

Despite all gains, connecting to an Internet service site and using it effectively still requires a careful assembly of properly configured, relatively complex hardware and software components. Your responsibility as a site operator is to make this easy for your users—easy enough to keep even relative neophytes from giving up and withdrawing their business.

20.1 Start-Up Documentation and Procedures

Once someone has decided to become a customer or user of your site, you should get them up and running as soon as possible (and certainly before they change their mind). If users enroll by telephone, try to accomplish the entire sign-up during the first call. This requires

- Getting the user's name, location, system type, and billing information.

- Setting up the user's account.

- Telling the user what user name and password to use.

- Agreeing on how the user will get setup instructions and any necessary software.

Unless you're operating in a corporate environment where all machines are the same, you'll need to develop instructions for several start-up scenarios. Each client operating system you support will require different software and instructions, for example.

Getting initial software and documentation to remote users can be a challenge. Mailing diskettes is a possibility, but most users would rather get up immediately, not in a day or two.

If the client's operating system includes SLIP or PPP support, you can refer the user to the operating system instructions for installing those options and make sure they know all the necessary phone numbers and access codes. If possible, transmit this information by FAX or download so that the new user doesn't have to call back for clarification.

Downloading files is a problem for users who don't already have SLIP or PPP software. If you support shell accounts, either through terminal servers or multi-serial-port software, users can download files using general asynchronous communication programs and protocols such as Xmodem, Ymodem, and Zmodem. Alternatively, you can distribute files using a conventional dial-up BBS system.

In a corporate LAN environment, the problem of how to download files should be nonexistent; users or local support analysts can install any required connectivity software over the network. Users who will dial into the corporate network from home and then access Internet applications can, given proper instructions, make their own floppies from sources on the LAN.

As to applications, you should at least identify a core set of supported applications for each platform and provide site-specific configuration instructions. For some applications, you can also provide preconfigured setup scripts that default to your site's host names.

Regardless of the setup procedures used, you should follow up on each new customer to make sure they're up and running to their satisfaction. At minimum, you should send them a "Welcome" E-Mail with "Read Receipt" and verify that you get the receipt. If you don't get the receipt within a day or so, you should contact the user by phone to see whether they're having difficulty.

20.2 Reference Documentation and FAQs

Your Web server provides the best way to publish tips, techniques, procedures, and general site information for your users. This is your most efficient means of distribution, and time spent preparing information this way is well worth the while. From a user standpoint, reference documentation and FAQs (Frequently Asked Questions) are then available at the click of a mouse 24 hours a day, 7 days a week.

The following is a list of information to consider publishing:

- Name, address, and ownership of your site.
- List of services provided and rates.
- Hours of operation and times reserved for scheduled maintenance.
- Policies on usage and content. Are any specific activities or content types prohibited? If so, what are the enforcement procedures and penalties?

- Legal statements. These describe the limits of liability you accept in return for providing access.
- Copies of all user start-up instructions.
- Names and IP addresses of hosts, DNS servers, and default gateways.
- List of supported and tested client applications.
- Instructions for acquiring and setting up client applications.
- Security and access procedures for user Web pages and user FTP directories.
- Telephone numbers and E-Mail addresses for technical support, problem reporting, billing, account changes, and so forth.
- List of recent changes.
- List of upcoming changes and planned outages.
- Pointers to other useful sites.

This list is far from mandatory; the nature of your site will greatly affect the information you publish. In addition, you'll undoubtedly publish and withdraw additional information as your site grows and matures.

20.3 Setting Expectations

Providing telephone or on-site technical support and user assistance can quickly become a no-win situation. The better support service you provide, the more your users will ask for. To resolve this dilemma, you must determine what level of support you can provide, promise that level to your users, and then consistently deliver it.

Your support commitment must, of course, be appropriate to your user base. It does no good to provide 8:00 A.M. to 5:00 P.M. support Monday through Friday if your customers mostly dial in evenings and weekends. Publish support times both you and your users can live with; then deliver consistently.

No site can keep its computers running forever. From time to time, you'll need to take systems down for hardware or software maintenance or upgrades. In addition, all operating systems gain stability from being rebooted on a periodic basis. Setting expectations for such outages is therefore another important policy. Choose an outage window that results in minimum user impact, publicize it, and provide a change notification for customers as well as site technicians.

Although you will probably choose not to provide 24-hour telephone support to individual users, you should have a notification and response plan for problems affecting the entire site. Be sure such planning includes a backup for yourself even if you're the site's only employee. For one thing, you'll eventually want a vacation or a day off. For another, some problems firmly resist solution by a single head. Finally, problems may arise at the end of a long day or simply take hours to resolve; when this happens, you need someone to take over in case of fatigue.

20.4 Good Surfing

The Web has come incredibly far in its first few years of existence—it's truly been a short, strange, incredibly exciting journey for everyone involved. That journey now includes you and your users.

The power of low-cost, rapid, one-to-many communication is now evident everywhere on the globe. The Web is certainly a new medium—vastly different from radio, television, telephone, and print—a medium available to everyone for both publishing and discovery. There can be no doubt that everything up to now is only a tiny fraction of what will come, and that among the torrent will be things we can't today begin to imagine.

Your role as a service provider is much more than unboxing computers, installing software, and stringing wires. You must be the enabling force, the visionary, the catapult for your users and employees. You will help invent whatever the Web will become. You may or may not get rich, but you and your users can certainly be famous (worldwide, no less). You both can certainly make a difference.

So, good luck in your pursuits. I hope you love a wild ride, because this new technology and new medium won't be slowing down any time soon.

Supplier List

The following list consists mostly of companies supplying products mentioned in the text; several other related and equally worthy products appear as well. The product categories given for each supplier are those that apply to this book; there is no attempt to list unrelated products.

There is no attempt to be comprehensive or to rate products against one another. Including such a list is impossible given the volatility of the Internet market and the lead times involved in publishing books.

Contact information was current at the time of authoring. In most cases, telephone numbers, FAX numbers, and E-Mail addresses are for product sales and information. Consult a supplier's Web site or your documentation for technical support.

■ 3Com   Network components
  5400 Bayfront Plaza
  PO Box 58145
  Santa Clara, CA 95052-8145
  Voice: (800) NET-3COM
  FAX: (408) 764-6740
  Web: http://www.3com.com/
  E-Mail: (many)

■ Apple Computer, Inc.   MacTCP
  1 Infinite Loop
  Cupertino, CA 95014
  Voice: (800) 776-2333
  FAX: (408) 974-9994
  Web: http://www.apple.com/
  E-Mail: (many)

■ **Arcada Software, Inc.**   Backup software
37 Skyline Drive, Bldg. 1101
Lake Mary, FL 32746
Voice: (800) 3ARCADA
FAX: (407) 333-7770
Web: http://www.arcada.com/
E-Mail: sales@arcada.com

■ **Ascend Communications, Inc.**   Routers
1275 Harbor Bay Parkway
Alameda, CA 94502
Voice: (800) 621-9578
FAX: (415) 688-4343
Web: http://www.ascend.com/
E-Mail: info@ascend.com

■ **Ashmount Research**   NSLOOKUP for Windows
9-10 Southampton Place
London WC1A 2EA, UK
Voice: +44-171-831-4000
FAX: +44-171-831-4400
Web: http://www.ashmount.com/
E-Mail: enquiries@ashmount.demon.co.uk

■ **Aspect Software Engineering, Inc.**   dbWeb Database Interface
2800 Woodlawn Drive, Suite 250
Honolulu, HI 96822
Voice: (808) 539-3782
FAX: (808) 539-3785
Web: http://www.aspectse.com
E-Mail: info@aspectse.com

■ **ATI Technologies, Inc.**   Graphics adapters
33 Commerce Valley Drive East
Thornhill, Ontario, Canada L3T 7N6
Voice: (905) 882-2600
FAX: (905) 882-2620
Web: http://www.atitech.ca/
E-Mail: sales@atitech.ca

■ **Attachmate Corporation**
3617 131st Ave. S.E.
Bellevue, WA 98006
Voice: (800) 426-6283
FAX: (206) 747-9924
Web: http://www.attachmate.com/
E-Mail: support@attachmate.com

Crosstalk for Windows
SLIP, PPP, TCP/IP software
   for PCs and Macintoshes

■ **Banyan Systems, Inc.**
120 Flanders Road
Westboro, MA 01581
Voice: (508) 898-1000
FAX: (508) 898-1755
Web: http://www.banyan.com/
E-Mail: www@banyan.com

LAN and TCP/IP software

■ **Castle Rock Computing**
20863 Stevens Creek Blvd., Suite 530
Cupertino, CA 95014
Voice: (408) 366-6540
FAX: (408) 252-2379
Web: http://www.castlerock.com/
E-Mail: sales@castlerock.com

SNMPc

■ **Cheyenne Software, Inc.**
3 Expressway Plaza
Roslyn Heights, NY 11577
Voice: (800) 243-9462
FAX: (516) 484-2489
Web: http://www.cheyenne.com
E-Mail: sales@cheyenne.com

ARCserve

■ **Cisco Systems, Inc.**
170 West Tasman Drive
San Jose, CA 95134-1706
Voice: (800) 859-2726
FAX: (408) 526-4100
Web: http://www.cisco.com/
E-Mail: cs-rep@cisco.com

Routers
Network components

■ **Coffler, Jeff**   NNS
                                                       Windows NT News server
   Web: http://www.ensta.fr/internet/windows_nt/news/NNS.html
   FTP: ftp://ftp.wa.com/local/ntnews/
   E-Mail: nns@jeck.wa.com

■**Compaq Computer Corporation**   Servers and PCs
   20555 SH 249
   Houston, TX 77070
   Voice: (800) 567-1616
   FAX: (713) 514-1740
   Web: http://www.compaq.com/
   E-Mail: (many)

■ **Conner Peripherals, Inc.**   Disks
   1650 Sunflower Avenue   Tape drives
   Costa Mesa, CA 92626   Backup software
   Voice: (800) 6-CONNER
   FAX: (714) 641-2590
   Web: http://www.conner.com/
   E-Mail: webmaster@conner.com

■ **Digi International**   Multi-serial-port adapters
   6400 Flying Cloud Drive   ISDN adapters
   Eden Prairie, MN 55344
   Voice: (800) 344-4273
   FAX: (612) 943-5398
   Web: http://www.digiboard.com
   E-Mail: sales@digibd.com

■ **e.g. Software, Inc.**   WebTrends HTTP
   319 SW Washington, Suite 706   Log Analyzer
   Portland, OR 97204
   Voice: (503) 294-7025
   FAX: (503) 294-7130
   Web: http://www.egsoftware.com/
   E-Mail: info@egSoftware.com

■ **EMWAC Computing Services**
30-38 George Square
Edinburgh EH8 9LJ, UK
Voice: +44-131-650-6565
FAX: +44-131-650-6464
Web: http://www.emwac.ed.ac.uk/
E-Mail: emwac@ed.ac.uk

Internet Toolchest

■ **Exabyte Corporation**
1685 38th Street
Boulder, CO 80301
Voice: (800) 392-2983
FAX: (303) 417-5500
Web: http://www.Exabyte.com/
E-Mail: sales@exabyte.com

Tape drives and accessories

■ **Frontier Technologies**
10201 North Port Washington Road
Mequon, WI 53092
Voice: (800) 929-3054
FAX: (414) 241-7084
Web: http://www.frontiertech.com
E-Mail: Info@Frontiertech.com

CyberJunction (Windows
    NT-based IPX to TCP/IP
    gateway)
TCP/IP applications

■ **Gandalf Technologies, Inc.**
130 Colonnade Road South
Nepean, Ontario, Canada
K2E 7M4
Voice: (800) GANDALF
FAX: (613) 274-6501
Web: http://www.Gandalf.ca/
E-Mail: http://www.gandalf.ca/contact/contact.html

ISDN Adapters

■ **Hewlett -Packard**
3000 Hanover Street
Palo Alto, CA 94304
Voice: 800-752-0900
FAX: (many)
Web: http://www.hp.com/
E-Mail: (many)

PCs, servers, and peripherals
UNIX workstations
Network components

■ **IBM**
Armonk, NY 10504
Voice: (800) IBM-3333
FAX: (many)
Web: http://www.ibm.com/
E-Mail: askibm@info.ibm.com

PCs, servers, and peripherals
UNIX workstations
Network components

■ **InterCon Systems Corporation**
950 Herndon Parkway
Herndon, VA 22070
Voice: (800) 468-7266
FAX: (703) 709-5555
Web: http://www.intercon.com/
E-Mail: sales@intercon.com

TCP/IP software
SLIP for Macintosh

■ **Internet Shopper Ltd.**
PO Box 6064
London SW12 9XG, UK
FAX: +44-181-673-2149
Web: http://www.net-shopper.co.uk/
E-Mail: ntmail-sales@net-shopper.co.uk

NTMail SMTP server

■ **Ipswitch, Inc.**
81 Hartwell Avenue
Lexington, MA 02173
Voice: (617) 676-5700
FAX: (617) 676-5710
Web: http://www.ipswitch.com
E-Mail: info@.ipswitch.com

IMail SMTP server

■ **L-Soft International, Inc.**
8401 Corporate Drive, Suite 380
Landover, MD 20785
Voice: (800) 399-5449
FAX: (301) 731-6302
Web: http://www.lsoft.com/listserv.html
E-Mail: sales@lsoft.com

LISTSERV

■ **MetaInfo, Inc.**   MetaInfo DNS
700 5th Ave., Suite 5500
Seattle, WA 98104
Voice: (206) 521-2600
FAX: (206) 467-9237
Web: http://www.metainfo.com/
E-Mail: info@metainfo.com
    dns-info@metainfo.com

■ **Microcom, Inc.**   Modems
500 River Ridge Drive   ISDN adapters
Norwood, MA 02062   Remote access software
Voice: (800) 822-8224
FAX: (617) 551-1021
Web: http://www.microcom.com/
E-Mail: (Choose "Contact Us" from Web page.)

■ **Microsoft Corporation**   Operating systems
One Microsoft Way   Productivity applications
Redmond, WA 98052-6399   Server applications
Voice: (800) 426-9400
FAX: (many)
Web: http://www.microsoft.com
E-Mail: (many)

■ **NetManage, Inc.**   TCP/IP applications
10725 North De Anza Blvd.
Cupertino, CA 95014
Voice: (408) 973-7171
FAX: (408) 257-6405
Web: http://www.netmanage.com/
E-Mail: sales@netmanage.com

■ **Netscape Communications Corporation** Web browsers and servers
501 E. Middlefield Road
Mountain View, CA 94043
Voice: (415) 528-2555
FAX: (415) 528-4124
Web: http://www.netscape.com/
E-Mail: info@netscape.com

■ **NetWin World**   DNEWS
PO Box 27574
Mt. Roskill
Aukland, New Zealand
Voice: +64-9636-7784
FAX: +64-9636-7784
Web: http://world.std.com/~netwin
E-Mail: netwin@world.std.com

■ **Novell, Inc.**   Netware
1555 North Technology Way
Orem, UT 84057
Voice: (801) 429-7000
FAX: (801) 429-5555
Web: http://www.novell.com
E-Mail: (many)

■ **O'Reilly & Associates**   WebSite
103A Morris Street
Sebastopol, CA 95472
Voice: (800) 998-9938
FAX: (707) 829-0104
Web: http://website.ora.com/
E-Mail: website@ora.com

■ **Pedro Mendes**   BLAT
Institute of Biological Sciences
University of Wales, Aberystwyth
Dyfed SY23 3DA, UK
FAX: +44-(0)-1970-622350
Web: http://gepasi.dbs.aber.ac.uk/pedro/prmhome.htm
E-Mail: prm@aber.ac.uk

■ **Performance Systems Intl.**   Internet services
(PSINet), Inc.
510 Huntmar Park Drive
Herndon, VA 22070
Voice: (800) 827-7482
FAX: (800) 329-7741
Web: http://www.psi.net
E-Mail: info@psi.com

■ **Process Software Corporation**   Purveyor HTTP server
959 Concord Street
Framingham, MA 01701
Voice: (800) 722-7770
FAX: (508) 879-0042
Web: http://www.process.com
E-Mail: sales@process.com

■ **QMS, Inc.**   Printers
One Magnum Pass
Mobile, AL 36618
Voice: (800) 523-2696
FAX: (many)
Web: http://www.qms.com
E-Mail: info@qms.com

■ **QUALCOMM**   Eudora Light
6455 Lusk Boulevard
San Diego, CA 92121-2779
Voice: (619) 587-1121
FAX: (619) 658-2100
Web: http://www.qualcomm.com
E-Mail: www-quest@qualcomm.com

■ **Quarterdeck Corporation**   IWareConnect
13160 Mindanao Way, 3rd Floor   (NLM TCP/IP gateway)
Marina Del Rey, CA 90292-9705
Voice: (310) 309-3700
FAX: (310) 309-4217
Web: http://www.quarterdeck.com/
E-Mail: info@quarterdeck.com

■ **RSA Data Security, Inc.**   Data security
100 Marine Parkway
Redwood City, CA 94065-1031
Voice: (415) 595-8782
FAX: (415) 595-1873
Web: http://www.rsa.com/
E-Mail: sales@rsa.com

■ **Software.com**
827 State Street
Santa Barbara, CA 93101
Voice: (805) 882-2470
FAX: (805) 882-2470
Web: http://www.software.com
E-Mail: info@software.com

post.office SNMP Mail server

■ **Sun Microsystems, Inc.**
2550 Garcia Avenue
Mountain View, CA 94043
Voice: (800) 821-4643
FAX: (many)
Web: http://www.sun.com
E-Mail: (many)

UNIX Workstations
Network management
Java language

■ **Xyplex, Inc.**
295 Foster Street
Littleton, MA 01460
Voice: (800) 338-5316
FAX: (508) 952-4702
Web: http://www.xyplex.com
E-Mail: info@xyplex.com

Dial-in com servers
Network components

HTML Fundamentals, Structure, and Syntax

HyperText Markup Language is a strange beast indeed. Designed as a simple, portable page description language, enhancements now appear almost daily as browser suppliers and Web page authors strain against HTML's limitations in pursuit of artistic advantage. Standards bodies are hopeless to match the pace.

The earliest use of HTML was for publishing scientific and technical papers. The structure of such documents is relatively simple—a few basic styles of text organized hierarchically into sections and chapters. The inventors of HTML therefore standardized on a handful of paragraph formats, six levels of headings, and a few simple constructs such as bulleted and numbered lists. Hypertext links provided document navigation. Tables, which appear frequently in paper versions of such documents, were a surprising omission.

As HTML has come into wider use, so has the desire for the more artistic elements of page design. Browser suppliers address this demand with an ever-increasing collection of formatting commands — commands that other browsers will ignore or handle differently. A second approach is presenting large page areas as bitmapped images. Bitmaps can deliver any desired appearance, but they can dramatically increase the time required to deliver a page.

Presenting every detail of HTML is a thankless and impossible task. Some documented features are already obsolete, and others will appear in the time before you read this. Eventually, HTML will become too complex for anyone to design by hand; hand-editing HTML will become as rare and difficult as creating PostScript.

This appendix provides a quick, elementary reference to HTML via Tables B.1 through B.8. For information on HTML forms, see Section 16.2.1. For information on HTML tables, see Section 16.2.2. If you need more detail, consult one of the many comprehensive HTML books or the following Web locations:

- **HyperText Markup Language 2.0 (RFC 1866)**
  ftp://ds.internic.net/rfc/rfc1866.txt
- **HyperText Markup Language Specification Version 3.0**
  http://www.w3.org/hypertext/WWW/MarkUp/html3/CoverPage.html
- **Netscape Extensions to HTML 2.0**
  http://www.netscape.com/assist/net_sites/html_extensions.html
- **Netscape Extensions to HTML 3.0**
  http://www.netscape.com/assist/net_sites/html_extensions_3.html
- **Microsoft HTML Extensions**
  http://www.microsoft.com/windows/ie/ie20html.htm
- **NCSA Beginner's Guide to HTML**
  http://www.ncsa.uiuc.edu/demoweb/html-primer.html
- **NCSA HTML Index**
  http://union.ncsa.uiuc.edu/HyperNews/get/www/html/code-index.html
- **Yahoo Computers and Internet:Internet:World Wide Web:HTML Editors**
  http://www.yahoo.com/Computers_and_Internet/Internet/World_Wide_Web/HTML_Editors/

Table B.1 HTML Structural Tags

Tag	Description
<HTML> </HTML>	Defines the beginning and end of an HTML document.
<HEAD> </HEAD>	Defines the head of an HTML document.
<BODY> </BODY>	Defines the body of an HTML document.

Table B.2 HTML Header Tags

Tag	Description
<!--text-->	Treats "text" as comments.
<BASE>	The file name that contains the current document.
<ISINDEX>	Specifies the page should accept user keywords for searching an index.
<LINK ATTRIBUTE>	Specifies a relationship to another document.
REV=relationship	The type of relationship.
HREF="URL"	The URL of the related file.
<META>	Identifies special information about a document.
HTTP-EQUIV="field"	Equates the element to an HTTP header field.
NAME="name"	Gives the element a name. If absent, the HTTP-EQUIV name applies.
CONTENT="value"	Specifies the element value.
<TITLE> </TITLE>	Denotes the title of a document. Browsers display the enclosed text outside the normal document area.

Table B.3 HTML Heading Style Tags

Tag	Description
<H1> </H1>	Displays enclosed text in the most prominent header style.
<H2> </H2>	Displays enclosed text in a less prominent style.
<H3> </H3>	Displays enclosed text in a less prominent style.
<H4> </H4>	Displays enclosed text in a less prominent style.
<H5> </H5>	Displays enclosed text in a less prominent style.
<H6> </H6>	Displays enclosed text in the least prominent header style.
<HR>	Horizontal rule.

Table B.4 HTML Paragraph Style Tags

Tag	Description
<P> </P>	Indicates the beginning and end of a paragraph. Use of </P> is rare given today's browers.
 	Line break (within paragraph).
<ADDRESS> </ADDRESS>	Displays enclosed text in a special format reserved for addresses (usually italic).
<BLOCKQUOTE> </BLOCKQUOTE>	Defines enclosed text as quoted from another source. Indents the left and right margins.
<PRE> </PRE>	Marks text displayed in a monospaced font. Line endings and multiple spaces are significant.

Table B.5 HTML List Element Tags

Tag	Description	Nesting Allowed
<UL> </UL>	Denotes the beginning and end of an unordered (bulleted) list.	Yes
<OL> </OL>	Denotes the beginning and end of an ordered (numbered) list.	Yes
<DIR> </DIR>	Marks a directory list of items (bulleted with multiple items on a line).	No
<MENU> </MENU>	Displays a menu of items. Similar to <UL> but more compact.	No
<LI>	Denotes the beginning of an item in a list.	
<DL> </DL>	Marks the beginning and end of a definition list.	
<DT>	Marks the beginning of a defined term; terminated by <DD>.	
<DD>	Marks the beginning of a definition; terminated by <DT> or </DL>.	

Table B.6 HTML Phrase Style Tags

Tag	Description
\<B\> \</B\>	Makes text bold.
\<CITE\> \</CITE\>	Indicates a citation from other material.
\<CODE\> \</CODE\>	Displays intervening text as a code fragment.
\<EM\> \</EM\>	Displays text with emphasis.
\<I\> \</I\>	Italicizes intervening text.
\<KBD\> \</KBD\>	Denotes text as keyboard characters.
\<SAMP\> \</SAMP\>	Marks text as sample output.
\<STRONG\> \</STRONG\>	Marks text for strong emphasis.
\<TT\> \</TT\>	Specifies a teletype (monospaced) font.
\<U\> \</U\>	Underlines intervening text.
\<VAR\> \</VAR\>	Indicates a placeholder variable.

Table B.7 HTML Anchor Tag Attributes (\<A "attributes"\> ... \</A\>)

Attribute	Description
HREF="#anchor_name"	Links this to anchor_name within this document.
HREF="URL"	Links this to URL.
HREF="URL#anchor_name"	Links this to anchor_name within URL.
HREF="URL?search_string"	Links this to search for search_string within URL.
NAME="anchor_name"	Defines an anchor at this spot.
TITLE="title"	Suggests a title for the destination resource.
METHODS="list"	Specifies a list of methods the client may use to access the destination.

Table B.8 HTML Image Tag Attributes (<IMG "attributes">)

Attribute	Description
SRC="URL"	Specifies the source (location) of the image.
ALIGN=	Aligns the image relative to the text baseline.
"TOP"	The top of the image aligns with the tallest other item in the same line.
"MIDDLE"	The center of the image aligns with the baseline of the line it occupies.
"BOTTOM"	The bottom of the image aligns with the baseline of the line it occupies.
ALT="text"	Text to use in place of the image, if necessary.
ISMAP	Indicates an active image map.

Archieving Fame and Glory

Building a capable and reliable Internet site is no guarantee of success; success ultimately depends on usage. Driving up usage requires identifying, attracting, and retaining users. This is equally true whether you're a publisher looking for people to receive your message or a provider looking for clients who wish to publish.

C.1 Developing Attractive Services and Image

The needs of your target market should drive the nature of the services you provide and the sales image you convey. These are decisions only you can make, and you must decide them in light of your mission or business plan. The point is to make such decisions deliberately and intelligently.

In an immediate sense, the people you most need to attract are those paying your bills: the subscribers or budget authorities who provide your cash. Some ways they'll judge your service include

- Direct personal experience, such as whether services are always available and exhibit consistent, acceptable performance.
- Usage statistics, such as Web hits, E-Mail message counts, and FTP download counts.
- Transaction counts, such as number and value of orders received.
- Anecdotal evidence, such as feedback they receive from customers, correspondents, and other users.

In addition to providing good access to paying customers, an Internet site must provide equally good but free access to every other user on the Internet. Access to and from other Internet users is generally the incentive for local users to sign up, remain, and keep paying.

The roles of content provider and service provider are distinct but closely related. *Content providers* seek an audience and a means of transmission to reach it. *Service providers* establish transmission facilities for resale to content providers. The role of service provider might at first seem entirely technical, but consider the case of commercial television; stations use expensive entertainment content to attract audiences for commercials. Internet search engines use the same concept; they attract users with popular free content so that they can sell transmission of unwanted, unrelated content (advertising).

If you're a content provider, the better you publicize your site and appeal to your audience's interest, the more successful you will be. As a service provider, your success depends on the success of your clients.

C.2 Getting Listed on Internet Search Engines

Services like Yahoo, Lycos, and WebCrawler provide one of the best ways for users to find content on the World Wide Web. Getting your site or your client's home page listed on these services is therefore a great way to attract interested viewers.

Services like Lycos and WebCrawler index content by starting with a relatively small list of "seed" URLs. The search engine gets these URLs, scans them to extract the text, and then stores text words in a large database. During the same scan, the search engine also detects URLs and (if they're not duplicates) adds them to the scan queue. This process continues until there are no more URLs to scan—that is, until the database provides keyword indexing to several million Web pages.

A surprising amount of the Web gets indexed automatically. If even one indexed page points to a page on your site, and if that page contains a pointer to your site's home page, then everything within your site's home menu tree will also get indexed.

Knowing this, you can ensure your entire site gets indexed by providing a menu structure that includes every page and by getting the main menu page listed as a seed. For this to work, however, you must not "break the chain." Search engines can't locate pages generated by CGI programs or referenced only on CGI-generated menus. This doesn't mean you should avoid CGI-generated menus; it just means you should provide additional seed pages or menus for any such pages you want indexed.

Other services, like Yahoo, require manual identification of each page indexed; this is less comprehensive but potentially more accurate (since someone manually prepares each entry and someone else reviews it):

- To add a site to Yahoo (www.yahoo.com), position to the page (such as "Computers and Internet:Internet:Internet Resources") that should index the new site and then click the "Add URL" icon at the top of the page.

- To add a site to Lycos (www.lycos.com), click the "Add Your Site" icon on the main page.

- To add a site to WebCrawler (www.webcrawler.com), click "Submit URLs" on the main page.

- To add a site to several search engines at once, browse the "Submit It!" site (http://www.submit-it.com).

C.3 Getting Links from Other Sites

If you'd like a pointer from another site to yours, don't be bashful. Simply send a message to the other site's webmaster and ask for a link. Most sites have a "webmaster" hypertext link on their home page for just such purposes. If another site asks for a listing on yours, ask the requesting site to list yours as well.

Don't be too hard on a site that doesn't provide reciprocal listings. If you maintain a jump page of products in a particular category, for example, suppliers who request a listing may understandably resist pointers on their site that direct customers to competing products. Some commercial sites also have policies against off-site pointers because other sites may, over time, add material they can't condone.

C.4 Headers, Addresses, and URLs

Every appearance of your domain name is a miniature advertisement. This includes the domain part of E-Mail addresses, your Web site address, SMTP headers, News headers, and so on. Don't overlook any opportunity to configure servers and clients to plaster your domain name around the Internet.

Signature files appended to E-Mail messages and News postings are another opportunity for publicity. Keep the length of your signature file down to a few lines, though, or you'll discover an in-box clogged with complaints.

C.5 Creating Awareness in Newsgroups

Various USENET newsgroups containing the word "announce" in their names exist solely for announcements. Consider posting to these newsgroups when you start a new site, virtual domain, or interest area. If the newsgroup doesn't allow direct posting, locate the required procedure in the newsgroup's FAQ.

Provided you have the time and knowledge, regular posting to a newsgroup can build worldwide recognition for yourself and your site. Who knows: This may even lead to magazine interviews, featured site listings, and book deals with major publishers. Stranger things have happened.

C.6 Monitoring Activity and Feedback

To avoid working and planning in a vacuum, you should develop indicators of interest and activity. Transaction counts from logs are certainly one source of data, but don't overlook other, less quantitative measures, such as the volume and nature of E-Mail you receive on a topic, follow-ons to your newsgroup postings, and telephone calls.

Content providers in particular need feedback to see which topics are popular, which are "working," and which aren't. As a service provider, you need to provide transaction counts for any client that wants them and copies of any feedback you receive regarding a client's content. Don't dismiss poor response to a content provider's material as not your problem; if the client's results don't improve, you will lose a paying customer.

APPENDIX D

Legal Issues

A number of serious legal issues confront Internet site operators. Watchdog groups, copyright owners, and the courts are concerned about improper distribution of information and other Internet crimes.

Watchdog groups and copyright owners usually attack service providers rather than originators. Service providers are easier (and more profitable) to attack than individuals who originate the questionable material; in addition, originators may be located overseas or may conceal their identity by using anonymous sites.

This appendix isn't an authoritative source of legal advice. The author is no lawyer. Nevertheless, Internet site operators need at least an awareness of what the issues are.

D.1 Legal Status—Service Provider or Publisher?

When illegal material passes through your site, someone is obviously liable. If the Internet site is a publisher of information, the site may be guilty of publishing material illegally. This is analogous to publishing false, stolen, or improper information in a book, magazine, newspaper, or telecast; the publisher has editorial responsibility even though the information came from outside sources.

Service providers, by contrast, aren't liable for every shred of information they handle. Telephone companies, the post office, and bookstores, for example, can't be sued for transmitting illegal material unless they knew or should have known the material or its transmission was illegal. Privacy laws may actually prevent service providers from detecting illegal activity.

In general, the more control you exert over the content of your site, the more you appear like a publisher and the more liable for illegal content you may be (even for material you choose not to review). The difficulty of reviewing all material passing through a site has led many operators to the conclusion they should exert no control over content at all.

Note that adopting a service provider stance is no basis for complacency. You can still be prosecuted for illegal acts you knew of or should have known of. Unfortunately, there is little guidance as to what means you should employ to learn of illegal acts.

D.2 Private versus Public Sites

Owners of privately held sites, such as informational Web servers run by corporations and government agencies, typically control content stringently and are obviously information publishers. Based on their corporate and site charter, they can strictly control the information posted without violating freedom of speech. In fact, stockholders or auditors may construe support of activities outside the organization's line of business as misuse of funds.

Public sites that offer service to anyone willing to pay the monthly rate are in quite a different position. For such sites to closely monitor their subscribers' activities may violate freedom of speech. The same may apply to restricting the activities of one interest group while permitting or encouraging others.

D.3 Location Issues

Geographic location is usually irrelevant on the Internet but highly relevant to the application of law. This leads to difficult problems when Internet activity is legal at one end of a connection but not at the other. If a file is illegal in location A and someone downloads it from location B (where it's legal), where did the crime occur? One interpretation holds the provider blameless because location A has no jurisdiction in the provider's location. Another viewpoint finds the provider guilty of transporting contraband across state or national borders. A third view sees the transaction as interstate commerce to which only federal or international laws apply.

Issues of this type usually involve sexually explicit materials, but other possibilities abound. Consider the possibility of off-shore gambling servers, for example, or electronic sale of lottery tickets across state lines.

Few courts seem inclined to absolve Internet and BBS sites of all responsibility simply because they operate across jurisdictions.

D.4 Types of Objectionable Materials

Opinion varies greatly on the nature of materials whose transmission may be improper. The following types appear questionable in at least some cases:

- Copyrighted material distributed without permission.
- Defamatory and libelous material.
- Explicit sexual material.
- Gambling transactions.
- Government-classified materials.
- Heavily encrypted data.
- Inflammatory or politically incorrect material.
- Material used in the planning or execution of a crime.
- Terrorist material.
- Trade secrets.

The issue with heavily encrypted data is this: Law-enforcement bodies object to any encryption they can't crack. They feel strong encryption interferes with their right—awarded by the courts—to wiretap electronic communication.

If you become aware of illegal material passing through your site, you should take action to halt it. As to what means and what level of scrutiny are appropriate for detecting illegal materials, however, your responsibilities are much less clear. At the very least, review exceptional activity that appears in activity logs.

If you're running a public site, you may want your user service contract to address liability for storing and transmitting illegal materials. That is, you may insist that each new user sign an agreement that liability for any illegal activities they engage in falls solely on them. Make sure, however, that such a clause doesn't prevent you from detecting, halting, or interfering with illegal activities.

D.5 Copyrights and Patents

The author of a work copyrights it simply by including a standard copyright statement. A copyright protects the specific expression of an idea but not the idea itself. There is no infringement if copyrighted work is sufficiently restated or reworked.[1]

---

[1]The author once received the advice, "If you steal from one source, it's plagiarism. If you steal from many, it's research."

If a copyright owner reserves exclusive rights of duplication and distribution, then for someone else to do so is a crime. Copying files from diskettes and zipping them up is not sufficient rework to avoid legalities. Reverse-engineering of software (writing new code that produces all the same results from all the same inputs), however, is legal. You can copy the behavior but not the code.

Patents protect ideas regardless of expression but are much harder to obtain; the inventor must prove the idea is new and register it with the government's patent office. Information supplied to obtain patents becomes public knowledge—a further deterrent if the inventor prefers to retain some information as trade secrets.

Patents have been rare in the personal computer industry for several reasons. First, patents can take a long time to secure and products may be obsolete before the patent comes through. Second, patents guarantee inventors a single-source market; this leads to resistance from buyers who demand competitive products to choose from. Finally, the PC industry tends to advance by having products imitate and improve on one another, and patents interfere with this process.

As a site operator, you must honor the copyrights of others by not publishing copyrighted materials yourself and by taking normal measures to prevent copyright abuse by users and public Internet users. In addition, you may wish to copyright material you publish yourself (such as site documentation or your own site's Web pages).

D.6 Guardianship of Client Data

If you provide electronic storage for materials belonging to others, you may be liable if those materials become lost or damaged. Users who pay to have HTML pages professionally authored, for example, will not be amused if their only copy gets destroyed in a hard-disk crash and you don't have a backup. This is another issue you should address in your service contract, perhaps making users solely responsible for restoring lost content. This doesn't mean you can abandon your backup plan or best efforts at restoral, though. Even if they can't sue you, unhappy users will surely take their business elsewhere.

A similar issue arises in the case of abandoned data—data no one has accessed for a long period of time or data belonging to users whose accounts lapse. Your service contract should spell out your rights to purge abandoned data without recourse from the user. Don't purge data without warning, though. State your purge policy publicly and, if possible, notify users in advance of any data you plan to delete.

D.7 Limits of Liability

Your user service contract should clearly indicate the limits of your liability in case of service interruptions, loss of client data, accidental disclosure of client data, and accidental disclosure of false, corrupted, or illegal data involving a client. If a client loses a million-dollar deal because your E-Mail server was down, you don't want him or her suing you for a million dollars in damages.

If possible, you should limit your liability to billing value—that is, to the amount the client originally agreed to pay for the service.

APPENDIX E

About the CD-ROM

\BLAT	Freeware command line mailer for Windows NT.
\DNEWS	DNEWS News Server for Windows NT (demo version).
\EUDORA	Freeware Eudora Lite E-Mail client from QUALCOMM, Inc.
\GO4MAINT	Gopher Maintenance Utility (for EMWAC Gopher Aliases).
\GSI386	EMWAC Gopher Server.
\HSI386	EMWAC HTTP Server.
\HTTP	Sample HTML files.
\IIS	Microsoft Internet Information Server.
\LISTSERV	LISTSERV E-Mail List server from L-Soft International. Obtain temporary key from www.lsoft.com.
\MAPTHIS	Map This! Image Map Editor. Freeware from Molly Penguin Software.
\METAINFO	Metainfo DNS 1.2 (demo version). Obtain temporary key from www.metainfo.com.
\NSLOOKUP	NSLOOKUP for Windows, from Ashmount Research (DNS diagnostic client).
\NTMAIL	NTMail SNMP Server and Listserver. Obtain temporary key from www.net-shopper.co.uk.
\SCRIPTS	Sample perl programs, Image Map files, Internet Database Connector (.idc) files, and HTML Extension (.htx) files.
\WEBSITE	O'Reilly WebSite 1.1 demonstration. Expires 60 days after installation.
\WEBTREND	WebTrends HTTP Log Analyzer (demo version from e.g. Software).
\WSI386	EMWAC WAIS Server.
\WTI386	EMWAC WAIS Toolkit.

Bibliography and References

Bean, Greg. *Internet Server Construction Kit for Windows*. New York: John Wiley & Sons, 1995.

Bradner, Scott O., and Allison Mankin, eds. *IPng Internet Protocol Next Generation*. Reading, Mass.: Addison-Wesley, 1996.

Chandler, David. *Running a Perfect Web Site*. Indianapolis, Ind.: Que., 1995.

Cheswick, William R., and Steven M. Bellovin. *Firewalls and Internet Security*. Reading, Mass.: Addison-Wesley, 1994.

Custer, Helen. *Inside Windows NT*. Redmond, Wash.: Microsoft Press, 1993.

December, John. *Presenting Java*. Indianapolis, Ind.: Sams.net, 1995.

Gilster, Paul. *The SLIP/PPP Connection*. New York: John Wiley & Sons, 1995.

Harper, Eric, Matt Arnett, and R. Paul Singh. *Building a Windows NT Internet Server*. Indianapolis, Ind.: New Riders Publishing, 1995.

Hunt, Craig. *TCP/IP Network Administration*. Sebastopol, Calif.: O'Reilly & Associates, 1992.

Hunt, Craig. *Networking Personal Computers with TCP/IP*. Sebastopol, Calif.: O'Reilly & Associates, 1995.

Liu, Cricket, Jerry Peek, Russ Jones, Bryan Buus, and Adrian Nye. *Managing Internet Information Services*. Sebastopol, Calif.: O'Reilly & Associates, 1994.

Marid, Johnathan R., Douglas Matthews, and Paul Jones. *The Web Server Book*. Chapel Hill, N.C.: Ventana Press, 1995.

Minasi, Mark, Christa Anderson, and Elizabeth Creegan. *Mastering Windows NT Server 3.5*. Alameda, Calif.: SYBEX, 1995.

net.Genesis, and Devra Hall. *Build a Web Site*. Rocklin, Calif.: Prima Publishing, 1995.

O'Reilly, Tim, and Grace Todina. *Managing uucp and Usenet.* Sebastopol, Calif.: O'Reilly & Associates, 1992.

Quarterman, John S., and Smoot Carl-Mitchell. *The Internet Connection—System Connectivity and Configuration.* Reading, Mass.: Addison-Wesley, 1994.

Schwartz, Randal L. *Learning Perl.* Sebastopol, Calif.: O'Reilly & Associates, 1993.

Sheldon, Ted, ed. *LAN Times Guide to Interoperability.* Berkeley, Calif.: Osborne McGraw-Hill, 1994.

Singh, Paul, Rick Fairweather, and Dan Laderman. *Connecting Netware to the Internet.* Indianapolis, Ind.: New Riders Publishing, 1995.

Wall, Larry, and Randal L. Schwartz. *Programming perl.* Sebastopol, Calif.: O'Reilly & Associates, 1991.

Glossary

ACK Acknowledgment—A packet or other network signal confirming that data has successfully arrived.

ACL Access Control List—A set of rules governing the ability of users to manipulate a file system.

ADSL Asynchronous Digital Subscriber Loop—An emerging technology that provides high bandwidth over short lengths of telephone wiring.

Archie An application that maintains a database of file names located on various FTP (archive) sites.

ARP Address Resolution Protocol—A procedure by which TCP/IP devices obtain data link addresses corresponding to a desired IP address. The originator emits a broadcast to the desired IP address, and that responder returns a packet containing its data link address.

ARPANET Advanced Research Projects Agency Network—The network that grew to become today's Internet. Operation began in 1969 with four nodes.

ATA AT Attachment—A hardware design that incorporated an IBM PC/AT-style disk controller with on-board drive electronics. This is synonymous with IDE.

ATA-2 An enhancement to ATA that provides faster PIO and DMA modes than original ATA. ATA-2 devices can also supply much more information about themselves as required for plug-and-play.

ATAPI AT Attachment Packet Interface—An extension of the AT Attachment specification that adds a SCSI-like packet interface. This supports attaching devices other than disk drives.

ATF Authenticated Firewall Traversal—Version 5 of SOCKS. This provides strong authentication, integrity, and privacy.

ATM Asynchronous Transfer Mode—A very high speed connection-oriented protocol using packets of exactly 53 bytes.

AVI Audio Video Interleave—A technology that allows a Windows PC to play animation and video clips.

AWK A special-purpose programming language that handles simple data-reformatting jobs with minimal code. Named for Aho, Weinberger, and Kernighan, the original developers.

Base64 An encoding scheme that considers 8-bit data 6 bits at a time. An ASCII character in the range 64 through 127 represents each 6-bit value.

BBS Bulletin Board System—A PC that provides dial-in clients with services like file transfer, mail, and discussion groups.

Binhex An encoding scheme—usually employed on Macintosh computers—that represents 8-bit data as valid 7-bit ASCII data.

BNC Bayonet Neill-Concelman—A knurled, twist-on connection used on coaxial cable such as thin Ethernet.

BOOTP Bootstrap Protocol—A networking standard that allows computers to obtain network parameters—based on their data link address —from a server elsewhere on the network.

BRI Basic Rate Interface—An ISDN class of service that provides two 64Kbps B-channels and one 16Kbps D-channel.

Bridge A device that segregates two networks based on data link addresses.

Broadcast An address to which every station on the network should respond. For Ethernet, this is an address of all ones. For TCP/IP, it's the network address followed by all zeros.

Browser A client World Wide Web application that displays HTML pages.

CA Certification Agency—An organization that issues digital IDs.

CATV Community Antenna Television—Strictly speaking, a cable television service that receives broadcasts using antennas in favorable sites and delivers the signal by cable to unfavorable sites. However, the acronym has come to mean cable television systems of all types.

CCITT International Consultative Committee on Telegraphy and Telephony—The international standards body responsible for telephony standards. CCITT headquarters is in France.

CDFS Compact Disk File System—The file system Windows NT uses for reading compact (CD-ROM) disks.

CERN European Laboratory for Particle Physics, Geneva, Switzerland—The birthplace of the World Wide Web. See http://www.cern.ch.

CGI Common Gateway Interface—A programming interface that virtually all HTTP servers support. Clients trigger program execution by submitting an appropriate URL; once started, the program receives input from its command line, from environment variables, or from standard input. CGI programs send response HTML by writing to standard output.

CICS Customer Information Control System—A teleprocessing monitor that runs on IBM mainframes.

CIR Committed Information Rate—The average bandwidth a Frame Relay provider guarantees to provide over a stated time period.

CNAME Canonical Name—An alias for a real host name in the Domain Name System.

CRC Cyclic Redundancy Check—A checksum computed both before and after transmitting data. Obtaining the same answer verifies no data was lost or corrupted.

CSLIP A version of SLIP that includes data compression.

CSU Channel Service Unit.

CTS Clear To Send—A pin on a serial port indicating whether a device is currently able to accept data.

Daemon A background process. The UNIX equivalent of a Windows NT service.

DARPA Defense Advanced Research Projects Agency—The government agency that funded ARPANET.

DAT Digital Audio Tape—A 4-millimeter tape format capable of storing 4 to 8 gigabytes of information.

Datagram The basic unit of data at the Internet network layer.

DBMS DataBase Management System—A software system that adds, changes, deletes, retrieves, and correlates keyed records.

DDE Dynamic Data Exchange—An inter-process communication method used between Windows programs running on the same computer.

DECnet A network protocol designed by Digital Equipment Corporation. DECnet replaces Ethernet addresses with its own structured addressing scheme.

DHCP Dynamic Host Configuration Protocol—An extended version of BOOTP that supports more configuration parameters and doesn't require configuring settings in advance for each data link address.

Digital ID An electronic document, signed with a Certification Agency's public key, certifying the authenticity of a given public key and distinguished name pair.

Distinguished name The official name of a person or an organization, qualified by enough well-known additional identifiers to make it unique in the world. "First National Bank" is not a distinguished name because there are many organizations so identified. Adding city, state or province, and country information distinguishes one such organization from others.

DLC Data Link Control—A protocol that provides application access to the data link network layer. Common uses include communication with Hewlett-Packard network printers, IBM mainframes, and IBM AS/400s.

DLCI Data Link Connection Identifier—An abbreviation for a given source and destination address pair. Using a DLCI shortens packet lengths in protocols such as ATM.

DLT Digital Linear Tape—A relatively new digital tape format providing greater speed and capacity than 8-millimeter or DAT formats.

DNS Domain Name System—A distributed database system that translates hierarchical host names to IP addresses (and vice versa).

DS0 A class of digital transmission service that provides 56Kbps of usable bandwidth over a dedicated line.

DSU Data Service Unit.

ECC Error Correcting Code—A parity scheme that not only detects but also corrects errors affecting a single bit.

EIDE A marketing term from Western Digital that incorporates ATA-2 and ATAPI.

EIR Excess Information Rate—The greatest throughput possibly available on a Frame Relay circuit.

EISA Extended Industry Standard Architecture—A 32-bit I/O bus developed by Compaq and eight other PC makers. This bus also accommodates 16-bit ISA expansion cards.

ELAN Emulated Local Area Network—A system that emulates a shared media network (such as Ethernet) using a circuit-switched network by automatically establishing circuits between devices as required.

EPS Encapsulated PostScript—A file format that transmits graphics as PostScript statements. EPS files frequently contain a "preview" version of the same graphic more suitable for monitor display.

Ethernet A shared media data link protocol Bob Metcalf invented at Xerox Palo Alto Research Center.

FAQ Frequently Asked Questions—A list of common questions and relevant answers. Distributing a FAQ should reduce repetitive queries.

FDDI Fiber Distributed Data Interface—A 100Mbps token ring LAN. It originally required fiber optics but now uses copper wire for short distances.

Firewall A computer that connects two networks using software that operates at the application layer. A common firewall scenario provides internal network users with access to the Internet but prevents Internet users from accessing the internal network.

Frame Relay A packet-switching technology with little error checking but very high speed. The packet nature of Frame Relay makes it less expensive than dedicated lines of the same speed.

freeWAIS A noncommercial version of WAIS supported by the Clearinghouse for Networked Information Discovery and Retrieval.

FTP File Transfer Protocol—A client-server application that transfers files from one computer to another. Commands originate at the client.

FTTC Fiber To The Curb—A metropolitan wiring plan that would install fiber optics near each home or other building but would continue using twisted pair for the actual subscriber connections.

FTTL Fiber To The Loop—A metropolitan wiring plan that would install fiber optics to local distribution points and then use twisted pair or coaxial cable for subscriber connections. Essentially, this involves less fiber and more copper than FTTC.

Gateway A display that controls traffic between two networks using factors above the network layer.

GDI Graphic Display Interface—The collection of Windows functions that creates images on the monitor or printer.

GIF Graphic Interchange Format—A bitmapped image file format invented by CompuServe.

Gopher A distributed document search and retrieval system that permits browsing, searching, and retrieving documents on any number of servers.

Gopherspace The sum of all Gopher information everywhere (or within some sphere).

HFC Hybrid Fiber Coaxial—A cable television technology that merges up to 750MHz of digital capacity with 50 to 75 channels of analog service.

HPFS High-Performance File System—An advanced file system IBM and Microsoft designed for use with OS/2.

HTML HyperText Markup Language—The page description language used for World Wide Web pages. HTML consists of plain ASCII text marked by angle-bracketed tags.

HTTP HyperText Transfer Protocol—The means by which browsers on the World Wide Web get pages from servers.

HTTPS Secure HTTP—A specification for authenticating and encrypting HTML requests and responses. This involves encrypting the body and adding new header types.

Hypertext A document that contains "hot spots" that, if clicked, invoke actions such as jumps to other documents.

ICMP Internet Control Message Protocol—A protocol, distinct from TCP and UDP, hosts and network devices use to report errors and other unusual situations.

IDE Integrated Drive Electronics—*See* ATA.

IETF Internet Engineering Task Force—The organization responsible for ongoing Internet design and enhancement.

IMAP Internet Message Access Protocol—A superset of POP that supports three modes of connection: online, offline, and disconnected. IMAP allows personal or shared mail folders to remain on the server, to be copied to a user computer, and then to be resynchronized.

Internet The world's largest computer network.

IP Internet Protocol—The scheme that controls how frames get transmitted over the network.

IP address A unique four-byte code that identifies each computer on the Internet. For human readability, IP addresses appear as four decimal numbers, 0 through 255, separated by periods.

IPX Internetwork Packet eXchange—The network layer protocol used natively by Novell Netware. IPX is roughly analogous to IP.

ISA Industry Standard Architecture—A hardware specification for PC system units. Its basis is the IBM PC-AT personal computer introduced in 1984.

ISAPI Internet Server Application Programming Interface—A specification that allows CGI programs to remain in memory between executions. In addition, ISAPI programs receive and send client data by means of highly efficient "call" interfaces.

ISDN Integrated Services Digital Network—A telephone service that provides digital (rather than analog) service. ISDN delivers bandwidth in channels of 64Kbps, of which 56Kbps is typically usable.

ISO International Standards Organization—An international standard-setting body active in computer networking.

ISP Internet Service Provider—An enterprise that sells Internet connectivity and related services.

JPEG Joint Photographic Experts Group—A bitmapped image file format offering high compression and 24-bit color with some loss in image quality.

Jughead Jonzy's Universal Gopher Hierarchy Excavation And Display—The program that indexes Gopher directories for searching by Veronica.

Kerberos (1) The watchdog of Hades, whose duty it was to guard the entrance. (2) A network authentication system that provides users and services with "tickets" that identify them to other services and users. It also provides secret keys for secure communication.

LCP Link Control Protocol—A procedure whereby PPP clients and servers negotiate packet formats and sizes, authenticate the user, verify proper link operation, and terminate the link when appropriate.

LEC LAN Emulation Client—Translates LAN address to and from ATM addresses. Opens ATM sessions based on demand.

LES LAN Emulation Server—A network service that maintains a database correlating LAN and ATM addresses.

Linux A public domain form of UNIX that runs on Intel architecture personal computers.

List server A network service that, upon receiving mail, resends the message to each recipient contained in a list.

LocalTalk A low-speed network used primarily with Apple Macintosh computers and Apple LaserWriter printers.

Loopback A term that denotes a computer talking to itself on a network. The loopback address, 127.0.0.0, is essentially each computer's internal nickname for itself.

LPD Line Printer Daemon—a print spooling service often used on UNIX and other TCP/IP-based hosts.

LPR A command that copies a file into a print queue on a host running LPD.

Lurker An Internet user who takes an interest in material published by others but who doesn't contribute, particularly in newsgroups.

LZH A compressed file archiving format handled by Haruyasu Yoshizaki's LHA program.

Mailslots A high-level interface for one-to-many communication between processes on remote machines. Systems communicating via mailslots send and receive messages as if writing to and receiving from a file system.

Maltshop A program that retrieves a list of known Gopher servers from an authoritative site, checks them for availability, and automatically creates Gopher pointers to the active ones.

MAPI Mail Application Programming Interface—A set of function calls that enable programs to invoke mail services through a standard programming interface.

MAU Multistation Access Unit—A wiring hub used with IBM token ring cabling.

MCA MicroChannel Architecture—A 32-bit PC expansion bus invented by IBM and used in its PS/2 line of computers.

MD5 An algorithm from RSA Data Security that produces a 128-bit "fingerprint" or "message digest" from any length message. A user can then encrypt the fingerprint with a public or secret key.

MDI Multiple Document Interface—A Microsoft Windows interface feature that supports one or more child windows within a single parent window.

MIB Management Information Base—A coded, hierarchical description of the SNMP features a device supports.

Microkernel The small, highly optimized core of a modern operating system.

MILNET A military version of the Internet formed in 1983.

MIS Management Information Systems—The function of providing computer and information services to an organization.

MNP Microcom Network Protocol—A set of error correction and compression algorithms invented and released into the public domain by Microcom, Inc.

MPEG Motion Picture Experts Group—A standard file format for full motion video and audio.

MTA Message Transfer Agent—A network service that stores and forwards messages to and from User Agents and other Message Transfer Agents.

Multicast An address sent to a group of stations on the network. Each station can program its network adapter to listen for specific multicast addresses it wants.

Mutex A switch, usually managed by an operating system, that only one task at a time may hold. Tasks asking for the same mutex thus become mutually exclusive.

MVS The operating system used on most IBM mainframes.

MX Mail Exchanger—A DNS record that translates the domain part of a mail address to the DNS name of a specific mail host.

NACK Negative Acknowledgment—A packet or other network signal reporting that data did not successfully arrive.

Named pipes A high-level interface for one-to-one communication between two processes on remote machines. Systems communicating via named pipes send and receive messages as if writing to and receiving from a file system.

NBNS NETBIOS Name Service—A TCP/IP network service that translates NETBIOS computer names to IP addresses.

NCP Network Control Protocol—A process that determines the transport protocols and related settings a PPP client and server will use.

NCSA National Center for Supercomputing Applications—The development site of Mosaic, the first graphical World Wide Web browser. NCSA developed accompanying server software as well.

NDIS Network Device Interface Specification—A layered architecture for network software. NDIS requires a MAC-layer driver specific to each network adapter in the system. The MAC-layer drivers report to a Protocol Manager that controls the flow of packets to and from network layer protocol drivers.

NetBEUI NETBIOS Extended User Interface—A nonroutable data link protocol that was once integral with NETBIOS.

NETBIOS Network Basic Input Output System—A collection of network services and programming interfaces invented by IBM for their original PC Network. Although once integral with the predecessor of today's NetBEUI, NETBIOS services now run on network protocols like TCP/IP, IPX/SPX, DECnet, and XNS as well.

NetDDE A form of DDE that allows processes on different computers to communicate over a network.

NETLOGON A Windows NT service that validates the user names and passwords of users wishing to use the system.

Netmask A string of binary digits that indicate (with 1-bits) which parts of a network address contain the network number. ANDing the netmask and the network address zeros out the host portion and leaves the network number.

Newsfeed A connection that transfers USENET News from one News server to another.

Newsgroup A topic category within the USENET News system. Newsgroups have hierarchical names such as comp.infosystems.www.servers.ms-windows.

Newsreader A client program for retrieving, reading, and posting USENET News articles.

NFS Network File System—A transparent network file sharing system most often used on UNIX systems.

NIC (1) Network Interface Card—An expansion card that provides a physical connection to a network. (2) Network Information Center—The source of public information and administrative control for a network.

NLM Netware Loadable Module—A background service that runs on a Novell Netware server.

NNRP Network News Reader Protocol— The procedure by which newsreaders communicate with USENET News servers over TCP/IP. This is a subnet of NNTP.

NNTP Network News Transfer Protocol—The procedure by which USENET News servers communicate over TCP/IP.

NSFNET For many years, the largest and fastest backbone network on the Internet. NSFNET no longer exists; commercial providers supply today's backbones.

NSLOOKUP A diagnostic program that queries DNS servers and displays results.

NTFS NT File System—An advanced file system Microsoft designed for use with Windows NT. NTFS supports very large volumes, access control lists, trans-action-based file system updates, and fault tolerance.

OLE Object Linking and Embedding— A software object model backed by Microsoft. OLE servers provide reusable functions, and OLE containers invoke them.

OSI Open System Interconnection—An ISO project to develop next-generation standards for connecting diverse systems.

Packet screener A router configured with highly specific rules that block unexpected or unwanted users and applications. This is a security measure.

PAD Packet Assembler/Disassembler—A device that provides entry to and exit from an X.25 network.

PASV A "proxy mode" in which an FTP client (rather than the server) initiates the data connections. This avoids problems validating remotely initiated connections in a secure environment.

PCI Personal Computer Interconnect—A 32-bit local PC bus developed by Intel.

PCMCIA Personal Computer Memory Card Industry Association—A specifi-cation for credit-card-sized expansion cards used mostly in laptop computers. The term *PC Card* is replacing PCM-CIA.

PDC Primary Domain Controller—The Windows NT server that holds the master copy of its domain's User Account Database.

PEM Privacy Enhanced Mail—A specifi-cation for handling authenticated and encrypted mail via SMTP. This involves encrypting the message body and adding new header types.

perl Practical Extraction and Report Language—An interpreted program-ming language invented by Larry Wall.

PGP Pretty Good Privacy—A public-domain encryption and authentication system that uses very long keys.

PIO Programmed Input/Output—A high-speed means to transfer data between an expansion card and a com-puter using I/O ports.

POP2 Post Office Protocol 2—A procedure for downloading mail from an SMTP mail server to a remote client.

POP3 Post Office Protocol 3—An enhanced procedure for downloading mail from an SMTP mail server to a remote client.

PPP Point-to-Point Protocol—A data link and network protocol designed for use over serial connections (such as dial-up modems).

PRI Primary Rate Interface—An ISDN class of service that provides 23 64Kbps B-channels and one 64Kbps D-channel.

Private key A secret password used to sign documents electronically. Recipients can only decipher private-key encrypted (digitally signed) documents if received intact and decrypted with a verifiable, widely available public key. Receiving confidential documents is a second use of private keys; in that scenario, the recipient uses a private key to decrypt data the sender encrypted with the recipient's public key.

PTR Identifies a Name Pointer Record in a DNS reverse zone database.

Public key A widely distributed password capable of decrypting data encrypted with a private (secret) key. The purpose isn't to keep the encrypted data secret, but to prove identity of the sender and unaltered document contents. Transmitting confidential documents is a second use of public keys; in that scenario, a sender encrypts the data with the recipient's public key and only the recipient (using the private key) can decrypt it.

PVC Permanent Virtual Circuit—A persistent link between two points of a connection-oriented network.

QIC Quarter Inch Cartridge— A medium-capacity digital tape format that accommodates up to 250MB per cartridge.

RAS Remote Access Service—A Windows NT service that supports dial-in and dial-out connections using modems, X.25 networks, and ISDN.

RDBMS Relational DBMS—A DBMS that stores all data in tables. All rows in the same table have the same fields ("columns"). The DBMS relates rows in different tables by joining them based on matching data values.

Replicator A Windows NT service that propagates new or changed files on one computer to others. A common use is replicating logon scripts from one server to all logon servers in a domain.

Resolver Software that queries a DNS server to translate computer names to IP addresses (or the reverse).

RFC Request For Comment—A document that describes a technology approved for Internet use. Proposed RFCs are Internet Drafts.

RMON Remote Monitor—A network management probe installed on a network segment. RMON probes collect statistics and packets for later analysis by a central monitoring console.

Router A multiport computer that examines network layer addresses of packets on a network and retransmits them on a different network if necessary.

RPC Remote Procedure Call—A subroutine call made on one computer but satisfied on another. A service broker of some kind typically decides which remote computer will execute the requested function.

RTS Request To Send—A pin on a serial port indicating whether a device has data available for sending.

SCSI Small Computer System Interface—An interface specification for input/output devices. SCSI accommodates up to eight devices on a single flexible bus.

SED A quick-and-dirty programming language traditionally used on UNIX. Perl has largely superseded SED.

Semaphore An indicator (software switch) accessed by several processes but managed by the operating system. For example, the operating system may suspend execution of one process until another process alters the semaphore or sets it to a required value.

SEPP Secure Electronic Payment Protocol—A credit card encryption and verification system developed by IBM, Netscape, GTE, CyberCash, and MasterCard. It was superseded in 1996 by SET.

SET Secure Electronic Transactions—A credit card encryption and verification system combining technology from SEPP and STT. Backers of SEPP and STT agreed to a single standard in 1996 under pressure from merchants, banks, and customers.

Sharename An external name assigned to a printer or a point in a server's file system.

SHTML SSI HTML—A file name extension that activates parsing (Server Side Includes) when delivering an HTML page.

SIMM Single Inline Memory Module—A small, printed circuit card that serves as a carrier for memory chips.

SLIP Serial Line Internet Protocol—A specification that supports IP (Internet Protocol) traffic over serial connections. SLIP isn't a complete protocol stack; for example, there are no Data Link addresses.

SMS System Management Server—A Microsoft network management product that includes a protocol analyzer. In a Microsoft Networking environment, it also provides hardware and software inventory, remote control, and remote software distribution.

SMTP Simple Mail Transfer Protocol—The accepted standard for transmitting Electronic Mail over the Internet. Messages consist of simple text files. Header lines are those preceding the first blank line; everything after the first blank line is the body.

Sniffer A line of protocol analyzers sold by Network General. Incorrectly, network analysts often call other protocol analyzers sniffers as well.

SNMP Simple Network Management Protocol—A scheme whereby network devices respond with statistics and other current data when queried. In addition, devices may initiate "trap" messages when specified events occur.

SOA Start Of Authority—The first record in a DNS zone database. This record specifies characteristics and defaults that pertain to the entire zone.

SOCKS A firewall mechanism whereby internal stations open circuits to a proxy server and then ask the proxy server to open sessions to outside hosts. This requires adding a SOCKS layer to the network stack of each client and minor modifications to applications.

SPAP Shiva Password Authentication Protocol—A procedure that verifies the identity of someone attempting to initiate a PPP connection.

Spoofing Deliberately using a false IP address. Intruders might do this to defeat filtering that tests for a particular organization's IP addresses.

SPX Sequenced Packet eXchange—The transport layer protocol used natively by Novell Netware. IPX is roughly analogous to TCP.

SSI Server Side Include—A feature for replacing marked portions of outgoing HTML with the contents of another file or with CGI program output.

SSL Secure Sockets Layer—A security service inserted between an application and the network stack.

STDIN The standard input file to a character-mode program. Standard input defaults to the console but can also receive input piped from another process.

STDOUT The standard output file from a character-mode program. Standard output defaults to the console but can also pipe into another process.

STT Secure Transaction Technology—A credit card encryption and verification system developed by Microsoft and Visa. It was superseded in 1996 by SET.

Subnet mask *See* Netmask.

SVC Switched Virtual Circuit—A dynamic link between two points of a connection-oriented network. End stations can open and terminate an SVC at will.

TCP Transmission Control Protocol—A transport layer protocol that provides reliable data delivery with end-to-end error detection and correction. TCP handles data in terms of segments.

Telco A telephone company.

Telenet A large public X.25 packet network now owned by Sprint.

Telnet An application that opens remote terminal sessions over a TCP/IP network.

TFTP Trivial File Transfer Protocol—An elementary file transfer system that provides no security at all. A common use for TFTP is downloading code to network devices as they boot. In such cases, an administrator typically configures TFTP for read-only access to a single directory.

TN3270 An application that opens remote terminal sessions to IBM mainframes over a TCP/IP network.

Tracert A diagnostic command that determines the route taken to a destination.

TSR Terminate and Stay Resident—An MS-DOS program that remains in memory after it ends. Such programs usually hook an interrupt before ending so that they regain control when certain system events occur.

TTL Time-To-Live—A limit after which data, events, or packets are no longer valid.

Tymnet A large public X.25 packet network.

UA User Agent—A client program, most often for sending and receiving E-Mail.

UADB User Account Database—A file that records user names, passwords, and other details about users authorized to use a Windows NT computer.

UDP User Datagram Protocol—A transport layer protocol that provides unreliable, connectionless delivery with low overhead. UDP deals with data as packets.

UNC Universal Naming Convention—A file name syntax in Microsoft Networking that provides access to remote files and directories without first mapping a drive letter. Such file names begin with \\<server>\<sharename>.

UPS Uninterruptible Power Supply—A power regulator containing rechargeable batteries. The batteries temporarily provide output power if conventional power fails.

URC Uniform Resource Characteristic— An object that contains data about a particular URN, such as the author, publisher, and revision date.

URI Uniform Resource Identifier—Meta-information that identifies a resource in any way. URL, URC, and URN are all URI types.

URL Uniform Resource Locator—The address to a specific resource's location. If you have a URL, you can retrieve the resource.

URN Uniform Resource Name—A string that uniquely and persistently identifies a resource on the network. A URN should stay the same regardless of the resource's location.

USENET A network of primarily UNIX machines that periodically connect via dial-up modem and transfer batches of files.

UUCP UNIX-to-UNIX Communication Protocol—An application that connects via serial port to its counterpart on another machine and then transfers or receives files.

UUencode An encoding scheme that considers 8-bit data 6 bits at a time. An ASCII character in the range 32 through 95 represents each 6-bit value. This allows binary (8-bit) files to pass through transmission systems that require 7-bit printable characters.

V.22bis A CCITT modem specification that provides for a 2400bps carrier with V.42, MNP4, or MNP5 error detection and compression.

V.32 A CCITT modem specification that provides for a 9600bps carrier with V.42, MNP4, or MNP5 error detection and compression.

V.32bis A CCITT modem specification that provides for a 14,400bps carrier with V.42 error detection and compression.

V.34 A CCITT modem specification that provides for a 28,800 bps carrier with V.42bis error detection and compression.

V.42 A CCITT specification for error detection and compression.

V.42bis An enhanced CCITT specification for error detection and compression.

VBX Visual Basic Extension—A drop-in code module that extends the capabilities of Visual Basic.

VCI Virtual Circuit Identifier—In ATM, a 3-byte abbreviation for the two 20-byte addresses (source and destination) participating in a virtual circuit. Transmitting a 3-byte VCI reduces overhead compared to transmitting two 20-byte addresses.

Veronica Very Easy Rodent-Oriented Netwide Index to Computerized Archives—A query mechanism for searching Gopherspace.

VESA Video Electronics Standards Association—Inventors of the first local bus used in PCs.

VFAT Virtual File Allocation Table—The file system used by Windows 95. VFAT accommodates file names longer than 8.3 by spreading long names among several directory entries.

VJ compression A method invented by Van Jacobson for compressing the headers of TCP/IP datagrams. This improves performance over low-speed serial links (such as PPP via modem).

VOD Video On Demand—A concept whereby cable television companies would transmit programs when subscribers asked for them. If operators install enough bandwidth for VOD, high bandwidth for data applications (such as Internet browsing) would be inconsequential by comparison.

VPI Virtual Path Identifier—In ATM, a 3-byte abbreviation for the two 20-byte addresses (source and destination) participating in a virtual circuit.

VXD Virtual Device Driver—A Microsoft Windows 32-bit device driver.

WAIS Wide Area Information Server—A widely established text indexing and search system.

Webmaster The individual responsible for proper ongoing operation of an HTTP server.

Whois A transaction that provides networkwide directory service to Internet users. To provide centralized lookup, Whois usually runs on relatively few specific machines.

WinCGI A specification that permits writing CGI programs in Visual Basic.

Because Visual Basic doesn't support piped standard input and standard output files, WinCGI uses physical files instead.

Winsock An implementation of Berkeley sockets ported to Microsoft Windows. Winsock provides a standard programming interface to any TCP/IP stack that supports it. Acceptance of Winsock has been nearly universal; virtually all Internet-related software for PCs now requires it.

World Wide Web A large, very loose collection of clients, networks, servers, and applications that support graphical hypertext browsing across the Internet. HTTP is the client-server network protocol, and HTML is the hypertext page description language.

WWW *See* World Wide Web.

X.25 A highly reliable packet network technology. Extensive error checking at each "hop" contributes to great reliability but introduces high latency and limits bandwidth.

Xmodem One of the first error-correcting file transfer protocols used among PCs.

XNS Xerox Networking System—A routable protocol developed by Xerox at Palo Alto Research Center. XNS was the protocol used by 3+Share, and it formed the basis for IPX/SPX.

XOFF An ASCII character (Ctrl-S, decimal 19) that a receiving device sends to a transmitting device to make it stop sending data.

XON An ASCII character (Ctrl-Q, decimal 17) that a receiving device sends to a transmitting device, allowing it to resume sending data.

XOVER A command newsreaders give news servers to retrieve the following information for a range of articles: subject, author, date, message id, references, byte count, and line count. This information allows the newsreader to build a threaded articles list.

Ymodem An error-correcting file transfer protocol used among PCs, usually over dial-up modem links.

Zmodem An error-correcting file transfer protocol used among PCs, usually over dial-up modem links.

Index

Account policies, setting user, 128–129
ACL (Access Control List), 137
Adding computers, 538–539
Address depletion, defined, 59
Addresses, multiple, 121
ADSL (Asynchronous Digital Subscriber Loop), 97
Aliasing, defined, 9, 258
Analog modems, 76
AnnotateDirectories, 225
Anonymous Logon user name and password, 382–383
APDA (Apple Programmers and Developers Association), 103
APIs (Application Programming Interfaces), 19, 79, 402
Applets, 457
Archie, 5
ARP (Address Resolution Protocol) cache, 61–62
Articles, defined, 301–302
@ sign, 258
ATAPI (AT Attachment Packet Interface), 43
ATM (Asynchronous Transfer Mode), 53, 91–95
    concepts, 91–92
    congestion management, 92
    LAN emulation, 92–95
    use for data applications, 92
Audit tracking, 130
Authoritative, defined, 181

Backbone sites, 32
Backup and recovery, 467–485
    backup strategies, 467–472
    installing a SCSI tape drive, 472–474
    ongoing management, 484–485
    running scheduled jobs, 481–484
    running Windows NT Backup, 474–481
    testing, 484
Backups, 521–522
Backup strategies, 467–472
    backup media and drives, 469–470
    backup retentions, 471
    backup software, 470–471
    how often to back up, 471
    media storage and rotation, 472
    what to back up, 467–469
Base64 encoding, 266
BBSs (Bulletin Board Systems), 29

BLAT, 483
    command line SMTP mailer for Windows NT, 423
    freeware program, 423
BNC (Bayonet Neill-Concelman) connectors, 99
BOOTP (Bootstrap Protocol), 81, 167–168
bps (bits per second), 76
BRI (Basic Rate Interface), 83
Bridges and routers, ISDN, 84
BrowseMaster, 25–27
Browsers, defined, 335
Buffered CGI, 404
BUS (Broadcast and Unknown Server), 94
Buses, system, 44–46
Business plans
    business and capacity plans, 38
    cost model, 37
    customer identification, 34–35
    customer needs, 35
    customer profiles and numbers, 35–36
    developing, 34–38
    marketing plan, 37–38
    product and pricing strategy, 37
    services required, 36
    support plan, 36
Bytecodes, 457
Byte versus octet, 59

CA (Certification Agency), 503
Cable modems, 96
Cable TV and telephone companies, 95–97
Capacity planning, 537
CATV (Community Antenna Television), 30
CCITT (International Consultative Committee on Telegraphy and Telephony), 75
CD-ROM
    drives, 126
    support, 44
CERN (European Laboratory for Particle Physics)
    format, 394
    servers, 391–392
Certificates
    digital, 511
    electronic, 510
CGI, writing standard programs, 426–428
    the <ISINDEX> tag, 429
    debugging programs, 426

grape.pl-passing form data, 413–426

hello.pl-introductory program, 406–409

iconlib.pl-passing input data, 409–413

Internet Server Application Programming Interface (ISAPI), 430–432

miscellaneous approaches, 432–434

Netscape Server Application Programming Interface (NSAPI), 429–430

notes on working with perl, 426

security concerns, 433–434

CGI (Common Gateway Interface), 4, 346, 402–434

  buffered, 404

  directory, 386

  programs, 568

  Windows, 404

  writing standard programs, 405–428

CGI programming languages, 404

  C or C++ console applications, 404

  perl (Practical Extraction and Report Language), 404

  Visual Basic, 404

CHKDSK commands, 124

CICS (Customer Information Control System), 439

CIR (Committed Information Rate), 90

Circuits

  dial-up, 75–82

  frame relay, 89–91

  X.25, 86–88

Circuit types, introduction to, 73–75

  dedicated circuits, 75

  packet services, 74–75

  switched circuits, 74

Circular definition, defined, 259

Client data, guardianship of, 574

  client.htm, 449

  client.htx, 452

  client.ide, 451

Client operating systems, 16–17

Client site programming

  JavaScript (Netscape), 457–459

  Java (Sun Microsystems), 456–457

  OLE controls and document objects, 459–460

Client software, 100–105

  DOS, 101

  Macintosh, 103–104

  OS/2, 104

  sources of, 100–104

  supporting, 104–105

  UNIX, 104

  Windows 3.1, 101–102

  Windows 95, 102

  Windows for Workgroups 3.11, 102

  Windows NT, 102

CNAME (Canonical Name) records, 187–188

CNIDR (Clearinghouse for Networked Information Discovery and Retrieval), 461

Commercial sites, 30

Communications

  providers, 31

  selecting, 73–105

Compression ratios, 76

Computers, and domain names, 115

Computers, intermediary, 342

  gateways, 342

  proxys, 342

  tunnels, 342

Computers, and security vendors, 33–34

Content management, 540–541

Content providers, 31, 568

Controllers, IDE (Integrated Drive Electronics), 42

Control message commands, 315

Copyrights and patents, 573–574

Cost centers, described, 37

CPU power, CGI exhausting, 40

CRC (cyclic redundancy checking), 92

CSLIP (Compression Serial Line Internet Protocol), 79

CTS (Clear To Send), 77

CyberJunction, 98

Databases

  design, 438

  general considerations, 439–440

  Microsoft IIS database connector, 442–456

  news overview (nov), 10

  preserving state information, 440

  record locking, 441–442

  and transaction processing, 436–456

DAT (Digital Audio Tape), 469

DBMS (DataBase Management System), 438

DDE (Dynamic Data Exchange), 404

Decryption, defined, 502
Dedicated circuits, 75
Default query handler, 461
Devices, NT-1, 84
DHCP (Dynamic Host Configuration
    Protocol), 24, 81, 98, 116–117
  administering, 171–175
  installing, 170–171
  installing and configuring, 167–178
  principles, 167–169
  using, 153–154
Dial-in routers, 78, 80–81
Dial-Out E-Mail Gateway, running, 276
Dial-up circuits, 75–82
  dial-in routers, 80–81
  introduction to SLIP and PPP, 79–80
  modem management, 77–78
  Windows NT Remote Access Service (RAS),
    81–82
Digests, defined, 288
Digital certificate, 511
Digital circuits, dedicated, 85
Digital connections, switched, 82–85
  Integrated Services Digital Network
    (ISDN), 82–84
  switched 56, 84–85
Digital IDs, 503–05
Digital signatures, solving problems with,
    502–503
Disk partitioning, 112–113
Disks
  choosing, 42–44
  fault tolerances for, 47–49
Disk space, allocating, 122–126
Disk striping, defined, 48
Distributions, defined, 316
DLCIs (Data Link Connection Identifiers), 89
DLLs (Dynamic Link Libraries), 101, 405, 430
DLT (Digital Linear Tape), 470
DNEWS, 318–319
  access.conf, 325–326
  dsnews.conf, 321–323
  installing, 320–326
  newsfeeds.conf, 323–325
DNS (Domain Name Service), 1, 11–12
  configuration, 270–273
  configuration files, 182
  configuring a DNS server, 181–182
  installing and configuring, 179–206

ongoing management, 206
operating concepts and standards, 180–189
relationship to WINS, 189
remembering names, 69
remembering numbers, 69
sample installation, 189–200
server boot files, 182–184
testing and problem resolution, 200–205
understanding, 70–71
zone database control statements, 184
zone database files, 184–189
zone database standard resource record
    formats, 184–185
zone database standard resource record
    types, 185–189
DNS (Domain Name Service) search order,
    118–119
Domain
  account structures, 126–128
  defined, 180
  parts, 258
  Windows NT, 25
Domain names, computer and, 115
DOS (disk operating system)
  based TCP/IP, 101
  pre-installing, 109
Drives, SCSI CD-ROM, 43
DSU/CSU (Data Service Unit/Channel Service
    Unit), 85, 89

ECC (Error Correcting Code), 49
EIR (Excess Information Rate), 90
EISA (Extended Industry Standard
    Architecture), 45
ELAN (emulated LAN), 94–95
Electronic certificates, 510
Electronic mail; See E-mail
Elevator seeking, defined, 42
E-mail, 8–9. *See also* Mail service
  architectures, 258
  fundamental transactions, 257
  gateways, 276
  protocols, SMTPs (Simple Mail Transport
    Protocols), 257–267
Emergency Repair, 44
EMWAC (European Microsoft Windows NT
    Academic Centre)
  HTTPS installing and configuring, 348–351
  ported WAIS to Windows NT, 461

EMWAC (European Microsoft Windows NT
Academic Centre) Gopher, 240–250
automating alias file maintenance, 248–250
configuring alias files for, 243–248
installing, 241–243
Encapsulation, defined, 57
Encryption and network security, 13
Encryption, defined, 502
Environmental management, 523–524
Equipment, selecting, 39–50, 523–545
axioms, 541–545
choosing a system bus, 44–46
choosing I/O buses, disks, and peripherals,
42–44
content management, 540–541
CPU type and speed, 39–41
environmental management, 523–524
fault tolerance and reliability, 47–49
network adapters, 46
procedural management, 539
sizing RAM, 41
specific recommendations, 49–50
technical management, 524–539
Errors, system crashing and recoverable, 49
Ethernet
10Base-2, 99
10Base-T, 99
thin, 99
Event logging, 535–537
ExitMessage, 225

Fallback servers, 70
FAQs (Frequently Asked Questions), 548–549,
570
FAT (File Allocation Table), 112
Fault tolerances, 47–49, 63
FDDI (Fiber Distributed Data Interface), 53
Files
LMHOSTS, 26
setting permissions, 136–138
system security, 14
Finger command, 493
Firewalls, 13, 494–496, 498
Flow control, defined, 76
Forcing an election, defined, 26
Frame relay circuits, 89–91
FTP (File Transfer Protocol), 5, 210, 490–492
access to services, 209
configuring parameters, 221–226

a connection-oriented protocol, 207
disk organization and management, 211
easy on CPU power, 40
installing and configuring, 207–236
internet conventions, 211–212
operating concepts and standards, 207–212
proxies, 497
security concerns, 209–210
session-oriented, 207–208
sites, 13
state-oriented, 208
unwanted activities, 211
FTP servers
content management, 236
enhancing security, 220–221
installing, 212–220
ongoing management, 235–236
space management, 235
testing and problem resolution, 234
FTP service
installing the Windows NT, 212–228
and Internet Information Server (IIS),
228–234
performance management, 227–228
remote management, 228
FTTC (Fiber To The Curb), 97
FTTL (Fiber To The Loop), 96
full.bat, 481

Gang of Nine (PC makers), 45
Gateways, 57–58
GIF (Graphic Interchange Format), 39, 76
Gopher
IIS, 250–256
IIS directories configuration for, 251–253
IIS logging and advanced configuration for,
253
installing and configuring, 237–256
installing and configuring EMWAC, 240–250
operating concepts and standards, 237–240
Gopher applications, 5–7
Gopherspace, defined, 6
grape.htm, 415–416
grape.pl htm, 417–423
Greeting message, 225
GROUP commands, 309
Groups
hunt, 78
rotary, 78

HAL (Hardware Abstraction Layer), 18
Handshakes
  defined, 76
  options, 76–77
  RTS/CTS, 76–77
Hardware, preparing and certifying, 107–110
  diagnostic shakedown, 109–110
  physical assembly and location, 107–109
  pre-installing MS-DOS, 109
Hardware reset commands, 49
HEAD commands, 310
Header types, news article, 313–315
hello.pl, 406–409
HFC (Hybrid Fiber Coaxial), 97
HGOPHER, 6
Hobbyist sites, 29–30
Home page hit counter, 435
Hosts
  defined, 56
  files, 179
HPFS (High-Performance File System), 137
htmindex.htm, 462
HTML (HyperText Markup Language),
    336–338
  format, 2
  forms and tables, 399–402
  server parsed, 434–436
  tables, 401–402
HTTP/1.1
  header types, 343–344
  response codes, 343–346
HTTP (HyperText Transfer Protocol), 1–4
  advanced features, 346–347
  clients, 335
  data directory management, 388–389
  HTTP/0.9, 339–340
  HTTP/1.0, 339–340
  HTTP/1.1, 339–341
  and HyperText Markup Language (HTML),
    336–338
  installing and configuring, 335–389
  installing and configuring EMWAC, 348–351
  ongoing management, 386–389
  operating concepts and standards, 335–347
  server, 2
  server installation, 348
  server user accounts, 386–388
  service start-up, 388

standards and versions, 339–346
  Uniform Resource Locators (URLs), 338–339
HTTPS (Secure HTTP), 33, 508
Hunt groups, 78

IAPs (Internet Access Providers), 96
IBM, invention of MCA (MicroChannel
    Architecture), 45
ICMP (Internet Control Message Protocol), 59
iconlib.pl, 409–413
IDC (Internet Database Connector), 442
IDE (Integrated Drive Electronics)
    controllers, 42
IETF (Internet Engineering Task Force), 60
IIS Gopher
  alias configuration, 253–256
  configuration for, 250–251
  configuring and managing, 250–256
  defining links to miscellaneous Gopher
    servers, 255
  defining menu names for local
    directories, 254–255
  defining menu names for local files, 254
  IIS Gopher type assignments, 255–256
  viewing existing Gopher tag information, 255
IIS (Internet Information Server)
  advanced configuration for FTP, 233–234
  database connectors, 442–456
    additional HTML extension (.htx)
      facilities, 455
    linking one IDC query to another, 453–455
    logging IIS activity, 443–445
    providing HTML form input to
      queries, 449–452
    summarizing log data, 445–449
  directories configuration for FTP, 230–231
  directories configuration for Gopher,
    251–253
  FTP service, 228–234
  installing, 160–164
  logging and advanced configuration for
    Gopher, 253
  logging configuration for FTP, 231–233
  messages configuration for FTP, 229
  securing pages with, 518
  service configuration for FTP, 229
  Web server, 382

IMAP (Internet Message Access Protocol), 267–268

Interfaces, defined, 54

Internal sites, 30

Internet

applications and support services, 1–14

application services, 1–11

conventions, 211–212

purpose of, 35

search engines, 568–569

security risks, 487–488

Internet Information Server (IIS), configuring Microsoft, 382–385

Internet Server Manager, 444

Internet sites, 20, 99–100

InterNIC (Internet Network Information Center), 12, 71, 181, 490

Inverse multiplexing, defined, 84

I/O buses, choosing, 42–44

I/O devices, SCSI, 42

IP (Internet Protocol). *See also* TCP/IP

addresses and parameter assignments, 81

defined, 57

routable versus nonroutable protocols, 60

routing, 121

IPX (Internetwork Packet eXchange), 498

ISA (Industry Standard Architecture), 44

ISAPI (Internet Server Application Programming Interface), 405, 430–432

callback functions, 431–432

extension control block, 431

ISDN (Integrated Services Digital Network), 30, 82–84

bridges and routers, 84

modems, 83

network adapters, 83

ISDN (Integrated Services Digital Network), classes of service, 83

Basic Rate Interface (BRI), 83

Primary Rate Interface (PRI), 83

ISPs (Internet Service Providers), 22, 29, 316, 318

IWareConnect, 98

Java, 432–433

JavaScript (Netscape), 457–459

Java (Sun Microsystems), 456–457

JPEG (Joint Photographic Experts Group) compressed format, 76

jstest.htm, 457–458

Jughead (Jonzy's Universal Gopher Hierarchy Excavation And Display), 8

Keys

private, 502

public, 502

Lab equipment setup, 41

LANs (Local Area Networks), 97–98

protocols, 56–57

and security, 98

Latency, defined, 74

LCP (Link Control Protocol), 157

Learning Perl (Schwartz), 426

Leased lines, 85

LEC (LAN Emulation Client), 94

LECS (LAN Emulation Configuration Server), 94

Legal issues, 571–575

copyrights and patents, 573–574

guardianship of client data, 574

limits of liability, 575

location issues, 572

private versus public sites, 572

service provider or publisher?, 571–572

types of objectionable materials, 573

LES (LAN Emulation Server), 94

Liability, limits of, 575

Lines

leased, 85

point-to-point, 85

private, 85

Listname

subscribe, 10

unsubscribe, 10

Lists

commands, 309

creating, 292–297

managers, 287, 289–292

List servers, 9–10

defined, 287

installing and configuring, 287–299

operating concepts and standards, 288

problem resolution and ongoing management, 298–299

sample installation, 288–297

LMHOSTS, 23, 26

Load balancing telephone lines, 78
Local part, 258
Locking
    optimistic, 441
    pessimistic, 441
    record, 441–442
LogAnonymous, 225–226
LogFileAccess, 225–226
Log file management, 519–521
LogNonAnonymous, 225–226
LowercaseFiles, 226
LPD (Line Printer Daemon), 116
Lurker, defined, 10–11

Macintosh
    operating system, 16–17
    running TCP/IP, 103–104
MAC (Media Access Control), 58
Maginot Line, 522
Mail exploders, defined, 287
Mailing lists, 287
Mail service. *See also* E-mail
    installing and configuring POP/SMTP,
        257–285
    ongoing management, 284–285
    testing and problem resolution, 282–284
Mailslots, 21
Maintenance, applying system, 164–165
Maltshop (program), 8
Marketing, defined, 37
Marketing services, 567–568
    being listed on internet search engines,
        568–569
    creating awareness in newsgroups, 570
    developing attractive services and image,
        567–568
    getting links from other sites, 569
    headers, addresses, and URLs, 569
    monitoring activity and feedback, 570
MaxClientsMessage, 224
MCA (MicroChannel Architecture), 45
MDI (Multiple Document Interface), 396–397
Message Transfer Agent, 257–260
MetaInfo DNS, 189–200
    configuring, 191–200
    modifying sample configuration files,
        196–200
    obtaining and installing, 190–191

reviewing sample configuration files,
    191–196
MIB (Management Information Base), 527
MIME (Multipurpose Internet Mail
    Extensions), 264–265
Mircosoft, configuring Internet Information
    Server (IIS), 382–385
MNP (Microcom Network Protocol), 75
Modems
    analog, 76
    banks, 77–78
    cable, 96
    ISDN, 83
    management, 77–78
MSCDEX (Microsoft CD-ROM Extensions),
    109
MsdosDirOutput, 222–224
MTA (Message Transfer Agent), 9, 257–260, 262
Multiple addresses on one network adapter,
    121, 140–144
Multitasking and elevator seeking, 42

Named pipes, 21–22
Name resolution by WINS clients, 25
NCPs (Network Control Protocols), 79
NCSA (National Center for Supercomputing
    Applications) servers, 391–392
NDIS (Network Device Interface Specification),
    58, 102
NetBEUI (NETBIOS Extended User Interface),
    21–22, 152–153
NETBIOS name resolution, 26–27
    b-node, 23
    h-node, 24
    m-node, 24
    p-node, 23
NETBIOS (Network Basic Input Output
    System), 20–21, 152–153, 167
    API, 21
    versus Internet names and name
        resolution, 23–25
Netscape
    Httpd server, 362
    server application functions, 430
Netscape Communications Server, 351–371
Netscape Navigator File, 365
Netscape Server Manager, 365
Netscape Servers, 512–516

Netstat commands, 68, 491
Netware servers (Novell), 16
Network adapters
  ISDN, 83
  multiple addresses on one, 121, 140–144
Network-level security protection, 494–498
Network Monitor Agent, 531
Networks
  monitors, 530–532
  packet-switched, 86–95
  security, 12–13
News, 10–11
News article header types, 313–315
Newsgroups, 10, 302
News overview (nov) database, 10
Newsreaders, defined, 10, 302
NFS (Network File System), 43
NLMs (Netware Loadable Modules), 16
NNRP (Network News Reader Protocol), 10
NNS, 319, 327–332
NNTP (Network News Transfer Protocol), 10,
    303–310
  commands, 310–311
  news article header types, 313–315
  server operation, 316–318
Nonroutable protocols, 60
NSAPI (Netscape Server Application
    Programming Interface), 429–430
NSLOOKUP programs, 201–204
NT-1 devices, 84
NTFS (NT File System), 18, 114
NTMail
  list definition parameters, 295–296
  preparing to run, 279–281
  3.0, 269–282

Octet versus byte, 59
ODBC (Open Data Base Connectivity) data
    source, 442
OLE (Object Linking and Embedding), 404,
    456, 459
Operating systems, weaknesses of, 15–17
  client operating systems, 16–17
  Macintosh, 16–17
  mainframe operating systems, 17
  minicomputer operating systems, 17
  Netware, 16
  OS/2, 16

UNIX, 15
Windows 3.1, 16–17
Windows 95, 16–17
O'Reilly WebSite, installing and configuring,
    371–381
OS/2 operating system, 16, 104
OSI (Open System Interconnection), 53, 269

Packet
  networks, 74
  services, 74–75
Packet-switched networks, 86–95
  frame relay circuits, 89–91
  X.25 circuits, 86–88
PAD (Packet Assembler/Disassembler), 86–87
Parts, SMTP address
  domain, 258
  local, 258
Password authentication, defined, 383
Passwords, 138, 210
Patents, 573–574
PCI (Personal Computer Interconnect)
    buses, 46
PCMCIA (Personal Computer Memory Card
    Industry Association), 78
PCT/SSL channel, secure, 385
PDC (Primary Domain Controller), 110, 126
PEM (Privacy Enhanced Mail), 506
Performance monitoring, 525–535
  protocol analyzers, 530–535
  SNMP management systems, 527–529
  Windows NT Performance Monitor, 525–526
Peripherals, choosing, 42–44
perl (Practical Extraction and Report
    Language), 404, 406–408, 426
Pessimistic locking, 441
PGP (Pretty Good Privacy), 506–508
Point-to-point lines, 85
POP (Post Office Protocol), 8, 262, 281–282
POP/SMTP alternatives, 267–269
  gateways from miscellaneous
    systems, 268–269
  Internet Message Access Protocol
    (IMAP), 267–268
  X.400, 269
POP/SMTP mail service, 257–285
Port number ranges, 67
  dynamically allocated ports, 67

UNIX-specific services, 67
well-known ports, 67
PPP (Point-to-Point Protocol), 79
Private keys, 502
Private lines, 85
Procedural management, 539
change control, 539
routine procedures, 539
Programming perl (Wall and Schwartz), 426
Promotions, cost-effective, 37–38
Protocols
connection-oriented, 207
defined, 54
LAN, 56–57
pull, 262
push, 262
routable versus nonroutable, 60
transport, 67
Providers
application service, 31
communications, 31
content, 31
segments, 29–30
service, 31
Providing an envelope, defined, 57
PTRs (Name Pointer Records), 188
Public information sites, 30
Public keys, 502
Pull protocol, 262
Push protocol, 262
PVCs (Permanent Virtual Circuits), 89, 91

QIC (Quarter Inch Cartridge) tapes, 469

RAID (Redundant Array of Inexpensive Disks)
concepts, 48
technology, 47
RAM (random-access memory), 39, 41
RAS (Remote Access Service), 27, 81
RAS (Remote Access Service), installing,
149–160
configuration and administration, 155
dialing out, 155–160
equipment, 149
managing dial-in services, 160
software, 149–155
Record locking, 441–442
Relationships, trust, 127

Replication partners, defined, 170
ResKit 3.51 FTP Configure, 226–227
Resolvers
built-in, 179
defined, 179
RFC 977 (Network News Transfer Protocol),
310
RFC 1036 (Standard for Interchange of
USENET Messages), 310, 315
RFC 1506, 269
RFCs (Requests For Comment), 72
RIP (Router Information Protocol), 64–65
RMON (remote monitor) probes, 489
Rotary groups, 78
Routable versus nonroutable protocols, 60
Router discovery, defined, 64
Routers, dial-in, 78, 80–81
RPC (Remote Procedure Call), 21
RTS/CTS, 76–77, 151
RTS (Request To Send), 77

Sales, defined, 37
scanner.htm, 392
scn_cern.map, 392
scn_ncsa.map, 394
SCSI CD-ROM drives, 43
SCSI I/O devices, 42
SCSI (Small Computer System Interface), 42
SCSI tape drive, installing a, 472–474
Search engines, 4–5
Internet, 568–569
WAIS, 460–464
WebCrawler, 4–5
WWWW (World Wide Web Worm), 4–5
Securing
pages with Netscape Servers, 512–516
page delivery, 511–519
Security, 487–522
backups, 521–522
computer vendors, 33–34
Web page delivery, 511–519
Security, dangerous applications, 490–493
File Transfer Protocols (FTP), 490–492
finger command, 493
Telnet, 492
Trivial File Transfer Protocols (TFTP), 492
X windows system, 492–493

Security, digital envelopes and signatures, 502–509
  digital certificates, 503–506
  securing HTTP transactions, 508–509
  securing Internet mail, 506–508
Security
  establishing a security policy and stance, 493–494
  file system, 14
  Internet security risks, 487–488
  LANs and, 98
  log file management, 519–521
  Maginot Line, 522
  methods of attack, 489–490
  motives for attack, 488–489
  securing electronic commerce, 509–511
Security, types of prevention, 494–509
  host-level security protection, 498–501
  network-level security protection, 494–498
Security
  user login, 14
  viruses, 521
Security protection, host-level, 498–501
  avoiding risky or unneeded protocols and services, 499
  closing back doors to system process authority, 501
  enforcing file system security, 501
  not advertising services, computer names, or user names, 499
  protecting privileged accounts, 500–501
  tightening user account security, 500
Segmentation, defined, 92
SEPP (Secure Electronic Payment Protocol), 509
Serial ports, 76
Server parsed HTML, 434–436
Servers
  CERN (European Laboratory for Particle Physics), 391–392
  fallback, 70
  NCSA (National Center for Supercomputing Applications), 391–392
Services, marketing, 567–568
Services, range of, 31–34
  credit card numbers, 33–34
  full service, 31–32
  limited service, 31–32

  partitioned data (pay-per-view), 34
  secure transactions, 33
  specialized services, 33–34
Services
  role of providers, 31
  Video On Demand, 95
Session, defined, 54
Session-oriented, defined, 207–208
SET (Secure Electronic Transactions), 509–511
Setup options, Windows NT, 110–121
  completing initial installation, 121
  computer and domain names, 115
  disk partitioning, 112–113
  file system, 114
  network settings, 115–117
SID (Security Identifier), 135–136
SIMMs (Single Inline Memory Modules), 49
Sites
  backbone, 32
  commercial, 30
  hobbyist, 29–30
  internal, 30
  measure of success, 30
  planning, 29–38
  public information, 30
SLIP (Serial Line Internet Protocol), 79
SMS (System Management Server), 530–531
SMTP, software configuration, 273–281
SMTP (Simple Mail Transfer Protocol), 8
  addresses, 258
  @ sign, 258
  installing and configuring, 257–285
  Mailer and BLAT, 423
  message forwarding, 257–262
  message structure, 262–267
  operating concepts and standards, 257–267
  and POP (Post Office Protocol), 262
  POP/SMTP alternatives, 267–269
  sample installation, 269–282
  sessions, 261
  software installation, 270
SMTP software configuration, 273–281
  environmental and routing settings, 273–278
  preparing to run NTMail, 279–281
SNMP (Simple Network Management Protocol), 81
  community, defined, 527
  service, 115

SOAs (Start Of Authority) records, 185–186
SOCKS source libraries, 498
SQL Server, 443–445
SSI (Server Side Include), 4, 346, 435–436
SSL (Secure Sockets Layer), 33, 385, 508–509
Standard input, 403
Standard output, 404
State-oriented, defined, 208
STDIN (Standard Input), 346
STDOUT (Standard Output), 346
STT (Secure Transaction Technology), 509
Subnets
    defined, 65–66
    masks, 65–66
Subscribe listname, 10
Support services, 11–14
    DNS (Domain Name System), 11–12
    file system security, 14
    network security, 12–13
    user login security, 14
SVCs (Switched Virtual Circuits), 91
Switched circuits, 74
System bus, choosing a, 44–46
System Management Server (SMS), 530–531

Tables, WebSite, 377–378
TCP/IP (Transmission Control
        Protocol/Internet Protocol). *See also* IP
    address resolution and routing, 61–65
    address structure, 59–60
    advantages of, 51–52
    and Domain Name System (DNS), 69–71
    fundamentals, 51–72
    how it stacks up, 53–59
    locating standards documents, 72
    networks, 167
    network software, 97–98
    origin of, 51–72
    port numbers and connections, 66–69
    registering a site, 71–72
    routing overview, 61–66
    services, 55–56
    settings, 117–121
    subnets, 65–66
    typical configuration settings, 69
TCP/IP configuration, advanced, 138–148
    multiple IP addresses per network
        adapter, 140–144

    multiple network adapters per system,
        139–140
    static IP routing, 144–148
TCP port 80, 376
Technical management, 524–539
    adding computers, 538–539
    capacity planning, 537
    event logging, 535–537
    performance monitoring, 525–535
Telephones
    companies, 95–97
    finding, 75
Telnet, 492
10Base-2 Ethernet, 99
10Base-T Ethernet, 99
Text-searching systems, 460
TFTP (Trivial File Transfer Protocols), 492
Threads, described, 10
Time stamping, 441
topten.htx, 448
topusers.idc, 453
Transport protocols, 56, 67
Trumpet Winsock
    obtaining, 103
    shareware, 101–102
Trust relationships, 127, 130–131

UADB (User Account Database), 28, 111,
        126–127
UA (User Agent) software, 257, 262
U interfaces, defined, 83
UNC (Universal Naming Convention), 21
UNIX
    as an Internet server, 17
    operating system, 15
    and port ranges, 67
    sendmail program, 258
    sources of client software, 104
    to-UNIX communication protocol, 8
    and USENET News Service, 301
    X window system, 492–493
Unsubscribe listname, 10
UPS (Uninterruptible Power Supply), 47
URLs (Uniform Resource Locators), 1, 338–339,
        568–569
USENET, news distributions, 316
USENET and UNIX machines, 301
USENET News, 10–11

USENET newsgroups, 570
USENET News service
  installing and configuring, 301–334
  installing DNEWS, 320–326
  installing NNS, 327–332
  Network News Transfer Protocol (NNTP),
    303–310
  NNTP news article header types, 313–315
  NNTP server operation, 316–318
  ongoing management, 332–334
  operating concepts and standards, 301–318
  sample installations, 318–332
  selected nonstandard news commands,
    311–313
  standard NNTP commands, 310–311
User accounts, creating, 126–138, 131–133
  creating groups, 133–134
  how many passwords?, 138
  managing audit tracking, 130
  managing trust relationships, 130–131
  managing user rights, 129–130
  miscellaneous user and group
    operations, 134–136
  setting file permissions, 136–138
  setting user account policies, 128–129
  Windows NT, domain account
    structures, 126–128
User accounts, setting up, 278–279
User Agent (UA) software, 257
Users
  login security, 14
  managing rights, 129–130
Users, support of, 547–550
  pursuing the Web, 550
  reference documentation and FAQs, 548–549
  setting expectations, 549–550
  start-up documentation and procedures,
    547–548
UUCP (UNIX-to-UNIX Communication
  Protocol), 8
UUencode encoding, 266

Vendors, computer security, 33–34
Veronica (Very Easy Rodent-Oriented Netwide
  Index to Computerized Archives), 7–8
VESA (Video Electronics Standards
  Association) 32-bit bus, 45–46
VFAT (Virtual File Allocation Table), 112

Video Electronics Standards Association, 45
Viruses, 521
Visual Basic, 432–433
VOD (Video On Demand) services, 95
VPI/VCI (Virtual Path Identifier/Virtual Circuit
  Identifier), 91
VXDs (Virtual Device Drivers), 102

WAIS (Wide Area Information Server), 4–5,
  460–464
  and miscellaneous search engines, 460–464
  and other search engines, 4–5
WAN (Wide Area Network) links, 233, 301
Web, delivering pages, 40
Web browsers, 1–2
WebCrawler search engines, 4–5
Web pages
  ensuring technical quality, 389
  securing delivery, 511–519
  securing pages with Internet Information
    Server (IIS), 518
  securing pages with Netscape Servers,
    512–516
  securing pages with WebSite, 516–518
Web servers, IIS, 382
Web services
  advanced, 391–465
  CGI (Common Gateway Interface), 402–434
  clickable image maps, 391–398
  client site programming, 456–460
  database and transaction processing, 436–456
  HTML forms and tables, 399–402
  performance issues, 465
  Server Side Includes (SSI), 434–436
  WAIS and miscellaneous search
    engines, 460–464
WebSite
  access log, 379
  directory listings, 378
  executing CGI programs, 381
  installing and configuring, 371–381
  running as a background service, 376
  search mechanism, 460
  securing pages with, 516–518
  starting, 376
  tables, 377–378
  translating client IP address to DNS, 379–380
  virtual domains feature, 376–377

WinCGI (Windows CGI), 404
Windows 3.1, 101–102
Windows 3.1 operating system, 16–17
Windows 95
    enhancement of TCP/IP–32, 102
    operating system, 16–17
Windows for Workgroups 3.11, 102
Windows networking browse lists,
        obtaining, 25–27
Windows NT, 102
  at an Internet site, 20
  ARP (Address Resolution Protocol)
    caches, 61–62
  and BLAT, 423
  computer accounts, 111
  configuring FTP parameters, 221–226
    Annotate Directories, 225
    ExitMessage, 225
    greeting message, 225
    LogAnonymous, 225–226
    LogFileAccess, 225–226
    LogNonAnonymous, 225–226
    LowercaseFiles, 226
    MaxClientsMessage, 224
    MsdosDirOutput, 222–224
  distributed administration, 22
  domain account structures, 126–128
  domains and workgroups, 25
  fault tolerance, 47–49
  file and print sharing, 22
  groups, 133–134
  installing and administering, 107–165
    advanced TCP/IP configurations, 138–148
    allocating disk space, 122–126
    applying system maintenance, 164–165
    creating user accounts, 126–138
    initial setup options, 110–121
    installing Internet Information Server
        (IIS), 160–164
    installing Remote Access Service
        (RAS), 149–160
    preparing and certifying
        hardware, 107–110
    repairing a partition, 114

    TCP/IP settings, 117–121
    testing and refining the installation, 122
  installing the FTP service, 212–228
  Remote Access Service (RAS), 81–82
  ResKit 3.51 FTP Configure, 226–227
  route tables, 65
  Server versus Workstation, 27–28
  stacks, 58
  strengths of, 17–20
    familiarity, 19–20
    microkernel architecture, 17–18
    multitasking, 18
    portability, 18
    reliability, 18–19
    scalability, 18
    security, 19
Windows NT Backup, running, 474–481
Windows NT Hardware Compatibility List, 44
Win I/O API, 21
WINS (Windows Internet Name Service), 24
  administering, 175–178
  DNS relationship to, 189
  installing, 167–168, 170–171
  name resolution by clients, 25
  principles, 169–170
  proxy agents, 121
  static mappings, 178
Winsock (Windows Sockets) API, 21, 22
Wnet (Win 32 Network) API, 21
WORM (Write Once Read Many) drives, 469
WWW (World Wide Web), 1–4
WWWW (World Wide Web Worm) index Web
        pages, 4–5

X.25, 269
X.25 circuits, 86–88
X.400, 269
XHDR commands, 310
XOVER commands, 10, 309–310
X windows system, 492–493

Zip compressed format, 76
Zone database files, 184–189
Zone, defined, 180–181

Addison-Wesley Developers Press publishes high-quality, practical books and software for programmers, developers, and system administrators.

Here are additional titles from A-W Developers Press that might be of interest to you. If you'd like to order any of these books, please visit your local bookstore or:

FAX us at: 800-367-7198

Call us at: 800-822-6339
(8:30 A.M. to 6:00 P.M. eastern
time, Monday through Friday)

Write to us at:
Addison-Wesley Developers Press
One Jacob Way
Reading, MA 01867

Reach us online at:
http://www.aw.com/devpress/

International orders, contact one of the following Addison-Wesley subsidiaries:

Australia/New Zealand
Addison-Wesley Publishing Co.
6 Byfield Street
North Ryde, N.S.W. 2113
Australia
Tel: 61 2 878 5411
Fax: 61 2 878 5830

Southeast Asia
Addison-Wesley
Singapore Pte. Ltd.
15 Beach Road
#05-09/10 Beach Centre
Singapore 189677
Tel: 65 339 7503
Fax: 65 338 6290

Latin America
Addison-Wesley Iberoamericana S.A.
Blvd. de las Cataratas #3
Col. Jardines del Pedregal
01900 Mexico D.F., Mexico
Tel: (52 5) 568-36-18
Fax: (52 5) 568-53-32
e-mail: ordenes@ibero.aw.com
 or: informaciona@ibero.aw.com

Europe and the Middle East
Addison-Wesley Publishers B.V.
Concertgebouwplein 25
1071 LM Amsterdam
The Netherlands
Tel: 31 20 671 7296
Fax: 31 20 675 2141

United Kingdom and Africa
Addison-Wesley Longman Group Limited
P.O. Box 77
Harlow, Essex CM 19 5BQ
United Kingdom
Tel: 44 1279 623 923
Fax: 44 1279 453 450

All other countries:
Addison-Wesley Publishing Co.
Attn: International Order Dept.
One Jacob Way
Reading, MA 01867 U.S.A.
Tel: (617) 944-3700 x5190
Fax: (617) 942-2829

If you'd like a free copy of our Developers Press catalog, contact us at: devpressinfo@aw.com

CGI Programming in C & Perl

Thomas Boutell
ISBN 0-201-42219-0, $34.95 w/CD-ROM

This book shows you how to create interactive, dynamically-generated Web pages with CGI programming in two practical languages: C, which has distinct performance advances, and Perl, one of the most popular choices for CGI today. You'll learn how to generate HTML pages and images on the fly, parse form submissions directly, and much more. The CD-ROM contains a complete range of CGI software libraries in both C and Perl, ready to plug into your Web site.

Web Weaving: Designing and Managing an Effective Web Site

Eric Tilton, Carl Steadman, and Tyler Jones
ISBN 0-201-48959-7, $24.95

Covering UNIX®, Windows®, and the Macintosh®, *Web Weaving* shows you how to install and configure Web servers, use authoring tools, implement security, and build structured, well-organized Web sites. The authors, experienced Webmasters, include tips for planning for growth, building in maintenance schemes, catering to your users' needs, and creating a logical, underlying infostructure.

Hooked on Java™: Creating Hot Web Sites with Java Applets

Arthur van Hoff, Sami Shaio, and Orca Starbuck,
Sun Microsystems, Inc.
ISBN 0-201-48837-X, $29.95 w/CD-ROM

Written by members of Sun's Java development team, *Hooked on Java* is a concise and practical introduction to using applets to add interactive capabilities to World-Wide Web sites.The CD-ROM contains a wealth of cool Java applets ready to plug into your home pages, examples of HTML pages that are already Java-enabled, Java source code, the Java Developer's Kit for Windows® 95, Windows NT, Solaris 2.x, and more.

The Internet Publishing Handbook For World-Wide Web, Gopher, and WAIS

Mike Franks
ISBN 0-201-48317-3, $22.95

The Internet Publishing Handbook takes you through the process of Internet publishing from beginning to end, using examples and advice gathered from Internet publishers around the world. You'll learn how to assess hardware and software server needs for your site; choose server setup options and features for World-Wide Web, Gopher, and WAIS; design HTML documents; implement digital cash, digital checks, charging, and more.

Growing and Maintaining a Successful BBS: The Sysop's Handbook

Alan D. Bryant
ISBN 0-201-48380-7, $39.95 w/CD-ROM

This book contains advice, tools, and tips from an industry expert on how to go from "up and running" to front runner BBS status. Alan Bryant's first book, *Creating Successful Bulletin Board Systems* covered the basics—this book takes you to the next level, covering topics such as discussions of why, when, and how you might choose to connect your BBS to the Internet; information on legal issues relevant to board content and sysop responsibility; online databases, and more.

Online Law: The SPA's Legal Guide to Doing Business on the Internet

Thomas J. Smedinghoff, Editor
ISBN 0-201-48980-5, $34.95

Written for the layperson, but extensively annotated for the experienced lawyer, *Online Law* provides clear guidance through the rapidly developing law of electronic commerce. Based on sound legal principles, this comprehensive handbook draws on the extensive knowledge of experienced attorneys at the forefront of today's emerging online legal issues.